If you're wondering why you need this new edition of *Voices of Dissent*, here are five good reasons!

1. Tom Engelhardt's "Militarism and the American Presidency" and Joseph G. Peschek's "The Obama Presidency and the Economic Crisis" explain why the Obama Administration has delivered much less change in both foreign and domestic policy than was promised in 2008.

2. Barbara Ehrenreich's "Kicking People When They're Down" explores poverty and material hardship in America and Matt Taibbi's "Wall Street's Big Win" reveals the inability of Congress to meaningfully regulate Wall Street in this era of economic crisis.

3. Paul Street and Anthony DiMaggio's "The Myth of the Tea Party" discusses the resurgence of conservatism in America through a critique of the Tea Party movement.

4. In an era of environmental awareness, Fred Magdoff and John Bellamy Foster's "Capitalism and the Environment" connects ecological challenges to the inner nature of capitalism and Naomi Oreskes and Erik Conway's "Merchants of Doubt" explains the politics behind climate change denial.

5. Noam Chomsky's "9/11 and the Imperial Mentality" discusses how U.S. imperialism since 9/11 has created an unrealistic understanding of conflicts around the world and of the United States' role in causing them.

PEARSON

Voices of Dissent
Critical Readings in American Politics

Ninth Edition

William F. Grover
Saint Michael's College

Joseph G. Peschek
Hamline University

PEARSON

Boston   Columbus   Indianapolis   New York   San Francisco   Upper Saddle River
Amsterdam   Cape Town   Dubai   London   Madrid   Milan   Munich   Paris   Montreal   Toronto
Delhi   Mexico City   São Paulo   Sydney   Hong Kong   Seoul   Singapore   Taipei   Tokyo

For our students—May you "occupy" the historic possibilities for real change by being voices of dissent.

Senior Acquisitions Editor: Vikram Mukhija
Editorial Assistant: Emily Sauerhoff
Executive Marketing Manager: Wendy Gordon
Senior Digital Media Editor: Paul DeLuca
Production Manager: Meghan DeMaio
Creative Director: Jayne Conte
Cover Designer: Suzanne Behnke
Cover Art: © Doug Armand/Getty Images
Project Coordination, Text Design, and Electronic Page Makeup: Sudip Sinha/PreMediaGlobal
Printer/Binder/Cover Printer: Courier Companies

Credits and acknowledgments borrowed from other sources and reproduced, with permission, in this textbook appear on page 344.

Library of Congress Cataloging-in-Publication Data

Voices of dissent: critical readings in American politics/[edited by] William F. Grover, Joseph G. Peschek. —9th ed.
   p. cm.
   ISBN 978-0-205-25171-1—ISBN 0-205-25171-4
1. United States—Politics and government.   I. Grover, William F., 1956-   II. Peschek, Joseph G.
JK21.V65 2012
320.973—dc23

2011052101

10 9 8 7 6 5 4 3 2 1—V013—16 15 14 13 12

ISBN 10: 0-205-25171-4
ISBN 13: 978-0-205-25171-1

Contents

Preface

What's New About This Edition?

In this ninth edition of *Voices of Dissent*, a third of the articles are new, offering coverage of issues and topics that have become of pronounced importance since the eighth edition. We have chosen fresh and stimulating readings that will widen and deepen students' understanding of contemporary American politics. We have given more extended attention to environmental politics and global climate change with new articles by Fred Magdoff and John Bellamy and by Naomi Oreskes and Erik Conway. Related questions of a normative nature are discussed by James Gustave Speth, who looks at competing concepts of happiness in the American tradition, and by Bill McKibben, who discusses economic and ecological sustainability in a concluding piece that we have edited and relocated from our previous edition. Challenges to the democratic functioning of political institutions during the Obama years are explored by Matt Taibbi, Joseph G. Peschek, and Saul Cornell in new articles on Congress and financial reform, the Obama presidency and the economic crisis, and the courts and constitutional interpretation. Political linkage processes are critically examined in new articles on the news media by Robert McChesney and John Nichols, John Atlas and Peter Dreier, and Bill Moyers. The much discussed Tea Party movement is put into perspective by Paul Street and Anthony DiMaggio, while the threat to democracy posed by the 2010 *Citizens United* Supreme Court decision is analyzed by Lawrence Lessig. Social divisions rooted in economic inequality, race, gender, and class are probed by Barbara Ehrenreich in a follow-up to her 2001 book *Nickel and Dimed* while Noam Chomsky provides a sobering perspective on how our "imperial mentality" continues to distort our understanding of world realities a decade after the 9/11 attacks. Taken together, both new and older selections challenge us to take on the tough work of revitalizing American democracy and make clear that far-reaching institutional and structural changes are essential if democracy is to be more than a hollow shell. We hope that you, as students and citizens, find this prospect both challenging and exciting.

Approach

In our view, *Voices of Dissent* continues to be the only reader on the market that fundamentally challenges the political and economic status quo in America. It provides a systematic series of critical perspectives on American politics that goes beyond the range of debate between mainstream liberalism and conservatism. In developing this book, we drew on some of the best examples of a diverse and energizing body of critical scholarship that is all too often overlooked in government courses. Political economy, and the tension between capitalism and democracy, is a recurrent theme in the selections. Other articles explore the ideological effects of the mass media, the ecological results of uncontrolled economic growth, and the dynamics of class, race, gender, and religious divisions in the United States—issues central to our political life early in the twenty-first century. American governmental institutions and political processes are treated in five central chapters, but only after they are placed in the context of underlying economic and social structures, as well as the more apparent constitutional arrangements, that shape their design and impact.

Goal and Audience

Our goal is to provide students with the intellectual tools to develop a sustained and integrated critique of the workings of U.S. democracy so that as citizens they can better contribute to a broader debate about the American future. We firmly believe that students today are open to a critical analysis of their political system and are eager to participate in a discussion about fresh alternatives. We also think that many instructors are interested in exposing their students and themselves to material that makes sense of the dissatisfaction with the status quo that registers daily in America today. Our book provides a set of readings to help accomplish these goals.

Voices of Dissent is designed for introductory college-level courses in American government. It could be used as a supplement to a variety of textbooks or in conjunction with several works that have a narrower focus. In our experience, some of the best opportunities for learning occur when alternative frameworks of analysis and explanation are matched against each other. For that reason, the pairing of our reader with a work that adopts a more conventional, or even sharply opposed, interpretation of American politics might prove quite stimulating.

Organization

We begin with a revised general introduction, "Why a *Critical* Reader?" Here we explain the intellectual and political orientation that shaped our selection of readings and contrast our outlook with what we call mainstream political science. The readings that follow are grouped into three sections. Part I looks at the broad structures that constrain and pattern American politics. The three chapters in this section look at democracy and political economy, ideology, and culture and the distinctive nature of the American state. Part II attends to the traditional subject matter of political processes and government institutions: the mass media, parties and elections, Congress, the presidency, and law and the courts. Many of the articles in this section are notable for relating familiar processes and institutions to the broader level of political analysis developed in Part I. Part III examines major political challenges facing the United States and explores visions for democratic revitalization in light of the critical analysis contained in the previous chapters.

Features

Voices of Dissent contains several features that make it an attractive and original resource. Our emphasis on the contextual centrality of corporate capitalism and individualist values should deepen students' understanding of the very meaning of politics. Article introductions relate selections to key political questions and overall themes of the book. Most chapters begin with a theoretical or conceptually oriented piece that identifies underlying issues relevant to the unconventional view of American politics this book has been designed to encourage. Our forty selections represent some of the best and most provocative writing on American politics, scholarly and journalistic, available today. Each article is followed by "Discussion Questions," which are meant to facilitate class dialog and debate.

We wish to thank the reviewers who made insightful comments and suggestions in previous editions. We also acknowledge the insight and encouragement of our editor at Pearson Longman, Reid Hester, and his staff, especially Emily Sauerhoff. Finally, we thank Pat Troxell and Glenace Edwall for their continuing support and helpful suggestions.

William F. Grover and Joseph G. Peschek

INTRODUCTION

Why a *Critical* Reader?

A long habit of not thinking a thing *wrong*, gives it a superficial appearance of being *right*.

—Thomas Paine, *Common Sense*

In January of 1776, Thomas Paine voiced Americans' growing aspirations for freedom and independence with his radical call for an end to the monarchical rule of the British Empire. His pamphlet *Common Sense* was a phenomenal success, with upwards of 150,000 copies printed, reaching an estimated one million people, unheard of numbers for his day. Paine's straightforward message found a receptive audience among ordinary people, whose often-inchoate opposition to the King was impeded by entrenched deference to royal authority. With fiery reasoning in support of dissent and republican government, he cut through the haze of "what was" and crystallized a vision of "what could be."

If a twenty-first century Thomas Paine were to issue a radical call for "common sense" today, would the public even be able to hear it? We wonder. As introductory students of politics, the lessons of eighteenth-century America may seem like ancient history as you ponder political life in the twenty-first century. The revolutions in political thinking that punctuated the end of the last century occurred elsewhere. We are now more than 20 years removed from such seismic shifts as the collapse of the Berlin Wall and the breakup of eastern Europe as a Soviet satellite, the coordination into a single market of the economies of the European Community nations, and the demise of Communism in Russia and, albeit more slowly, in China. India, China, and some other Asian nations now stand poised to challenge the United States economically as they compete for a greater share of the world's resources and flourish as producers of jobs and investment opportunities. Religious fundamentalism is spreading at an alarming rate worldwide, with dramatic impacts on political structures. Historic world events have swept away the political, economic, military, and ideological basis of the Cold War, and with it much of what we knew as foreign affairs in the post–World War II period. Even in the face of such breathtakingly rapid transformations, we have been treated to a predictable chorus of political pundits and "experts" in the mass media reassuring us that recent history confirms the universal appeal and unquestionable rightness of American versions of democracy and corporate capitalism. Despite everything, the tide of history still moves our way, we are told. Why swim against it?

SHIFTING TIMES/ENDURING STRUCTURE

This ninth edition of *Voices of Dissent* carries on our call to you as students to swim against the tide and challenge the received wisdom of the day. The sentiments in the previous section speak of changes of historic magnitude. If anything, the changes we began to highlight in the first edition of our anthology have only accelerated since then. Thus, we continue to live in exciting yet crisis-filled times. As this edition goes to press, the United States remains mired in economic problems of an extremely serious nature. After the midterm elections of 2010, the terms of discussion about economic policy among political elites centered increasingly on deficit reduction and spending cuts, rather than on job creation and reviving economic growth. This austerity-oriented shift to the right in political discourse went against the advice of many mainstream economists, who worried about a reversion to pre-Keynesian thinking, and the public's consistently expressed preferences for job creation policies and support for tax increases on the wealthy to reduce the deficit. This represents a remarkable comeback for a business-oriented ideology that had seemingly been discredited by the economic crisis. Testifying before the House Committee on Oversight and Government Reform less than two weeks before the election, a befuddled former chair of the Federal Reserve, Alan Greenspan, admitted to being in "a state of shocked disbelief" at the inability of banks to regulate themselves:

> I made a mistake in presuming that the self-interest of organizations, specifically banks and others, were such as that they were best capable of protecting their own shareholders and their equity in the firms.

Greenspan, who had chaired the Fed for 18 years before retiring in 2006, was used to being treated with deference, as something of a conservative free market sage. Facing criticism from committee chair Rep. Henry Waxman (D-CA), Greenspan was asked to clarify his position. Waxman pressed him, "In others words, you found that your view of the world, your ideology, was not right, it was not working?" "Absolutely, precisely," Greenspan responded. "You know, that's precisely the reason I was shocked, because I have been going for 40 years or more with the very considerable evidence that it was working exceptionally well." This level of shock and the potential to rethink old economic assumptions prompted Congress to approve a mind-boggling $700 billion bailout for the financial sector, and shortly thereafter craft a special $17.4 billion loan plan to rescue the domestic automobile industry. It appeared that the very corporate economic actors whose poor decisions were bringing the country to its knees were being rewarded with astronomical handouts from Congress and the president. Wall Street was getting help while Main Street languished. With President Bush on the way out and president-elect Obama waiting in the wings, the economic outlook was grim. The hope for "change" that inspired so many Obama supporters was being fundamentally challenged before he even had a chance to take office.

In 2008, Barack Obama was elected as the country's first African American president. His historic victory electrified the nation—and the world—with his constant theme of "Change you can believe in!" as a backdrop. Hope and optimism abounded. A sense of relief—something akin to global catharsis—immediately followed Obama's 2008 electoral victory, as the Bush presidency staggered toward its end amidst a straining global economy facing the worst recession since the Great Depression. The sense of hope associated with Obama's victory has long since been tinged with disappointment on the part of many of his early supporters. In 2008, liberal and progressive voters hoped that the crisis of capitalism would lead to a sharp break with corporate-friendly "neoliberal" public policies, perhaps in the form of a "New New Deal." On the domestic policy front,

President Obama persuaded Congress to pass important and in some ways historic legislation in the areas of economic stimulation, banking and financial regulation, and health care reform. Yet in each case, Obama's centrist approach, combined with his quest to win "business confidence" and the clout of powerful private economic interests, produced much less change from the neoliberalism of his predecessors than had been promised.

It should have been clear from the cabinet picks that he unveiled after the election that Obama was proposing to staff his administration with "pragmatic" and "non-ideological" policy elites drawn from the center-right of his party. While liberal and conservative media elites uniformly praised such "hard-headed" choices, many voters and analysts outside the mainstream wondered aloud if the soaring rhetoric of the presidential campaign and the exciting promise of "change" was being diverted into the creation of what looked a lot like a reunion of Bill Clinton's administration from the 1990s—tilting toward powerful pro-corporate, pro-financial sector advisors. Perhaps like FDR, Obama would need powerful grassroots movement for reform to push him beyond conventional policy potions. As political scientist Frances Fox Piven reminded us:

> FDR became a great president because the mass protests among the unemployed, the aged, farmers and workers forced him to make choices he would otherwise have avoided. He did not set out to initiate big new policies . . . But the rise of protest movements forced the new president and the Democratic Congress to become bold reformers.

Piven offers a more sobering view of the prospects for an Obama presidency—hope without illusions, excitement tempered by the insight that an engaged citizenry will be needed to keep the new president on course for deep changes. It remains to be seen if the Occupy Wall Street (OWS) movement, which emerged in the fall of 2011 and demonstrated unexpected staying power, will help to shift political discussion in a more progressive discussion during the presidential campaign of 2012.

As if a shattered economy wasn't a big enough challenge for Obama to confront, the new president inherited wars on two fronts, in Iraq and Afghanistan, where Obama decided on a military escalation. For years, President George W. Bush kept the nation on a war footing. His initial reasons for entering the war in Iraq have long since evaporated, having been exposed as either miscalculations based on highly selective reading of intelligence or deliberate distortions. Growing legions of people of differing political persuasions acknowledge the unjustifiable nature of this war, while its continuation exerts tremendous pressure on our political and financial systems. And the expansion of this conflict into Afghanistan promises more conflict and heightened instability around the world. The framing events for this challenge to our political principles, of course, are the horrendous terrorist attacks of September 11, 2001, which precipitated the U.S. bombing of Afghanistan, the war in Iraq, and the larger ongoing "war on terror," which have been justified and fought largely under the sway of the unilateral exercise of executive power. As political analysts, we cannot escape the need to address myriad issues that flow out of circumstances that have seared themselves into the consciousness of the nation. The "war on terror" has been the ubiquitous theme of President Bush and the media. We have been told on an almost daily basis that 9-11 "changed everything" in American politics. We are now skeptical of that assertion. As renowned linguist and political analyst Noam Chomsky puts it in his best seller *9-11*:

> The horrifying atrocities of September 11 are something quite new in world affairs, not in their scale and character, but in the target. For the United States, this is the first time since the War of 1812 that the national territory has been under attack, or even threatened. . . . For the first time, the guns have been directed the other way. That is a dramatic change.

What hasn't changed, Chomsky reminds us, are the fundamental objectives of U.S. foreign policy. Supported as they always have been by massive use of state-sponsored violence and neglect of international law, these objectives reflect the structure of corporate, military, and political power in America. Indeed, the events of 9-11 and the "war on terror" have solidified that structure and obstructed potential challenges to it. While the Obama administration has made adjustments to the policies of the Bush administration, it has not fundamentally challenged any aspect of that structure—in domestic or foreign affairs, as several articles in *Voices of Dissent* make clear. In such troubling times, we desperately need contemporary Thomas Paines to meet the challenges posed by these times of crisis. While dissenters risk being labeled "unpatriotic," it's a risk that must be taken in a true democracy. For structures of power endure.

DEMOCRACY AND ITS DISCONTENTS

The American political landscape has shifted significantly since President Barack Obama came to power in 2008. Democrats had controlled both houses of Congress since the 2006 midterm elections, with their margins growing in 2008 as President Obama took over amidst public disillusionment with the wars in Iraq and Afghanistan, and worries (verging on panic) about the deep economic recession, growing joblessness, lack of adequate health care, vanishing pension security, and global environmental crises. Those margins vanished, however, in the 2010 midterm, with voters punishing Democrats as the nation remained mired in the "Great Recession," ongoing wars in Iraq and Afghanistan, little movement on a domestic legislative agenda, and backlash heating up over the health care reform bill and the growing budget deficit and national debt. As a result, Republicans regained control of the House, and the Democrats barely clung to a slim majority in the Senate, well short of the 60 votes needed for a filibuster-proof majority. With this reassertion of power, the GOP (Grand Old Party) became what many observers referred to as "the party of *no*." All hope for bipartisan consensus on domestic and foreign policy initiatives—the hallmark of Obama approach to governing—was futile from this point onward, culminating in the fiasco over the extension of the debt ceiling in the late summer of 2011, wherein House and Senate Republicans were able to hold the country hostage with the threat of national bankruptcy as Tea Party–inspired leaders extracted $2.5 trillion in budget cuts over the next 10 years as part of congressional deficit reduction package. Not that Democrats had been fighting all that hard to challenge Republican intransigence, having agreed to an extension of the Bush-era tax cuts for the wealthy in December of 2010 even while the Democrats still had majorities in both house of Congress at that time. Programs for the poor and vulnerable were to be cut; increased tax revenue from the wealthiest Americans was a non-starter, even though their tax rates were at historic lows, a major contributing factor to the budget deficit in the first place.

The rightward framing of the economic debate promises to carry over into the 2012 presidential election, as the GOP obstruction and Democratic lack of vision play out against the backdrop of unprecedented voter dissatisfaction. Polls in October of 2011 revealed the depth of this discontent. One *New York Times*/CBS News poll found Americans' distrust of government at 89 percent, its highest disapproval level ever. Another CBS News poll found public approval of the job Congress is doing at an all-time low of 9 percent. In fact, in that poll, Americans gave higher rating to polygamy, pornography, and "the

U.S. going Communist." The failure one month later of the bipartisan congressional supercommittee to agree on a plan for budget cuts and tax increases only added to this dim view of politics and politicians. For Republicans, it was a self-fulfilling prophecy: Make sure nothing gets done and then blame the Obama administration for lack of leadership on the nation's pressing problems. For Democrats, it was a frustration: President Obama fails to live up to his promise of change and hope by not pursuing progressive policies, while trying to reach a hopeless compromise with the other party that wants part of compromise. The resulting political stalemate and economic hard times get blamed on the incumbent president while GOP prospects for retaking the White House grow stronger.

While presidential elections can help bring the need for serious alternatives into sharper relief, the 2012 race is shaping up to be an ugly, expensive affair with little enthusiasm amongst potential voters. In 2004, a rise in turnout among evangelical Christians and young first-time voters led to an improved turnout rate of about 59 percent, and that upward trend continued in 2008 with turnout edging above 61 percent, the highest turnout for a U.S. election in 40 years. Although America fancies itself as the greatest democracy on earth, even with a record 131 million voters going to the polls in the hotly contested 2008 race, the United States still remains mired at or near the bottom of all industrialized nations in terms of voter participation. And virtually all predictions are for much lower turnout in 2012 as disillusioned voters—particularly young people who generated so much energy and electoral clout for Obama in 2008—are expected to stay home. Moreover, in the wake of the 2010 Supreme Court decision in the *Citizens United v. Federal Election Commission* case, the 2012 presidential contest promises to top all records for campaign spending. The *Citizens United* decision effectively struck down all limits on independent campaign expenditures by political action committees, opening the way for a fresh torrent of corporate money with their newly reaffirmed status as "persons" whose "free speech" (campaign spending) is constitutionally protected. This continues an ominous trend in American electoral campaigns. While campaign finance was reformed through the 2002 McCain–Feingold Act targeting soft money, the cash flow to campaigns has been rerouted and continues to grow. Indeed, the 2008 campaign may have contributed to the effective dismantlement of the system of partially publicly financed presidential campaigns, as candidate Obama declined to accept any public funds, spending a record $740 million of privately raised funds. His stated goal for the 2012 race was to become the first $1 billion presidential candidate in history. Any serious approach to the revitalization of American democracy must make systematic electoral reform a priority. Widespread popular alienation from politics enables the influence of corporate business on government policy to grow, threatening to turn America into a plutocracy and make democracy an endangered species. As Ralph Nader has pointed out, "This control by the corporate government over our political government is creating a widening *democracy gap*. Active citizens are left shouting their concerns over a deep chasm between them and their government."

This chasm manifests itself in countless ways, occasionally bringing the subterranean issue of class inequality starkly to the surface. For instance, in the summer of 2005, one of the worst natural disasters in American history occurred as Hurricane Katrina devastated New Orleans. Katrina's force was compounded by social and political disasters that lay bare the class and racial divisions of U.S. society. Americans were stunned by the lack of responsiveness by local, state, and national authorities, and the city still struggles to recover. Many other domestic issues and trends are troubling as well—particularly when read against the backdrop of the most severe economic crisis since the Great Depression and persisting well after the 1999–2009 period characterized by *Business Week* as "the lost decade for jobs." These persistent problems include the growing gap between the rich and the poor, with the top 1 percent of households now owning more wealth than the bottom 95 percent, leaving the country with class divisions based on income and wealth reminiscent of the late nineteenth century; with that gap illustrated another way, the top 400 individuals in America now own more wealth than the bottom 150 million people combined; the loss of millions of jobs during the Great Recession—job loss far greater than during any other post–World War II economic downturn—with the unemployment rate still above 9 percent nationally throughout 2011, and with more than 14 million Americans unemployed and 9 million others involuntarily working part time; an essentially stagnant standard of living for working and middle-class Americans over the last three decades; the soaring wage differential between CEOs and average factory workers, which resulted in CEOs in 2008 earning about 344 times what an average worker earned, up from 1980 when CEOs made 41 times as much; the health care crunch that has left at least 47 million Americans without any medical coverage and an equal number with woefully inadequate coverage; the persistence of poverty (especially among children—22 percent now live below the poverty line), with the overall poverty rate in 2010 of about 16 percent (or 49 million people) and an additional 51 million now classified as "near poor"; lingering racism and sexism as barriers to basic equality; and the crisis of environmental degradation, which is reaching potentially cataclysmic proportions globally as the United States continues to lag behind international efforts to curb climate change.

Other, more hopeful signs of discontent have emerged, albeit sporadically, in the past dozen years. In Seattle in November of 1999, and again in Washington, DC, in April of 2000, tens of thousands of people from around the world came together to voice growing opposition to the World Trade Organization and other global financial institutions whose decisions set the rules of economic life far removed from citizen input. This nascent social movement—uniting students, environmentalists, working people, and other activists against the elite agenda of corporate capital—has shed light on the often secretive world of international economic decision making, raising deep doubts about the presumed wisdom of globalization. In February 2003, millions of people around the globe protested against the impending U.S. invasion of Iraq—the largest one-day protest in the history of the world. In January 2007, hundreds of thousands of citizens gathered on the National Mall in Washington to demand an end to the ongoing Iraq War. And of course, in the fall of 2011, the OWS movement exploded around the United States. Beginning in Zuccotti Park near Wall Street, the movement spread to 70 major U.S. cities and hundreds of others, with sympathy movements around the world as well. With its galvanizing slogan of "We are the 99%," OWS has shed unprecedented light on the staggering gap between the rich and the rest of us, achieving the feat of moving class and inequality on to the agenda of "legitimate" political discourse—a rarity in American politics. The sometimes shocking police response to OWS attests to the militarization of the domestic police function, a stark reminder of what's at stake when the political narrative shifts to the core structural issue of corporate/class power in American politics. While it remains to be seen whether the OWS movement will have a lasting impact, we strongly believe that the American political system today retains a superficial appearance of rightness, a veneer of public ritual and familiarity beneath which lies tremendous private (and increasingly public) discontent. Moreover, we sense students and teachers are interested in a challenging analysis of American politics that includes alternatives to conventional liberal and conservative approaches, which, we are all taught, mark the limits of "legitimate" debate. In our text, we ask you to move beyond these socialized limits in an attempt to span the "democracy gap."

THREE POSSIBLE RESPONSES

These and a host of other problems confront the student of politics. In the face of such formidable dilemmas, you are left with a few possible responses. One common response is *resignation*, expressed in such adages as "you can't fight city hall" and "don't rock the boat." Many students tell us they can see basic injustices but feel powerless to change anything. The continuing durability of this view is ironic, though, given the sweeping and rapid changes that have taken place elsewhere in the world in recent years.

Another response available to you is the *pluralist* interpretation of political life, which encourages piecemeal problem solving and an incremental view of change. Closely linked to an inherited cultural assumption about politics and power, the pluralist model of politics dominates contemporary political science. Pluralism rests on the view of society as a collection of groups that compete over various policy areas. Through these groups, or acting as individuals through other democratic freedoms such as voting rights, representative institutions, and civil liberties, people can negotiate and compromise in an open political process. Group conflict is considered fair as long as the government serves as an unbiased umpire, maintaining a level-playing field for all groups. Power is said to be diffuse so that no one group has unfair advantages. When necessary, reforms occur as groups succeed (or fail) in having their ideas triumph over competing ideas. And the end result of this pluralist interaction is understood to reasonably approximate "the public interest." On a pluralist reading of politics, the system may have its flaws, but none are so fatal that the system itself is called into question. The pluralist understanding of American politics is a relatively comfortable one, for it allows students to retain the belief that the political process is open enough, and sufficiently fluid, to adapt to virtually any contingency without changing the basic power relations of the political economy. Moreover, pluralists define *politics* narrowly—as what *government* does—so that the model overlooks other arenas of power, among them corporate capital.

We contend that neither resignation nor pluralist incrementalism will help you make sense of the American political landscape. A third, more *critical* approach is warranted, one that challenges existing power relations. As currently practiced, politics speaks largely to the concerns of the already wealthy and influential. The political system does not offer the hope of a better life for most Americans, but rather leaves unquestioned a structure of power and privilege that endures regardless of which party controls Congress and the White House. In American political history, this kind of critical questioning often has been championed through the collective action of social movements, a point emphasized by many authors in this volume.

A CRITICAL VIEW? BUT I'M NOT A "RADICAL!"

Our anthology seeks to contribute to the ongoing discussion about the need to rethink and broaden the range of political and economic options facing the country. For many of you, this may be your first exposure to dissenting political orientations, which are marginalized, or rendered invisible, in the mass media and most college textbooks. Within political science, the field of American politics is awash in textbooks and readers that assume an orthodox pluralist perspective or provide a small sampling of differing viewpoints (though uniformly still heavily weighted toward the mainstream) on a series of issues of the day. Against this current, we adopt a critical stance, which challenges conventional self-congratulatory accounts of the American political system. We draw articles from the rich literature of radical scholarship, along with selected mainstream pieces, which add texture to the more critical interpretation.

While there are many ways to use our reader in introductory courses, we believe it may be most useful as an analytic complement to any of the myriad conventional textbooks on the market. It is through the competition of ideas that you will develop your capacity to think freely and critically. Our alternative perspective—which questions the very roots of political, economic, and ideological power in the United States—grows out of a positive belief that the current distribution of power and resources seriously impedes freedom, equality, and democracy, in the fullest sense of these terms. As proponents of real political participation and social justice, we critique the system in order to improve it when possible and change it when necessary.

With these thoughts in mind, we frankly hope that the ninth edition of *Voices of Dissent* will make you feel uncomfortable, shake you up a bit, and ultimately stimulate you to ask deep questions about the American political and economic system. Our goal in this sense is a radical one, for we ask that in your study of American politics you "go to the root causes," the very definition of the word *radical*. A nation is not a healthy democracy simply because its politicians, corporate leaders, and the mass media constantly say it is or because other forms of more authoritarian control have tumbled down worldwide. And the democratic ideal is not close to being realized if the people continually are asked to settle for a political system that is merely "pretty good," or if at election time, voters find themselves holding their noses and voting for the "lesser of two evils," or if the answers to our problems are assumed to lie in policies of a "moderate" direction. For, the legacy of Thomas Paine also reminds us:

> A thing moderately good is not so good as it ought to be. Moderation in temper is always a virtue; but moderation in principle is always a vice. (1792 letter)

A truly healthy polity can thrive only when ordinary people have meaningful control over the decisions that directly affect their lives. Ralph Nader refers to such control as "deep democracy," which facilitates people's best efforts to achieve social justice and self-reliance. Democracy in the fullest sense should provide the societal context within which people's "instinct for freedom" can flourish, as Noam Chomsky has written in *Language and Politics:*

> I would like to believe that people have an instinct for freedom, that they really want to control their own affairs. They don't want to be pushed around, ordered, oppressed, etc., and they want a chance to do things that make sense, like constructive work in a way that they control, or maybe control together with others. I don't know any way to prove this. It's really a hope about what human beings are like—a hope that if social structures change sufficiently, those aspects of human nature will be realized.

We share the hope of these two modern-day Thomas Paines, a hope that is animated by a spirit Paine would have appreciated. The realization of this hope—and the empowerment that would accompany it—is what informed, truly democratic citizenship is supposed to be about. We welcome feedback from students and teachers so we may learn whether this reader has helped you develop the analytic skills necessary to bring this hope closer to fruition.

PART I

STRUCTURE

If the foundation of your house is cracked and starting to weaken, it makes little sense to address the problem by applying a fresh coat of paint that would merely conceal the underlying reality of decay. In our view, the American political system is a lot like a house with an unstable foundation. Although the possibility of collapse certainly is not imminent, the structure of the American political economy, and the ideology that sustains it, is showing signs of severe stress. Moreover, this structure belies the cherished pluralist assumption (discussed in our Introduction) that our political system is one of open, fluid competition among groups. The inherent structural advantages, and disadvantages, accorded various groups significantly bias the political and economic system toward the interests of those who wield great power.

At the outset, we must acknowledge that the concept of *structure* is itself quite muddled. Mainstream political scientists often use the term *structure* in a shallow sense when discussing institutions of government, thus equating structure with the formal machinery of politics. This reduces structure to the institutional balance of power among the executive, legislative, and judicial branches of government. While these institutional interactions obviously merit our attention, the structure-as-institutions approach ignores the deeper structure of power within which institutions operate.

In Part I, we explore this deep structure of American politics, with three chapters focusing on the primary structural components of political economy, ideology, and state-constitutional arrangements. Taken as a whole, these components challenge you to consider whether tensions inherent in the relationship between democracy as a political concept and capitalism as a form of economic organization may in fact constitute a *problem* for the nation, not the solution to our problems, as we are socialized to believe. Are capitalism and a meaningful degree of democracy really compatible, or is capitalist democracy an oxymoron? Does our political culture enable us to consider carefully a wide range of alternative policy directions in the United States? If not, are we as "free" as we like to think? Why is the power of the state so closely connected to the private power of large economic entities? Does the U.S. Constitution strengthen this connection or provide ways to challenge it? To what extent have social movements been able to constrain and change this structure? These and many other troubling questions flow from a close reading of the selections in Part I.

Together, these three structural components form the basic context—the playing field—within which political institutions operate. Understanding this structure will help you make sense of what government institutions do and why problems so often seem to persist regardless of what policies are pursued in Washington. And it will help you come to grips with the pressures that impinge upon the foundations of American politics.

CHAPTER 1

Democracy and Political Economy

Politics is much more than government. Underlying this book of readings is the conviction that politics involves all relationships of power, whether they be economic, social, or cultural, as well as the interrelationship of government institutions. In their accounts of American politics, many political scientists focus on the Constitution and the three branches of government it established well over two hundred years ago. We include these traditional subjects but place them in a broader context that, in our view, will help you to better understand their actual workings and significance. Given our approach, it should not seem strange that we begin a book on American politics with what appears to be an economic focus.

Our first set of readings emphasizes the closely interwoven connection between democracy and political economy and the importance of understanding our capitalist system if we are to understand our politics. In the late eighteenth century, political economy was a commonsense way of thinking for Alexander Hamilton and other Founding Fathers, as we will see in Chapter 3. But in the twentieth century, the study of economics and politics became institutionally separated in American colleges and in academic discourse, more generally. In recent years this conceptual chasm has been challenged from a variety of perspectives. The selections in Chapter 1 represent a revival of a broader, integrated analysis of American politics that challenges us to think critically about the relationship of capitalism and democracy. All of the authors in this chapter should help you to see politics as much broader than what goes on in government and as powerfully shaped and constrained by the dynamics of our economy. When this is understood it is difficult to be satisfied with a definition of democracy confined to the presence of elections and formal rights.

1   *Frances Moore Lappé*

THE STRAIGHTJACKET OF THIN DEMOCRACY

Democracy—is there a principle more celebrated in the American political imagination? Generally speaking, Americans think they know exactly what democracy is and assume they live in the most vibrant democracy imaginable. But at the risk of sounding absurd, what IS democracy? In this opening article, internationally renowned author and economic development activist Frances Moore Lappé explores the dominant concept of democracy within U.S. political culture and argues that it is, at best, a "thin" version of democracy. Drawing on her 2007 book Getting a Grip: Clarity, Creativity and Courage in a World Gone Mad *(her 16th), Lappé outlines two major "pitfalls" and four "deeper dangers" of Thin Democracy, which focuses on elections and a market economy as the only relevant factors. Lappé wants us to ponder the "mental straightjacket" Thin Democracy has become in our consciousness, with its negative assumption about human nature and the resulting powerlessness such an assumption engenders. She wants us to return to the empowering potential of democracy's original promise. Indeed, she thinks the future of the world depends on a rejection of this Thin Democracy.*

Why are we as societies creating a world that we as individuals abhor?

This is the question that's propelled my life for decades now. It *is* really bewildering. We know that no human being actually gets up in the morning vowing, "Yeah, today I'm going to make sure another child dies needlessly of hunger," or muttering, "Sure, I'll do my part to heat the planet and obliterate entire species."

Yet each day over twenty-five thousand young children die of hunger and poverty, and roughly one hundred more species are forever gone. And the crises are not abating; they just keep

Source: Frances Moore Lappé, *Getting a Grip: Clarity, Creativity and Courage in a World Gone Mad,* Cambridge, MA: Small Planet Media, 2007, pp. 3–18.

whacking us: global climate chaos, terrorism, racial and religious divides, life-stunting poverty, pandemic disease . . . and now our own government's betrayal of constitutional principle.

Again . . . *why*?

I think for a lot of us, there is no real answer. Things just keep happening. We know *we're* not in control, and it seems like nobody is.

Sure, some people believe the problem is just us—human beings are just screwed up. Whether you call it original sin or simple selfishness, it's just who we are. Others are more targeted in assigning blame. For them, the root cause of our planet's crises is those *particular* people . . . the evil ones. Osama bin Laden, George W. Bush, Saddam Hussein, Dick Cheney. Still others believe we have no choice. We must conform to the now-proven economic laws of the global marketplace or suffer an even worse fate.

For all their many differences, the consequences of these views are similar. They leave us powerless. With no grip on how things got so bad, we have no clue as to where to start to correct them. So we're tempted to seize on any gesture of charity or any burst of protest—any random act of sanity. For a moment, at least, we can feel less useless in the face of the magnitude of the crises. Ultimately, though, acts of desperation contribute to our despair if we're unable to link our specific acts to real solutions.

Feeling powerless, we're robbed of energy and creativity, with hearts left open to fear and depression. No wonder the World Health Organization tells us depression is now the fourth leading cause of lost productive life worldwide—expected to jump to second place in fifteen years. Or that suicides worldwide now exceed homicides by 50 percent.

But what if . . . what if . . . together with our friends, family, and acquaintances, we could probe the root causes of the biggest threats to our planet. What if we were able to grasp something of the common origins of these threats and then identify powerful entry points to interrupt them? And more than that, what if we could then feel we are shifting the destructive underlying patterns towards health?

Now, that's power. Our power.

PEELING AWAY THE LAYERS

Over the years, I've come to sense that blaming the evil other stumbles on what logicians call an attribution error, the misplaced identification of cause. And it's a pretty serious error, for it releases us from asking really helpful questions: What is it about the current order we ourselves are creating that elicits so much pain and destruction? And peeling to the next layer: What are our own unexamined assumptions and beliefs that leave us feeling so powerless?

In the late nineteenth century, for example, Indians outnumbered the British civil servants ruling them by three hundred thousand to one. Yet Indians' widespread belief in their powerlessness continued until Gandhi and others re-framed reality, revealing the power that was theirs all along. In 1930, Indians declared independence and, sparked by Gandhi's example, thousands walked over two hundred miles to the sea to protest the British salt tax. Within seventeen years, the Indian people had ousted their colonial rulers.

It's pretty easy to see how mental concepts—ideas about reality—disempower others, whether it's belief in a ruler's "divine right" or a conviction about the inferiority of a lower caste. It's much harder to perceive the mental straightjackets we ourselves don every day.

Our future, though, may well depend on giving it a try.

In *The Anatomy of Human Destructiveness*, social philosopher Erich Fromm observes that all human beings carry within us "frames of orientation" through which we make sense of the world. They determine—often literally—what we can see, what we believe humans are made of, and therefore what we believe is possible. In other words, just about everything.

Now this trait might be just fine . . . *if* our frames are life-serving, but, Fromm warns, they aren't always. To stir us to realize the danger within this unique aspect of our humanness—our filtering through socially determined frames—Fromm came up with this mind-bending declaration: "It is man's humanity that makes him so inhuman."

Cultures live or die, Fromm is telling us, not by violence, or by chance, but ultimately by ideas. And unfortunately for our precious planet, much of the world appears locked within sets of ideas, including our ideas about democracy, that actually contribute to our "inhumanity"—whether that means inflicting or ignoring the suffering and loss mounting worldwide.

Please see what I call a *Spiral of Powerlessness*. It is the scary current of limiting beliefs and consequences in which I sense we're trapped.

Its premise is "lack."

There isn't enough of anything, neither enough "goods"—whether jobs or jungles—nor enough "goodness" because human beings are, well, pretty bad. These ideas have been drilled into us for centuries, as world religions have dwelt on human frailty, and Western political ideologies have picked up similar themes.

"*Homo homini lupus* [we are to one another as wolves]," wrote the influential seventeenth-century philosopher Thomas Hobbes. Repeating a Roman aphorism—long before we'd learned how social wolves really are—Hobbes reduced us to cutthroat animals.

> *Private interest . . . is the only immutable point in the human heart.*
>
> —ALEXIS DE TOCQUEVILLE,
> *DEMOCRACY IN AMERICA*, 1835

From that narrow premise, it follows that it's best to mistrust deliberative problem-solving, distrust even democratic government, and grasp for an infallible law—the market!—driven by the only thing we can really count on, human selfishness. From there, wealth concentrates and suffering increases, confirming the dreary premises that set the spiral in motion in the first place.

What this downward spiral tells me is that we humans now suffer from what linguists call "hypocognition," the lack of a critical concept we need to thrive. And it's no trivial gap! Swept into the vortex of this destructive spiral, we're missing an understanding of democracy vital and compelling enough to create the world we want.

Democracy? Why start there?

Democracy is *the* problem-solving device much of the world now embraces as the way to meet common needs and solve common problems. So if our definition of democracy is flawed, we are in big trouble.

ELECTIONS PLUS A MARKET . . . THAT'S DEMOCRACY?

To see what's missing, let's explore a bit more the dominant conception of reality in which our nation's culture, especially our view of democracy, is grounded. As just noted, its foundational premise is scarcity—there just isn't enough of *anything*—from love to jobs to parking spots. In such a world, only one type of person thrives. So if you peel away all the fluff, humans must have evolved as competitive materialists, elbowing one another out in a giant scramble over scarce stuff.

Absorbing this shabby caricature of humanity, we understandably see ourselves as incapable of making a success of democratic deliberation—assuming a selfish nature, we're sure somebody will always muck it up. Not to fret, though. We've been assured with ever-greater intensity since the 1980s that if real democracy—deliberating together to shape a common purpose and strategies—is suspect, there's a perfect solution: Just turn over our fate to an impersonal law that will settle things for us. Privatize and commoditize all that we can—from health care to prison management to schools—in order to take full advantage of what Ronald Reagan called "the magic of the market."

And government? It's something done *to* us or *for* us by taking "our money," so the less of it the better.

From these assumptions, it is easy to see why most Americans grow up absorbing the notion that democracy boils down to just two things—elected government and a market economy. Since in the United States we have both, there isn't much for us to do except show up at the polls and shop.

I like to call this stripped-down duo Thin Democracy because it is feeble.

We breathe in this definition like invisible ether, so it's easy to jump over an unpleasant fact: Real democracy and our peculiar variant of a market economy are based on opposing principles. Democracy derives from the Greek: *demos* (people) plus *kratos* (rule). Thus democracy depends on the wide dispersion of power so that each citizen has both a vote and a voice. But our particular market economy, driven by one rule—that is, highest return to shareholder and corporate chiefs—moves inexorably in the opposite direction. By continually returning wealth to wealth, a one-rule economy leads to an ever-increasing concentration of power.

LIZZIE'S LESSONS

In the early 1900s, Lizzie Maggie tried to warn us. Lizzie was a concerned Quaker, worried that one-rule capitalism would do us in. So she came up with a board game she hoped would entertain us but also serve as an object lesson: It may take all night, but the rules of the game eventually drive property into the hands of one player, ending the fun for everybody.

Well, Lizzie's idea got into the hands of Parker Brothers. They called it Monopoly, and the rest, as they say, is history—history that, in this case, reveals just what Maggie was trying to tell us about one-rule economics. Just five companies sell well over half of all toys in America. More generally, in 1955, sales of the top five hundred corporations equaled one-third of the U.S. gross domestic product. They now account for two-thirds.

As corporate wealth concentrates, so does private: Here in the United States, between 1979 and 2001, family income among the wealthiest 5 percent leapt by 81 percent, but families in the bottom 20 percent saw virtually no gain. The gap separating America's average CEO's compensation and average worker's pay has widened tenfold in a generation, so today the CEO earns as much by lunchtime on the first day of the year as a minimum wage worker earns the entire year.

In the United States over the last four years, the share of economic growth going to corporate profits increased by over two-thirds, while the share rewarding workers fell, even as their productivity continued to rise. Today America's biggest employer, Wal-Mart, pays its workers in inflation-adjusted dollars only 40 percent as much as the biggest employer in 1969, GM, paid its employees—not to mention the workers' benefits now stripped away.

For the first time, the four hundred richest Americans are all billionaires, with combined wealth of $1.25 trillion, roughly comparable to the total annual income of half the world's people. Worldwide, the number of billionaires is exploding. Growing eight times faster than the global economy, it is now at 946 people with a total wealth almost 40 percent greater than the entire GDP of China.

So we didn't learn from Lizzie. We didn't get it—that to keep the game going, we citizens have to devise rules to ensure that wealth continually circulates. Otherwise, it all ends up in one player's pile. (In my household, it was usually my brother's!)

Yet under the spell of one-rule economics, most economists ignore this truth, as well as new jaw-dropping evidence that markets, by themselves, don't create livable societies.

Worldwide, during the 1990s, every one hundred dollars in economic growth reduced the poverty of the world's billion poorest people by just *sixty pennies*.

Denial runs so deep, though, that the pro-corporate British journal, *The Economist*, apparently with a straight face, can describe inequality deepening worldwide as a "snag" in the system. And well-meaning academics, with Columbia University's Jeffrey Sachs in the lead, can rally us to end global poverty by exporting our assumed-to-be successful economic model to them.

So we remain blind to Thin Democracy's pitfalls.

THIN DEMOCRACY'S PITFALLS

Death to Open Markets

Despite the myth of competitive capitalism, writes economist James Galbraith, "[C]orporations exist to control markets and often to replace them." Two companies have succeeded in controlling roughly three-fourths of the global grain trade; one, Monsanto, accounts for 88 percent of the area planted worldwide with genetically modified seed and/or seed with biotech traits. Six corporations control most global media, from publishing to movies, and five control almost two-thirds of U.S. gasoline sales.

In our one-rule economy, concentrated economic power is inevitable, destroying the very open, competitive market that was the rationale for the whole set-up to begin with. Wasn't it? Competitive, fair markets cannot be sustained, it turns out, outside of a genuinely democratic polity.

Just as with the protection of civil liberties, open markets depend on *us*, on our creating and continually monitoring rules that keep them open. Corporations want the opposite; they seek control over markets to ensure highest returns—not because they're run by bad people, but because the rules we've set up encourage them to.

History bears out this truth: it was only when Americans did step up to the plate, especially in the period from 1933 to 1945, and created fairness rules—including the right of workers to organize, Social Security, and a legal minimum wage—that our country experienced a dramatic narrowing of the gap between most of us and a tiny minority at the top. The approach fostered broad-based economic prosperity for decades: Our median family income grew four times faster between 1947 and 1973 than it has since—as America has forsaken Lizzie's commonsense insight.

Unfortunately, Thin Democracy's pitfalls don't stop here.

Warping of Politics

Concentrated economic power, flowing inevitably from a one-rule economy, ends up infecting and warping our political system, as well. Sixty-one lobbyists now walk the corridors of power in Washington, D.C., for every one person we citizens have elected to represent our interests there.

> *[T]he liberty of a democracy is not safe if the people tolerate the growth of private power to the point where it becomes stronger than their democratic state itself. That, in its essence, is fascism . . .*
>
> —FRANKLIN DELANO ROOSEVELT, 1938

When citizens are outnumbered sixty-one to one, private power supersedes public power—as FDR warned us seven decades ago. Little wonder! To pick just a few frightening examples:

- for almost six years after 9/11, the chemical industry lobby was able to resist measures needed to secure fifteen thousand chemical plants against attack.
- while five thousand Americans die annually from food-borne illnesses, the food industry is able to block mandatory recalls.
- ex-oil lobbyist Philip Cooney was so tight with the Bush White House that he edited official reports to downplay climate change.
- pharmaceutical lobbyists helped craft a healthcare law that forbids Medicare to negotiate drug prices—while we pay double what Europeans do for identical drugs.

So more and more Americans feel their democracy has been stolen, and they know by whom. Ninety percent of us agree that corporations have too much influence in Washington.

DEEPER DANGERS

More than unworkable, Thin Democracy is dangerous. The power it gives corporations to put their own short-term gain ahead of our survival is only one danger.

The Fragility of Centralized Power

Contrary to lessons drummed into us, concentrated power is often not resilient, efficient, or smart. The Inca and the Aztecs, huge civilizations, fell to conquistadors in no time, while the leaderless, decentralized Apaches fended off harsh attacks for two centuries. Concentrated power often isolates itself and thus fails to learn. Think only of the, "I'm in the decider" bunker stance of the Bush White House that led the U.S. into Iraq, one of our country's most horrific foreign policy blunders.

Missing Problem Solvers

The flipside is that the centralized power of Thin Democracy leaves most of us feeling powerless, robbing the planet of just the problem solvers we most need. It encourages us to look to the "market" or to CEOs or to government higher-ups for answers, but our planet's problems are too complex, pervasive, and interconnected to be addressed from the top down. Solutions depend on the insights, experience, and ingenuity of people most affected—all thwarted when citizens are cut out and manipulated, and when decisions get made secretly by the few.

Put slightly differently, solutions require in-the-moment inventiveness and widespread behavior changes, and both depend on the engagement and "buy-in" of citizens. So Thin Democracy undermines precisely the broad-based commitment our world so desperately needs.

Misaligned with Our Nature

Thin Democracy can't create healthy societies because it is misaligned with human nature in two ways. Denying our rich complexity, it fails to tap the best in us and fails to protect us from the worst.

By "best" I mean several innate needs and capacities. They include our needs to connect with others, for basic fairness, and for efficacy,

as well as the need to feel that our lives matter, which for many people means contributing to something grander than our own survival.

Forcing us to buy these needs, Thin Democracy fuels paralyzing despair and alienation.

Ironically, Thin Democracy doesn't register our really negative potential, either. Let me be clear. I don't mean the capacity of a tiny minority of us; I mean the vast majority. The Holocaust doesn't prove what a crazed dictator and some sadistic guards will do. Actually, it proves the depravity most normal people will express, given the "right" conditions.

To bring home this unhappy truth, British historian Christopher Browning reports that as late as March, 1942, the vast majority—75 to 80 percent—of all victims of the Holocaust were still alive, but "a mere eleven months later" most were dead.

These murders happened, Browning says, because "ordinary" people became killers. He tells, for example, of Reserve Battalion 101—about five hundred men from Hamburg, Germany, many of whom were middle-aged reservists drafted in the fall of 1939. From working and lower middle-classes, these men with no military police experience were sent to Poland on a bloody mission—the total extermination of Jews in Poland's many remote hamlets.

Within four months, they had shot to death, at point-blank range, at least thirty-eight thousand Jews and had another forty-five thousand deported to the concentration camp at Treblinka.

"Though almost all of them—at least initially—were horrified and disgusted," over time, social modeling processes took their toll, as did guilt-induced persuasion by buddies who did the killing, until up to 90 percent of the men in Battalion 101 were involved in the shootings.

I first learned about Battalion 101 from Philip Zimbardo. You might recognize the name. Zimbardo is the professor who organized the infamous "prison experiment" at Stanford in 1971. He put young people who'd "tested normal" into a mock prison setting where they were divided into prisoners and guards, dressed for their roles, and told the experiment would last two weeks.

But on the sixth day, Zimbardo abruptly halted the experiment. He had to. Using some techniques eerily similar to those in Abu Ghraib prison over three decades later, the "guards" had begun brutalizing their "prisoners" causing severe emotional breakdown. Professor Zimbardo has since acknowledged that one reason he stopped the experiment is that his girlfriend told him he himself had begun behaving like a warden—"more concerned," as he put it later, "about the security of 'my prison' than the needs of the young men entrusted to my care . . ."

In the last one hundred years, humans have killed roughly forty million other humans not in war, as we normally define it, but in massive assaults on civilians, from the fifteen million lost in the Russian Gulag to almost one million in Rwanda. Whether we're talking about a psychologist's carefully designed experiment or the current genocide in Darfur, the inescapable proof is in: Decent people do evil things under the "right conditions."

And what is one condition certain to bring forth brutality? Extreme power imbalances that arise inevitably in a range of social orders. One of these is Thin Democracy.

Failure to Bring Meaning

Finally, Thin Democracy is dangerously vulnerable because its materialistic premise can't satisfy our higher selves' yearning for transcendent meaning.

Thin Democracy's narrow, insulting assumptions about human nature cannot sustain dedication and sacrifice. Many U.S. soldiers now risk their lives in war, believing they're serving a high calling. But the built-in logic of one-rule economics mocks their idealism. Since 9/11, thousands of American soldiers have made the ultimate sacrifice in Iraq, while executives of U.S. armament corporations have made a killing, doubling their own compensation.

At the same time, Thin Democracy's demeaning materialism and its concentrated wealth help to swell the numbers of excluded people who feel humiliated and angry. Understandably, these feelings open some hearts to extremist, violent ideologies—both religious and secular—that claim high moral ground and offer adherents everlasting glory.

"My grandmother's gone to heaven because she shot the Israelis," explained six-year-old Israa, as she played beneath a photo of seventy-year-old Fatima Najar, who blew herself up in Gaza in 2006. Young men have long seemed most susceptible to violent ideologies, but a sixty-five-year-old in Gaza told the British *Observer*, "I know at least twenty of us [elder women] who want to put on the [suicide bomber's] belt." They've "found a use for themselves," she said.

How deep runs our need to feel useful, a need unmet for so many people in today's world. Ultimately, Thin Democracy can't hold a candle to the fanatics' uplifting, absolutist visions—right or left. In all, Thin Democracy gives democracy itself a bad name.

DISCUSSION QUESTIONS

1. Lappé describes our dominant mental image of democracy as "thin." Explain in what sense democracy, as we tend to think of it, can be viewed as "thin." Discuss how we might make democracy "thicker," or stronger.
2. According to Lappé's analysis, the popular board game Monopoly explains a lot about what is wrong with American democracy. How can economic assumptions and economic power inhibit democracy as a *political* ideal?

2 Susan George

A SHORT HISTORY OF NEO-LIBERALISM

For more than 30 years, discussion of politics and public policy in the U.S. and other democratic capitalist countries has been dominated by the ideology of neo-liberalism. As political economist Susan George explains, neo-liberalism advocates letting "the market" decide crucial social and political questions. Government social protections are to be slashed and corporations are to be empowered through greater freedom from regulation and taxation. In this article, which originated as a 1999 lecture in Thailand, George provides a brief history of neo-liberalism, noting that it represents a departure from the Keynesian and social democratic policy approaches that were dominant for several decades after World War II. One of George's key points is that neo-liberalism is not a "natural" or foreordained policy approach. It is a political and ideological perspective that has been promoted by a well-funded network of conservative think tanks, research institutes, and publications. Here in the U.S. the pro-corporate structures of neo-liberalism profoundly affect the policy approaches of both Republicans and Democrats, certainly including the Obama administration. For George, understanding neo-liberalism demands that we recognize clearly its winners and losers and its view of democracy as an "encumbrance"—resulting in nothing short of the "demolition of society."

The conference organizers have asked me for a brief history of neo-liberalism which they title "Twenty Years of Elite Economics." I'm sorry to tell you that in order to make any sense, I have to start even further back, some 50 years ago, just after the end of World War II.

In 1945 or 1950, if you had seriously proposed any of the ideas and policies in today's standard neo-liberal toolkit, you would have been laughed off the stage at or sent off to the insane asylum. At least in the Western countries, at that time, everyone was a Keynesian, a social democrat or a social-Christian democrat or some shade of Marxist. The idea that the market should be allowed to make major social and political decisions; the idea that the State should voluntarily reduce its role in the economy, or that corporations should be given total freedom, that trade unions should

Source: Lecture at the Conference on Economic Sovereignty in a Globalizing World, Bangkok, Thailand, March 24–26, 1999.

be curbed and citizens given much less rather than more social protection—such ideas were utterly foreign to the spirit of the time. Even if someone actually agreed with these ideas, he or she would have hesitated to take such a position in public and would have had a hard time finding an audience.

However incredible it may sound today, particularly to the younger members of the audience, the IMF and the World Bank were seen as progressive institutions. They were sometimes called Keynes's twins because they were the brainchildren of Keynes and Harry Dexter White, one of Franklin Roosevelt's closest advisors. When these institutions were created at Bretton Woods in 1944, their mandate was to help prevent future conflicts by lending for reconstruction and development and by smoothing out temporary balance of payments problems. They had no control over individual government's economic decisions nor did their mandate include a license to intervene in national policy.

In the Western nations, the Welfare State and the New Deal had got underway in the 1930s but their spread had been interrupted by the war. The first order of business in the post-war world was to put them back in place. The other major item on the agenda was to get world trade moving— this was accomplished through the Marshall Plan which established Europe once again as the major trading partner for the U.S., the most powerful economy in the world. And it was at this time that the strong winds of decolonization also began to blow, whether freedom was obtained by grant as in India or through armed struggle as in Kenya, Vietnam and other nations.

On the whole, the world had signed on for an extremely progressive agenda. The great scholar Karl Polanyi published his masterwork, *The Great Transformation* in 1944, a fierce critique of nineteenth-century industrial, market-based society. Over 50 years ago Polanyi made this amazingly prophetic and modern statement: "To allow the market mechanism to be sole director of the fate of human beings and their natural environment . . . would result in the demolition of society." However, Polanyi was convinced that such a demolition could no longer happen in the post-war world because, as he said, "Within the nations we are witnessing a development under which the economic system ceases to lay down the law to society and the primacy of society over that system is secured."

Alas, Polanyi's optimism was misplaced—the whole point of neo-liberalism is that the market mechanism should be allowed to direct the fate of human beings. The economy should dictate its rules to society, not the other way around. And just as Polanyi foresaw, this doctrine is leading us directly towards the "demolition of society."

So what happened? Why have we reached this point half a century after the end of the Second World War? Or, as the organizers ask, "Why are we having this conference right now?" The short answer is "Because of the series of recent financial crises, especially in Asia". But this begs the question—the question they are really asking is "How did neo-liberalism ever emerge from its ultra-minoritarian ghetto to become the dominant doctrine in the world today?" Why can the IMF and the Bank intervene at will and force countries to participate in the world economy on basically unfavorable terms? Why is the Welfare State under threat in all the countries where it was established? Why is the environment on the edge of collapse and why are there so many poor people in both the rich and the poor countries at a time when there has never existed such great wealth? Those are the questions that need to be answered from an historical perspective.

As I've argued in detail in the U.S. quarterly journal *Dissent*, one explanation for this triumph of neo-liberalism and the economic, political, social and ecological disasters that go with it is that neo-liberals have bought and paid for their own vicious and regressive "Great Transformation". They have understood, as progressives have not, that ideas have consequences. Starting from a tiny embryo at the University of Chicago with the philosopher-economist Friedrich von Hayek and his students like Milton Friedman at its nucleus, the neo-liberals and their funders have created a huge international network of foundations, institutes, research centers, publications, scholars, writers and public relations hacks to develop, package and push their ideas and doctrine relentlessly.

They have built this highly efficient ideological cadre because they understand what the Italian Marxist thinker Antonio Gramsci was talking about when he developed the concept of cultural hegemony. If you can occupy peoples' heads, their hearts and their hands will follow. I do not have time to give you details here, but believe me, the ideological and promotional work of the right has been absolutely brilliant. They have spent hundreds of millions of dollars, but the result has been worth every penny to them because they have made neo-liberalism seem as if it were the natural and normal condition of humankind. No matter how many disasters of all kinds the neo-liberal system has visibly created, no matter what financial crises it may engender, no matter how many losers and outcasts it may create, it is still made to seem inevitable, like an act of God, the only possible economic and social order available to us.

Let me stress how important it is to understand that this vast neo-liberal experiment we are all being forced to live under has been created by people with a purpose. Once you grasp this, once you understand that neo-liberalism is not a force like gravity but a totally artificial construct, you can also understand that what some people have created, other people can change. But they cannot change it without recognizing the importance of ideas. I'm all for grassroots projects, but I also warn that these will collapse if the overall ideological climate is hostile to their goals.

So, from a small, unpopular sect with virtually no influence, neo-liberalism has become the major world religion with its dogmatic doctrine, its priesthood, its law-giving institutions and perhaps most important of all, its hell for heathen and sinners who dare to contest the revealed truth. Oskar Lafontaine, the ex-German Finance Minister whom the *Financial Times* called an "unreconstructed Keynesian" has just

been consigned to that hell because he dared to propose higher taxes on corporations and tax cuts for ordinary and less well-off families.

Having set the ideological stage and the context, now let me fast-forward so that we are back in the twenty year time frame. That means 1979, the year Margaret Thatcher came to power and undertook the neo-liberal revolution in Britain. The Iron Lady was herself a disciple of Friedrich von Hayek; she was a social Darwinist and had no qualms about expressing her convictions. She was well known for justifying her program with the single word TINA, short for There Is No Alternative. The central value of Thatcher's doctrine and of neo-liberalism itself is the notion of competition—competition between nations, regions, firms and of course between individuals. Competition is central because it separates the sheep from the goats, the men from the boys, the fit from the unfit. It is supposed to allocate all resources, whether physical, natural, human or financial with the greatest possible efficiency.

In sharp contrast, the great Chinese philosopher Lao Tzu ended his *Tao-te Ching* with these words: "Above all, do not compete." The only actors in the neo-liberal world who seem to have taken his advice are the largest actors of all, the Transnational Corporations. The principle of competition scarcely applies to them; they prefer to practice what we could call Alliance Capitalism. It is no accident that, depending on the year, two-thirds to three-quarters of all the money labeled "Foreign Direct Investment" is not devoted to new, job-creating investment but to Mergers and Acquisitions which almost invariably result in job losses.

Because competition is always a virtue, its results cannot be bad. For the neo-liberal, the market is so wise and so good that like God, the Invisible Hand can bring good out of apparent evil. Thus Thatcher once said in a speech, "It is our job to glory in inequality and see that talents and abilities are given vent and expression for the benefit of us all." In other words, don't worry about those who might be left behind in the competitive struggle. People are unequal by nature, but this is good because the contributions of the well-born, the best-educated, the toughest, will eventually benefit everyone. Nothing in particular is owed to the weak, the poorly educated, what happens to them is their own fault, never the fault of society. If the competitive system is "given vent" as Margaret says, society will be the better for it. Unfortunately, the history of the past twenty years teaches us that exactly the opposite is the case.

In pre-Thatcher Britain, about one person in ten was classed as living below the poverty line, not a brilliant result but honorable as nations go and a lot better than in the pre-War period. Now one person in four, and one child in three is officially poor. This is the meaning of survival of the fittest: people who cannot heat their houses in winter, who must put a coin in the meter before they can have electricity or water, who do not own a warm waterproof coat, etc. I am taking these examples from the 1996 report of the British Child Poverty Action Group. I will illustrate the result of the Thatcher-Major "tax reforms" with a single example: During the 1980s, 1 percent of taxpayers received 29 percent of all the tax reduction benefits, such that a single person earning half the average salary found his or her taxes had gone up by 7 percent, whereas a single person earning 10 times the average salary got a reduction of 21 percent.

Another implication of competition as the central value of neo-liberalism is that the public sector must be brutally downsized because it does not and cannot obey the basic law of competing for profits or for market share. Privatization is one of the major economic transformations of the past twenty years. The trend began in Britain and has spread throughout the world.

Let me start by asking why capitalist countries, particularly in Europe, had public services to begin with, and why many still do. In reality, nearly all public services constitute what economists call "natural monopolies." A natural monopoly exists when the minimum size to guarantee maximum economic efficiency is equal to the actual size of the market. In other words, a company has to be a certain size to realize economies of scale and thus provide the best possible service at the lowest possible cost to the consumer. Public services also require very large investment outlays at the beginning—like railroad tracks or power grids—which does not encourage competition either. That's why public monopolies were the obvious optimum solution. But neo-liberals define anything public as ipso facto "inefficient".

So what happens when a natural monopoly is privatized? Quite normally and naturally, the new capitalist owners tend to impose monopoly prices on the public, while richly remunerating themselves. Classical economists call this outcome "structural market failure" because prices are higher than they ought to be and service to the consumer is not necessarily good. In order to prevent structural market failures, up to the mid-1980s, the capitalist countries of Europe almost universally entrusted the post office, telecoms, electricity, gas, railways, metros, air transport and usually other services like water, rubbish collection, etc. to state-owned monopolies. The U.S.A. is the big exception, perhaps because it is too huge geographically to favor natural monopolies.

In any event, Margaret Thatcher set out to change all that. As an added bonus, she could also use privatization to break the power of the trade unions. By destroying the public sector where unions were strongest, she was able to weaken them drastically. Thus between 1979 and 1994, the number of jobs in the public sector in Britain was reduced from over 7 million to 5 million, a drop of 29 percent. Virtually all the jobs eliminated were unionized jobs. Since private sector employment was stagnant during those fifteen years, the overall reduction in the number of British jobs came to 1.7 million, a drop of 7 percent compared to 1979. To neo-liberals, fewer workers is always better than more because workers impinge on shareholder value.

As for other effects of privatization, they were predictable and predicted. The managers of the newly privatized enterprises, often exactly the same people as before, doubled or tripled their own salaries. The government used taxpayer money to wipe out debts and recapitalize firms before putting them on the market—for example, the water authority got 5 billion pounds of debt relief plus 1.6 billion pounds called the "green dowry" to make the bride more attractive to prospective buyers. A lot of Public Relations fuss was made about how small stockholders would have a stake in these companies—and in fact 9 million Brits did buy shares—but half of them invested less than a thousand pounds and most of them sold their shares rather quickly, as soon as they could cash in on the instant profits.

From the results, one can easily see that the whole point of privatization is neither economic efficiency nor improved services to the consumer but simply to transfer wealth from the public purse—which could redistribute it to even out social inequalities—to private hands. In Britain and elsewhere, the overwhelming majority of privatized company shares are now in the hands of financial institutions and very large investors. The employees of British Telecom bought only 1 percent of the shares, those of British Aerospace 1.3 percent, etc. Prior to Ms. Thatcher's onslaught, a lot of the public sector in Britain was profitable. Consequently, in 1984, public companies contributed over 7 billion pounds to the treasury. All that money is now going to private shareholders. Service in the privatized industries is now often disastrous—the *Financial Times* reported an invasion of rats in the Yorkshire Water system and anyone who has survived taking Thames trains in Britain deserves a medal.

Exactly the same mechanisms have been at work throughout the world. In Britain, the Adam Smith Institute was the intellectual partner for creating the privatization ideology. USAID and the World Bank have also used Adam Smith experts and have pushed the privatization doctrine in the South. By 1991 the Bank had already made 114 loans to speed the process, and every year its Global Development Finance report lists hundreds of privatizations carried out in the Bank's borrowing countries.

I submit that we should stop talking about privatization and use words that tell the truth: we are talking about alienation and surrender of the product of decades of work by thousands of people to a tiny minority of large investors. This is one of the greatest hold-ups of ours or any generation.

Another structural feature of neo-liberalism consists in remunerating capital to the detriment of labor and thus moving wealth from the bottom of society to the top. If you are, roughly, in the top 20 percent of the income scale, you are likely to gain something from neo-liberalism and the higher you are up the ladder, the more you gain. Conversely, the bottom 80 percent all lose and the lower they are to begin with, the more they lose proportionally.

Lest you thought I had forgotten Ronald Reagan, let me illustrate this point with the observations of Kevin Phillips, a Republican analyst and former aide to President Nixon, who published a book in 1990 called *The Politics of Rich and Poor*. He charted the way Reagan's neo-liberal doctrine and policies had changed American income distribution between 1977 and 1988. These policies were largely elaborated by the conservative Heritage Foundation, the principal think-tank of the Reagan administration and still an important force in American politics. Over the decade of the 1980s, the top 10 percent of American families increased their average family income by 16 percent, the top 5 percent increased theirs by 23 percent, but the extremely lucky top 1 percent of American families could thank Reagan for a 50 percent increase. Their revenues went from an affluent $270,000 to a heady $405,000. As for poorer Americans, the bottom 80 percent all lost something; true to the rule, the lower they were on the scale, the more they lost. The bottom 10 percent of Americans reached the nadir: according to Phillips's figures, they lost 15 percent of their already meager incomes: from an already rock-bottom average of $4,113 annually, they dropped to an inhuman $3,504. In 1977, the top 1 percent of American families had average incomes 65 times as great as those of the bottom 10 percent. A decade later, the top 1 percent was 115 times as well off as the bottom decile.

America is one of the most unequal societies on earth, but virtually all countries have seen inequalities increase over the past twenty years because of neo-liberal policies. UNCTAD published some damning evidence to this effect in its 1997 Trade and Development Report based on some 2600 separate studies of income inequalities, impoverishment and the hollowing out of the middle classes. The UNCTAD team documents these trends in dozens of widely differing societies, including China, Russia and the other former Socialist countries.

There is nothing mysterious about this trend towards greater inequality. Policies are specifically designed to give the already rich more disposable income, particularly through tax cuts and by pushing down wages. The theory and ideological justification for such measures is that higher incomes for the rich and higher profits will lead to more investment, better allocation of resources and therefore more jobs and welfare for everyone. In reality, as was perfectly predictable, moving money up the economic ladder has led to stock market bubbles, untold paper wealth for the few, and the kind of financial crises we shall be hearing a lot about in the course of this conference. If income is redistributed towards the bottom 80 percent of society, it will be used for consumption and consequently benefit employment. If wealth is redistributed towards the top, where people already have most of the things they need, it will go not into the local or national economy but to international stockmarkets.

As you are all aware, the same policies have been carried out throughout the South and East under the guise of structural adjustment, which is merely another name for neo-liberalism. I've used Thatcher and Reagan to illustrate the policies at the national level. At the international level, neo-liberals have concentrated all their efforts on three fundamental points:

- free trade in goods and services
- free circulation of capital
- freedom of investment

Over the past twenty years, the IMF has been strengthened enormously. Thanks to the debt crisis and the mechanism of conditionality, it has moved from balance of payments support to being quasi-universal dictator of so-called "sound" economic policies, meaning of course neo-liberal ones. The World Trade Organization was finally put in place in January 1995 after long and laborious negotiations, often rammed through parliaments which had little idea what they were ratifying. Thankfully, the most recent effort to make binding and universal neo-liberal rules, the Multilateral Agreement on Investment, has failed, at least temporarily. It would have given all rights to corporations, all obligations to governments and no rights at all to citizens.

The common denominator of these institutions is their lack of transparency and democratic accountability. This is the essence of neo-liberalism. It claims that the economy should dictate its rules to society, not the other way around. Democracy is an encumbrance, neo-liberalism is designed for winners, not for voters who, necessarily encompass the categories of both winners and losers.

I'd like to conclude by asking you to take very seriously indeed the neo-liberal definition of the loser, to whom nothing in particular is owed. Anyone can be ejected from the system at any time—because of illness, age, pregnancy, perceived failure, or simply because economic circumstances and the relentless transfer of wealth from top to bottom demand it. Shareholder value is all. Recently the *International Herald Tribune* reported that foreign investors are "snapping up" Thai and Korean companies and banks. Not surprisingly, these purchases are expected to result in "heavy layoffs."

In other words, the results of years of work by thousands of Thais and Koreans is being transferred into foreign corporate hands. Many of those who labored to create that wealth have already been, or soon will be left on the pavement. Under the principles of competition and maximizing shareholder value, such behavior is seen not as criminally unjust but as normal and indeed virtuous.

I submit that neo-liberalism has changed the fundamental nature of politics. Politics used to be primarily about who ruled whom and who got what share of the pie. Aspects of both these central questions remain, of course, but the great new central question of politics is, in my view, "Who has a right to live and who does not." Radical exclusion is now the order of the day, I mean this deadly seriously.

I've given you rather a lot of bad news because the history of the past twenty years is full of it. But I don't want to end on such a depressing and pessimistic note. A lot is already happening to counter these life-threatening trends and there is enormous scope for further action.

This conference is going to help define much of that action which I believe must include an ideological offensive. It's time we set the agenda instead of letting the Masters of the Universe set it at Davos. I hope funders may also understand that they should not be funding just projects but also ideas. We can't count on the neo-liberals to do it, so we need to design workable and equitable international taxation systems, including a Tobin Tax on all monetary and financial market transactions and taxes on Transnational Corporation sales on a pro-rata basis. I expect we will go into detail on such questions in the workshops here. The proceeds of an international tax system should go to closing the North-South gap and to redistribution to all the people who have been robbed over the past twenty years.

Let me repeat what I said earlier: neo-liberalism is not the natural human condition, it is not supernatural, it can be challenged and replaced because its own failures will require this. We have to be ready with replacement policies which restore power to communities and democratic states while working to institute democracy, the rule of law and fair distribution at the international level. Business and the market have their place, but this place cannot occupy the entire sphere of human existence.

Further good news is that there is plenty of money sloshing around out there and a tiny fraction, a ridiculous, infinitesimal proportion of it would be enough to provide a decent life to every person on earth, to supply universal health and education, to clean up the environment and prevent further destruction to the planet, to close the North-South gap—at least according to the UNDP which calls for a paltry $40 billion a year. That, frankly, is peanuts.

Finally, please remember that neo-liberalism may be insatiable but it is not invulnerable. A coalition of international activists only yesterday obliged them to abandon, at least temporarily, their project to liberalize all investment through the MAI. The surprise victory of its opponents infuriated the supporters of corporate rule and demonstrates that well–organized network guerillas can win battles. Now we have to regroup our forces and keep at them so that they cannot transfer the MAI to the WTO.

Look at it this way. We have the numbers on our side, because there are far more losers than winners in the neo-liberal game. We have the ideas, whereas theirs are finally coming into question because of repeated crisis. What we lack, so far, is the organization and the unity which in this age of advanced technology we can overcome. The threat is clearly transnational so the response must also be transnational. Solidarity no longer means aid, or not just aid, but finding the hidden synergies in each other's struggles so that our numerical force and the power of our ideas become overwhelming. I'm convinced this conference will contribute mightily to this goal and I thank you all for your kind attention.

DISCUSSION QUESTIONS

1. According to George, in what ways does neo-liberalism amount to a kind of "elite economics"?
2. George says that "neo-liberalism is not the natural human condition." What is her explanation for how and why neo-liberal ideas became influential? In what ways might neo-liberalism be politically vulnerable?

3 *Dan Clawson, Alan Neustadtl, and Mark Weller*

WHY DOES THE AIR STINK?
Corporate Power and Public Policy

How is economic power translated into political influence? Sociologists Dan Clawson, Alan Neustadtl, and Mark Weller explore this fundamental question through their examination of corporate political action committees (PACs) on public policy. Uniquely drawing on interviews with PAC directors, they demonstrate how campaign contributions win "access" to members of Congress, resulting in loopholes and regulatory rules favorable to business. Clawson, Neustadtl, and Weller base their analysis of corporate PACs on a "field theory of power." Focus on this concept and consider its usefulness in understanding business "hegemony" in our political system. In a concluding section, the authors itemize the enormous public impact of private corporate power by providing a detailed list of decisions made by business companies in the United States. One implication of this analysis is that even if PACs were banned, business decisions would have a greater impact on our lives than most government decisions have, barring significant change in our economic system. While the specific example they use—debates in the 1990s over revision of the Clean Air Act—is dated, the authors' core points about business power are relevant and useful as President Barack Obama nears the end of his first term.

Everybody wants clean air. Who could oppose it? "I spent seven years of my life trying to stop the Clean Air Act," explained the vice president of a major corporation that is a heavy-duty polluter. Nonetheless, he was perfectly willing to make campaign contributions to members who voted for the Act:

How a person votes on the final piece of legislation often is not representative of what

they have done. Somebody will do a lot of things during the process. How many guys voted against the Clean Air Act? But during the process some of them were very sympathetic to some of our concerns.

In the world of Congress and political action committees things are not always what they seem. Members of Congress all want to vote for clean

Source: Dan Clawson, Alan Neustadtl, and Mark Weller, *Dollars and Votes: How Business Campaign Contributions Subvert Democracy*, Philadelphia: Temple University Press, 1998, pp. 6–12, 21–26, and 188–191.

air, but they also want to get campaign contributions from corporations, and they want to pass a law that business will accept as "reasonable." The compromise solution is to gut the bill by crafting dozens of loopholes. These are inserted in private meetings or in subcommittee hearings that don't get much (if any) attention in the press. Then the public vote on the final bill can be nearly unanimous. Members of Congress can reassure their constituents and their corporate contributors: constituents, that they voted for the final bill; corporations, that they helped weaken it in private. Clean air, and especially the Clean Air Act of 1990, can serve as an introduction to the kind of process we try to expose.

The public strongly supports clean air, and is unimpressed when corporate officials and apologists trot out their normal arguments—"corporations are already doing all they reasonably can to improve environmental quality," "we need to balance the costs against the benefits," "people will lose their jobs if we make controls any stricter." The original Clean Air Act was passed in 1970, revised in 1977, and not revised again until 1990. Although the initial goal was to have us breathing clean air by 1975, the deadline has been repeatedly extended—and the 1990 legislation provides a new set of deadlines to be reached sometime in the distant future.

Corporations control the production process unless the government specifically intervenes. Therefore, any delay in government action leaves corporations free to do as they choose; business often prefers a weak, ineffective, and unenforceable law. The laws have not only been slow to come, but corporations have also fought to delay or subvert implementation. The 1970 law ordered the Environmental Protection Agency (EPA) to regulate the hundreds of poisonous chemicals that are emitted by corporations, but, as William Greider notes, "In twenty years of stalling, dodging, and fighting off court orders, the EPA has managed to issue regulatory standards for a total of seven toxics."

Corporations have done exceptionally well politically, given the problem they face: The

interests of business are diametrically opposed to those of the public. Clean air laws and amendments have been few and far between, enforcement is ineffective, and the penalties minimal. On the one hand, corporations *have* had to pay billions for clean-ups; on the other hand, the costs to date are a small fraction of what would be needed to actually clean up the environment.

This corporate struggle for the right to pollute takes place on many fronts. The most visible is public relations: the Chemical Manufacturers Association took out a two-page Earth Day ad in the *Washington Post* to demonstrate its concern; coincidentally, the names of many of the corporate signers of this ad appear on the EPA's list of high-risk producers. Another front is expert studies that delay action while more information is gathered. The federally funded National Acid Precipitation Assessment Program took ten years and $600 million to figure out whether acid rain was in fact a problem. Both business and the Reagan administration argued that nothing should be done until the study was completed. Ultimately, the study was discredited: The "summary of findings" minimized the impact of acid rain, even though this did not accurately represent the expert research in the report. But the key site of struggle was Congress. For years, corporations successfully defeated legislation. In 1987 utility companies were offered a compromise bill on acid rain, but they "were very adamant that they had beat the thing since 1981 and they could always beat it," according to Representative Edward Madigan (Republican-Illinois). The utilities beat back all efforts at reform through the 1980s, but their intransigence probably hurt them when revisions finally came to be made.

The stage was set for a revision of the Clean Air Act when George Bush, "the environmental president," was elected, and George Mitchell, a strong supporter of environmentalism, became the Senate majority leader. But what sort of clean air bill would it be? "What we wanted," said Richard Ayres, head of the environmentalists' Clean Air Coalition, "is a health based standard—one-in-1-million cancer risk," a standard that would require corporations to clean up their plants until the cancer risk from their operations was reduced to one in a million. "The Senate bill still has the requirement," Ayres said, "but there are forty pages of extensions and exceptions and qualifications and loopholes that largely render the health standard a nullity." Greider reports, for example, "According to the EPA, there are now twenty-six coke ovens that pose a cancer risk greater than 1 in 1000 and six where the risk is greater than 1 in 100. Yet the new clean-air bill will give the steel industry another thirty years to deal with the problem."

This change from what the bill was supposed to do to what it did do came about through what corporate executives like to call the "access" process. The principal aim of most corporate campaign contributions is to help corporate executives gain "access" to key members of Congress and their staffs. In these meetings, corporate executives (and corporate PAC money) work to persuade the members of Congress to accept a predesigned loophole that will sound innocent but effectively undercut the stated intention of the bill. Representative John D. Dingell (Democrat-Michigan), who was chair of the House Committee, is a strong industry supporter; one of the people we interviewed called him "the point man for the Business Roundtable on clean air." Representative Henry A. Waxman (Democrat-California), chair of the subcommittee, is an environmentalist. Observers had expected a confrontation and contested votes on the floor of the Congress.

The problem for corporations was that, as one Republican staff aide said, "If any bill has the blessing of Waxman and the environmental groups, unless it is totally in outer space, who's going to vote against it?" But corporations successfully minimized public votes. Somehow, Waxman was persuaded to make behind-the-scenes compromises with Dingell so members, during an election year, didn't have to side publicly with business against the environment. Often the access process leads to loopholes that protect a single corporation, but for "clean" air most of the special deals targeted not specific companies but entire industries. The initial bill, for example, required cars

to be able to use carefully specified, cleaner fuels. But the auto industry wanted the rules loosened, and Congress eventually incorporated a variant of a formula suggested by the head of General Motors' fuels and lubricants department.

Nor did corporations stop fighting even after they gutted the bill through amendments. Business pressed the EPA for favorable regulations to implement the law: "The cost of this legislation could vary dramatically, depending on how EPA interprets it," said William D. Fay, vice president of the National Coal Association, who headed the hilariously misnamed Clean Air Working Group, an industry coalition that fought to weaken the legislation. As one EPA aide working on acid rain regulations reported, "We're having a hard time getting our work done because of the number of phone calls we're getting from corporations and their lawyers."

Corporations trying to get federal regulators to adopt the "right" regulations don't rely exclusively on the cogency of their arguments. They often exert pressure on a member of Congress to intervene for them at the EPA or other agency. Senators and representatives regularly intervene on behalf of constituents and contributors by doing everything from straightening out a social security problem to asking a regulatory agency to explain why it is pressuring a company. This process—like campaign finance—usually follows rules of etiquette. In addressing a regulatory agency, the senator does not say, "Lay off my campaign contributors or I'll cut your budget." One standard phrasing for letters asks regulators to resolve the problem "as quickly as possible within applicable rules and regulations." No matter how mild and careful the inquiry, the agency receiving the request is certain to give it extra attention; only after careful consideration will they refuse to make any accommodation.

Soft money—unregulated megabuck contributions—also shaped what happened to air quality. Archer Daniels Midland argued that increased use of ethanol would reduce pollution from gasoline; coincidentally, ADM controls a majority of the ethanol market. To reinforce its arguments, in the 1992 election ADM gave $90,000 to Democrats and $600,000 to Republicans, the latter supplemented with an additional $200,000 as an individual contribution from the company head, Dwayne Andreas. Many environmentalists were skeptical about ethanol's value in a clean air strategy, but President Bush issued regulations promoting wider use of ethanol; we presume he was impressed by the force of ADM's 800,000 Republican arguments. Bob Dole, the 1996 Republican presidential candidate, helped pass and defend special breaks for the ethanol industry; he not only appreciated ADM's Republican contributions, but presumably approved of the more than $1 million they gave to the American Red Cross during the period when it was headed by his wife, Elizabeth Dole. What about the post-1994 Republican-controlled Congress, defenders of the free market and opponents of government giveaways? Were they ready to end this subsidy program, cracking down on corporate welfare as they did on people welfare? Not a chance. In 1997, the Republican chair of the House Ways and Means Committee actually attempted to eliminate the special tax breaks for ethanol. Needless to say, he was immediately put in his place by other members of the Republican leadership, including Speaker Newt Gingrich and most of the Senate, with the subsidy locked in place for years to come, in spite of a General Accounting Office report that "found that the ethanol subsidy justifies none of its political boasts." The Center for Responsive Politics calculated that ADM, its executives and PAC, made more than $1 million in campaign contributions of various types; the only thing that had changed was that in 1996, with a Democratic president, this money was "divided more or less evenly between Republicans and Democrats."

The disparity in power between business and environmentalists looms large during the legislative process, but it is enormous afterward. When the Clean Air Act passed, corporations and industry groups offered positions, typically with large pay increases, to congressional staff members who wrote the law. The former congressional staff members who now work for corporations both know how to evade the law and can persuasively claim to EPA that they know what Congress

intended. Environmental organizations pay substantially less than Congress and can't afford large staffs. They are seldom able to become involved in the details of the administrative process or to influence implementation and enforcement.

Having pushed Congress and the Environmental Protection Agency to allow as much pollution as possible, business then went to the Quayle council for rules allowing even more pollution. Vice President J. Danforth Quayle's council, technically known as the "Council on Competitiveness," was created by President Bush specifically to help reduce regulations on business. Quayle told the *Boston Globe* "that his council has an 'open door' to business groups and that he has a bias against regulations." During the Bush administration, this council reviewed, and could override, all regulations, including those by the EPA setting the limits at which a chemical was subject to regulation. The council also recommended that corporations be allowed to increase their polluting emissions if a state did not object within seven days of the proposed increase. Corporations thus have multiple opportunities to win. If they lose in Congress, they can win at the regulatory agency; if they lose there, they can try again at the Quayle council (or later equivalent). If they lose there, they can try to reduce the money available to enforce regulations, or tie the issue up in the courts, or plan on accepting a minimal fine.

The operation of the Quayle council probably would have received little publicity, but reporters discovered that the executive director of the Council, Allan Hubbard, had a clear conflict of interest. Hubbard chaired the biweekly White House meetings on the Clean Air Act. He owned half of World Wide Chemical, received an average of more than $1 million a year in profits from it while directing the Quayle council, and continued to attend quarterly stockholder meetings. According to the *Boston Globe*, "Records on file with the Indianapolis Air Pollution Control Board show that World Wide Chemical emitted 17,000 to 19,000 pounds of chemicals into the air" in 1991. At that time the company did "not have the permit required to release the emissions," was "putting out nearly four times the allowable emissions without a permit, and could be subject to a $2,500-a-day penalty," according to David Jordan, director of the Indianapolis Air Pollution Board.

This does not, however, mean that business always gets exactly what it wants. In 1997, the Environmental Protection Agency proposed tough new rules for soot and smog. Business fought hard to weaken or eliminate the rules: hiring experts (from pro-business think tanks) to attack the scientific studies supporting the regulations and putting a raft of lobbyists ("many of them former congressional staffers," the *Washington Post* reported) to work securing the signatures of 250 members of Congress questioning the standards. But the late 1990s version of these industry mobilizations adds a new twist—creating a pseudo-grassroots campaign. For example, business, operating under a suitably disguised name (Foundation for Clean Air Progress), paid for television ads telling farmers that the EPA rules would prohibit them from plowing on dry windy days, with other ads predicting the EPA rules "would lead to forced carpooling or bans on outdoor barbecues—claims the EPA dismisses as ridiculous." Along with the ads, industry worked to mobilize local politicians and business executives in what business groups called a "grass tops" campaign.

Despite a massive industry campaign, EPA head Carol Browner remained firm, and President Clinton was persuaded to go along. Of course, industry immediately began working on ways to undercut the regulations with congressional loopholes and exceptions—but business has suffered a defeat, and proponents of clean air (that is, most of the rest of us) had won at least a temporary and partial victory. And who leads the struggles to overturn or uphold these regulations? Just as before, Dingell and Waxman; Republicans "are skittish about challenging" the rules publicly, "so they gladly defer to Dingell as their surrogate." Dingell's forces have more than 130 cosponsors (about one-third of them Democrats) for a bill to, in effect, override the EPA standards.

In business-government relations most attention becomes focused on instances of scandal. The real issue, however, is not one or another scandal or conflict of interest, but rather the *system* of business-government relations, and especially of campaign finance, that offers business so many opportunities to craft loopholes, undermine regulations, and subvert enforcement. Still worse, many of these actions take place beyond public scrutiny.

WHAT IS POWER?

Our analysis is based on an understanding of power that differs from that usually articulated by both business and politicians. The corporate PAC directors we interviewed insisted that they have no power:

> If you were to ask me what kind of access and influence do we have, being roughly the 150th largest PAC, I would have to tell you that on the basis of our money we have zero. . . . If you look at the level of our contributions, we know we're not going to buy anybody's vote, we're not going to rent anybody, or whatever the clichés have been over the years. We know that.

The executives who expressed these views clearly meant these words sincerely. Their statements are based on roughly the same understanding of "power" that is current with political science, which is also the way the term was defined by Max Weber, the classical sociological theorist. Power, in this common conception, is the ability to make someone do something against their will. If that is what power means, then corporations rarely have any in relation to members of Congress, nor does soft money give the donor power over presidents. As one senior vice president said to us: "You certainly aren't going to be able to buy anybody for $500 or $1,000 or $10,000—it's a joke." Soft money donations of a million dollars might seem to change the equation, but we will argue they do not: Just as $10,000 won't buy a member of Congress, $1,000,000 won't buy a president. In this regard we agree with the corporate officials we interviewed: A corporation is not in a position to say to a member of Congress, "Either you vote for this bill, or we will defeat your bid for reelection." Rarely do they even say: "You vote for this bill or you won't get any money from us."

This definition of power as the ability to make someone do something against their will is what Steven Lukes calls a "one-dimensional" view of power. A two-dimensional view recognizes the existence of nondecisions: A potential issue never gets articulated or, if articulated by someone somewhere, never receives serious consideration. For example, in 1989 and 1990, one of the major political battles, and a focus of great effort by corporate PACs, was the Clean Air Act. Yet twenty or thirty years earlier, before the rise of the environmental movement, pollution was a nonissue: it simply was not considered, although its effects were, in retrospect, of great importance. In one of Sherlock Holmes stories, the key clue is that the dog didn't bark. A two-dimensional view of power makes the same point: The most important clue in some situation may be that no one noticed power was exercised—because there was no overt conflict.

Even this model of power is too restrictive, however, because it still focuses on discrete decisions and nondecisions. Tom Wartenberg calls these "interventional" models of power, and notes that, in such models "the primary locus of power . . . is a specific social interaction between two social agents." Such models do not recognize "the idea that the most fundamental use of power in society is its use in structuring the basic manner in which social agents interact with one another." Wartenberg argues, instead, for a "field theory" of power that analyzes social power as a force similar to a magnetic field. A magnetic field alters the motion of objects susceptible to magnetism. Similarly, the mere presence of a powerful social agent alters the social space for others and causes them to orient themselves toward the powerful agent. For example, one of the executives we interviewed took it for granted that "if we go see the congressman who represents [a city where the company has a major plant], where 10,000 of our employees are also his constituents, we don't need a PAC to go see him." The corporation is so important in that area that the member has to orient himself in relation to the corporation and its concerns. In a different sense, the very act of accepting a campaign contribution changes the way a member relates to a PAC, creating a sense of obligation, a need to reciprocate. The PAC contribution has altered the member's social space, his or her awareness of the company and wish to help it, even if no explicit commitments have been made.

BUSINESS IS DIFFERENT

Power, we would argue, is not just the ability to force someone to do something against their will; it is most effective (and least recognized) when it shapes the field of action. Moreover, business's vast resources, influence on the economy, and general legitimacy place it on a different footing from other campaign contributors. Every day a member of Congress accepts a $1,000 donation from a corporate PAC, goes to a committee hearing, proposes "minor" changes in a bill's wording, and has those changes accepted without discussion or examination. The changes "clarify" the language of the bill, legalizing higher levels of pollution for a specific pollutant, or exempting the company from some tax. The media do not report on this change, and no one speaks against it. On the other hand, if a PAC were formed by Drug Lords for Cocaine Legalization, no member would take their money. If a member introduced a "minor" wording change to make it easier to sell crack without bothersome police interference, the proposed change would attract massive attention, the campaign contribution would be labeled a scandal, the member's political career would be ruined, and the changed wording would not be incorporated into the bill. Drug Lords may make an extreme example, but approximately the same holds true for many groups: At present, equal rights for gays and lesbians could never be a minor and unnoticed addition to a bill with a different purpose.

Even groups with great social legitimacy encounter more opposition and controversy than business faces for proposals that are virtually without public support. One example is the contrast between the largely unopposed commitment of tens or hundreds of billions of dollars for the savings and loan bailout, compared to the sharp debate, close votes, and defeats for the rights of men and women to take *unpaid* parental leave. The classic term for something non-controversial that everyone must support is "a motherhood issue," and while it costs little to guarantee every woman the right to an *un*paid parental leave, this measure nonetheless generated intense scrutiny and controversy—going down to defeat under President Bush, passing under President Clinton, and then again becoming a focus of attack after the 1994 Republican takeover of Congress. Few indeed are the people publicly prepared to defend pollution or tax evasion. Nevertheless, business is routinely able to win pollution exemptions and tax loopholes. Although cumulatively some vague awareness of these provisions may trouble people, most are allowed individually to pass without scrutiny. *No* analysis of corporate political activity makes sense unless it begins with a recognition of this absolutely vital point. The PAC is a vital element of corporate power, but it does not operate by itself. The PAC donation is always backed by the wider power and influence of business.

Corporations are unlike other "special interest" groups not only because business has far more resources, but also because of its acceptance and legitimacy. When people feel that "the system" is screwing them, they tend to blame politicians, the government, the media—but rarely business. In terms of campaign finance, while much of the public is outraged at the way money influences elections and public policy, the issue is almost always posed in terms of politicians, what they do or don't do. This is part of a pervasive double standard that largely exempts business from criticism. We, however, believe it is vital to scrutinize business as well.

We did two dozen radio call-in shows after the appearance of our last book, *Money Talks*. On almost every show, at least one call came from someone outraged that members of Congress had recently raised their pay to $125,100. (For 1998, it will be about $137,000.) Not a single person even mentioned corporate executives' pay. *Business Week* calculated that in 1996 corporate CEOs were paid an average of $5.8 million (counting salary, bonuses, and stock option grants), or more than 200 times the average worker's pay, and more than 40 times what members of Congress are paid. More anger is directed at Congress for delaying new environmental laws than at the companies who fight every step of the way to stall and subvert the legislation. When members of Congress do favors for large campaign contributors, anger is directed at the senators who went along, not at the business owner who paid the money (and usually initiated the pressure). The public focuses on the member's receipt of thousands of dollars, not on the business's receipt of millions (or hundreds of millions) in tax breaks or special treatment. It is a widely held belief that "politics is dirty." But little public comment and condemnation is generated when companies get away—quite literally—with murder. This disparity is evidence of business's success in shaping public perceptions. Lee Atwater, George Bush's 1988 campaign manager, saw this as a key to Republican success:

> In the 1980 campaign, we were able to make the establishment, insofar as it is bad, the government. In other words, big government was the enemy, not big business. If the people think the problem is that taxes are too high, and the government interferes too much, then we are doing our job. But, if they get to the point where they say that the real problem is that rich people aren't paying taxes, . . . then the Democrats are going to be in good shape.

We argue that corporations are so different, and so dominant, that they exercise a special kind of power, what Antonio Gramsci called hegemony. Hegemony can be regarded as the ultimate example of a field of power that structures what people and groups do. It is sometimes referred to as a worldview, a way of thinking about the world that influences every action, and makes it difficult to even consider alternatives. But in Gramsci's analysis it is much more than this, it is a culture and set of institutions that structure life patterns and coerce a particular way of life. Susan Harding gives the example of relations between whites and blacks in the South prior to the 1960s. Black inferiority and subservience were not simply ideas articulated by white racists, they were incorporated into a set of social practices: segregated schools, restrooms, swimming pools, restaurants; the black obligation to refer to white men as "Mister"; the prohibition on referring to black men as "Mister"; the use of the term "boy" for black males of any age and social status; the white right to go to the front of any line or to take the seat of any African American, and so on. Most blacks recognized the injustice and absurdity of these rules, but this did not enable them to escape, much less defy, them. White hegemony could not be overthrown simply by recognizing its existence or articulating an ideal of, equality; black people had to create a movement that transformed themselves, the South, and the nation as a whole.

Hegemony is most successful and most powerful, when it is unrecognized. White hegemony in the South was strong but never unrecognized and rarely uncontested. White southerners would have denied, probably in all sincerity, that they exercised power: "Why our nigras are perfectly happy that's the way they want to be treated." But many black southerners would have vigorously disputed this while talking to each other. In some sense, gender relations in the 1950s embodied a hegemony even more powerful than that of race relations. Betty Friedan titled the first chapter of *The Feminine Mystique* "The Problem That Has No Name," because women literally did not have a name for, did not recognize the existence of, their oppression. Women as well as men denied the existence of inequality or oppression, denied the systematic exercise of power to maintain unequal relations.

We argue that today business has enormous power and exercises effective hegemony, even though (perhaps because) this is largely undiscussed and unrecognized. *Politically*, business power today is similar to white treatment of blacks in 1959—business may sincerely deny its power, but many of the groups it exercises power over recognize it, feel dominated, resent this, and fight the power as best they can. At least until very recently, *economically*, business power was more

like gender relations in 1959: Virtually no one saw this power as problematic. The revived labor movement is beginning to change this, and there are signs that a movement is beginning to contest corporate power. Nonetheless, if the issue is brought to people's attention, many still don't see a problem: "Well, so what? How else could it be? Maybe we don't like it, but that's just the way things are."

Hegemony is never absolute. African Americans and women both were (and are) forced to live in disadvantaged conditions, but simultaneously fought for dignity and respect. Unusual individuals always violated conventions and tested limits. A hegemonic power is usually opposed by a counterhegemony. Thus, while children in our society are taught to compete with each other to earn the praise of authority figures, and while most children engage in this process much of the time, it is also true that the "teacher's pet" is likely to face ostracism. We hope this book makes a small contribution to weakening business hegemony and to developing a counterhegemony.

The primary power of the wealthy is not exercised by individuals or even by families. Power in our society is based in institutions, not individuals, and the power of wealth is channeled through corporations. There are more than 200,000 industrial corporations in the United States, but all companies are *not* created equal: The 500 largest industrials control three-quarters of the sales, assets, and profits of *all* industrial corporations. More than 250 of these companies had revenues of more than $5 billion. Similarly, in the service sector, 500 firms control a disproportionate share of the resources. The dominance of these corporations means that a handful of owners and top executives, perhaps one-hundredth of one percent of the U.S. population, or 25,000 individuals, have the power to make decisions that have a huge impact on all of our lives. Collectively these people exercise incalculable power, making decisions with more impact on most of our lives than those made by the entire elected government.

Consider for a moment those decisions that virtually everyone in our society agrees should be made by business. Consider, for this exercise, only those decisions on which there is broad bipartisan political agreement; exclude anything that would generally be considered ethically or legally dubious and anything where a significant fraction of elected officials dispute business's right. Exclude, as well, any actions that are taken only through business's influence on government, and confine your attention to the decisions made in operating businesses. Remember that any decision made by "business" is primarily determined by the 25,000 individuals at the top of the corporate ladder, since their companies control about three-quarters of *all* corporate sales, assets, employees, and profits.

BUSINESS DECISIONS

What are some of these decisions? A brief and partial list indicates their scope:

Decisions about Employment

- the number of people employed.
- when to have layoffs.
- the number of hours people work.
- when work begins in the morning and ends in the afternoon.
- whether to phase out full-time jobs and replace them with part-time, lower-wage, no-benefits jobs. In 1997, UPS workers and the Teamsters Union successfully contested the company's increasingly heavy reliance on part-timers, but it was big news that a union even attempted to raise the issue, much less that they were able to win.
- whether or not there is overtime, and whether it is compulsory.
- whether to allow flextime and job-sharing.
- the skill level of the jobs. Does the company make an effort to use lots of skilled workers paid good wages or is it always trying to de-skill positions and replace skilled workers with unskilled?
- the educational (and other) requirements for employment. Are certain educational levels *necessary* in order to be hired, or are they simply helpful? Are exconvicts or former mental patients eligible for all jobs or only some? What about the handicapped?

- whether the firm *de facto* discriminates in favor of men and whites or makes an active effort to recruit and promote minorities and women.
- workers' rights on the job. For example, do they have free speech? A worker at a Coca-Cola plant was given a three-day suspension (without pay) because his wife brought him a lunch with a soda from Burger King, at a time when Burger King sold Pepsi. It is totally legal to penalize an employee for this or many other such actions.
- job safety. In one of the most extreme examples, a worker was killed while performing a dangerous task. Almost immediately thereafter another worker was ordered to do the same job and refused because he said conditions were unsafe and had not been remedied. The company fired him for this refusal, and the Supreme Court upheld the firing.
- (within limits) whether or not a union is recognized; whether the union and the workers are treated with dignity and respect; how bitterly and viciously the union is resisted.

Investment Decisions

- decisions about whether to expand a plant, and if so, which plant to expand.
- whether to merge the corporation and "downsize" workers. Recently, a number of corporations have laid off thousands of employees, blighting communities and individual lives, at the same time giving huge bonuses to the top executives.
- whether to contract out jobs.
- whether to close down a plant; when and how to do so. Virtually no one questions a company's absolute right (in the United States, not in Europe) to shut down if it chooses to do so, no matter what the effect on the workers and communities.
- where to open new plants. The company has every right to bargain for the best deal it can get. Deals can include tax abatements and implicit agreements to ignore labor or pollution laws.

Product and Marketing

- the products produced, including whether to introduce a new product and whether to discontinue an old stand-by.
- the design, both functional and aesthetic.
- the relative attention to different considerations: in a new car, how important is styling? sex appeal? fuel efficiency? safety? durability?
- the quality of the goods produced. Are they made to last, with high standards throughout, or are they just made to look good in the store and for the first month of use?
- the price for which goods are sold.
- the character of the advertising used to promote the product. Does it stress the significant features of the product, or distract through sex and extraneous symbols?
- the amount spent on advertising—90 percent of the commercials on prime time television are sponsored by the nation's 500 largest corporations.
- the places where ads appear—in left-wing journals? in right-wing journals? on television? on which programs?

Community and Environment

- the level of pollution in the workplace: air, heat, noise, chemicals, and so on.
- the level of pollution in the outside environment. Beginning in the 1970s, for pollution both in the workplace and in the larger community, the government set maximum limits for a few items, but companies are completely free to do better than these standards. No government regulation prevents companies from setting and meeting tougher standards of their own devising. For example, in July 1991, a railroad tanker car derailed, tumbled into the Sacramento River, ruptured, and spilled pesticide. The pesticide was not listed as a regulated substance, and therefore the railroad was not required to carry it in a double-hulled tanker, though it could have chosen to do so. Though the pesticide was unregulated, it *was* strong enough to kill virtually all the fish in the river, formerly famous for its trout.
- the degree of consideration for the community: Does the company make an effort to be a good neighbor? Does it contribute to local charities? Support local initiatives?

This by no means exhausts the list of decisions that companies are allowed to make. Not only allowed to make, but expected and, in many cases, required to make. There is some regulation of business decisions at the margin, with possible regulation for issues such as: Can a company pull up stakes and leave town with no more than a day's notice? Can it dump raw wastes in the river? Can it make dubious claims in its advertising? For the most part, however, corporations are free to make decisions about their economic operations.

If the government fails to act, big business can do as it wishes.

DISCUSSION QUESTIONS

1. Consider the discussion of hidden versus blatant power and relate this to the manner in which business exercised its privileged position through the Clean Air Act negotiations.
2. What comparisons may be drawn, if any, between white hegemony (prior to the 1960s) and corporate hegemony today?
3. If corporations that are so central to the structure of our economy do constitute a "field of power," can their hegemony be reconciled with our "democracy"?

CAPITALISM AND THE ENVIRONMENT

Intensifying examples of extreme weather in the United States, including drought, heavy precipitation, heat waves, and devastating tornadoes, have brought home to Americans the reality that the Earth is in serious danger. While climate change deniers are well represented in the U.S. political system, environmentalists understand that it is necessary to make significant changes in how our economic system functions if we are to head off planetary disaster. Fred Magdoff and John Bellamy Foster are editors of the socialist magazine Monthly Review, *whose first issue in 1949 featured an article by physicist Albert Einstein titled "Why Socialism?" In this article they argue that environmental problems are not essentially caused by ignorance or greed. Rather, "ecological destruction is built into the inner nature and logic of our present system of production." They go on to detail the ways in which capitalism as such is in conflict with environmental sustainability, as well as social justice. In response to proponents of "green" capitalism, they criticize a number of technical proposals for limiting ecological damage without fundamentally changing the economic system, such as "cap and trade" schemes. Magdoff and Foster believe that a sustainable future requires that social and political movements opposing the "logic of capital" grow stronger and achieve new connections, within the United States and globally.*

For those concerned with the fate of the earth, the time has come to face facts: not simply the dire reality of climate change but also the pressing need for social-system change. The failure to arrive at a world climate agreement in Copenhagen in December 2009 was not simply an abdication of world leadership, as is often suggested, but had deeper roots in the inability of the capitalist system to address the accelerating threat to life on the planet. Knowledge of the nature and limits of capitalism, and the means of transcending it, has therefore become a matter of survival.

THE PLANETARY ECOLOGICAL CRISIS

There is abundant evidence that humans have caused environmental damage for millennia. Problems with deforestation, soil erosion, and salinization of irrigated soils go back to antiquity.

Source: Fred Magdoff and John Bellamy Foster, "What Every Environmentalist Needs to Know About Capitalism," *Monthly Review*, January 2010, Volume 61, Number 10, pages 1–30. Online location: http://monthlyreview.org/2010/03/01/what-every-environmentalist-needs-to-know-about-capitalism

What is different in our current era is that there are many more of us inhabiting more of the earth, we have technologies that can do much greater damage and do it more quickly, and we have an economic system that knows no bounds. The damage being done is so widespread that it not only degrades local and regional ecologies, but also affects the planetary environment.

There are many sound reasons that we, along with many other people, are concerned about the current rapid degradation of the earth's environment. Global warming, brought about by human-induced increases in greenhouse gases (CO_2, methane, N_2O, etc.), is in the process of destabilizing the world's climate—with horrendous effects for most species on the planet and humanity itself now increasingly probable. Each decade is warmer than the one before, with 2009 tying as the second warmest year (2005 was the warmest) in the 130 years of global instrumental temperature records. Climate change does not occur in a gradual, linear way, but is non-linear, with all sorts of amplifying feedbacks and tipping points. There are already clear indications of accelerating problems that lie ahead. These include:

- Melting of the Arctic Ocean ice during the summer, which reduces the reflection of sunlight as white ice is replaced by dark ocean, thereby enhancing global warming. Satellites show that end-of-summer Arctic sea ice was 40 percent less in 2007 than in the late 1970s when accurate measurements began.

- Eventual disintegration of the Greenland and Antarctic ice sheets, set in motion by global warming, resulting in a rise in ocean levels. Even a sea level rise of 1–2 meters would be disastrous for hundreds of millions of people in low-lying countries such as Bangladesh and Vietnam and various island states. A sea level rise at a rate of a few meters per century is not unusual in the paleoclimatic record, and therefore has to be considered possible, given existing global warming trends. At present, more than 400 million people live within five meters above sea level, and more than one billion within twenty-five meters.

- The rapid decrease of the world's mountain glaciers, many of which—if business-as-usual greenhouse gas emissions continue—could be largely gone (or gone altogether) during this century. Studies have shown that 90 percent of mountain glaciers worldwide are already visibly retreating as the planet warms. The Himalayan glaciers provide dry season water to countries with billions of people in Asia. Their shrinking will lead to floods and acute water scarcity. Already the melting of the Andean glaciers is contributing to floods in that region. But the most immediate, current, and long-term problem, associated with disappearing glaciers—visible today in Bolivia and Peru—is that of water shortages.

- Devastating droughts, expanding possibly to 70 percent of the land area within several decades under business as usual; already becoming evident in northern India, northeast Africa, and Australia.

- Higher levels of CO_2 in the atmosphere may increase the production of some types of crops, but they may then be harmed in future years by a destabilized climate that brings either dry or very wet conditions. Losses in rice yields have already been measured in parts of Southeast Asia, attributed to higher night temperatures that cause the plant to undergo enhanced nighttime respiration. This means losing more of what it produced by photosynthesis during the day.

- Extinction of species due to changes in climate zones that are too rapid for species to move or adapt to, leading to the collapse of whole ecosystems dependent on these species, and the death of still more species. (See below for more details on species extinctions.)

- Related to global warming, ocean acidification from increased carbon absorption is threatening the collapse of marine ecosystems. Recent indications suggest that ocean acidification may, in turn, reduce the carbon-absorption efficiency of the ocean. This means a potentially faster build-up of carbon dioxide in the atmosphere, accelerating global warming.

While global climate change and its consequences, along with its "evil twin" of ocean acidification (also brought on by carbon emissions), present by far the greatest threats to the earth's species, including humans, there are also other severe environmental issues. These include contamination of the air and surface waters with industrial pollutants. Some of these pollutants (the metal mercury, for example) go up smoke stacks to later fall and contaminate soil and water, while others are leached into surface waters from waste storage facilities. Many ocean and fresh water fish are contaminated with mercury as well as numerous industrial organic chemicals. The oceans contain large "islands" of trash—"Light bulbs, bottle caps, toothbrushes, Popsicle sticks and tiny pieces of plastic, each the size of a grain of rice, inhabit the Pacific garbage patch, an area of widely dispersed trash that doubles in size every decade and is now believed to be roughly twice the size of Texas."

In the United States, drinking water used by millions of people is polluted with pesticides such as atrazine as well as nitrates and other contaminants of industrial agriculture. Tropical forests, the areas of the greatest terrestrial biodiversity, are being destroyed at a rapid pace. Land is being converted into oil palm plantations in Southeast Asia—with the oil to be exported as a feedstock for making biodiesel fuel. In South America, rainforests are commonly first converted to extensive pastures and later into use for export crops such as soybeans. This deforestation is causing an estimated 25 percent of all human-induced release of CO_2. Soil degradation by erosion, overgrazing, and lack of organic material return threatens the productivity of large areas of the world's agricultural lands.

We are all contaminated by a variety of chemicals. A recent survey of twenty physicians and nurses tested for sixty-two chemicals in blood and urine—mostly organic chemicals such as flame retardants and plasticizers—found that

> each participant had at least 24 individual chemicals in their body, and two participants had a high of 39 chemicals detected . . . .

All participants had bisphenol A [used to make rigid polycarbonate plastics used in water cooler bottles, baby bottles, linings of most metal food containers—and present in the foods inside these containers, kitchen appliances etc.], and some form of phthalates [found in many consumer products such as hair sprays, cosmetics, plastic products, and wood finishers], PBDEs [polybrominated diphenyl ethers used as flame retardants in computers, furniture, mattresses, and medical equipment] and PFCs [perfluorinated compounds used in non-stick pans, protective coatings for carpets, paper coatings, etc.].

Although physicians and nurses are routinely exposed to larger quantities of chemicals than the general public, we are all exposed to these and other chemicals that don't belong in our bodies, and that most likely have negative effects on human health. Of the 84,000 chemicals in commercial use in the United States, we don't even have an idea about the composition and potential harmfulness of 20 percent (close to 20,000)—their composition falls under the category of "trade secrets" and is legally withheld.

Species are disappearing at an accelerated rate as their habitats are destroyed, due not only to global warming but also to direct human impact on species habitats. A recent survey estimated that over 17,000 animals and plants are at risk of extinction. "More than one in five of all known mammals, over a quarter of reptiles and 70 percent of plants are under threat, according to the survey, which featured over 2,800 new species compared with 2008. 'These results are just the tip of the iceberg,' said Craig Hilton-Taylor, who manages the list. He said many more species that have yet to be assessed could also be under serious threat." As species disappear, ecosystems that depend on the multitude of species to function begin to degrade. One of the many consequences of degraded ecosystems with fewer species appears to be greater transmission of infectious diseases.

It is beyond debate that the ecology of the earth—and the very life support systems on which humans as well as other species depend—is under sustained and severe attack by human activities. It is also clear that the effects of continuing down the same path will be devastating. As James Hansen, director of NASA's Goddard Institute for Space Studies, and the world's most famous climatologist, has stated: "Planet Earth, creation, the world in which civilization developed, the world with climate patterns that we know and stable shorelines, is in imminent peril....The startling conclusion is that continued exploitation of all fossil fuels on Earth threatens not only the other millions of species on the planet but also the survival of humanity itself—and the timetable is shorter than we thought." Moreover, the problem does not begin and end with fossil fuels but extends to the entire human-economic interaction with the environment.

One of the latest, most important, developments in ecological science is the concept of "planetary boundaries," in which nine critical boundaries/thresholds of the earth system have been designated in relation to: (1) climate change; (2) ocean acidification; (3) stratospheric ozone depletion; (4) the biogeochemical flow boundary (the nitrogen cycle and the phosphorus cycles); (5) global freshwater use; (6) change in land use; (7) biodiversity loss; (8) atmospheric aerosol loading; and (9) chemical pollution. Each of these is considered essential to maintaining the relatively benign climate and environmental conditions that have existed during the last twelve thousand years (the Holocene epoch). The sustainable boundaries in three of these systems—climate change, biodiversity, and human interference with the nitrogen cycle—may have already been crossed.

COMMON GROUND: TRANSCENDING BUSINESS AS USUAL

We strongly agree with many environmentalists who have concluded that continuing "business as usual" is the path to global disaster. Many people have determined that, in order to limit the ecological footprint of human beings on the earth, we need to have an economy—particularly in the rich countries—that doesn't grow, so as to be able to stop and possibly reverse the increase in pollutants released, as well as to conserve non-renewable resources and more rationally use renewable resources. Some environmentalists are concerned that, if world output keeps expanding and everyone in developing countries seeks to attain the standard of living of the wealthy capitalist states, not only will pollution continue to increase beyond what the earth system can absorb, but we will also run out of the limited non-renewable resources on the globe. *The Limits to Growth* by Donella Meadows, Jorgen Randers, Dennis Meadows, and William Behrens, published in 1972 and updated in 2004 as *Limits to Growth: The 30-Year Update*, is an example of concern with this issue. It is clear that there are biospheric limits, and that the planet cannot support the close to 7 billion people already alive (nor, of course, the 9 billion projected for mid-century) at what is known as a Western, "middle class" standard of living. The Worldwatch Institute has recently estimated that a world which used biocapacity per capita at the level of the contemporary United States could only support 1.4 billion people. The primary problem is an ancient one and lies not with those who do not have enough for a decent standard of living, but rather with those for whom enough does not exist. As Epicurus said: "Nothing is enough to someone for whom enough is little." A global social system organized on the basis of "enough is little" is bound eventually to destroy all around it and itself as well.

Many people are aware of the need for social justice when solving this problem, especially because so many of the poor are living under dangerously precarious conditions, have been especially hard hit by environmental disaster and degradation, and promise to be the main victims if current trends are allowed to continue. It is clear that approximately half of humanity—over three billion people, living in deep poverty and subsisting on less than $2.50 a day—need to have access to the requirements for a basic human existence such as decent housing, a secure food supply, clean water, and medical care. We whole-heartedly agree with all of these concerns.

Some environmentalists feel that it is possible to solve most of our problems by tinkering with our economic system, introducing greater energy efficiency and substituting "green" energy sources for fossil fuels—or coming up with technologies to ameliorate the problems (such as using carbon capture from power plants and injecting it deep into the earth). There is a movement toward "green" practices to use as marketing tools or to keep up with other companies claiming to use such practices. Nevertheless, within the environmental movement, there are some for whom it is clear that mere technical adjustments in the current productive system will not be enough to solve the dramatic and potentially catastrophic problems we face.

Curtis White begins his 2009 article in *Orion*, entitled "The Barbaric Heart: Capitalism and the Crisis of Nature," with: "There is a fundamental question that environmentalists are not very good at asking, let alone answering: 'Why is this, the destruction of the natural world, happening?' " It is impossible to find real and lasting solutions until we are able satisfactorily to answer this seemingly simple question.

It is our contention that most of the critical environmental problems we have are either caused, or made much worse, by the workings of our economic system. Even such issues as population growth and technology are best viewed in terms of their relation to the socioeconomic organization of society. Environmental problems are not a result of human ignorance or innate greed. They do not arise because managers of individual large corporations or developers are morally deficient. Instead, we must look to the fundamental workings of the economic (and political/social) system for explanations. It is precisely the fact that ecological destruction is built into the inner nature and logic of our present system of production that makes it so difficult to solve.

In addition, we shall argue that "solutions" proposed for environmental devastation, which

would allow the current system of production and distribution to proceed unabated, are not real solutions. In fact, such "solutions" will make things worse because they give the false impression that the problems are on their way to being overcome when the reality is quite different. The overwhelming environmental problems facing the world and its people will not be effectively dealt with until we institute another way for humans to interact with nature—altering the way we make decisions on what and how much to produce. Our most necessary, most rational goals require that we take into account fulfilling basic human needs, and creating just and sustainable conditions on behalf of present and future generations (which also means being concerned about the preservation of other species).

CHARACTERISTICS OF CAPITALISM IN CONFLICT WITH THE ENVIRONMENT

The economic system that dominates nearly all corners of the world is capitalism, which, for most humans, is as "invisible" as the air we breathe. We are, in fact, largely oblivious to this worldwide system, much as fish are oblivious to the water in which they swim. It is capitalism's ethic, outlook, and frame of mind that we assimilate and acculturate to as we grow up. Unconsciously, we learn that greed, exploitation of laborers, and competition (among people, businesses, countries) are not only acceptable but are actually good for society because they help to make our economy function "efficiently."

Let's consider some of the key aspects of capitalism's conflict with environmental sustainability.

Capitalism Is a System That Must Continually Expand

No-growth capitalism is an oxymoron: when growth ceases, the system is in a state of crisis with considerable suffering among the unemployed. Capitalism's basic driving force and its whole reason for existence is the amassing of profits and wealth through the accumulation (savings and investment) process. It recognizes no limits to its own self-expansion—not in the economy as a whole; not in the profits desired by the wealthy; and not in the increasing consumption that people are cajoled into desiring in order to generate greater profits for corporations. The environment exists, not as a place with inherent boundaries within which human beings must live together with earth's other species, but as a realm to be exploited in a process of growing economic expansion.

Expansion Leads to Investing Abroad in Search of Secure Sources of Raw Materials, Cheaper Labor, and New Markets

As companies expand, they saturate, or come close to saturating, the "home" market and look for new markets abroad to sell their goods. In addition, they and their governments (working on behalf of corporate interests) help to secure entry and control over key natural resources such as oil and a variety of minerals. We are in the midst of a "land-grab," as private capital and government sovereign wealth funds strive to gain control of vast acreage throughout the world to produce food and biofuel feedstock crops for their "home" markets. It is estimated that some thirty million hectares of land (roughly equal to two-thirds of the arable land in Europe), much of them in Africa, have been recently acquired or are in the process of being acquired by rich countries and international corporations.

A System That, by Its Very Nature, Must Grow and Expand Will Eventually Come Up Against the Reality of Finite Natural Resources

The irreversible exhaustion of finite natural resources will leave future generations without the possibility of having use of these resources. Natural resources are used in the process of production—oil, gas, and coal (fuel), water (in industry and agriculture), trees (for lumber and paper), a variety of mineral deposits (such as iron ore, copper, and bauxite), and so on. Some resources, such as forests and fisheries, are of a finite size, but can be renewed by natural processes if used in a planned system that is flexible enough to change as conditions warrant. Future use of other resources—oil and gas, minerals, aquifers in some desert or dryland areas (prehistorically deposited water)—are limited forever to the supply that currently exists. The water, air, and soil of the biosphere can continue to function well for the living creatures on the planet only if pollution doesn't exceed their limited capacity to assimilate and render the pollutants harmless.

A System Geared to Exponential Growth in the Search for Profits Will Inevitably Transgress Planetary Boundaries

The earth system can be seen as consisting of a number of critical biogeochemical processes that, for hundreds of millions of years, have served to reproduce life. In the last 12 thousand or so years the world climate has taken the relatively benign form associated with the geological epoch known as the Holocene, during which civilization arose. Now, however, the socioeconomic system of capitalism has grown to such a scale that it overshoots fundamental planetary boundaries—the carbon cycle, the nitrogen cycle, the soil, the forests, the oceans. More and more of the terrestrial (land-based) photosynthetic product, upwards of 40 percent, is now directly accounted for by human production. All ecosystems on earth are in visible decline. With the increasing scale of the world economy, the human-generated rifts in the earth's metabolism inevitably become more severe and more multifarious. Yet, the demand for more and greater economic growth and accumulation, even in the wealthier countries, is built into the capitalist system. As a result, the world economy is one massive bubble.

There is nothing in the nature of the current system, moreover, that will allow it to pull back before it is too late. To do that, other forces from the bottom of society will be required.

Capitalism Is Not Just an Economic System—It Fashions a Political, Judicial, and Social System to Support the System of Wealth and Accumulation

Under capitalism people are at the service of the economy and are viewed as needing to consume more and more to keep the economy functioning. . . . The notion of responsibility to others and to community, which is the foundation of ethics, erodes under such a system. In the words of Gordon Gekko—the fictional corporate takeover artist in Oliver Stone's film *Wall Street*—"Greed is Good." Today, in the face of widespread public outrage, with financial capital walking off with big bonuses derived from government bailouts, capitalists have turned to preaching self-interest as the bedrock of society from the very pulpits. On November 4, 2009, Barclay's Plc Chief Executive Officer John Varley declared from a wooden lectern in St. Martin-in-the-Fields at London's Trafalgar Square that "Profit is not Satanic." Weeks earlier, on October 20, 2009, Goldman Sachs International adviser Brian Griffiths declared before the congregation at St. Paul's Cathedral in London that "the injunction of Jesus to love others as ourselves is a recognition of self-interest."

Wealthy people come to believe that they deserve their wealth because of hard work (theirs or their forbearers) and possibly luck. The ways in which their wealth and prosperity arose out of the social labor of innumerable other people are downplayed. They see the poor—and the poor frequently agree—as having something wrong with them, such as laziness or not getting a sufficient education. The structural obstacles that prevent most people from significantly bettering their conditions are also downplayed. This view of each individual as a separate economic entity concerned primarily with one's (and one's family's) own well-being, obscures our common humanity and needs. People are not inherently selfish but are encouraged to become so in response to the pressures and characteristics of the system. After all, if each person doesn't look out for "Number One" in a dog-eat-dog system, who will?

Capitalism is unique among social systems in its active, extreme cultivation of individual self-interest or "possessive-individualism." Yet the reality is that non-capitalist human societies have thrived over a long period—for more than 99 percent of the time since the emergence of anatomically modern humans—while encouraging other traits such as sharing and responsibility to the group. There is no reason to doubt that this can happen again.

The incestuous connection that exists today between business interests, politics, and law is reasonably apparent to most observers. These include outright bribery, to the more subtle sorts of buying access, friendship, and influence through campaign contributions and lobbying efforts. In addition, a culture develops among political leaders based on the precept that what is good for capitalist business is good for the country. Hence, political leaders increasingly see themselves as political entrepreneurs, or the counterparts of economic entrepreneurs, and regularly convince themselves that what they do for corporations to obtain the funds that will help them get reelected is actually in the public interest. Within the legal system, the interests of capitalists and their businesses are given almost every benefit.

Given the power exercised by business interests over the economy, state, and media, it is extremely difficult to effect fundamental changes that they oppose. It therefore makes it next to impossible to have a rational and ecologically sound energy policy, health care system, agricultural and food system, industrial policy, trade policy, education, etc.

CHARACTERISTICS OF CAPITALISM IN CONFLICT WITH SOCIAL JUSTICE

The characteristics of capitalism discussed above—the necessity to grow; the pushing of people to purchase more and more; expansion abroad; use of resources without concern for future generations; the crossing of planetary boundaries; and the predominant role often exercised by the economic system over the moral, legal, political, cultural forms of society—are probably the characteristics of capitalism that are most harmful for the environment. But there are other characteristics of the system that greatly impact the issue of social justice. It is important to look more closely at these social contradictions imbedded in the system.

As the System Naturally Functions, a Great Disparity Arises in Both Wealth and Income

There is a logical connection between capitalism's successes and its failures. The poverty and misery of a large mass of the world's people is not an accident, some inadvertent byproduct of the system, one that can be eliminated with a little tinkering here or there. The fabulous accumulation of wealth—as a direct consequence of the way capitalism works nationally and internationally—has simultaneously produced persistent hunger, malnutrition, health problems, lack of water, lack of sanitation, and general misery for a large portion of the people of the world. The wealthy few resort to the mythology that the grand disparities are actually necessary. For example, as Brian Griffiths, the advisor to Goldman Sachs International, quoted above, put it: "We have to tolerate the inequality as a way to achieving greater prosperity and opportunity for all." What's good for the rich also—according to them—coincidentally happens to be what's good for society as a whole, even though many remain mired in a perpetual state of poverty.

Goods and Services Are Rationed According to Ability to Pay

The poor do not have access to good homes or adequate food supplies because they do not have "effective" demand—although they certainly have biologically based demands. All goods are commodities. People without sufficient effective demand (money) have no right in the capitalist system to any particular type of commodity—whether it is a luxury such as a diamond bracelet or a huge McMansion, or whether it is a necessity of life such as a healthy physical environment, reliable food supplies, or quality medical care. Access to all commodities is determined, not by desire or need, but by having sufficient money or credit to purchase them. Thus, a system that, by its very workings produces inequality and holds back workers' wages, ensures that many (in some societies, most) will not have access to even the basic necessities or to what we might consider a decent human existence.

It should be noted that, during periods when workers' unions and political parties were strong, some of the advanced capitalist countries of Europe instituted a more generous safety net of programs, such as universal health care, than those in the United States. This occurred as a result of a struggle by people who demanded that the government provide what the market cannot—equal access to some of life's basic needs.

Capitalism Is a System Marked by Recurrent Economic Downturns

In the ordinary business cycle, factories and whole industries produce more and more during a boom—assuming it will never end and not wanting to miss out on the "good times"—resulting in overproduction and overcapacity, leading to a recession. In other words, the system is prone to crises, during which the poor and near poor suffer the most. Recessions occur with some regularity, while depressions are much less frequent. Right now, we are in a deep recession or mini-depression (with 10 percent official unemployment), and many think we've averted a full-scale depression by the skin of our teeth. All told, since the mid-1850s there have been thirty-two recessions or depressions in the United States (not including the current one)—with the average contraction since 1945 lasting around ten months and the average expansion between contractions lasting about six years. Ironically, from the ecological point of view, major recessions—although causing great harm to many people—are actually a benefit, as lower production leads to less pollution of the atmosphere, water, and land.

PROPOSALS FOR THE ECOLOGICAL REFORMATION OF CAPITALISM

There are some people who fully understand the ecological and social problems that capitalism brings, but think that capitalism can and should be reformed. According to Benjamin Barber: "The struggle for the soul of capitalism is . . . a struggle between the nation's economic body and its civic soul: a struggle to put capitalism in its proper place, where it serves our nature and needs rather than manipulating and fabricating whims and wants. Saving capitalism means bringing it into harmony with spirit—with prudence, pluralism and those 'things of the public' . . . that define our civic souls. A revolution of the spirit." William Greider has written a book titled *The Soul of Capitalism: Opening Paths to a Moral Economy*. And there are books that tout the potential of "green capitalism" and the "natural capitalism" of Paul Hawken, Amory Lovins, and L. Hunter Lovins. Here, we are told that we can get rich, continue growing the economy, and increase consumption without end—and save the planet, all at the same time! How good can it get? There is a slight problem—a system that has only one goal, the maximization of profits, has no soul, can never have a soul, can never be green, and, by its very nature, it must manipulate and fabricate whims and wants.

There are a number of important "out of the box" ecological and environmental thinkers and doers. They are genuinely good and well-meaning people who are concerned with the health of the planet, and most are also concerned with issues of social justice. However, there is one box from which they cannot escape—the capitalist economic system. Even the increasing numbers of individuals who criticize the system and its "market failures" frequently end up with "solutions" aimed at a tightly controlled "humane" and non-corporate capitalism, instead of actually getting outside the box of capitalism. They are unable even to think about, let alone promote, an economic system that has different goals and decision-making processes—one that places primary emphasis on human and environmental needs, as opposed to profits.

Corporations are outdoing each other to portray themselves as "green." You can buy and wear your Gucci clothes with a clean conscience because the company is helping to protect rainforests by using less paper. *Newsweek* claims that corporate giants such as Dell, Hewlett-Packard, Johnson & Johnson, Intel, and IBM are the top five green companies of 2009 because of their use of "renewable" sources of energy, reporting greenhouse gas emissions (or lowering them), and implementing formal environmental policies and good reputations. You can travel wherever you want, guilt-free, by purchasing carbon "offsets" that supposedly cancel out the environmental effects of your trip.

Let's take a look at some of the proposed devices for dealing with the ecological havoc without disturbing capitalism.

Better Technologies That Are More Energy Efficient and Use Fewer Material Inputs

Some proposals to enhance energy efficiency—such as those to help people tighten up their old homes so that less fuel is required to heat in the winter—are just plain common sense. The efficiency of machinery, including household appliances and automobiles, has been going up continually, and is a normal part of the system. Although much more can be accomplished in this area, increased efficiency usually leads to lower costs and increased use (and often increased size as well, as in automobiles), so that the energy used is actually increased. The misguided push to "green" agrofuels has been enormously detrimental to the environment. Not only has it put food and auto fuel in direct competition, at the expense of the former, but it has also sometimes actually decreased overall energy efficiency.

Nuclear Power

Some scientists concerned with climate change, including James Lovelock and James Hansen, see nuclear power as an energy alternative, and as a partial technological answer to the use of fossil fuels; one that is much preferable to the growing use of coal. However, although the technology of nuclear energy has improved somewhat, with third-generation nuclear plants, and with the possibility (still not a reality) of fourth-generation nuclear energy, the dangers of nuclear power are still enormous—given radioactive waste lasting hundreds and thousands of years, the social management of complex systems, and the sheer level of risk involved. Moreover, nuclear plants take about ten years to build and are extremely costly and uneconomic. There are all sorts of reasons, therefore (not least of all, future generations), to be extremely wary of nuclear power as any kind of solution. To go in that direction would almost certainly be a Faustian bargain.

Large-Scale Engineering Solutions

A number of vast engineering schemes have been proposed either to take CO_2 out of the atmosphere or to increase the reflectance of sunlight back into space, away from earth. These include: *Carbon sequestration schemes* such as capturing CO_2 from power plants and injecting it deep into the earth, and fertilizing the oceans with iron so as to stimulate algal growth to absorb carbon; and *enhanced sunlight reflection* schemes such as deploying huge white islands in the oceans, creating large satellites to reflect incoming sunlight, and contaminating the stratosphere with particles that reflect light.

No one knows, of course, what detrimental side effects might occur from such schemes. For example, more carbon absorption by the oceans could increase acidification, while dumping sulphur dioxide into the stratosphere to block sunlight could reduce photosynthesis.

Also proposed are a number of low-tech ways to sequester carbon such as increasing reforestation and using ecological soil management to increase soil organic matter (which is composed mainly of carbon). Most of these should be done for their own sake (organic material helps to improve soils in many ways). Some could help to reduce the carbon concentration in the atmosphere. Thus reforestation, by pulling carbon from the atmosphere, is sometimes thought of as constituting negative emissions. But low-tech solutions cannot solve the problem given an expanding system—especially considering that trees planted now can be cut down later, and carbon stored as soil organic matter may later be converted to CO_2 if practices are changed.

Cap and Trade (Market Trading) Schemes

The favorite economic device of the system is what are called "cap and trade" schemes for limiting carbon emissions. This involves placing a cap on the allowable level of greenhouse gas emissions and then distributing (either by fee or by auction) permits that allow industries to emit carbon dioxide and other greenhouse gases. Those corporations that have more permits than they need may sell them to other firms wanting additional permits to pollute. Such schemes invariably include "offsets" that act like medieval indulgences, allowing corporations to continue to pollute while buying good grace by helping to curtail pollution somewhere else—say, in the third world.

In theory, cap and trade is supposed to stimulate technological innovation to increase carbon efficiency. In practice, it has not led to carbon dioxide emission reductions in those areas where it has been introduced, such as in Europe. The main result of carbon trading has been enormous profits for some corporations and individuals, and the creation of a subprime carbon market. There are no meaningful checks of the effectiveness of the "offsets," nor prohibitions for changing conditions sometime later that will result in carbon dioxide release to the atmosphere.

What Can Be Done Now?

In the absence of systemic change, there certainly are things that have been done and more can be done in the future to lessen capitalism's negative effects on the environment and people. There is no particular reason why the United States can't have a better social welfare system, including universal health care, as is the case in many other advanced capitalist countries. Governments can pass laws and implement regulations to curb the worst environmental problems. The same goes for the environment or for building affordable houses. A carbon tax of the kind proposed by James Hansen, in which 100 percent of the dividends go back to the public, thereby encouraging conservation while placing the burden on those with the largest carbon footprints and the most wealth, could be instituted. New coal-fired plants (without sequestration) could be blocked and existing ones closed down. At the world level, contraction and convergence in carbon emissions could be promoted, moving to uniform world per capita emissions, with cutbacks far deeper in the rich countries with large per capita carbon footprints. The problem is that very powerful forces are strongly opposed to these measures. Hence, such reforms remain at best limited, allowed a marginal existence only insofar as they do not interfere with the basic accumulation drive of the system.

Indeed, the problem with all these approaches is that they allow the economy to continue on the same disastrous course it is currently following. We can go on consuming all we want (or as much as our income and wealth allow), using up resources, driving greater distances in our more fuel-efficient cars, consuming all sorts of new products made by "green" corporations, and so on. All we need to do is support the new "green" technologies (some of which, such as using

agricultural crops to make fuels, are actually not green!) and be "good" about separating out waste that can be composted or reused in some form, and we can go on living pretty much as before—in an economy of perpetual growth and profits.

The very seriousness of the climate change problem arising from human-generated carbon dioxide and other greenhouse gas emissions has led to notions that it is merely necessary to reduce carbon footprints (a difficult problem in itself). The reality, though, is that there are numerous, interrelated, and growing ecological problems arising from a system geared to the infinitely expanding accumulation of capital. What needs to be reduced is not just *carbon footprints*, but *ecological footprints*, which means that economic expansion on the world level and especially in the rich countries needs to be reduced, even cease. At the same time, many poor countries need to expand their economies. The new principles that we could promote, therefore, are ones of sustainable human development. This means enough for everyone and no more. Human development would certainly not be hindered, and could even be considerably enhanced for the benefit of all, by an emphasis on sustainable human, rather than unsustainable economic development.

Another Economic System Is Not Just Possible—It's Essential

The foregoing analysis, if correct, points to the fact that the ecological crisis cannot be solved within the logic of the present system. The various suggestions for doing so have no hope of success. The system of world capitalism is clearly unsustainable in: (1) its quest for never ending accumulation of capital leading to production that must continually expand to provide profits; (2) its agriculture and food system that pollutes the environment and still does not allow universal access to a sufficient quantity and quality of food; (3) its rampant destruction of the environment; (4) its continually recreating and enhancing of the stratification of wealth within and between countries; and (5) its search for technological magic bullets as a way of avoiding the growing social and ecological problems arising from its own operations.

The transition to an ecological—which we believe must also be a socialist—economy will be a steep ascent and will not occur overnight. This is not a question of "storming the Winter Palace." Rather, it is a dynamic, multifaceted struggle for a new cultural compact and a new productive system. The struggle is ultimately against the *system of capital*. It must begin, however, by opposing the *logic of capital*, endeavoring in the here and now to create in the interstices of the system a new social metabolism rooted in egalitarianism, community, and a sustainable relation to the earth. The basis for the creation of sustainable human development must arise *from within* the system dominated by capital, *without being part of it,* just as the bourgeoisie itself arose in the "pores" of feudal society. Eventually, these initiatives can become powerful enough to constitute the basis of a revolutionary new movement and society.

DISCUSSION QUESTIONS

1. Magdoff and Foster argue that the "logic" of capitalism as an economic system is in conflict with the environment. Which characteristics of capitalism do they identify to support this claim? Are you convinced that a fundamentally different economic system is necessary if ecological catastrophe is to be avoided?

2. Magdoff and Foster discuss several proposals for the ecological reform of capitalism. What are their criticisms of these proposals? Do you agree that "green" capitalism is a contradiction in terms?

CHAPTER 2

Ideology and Political Culture

Politics is "in here"—within ourselves—as well as "out there," inside of government institutions. Each of us perceives the world by way of an *ideology,* a socially produced and culturally reinforced mental map made up of values, beliefs, and assumptions about why the world is the way it is and what, if anything, should be done about it. Rooted in the history and culture of our society, political ideology has a taken-for-granted naturalness about it such that we are usually not conscious of its grip on us. When left unchallenged, our received ideology impedes our capacity for independent thought and serves as a powerful force for social control. One of the goals of a liberal education should be to see our underlying beliefs and values for what they are, and to understand the selectiveness of our ideology in what it discloses and affirms and in what it conceals and denies. The readings in this chapter address the nature and limitations of American political culture and ideology.

Any number of interpreters of U.S. history have identified *liberalism* as the dominant and unrivaled American ideology. Cut off from European brands of aristocratic conservatism on one hand and working-class socialism on the other, Americans emphasized the values of individualism, private property, the free market, and limited government that had emerged in seventeenth- and eighteenth-century English thought, most notably in John Locke's *Second Treatise of Government* (1690). In this classical sense, liberalism is a broad set of ideas that encompasses both "liberal" and "conservative" positions today, a point that helps explain how limited our spectrum of political viewpoints actually is. As it developed out of the shadows of the feudal era, liberalism seemed to represent a great advance in human freedom. But given the interdependent nature of our increasingly multicultural world, how well do liberal individualism and the private market economy it legitimates prepare us for confronting the challenges of the twenty-first century?

5 *Jennifer L. Hochschild*

WHAT IS THE AMERICAN DREAM?

In this selection, political scientist Jennifer Hochschild examines the four basic tenets of the American dream. The dream is rooted in a variation of philosopher John Locke's fantasy frontier, a state of nature where anyone is almost guaranteed to be able to achieve any success with enough personal determination. Hochschild discusses the myriad of ways American history and popular culture have portrayed the "almost-promise" of success, and the equally haunting power of the fear of failure. Having articulated the virtues of the American dream and its ascendance to the level of a seductive ideology, she then assesses the flaws inherent in the dream's four key tenets. Particularly troubling is the nightmarish quality of the dream for those who fail to achieve it, who are subsequently devalued by society and who, often, devalue themselves. Hochschild finds that the dream, taken as a whole, is overly (and unnecessarily) individualistic, fixated on an extremely narrow definition of "success," and analytically deceptive in that it encourages an emphasis on traits of individuals rather than political, economic, and social structures. Moreover, our political culture offers few alternative ideologies against which to evaluate the strengths and weaknesses of our own. Thus, the individually focused, nonstructural tendencies of the ideology of the American dream make it that much harder for U.S. citizens to fully understand themselves and the political world they inhabit.

"In the beginning," wrote John Locke, "all the world was *America*." Locke was referring specifically to the absence of a cash nexus in primitive society. But the sentence evokes the unsullied newness, infinite possibility, limitless resources that are commonly understood to be the essence of the "American dream." The idea of the American dream has been attached to everything from religious freedom to a home in the suburbs, and it has inspired emotions ranging from deep satisfaction to disillusioned fury. Nevertheless, the phrase elicits for most Americans some variant of Locke's fantasy—a new world where anything can happen and good things might. . . .

Source: Jennifer L. Hochschild, *Facing Up to the American Dream: Race, Class and the Soul of the Nation,* Princeton, NJ: Princeton University Press, 1995, pp. 15–38.

THE MEANING OF SUCCESS

The American dream consists of tenets about achieving success. Let us first explore the meaning of "success" and then consider the rules for achieving it.

People most often define success as the attainment of a high income, a prestigious job, economic security. My treatment is no exception. But *pace* President Reagan, material well-being is only one form of accomplishment. People seek success from the pulpit to the stage of the Metropolitan Opera, from membership in the newest dance club to membership in the Senate. Success can be as amorphous and encompassing as "a right to say what they wanta say, do what they wanta do, and fashion a world into something that can be great for everyone."

Different kinds of success need not, but often do, conflict. A classic plot of American family sagas is the children's rejection of the parents' hard-won wealth and social standing in favor of some "deeper," more meaningful form of accomplishment. The rejection may be reversed, as Cotton Mather sadly reported:

> There have been very fine settlements in the north-east regions; but what is become of them? . . . One of our ministers once preaching to a congregation there, urged them to approve themselves a religious people from this consideration, "that otherwise they would contradict the main end of planting this wilderness"; whereupon a well-known person, then in the assembly, cryed out, "Sir, you are mistaken: you think you are preaching to the people at the [Plymouth] Bay; our main end was to catch fish."

Mather "wished that something more excellent had been the main end of the settlements in that brave country," but the ideology of the American dream itself remains agnostic as to the meaning of "something more excellent."

A definition of success involves measurement as well as content. Success can be measured in at least three ways, with important normative and behavioral consequences. First, it can be *absolute*. In this case, achieving the American dream implies reaching some threshold of well-being, higher than where one began but not necessarily dazzling. As Bruce Springsteen puts it, "I don't think the American dream was that everybody was going to make . . . a billion dollars, but it was that everybody was going to have an opportunity and the chance to live a life with some decency and some dignity and a chance for some self-respect."

Second, success can be *relative*. Here achieving the American dream consists in becoming better off than some comparison point, whether one's childhood, people in the old country, one's neighbors, a character from a book, another race or gender—anything or anyone that one measures oneself against. Relative success implies no threshold of well-being, and it may or may not entail continually changing the comparison group as one achieves a given level of accomplishment. A benign version of relative success is captured by James Comer's "kind of competition . . . we had . . . going on" with "the closest friends that we had":

> When we first met them, we had a dining room and they didn't. They went back and they turned one of their bedrooms into a dining room . . . After that we bought this big Buick car. And we came to their house and they had bought another car. She bought a fur coat one year and your dad bought me one the next. But it was a friendly thing, the way we raced. It gave you something to work for, to look forward to. Every year we tried to have something different to show them what we had done, and they would have something to show us.

William Byrd II articulated a more malign version in 1736: slaves "blow up the pride, and ruin the industry of our white people, who seeing a rank of poor creatures below them, detest work for fear it should make them look like slaves."

Success can, alternatively, be *competitive*— achieving victory over someone else. My success implies your failure. Competitors are usually people, whether known and concrete (opponents in a tennis match) or unknown and abstract (all other applicants for a job). *U.S. News and World Report,* in an article celebrating "SUCCESS! The Chase Is Back in Style Again," graphically illustrates the relationship among competitors in the business world. An opponent may, however, be entirely impersonal. John Henry, "the steel-drivin' man," is famed for beating a machine, and Paul Bunyan for taming the primeval forest.

TENETS OF SUCCESS

The American dream that we were all raised on is a simple but powerful one—if you work hard and play by the rules you should be given a chance to go as far as your God-given ability will take you.

—PRESIDENT BILL CLINTON,
SPEECH TO DEMOCRATIC LEADERSHIP
COUNCIL, 1993

In one sentence, President Clinton has captured the bundle of shared, even unconsciously presumed, tenets about achieving success that make up the ideology of the American dream. Those tenets answer the questions: Who may pursue the American dream? In what does the pursuit consist? How does one successfully pursue the dream? Why is the pursuit worthy of our deepest commitment?

The answer to "who" in the standard ideology is "everyone, regardless of ascriptive traits, family background, or personal history." The answer to "what" is "the reasonable anticipation, though not the promise, of success, however it is defined." The answer to "how" is "through actions and traits under one's own control." The answer to "why" is "true success is associated with virtue." Let us consider each rule in turn.

Who May Pursue Success?

The first tenet, that everyone may always pursue their dream, is the most direct connotation of Locke's "in the beginning. . . ." But the idea extends beyond the image of a pristine state of nature waiting for whoever "discovers" it. Even in the distinctly nonpristine, nonnatural world of Harlem or Harlan County, anyone can pursue a dream. A century ago, one moved to the frontier to hide a spotted past and begin afresh; Montana frontierswomen "never ask[ed] women where they come from or what they did before they came to live in our neck of the woods. If they wore a wedding band and were good wives, mothers, and neighbors that was enough for us to know."

But seldom, say Americans, does one need to take such dramatic steps; fewer than one-fifth see race, gender, religion, or class as very important for "getting ahead in life." Even two-thirds of the poor are certain that Americans like themselves "have a good chance of improving our standard of living," and up to three times as many Americans as Europeans make that claim. In effect, Americans believe that they can create a personal ministate of nature that will allow them to slough off the past and invent a better future.

What Does One Pursue?

The second tenet, that one may reasonably anticipate success, is less straightforward. "Reasonable anticipation" is far from a guarantee, as all children on the morning of their birthday know. But "reasonable anticipation" is also much more than simply longing; most children are fairly sure of getting at least some of what they wish for on their birthday. On a larger scale, from its inception America has been seen by many as an extravagant birthday party:

Seagull: A whole countrie of English is there, man, . . . and . . . the Indians are so in love with 'hem that all the treasure they have they lay at their feete . . . Golde is more plentiful there than copper is with us. . . . Why, man, all their dripping pans and their chamberpots are pure golde; and all the chaines with which they chaine up their streets are massie golde; all the prisoners they take are fettered in golde; and for rubies and diamonds they goe forthe on holy dayes and gather 'hem by the sea shore to hang on their childrens coats.

Presumably few Britons even in 1605 took this message literally, but the hope of abundant riches—whether material, spiritual, or otherwise—persists.

Thus Americans are exhorted to "go for it" in their advertisements as well as their commencement addresses. And they do; three-quarters of Americans, compared with only one-third of Britons, West Germans, and Hungarians (and fewer Dutch), agree that they have a good chance of improving their standard of living. Twice as many Americans as Canadians or Japanese think future generations of their nationality will live better than the present generation.

How Does One Pursue Success?

The third premise, for those who do not take Seagull literally, explains how one is to achieve the success that one anticipates. Ralph Waldo Emerson is uncharacteristically succinct on the point: "There is always a reason, *in the man,* for his good or bad fortune, and so in making money." Other nineteenth-century orators exhorted young men to

Behold him [a statue of Benjamin Franklin], . . . holding out to you an example of diligence, economy and virtue, and personifying the triumphant success which may await those who follow it! Behold him, ye that are humblest and poorest . . . —lift up your heads and look at the image of a man who rose from nothing, who owed nothing to parentage or patronage, who enjoyed no advantages of early education, which are not open,—a hundredfold open,—to yourselves, who performed the most menial services in the business in which his early life was employed, but who lived to stand before

Kings, and died to leave a name which the world will never forget.

Lest we smile at the quaint optimism (or crude propaganda) of our ancestors, consider a recent advertisement from Citicorp Bank. This carefully balanced group of shining faces— young and old, male and female, black, Latino, Nordic, and Asian—all gazing starry-eyed at the middle distance over the words "THE WILL TO SUCCEED IS PART OF THE AMERICAN SPIRIT" conveys the message of the third tenet in no uncertain terms.

This advertisement is well aimed; surveys unanimously show Americans' strong support for rewarding people in the marketplace according to their talents and accomplishments rather than their needs, efforts, or simple existence. And Americans mostly believe that people are in fact rewarded for their acts. In 1952 fully 88 percent of Americans agreed that "there is plenty of opportunity and anyone who works hard can go as far as he wants"; in 1980, 70 percent concurred.

Comparisons across space yield the same results as comparisons across time. In a 1973 survey of youth in ten nations, only Swedes and British disagreed more than did Americans that a man's [sic] future is "virtually determined" by his family background. A decade later only 31 percent of Americans agreed that in their nation "what you achieve in life depends largely on your family background," compared with over 50 percent of Austrians and Britons, and over 60 percent of Italians. Most pointedly, half of American adolescents compared with one-fourth of British adolescents agreed in 1972 that "people get to be poor . . . [because] they don't work hard enough."

Americans also believe more than do Europeans that people ought not to be buffered from the consequences of their actions, so long as they have a fair start in life. Thus up to four times as many more Americans think college opportunities should be increased, but roughly half as many think the government should reduce the income disparity between high- and low-income citizens, or provide jobs or income support for the poor.

Why Is Success Worth Pursuing?

Implicit in the flows of oratory and survey responses is the fourth tenet of the American dream, that the pursuit of success warrants so much fervor because it is associated with virtue. "Associated with" means at least four things: virtue leads to success, success makes a person virtuous, success indicates virtue, or apparent success is not real success unless one is also virtuous.

That quintessential American, Benjamin Franklin, illustrates three of these associations: the *Autobiography* instructs us that "no Qualities were so likely to make a poor Man's Fortune as those of Probity & Integrity." Conversely, "Proverbial Sentences, chiefly such as inculcated Industry and Frugality," are included in *Poor Richard's Almanack* as "the Means of procuring Wealth and thereby securing Virtue, it being more difficult for a Man in Want to act always honestly, as . . . *it is hard for an empty Sack to stand upright.*" Finally, mere wealth may actually impede true success, the attainment of which requires a long list of virtues: "Fond *Pride of Dress*, is sure a very Curse; E'er *Fancy* you consult, consult your Purse"; "A Ploughman on his Legs is higher than a Gentleman on his Knees"; and "Pride that dines on Vanity sups on Contempt."

Americans have learned Franklin's lessons well: they distinguish between the worthy and unworthy rich, as well as the deserving and undeserving poor. For example, most Americans characterize "yuppies" as people who "play fashionable games" and "eat in trendy restaurants," and on the whole they enjoy watching such forms of conspicuous consumption. But they also characterize yuppies as selfish, greedy, inclined to flaunt their wealth, and imbued with a false sense of superiority. These traits they mostly find unacceptable. Overall, Americans overwhelmingly deplore the 1980s sentiment of "making it fast while you can regardless of what happened to others." This is not simply a reaction against the Reagan years. In surveys throughout the 1970s, four in ten Americans deemed honesty to be the most important quality for a child to learn, compared with 2 percent proclaiming that a child should try hard to succeed. Virtually all Americans require that their friends be "honest" and "responsible"—core components of the third and fourth tenets.

Americans also focus more on virtue than do citizens of other nations, at least in their self-descriptions. A survey of youth in ten nations found that more Americans than people in any other country described their chief goal in life as "sincerity and love between myself and others," and in only one other nation (the Philippines) did more youth seek "salvation through faith." Conversely, only in Sweden did fewer youths seek "money and position," and only in three other countries did fewer seek "freedom from restrictions." More Americans than Europeans gain strength from religion, report prayer to be an important part of their daily life, and agree that there are universally applicable "clear guidelines about what is good or evil." In short, "this country succeeds in living a very sinful life without being deeply cynical. That is the difference between Europe and America, and it signifies that ethics *means* something here."

The American Dream as Fantasy

We must beware reducing the dream to its components; as a whole it has an evocative resonance greater than the sum of its parts. The theme of most Walt Disney movies boil down to the lyrics in *Pinocchio:* "When you wish upon a star, makes no difference who you are, your dreams come true." It is no coincidence that Disney movies are so durable; they simply update Locke's fantasy. And the global, amorphous vision of establishing a city upon the hill, killing the great white whale, striking a vein of gold, making the world safe for democracy—or simply living a life of decency and dignity—underlies all analyses of what success means or what practices will attain it.

VIRTUES OF THE AMERICAN DREAM

Combining the amorphous fantasy or the more precise tenets of the American dream with the various meanings of success shows the full richness—and seductiveness—of the ideology. If one measures success absolutely and accepts a wide array of indicators of success, the ideology portrays America as a land of plenty, and Americans as "people of plenty." This is the great theme of one of the most powerful children's sagas ever written in America, the *Little House in the Big Woods* series. Decades (and nine volumes) of grasshopper plagues, ferocious blizzards, cheating and cowardly railroad bosses, even hostile Indians cannot prevent Pa and his girls from eventually "winning their bet with Uncle Sam" and becoming prosperous homesteaders. In the words of one of Pa's songs:

> I am sure in this world there are plenty
> of good things enough for us all. . . .
> It's cowards alone that are crying
> And foolishly saying, "I can't."
> It is only by plodding and striving
> And laboring up the steep hill
> Of life, that you'll ever be thriving,
> Which you'll do if you've only the will.

If success is measured competitively and defined narrowly, however, the ideology portrays a different America. Hard work and virtue combined with scarce resources produce a few spectacular winners and many dismissible losers. This is the theme of John Rockefeller's turn-of-the-century Sunday school address:

> The growth of a large business is merely a survival of the fittest. . . . The American Beauty rose can be produced in the splendor and fragrance which bring cheer to its beholder only by sacrificing the early buds which grow up around it. This is not an evil tendency in business. It is merely the working out of a law of nature and a law of God.

The *Little House* series has sold well over four million copies; Americans prefer the self-image of universal achievement to that of a few stalwarts triumphing over weaker contenders. What matters most, however, is not any single image but rather the elasticity and range of the ideology of the American dream. People can encourage themselves with soft versions, congratulate themselves with harder ones, and exult with the hardest, as their circumstances and characters warrant.

Thus the American dream is an impressive ideology. It has for centuries lured people to America and moved them around within it, and it has kept them striving in horrible conditions against impossible odds. Most Americans celebrate it unthinkingly, along with apple pie and motherhood; criticism typically is limited to imperfections in its application. But like apple pie and motherhood, the American dream turns out upon closer examination to be less than perfect. Let us look, then, at flaws intrinsic to the dream.

FLAWS IN THE TENETS OF THE AMERICAN DREAM

The First Tenet

The first tenet, that everyone can participate equally and can always start over, is troubling to the degree that it is not true. It is, of course, never true in the strongest sense; people cannot shed their existing selves as snakes do their skin. So the myth of the individual mini-state of nature is just that—a fantasy to be sought but never achieved.

Fantasies are fine so long as people understand that that is what they are. For that reason, a weaker formulation of the first tenet—people start the pursuit of success with varying advantages, but no one is barred from the pursuit—is more troubling because the gap between ideological claim and actual fact is harder to recognize. As a factual claim, the first tenet is largely false; for most of American history, women of any race and men who were Native American, Asian, black, or poor were barred from all but a narrow range of "electable futures." Ascriptive constraints have arguably been weakened over time, but until recently no more than about a third of the population was able to take seriously the first premise of the American dream.

This flaw has implications beyond the evident ones of racism and sexism. The emotional potency of the American dream has made people who *were* able to identify with it the norm for everyone else. White men, especially European immigrants able to ride the wave of the Industrial Revolution (and to benefit from the absence of competition from the rest of the population) to comfort or even prosperity, are the epitomizing demonstration of America as the bountiful state of nature. Those who do not fit the model disappear from the collective self-portrait. Thus the irony is doubled: not only has the ideal of universal participation been denied to most Americans, but also the very fact of its denial has itself been denied in our national self-image.

This double irony creates deep misunderstandings and correspondingly deep political tensions. Whites increasingly believe that racial discrimination is slight and declining, and blacks increasingly believe the opposite. But this form of racial conflict is not unique. For example, surveys show that more women than men believe that women are discriminated against in employment and wages, in "being able to combine family and work," and in their overall chance to pursue their dreams. Similarly, regardless of when the survey was conducted, more men than women believe that women are better off now than a decade earlier with regard to these issues. Not surprisingly, bitter disagreements about the need for affirmative action, policies to stem sexual harassment, family leave policies, and the like ensue.

The Second Tenet

The flaws of the second tenet of the American dream, the reasonable anticipation of success, stem from the close link between anticipation and expectation. That link presents little problem so long as there are enough resources and opportunities that everyone has a reasonable chance of having some expectations met. Indeed, panegyrics to the American dream always expound on the bounty and openness of the American continent. Governor James Glen typified eighteenth-century entrepreneurs of colonization by promising that

> Adventurers will be pleased to find a Change from Poverty and Distress to Ease and Plenty; they are invited to a Country not yet half settled, where the Rivers are crowded with Fish, and the Forests with Game; and no Game-Act to restrain them from enjoying those Bounties of Providence, no heavy Taxes to impoverish them, nor oppressive Landlords to snatch the hard-earned Morsel from the Mouth of Indigence, and where Industry will certainly inrich them.

Three centuries later, the message was unchanged:

> All my life I am thinking to come to this country. For what I read in the magazines, and the movies. . . . I would have a beautiful castle in the U.S. I will have a thousand servant. I will have five Rolls-Royces in my door. . . . We thinking everybody has this kind of life. . . . I have this kind of dream.

These fantasies are innocuous so long as resources roughly balance dreams for enough people enough of the time. But if they do not—worse yet, if they used to but do no longer—then the dream rapidly loses its appeal. The circumstances that cause resources no longer to balance dreams vary, from an economic downturn to a rapid increase in the number of dreamers to a narrowing of the grounds on which success is publicly recognized. The general point, however, always holds: no one promises that dreams will be fulfilled, but the distinction between the right to dream and the right to succeed is psychologically hard to maintain and politically always blurred. It is especially hard to maintain because the dream sustains Americans against daily nightmares only if they believe that they have a significant likelihood, not just a formal chance, of reaching their goals.

In short, the right to aspire to success works as an ideological substitute for a guarantee of success only if it begins to approach it. When people recognize that chances for success are slim or getting slimmer, the whole tenor of the American dream changes dramatically for the worse.

The general problem of scarcity varies depending on how people measure success and how broadly they define possible goals. It is most obvious and acute for those focused on competitive success in only a few arenas; by definition resources and opportunities are insufficient to satisfy all dreamers in such a case. But it may be more problematic for those who measure success relatively or who admit a wide array of outcomes into their picture of success. After all, there are more such people and they have no a priori reason to assume that many will fail.

The problem of scarcity may be most devastating, however, for people anticipating absolute success or for people willing to see success almost anywhere. They, after all, have the least reason to expect failure. Losers of this type have an unmatched poignancy: "I don't dream any more like I used to. I believed that in this country, we would have all we needed for the decent life. I don't see that any more."

Conversely, the availability of resources and opportunities may shape the kind of success that Americans dream of. If resources are profoundly scarce (as in a famine) or inherently limited (as in election to the presidency), people almost certainly envision competitive success in that arena. If resources are moderately scarce, people will be concerned about their position relative to that of others, but will not necessarily see another's gain as their loss. When resources and opportunities seem wide open and broadly defined—anyone can achieve salvation, get an "A" on the exam, claim 160 acres of western prairie—people are most free to pursue their idiosyncratic dreams and to measure their achievement by their own absolute standard.

This logic suggests a dynamic: as resources become tighter or success is more narrowly defined, Americans are likely to shift their understanding of success from absolute to relative to competitive. Before the 1980s, claims one journalist, "there was always enough to go around, plenty

of places in the sun. It didn't even matter much about the rich—so long as everyone was living better, it seemed the rich couldn't be denied their chance to get richer." But "today [in 1988] that wave [of prosperity] has crested. . . . Now when the rich get richer, the middle class stagnates—and the poor get decidedly poorer. If left unchecked, a polarization of income . . . is likely to provoke consequences that will affect America's politics and power, to say nothing of its psyche."

The risks of anticipating success do not stop with anticipation. Attaining one's dreams can be surprisingly problematic. From William Shakespeare to William Faulkner, writers have limned the loneliness of being at the top, the spiritual costs of cutthroat competition, the shallowness of a society that rewards achievement above all else. Alexis de Tocqueville characteristically provides one of the most eloquent of such admonitions:

> Every American is eaten up with longing to rise. . . . In America I have seen the freest and best educated of men in circumstances the happiest in the world; yet it seemed to me that a cloud habitually hung on their brow, and they seemed serious and almost sad even in their pleasures. The chief reason for this is that . . . [they] never stop thinking of the good things they have not got. . . . They clutch everything but hold nothing fast, and so lose grip as they hurry after some new delight.

The obsession with ever more material success threatens the body politic as well as the individual soul:

> When the taste for physical pleasures has grown more rapidly than either education or experience of free institutions, the time comes when men are carried away and lose control of themselves at sight of the new good things they are ready to snatch. . . . There is no need to drag their rights away from citizens of this type; they themselves voluntarily let them go. . . . The role of

government is left unfilled. If, at this critical moment, an able and ambitious man once gets power, he finds the way open for usurpations of every sort.

Not only nineteenth-century romantics cautioned against the failures of success. Today psychotherapists specialize in helping "troubled winners" or the "working wounded," for whom "a life too much devoted to pursuing money, power, position, and control over others ends up being emotionally impoverished." In short, material—and perhaps other forms of—success is not all it's cracked up to be, even (or especially) in a nation where it is the centerpiece of the pervasive ideology.

The problems of success, however, pale beside the problems of failure. Because success is so central to Americans' self-image, and because they expect as well as hope to achieve, Americans are not gracious about failure. Others' failure reminds them that the dream may be just that—a dream, to be distinguished from waking reality. Their own failure confirms that fear. As Zora Neale Hurston puts it, "there is something about poverty that smells like death."

Furthermore, the better the dream works for other people, the more devastating is failure for the smaller and smaller proportion of people left behind. In World War II, members of military units with a high probability of promotion were less satisfied with advancement opportunities than members of units with a much lower probability of promotion, because failure to be promoted in the former case was both more salient and more demonstrably a personal rather than a systemic flaw. The "tunnel effect" is a more nuanced depiction of this phenomenon of relative deprivation. The first stage is one of relative gratification, in which others' success enhances one's own well-being. After all, drivers in a traffic jam in a tunnel are initially pleased when cars in the adjacent lane begin to move "because advances of others supply information about a more benign external environment; receipt of this information produces gratification; and this gratification overcomes, or at least suspends, *envy*." At some point,

however, those left behind come to believe that their heightened expectations will not be met; not only are their hopes now dashed, but they are also worse off than when the upward mobility began. "Nonrealization of the expectation ['that my turn to move will soon come'] will at some point result in my 'becoming furious.'" And one is still stuck in the tunnel. In short, the ideology of the American dream includes no provision for failure; a failed dream denies the loser not only success but even a safe harbor within which to hide the loss.

The Third Tenet

Failure is made more harsh by the third premise of the American dream—the belief that success results from actions and traits under one's own control. Logically, it does not follow that if success results from individual volition, then failure results from lack of volition. All one needs in order to see the logical flaw here is the distinction between necessary and sufficient. But that distinction is not obvious or intuitive, and in any case the psychologic of the American dream differs from strict logic. In the psychologic, if one may claim responsibility for success, one must accept responsibility for failure.

Americans who do everything they can and still fail may come to understand that effort and talent alone do not guarantee success. But they have a hard time persuading others. After all, they are losers—why listen to them? Will we not benefit more by listening to winners (who seldom challenge the premise that effort and talent breed success)?

The Fourth Tenet

Failure, then, is unseemly for two reasons: it challenges the blurring between anticipation and promise that is the emotional heart of the American dream, and people who fail are presumed to lack talent or will. The coup de grace comes from the fourth tenet of the dream, the association of success with virtue. By the psychologic just described, if success implies virtue, failure implies sin.

American history and popular culture are replete with demonstrations of the connection between failure and sin. In the 1600s, indentured servants—kidnapped children, convicts, and struggling families alike—were described by earlier immigrants as "strong and idle beggars, vagabonds, egyptians, common and notorious whoores, theeves, and other dissolute and lousy persons." Nineteenth-century reformers concurred: fallen women are typically "the daughters of the ignorant, depraved, and vicious part of our population, trained up without culture of any kind, amidst the contagion of evil example, and enter upon a life of prostitution for the ratification of their unbridled passions, and become harlots altogether by choice."

Small wonder that in the late twentieth century even the poor blame the poor for their condition. Despite her vivid awareness of exploitation by the rich, an aging cleaning woman insists that many people are poor because they "make the money and drink it all up. They don't care about the kids or the clothes. Just have a bottle on that table all the time." Losers even blame themselves: an unemployed factory worker, handicapped by a childhood accident, "wish[es] to hell I could do it [save money for his children]. I always said for years, 'I wanna get rich, I wanna get rich.' But then, phew! My mind doesn't have the strong will. I say, 'Well, I'm *gonna* do it.' Only the next day's different." These people are typical. In 1985, over 60 percent of poor people but only 45 percent of the nonpoor agreed that "poor young women often have babies so they can collect welfare." Seven years later, the same proportions of poor and well-off agreed that welfare recipients "are taking advantage of the system."

The equation of failure with evil and success with virtue cannot be attributed to poor education or low status. College students "who learned that a fellow student had been awarded a cash prize as a result of a random drawing were likely to conclude that he had in fact worked especially hard." In another experiment, subjects rated a presumed victim of electric shocks who was randomly selected to receive compensation for her pain more favorably than a victim who would not be compensated. "The sight of an innocent person suffering without possibility of reward or compensation motivated people to devalue the attractiveness of the victim in order to bring about a more appropriate fit between her fate and her character." Devaluing losers allows people to maintain their belief that the world is fundamentally just, even when it patently is not.

Losers are obviously harmed by the association of success with virtue. But the association creates equally important, if less obvious, problems for winners. Fitzwilliam Darcy, in Jane Austen's *Pride and Prejudice,* epitomizes the defect of pride: if I believe that virtue produced my success, or that success has made me even more virtuous, I am likely to become insufferably smug. That may not bother me much, but the fact that people around me feel the same way will. In addition, this equation raises the stakes very high for further rounds of endeavor. If I continue to win, all is well; if I falter, I lose my *amour propre* as well as my wealth or power. Alternatively, if I recognize that I partly owe my success to lying to a few clients, evading a few taxes, cheating a few employees, then I am likely to feel considerable guilt. This guilt might induce reform and recompense, but it may instead induce drinking to assuage the unease, persecuting other nonvirtuous winners, striving to show that losers are even more sinful, or simple hypocrisy.

These problems intensify when patterns of group success rather than the idiosyncrasies of individual success are at issue. When members of one group seem disproportionately successful, that group acquires a halo of ascribed virtue. Consider a 1907 article by Burton J. Hendrick on "The Great Jewish Invasion" in *McClure's Magazine.* The author's name, the publication, the date, and the title all lead one to expect an (at best, thinly veiled) anti-Semitic diatribe. The first few pages seem to confirm that expectation, with their claims that "the real modern Zion, greater in numbers and wealth and power than the old, steadily gathers on Manhattan Island," and that "the Jews are active, and invariably with success, in practically every business, professional, and intellectual field. The New Yorker constantly rubs shoulders with Israel." These feats are all the more "remarkable" because "the great mass of its [New York's] Jews are not what are commonly regarded as the most enlightened of their race" since they come from eastern Europe. After all, "no people have had a more inadequate preparation, educational and economic, for American citizenship."

Yet the article goes on to describe in careful and admiring detail how these dirt-poor, ignorant, orthodoxly non-Christian immigrants work, save, cooperate, sacrifice for their children—and end up wealthy beyond anyone's wildest imaginings. Nor are they merely money-grubbers; Russian Jews are "individualist[s]," the "city's largest productive force and the greatest contributor to its manufacturing wealth," demonstrating "intense ambition," abstinence, and foresight. In his highest accolade, Mr. Hendrick even insists that the Russian Jew's

> enthusiasm for America knows no bounds. He eagerly looks forward to the time when he can be naturalized. . . . The rapidity with which the New York Jew adopts the manners and trappings of Americans almost disproves his ancient heritage as a peculiar people. . . . Better than any other element, even the native stock, do they meet the two supreme tests of citizenship: they actually go to the polls, and when once there, vote independently.

In short, in one generation the east European Jewish immigrant has gone from an unassimilable, bovine drag on the American spirit to the epitome of all the American virtues. Nothing succeeds like success.

The contemporary equivalent of Mr. Hendrick's amazing Jews are Southeast Asians. A century ago, Chinese and Japanese immigrants could hardly be derogated enough. Now newspapers have a seemingly endless supply of rags-to-riches stories about destitute boat people whose daughter became the high school valedictorian a scant five years later and is now a pre-med student at Stanford. Such success is inevitably attributed to hard work, self-discipline, family support, and refusal to follow the bad example set by American-born peers. This portrayal is so ubiquitous that spokespeople for Asian immigrants feel impelled to insist publicly that not *all* Asians escape poverty, crime, and discrimination, and that even the successful pay a heavy emotional cost.

It would be churlish to argue that excessive praise is as bad as racism or ethnic slurs. But newly anointed groups are too often used to cast aspersions on some despised group that has not managed to fulfill the American dream. In Burton Hendrick's case, the main negative reference group is the Irish, who drink and gamble, yield their productive jobs to Jews, and—worst of all—band together in labor unions, in the "Irish vote," and in political party machines. In the case of immigrant Asians, the usual (if slightly more subtle) message is "Why can't African Americans do the same thing? At least they speak English when they start school." This dynamic adds yet another component to the nightmare of a failed American dream. Members of a denigrated group are disproportionately likely to fail to achieve their goals; they are blamed as individuals (and perhaps blame themselves) for their failure; and they carry a further stigma as members of a nonvirtuous (thus appropriately denigrated) group.

This effect of the fourth tenet can be taken a further, and most dangerous, step. For some Americans always, and for many Americans in some periods of our history, virtuous success has been defined as the dominance of some groups over others. This phenomenon extends the idea of competitive success from individual victories to collective hierarchies. If women are weak and emotional, it is *right* for men to control their bodies and wealth; if blacks are childlike pagans, it is *right* for whites to ensure their physical and spiritual survival through enslavement and conversion; if citizens of other nations refuse to recognize the value of capitalism and free elections, it is *right* for Americans to install a more enlightened government in their capitol. I find it hard to present these sentiments with a straight face, but they have arguably done almost as much as the American dream to shape Americans' beliefs, practices, and institutions.

FLAWS IN THE AMERICAN DREAM TAKEN AS A WHOLE

Atomistic Individualism

Not only each tenet, but also the ideology of the American dream as a whole, is flawed. One problem stems from the radical individualism often associated with the dream (although the ideology entails nothing that prohibits groups from pursuing collective success). Achievers mark their success by moving away from the tenement, ghetto, or holler of their impoverished and impotent youth, thus speeding the breakup of their ethnic community. This is a bittersweet phenomenon. The freedom to move up and out is desirable, or at least desired. But certainly those left behind, probably those who leave, and arguably the nation as a whole lose when groups of people with close cultural and personal ties break those ties in pursuit of or after attaining "the bitch-goddess, success." The line between autonomy and atomism is hard to draw.

American culture is full of stories about the mixed effects of success on communities and their residents. A Polish-American folk song tells of a man who emigrated to America, worked for three years in a foundry, returned home with "gold and silver," but found that "my children did not know me, for they fled from me, a stranger." The emancipated children may be as pained as the abandoned parents, as illustrated by the five brothers who complained to the *Jewish Daily Forward* in 1933:

> Imagine, even when we go with our father to buy something in a store on Fifth Avenue, New York, he insists on speaking Yiddish. We are not ashamed of our parents, God forbid, but they ought to know where it's proper and where it's not. If they talk Yiddish among themselves at home, or to

us, it's bad enough, but among strangers and Christians? Is that nice?

Only irresponsible romanticism permits the wish that peasants and villagers would opt for tradition rather than opportunity. It is surely significant that across the world and throughout centuries, they almost never do. But one can still regret what is lost. And Thomas Hooker's warning cannot be shrugged off: "For if each man may do what is good in his owne eyes, proceed according to his own pleasure, so that none may crosse him or controll him by any power, there must of necessity follow the distraction and desolation of the whole."

Narrowing "Success"

William James followed his comment on "the moral flabbiness born of the exclusive worship of the bitch-goddess, success" with the less well-known observation that "that—with the squalid cash interpretation put on the word success—is our national disease." It was at best indecorous for a man as wealthy and prestigious as William James to castigate others' pursuit of wealth or inattentiveness to philosophy. But his concern is warranted. The American dream is susceptible to having the open-ended definition of success, which can equally include salvation or writing the great American novel, narrowed to wealth, job status, or power. Well-educated women (not to speak of men) are embarrassed to admit that they would rather raise happy children than practice corporate law; environmentalists worry that the value of a beautiful forest cannot be monetized and therefore will not be considered in regulatory decisions. Even high school seniors, for whom "having lots of money" has become increasingly important over the past two decades, overwhelmingly and increasingly agree that "people are too much concerned with material things these days."

Sometimes market values colonize, rather than submerge, other values. Economists designing environmental regulations assign monetary value to a stand of redwood trees, thereby cheapening (note the metaphor) the meaning of the primeval forest in the eyes of environmentalists. Some feminists seek to enhance the status of women by calculating the wages due to housework and including them in the gross national product; other feminists see this move as turning loving wives and mothers into calculating *homo economici.* The problem in these and similar cases is not that the assignment of monetary worth is too high or low, but that the very process of assigning monetary worth reduces an array of values to a single thin one.

Only sentimentalism allows one to value the purity of artistic poverty over the sordidness of corporate wealth unless one made the choice after experiencing both states. But it is a serious flaw in the American dream if those who envision success in artistic or religious or altruistic terms must defend their vision as well as fight to achieve their chosen goals. Nothing in the ideology requires reducing success to money and power, but the ideology is so vulnerable to the reduction that that point must count as an internal flaw, not merely as grounds for an external attack.

The Ideology as Deception

I have argued that the American dream need not be individualistic in the narrow sense, given that one can under its rubric pursue success for one's family or community as well as for oneself. But it is highly *individual,* in that it leads one to focus on people's behaviors rather than on economic processes, environmental constraints, or political structures as the causal explanation for social orderings. That focus is not itself a flaw; it is simply an epistemological choice with methodological implications for the study of American politics. But to the degree that the focus carries a moral message, it points to a weakness at the very heart of the dream.

The idea of the blank slate in the first tenet, the almost-promise of success of the second, the reliance on personal attributes in the third, the

association of failure with sin in the fourth—all these elements of the dream make it extremely difficult for Americans to see that everyone cannot simultaneously attain more than absolute success. Capitalist markets require some firms to fail; elections require some candidates and policy preferences to lose; status hierarchies must have a bottom in order to have a top. But the optimistic language of and methodological individualism built into the American dream *necessarily* deceive people about these societal operations. We need not invoke hypocrites out of Mark Twain or "blue-eyed white devils" in order to understand why some people never attain success; hypocrisy or bias only enter the picture in determining *who* fails. But our basic institutions are designed to ensure that some fail, at least relatively, and a dream does nothing to help Americans cope with or even to recognize that fact.

Few Alternative Visions

All ideologies are designed to put the best possible face on the social structure within which they operate, and all privilege some values over others. So all the flaws I have described, damning though they may seem, must themselves be judged in light of the comparable flaws of other ideological formations. That point is intended to soften slightly the critique of the American dream, but it also raises a final problem with it.

Americans have few alternative ideologies against which to measure the distinctive virtues and flaws of the American dream. Alternatives are not completely absent: Thoreau's *Walden* has long been recognized as a sharp political challenge couched in a literary classic. "Country-party" or labor republicanism, Protestant fundamentalism, and ascriptive Americanism similarly have deep roots and on occasion strong adherents and powerful institutional manifestations. But most Americans honor these alternative visions more in the breach than in the observance, if then. *Walden* is read by more students majoring in English than in political science. "Small is beautiful" and "social limits to growth" are slogans for a few, but warnings to many more. And many possible visions—within-class solidarity and cross-class warfare, a military or theocratic polity pursuing collective glory, small cooperative enterprises living lightly on the land—are barely visible in the American political spectrum. In short, the political culture of the U.S. is largely shaped by a set of views in which the American dream is prominent, and by a set of institutions that make it even more prominent than views alone could do.

Tocqueville assured his readers that "up to now the Americans have happily avoided all the reefs I have just charted." Some Americans continue, 150 years later, to sail free, and perhaps they always will. But some have wrecked, and some have never gotten anywhere near the boat. For those afloat, the ideology of the American dream is a vindication, a goad to further efforts, a cause for celebration—and also grounds for anxiety, guilt and disillusionment. For the shipwrecked and drifters, the dream is a taunt, a condemnation, an object of fury—and also grounds for hope; renewed striving, and dreams for one's children.

DISCUSSION QUESTIONS

1. According to Hochschild, what are the key tenets of success in the American dream, and in what ways might the American definition of success be considered narrow?
2. In what sense is the American dream a "fantasy"? How is this fantasy reinforced by American life and culture?
3. What does Hochschild mean by "atomistic individualism" and why does she consider it a flaw?

6 *James Gustave Speth*

HAPPINESS AND THE AMERICAN DREAM

From the very beginning, the American political tradition has not been monolithic or consistent, containing as it does several core contradictions that contend for preeminence in our political, economic, and cultural lives. Here environmental Law Professor James Gustave (Gus) Speth focuses his attention on these differing visions of what constitutes the "American Dream," particularly as it relates to how we envision happiness and human fulfillment. Drawing on an array of recent scholarship, Speth traces these competing visions from the Founders through our twenty-first century political world. At their core, each of the three sets of "dueling dualities" contains a vision of an individualistic and materialistic notion of the pursuit of happiness at odds with a notion steeped in the common good and shared values—a crude version of capitalism at odds with a more vibrant and democratic civic life. How these clashing visions play out politically says a lot about where we are as a nation, and this discord profoundly impacts the kinds of public policies pursued in the name of improving the lives of American citizens. Moreover, the way we move toward one end or the other of these dual visions contributes significantly to defining the contours of our nation's hopes and dreams.

Throughout our history, there have been alternative, competing visions of the "good life" in America. The story of how these competing visions played out in our history is prologue to an important question: What is the American Dream and what is its future?

The issue came up in the early Republic, offspring of the ambiguity in Jefferson's declaration that we have an unalienable right to "the pursuit of happiness." Darrin McMahon in his admirable book, *Happiness: A History*, will be our guide here. McMahon locates the origins of the "right to happiness" in the Enlightenment. "Does not everyone have a right to happiness? asked . . . the entry on that subject in the French encyclopedia edited by Denis Diderot. Judged by the standards of the preceding millennium and a half, the question was extraordinary: a *right* to happiness? And

Source: James Gustav Speth, "What is the American Dream? Dueling Dualities in the American Tradition." *Grist.org*, June 24, 2011. Online location: http://www.grist.org/politics/2011-06-24-what-is-the-american-dream-dueling-dualities-in-the-american-tra

yet it was posed rhetorically, in full confidence of the nodding assent of enlightened minds." It was in 1776, the year of the Declaration of Independence, that Jeremy Bentham would write his famous principle of utility: "It is the greatest happiness of the greatest number that is the measure of right and wrong."

Thus, when Thomas Jefferson drafted the Declaration in June of that memorable year, the words "the pursuit of happiness" came naturally to him, and the language sailed through the debates of June and July without dissent. McMahon believes this lack of controversy stemmed in part from the fact that the "pursuit of happiness" phrase brought together ambiguously two very different notions: the idea from John Locke and Jeremy Bentham that happiness was the pursuit of personal pleasure and the older Stoic idea that happiness derived from active devotion to the public good and from civic virtue, which have little to do with personal pleasure.

"The 'pursuit of happiness,'" McMahon writes, "was launched in different, and potentially conflicting, directions from the start, with private pleasure and public welfare coexisting in the same phrase. For Jefferson, so quintessentially in this respect a man of the Enlightenment, the coexistence was not a problem." But Jefferson's formula almost immediately lost its double meaning in practice, McMahon notes, and the right of citizens to pursue their personal interests and joy won out. This victory was confirmed by waves of immigrants to America's shores, for whom America was truly the land of opportunity. "To pursue happiness in such a land was quite rightly to pursue prosperity, to pursue pleasure, to pursue wealth."

It is in this jettisoning of the civic virtue concept of happiness in favor of the self-gratification side that McMahon finds the link between the pursuit of happiness and the rise of American capitalism in the nineteenth and twentieth centuries. Happiness, he writes, "continued to entice with attractive force, providing a justification for work and sacrifice, a basis for meaning and hope that only loomed larger on the horizon of Western

democracies." "If economic growth was now a secular religion," McMahon observes, "the pursuit of happiness remained its central creed, with greater opportunities than ever before to pursue pleasure in comfort and things." Max Weber saw this transformation first hand. "Material goods," he observed in *The Protestant Ethic and the Spirit of Capitalism*, "have gained an increasing and finally an inexorable power over the lives of men as at no previous period in history."

The story of the pursuit of happiness in America is thus a story of its close alliance with capitalism and consumerism. But in recent years, many researchers have begun to see this relationship as one of misplaced allegiance. Has the pursuit of happiness through growth in material abundance and possessions actually brought Americans happiness? That is a question more for science than for philosophy, and the good news is that social scientists have in fact recently turned abundantly to the subject. A new field, positive psychology, the study of happiness and subjective well-being, has been invented, and there is now even a professional *Journal of Happiness Studies*.

Imagine, if you will, two very different alternatives for affluent societies. In one, economic growth, prosperity and affluence bring steadily increasing human happiness, well-being and satisfaction. In a second, prosperity and happiness are not correlated, and, indeed, prosperity, beyond a certain point, is associated with the growth of important social pathologies. Which scenario provides a closer fit to reality?

What the social scientists in this new field are telling us is of fundamental importance. Two of the leaders in the field, Ed Diener and Martin Seligman, carried out a review of the now-voluminous literature on well-being in their 2004 article, "Beyond Money: Toward an Economy of Well-Being." In what follows, I will draw upon this article and other research.

The overall concept that is gaining acceptance among researchers is "subjective well being," i.e., a person's own opinion of his or her well being. Subjects in surveys are frequently asked, on a scale of one to 10, how satisfied are you with your life? Most well-being surveys today ask individuals how happy or satisfied they are with their lives in general, how satisfied they are in particular contexts (e.g., work, marriage), or how much they trust others, and so on.

A good place to begin is with the studies that compare levels of happiness and life satisfaction among nations at different stages of economic development. They find that the citizens of wealthier countries do report higher levels of life satisfaction, although the correlation is rather poor and is even poorer when factors such as quality of government are statistically controlled. Moreover, this positive relationship between national well-being and national per capita income virtually disappears when one looks only at countries with GDP per capita over $10,000 per year. In short, once a country achieves a moderate level of income, further growth does not significantly improve perceived well-being.

Diener and Seligman report that peoples with the highest well-being are not those in the richest countries but those who live where political institutions are effective and human rights protected, where corruption is low, and mutual trust high.

Even more challenging to the idea that well-being increases with higher incomes is extensive time series data showing that throughout almost the entire post-World War II period, as incomes skyrocketed in the United States and other advanced economies, reported life satisfaction and happiness levels stagnated or even declined slightly.

But that is not all. Diener and Seligman note that, "Even more disparity [between income and well-being] shows up when ill-being measures are considered. For instance, depression rates have increased 10-fold over the same 50-year period, and rates of anxiety are also rising . . . [T]he average American child in the 1980s reported greater anxiety than the average child receiving psychiatric treatment in the 1950s. There is [also] a decreasing level of social connectedness in society, as evidenced by declining levels of trust in other people and in governmental institutions." Numerous studies also stress that nothing is more devastating to well-being than losing one's job and unemployment.

Instead of income, Diener and Seligman stress the importance of personal relationships to happiness: "The quality of people's social relationships is crucial to their well-being. People need supportive, positive relationships and social belonging to sustain well-being . . . [T]he need to belong, to have close and long-term social relationships, is a fundamental human need . . . People need social bonds in committed relationships, not simply interactions with strangers, to experience well-being."

In short, what the social scientists are telling us is that as of today, in Ed Diener's words, "materialism is toxic for happiness." Whether the pursuit of happiness through evermore possessions succeeded earlier in our history, it no longer does.

Norton Garfinkle traces another dueling duality in the American tradition, one reflected in the title of his helpful book, *The American Dream vs. the Gospel of Wealth*. Although the phrase "the American Dream" entered the language thanks to James Truslow Adams and his 1931 book, *The Epic of America*, Garfinkle argues that the force of the concept, if not the phrase, derives from President Lincoln. "More than any other president," Garfinkle believes, "Lincoln is the father of the American Dream that all Americans should have the opportunity through hard work to build a comfortable middle class life. For Lincoln, liberty meant above all the right of individuals to the fruits of their own labor, seen as a path to prosperity. 'To [secure] to each laborer the whole product of his labor, or as nearly as possible,' he wrote, 'is a most worthy object of any good government.'"

"The universal promise of opportunity," Garfinkle writes, "was for Lincoln the philosophical core of America: it was the essence of the American system. 'Without the *Constitution* and the *Union*,' he wrote, 'we could not have attained . . . our great prosperity.' But the Constitution and the Union were not the 'primary cause' of America, Lincoln believed. 'There is something,' he continued, 'back of these, entwining itself more closely about the human heart . . . This is the just and generous and prosperous system which opens the way to all, gives hope to all, and consequent energy and progress and improvement of condition to all.' This was, for Lincoln, the American Dream, the raison d'être of America, and the unique contribution of America to world history."

Although Garfinkle does not bring it out, I believe James Truslow Adams' vision of the American Dream is at least as compelling as that of Lincoln. Adams used the phrase, "the American dream," to refer, not to getting rich or even especially to a secure, middle class lifestyle, though that was part of it, but primarily to something finer and more important: "It is not a dream of motor cars and high wages merely, but a dream of a social order in which each man and each woman shall be able to attain to the fullest stature of which they are innately capable, and be recognized by others for what they are, regardless of the fortuitous circumstances of birth or position." That American Dream is well worth carrying with us into the future.

The competing vision, the Gospel of Wealth, found its origins in the Gilded Age. In his 1889 book, *The Gospel of Wealth*, Andrew Carnegie espoused a widely held philosophy that drew on Social Darwinism and, though less crudely expressed, has many adherents today. To Carnegie, the depressed conditions of late 19th century American workers and the limited opportunities they faced were prices to be paid for the abundance economic progress made possible. Carnegie was brutally honest in his views: "The price which society pays for the law of competition, like the price it pays for cheap comforts and luxuries, is also great; but the advantages of this law are also greater still than its cost—for it is to this law that we owe our wonderful material development, which brings improved conditions in its train. But, whether the law be benign or not, . . . it is here, we cannot evade it; no substitutes for it have been found; and while the law may be sometimes hard for the individual, it is

best for the race, because it insures the survival of the fittest in every department. We accept and welcome, therefore, as conditions to which we must accommodate ourselves, great inequality of environment; the concentration of business, industrial and commercial, in the hands of a few; and the law of competition between these, as being not only beneficial, but essential to the future progress of the race. Having accepted these, it follows that there must be great scope for the exercise of special ability in the merchant and in the manufacturer who has to conduct affairs upon a great scale. That this talent for organization and management is rare among men is proved by the fact that it invariably secures enormous rewards for its possessor."

Garfinkle recounts the many ways Carnegie's Gospel stood Lincoln's vision on its head: "Whereas in Lincoln's America, the underlying principle of economic life was widely shared equality of opportunity, based on the ideals set forth in the Declaration of Independence, in Carnegie's America the watchword was inequality and the concentration of wealth and resource in the hands of the few. Whereas in Lincoln's America, government was to take an active role in clearing the path for ordinary people to get ahead, in Carnegie's America, the government was to step aside and let the laws of economics run their course. Whereas in Lincoln's America, the laborer had a right to the fruits of his labor, in Carnegie's America the fruits went disproportionately to the business owner and investor as the fittest. Whereas in Lincoln's America, the desire was to help all Americans fulfill the dream of the self-made man, in Carnegie's America, it was the rare exception, the man of unusual talent that was to be supported."

Since the Reagan Revolution, of course, the Gospel of Wealth has returned with a vengeance. Income and wealth have been reconcentrated in the hands of the few at levels not seen since 1928, American wages have flatlined for several decades, the once-proud American middle class is fading fast, and government action to improve the prospects of average Americans is widely disparaged.

Indeed, government has pursued policies leading to the dramatic decline in both union membership and good American jobs. In a sample of its 20 peer OECD countries, the United States today has the lowest social mobility, the greatest income inequality, and the most poverty.

A third historical duality in envisioning America is that between an American lifestyle that revolves around consumption and one that embraces plain and simple living. In her important book, *The Consumers' Republic*, Lizabeth Cohen traces the rise of mass consumption in America to policies adopted after World War II: "Americans after World War II saw their nation as the model for the world of a society committed to mass consumption and what were assumed to be its far-reaching benefits. Mass consumption did not only deliver wonderful things for purchase—the televisions, air conditioners, and computers that have transformed American life over the last half century. It also dictated the most central dimensions of postwar society, including the political economy (the way public policy and the mass consumption economy mutually reinforced each other), as well as the political culture (how political practice and American values, attitudes, and behaviors tied to mass consumption became intertwined)."

However, Cohen also documents that, whatever its blessings, American consumerism has had profound and unintended consequences on broader issues of social justice and democracy. She notes that "the Consumers' Republic did not unfold quite as policymakers intended . . . the Consumers' Republic's dependence on unregulated private markets wove inequalities deep into the fabric of prosperity, thereby allowing, intentionally or not, the search for profits and the exigencies of the market to prevail over higher goals. Often the outcome dramatically diverged from the stated objective to use mass markets to create a more egalitarian and democratic American society . . . [T]he deeply entrenched convictions prevailing in the Consumers' Republic that a dynamic, private, mass consumption marketplace could float all boats and that a growing economy

made reslicing the economic pie unnecessary predisposed Americans against more redistributive actions . . .

"Most ironic perhaps, the confidence that a prospering mass consumption economy could foster democracy would over time contribute to a decline in the most traditional, and one could argue most critical, form of political participation—voting—as more commercialized political salesmanship replaced rank-and-file mobilization through parties."

The creation of the Consumers' Republic represented the triumph of one vision of American life and purpose. But there has been a competing vision, what historian David Shi calls the tradition of "plain living and high thinking," a tradition that began with the Puritans and the Quakers. In his book, *The Simple Life*, Shi sees in American history a "perpetual tension . . . between the ideal of enlightened self-restraint and the allure of unfettered prosperity. From colonial days, the mythic image of America as a spiritual commonwealth and a republic of virtue has survived alongside the more tantalizing view of the nation as an engine of economic opportunities, a festival of unfettered individualism, and a cornucopia of consumer delights."

"The concept [of the simple life] arrived with the first settlers, and it has remained an enduring—and elusive—ideal . . . Its primary attributes include a hostility toward luxury and a suspicion of riches, a reverence for nature and a preference for rural over urban ways of life and work, a desire for personal self-reliance through frugality and diligence, a nostalgia for the past, a commitment to conscientious rather than conspicuous consumption, a privileging of contemplation and creativity, an aesthetic preference for the plain and functional, and a sense of both religious and ecological responsibility for the just uses of the world's resources."

In the end, these three dueling dualities in the American tradition—competing over the meaning of happiness, the path to prosperity, the centrality of consumerism—tell much the same story: the vision of an America where the pursuit of happiness is sought in the growth of civic virtue and in devotion to the public good, where the American dream is steadily realized as the average American achieves his or her human potential and the benefits of economic activity are widely shared, and where the virtues of simple living, self-reliance and reverence for nature predominate, that vision has not prevailed and has instead been overpowered by the rise of commercialism, consumerism, and a particularly ruthless variety of winner-take-all capitalism.

These American traditions may not have prevailed to date, but they are not dead. They await us, and indeed they are today being awakened across this great land. New ways of living and working, sharing and caring are emerging across America. They beckon us with a new American Dream, one rebuilt from the best of the old, drawing on the best of who we were and are and can be.

There is an America beyond despair, and it is fueling these developments. Ask a parent, ask yourself, what America would you like for your grandchildren and their children, and the odds are good that in the reply, the outpouring of hope, a new America unfolds.

DISCUSSION QUESTIONS

1. Identify and discuss the dueling dualities of the American Dream and the related concept of happiness. Where did they come from? What is gained, and what is lost, by defining the dream of happiness in each version?
2. What policy debates today reflect these dueling notions of happiness and the American Dream? Explain. Do our two major political parties reflect these "dueling dualities"? Or would we need a new political party to articulate a version of the American Dream "worth carrying with us into the future"?
3. Compare and contrast the dilemmas of the American Dream as enumerated in Jennifer Hochschild's article (No. 5) and in this selection by Speth. Do their arguments reinforce each other or are they at odds in some ways? Explain.

7 *Ira Chernus*

THE THEOLOGY OF AMERICAN EMPIRE

In this selection, Professor of Religious Studies and author Ira Chernus searches for the roots of U.S. foreign policy. He finds them in, of all places, Christian theology, a foundation "hidden underground." He cites the work of twentieth-century theologian Reinhold Niebuhr as the touchstone for this theological perspective, with his dark view of human nature based in original sin. Although sharing some affinity with Niebuhr, today's neo-conservative policy makers have distorted his "realism" to suit their own ends. Neoconservatives assert that while all people may be sinners, not all nations are; thus, they assert a hierarchy of nations within which America's enemies are on the bottom and America is on top with its allegedly pure motives. This "good versus evil" passion play leads to a mythic world-view where America stands tall with moral certainty and clarity—"the world's chosen people"—with reality only creeping in when U.S. military intervention doesn't follow this heavenly script. While Chernus notes some variations on these assumptions among foreign policy planners, the "main-stream foreign policy elite" have adopted the basic story of this script, while differing on some of the means for achieving the same ends of American global dominance wrapped in moral idealism. Chernus makes the case for the need for America to embrace "different moral certainties" and a "dif-ferent narrative," in order to redefine national security altogether. If we can forge a new way of thinking about national interests within our politi-cal culture, we might have a chance to create a more peaceful, integrated global system.

American foreign policy is built on a deep foundation of Christian theology. Some of the people who make our foreign policy may understand that foundation. Most probably aren't even aware of it. But foundations are hidden underground. You can stand above them, and even take a strong stand upon them, without knowing they are there. When it comes to foreign policy, we are

Source: "Ira Chernus, "The Theology of American Empire" (Washington, DC: Foreign Policy In Focus, September 26, 2007).

all influenced by theological foundations that we rarely see.

For example, few Americans have read the work of Reinhold Niebuhr, the most influential American theologian of the twentieth-century. Many have never even heard the name. Yet Niebuhr's thought affects us all. In the 1930s, he launched an attack on the liberal Christianity of the Social Gospel, a movement that powerfully influenced U.S. foreign policy in the first third of the twentieth-century. The liberals were starry-eyed fools, Niebuhr charged, because they trusted people to be reasonable enough to resolve international conflicts peacefully. They forgot the harsh reality of original sin.

Niebuhr wrapped that traditional notion of sin in a new intellectual package and sold it successfully, not only to theologians but to the foreign policy elite. Since the 1940s, foreign policy has largely been reduced to an endless round of debates about how to apply Niebuhr's "realism." Policymakers who still tried to follow the Social Gospel path have been marginalized and stigmatized with the harshest epithet a Niebuhrian can hurl: "unrealistic."

It's a Jungle Out There

Many policymakers, like much of the public at large, have come to find a strange comfort in the world as Niebuhr described it. They see a jungle where evildoers, who are all around, must be hunted down and destroyed. Though frightening, this world can easily become the stage for simplistic dramas of good against evil. And the moral certainty of being on the side of good—the side of God—can provide a sense of security that more than makes up for the constant terror. That was not what Niebuhr had in mind. But as he found out so painfully, once you let ideas loose in the world, you can't control what others do with them.

Niebuhr would have been pained to see what the neoconservatives have done with his ideas. Their theory starts out from his own premise: All people are born naturally selfish and impulsive. The godfather of neoconservatism, Irving Kristol, was (like most of the early neocons) an intellectual—a teacher, writer, and editor—and (like many of the early neocons) a Jew. But he turned to Christian theology to describe his Niebuhrian view of human nature: "Original sin was one way of saying this, and I had no problem with that doctrine." Selfish impulses, when they get out of control, can tear society apart, he warned. To preserve social order we need a fixed moral order. We therefore need a clear sense of the absolute difference between good and bad, strict rules that tell us what is good, and powerful institutions that can get people to obey those rules.

According to this worldview, organized religion has been the most effective institution to promote moral absolutes and self-control. Religion now needs to be strengthened to stave off a rising tide of moral relativism that, along with secular humanism, is breaking down the bulwarks of social order and threatening to release a flood of selfish impulse to drown us all in chaos. A favorite neoconservative columnist, Charles Krauthammer, complains that American mass culture, dominated by skepticism and pleasure, is an "engine of social breakdown." The best antidote would be a "self-abnegating religious revival." Since that is not likely to happen, Krauthammer admits, the best place to recover moral discipline and will power is in foreign affairs: America must find the will to exercise its strength and become "confident enough to define international morality in its own, American terms."

Original Sin Goes global

When neoconservatives apply their views to international relations, they deviate from Niebuhr's teaching. All people may be sinners, they imply, but not all nations. They assume an (often vaguely defined) hierarchy of nations. At the bottom are the enemies of America, consistently described as chaotic, irrational monsters who are incapable of self-control and bent on provoking instability and evil for its own sake. Above them are neutral nations and then U.S. allies near the top of the pyramid. At the top is the United States, in a class by itself because its national motives are good and pure, somehow untainted by original sin.

Neoconservatives insist on this hierarchy, with its dramatic contrast between the good United States and its evil enemies, because it gives them the sense of moral clarity and certainty that they rely on to hold back the relativism they fear. They bolster their sense of certainty by reducing international affairs to simplistic myths: black-and-white tales of absolute good versus absolute evil. (Here I use the word "myth" in its religious sense of a narrative story that expresses a community's worldview and basic values.) George W. Bush tapped into this mythic world when he said that the war on terrorism is "a monumental struggle between good and evil. But good will prevail." The outcome is certain, according to Bush, because "we all know that this is one nation, under God." But Americans must do their world-ordering job pretty much alone, since other nations and international institutions are too self-ish to be trusted. The United States must rely primarily on military might, since the only language that the sinful evildoers understand is force.

The neoconservatives did not invent this myth. It goes back to the Puritan belief in "the new Israel" and Americans as God's chosen people, with the special privilege and responsibility of bringing order to a sinful, chaotic world. Most Americans are still likely to see their nation as the global hero fulfilling that sacred task. Only the United States, they believe in a great leap of faith, is moved by an unselfish desire to serve the good of all humanity by spreading ordered liberty.

Throughout the Cold War era, across the political spectrum, there was no doubting the name of the threatening evil: Communism. After a decade of drift and uncertainty in the 1990s, the September 11 attacks, despite their horror, allowed the nation to breathe easier, at least in terms of the theology of foreign policy. Once again, it seemed that everyone agreed on the name of the monstrous sinners, the source of insta-bility. Rudolph Giuliani could have been speak-ing for most Americans when he explained that the cultural payoff of the war on terrorism was

moral stability: "The era of moral relativism . . . must end. Moral relativism does not have a place in this discussion." That crusading tone of cer-tainty gave Bush and the neoconservatives a very free hand in the early post-September 11 days, when they launched the invasion of Afghanistan. The administration then invaded Iraq with the approval of 75% of the U.S. public and nearly all the foreign policy elite.

IRAQ WAR

The myth of U.S. moral and global supremacy—Americans as the world's chosen people—went largely unchallenged until the U.S. venture in Iraq went sour. The myth says that the good guys are supposed to win every time, because they are good. When the myth does not get played out in reality, people start to complain. If you look at the current debate about Iraq from the standpoint of myth and theology, the complainers fall into three broad groups.

First there is the mainstream of the foreign policy elite, made up of Democrats and more moderate Republicans. They complain that the Bush administration is pursuing the right goals but using the wrong tactics. That's because the elite still hold on to some shreds of the old Social Gospel view. They give most of the world a bit more credit for rationality; they fear the impulses of original sin a bit less. So they see military strength as one of several ways to secure Amer-ica's global hegemony. They are more willing to take a multilateral approach and use the carrot as well as the stick—to pull diplomatic and eco-nomic levers before calling out the troops.

But these differences, though they can be very important, are largely ones of degree and tactics. Across the board, members of the foreign policy establishment, even the liberal Democrats, still give a very respectful (sometimes slavish) hearing to the great theologian Niebuhr. But they apply his "realistic" view of original sin only to other nations. The liberals among the elite, too, want their sense of moral clarity and certainty reas-sured by seeing it played out in a global drama of good against evil. So they make a huge exception for the supposedly pure and innocent motives of their own nation, the chosen people. They believe that the U.S. has a higher moral standing, which gives us the right and duty to rule. That's how they can justify the most ruthless policies against anyone who stands in their way.

The bipartisan elite may not value the display of American strength as an end in itself, the way neoconservatives do. They are willing to risk a short-term appearance of weakness in one place in order to bolster long-term U.S. strength everywhere else. But long-term strength (including a long-term military presence in Iraq) is still crucial, because they feel a sacred calling to enforce "stability"—their favorite code word for a single global order that protects U.S. interests—everywhere and forever.

The second group of war critics is on the right. A growing number of traditional conservatives criticize the administration and the bipartisan establishment for betraying genuine Niebuhrian "realism." These hard-core "realists" want the United States to recognize that it too is a sinful nation, limited in its goodness as well as its resources, all too likely to overreach and eventually destroy itself if it doesn't scale back its hubristic dream of enduring empire.

Thus the right-wing "realists" become strange bedfellows with the third group of war critics, the left-wingers, who, starting from very different principles, arrive at the same anti-imperialist conclusions. Though most of them don't know it, what makes leftists leftist is that they still champion many of the basic values of the Social Gospel movement. They do not accept the doctrine of original sin; they don't think people are inherently doomed to be selfish and unreasonable. They assume that the vast majority of people, if treated decently and given decent living conditions, will respond by being decent people. For the left, order and stability are not as important as human growth, creativity, and transformation. The key to a better world is not strength and dominance, but sharing and cooperation. And leftists often assume—or at least

hope—that the long-term trend of history is leading to that better world, a view that is rooted in the biblical hope for redemption.

IN MIDDLE AMERICA

Leftists who are consistent extend their Social Gospel view to its logical conclusion: There are no monsters—no inherently bad people—only bad conditions. So the good guys versus bad guys myth always distorts reality. But a surprising number of leftists sacrifice logical consistency for the emotional pleasure of the traditional myth. For them, of course, the monsters are the Bush administration, the neoconservatives, sometimes the mainstream Democrats too, and always, above all, the corporate elite whose hand they see behind every gesture of U.S. imperialism.

This left-wing version of the myth does not play very well in middle America, or even on the coasts apart from a few ultra-liberal enclaves. The hardcore "realist" view may get slightly higher ratings, but not much. Most Americans still demand a heavy dose of moral idealism in their foreign policy. They want to continue believing in the myth of American innocence. They won't give in to a full-blown Niebuhrian pessimism about human nature—at least not when it comes to American humans. And they don't want to believe that the economic and political leaders of their nation are utterly cynical "realists," devoid of ideals, caring only about money and power.

So the mass of the citizenry, sick and tired of losing in Iraq, swing in line behind the only critical voice they can support: the foreign policy elite. The public criticizes the administration for its inept effort in Iraq. But most citizens don't raise any questions about the long-term goals or the theological premises underlying them.

Only when something looks broken do people think about fixing it. The last time the U.S. foreign policy system broke down was when the United States suffered defeat in Vietnam. However, after a short period of radical questioning, a powerful reaction set in, fueled by the deep and widespread need for idealism and moral certainty. The neoconservatives got control of the public conversation in the late 1970s because they recognized that need and offered a Cold War myth that satisfied it.

The same need for moral clarity arose after September 11, but it's been bitterly betrayed by the failure in Iraq. How can we avoid a similar neoconservative reaction as we question the underpinnings of U.S. foreign policy in the years to come? And if the Iraq debacle boots the neoconservatives out of power for good, how can we use this window of opportunity to challenge the most powerful alternative view, the bipartisan establishment consensus? From the outset it won't help to scorn the average citizen's idealistic view of America. That's like wishing away the Rocky Mountains. Claiming that this worldview is unrealistic would be caving in to a simplistic Niebuhrian "realism." After all, we on the left believe in our own idealism. We are happy to hear right-wing "realists" argue that Americans are no more idealistic than anyone else. But we forget that Americans are no less idealistic either. That includes even the most powerful leaders of the nation. Rather than demonizing them and dismissing their claim to good intentions outright, we would do better to look for common values that we can all agree on and then find progressive programs that can put those values into practice.

DIFFERENT MORAL CERTAINTIES

Just about all Americans, from Bush and Cheney and the CEOs of Exxon and Lockheed-Martin on down, sincerely want the nation to be secure. As long as our notions of security are built on the myth of well-meaning Americans versus ever-threatening evildoers who embody original sin, we can never dispense with the evildoers. They are as necessary in U.S. foreign policy as sin is in Niebuhr's theology. They always have to be out there threatening us, in our imaginations at least, in order for our pursuit of national security to make any sense at all.

The bipartisan consensus on U.S. foreign policy calls for us to be powerful enough to dominate them. But every step we take to dominate

only antagonizes more people and makes some of them really want to harm us. As long as we keep on this self-defeating road, we are not a national security state. We are a national insecurity state. So, we need to redefine national security in a way that meets people's need for a second value that so many of us share: moral certainty. This involves a faith in some rock-bottom kind of goodness in the world, which many Americans believe has a special home here in the United States.

There is a special kind of goodness, rooted in a special kind of theology, that does have an old and honored home here—the goodness of nonviolence. There have always been Christians who were certain that the only moral way to treat others, even enemies, is with love, not violence. They knew it because Jesus said it, right there in the Bible. In nineteenth-century America, the abolitionists and Thoreau turned the theology of nonviolence into a homegrown strategy for political change.

Martin Luther King, Jr. took this strategy a crucial step further. He preached that it's the government's role to help bring all people together in what he called "the beloved community" (something very much like what the Social Gospel called the Kingdom of God). Every government policy should promote "the mutually cooperative and voluntary venture of man to assume a semblance of responsibility for his brother [and sister]"—the responsibility to help every person fulfill their God-given potential.

In King's words, no matter how bad a person's behavior, "the image of God is never totally gone." So, government must serve everyone, everywhere. No one can be written off as a monstrous evildoer, sinful beyond redemption. That was a moral certainty for King, an essential foundation of his religious faith. King knew all about moral clarity and certainty. He was willing to die for the truths he believed in so firmly. But he was not willing to kill.

A DIFFERENT NARRATIVE

With King as our guide, we could have a distinctly American foreign policy based on the conviction of absolute moral certainty we find in the Social

Gospel and nonviolence traditions. Our goal would always be to move the world one step closer to becoming a universal beloved community. We would no longer act out the myth of good versus evil. We would not demonize a bin Laden or Saddam—or a Bush or Cheney. We would recognize that when people do bad things, their actions grow out of a global network of forces that we ourselves have helped to create. King said it most eloquently: "We are caught in an inescapable network of mutuality, tied in a single garment of destiny."

We can never stand outside the network of mutuality, as if we were the Lone Ranger arriving on the scene to destroy an evil we played no part in creating. Just as Bush is tied to Osama, so each of us is tied to all those who do things that outrage us. We cannot simply destroy them and think that the outrages have been erased. To right the wrongs of the world, we must start by recognizing our own responsibility for helping to spawn those wrongs. Indeed, fixing our own part in the wrongs we see all over the world may be all that we can do.

But in the case of the United States in 2007, that alone would be more than a full time job for our foreign policy. We would have to, among other things:

- end the occupation that creates a breeding ground for violent jihadis in Iraq and Afghanistan;

- reverse the policy of supporting authoritarian regimes in the Middle East;
- stop participating in the mad rush for power and resources in Africa, which breeds disasters like Rwanda and Darfur;
- withdraw support for the corporations and financiers who would strangle the emerging popular democracies in Latin America;
- and treat everyone as our brothers and sisters, even the leaders of North Korea and Cuba and Iran.

In short, we would have to create a new notion of "national interest" based on the moral certainty that we are all threads in a network of mutuality that is the foundation of our national as well as individual life. Since our foundation is infinite and eternal, no one can threaten to destroy it, or us. Embracing that principle as the basis of foreign policy could set us on the road to a radically new way of thinking about genuine national security.

If that's not something all Americans can agree on, at least it's a program that gets the debate down to our most basic assumptions. This is a democracy. If the people want a religion-laden foreign policy based on the doctrine of original sin and the myth of good against evil, it's what we should have. But at least we should all talk about it together, openly and honestly.

DISCUSSION QUESTIONS

1. Chernus contends that "when it comes to foreign policy, we are all influenced by theological foundations that we rarely see." Discuss the particulars of, and offer your own comments on, the theological foundations Chernus lays bare.
2. According to Chernus, "If people want a religion-laden foreign policy based on the doctrine of original sin and the myth of good against evil, it's what we should have. But at least we should all talk about it together, openly and honestly." From his perspective, what's *wrong* with foreign policy rooted in theology? Why do you think such roots tend not to be openly discussed?

THE GREATEST NATION ON EARTH

Since the terrorist attacks of September 11, 2001, journalism professor and political activist Robert Jensen has been a leading voice in the effort to rethink the notion of patriotism in the United States. His perspective begins with the simple and honest recognition of our place in the world: U.S. citizens are citizens of the empire. His book Citizens of the Empire lays bare the reality of global empire that underlies the pursuit of U.S. foreign policy regardless of which party occupies the White House, and regardless of the flowery principles offered in the name of justifying the exercise of power. The following selection addresses one of the three key political slogans that frame public discussion of the U.S. role in the world—the common invocation that the United States is the greatest nation on earth. Jensen contends that while this rhetorical principle permeates our political discourse, and appears as an unassailable truth because of its ubiquity, "any claim to being the greatest nation is depraved and dangerous, especially when made in the empire." He proceeds to unravel the many strands of this assertion of greatness, pointing out with clear examples the moral dangers of such claims. His argument will not be familiar to you and may, in fact, make you angry. His call for us to imagine a political world where all people are valued equally presents us with a challenge—a challenge to take our professed values seriously enough to apply them uniformly in a balanced way, for "if we are to be a moral people, everything about the United States, like everything about any country, needs to be examined and assessed."

In any debate, the person who has the power to set the framework and define the terms has an enormous advantage. Part of the struggle for the antiwar movement, and those taking critical positions more generally, is to avoid being trapped in the rhetoric of the dominant culture.

Especially since 9/11, through the wars in Afghanistan and Iraq, there have been three

Source: Robert Jensen, *Citizens of the Empire: The Struggle to Claim Our Humanity,* San Francisco: City Lights Books, 2004, pp. 1–17.

crucial rhetorical frameworks that have been difficult to challenge in public. All of them are related,
but each has to be deconstructed separately. First
is the assertion that the United States is the greatest nation on earth. Second is the claim that one
must support the troops because they defend our
freedom. Third is the assumption that patriotism
is a positive value. Anyone who challenges any of
these in public in the contemporary United States
risks being labeled irrelevant, crazy, or both. But
all three claims must be challenged if there is to
be progressive political change.

My critique does not dictate a single political
strategy for dealing with these rhetorical frameworks in public. With different audiences and in
different situations, different strategies will be
appropriate. But it is crucial to be clear about why
these ideas are dangerous. Embedded in each are
moral and political assertions and assumptions
that have to be resisted, which should make progressive political people cautious about buying
into the frameworks at all. I will suggest that it's
important not just to criticize the dominant culture's version of each claim but to step back and
critique the framework itself.

One of the requirements for being a mainstream American politician, Republican or Democrat, is the willingness to repeat constantly the
assertion that the United States is "the greatest
nation on earth," maybe even "the greatest nation
in history." At hearings for the House Select
Committee on Homeland Security on July 11,
2002, Texas Republican Dick Armey described the
United States as "the greatest, most free nation
the world has ever known." California Democrat Nancy Pelosi declared that America is "the
greatest country that ever existed on the face of
the earth." Even other nations that want to play
ball with the United States have caught on. When
George W. Bush visited our new favored ally in
the Persian Gulf, Qatar, the *Al-Watan* newspaper described it as "A visit by the president of the
greatest nation."

I want to offer a different assessment: Any
claim to being the greatest nation is depraved and
dangerous, especially when made in the empire.

SIGN OF PATHOLOGY

Imagine your child, let's call him Joe, made the
declaration, "I am the greatest ten-year-old on
earth." If you were a loving parent, interested in
helping your child develop into a decent person,
what would you say? Let's assume you believe Joe
to be a perfectly lovely boy, maybe even gifted in
many ways. Would you indulge him in that fantasy? Most of us would not.

Instead, you would explain to Joe that however special he is, he is one of millions of ten-
year-olds on the planet at that moment, and
that—if there were a measure of greatness that
could take into account all relevant attributes and
abilities—the odds are against Joe coming out on
top. But more important than that, you would
explain to Joe that people are a wonderfully complex mix of many characteristics that are valued
differently by different people, and that it would
be impossible to make any sensible assessment of
what makes one person the greatest. Even if you
reduced it to a single item—let's say the ability to
solve mathematical problems—there's no imaginable way to label one person the greatest. That's
why people have so much fun arguing about, for
example, who is the greatest hitter in baseball
history. There's no way to answer the question
definitively, and no one really expects to ever win;
the fun is in the arguing.

Now, if Joe makes it to adulthood and continues to claim he is the greatest, we would come to
one of two conclusions (assuming he's not saying
it just to hype the sales of his book or sell tickets to some event): Either he is mentally unstable
or he's an asshole. That is, either he believes it
because there's something wrong with him cog-
nitively and/or emotionally, or he believes it
because he's an unpleasant person. It's painfully
obvious that the best evidence that Joe is not the
greatest is his claim to be that, for we can observe
that throughout history people who have something in them that we might call "greatness" tend
not to proclaim their own superiority.

So, we would want to put the brakes on
young Joe's claim to greatness as soon as possible

because of what tends to happen to people who believe they are the greatest: They lose perspective and tend to discount the feelings and legitimate claims of others. If I am so great, the reasoning goes, certainly my view of the world must be correct, and others who disagree with me—because they lack my greatness—must simply be wrong. And if they are wrong, well, I'm certainly within my rights as the greatest to make sure things turn out the way that I know (by virtue of my greatness) they should. The ability to force others to accept the decisions of those with greatness depends, of course, on power. If Joe takes positions in society that give him power, heaven help those below him.

All these observations are relevant to national assertions of greatness. Such claims ignore the complexity of societies and life within them. Even societies that do great things can have serious problems. We are all aware that a person with admirable qualities in one realm can have quite tragic flaws in another. The same is true of nations. Constant claims to being the greatest reveal a pathology in the national character. Crucially, that pathology is most dangerous in nations with great economic or military power (which tend to be the ones that most consistently make such claims). That is, the nations that claim to be great are usually the ones that can enforce their greatness through coercion and violence.

Nothing in this argument denies the ways that children or nations sometimes do great things. It is rather the claim to uniqueness in one's greatness that is at issue.

WHAT IS GREATNESS?

Let's assume, for the sake of discussion, that determining which nation on earth is the greatest would be a meaningful and useful enterprise. On what criteria would we base the evaluation? And how would the United States stack up? In other words, what is greatness?

We might start with history, where we would observe that the histories of nation-states typically are not pretty. At best, it's a mixed bag. The

United States broke away from a colonial power ruled by a monarch, espousing the revolutionary political ideal of democratic rights for citizens. Even though the Founding Fathers' definition of "citizen" was narrow enough to exclude the vast majority of the population, that breakthrough was an inspirational moment in human history. That's why, when declaring an independent Vietnam in 1945, Ho Chi Minh borrowed language from the U.S. Declaration of Independence.

But from the beginning the new American experiment was also bathed in blood. The land base of the new nation was secured by a genocide that was almost successful. Depending on the estimate one uses for the precontact population of the continent (the number of people here before Columbus)—12 million is a conservative estimate—the extermination rate was from 95 to 99 percent. That is to say, by the end of the Indian wars at the close of the nineteenth century, the European invaders had successfully eliminated almost the entire indigenous population (or the "merciless Indian Savages" as they are labeled in the Declaration of Independence). Let's call that the first American holocaust.

The second American holocaust was African slavery, a crucial factor in the emergence of the textile industry and the industrial revolution in the United States. Historians still debate the number of Africans who worked as slaves in the New World and the number who died during the process of enslavement in Africa, during the Middle Passage, and in the New World. But it is safe to say that tens of millions of people were rounded up and that as many as half of them died in the process.

Some would say greatness is not perfection but the capacity for critical self-reflection, the ability to correct mistakes, the constant quest for progressive change. If that were the case, then a starting point would be honest acknowledgment of the way in which the land base and wealth of the nation had been acquired, leading to meaningful attempts at reparations for the harm caused along the way. Have the American people taken serious steps in that direction on these two fundamental questions regarding indigenous and African peoples? Is the privilege of running casinos on reservation land a just resolution of the first holocaust? Are the Voting Rights and Civil Rights Acts an adequate solution to the second? Can we see the many gains made on these fronts, yet still come to terms with lingering problems?

And what of the third American holocaust, the building of the American empire in the Third World? What did the nation that finally turned its back on slavery turn to?

—The Spanish-American War and the conquest of the Philippines, at a cost of at least 200,000 Filipino lives.

—The creation of a U.S.-dominated sphere in Central America backed by regular military incursions to make countries safe for U.S. investment, leading to twentieth-century support for local dictatorships that brutalized their populations, at a total cost of hundreds of thousands of dead and whole countries ruined.

—The economic and diplomatic support of French efforts to recolonize Vietnam after World War II and, after the failure of that effort, the U.S. invasion of South Vietnam and devastation of Laos and Cambodia, at a cost of 4 million Southeast Asians dead and a region destabilized.

We could list every immoral and illegal U.S. intervention into other nations, which often had the goal of destroying democratically elected governments, undermining attempts by people to throw off colonial rule, or ensuring that a government would follow orders from Washington. But the point is easily made: Subjecting claims of American greatness to historical review suggests a more complex story. The United States has made important strides in recent decades to shed a brutal racist history and create a fairer society at home, though still falling short of a truly honest accounting and often leaving the most vulnerable in seemingly perpetual poverty. At the same time, U.S. policy abroad has been relentlessly barbaric.

Such an examination would lead to some simple conclusions: The United States was founded on noble principles that it has advanced and, often at the same time, undermined. As the United States has emerged as a world power with imperial ambitions—and we rest now at a place where commentators from all points on the political spectrum use the term "empire" to describe the United States, often in a celebratory fashion—we have much to answer for. Historically, empires are never benevolent, and nothing in history has changed that should lead to the conclusion that the United States will be the first benevolent empire. Unless, of course, one believes that God has a hand in all this.

WHAT'S GOD GOT TO DO WITH IT?

During the 2000 presidential campaign, George W. Bush was trying to recover from his association with the painfully public bigotry of Bob Jones University. On matters of racism, it's impossible—even for politicians—to make claims about America's heroic history. But in remarks at the Simon Wiesenthal Center and the Museum of Tolerance, Bush said, "For all its flaws, I believe our nation is chosen by God and commissioned by history to be the model to the world of justice and inclusion and diversity without division."

This invocation of a direct connection to God and truth—what we might call the "pathology of the anointed"—is a peculiar and particularly dangerous feature of American history and the "greatest nation" claims. The story we tell ourselves goes something like this: Other nations throughout history have acted out of greed and self-interest, seeking territory, wealth, and power. They often did bad things in the world. Then came the United States, touched by God, a shining city on the hill, whose leaders created the first real democracy and went on to be the beacon of freedom for people around the world. Unlike the rest of the world, we act out of a cause nobler than greed; we are both the model of, and the vehicle for, peace, freedom, and democracy in the world.

That is a story that can be believed only in the United States by people sufficiently insulated from the reality of U.S. actions abroad to maintain such illusions. It is tempting to laugh at and dismiss these rhetorical flourishes of pandering politicians, but the commonness of the chosen-by-God assertions—and the lack of outrage or amusement at them—suggests that the claims are taken seriously both by significant segments of the public and the politicians. Just as it has been in the past, the consequences of this pathology of the anointed will be borne not by those chosen by God, but by those against whom God's-chosen decide to take aim.

What stance on these matters would leaders who took seriously their religious tradition take? Scripture, for those who believe it to be an authority, is—as is typical—mixed on these matters. But certainly one plausible reading of that text would lead one not to claims of greatness but of humility. As one of the Old Testament prophets, Micah, put it: "What does the Lord require of you but to do justice, and to love kindness, and to walk humbly with your God?" (Micah 6:8).

In the second presidential debate on October 11, 2000, Bush himself made this point. When asked how he would try to project the United States around the world, Bush used the word "humble" five times:

> It really depends upon how our nation conducts itself in foreign policy. If we're an arrogant nation, they'll resent us, if we're a humble nation but strong, they'll welcome us. And our nation stands alone right now in the world in terms of power, and that's why we've got to be humble and yet project strength in a way that promotes freedom.
>
> We're a freedom-loving nation. And if we're an arrogant nation, they'll view us that way, but if we're a humble nation, they'll respect us.
>
> I think the United States must be humble and must be proud and confident of our values, but humble in how we treat nations that are figuring out how to chart their own course.

Although all available evidence suggests Bush and his advisers (or any other U.S. president, for that matter) were not serious about pursuing a foreign policy based in humility, his comments were sensible. Humility, it is important to remember, does not mean humiliation; it is a sign of strength, not weakness. It means recognizing that the United States is one nation among many; that the only way to security is to work together democratically with other nations; and that multilateral institutions must be strengthened and we must be willing to accept the decisions of such bodies, even when they go against us.

In other words, the exact opposite of the path that the Bush administration has pursued.

BLAME AMERICA FIRST?

When one points out these kinds of facts and analyses, which tend to get in the way of the "greatest nation" claims, a standard retort is, "Why do you blame America first?" Though it is a nonsensical question, the persistence and resonance of it in the culture requires a response.

First, it should not be controversial that when assessing the effects of actions, one is most clearly morally responsible for one's own actions. Depending on the circumstances, I may have obligations to act to curtail someone else's immoral behavior, but without question I have an obligation to curtail my own immoral behavior. In some circumstances, if someone else's immoral behavior is so egregious that the harm it does to others requires immediate intervention and such intervention is feasible in the real world, then there can be cases in which I have cause to temporarily put on hold an assessment of my own behavior to stop the greater evil. But such cases are rare, and the human tendency to rationalize our own bad behavior should give us pause whenever we claim that the greater good requires us to focus on the mistakes other people make before we tackle our own.

So, in place of the common phrase "judge not and ye shall not be judged," perhaps the rule should be "invite judgment of yourself by others, come to judgment about your behavior, commit to not repeating immoral behavior, repair to the degree possible the damage done by previous immoral acts, and keep an eye on others to help them in the same process."

There is no reason that the same logic that applies to us as individuals should not apply to us collectively as citizens of a nation. From such a vantage point, the emptiness of the accusation that one shouldn't "blame America first" becomes clear. America should be blamed first, if and when America is blameworthy. If the United States has engaged in behavior that cannot be morally justified—such as the invasion of another country to overthrow its legally elected democratic government for the self-interested material gain of some segment of U.S. society—whom else should we blame? Because people often use the term "blame" in a way to redirect accountability (when Johnny blames Joey for breaking the toy, we suspect that Johnny actually had something to do with the accident himself), the phrase is designed to divert people from an honest assessment. A better formulation would be, "Why do you hold America accountable first?" In that case, the obvious answer—we should hold America accountable first when America is responsible—is somewhat easier for a reasonable person to see.

That does raise the question, of course, of who is a reasonable person. We might ask that question about, for example, George H. W. Bush, the father. In 1988, after the U.S. Navy warship *Vincennes* shot down an Iranian commercial airliner in a commercial corridor, killing 290 civilians, the then-vice president said, "I will never apologize for the United States of America. I don't care what the facts are."

Whether the firing was an understandable reaction to the misidentification of the Iranian aircraft (as apologists claim), a deliberate act to send Iran a message about U.S. intentions in the region (as some suspect), or the responsibility primarily of a hyperaggressive, trigger-happy commander (as others argue), Bush's declaration is an extraordinarily blunt admission that he does not adhere to even minimal moral standards. The grotesqueness of the episode was only compounded by the fact that Bush later awarded the ship's commander a Legion of Merit award for

"exceptionally meritorious conduct in the performance of outstanding service." We could call it the "blame America never" approach.

THE FACTS MATTER

My position does not lead to a blanket denunciation of the United States, our political institutions, or our culture. I simply put forward the proposition that facts matter. If we are to be moral people, everything about the United States, like everything about any country, needs to be examined and assessed. People often tell me, "You assume that everything about the United States is bad." But, of course, I do not assume that; it would be as absurd as the assumption that everything about the United States is good. After a lecture in which I outlined some of the important advances in the law of free speech in the United States but was also critical of contemporary U.S. foreign policy, someone in the audience asked, "Is there anything about America that you like?" Yes, I said, there is much I like—for example, the advances in the law of free speech that I just spent considerable time describing and celebrating. For some reason, honest assessments of both the successes and failures of the United States are seen as being hypercritical and negative.

The facts do matter, of course. And the "greatest nation on earth" mantra tends to lead us to get the facts wrong. Take the question of foreign aid. One would assume that the greatest nation on earth, which also happens to be the wealthiest nation on the planet with the largest economy, gives generously to nations less fortunate. And, in fact, many Americans do assume that. Unfortunately, it's wrong. Political journalist William Finnegan summarizes the polling data:

Americans always overestimate the amount of foreign aid we give. In recent national polls, people have guessed, on average, that between 15 and 24 percent of the federal budget goes for foreign aid. In reality, it is less than 1 percent. The U.N. has set a foreign-aid goal for the rich countries of .7 percent of gross national product. *A few countries have attained that modest goal, all of them Scandinavian. The U.S. has never come close, indeed, it comes in dead last, consistently, in the yearly totals of rich-country foreign aid as a percentage of GNP.* In 2000, we gave .1 percent. President Bush's dramatic proposal, post-September 11, to increase foreign aid to $15 billion looks rather puny next to the $48 billion increase in this year's $379 billion military budget.

So, on this count, are the Scandinavian nations the greatest on earth? They also seem to have the edge on us in providing health care to their citizens. Here's the assessment of two prominent U.S. medical researchers:

The absence of universal access in the United States is a global scandal. No other highly industrialized country has so many citizens totally without access to even the most rudimentary health care. Consider these facts: there are almost twice as many people in the U.S. without access to health care than the entire population of Scandinavia where access is a universal right.

One might think that the greatest nation on earth would not leave its most vulnerable citizens without reliable access to health care. There will be, of course, disagreement on how to best achieve that, but it seems not to be a serious goal among the dominant political players in the United States.

So, we score higher on legal guarantees of freedom of speech but lower on guarantees of health care compared with other developed countries. Our history and contemporary foreign policy suggest that self-interest and greed usually trump concern for human rights and democracy. Yet the existence of a democratic process at home—the product of much struggle by the forces interested in progressive change—should leave us with hope that we can change the course of that policy through long-term, dedicated efforts. But to do that, honest reflection on the record is required. And it matters. It really matters. It is one thing for small and powerless nations to have delusions of grandeur; they can't do much damage outside their own borders. It is quite another thing for the nation with the most destructive military capacity in the history of the world—and a demonstrated willingness to use it to achieve self-interested goals—to play the "greatest nation on earth" game. To the degree that the game diminishes people's ability to assess facts, reach honest conclusions, and take moral action based on those conclusions, it increases the risk of people everywhere. It makes it easier for leaders to justify wars of conquest and mask the reasons for those wars. It's easy for a vice president to say, as Dick Cheney did in a speech in 2002:

America is again called by history to use our overwhelming power in defense of our freedom. We've accepted that duty, certain of the justice of our cause and confident of the victory to come. For my part, I'm grateful for the opportunity to work with the president who is making us all proud upholding the cause of freedom and serving the greatest nation on earth.

DISCUSSION QUESTIONS

1. Discuss the ways in which you've been raised to buy into the notion that we live in the greatest country in the world. How does this process work? Is it healthy for us as free thinkers?
2. Explain the many dangers that Jensen sees arising from the constant assertion of America's "greatness." How does Jensen respond to potential critics of his thesis?
2. Explain how a person in a foreign country might respond to Jensen's perspective about America's claims of greatness?

CHAPTER 3

Constitutional and State Structures

Few, if any, American documents are worshiped as much as the Constitution. Political leaders across the ideological spectrum pay tribute to the 1787 parchment and its twenty-seven amendments as the bedrock of our political institutions and the sentry of our civil liberties. Not without reason, many Americans see more than two hundred years of constitutional government as a unique achievement in the modern world. Former president Ronald Reagan, for his part, discerned in the Founders' creation "a sureness and originality so great that I can't help but perceive the guiding hand of God, the first political system that insisted that power flows from the people to the state, not the other way around." But does the U.S. Constitution deserve such veneration?

Taken together, the articles in this chapter offer an analysis of the U.S. Constitution and the state it helped to establish that challenges this posture of self-congratulation. Familiar features like the separation of powers, checks and balances, and federalism are related to the Framers' concerns about democratic threats to property rights and to their vision of a new political economy energized by men of commerce and finance. These articles suggest that the Constitution often has been irrelevant or even an obstacle to democratic advances and that, at the least, we should avoid making the document a patriotic fetish.

9 *Joshua Cohen and Joel Rogers*

AMERICAN EXCEPTIONALISM AND THE POLITICS OF FRAGMENTATION

Joshua Cohen and Joel Rogers situate the Constitution within the broader context of the "exceptional" nature of the American state, which lacks the class-based politics that characterizes other advanced capitalist democracies. They argue that the basic structures of our polity, including its constitutional framework, encourage fragmentation among people of ordinary means and raise their costs of collective action. When this pattern becomes entrenched, popular control of public policy is constrained and the inequalities flowing from the economy are difficult to challenge. Students may want to focus on two aspects of Cohen and Rogers's piece. First, locate the six historical factors that, in their view, have contributed to the fragmentation of democratic politics. Second, consider their claim that the "essence of politics is collective action." Doesn't this cut across the grain of our "look out for number one" culture? Perhaps the ideology of liberal individualism, one of the focal points of articles in Chapter 2, is itself a factor that limits meaningful democratic action.

The essence of politics is collective action—different people acting together for the achievement of common aims. There are many conditions for such action—including common interests, an awareness of those interests, a willingness to cooperate with one another, and the ability to sustain the costs of that cooperation.

On all these dimensions and others, the structure of the U.S. political system tends to constrain collective action by people of ordinary means. Most importantly, *American political conflict and bargaining is extremely fragmented*. Instead of bringing people together, the basic structures of American politics tend to keep them separate and divided, while encouraging the pursuit of narrower interests. This division raises the costs of coordination. Its effects are most sharply pronounced among those who have few resources to begin with—that is, among those whose "strength is in numbers," and not in their wallets.

Reflecting these tendencies to fragmentation, ordinary people in the U.S. are among the most politically disorganized in the world. Most strikingly, perhaps, the U.S. is virtually unique

Source: Joshua Cohen and Joel Rogers, *Rules of the Game: American Politics and the Central America Movement*, Boston: South End Press, 1986, pp. 4–16.

among advanced industrial capitalist democracies in never having had a labor party or socialist movement of significant strength and duration. To this day, conventional political debate here is not marked by the sort of class-based cleavages and terms ("workers" versus "capitalists") characteristic of the political systems of Italy, France, Germany, England, and indeed most of the advanced industrial world. This peculiar absence of class politics in the U.S.—one instance of the general fragmentation of the U.S. political system—is called "American exceptionalism."

. . . What generates these conditions in the first place? As might be expected, the answer is that over the course of U.S. history many factors have contributed, and that the importance of particular factors, and their interaction with others, has shifted over the course of U.S. history. Such historical variation and political complexity pose severe problems in providing an adequate rendering of American exceptionalism—problems which, we should emphasize, we do not pretend to solve here. These important complexities aside, however, there are six basic factors which can be identified as having contributed throughout *all* of U.S. history. Reinforcing one another, and given varied political expression, they have always been central to producing, and reproducing, the politics of fragmentation.

CONSTITUTIONAL DESIGN

The basic founding document of the U.S., the Constitution, mandates a fragmented government structure. This has permitted, within a single nation, considerable political experimentation, particularly at the local level, and has helped ensure certain limits on the abuse of centralized powers. But the clear effect of constitutional fragmentation has also been to limit the potential for political cooperation among people of ordinary means, and this was something that the architects of the constitutional system, the "founding fathers," clearly recognized and desired.

In *The Federalist Papers,* for example, James Madison explained that a fragmented system would help cure "the mischiefs of faction," whose most common source was the distribution of property ownership:

> Those who hold and those who are without property have ever formed distinct interests in society. Those who are creditors, and those who are debtors, fall under a like discrimination. . . . The regulation of these various and interfering interests forms the principal task of modern legislation and involves the spirit of party and faction in the necessary and ordinary operations of government.

Madison was particularly concerned that a "majority faction" composed of those owning little property might come together to challenge inequalities in wealth and income. He saw two ways to prevent its formation:

> Either the existence of the same passion or interest in a majority at the same time must be prevented, or the majority, having such coexistent passion or interest, must be rendered, by their number and local situation, unable to concert and carry into effect schemes of oppression.

In the constitutional scheme they eventually agreed upon, Madison and the other framers accordingly sought both to prevent majorities from forming common programs, and to impose barriers to the implementation of those programs, should they be formed. The most straightforward way this was done was by weakening and dividing the American state.

The Constitution, for example, mandates a *separation of powers* at the national level. The legislative, executive, and judicial functions are each assigned to distinct branches of government, and each branch is given powers to block the activities of the other two. While the power of the judiciary to curtail Congressional or Presidential action is great, probably the most important separation and source of blockage is that between executive and legislative authority. In contrast to parliamentary systems of representation, where the leader of the dominant party (or coalition of parties) in the legislature is also the chief executive of government, the U.S. Constitution mandates separate elections for Congress and the Presidency. This has commonly meant that the President comes from a party that does not command a majority within the legislature. Such differences between the executive and the legislature typically generate barriers to concerted national policy—except of course in those cases (foreign affairs being the source of most examples) where "bipartisan consensus" obtains between the major parties.

Additionally limiting the effectiveness of the national government, and limiting the potential for the emergence of majoritarian factions, is the principle of *federalism*. This means that public power is shared between the national government and the states. By contrast with "unified" governments, where subnational units are extensions of a central authority, the United States is a "divided" government, in which the states enjoy powers independent of the Federal government. Competing with the Federal government and one another, the fifty states produce wide variations in policy on basic issues, and reinforce political diversity and division. . . .

Even within national government, moreover, federalism shapes the perspective and interests of Congress. Candidates for Congress are not selected by national parties, but by state and local organizations. Members are then elected by local constituencies, and to stay in Congress they must satisfy the interests of those constituencies. Local interests are thus represented both in state governments and the national legislature. In fact, aside from the Presidency (and even there the case is ambiguous), there is no Federal office or body whose members are selected by exclusively national criteria. As House Speaker Tip O'Neill often points out, in the U.S. "*all* politics is local politics."

One effect of this is to immensely complicate the consideration of national issues, and to introduce yet additional barriers in generating coherent national policies. A closely related effect is

the *discouragement* of attempts at such national coordination, and the *encouragement* of a local or regional orientation in political action. This orientation, in turn, tends to solidify differences and divisions among people located in different places.

GEOGRAPHY AND NATURAL RESOURCES

In comparative terms, the United States has always been an enormous country, larger at its founding than all other countries of the time except Russia, and today, more than 200 years later, still larger than all countries but the Soviet Union, Canada, and China. Early on, the framers recognized that sheer size, like constitutional divisions, would tend to impose barriers to the existence and formation of mischievous majority factions. Rejecting the received wisdom in political theory, *The Federalist Papers* extolled the virtues of a "large commercial republic." Size would encourage a diversity of interests, and that diversity would in turn pose barriers to the existence and coordination of any stable popular majority.

In addition to encouraging diversity, the great size of the land, which for long periods had an open frontier, helped to provide a safety valve for social unrest. Those who did not like it in one place—and were not slaves—could simply leave. The widespread availability of free or very cheap land, moreover, facilitated widespread land *ownership*. This helped confirm Americans' status as a race of independent and free (white) men, and provided a ballast of popular support for a private property regime.

The repeated acquisition of new land helped prolong the period of an open frontier. Even after the rate of acquisition slowed, however, and even after the frontier was closed, the U.S. would also enjoy comparatively low population densities. Combined with the sheer size of the country, the sparse settlement of the land in turn meant that its different inhabitants could afford to operate in relative isolation from one another. This in turn encouraged extremely diverse, and largely uncoordinated, forms of political organization, giving further substance to the constitutional fragmentation of American politics.

Political fragmentation was also encouraged by America's strategic isolation. For most of its history—at least from the peace with Britain that concluded the War of 1812 to the Japanese attack on Pearl Harbor in 1941—the U.S. enjoyed a long unbroken period of strategic isolation, during which thousands of miles of ocean provided a bar to credible attack from abroad. It could thus develop without much concern for the activities of other nations, and could afford the highly decentralized political system that more threatened nations could not.

Finally, in addition to being big and isolated, the U.S. enjoyed (and continues to enjoy) tremendous advantages of climate and natural resources. Even leaving aside the productive activities of men and women, it is truly the richest nation on earth. Virtually all of the country is located in the temperate zone, which is ideal for agriculture and industry. Early settlers found vast deposits of timber and basic minerals, some of the best farmland on earth, apparently limitless water resources for farming and industry, and extended systems of lakes and rivers that eased the flow of trade. Once these resources were taken from their Native American owners, this was an almost perfect setting for economic development, which proceeded quickly.

By providing the basis for a comparatively high standard of living, these natural endowments tended to discourage efforts at collective organization along class lines. Throughout almost all of American history, and even after they had changed from a race of independent farmers to a population of wage and salary workers, ordinary people in the U.S. were paid more, and lived far better, than their counterparts in Western Europe and the rest of the developed world. In this relatively affluent environment, and especially given all the other social and political incentives to seek private gains, the appeal of collective organization was diminished. As the German economist Werner Sombart once overstated the point,

"Socialist utopias came to nothing on roast beef and apple pie."

UNEVEN ECONOMIC DEVELOPMENT

The very rapid emergence of the U.S. as a major economic power concealed tremendous differences within the U.S. in the level and scope of economic activity. It was only after the Civil War that capitalism was firmly established as the exclusive mode of economic production in the U.S., and only after World War II, with the industrial development of the South, that it was possible to speak of a truly national industrial economy. This unevenness, combined with the tremendous diversity of American economic activity, encouraged different and competing interests in different regions of the country. An incalculably large part of American politics—from immigration to energy policy—is and always has been concerned with managing these differences.

Like so many other dynamics of American politics, this phenomenon of regional diversity was most dramatically highlighted by the Civil War. In that effort, infant industry and finance in the Northeast and Midwest joined with independent farming interests to crush the plantation South, initiating a period of economic and political subordination that would last well into the twentieth century. The long deflation that followed the war (like most major wars, it had been paid for by printing money) eventually ignited the great agrarian protest movement of the Populists, which drew particular strength from independent farmers in the South, Midwest, and West. But within a generation of the close of the war predominantly Northeastern industrial and financial interests had crushed the Populists as well, and were busy rolling back political organization, and even electoral participation, among the dependent classes.

Such dramatic events aside, and even after the great levelling of regional differences that has occurred over the past forty years, uneven and diverse economic development tends to fragment

U.S. politics. Among elites, the enduring vitality of regional splits is evident in phenomena like the "Sagebrush Rebellion," which pits Western business interests against the Northeast in a battle over environmental regulation and Federal land management in the West. Among nonelites, it is evident in the difficulties northern workers have encountered from their southern counterparts in responding to "runaway" shops down South. Regional economic differences continue to slow concerted national responses to problems, and to divide ordinary people with potentially shared interests from one another.

RACISM

The first black slaves were brought to America in the early 1600s. By the time of the Declaration of Independence in 1776, slavery was established in all thirteen colonies. Oppressive relations between whites and blacks in America are as old as the country itself.

The history since is familiar, or should be. Shortly after the Revolution, the "First Emancipation" began in New England, as state after state abolished slavery, or phased it out. The most substantial black populations, however, were located in the South, and this "emancipation" stopped at Virginia. Growing tensions between the slave and non-slave states, which were importantly tensions between a precapitalist plantation economy and the imperatives of free capitalist development, eventually erupted in the Civil War. Ostensibly the war freed the slaves, but with the collapse of "radical" efforts to reconstruct the South in the postwar period, an elaborate system of oppressive and segregationist race relations was soon reestablished.

It would not be until well into the twentieth century—when the combined push of the mechanization of southern agriculture, and the pull of labor-starved northern industry in World War II, brought millions of blacks north—that racism began to be seriously addressed on a national scale. And it would not be until the 1960s, and only then under the pressures of massive protest

and civil disobedience, that the major legal components of discrimination would be broken down. The fight over *de facto* discrimination—in housing, education, employment, and other essentials—continues, and blacks and whites in this country continue to live very different sorts of lives.

Volumes have been written on American racism. Suffice it to say here that there is no more persistent form of division in American politics, and none more debilitating to popular democratic politics. In the pre-Civil War period, the small number of "freemen" who trickled North were almost universally excluded from early worker organizations. In the late nineteenth century, each of the great attempts at forging classwide ties in labor failed to confront the race question, giving force to endless employer strategies of "divide and conquer" between antagonistic racial groups. In the twentieth century, at the peak of worker organization immediately after World War II, the failure to press the issue of racial equality by organizing the South defined the limits of labor's national power for a generation, and hastened its decline. And even today, 120 years after the close of the Civil War, racial animosity and fear, and the forms and habits of political association based on them, continue to impede the construction of a truly popular democratic coalition. The racial and ethnic tensions which marked the Rainbow Coalition's effort in 1984 provide ample evidence on this point.

ETHNIC AND RELIGIOUS DIVISIONS

At least until the turn of the twentieth century, the great natural wealth of the U.S., along with its rapid economic development and low population density, produced chronic labor shortages. The solution to this problem was provided by immigrant labor.

Over 1820–1830, only a little over 150,000 immigrants came to the U.S. Three decades later, over 1851–1860, the inflow had risen to 2.6 million. By 1881–1890, as the U.S. entered a peak phase in industrialization, the number doubled to 5.2 million. And at its high point, over 1901–1910, it rose to 8.7 million, or better than 10 percent of the resident population. In today's terms, that would amount to roughly 25 million new workers over the course of the 1980s.

Given all the other constraints on popular action, the fact that the population of the U.S. was comprised of people from diverse cultural backgrounds—while surely one of the appealing features of American society—contributed to the general fragmentation of U.S. politics and the weakness of worker organization within it. Coming to a vast land, with a decentralized political structure, successive waves of immigrants took up residence in communities that were often isolated from one another, and developed political commitments and organizations peculiar to individual locales. The deeply ethnic character of much local American politics—Slavs in the Midwest, Irish in Boston, Jews in New York—can be traced to this experience. The fact that the system was sufficiently porous and diffuse to permit such localized expressions, in turn, tended to consolidate patterns of organizational isolation along ethnic grounds. The myth of the American "melting pot" was only that—a myth. In all sorts of ways, immigrants found that they could preserve ethnic identities in the new land. But the maintenance of these diverse identities also tended to undermine attempts to forge alliances among workers that cut across ethnic differences.

Complementing the barriers of language and custom, and immensely important throughout American politics, were the deep religious splits with which ethnic divisions were commonly associated. In part because Americans never had to struggle for land or political rights against an entrenched church, the U.S. has always been a deeply religious country, and throughout its history religion has often served as an organizing metaphor for political action. Popular support for the Revolutionary War, for example, was fueled by the "First Great Awakening" of Protestant religious fervor; and black churches have long supplied the backbone of struggles for civil rights.

Even more often, however, religious differences have served to undermine or distort popular democratic politics. The arrival of waves of Irish Catholic immigrants in the 1850s, for example, led to the nativist backlash of the "Know Nothing" movement, and helped trigger the realignment of political parties that issued in the modern Republican and Democratic parties. This divided workers along Protestant/Catholic lines, reflected not only in the parties but in all manner of popular organizations. And just as the U.S. was entering the second great phase of industrialization in the late nineteenth century, a tidal wave of new immigrants from southern and eastern Europe introduced yet additional divisions into emergent worker organizations. Ably exploited by employers, ethnic and religious cleavages repeatedly wrecked efforts at working class solidarity.

STATE REPRESSION

Despite the many structural barriers to their coordination, ordinary Americans have often banded together to attempt to improve their condition. With some rare and notable exceptions, these efforts have met with physical violence, imprisonment, brutally applied court sanctions, or more subtle forms of harassment and intimidation sponsored by the state. Such state repression makes for a long history, coextensive with the history of the United States. It runs roughly from the 1786 suppression of the protests of indebted farmers in Massachusetts (Shays's Rebellion), through the labor injunctions that helped wreck worker organizations in the late nineteenth century, to the Reagan administration's surveillance of Central America activists, and prosecution of church groups offering sanctuary to refugees from U.S. policies in that region.

Over the last 200 years, there have been too many government sponsored shootings, beatings, lynchings, police spies, agents provocateurs, goons, scabs, rigged trials, imprisonments, burglaries, and illegal wiretaps to permit easy summary here. Once again we only note the obvious. By raising the costs of political action to individuals—in money, physical pain, imprisonment, or the destruction of their personal lives—repression makes it less likely that individuals will be willing to engage in collective political activity at all. And this is especially true for those individuals, comprising the most obvious mischievous faction, who can least afford those costs, since they have little "property" or other resources of their own.

Over the course of U.S. history, these six basic factors—constitutional design, geography and natural resources, uneven economic development, racism, ethnic and religious divisions, and state repression—have repeatedly constrained popular democratic action in the U.S. As indicated earlier, appreciating the interaction of these different factors at different times would require discussion of the peculiarities of particular circumstances and periods, and of the ways in which these divisions were themselves institutionalized and given political expression. This, again, we cannot do here. What is important to recognize, however, is that these sources of divisions are enduring and ongoing features of U.S. politics, and not merely of historical interest. They operate now, as well as having operated in the past.

DISCUSSION QUESTIONS

1. Cohen and Rogers state that "ordinary people in the United States are among the most politically disorganized in the world." What evidence of this do the authors provide and how does that relate to the issue of "American exceptionalism"?
2. Have the six basic factors contributing to American exceptionalism been equally important in U.S. history? Which are most important today?

10 *Kenneth M. Dolbeare and Linda Medcalf*

THE DARK SIDE OF THE CONSTITUTION

In a wide-ranging essay, written for the constitutional bicentennial in 1987, Kenneth Dolbeare and Linda Medcalf explore what they call the "dark side" of the Constitution, critically examining its meaning and values while relating them to contemporary political ills. Writing in the spirit of historian Charles Beard, whose 1913 book An Economic Interpretation of the Constitution *was a path-breaking critical study, they detail the Framers' concern for the protection of property, placing their fear of democracy in the context of such threatening events as Shays's Rebellion among farmers in western Massachusetts. The Constitution is read in light of the top-down model of political economy espoused by Alexander Hamilton and initially implemented during his tenure as Treasury Secretary in the 1790s. Dolbeare and Medcalf argue that current problems like policy gridlock, low voter turnout, and the general lack of political responsiveness are direct results of the hegemony of Hamiltonian principles in the twentieth century, and outline measures that might help to reverse the de-democratization of American politics.*

The golden glow of the Constitution's bicentennial celebration—already well launched—threatens to blind us all at a time when Americans most need to see clearly. We do not refer to the harmless factual errors and the merely misleading exaggerations that accompany this latest patriotic spectacular. Our national myopia is far more serious. In the midst of institutional paralysis, an urgent but unaddressed policy agenda, and the protracted withdrawal of the American public from "public" affairs, we continue to celebrate the Constitution as an unrivaled political achievement. When we most need to critically examine our fundamental structures, we embark on a laudatory extravaganza—and do so with full scholarly support.

But, from its inception, there has been a dark side to the United States Constitution that accounts in part for many of the acknowledged ills of contemporary American politics. Low

Source: Kenneth M. Dolbeare and Linda Medcalf, "The Dark Side of the Constitution." *The Case Against the Constitution: From the Antifederalists to the Present*, Kenneth M. Dolbeare and John F. Manley, eds., Armonk, NY: M.E. Sharpe, 1987, pp. 120–124, 126–133, and 136–141.

voter turnout, lack of confidence in government, the decline of the political parties, institutional deadlock and indecisiveness, the pervasiveness of protest, frustration, and resentment—all these can be traced to the deliberate anti-democratic design of our founding document and the way it was completed by Alexander Hamilton's nation-building program.

In effect, the Framers, and Alexander Hamilton in particular, wrought too well. Their chief ambition—a strong and stable political economy insulated from popular control—is now threatened by the consequences of the very methods chosen to achieve that goal 200 years ago.

There is no news in the point that the men of 1787 sought to protect property and contain democracy. They have more than amply testified to this themselves. It is only later celebrants who have sought to make the Framers into "realistic" architects of a neutral political system; the Framers, and their opponents, knew better. But the celebrants have written history, and held office, in a country where democracy became a vital symbol. It became increasingly necessary to change the definition of democracy, in order to fit the reality of the limitations on popular impact that the Framers so artfully designed. Just as the proponents of the Constitution preempted the label "Federalist," turning it into its opposite, the celebrants of the Constitution worked similar magic with the word "democracy."

Alexander Hamilton's vital contributions to the development of a strong central government have been noted often, although by a minority of commentators. The crucial contract clause, several key Federalist essays, ratification in New York, and the various programs on credit, funding, the bank, and manufacturing are all recognized as major contributions to the development of the new nation. However, these are usually seen episodically, as independent events or specific isolated achievements in a context evolving in response to many other initiatives. Few have adequately appreciated Hamilton's grand design in its entirety, understood it as an agenda partially completed by the convention and partially by Hamilton later, or recognized its full realization in our twentieth-century history and contemporary situation. Instead, the utterly unrealized Jeffersonian image, more consistent with our attachment to "democracy," has dominated our national self-conception and our national rhetoric.

Inherent in Hamilton's grand design is a set of political implications with profound importance. He created an intricate central government machine that encouraged and rewarded behavior appropriate to his vision of a national commercial-financial-industrial economy—the entrepreneurial, productive, growth-oriented behavior that was to define our economic, political, and cultural life and identity for centuries. It was our first "industrial policy," incubating capitalism as a crucial by-product.

Hamilton also insulated the machine against the possibility that popular majorities or political chicanery might alter the outcomes he deemed essential to the creation of a great nation. In the process, by building upon the dark side of the Constitution, the Framers' property-protecting provisions and fear of democracy, Hamilton succeeded in almost completely removing the *substance* of public policy from popular hands. We live amidst the consequences today.

In this paper, we first review briefly the Framers' intentions and actions regarding the protection of property, both absolutely and from the interference of popular majorities. We shall see, as have many historians and political scientists before us, that the Framers were both class conscious and thorough in their efforts.

Then we explore Hamilton's grand design, its political implications, and the protection he added to assure that his system would be insulated in multiple ways against popular impact. Hamilton wove a web that deliberately deflected popular preferences away from the most sensitive and crucial areas of public policy—financial affairs, and the nature and distribution of wealth in the country. More specifically, he developed major expansive constitutional doctrines and set up the power of judicial review. One of the most important and intended results was the ensuing heavy reliance upon the law and the courts as decision makers, and a governing role for the legal profession. This erected an ostensibly neutral and objective shield that first obscured what was happening and then made it seem natural and inevitable.

Finally, we show how this system, in its twentieth-century maturity, has come to threaten the very political stability and productive national economy that were the Framers' and Hamilton's goals. What the more knowingly purposeful defenders of this system did when faced with the inescapable prospect of popular participation was *first* to build a maze of multiple limits on the effects of that participation, and *second,* to remove the substance of key policies into another, more remote, decision-making system. What its subsequent defenders have done is to triumphantly label the result "democracy."

Ironically, the great republican experiment has been converted into something like what the Framers feared almost as much as democracy— an absolutist monarchy complete with ongoing baronial struggles for court power and privilege, subject only to the occasional disturbance of crowds running in the streets. In the discouraging character and prospects of our contemporary politics, therefore, we have not experienced the *perversion* of the Framers' intent so much as we have seen the *fulfillment* of the dark side of the Constitution.

I. THE FRAMERS' CONSTITUTION

The Framers' Attitudes

As is well known, only a few of the delegates to the convention of 1787 were distinguished by concern for the rights and goals of popular majorities. Most of these dropped out or ended up among the Antifederalists in opposition to ratification. The general attitude of the main body of Framers can be summarized in the phrase "too

much democracy." As James Madison put it in *Federalist No. 10*:

> Complaints are everywhere heard from our most considerate and virtuous citizens, equally the friends of public and private faith and of public and personal liberty, that our governments are too unstable, that the public good is disregarded in the conflicts of rival parties, and that measures are too often decided, not according to the rules of justice and the rights of the minor party, but by the superior force of an interested and overbearing majority.

Or, as Hamilton wrote in *Federalist No. 15*: "There are material imperfections in our national system and . . . something is necessary to be done to rescue us from impending anarchy."

Concerns focused on "a rage for paper money, for an abolition of debts, for an equal division of property, or for any other improper or wicked project." All these improper projects and unjust legislation, of course, sprang from the state legislatures, where "men of more humble, more rural origins, less educated, and with more parochial interests" held sway. Even Jefferson could not support such an excess: "173 despots would surely be as oppressive as one," he wrote. "An *elective despotism* was not the government we fought for." Shays's Rebellion was much on the delegates' minds, and for many, provided the final straw. As Gordon Wood points out:

> Finally, when even Massachusetts with its supposedly model constitution [one of the less democratic of the states] experienced popular excesses, including Shays's Rebellion and the subsequent legislative "tyranny" of Shaysite sympathizers, many leaders were ready to shift the arena of constitutional change from the states to the nation.

The Framers' contemporaries were well aware of the backgrounds and biases of those who drafted our founding document. The Antifederalist writings of the period are full of accusations on this count. According to Jackson Turner Main, "the criticism that the Constitution favored the few at the expense of the many was almost universal." In the words of one prominent Antifederalist: "It changes, totally changes, the form of your present government. From a well-digested, well-formed democratic, you are at once rushing into an aristocratic government." The late Herbert Storing, who collected and edited the Antifederalist writings, called this "the underlying theme of a vast quantity of the specific criticism by the Anti-Federalists of the proposed Constitution."

"The Federal Farmer," a prominent opponent of the Constitution, argued that the state conventions should revise and amend the proposed Constitution as needed, before ratification. Otherwise, the liberty of free men will be lost to those who "avariciously grasp at all power and property." An aristocratic group had

> taken the political field, and with its fashionable dependents, and the tongue and the pen, is endeavouring to establish in great haste, a politer kind of government. . . . The fact is, these aristocrats support and hasten the adoption of the proposed constitution, merely because they think it is a stepping stone to their favorite object. I think I am well founded in this idea; I think the general politics of these men support it, as well as the common observation among them.

In addition, the "Federal Farmer" asserted,

> This system promises a large field of employment to military gentlemen, and gentlemen of the law; and . . . it will afford security to creditors, to the clergy, salary-men and others depending on money payments.
>
> [Once] power is transferred from the many to the few, all changes become extremely difficult; the government, in this case, being beneficial to the few, they will be exceedingly artful and adroit in preventing any measures which may lead to a change.

"Centinel," in his letters in opposition, was even more forceful, terming the effort to foist the Constitution on unsuspecting citizens "a most daring attempt to establish a despotic aristocracy among freemen, that the world has ever witnessed." He added:

> From this investigation into the organization of this government, it appears that it is devoid of all responsibility or accountability to the great body of the people, and that so far from being a regular balanced government, it would be in practice a *permanent ARISTOCRACY*.

The Lure of the New Economy

As early as 1785, Hamilton and others had more in mind than merely the containment of democracy. They began to envision a new kind of commercial economy that would replace production for one's own use with production for sale elsewhere. Trade, transportation, and accompanying financial opportunities would be vastly expanded on a national scale. Eventually, such a national market and exchange system would penetrate parochial communities and replace the almost subsistence-level agricultural economies characteristic of all but the seacoast towns and cosmopolitan centers of the time.

But there would be no national commercial economy unless the Articles of Confederation could be replaced by some more powerful central government. That central government would not only put the brakes on the pernicious projects of the local majorities, but would protect the "property"—the contracts, bonds, paper, credit, etc.—essential to a commercial economy. Such a government would defend the hard money that made for a sound economy, promote the national market through uniform laws and otherwise overcome state protectionism, use import regulations both for taxes and to protect American goods against British competition, and establish sound credit in the international commercial community.

There were two prospective opponents whose interests would be directly damaged by such a new government. One was the mass of heavily indebted back-country farmers still stirred by the Revolutionary dream of equality and individual rights. The other was the state legislatures whose support the farmers sought in their struggle against their creditors and others of the "better people," and which would have had ample institutional reasons to be opposed to any strengthening of the center. An adequate new government would have to control both these threats.

The public campaign for the new government began with the call to the Annapolis Convention in 1786, though its origins are visible much earlier in the correspondence and speeches of advocates. A rather full reform proposal came from Hamilton as early as September 3, 1780, in his letter to James Duane, in which he stated that "The first step must be to give Congress powers competent to the public exigencies." In its call for the Annapolis Convention, the Virginia Legislature was more specific:

To take into consideration the *trade* and *commerce* of the United States; to consider how far an uniform system, in their commercial intercourse and regulations, might be necessary to their common interest and permanent harmony, and to report to the several States such an act relative to this great object, as when unanimously ratified by them, would enable the United States, in Congress assembled, effectually to provide for the same.

As is well known, the Annapolis Convention was attended by only twelve delegates from five states. Among them was Alexander Hamilton, who seized the opportunity to issue the call for the constitutional convention, as follows:

Your Commissioners cannot forbear to indulge an expression of their earnest and unanimous wish, that speedy measures may be taken, to effect a general meeting of the States, in a future Convention, for the same and such other purposes, as the situation of public affairs, may be found to require. . . .

In this persuasion your Commissioners submit an opinion, that the Idea of extending the powers of their Deputies, to other objects, than those of Commerce . . . will deserve to be incorporated into that of a future Convention. . . .

That there are important defects in the system of the Federal Government is acknowledged by the Acts of all those States, which have concurred in the present Meeting; That the defects, upon a closer examination, may be found greater and more numerous, than even these acts imply, is at least so far probable . . . as may reasonably be supposed to merit a deliberate and candid discussion. . . .

Your Commissioners . . . beg leave to suggest their unanimous conviction, that it may essentially tend to advance the interests of the union, if the States, by whom they have been respectively delegated, would themselves concur, and use their endeavours to procure the concurrence of the other States, in the appointment of Commissioners, to meet at Philadelphia on the second Monday in May next, to take into consideration the situation of the United States, to devise such further provisions as shall appear to them necessary to render the constitution of the Federal Government adequate to the exigencies of the Union. . . .

Shays's Rebellion, that heroic and desperate act by a handful of farmers, is surely the dominant symbol of the period and in many ways the real source of the Constitution. It was the frightening, triggering event that caused a particular selection of delegates to be appointed by their legislatures, induced them to spend a hot summer at an uncertain task in Philadelphia, and provided the context for their work and its later reception. For Hamilton and his cause, it was a godsend. For the convention, it was the ever present threat that led to acceptance of several of the preventive provisions of the Constitution.

For us, Shays's Rebellion may serve to synthesize and express the two streams of thinking that led to the Constitution. The need to protect property and contain democracy could hardly be made more compelling. The need for a powerful central government that could protect commercial interests against citizens, if necessary, is indelibly clear. The basic principles that would have to be enforced in order to prevent such incidents were precisely those that would help to build the new national commercial economy.

The Framers' Constitution responds to both of these concerns, but leaves a substantial part of the second less explicit, and thus subject to Hamilton's later completion in the first administration. While there was little or no disagreement about the need to protect property and contain democracy, some delegates (particularly from the South) certainly would have had reservations about the new national economy and its implications for central government power if they had fully realized what was happening. The convention avoided potential conflict by leaving some provisions incomplete or undefined, in effect passing the responsibility to the first Congress.

In effect, several Framers (Hamilton central among them) were calling for the country—or at least its decisive elites—to make a crucial choice. The choice they advocated was to move from the current mostly agricultural economy (large plantations in the South, and small farms throughout the country) to a national commercial economy in which trade and finance would be dominant. They did not make this call openly, of course, and perhaps some of them did not grasp its totality or significance. Small wonder that their opponents did not see and oppose their design in explicit ways.

The Constitution as Synthesis

The Constitution's many provisions limiting the potential impact of popular majorities are too well known to require extensive comment. They range broadly from the design of basic structures, to methods of constituting the government, to limits on its powers. Examples in each category are separation of powers and checks and balances,

the various forms of insulating elections, and prohibitions against specific acts that might impinge upon property rights.

More interesting and perhaps less familiar—at least in their totality as a means of instituting a new economy—are the several provisions that create and defend the new national commercial economy through central government power. Many of these provisions were unselfconsciously promoted under the rubric of "protection of property." They were meant to insure that "the rules of justice and the rights of the minor party," as Madison said, would be maintained, even in the face of the "superior force of an interested and overbearing majority." Many do double duty as limits on popular majorities, *but that is exactly the point*. The new economy *necessitated* a national political system in which commercial and financial interests were assured that new and potentially unpopular rules and practices would nevertheless be enforced reliably and consistently—and, it was hoped, be accepted under the more widespread acceptance of the necessity of protection for property rights.

The powers granted to the Congress in Article I, Section 8 and denied to the states in Section 10 amount to the framework for a new fiscal and commercial public policy. Congress gains the power to declare what shall constitute money and to control its value, while the states are forbidden to coin money, emit bills of credit, or allow anything but gold and silver coin in payment of debts. As a result, the states (and their "too democratic" legislatures) were prevented from issuing paper money or defining what might serve as legal tender for the payment of debts, and the gold and silver preferred by bankers and creditors would continue as the basis of the economy.

The Congress also acquired effective taxing powers, and with them the potential to become a creditworthy engine of economic development. Paying existing debts would make it possible to borrow more, to stabilize the currency, and to encourage investment and expansion in various ways. Vital among these tax powers was the power to impose duties and imposts. These are not only the easiest way to collect taxes, but also a means to manage access to the American market—whether to protect infant American industries or to open up other nations' markets. By contrast with the new powers of Congress and the past practice of the states alike, the states were firmly and completely excluded from all such powers (except for the strictly limited purposes of inspections).

The centrality of the famous "commerce clause" to the creation of the new national economy can hardly be debated, even if the question of exclusivity remains at issue today. Hamilton and some of the Framers would undoubtedly have preferred that the mere presence of this provision be understood to preclude the states from acting in the field of interstate commerce at all. But it is not a serious obstacle to their ends that the states be allowed to employ their police or regulatory powers in this area when the Congress has not fully occupied the field or acted in ways that conflict with such state legislation. More important to the creation of the new economy were the requirements for uniformity on the part of national laws pertaining to commerce.

Finally, the contract clause must be appreciated as something more than a prohibition that would assure creditors against any future Shays-type rebellions. Article I, Section 10 includes the prohibition against state laws impairing the obligations of contract as one of a long series of limitations starting with "No states shall. . . ." Clearly, this would render unconstitutional and void any state law that changed the terms of repayment of any existing private contract. By making such contracts into fixed "givens" of economic life, it also tended to discourage popular majorities from seeking redress of economic grievances from their state legislatures.

In Hamilton's hands, the clause applied equally to *public* contracts, so that state legislatures would lose the long-standing sovereign privilege of changing or withdrawing prior grants or franchises. Stability and predictability would be assured, but at the cost of legislative responsiveness to shifting popular preferences.

As Forrest McDonald has shown, this clause may also be distinguished as having been inserted in the Constitution through something like a Hamiltonian coup. At least we know that the convention had twice rejected the principle, and that it was re-inserted by the five-member Committee of Style at the last moment and (apparently) accepted without argument by a weary convention. McDonald makes the case that Hamilton was the only one of the five to grasp the potential in such a clause and therefore must have brought about its last-minute inclusion almost single-handedly.

These primarily economic provisions only sketch the outline of the Framers' intent. They do not by any means constitute the Constitution's entire commitment to the support of the new commercial economy. There are many other provisions that, when taken together, add up to some extensive buttressing of that economy. These include the privileges and immunities of state citizens (to do business in other states), full faith and credit requirements (so that contracts could be enforced and debtors pursued), authorization for a federal court system (for some of the same purposes), and the guarantee and supremacy clauses.

In the United States of the 1780s, it would have been politically difficult, if not impossible, to devise a government that was not, at the least, republican. The Framers had to devise a document with at least the appearance of some democracy, and which could be defended as "republican." Thus, the Constitution does have "democratical" features. However, between the fear of the majority and the desire to protect the newly developing property of the commercial classes, the Framers found it necessary to create a document with a darker side, as we have outlined.

The spare and often ambiguous language of the Constitution was ideally suited to Hamilton's interpretation and expansion. It is Hamilton's interpretations, such as that involving the necessary and proper clause and the creation of the bank, and his expansions, such as in the development of the power of judicial review, that really brought the new national commercial economy into life in the Constitution.

The Framers sketched an outline, but Hamilton made it real. Commercial property and its developing economic relations were protected, and, by the completion of Hamilton's program, removed from the public policy agenda. The ability to change the economy, to deal with substantive public policy issues such as the distribution of wealth and fiscal and monetary measures, was effectively removed from popular control. The "majority" was now contained.

II. HAMILTON'S GRAND DESIGN AND LEGISLATIVE PROGRAMS

As a constitutional architect of vision and purpose, no American compares with Alexander Hamilton. From his earliest critiques of the Articles to the legal cases he argued after leaving the Cabinet, Hamilton pursued a single comprehensive image of a future economy and a government that would promote and defend it. If one person can be singled out, surely Hamilton—not Madison—was the primary driving force behind the origin, character, and ultimate meaning of the American Constitution.

Hamilton's Federalist essays are widely known for their emphasis on the weakness of the Articles and the contrasting need for energy in government, taxing powers to maintain that government's creditworthiness, a strong executive, direct application of national laws to individuals, and the like. All of these reflect characteristic Hamiltonian principles, and together they indicate a direction for the new system.

But the Hamiltonian design comes into its clearest focus from two other major sources which represent the main thrust of his efforts to complete the work of the convention. The first of these is the set of Reports and accompanying legislation and opinions that Hamilton authored as Secretary of the Treasury. The other is *Federalist No. 78* and its argument for the power of judicial review, a bold and in many respects original expansion of central government power which helped to raise the courts, the law, and the legal profession to a governing role unprecedented then and unequaled elsewhere today.

.   .   .

What Hamilton demonstrated in these Reports was a clear conception of the national government's capacity to serve as the manipulator of an array of carrots and sticks that would move the economy in desirable directions. Hamilton was also clear about who should determine what those desirable directions might be, and who should benefit from such purposeful action. Men of commercial foresight and experience, and probably of property, should hold such powers, and use them for mutual—and hence national—benefit. Most of all, no such system could tolerate significant popular involvement or impact.

Hamilton's design, let us acknowledge, was intended to build national strength and grandeur, on the model of the British Empire he so much admired. In practical terms, it added up to a new set of legal concepts, new financial principles and methods at the national level, and a new overall developmental role for the national government. His incipient commercial-financial economy (soon to emerge, with industrialization, as capitalism) required changing a number of key legal principles long established in the pre-commercial common law. It required creative use of the national debt, deliberate management of the currency, purposeful industrial policy, and conscious inducements in the form of grants of rights to the vast lands inexpensively acquired by the national government through treaties and conquest.

Most of all, Hamilton's design required insulation against reactions from all sides, and particularly against popular efforts to change the patterns of wealth distribution that this design would accomplish. Hamilton's answer to this compelling need was twofold.

First, as we have just seen, he placed the reins of power as far from the people as he could—in a centrally guided financial and development system that would be as hard to identify as it would be to reach and change. Hamilton's system had an early demonstration while he was Secretary of the Treasury, and was legitimated by Jefferson's failure to demolish it while in office. But it was visible only in isolated pieces—growing, merging, self-validating pieces like the restoration and refinement of the Bank, the development of the tariff and internal improvements and the income tax, the vigorous use of judicial review, the triumph of the legal profession—until its full flowering in the Progressive-New Deal Era.

Hamilton stood for an economy that would be dynamic, responsive to opportunities, and oriented to long-term growth. That economy required far-sighted elites to assure that the government would offer incentives for development, stabilize its context, and control its excesses. Government could also serve by providing a means of deflecting or absorbing popular complaints. For all of these goals, the government had to be big, powerful, highly centralized, and removed from the people—but apparently highly responsive to them. Herbert Croly aptly named the twentieth-century version of Hamilton's design "a Hamiltonian government for Jeffersonian ends." Thus the two ever-contending strands of American political thought—our two major images of the desirable American political economy—came to an ultimate merger. Together, they gave credence to labeling Hamilton's national government with the venerable Jeffersonian symbol of "democracy."

The *second* means by which Hamilton sought insulation from popular impact was through transferring as much policymaking as possible into the far less visible and apparently neutral and mechanical hands of courts and lawyers. This strategy encompassed not only the usual and often discretionary law-enforcing role of courts, but more significantly a deliberate lawchanging function and—most important of all—a major policymaking role for the Supreme Court at least equal to that of the other branches.

· · ·

The effect of Hamilton's various efforts in this area was to raise courts, the law, and the legal profession into a covert policy-making system representing his best hope of protecting the national economy from popular interference. He was apparently willing to pay the price of the law's rigidities and tendency toward backward-looking in order to insulate the economy and its distribution patterns in this way. But the price paid by the people—and ultimately by the constitutional system itself—has yet to be calculated.

III. THE CONSEQUENCES OF THE DARK SIDE

Any list of the basic problems of current American politics would surely include institutional deadlock, the decline of the political parties, domination by special interests, the multiplicity and complexity of issues, television's role in diverting attention away from public policy, and the deplorable levels of knowledge and interest on the part of most citizens. For each problem, there are one or more standard explanations.

Most of the explanations (and prescriptions for improvement when the situation is not deemed totally hopeless) take one of two forms. The first involves a focus on specific causal factors, i.e., the effects of incumbency, patterns of campaign contributions, the candidate focus of the media, and so forth. The second is more or less an inventory of the incurable failures of the American people: low and declining turnout at elections, ignorance and self-interestedness, an enduring spectator orientation, apparent manipulability by money and media, and an inability to grasp and act on issues.

These standard explanations amount to a massive exercise in blaming the victim. More important, the situation is actually *worse,* and much more fundamental, than generally suggested. We have no quarrel with the list of problems. If anything, we would lengthen and deepen any such list, and would predict that many others will soon be doing so. The United States is already beginning to emerge from the self-congratulatory stupor of the early 1980s. Realism will be in vogue again by the next recession.

Many of the problems of our politics have their origins in the deliberate design of the Constitution, particularly as it was developed by Hamilton. The problems are *real*. The people's response to them is *rational*. What is missing is recognition that the roots of the problem lie in Hamilton's very success.

Today's national government is highly centralized, a huge and distant bureaucracy related in a merely episodic manner to gridlocked and unresponsive policy-making institutions. The web of special interests is a pragmatic answer, albeit one that represents only the most powerful few. Media and money call the tune for parties and candidates. People may quite rationally decide not to study issues or to participate in such a system.

What has brought about this set of problems and popular response? One absolutely fundamental cause is Hamilton's successful removal of the substance of policy from popular reach. The major pieces of Hamilton's design—the financial system and the legal system—were put in place in the late 1700s and early 1800s by Hamilton and his followers. They became fully integrated and coherently employed in the Progressive Era, from which the rise of the truly centralized Hamiltonian state can be dated.

These two major pieces of Hamilton's design, however, had more than proved their value in the nineteenth century. Each served effectively to obscure unpopular basic national policies from visibility, displace and eventually absorb popular complaints within apparently neutral and objective machines, and frustrate even quite determined popular movements. As Morton Horwitz has shown, the legal system took on its economic role as covert redistributor and allocator of financial burdens as early as the 1820s and 1830s. As opponents of the Bank alleged from the start, and as Goodwyn, Sharkey and others have shown with respect to the financing of the Civil War, the financial system effectively enriched the wealthy while putting the burden on the working and later the middle classes.

When the high point of judicial review was reached in the early 1890s and successfully defended in the election of 1896, the full Hamiltonian legal system was in place. The Supreme Court's power was confirmed; the multitude of state courts were encouraged; and the governing role of an increasingly elite and corporate-oriented Bar was further legitimated. Passage of the Federal Reserve Act offered a final financial link and means of leverage for the same corporate banking-legal community.

Once this system was consolidated in the First World War, participation could actually be encouraged because there was little chance that popular majorities could do much damage. If the basic defenses erected by the Framers did not work, then surely Hamilton's system would divert and absorb popular efforts until they were harmless. Nevertheless, the "better people" were still fearful, not just because of the near-success of labor and the Populists in the 1890s, but also because of the growing ranks of immigrants. Thus, deliberate repression sought to discourage lower-class opposition and electoral participation for a decade or more, just as Hamilton's system was crystallizing. A newly refurbished ("democratic") rationalizing ideology was soon bolstered by powerful new means of communication and indoctrination.

The net result of all these efforts was dramatic decline in electoral turnout in the twentieth century.

Women were added to the eligible electorate in 1920, and blacks and many immigrants had been effectively subtracted in the previous decades, so that turnout percentages are not strictly comparable. However, it is still a shock to realize that elections in the 1880s and 1890s generally had turnout levels over 70 percent and often exceeding 80 percent. Today, when women have had 60 years of experience with the franchise and a whole new generation of black voters has entered the active electorate, we count ourselves lucky to attract more than half of the eligible electorate to the polls.

Where have all the voters gone? They have caught on that the system is rigged. Popular majorities' efforts to change either the distribution of wealth and power or the basic policies that seem necessary to maintain that structure of wealth and power simply don't seem possible. To be sure, decades of accomplishment by the ideological defenders and celebrants of this system have encouraged Americans to accept it as "democracy." Americans learn to want or, more likely, consider inevitable whatever is produced, to settle for various diversionary satisfactions, and/or to fear change and even suspect that those who do seek change must have self-interested and unpatriotic motives. These are ideological rationalizations for the central fact that the Hamiltonian Constitution excludes people from directly affecting important public policy outcomes.

This is not to say that there is no history of popular impact on government, or that the Supreme Court is merely a tool of the corporations. Either such caricature of our argument would be silly. What is important is that popular impact, such as it is, can be made effective only in very limited ways through the electoral process. For the most part, it must come through disruption—riots, massive strikes, demonstrations involving the threat of violence, and other attacks on the social order itself. What does it mean for a popular government that its people are politically effective only when they threaten to destroy it?

The Supreme Court has made many decisions, particularly in the middle years of this century, that advanced basic democratic rights. But that was a result of judicial appointments, not an attribute of the institution. The Supreme Court has, and can, and may well again, make precisely the opposite kinds of decisions. What does it mean for a popular government that its basic policies can be set by a transitory majority drawn from a body of nine life-appointed lawyers?

What we are saying is that the Framers' two major goals are threatened today by the success with which Hamilton and his followers implemented those goals. We do not have a stable political economic system, and we do not have the capacity to make the choices necessary to assure a strong and successful American political economy.

Our political system works by fits and starts. It is neither responsive nor accountable and it lacks solid grounding in the body of its people. It sits and waits for the next crisis. Unfortunately, to solve that crisis, it may have to transform itself into something that will be *very* difficult to rationalize as "democracy."

We have not addressed the great issues of nuclear war, planetary survival, or even American economic viability in a drastically changing world economy—not because the people don't care, but because there is no linkage between the people's felt needs and their policymakers. No such basic policies can be implemented, even if policymakers were to concur, without the sustained support of some major portion of the people.

To solve our problems, or merely to fulfill the Framers' goals in the wholly different conditions of our times, we will have to come to terms with Hamilton's Constitution in a realistic manner. Perhaps the best way to honor the Framers' work is not to join in obfuscating celebrations, but to act as they did under like circumstances.

We might start by critically exploring the ways in which today's analogue of the Articles of Confederation is defective in achieving goals that are necessary and desirable for the *future*. Obviously, like the Framers, we would have to address basic principles of social order and purpose—if we have not completely forgotten how to do so. (That we *have* forgotten is strongly suggested by the nature of the proposals currently offered for constitutional "reform.")

Curing the defects of Hamilton's Constitution may not be possible, for many reasons. It may be that patterns of material advantage, or the depth of the problems we face, or the sheer size of the country, make it practically impossible. Or our situation may be even worse: perhaps generations of structural deflection—of elites as well as of the general public—from considering the Constitution in a realistic manner has made it impossible for us to do so now. Decades of cultural lowering of the criteria of democracy may have made it impossible for us to recapture its fuller definition and potential.

If there is a route out of our crisis, it lies in deliberately reversing Hamilton's strategy. That is, we must seek to re-engage the people in their government, and particularly in ways that enable them to have direct impact on the substance of important public policies. Without regard to what might be "realistic" or "practical" in light of today's power distribution, or to questions of strategy, the kinds of measures to which consideration might be given are of the following order:

a. Radical decentralization, perhaps to some regional system, reserving only a few global functions for the national government, to put government within reach of the people;

b. Removing the incumbent character of the national government by putting limits on the number of terms that Representatives and Senators can serve;

c. Reducing the role of money by requiring free television time for public affairs issues, party deliberations and arguments, and candidates' presentations;

d. Sharply contracting the policy-making role of courts and lawyers by transferring jurisdiction of constitutional and major policy issues to openly political forums;

e. Instituting mechanisms for direct action— the old initiative and referendum in modern form, with encouragement and provision of educational opportunities and some screen for levels of information;

f. Making registration immediate and eligibility for voting open to all, if necessary by decentralized computer access;

g. Reviving the parties by starting at the local and state levels and providing a series of thresholds through which, by showing increasing levels of popular participation, parties might increasingly acquire control over campaign funding and nominations;

h. Overhauling the public education system to make public affairs a vital and exciting part of the curriculum, welcome controversy, and set future-oriented public service once again at the center of the aspirations of all citizens.

These suggestions are only a start, intended to illustrate the combined fundamental-and-electoral level at which rethinking must begin. They are easily caricatured, and of course they are not "realistic." The point is that institutional tinkering will not suffice.

When problems such as we have described are real, remedies must be radical; that is the lesson the Framers taught in 1787. Only when the people are re-engaged in a government within their reach will Hamilton's damage be undone. At that point, we can proceed to build upon his successes, and seek to truly achieve the stable political system and productive economy that were his vision for the new nation. Only the bright hope of a new twenty-first-century vision can finally transcend the dark side of our much-celebrated eighteenth-century Constitution.

DISCUSSION QUESTIONS

1. According to Dolbeare and Medcalf, how is the dark side of the Constitution related to Alexander Hamilton's model of political economy?
2. To what extent are the current problems of American politics rooted in the design of our Constitution and to what extent do they have other causes?

11 *Brooke Allen*

OUR GODLESS CONSTITUTION

One of the axioms of American political culture is that our eighteenth-century Founding Fathers were deeply religious, weaving Christian principles into the political fabric of the nation. In this brief historical survey, scholar and literary critic Brooke Allen debunks this assumption as myth. Rather than pious Christians fashioning the nation in the image of God, Allen depicts many of our key Founders—George Washington, Thomas Jefferson, John Adams, Thomas Paine, Benjamin Franklin, James Madison—as at best religious skeptics, more deeply wed to Enlightenment rationality than any religious dogma. Our Constitution, The Federalist Papers, and other founding documents make scant reference to God and virtually none to Jesus. Widespread fear of the oppressive potential of what we today would call religious fundamentalism relegated theological pronouncements to a mostly minor, mostly rhetorical role in our constitutional framework and early political discourse as a nation. Understanding why religion was viewed so skeptically—and why that skepticism ordinarily is not part of our national story—sheds light on our constitutional background and on the ideological conditioning we receive as part of our political culture.

Our Constitution makes no mention whatever of God. Our nation was founded not on Christian principles but on Enlightenment ones. God only entered the picture as a very minor player, and Jesus Christ was conspicuously absent. The omission was too obvious to have been anything but deliberate, in spite of Alexander Hamilton's flippant responses when asked about it: According to one account, he said that the new nation was not in need of "foreign aid"; according to another, he simply said "we forgot." But as Hamilton's biographer Ron Chernow points out, Hamilton never forgot anything important.

In the eighty-five essays that make up *The Federalist,* God is mentioned only twice (both times by Madison, who uses the word, as Gore Vidal has remarked, in the "only Heaven knows" sense). In the Declaration of Independence, He

Source: Brooke Allen, "Our Godless Constitution," *The Nation,* Volume 280, Number 7, February 21, 2005, pp. 15–20.

gets two brief nods: a reference to "the Laws of Nature and Nature's God," and the famous line about men being "endowed by their Creator with certain inalienable rights." More blatant official references to a deity date from long after the founding period: "In God We Trust" did not appear on our coinage until the Civil War, and "under God" was introduced into the Pledge of Allegiance during the McCarthy hysteria in 1954.

In 1797 our government concluded a "Treaty of Peace and Friendship between the United States of America and the Bey and Subjects of Tripoli, or Barbary," now known simply as the Treaty of Tripoli. Article 11 of the treaty contains these words:

> As the Government of the United States . . . is not in any sense founded on the Christian religion—as it has in itself no character of enmity against the laws, religion, or tranquillity of Musselmen—and as the said States never have entered into any war or act of hostility against any Mehomitan nation, it is declared by the parties that no pretext arising from religious opinions shall ever produce an interruption of the harmony existing between the two countries.

This document was endorsed by Secretary of State Timothy Pickering and President John Adams. It was then sent to the Senate for ratification; the vote was unanimous. It is worth pointing out that although this was the 339th time a recorded vote had been required by the Senate, it was only the third unanimous vote in the Senate's history. There is no record of debate or dissent. The text of the treaty was printed in full in the Philadelphia Gazette and in two New York papers, but there were no screams of outrage, as one might expect today.

The Founding Fathers were not religious men, and they fought hard to erect, in Thomas Jefferson's words, "a wall of separation between church and state." John Adams opined that if they were not restrained by legal measures, Puritans—the fundamentalists of their day—would "whip and crop, and pillory and roast." The historical

epoch had afforded these men ample opportunity to observe the corruption to which established priesthoods were liable, as well as "the impious presumption of legislators and rulers," as Jefferson wrote, "civil as well as ecclesiastical, who, being themselves but fallible and uninspired men, have assumed dominion over the faith of others, setting up their own opinions and modes of thinking as the only true and infallible, and as such endeavoring to impose them on others, hath established and maintained false religions over the greatest part of the world and through all time."

If we define a Christian as a person who believes in the divinity of Jesus Christ, then it is safe to say that some of the key Founding Fathers were not Christians at all. Benjamin Franklin, Thomas Jefferson and Tom Paine were deists—that is, they believed in one Supreme Being but rejected revelation and all the supernatural elements of the Christian Church; the word of the Creator, they believed, could best be read in Nature. John Adams was a professed liberal Unitarian, but he, too, in his private correspondence seems more deist than Christian.

George Washington and James Madison also leaned toward deism, although neither took much interest in religious matters. Madison believed that "religious bondage shackles and debilitates the mind and unfits it for every noble enterprize." He spoke of the "almost fifteen centuries" during which Christianity had been on trial: "What have been its fruits? More or less in all places, pride and indolence in the Clergy, ignorance and servility in the laity, in both, superstition, bigotry, and persecution." If Washington mentioned the Almighty in a public address, as he occasionally did, he was careful to refer to Him not as "God" but with some nondenominational moniker like "Great Author" or "Almighty Being." It is interesting to note that the Father of our Country spoke no words of a religious nature on his deathbed, although fully aware that he was dying, and did not ask for a man of God to be present; his last act was to take his own pulse, the consummate gesture of a creature of the age of scientific rationalism.

Tom Paine, a polemicist rather than a politician, could afford to be perfectly honest about his religious beliefs, which were baldly deist in the tradition of Voltaire: "I believe in one God, and no more; and I hope for happiness beyond this life. . . . I do not believe in the creed professed by the Jewish church, by the Roman church, by the Greek church, by the Turkish church, by the Protestant church, nor by any church that I know of. My own mind is my own church." This is how he opened *The Age of Reason*, his virulent attack on Christianity. In it he railed against the "obscene stories, the voluptuous debaucheries, the cruel and torturous executions, the unrelenting vindictiveness" of the Old Testament, "a history of wickedness, that has served to corrupt and brutalize mankind." The New Testament is less brutalizing but more absurd, the story of Christ's divine genesis a "fable, which for absurdity and extravagance is not exceeded by any thing that is to be found in the mythology of the ancients." He held the idea of the Resurrection in especial ridicule: Indeed, "the wretched contrivance with which this latter part is told, exceeds every thing that went before it." Paine was careful to contrast the tortuous twists of theology with the pure clarity of deism. "The true deist has but one Deity; and his religion consists in contemplating the power, wisdom, and benignity of the Deity in his works, and in endeavoring to imitate him in every thing moral, scientifical, and mechanical."

Paine's rhetoric was so fervent that he was inevitably branded an atheist. Men like Franklin, Adams and Jefferson could not risk being tarred with that brush, and in fact Jefferson got into a good deal of trouble for continuing his friendship with Paine and entertaining him at Monticello. These statesmen had to be far more circumspect than the turbulent Paine, yet if we examine their beliefs it is all but impossible to see just how theirs differed from his.

Franklin was the oldest of the Founding Fathers. He was also the most worldly and sophisticated, and was well aware of the Machiavellian principle that if one aspires to influence the masses, one must at least profess religious sentiments. By his own definition he was a deist, although one French acquaintance claimed that "our free-thinkers have adroitly sounded him on his religion, and they maintain that they have discovered he is one of their own, that is that he has none at all." If he did have a religion, it was strictly utilitarian: As his biographer Gordon Wood has said, "He praised religion for whatever moral effects it had, but for little else." Divine revelation, Franklin freely admitted, had "no weight with me," and the covenant of grace seemed "unintelligible" and "not beneficial." As for the pious hypocrites who have ever controlled nations, "A man compounded of law and gospel is able to cheat a whole country with his religion and then destroy them under color of law"— a comment we should carefully consider at this turning point in the history of our Republic.

Here is Franklin's considered summary of his own beliefs, in response to a query by Ezra Stiles, the president of Yale. He wrote it just six weeks before his death at the age of 84:

> Here is my creed. I believe in one God, Creator of the universe. That he governs it by his providence. That he ought to be worshipped. That the most acceptable service we render to him is doing good to his other children. That the soul of Man is immortal, and will be treated with justice in another life respecting its conduct in this. These I take to be the fundamental points in all sound religion, and I regard them as you do in whatever sect I meet with them.
>
> As for Jesus of Nazareth, my opinion of whom you particularly desire, I think his system of morals and his religion, as he left them to us, the best the world ever saw or is likely to see; but I apprehend it has received various corrupting changes, and I have, with most of the present dissenters in England, some doubts as to his divinity; though it is a question I do not dogmatize upon, having never studied it, and think it needless to busy myself with now, when I expect soon an opportunity of knowing the

truth with less trouble. I see no harm, however, in its being believed, if that belief has the good consequence, as it probably has, of making his doctrines more respected and better observed, especially as I do not perceive that the Supreme takes it amiss, by distinguishing the unbelievers in his government of the world with any particular marks of his displeasure.

Jefferson thoroughly agreed with Franklin on the corruptions the teachings of Jesus had undergone. "The metaphysical abstractions of Athanasius, and the maniacal ravings of Calvin, tinctured plentifully with the foggy dreams of Plato, have so loaded [Christianity] with absurdities and incomprehensibilities" that it was almost impossible to recapture "its native simplicity and purity." Like Paine, Jefferson felt that the miracles claimed by the New Testament put an intolerable strain on credulity. "The day will come," he predicted (wrongly, so far), "when the mystical generation of Jesus, by the supreme being as his father in the womb of a virgin, will be classed with the fable of the generation of Minerva in the brain of Jupiter." The Revelation of St. John he dismissed as "the ravings of a maniac."

Jefferson edited his own version of the New Testament, "The Life and Morals of Jesus of Nazareth," in which he carefully deleted all the miraculous passages from the works of the Evangelists. He intended it, he said, as "a document in proof that I am a real Christian, that is to say, a disciple of the doctrines of Jesus." This was clearly a defense against his many enemies, who hoped to blacken his reputation by comparing him with the vile atheist Paine. His biographer Joseph Ellis is undoubtedly correct, though, in seeing disingenuousness here: "If [Jefferson] had been completely scrupulous, he would have described himself as a deist who admired the ethical teachings of Jesus as a man rather than as the son of God. (In modern-day parlance, he was a secular humanist.)" In short, not a Christian at all.

The three accomplishments Jefferson was proudest of—those that he requested be put on his tombstone—were the founding of the University of Virginia and the authorship of the Declaration of Independence and the Virginia Statute for Religious Freedom. The latter was a truly radical document that would eventually influence the separation of church and state in the U.S. Constitution; when it was passed by the Virginia legislature in 1786, Jefferson rejoiced that there was finally "freedom for the Jew and the Gentile, the Christian and the Mohammeden, the Hindu and infidel of every denomination"—note his respect, still unusual today, for the sensibilities of the "infidel." The University of Virginia was notable among early-American seats of higher education in that it had no religious affiliation whatever. Jefferson even banned the teaching of theology at the school.

If we were to speak of Jefferson in modern political categories, we would have to admit that he was a pure libertarian, in religious as in other matters. His real commitment (or lack thereof) to the teachings of Jesus Christ is plain from a famous throwaway comment he made: "It does me no injury for my neighbor to say there are twenty gods or no god. It neither picks my pocket nor breaks my leg." This raised plenty of hackles when it got about, and Jefferson had to go to some pains to restore his reputation as a good Christian. But one can only conclude, with Ellis, that he was no Christian at all.

John Adams, though no more religious than Jefferson, had inherited the fatalistic mindset of the Puritan culture in which he had grown up. He personally endorsed the Enlightenment commitment to Reason but did not share Jefferson's optimism about its future, writing to him, "I wish that Superstition in Religion exciting Superstition in Politicks . . . may never blow up all your benevolent and phylanthropic Lucubrations," but that "the History of all Ages is against you." As an old man he observed, "Twenty times in the course of my late reading have I been upon the point of breaking out, 'This would be the best of all possible worlds, if there were no religion in it!' " Speaking ex cathedra, as a relic of the founding generation, he expressed his admiration for the

Roman system whereby every man could worship whom, what and how he pleased. When his young listeners objected that this was paganism, Adams replied that it was indeed, and laughed.

In their fascinating and eloquent valetudinarian correspondence, Adams and Jefferson had a great deal to say about religion. Pressed by Jefferson to define his personal creed, Adams replied that it was "contained in four short words, 'Be just and good.'" Jefferson replied, "The result of our fifty or sixty years of religious reading, in the four words, 'Be just and good,' is that in which all our inquiries must end; as the riddles of all priesthoods end in four more, 'ubi panis, ibi deus.' What all agree in, is probably right. What no two agree in, most probably wrong."

This was a clear reference to Voltaire's *Reflections on Religion*. As Voltaire put it:

There are no sects in geometry. One does not speak of a Euclidean, an Archimedean. When the truth is evident, it is impossible for parties and factions to arise. . . . Well, to what dogma do all minds agree? To the worship of a God, and to honesty. All the philosophers of the world who have had a religion have said in all ages: "There is a God, and one must be just." There, then, is the universal religion established in all ages and throughout mankind. The point in which they all agree is therefore true, and the systems through which they differ are therefore false.

Of course all these men knew, as all modern presidential candidates know, that to admit to theological skepticism is political suicide. During Jefferson's presidency a friend observed him on his way to church, carrying a large prayer book. "You going to church, Mr. J," remarked the friend. "You do not believe a word in it." Jefferson didn't exactly deny the charge. "Sir," he replied, "no nation has ever yet existed or been governed without religion. Nor can be. The Christian religion is the best religion that has been given to man and I as chief Magistrate of this nation am bound to give it the sanction of my example. Good morning Sir."

Like Jefferson, every recent President has understood the necessity of at least paying lip service to the piety of most American voters. All of our leaders, Democrat and Republican, have attended church, and have made very sure they are seen to do so. But there is a difference between offering this gesture of respect for majority beliefs and manipulating and pandering to the bigotry, prejudice and millennial fantasies of Christian extremists. Though for public consumption the Founding Fathers identified themselves as Christians, they were, at least by today's standards, remarkably honest about their misgivings when it came to theological doctrine, and religion in general came very low on the list of their concerns and priorities—always excepting, that is, their determination to keep the new nation free from bondage to its rule.

DISCUSSION QUESTIONS

1. Focusing on a few of our more famous Founding Fathers, identify their major objections to the intersection of religion and political life. How would you describe them religiously?
2. In the penultimate paragraph, Allen points out that politicians—then and now—know that to acknowledge any personal skepticism about religion amounts to "political suicide." Given how untethered our Founding Fathers were to theological precepts, speculate about why being skeptical about religion—or being non-religious—is political suicide.

12 *Howard Zinn*

SOME TRUTHS ARE NOT SELF-EVIDENT

Writing during the bicentennial celebrations of 1987, historian and political scientist Howard Zinn makes a case that the Constitution is of minor importance in determining the degree of justice, liberty, and democracy in our society. While not denying the symbolic and moral weight of the Constitution, Zinn contends that social movements and citizen action have been far more significant in the realization of democratic values over the course of American history. He provides examples from the areas of racial equality, freedom of speech, economic justice, sexual equality, and questions of war and peace to support his claim that a "mere document" like the Constitution "is no substitute for the energy, boldness, and concerted action of the citizens."

This year [1987] Americans are talking about the Constitution but asking the wrong questions, such as, Could the Founding Fathers have done better? That concern is pointless, 200 years after the fact. Or, Does the Constitution provide the framework for a just and democratic society today? That question is also misplaced, because the Constitution, whatever its language and however interpreted by the Supreme Court, does not determine the degree of justice, liberty or democracy in our society.

The proper question, I believe, is not how good a document is or was the Constitution but, What effect does it have on the quality of our lives? And the answer to that, it seems to me, is, Very little. The Constitution makes promises it cannot by itself keep, and therefore deludes us into complacency about the rights we have. It is conspicuously silent on certain other rights that all human beings deserve. And it pretends to set limits on governmental powers, when in fact those limits are easily ignored.

I am not arguing that the Constitution has no importance; words have moral power and principles can be useful even when ambiguous. But, like other historic documents, the Constitution is of minor importance compared with the actions that citizens take, especially when those actions are joined in social movements. Such movements have worked, historically, to secure the rights our human sensibilities tell us are self-evidently ours, whether or not those rights are "granted" by the Constitution.

Source: Howard Zinn, "Some Truths Are Not Self-Evident." *The Nation,* Volume 245, Number 3, August 1–8, 1987, pp. 87–88.

Let me illustrate my point with five issues of liberty and justice:

First is the matter of racial equality. When slavery was abolished, it was not by constitutional fiat but by the joining of military necessity with the moral force of a great antislavery movement, acting outside the Constitution and often against the law. The Thirteenth, Fourteenth and Fifteenth Amendments wrote into the Constitution rights that extra-legal action had already won. But the Fourteenth and Fifteenth Amendments were ignored for almost a hundred years. The right to equal protection of the law and the right to vote, even the Supreme Court decision in *Brown v. Board of Education* in 1954 underlining the meaning of the equal protection clause, did not become operative until blacks, in the fifteen years following the Montgomery bus boycott, shook up the nation by tumultuous actions inside and outside the law.

The Constitution played a helpful but marginal role in all that. Black people, in the political context of the 1960s, would have demanded equality whether or not the Constitution called for it, just as the antislavery movement demanded abolition even in the absence of constitutional support.

What about the most vaunted of constitutional rights, free speech? Historically, the Supreme Court has given the right to free speech only shaky support, seesawing erratically by sometimes affirming and sometimes overriding restrictions. Whatever a distant Court decided, the real right of citizens to free expression has been determined by the immediate power of the local police on the street, by the employer in the workplace and by the financial limits on the ability to use the mass media.

The existence of a First Amendment has been inspirational but its protection elusive. Its reality has depended on the willingness of citizens, whether labor organizers, socialists or Jehovah's Witnesses, to insist on their right to speak and write. Liberties have not been given; they have been taken. And whether in the future we have a right to say what we want, or air what

we say, will be determined not by the existence of the First Amendment or the latest Supreme Court decision but by whether we are courageous enough to speak up at the risk of being jailed or fired, organized enough to defend our speech against official interference and can command resources enough to get our ideas before a reasonably large public.

What of economic justice? The Constitution is silent on the right to earn a moderate income, silent on the rights to medical care and decent housing as legitimate claims of every human being from infancy to old age. Whatever degree of economic justice has been attained in this country (impressive compared with others, shameful compared with our resources) cannot be attributed to something in the Constitution. It is the result of the concerted action of laborers and farmers over the centuries, using strikes, boycotts and minor rebellions of all sorts, to get redress of grievances directly from employers and indirectly from legislators. In the future, as in the past, the Constitution will sleep as citizens battle over the distribution of the nation's wealth, and will be awakened only to mark the score.

On sexual equality the Constitution is also silent. What women have achieved thus far is the result of their own determination, in the feminist upsurge of the nineteenth and early twentieth centuries, and the more recent women's liberation movement. Women have accomplished this outside the Constitution, by raising female and male consciousness and inducing courts and legislators to recognize what the Constitution ignores.

Finally, in an age in which war approaches genocide, the irrelevance of the Constitution is especially striking. Long, ravaging conflicts in Korea and Vietnam were waged without following Constitutional procedures, and if there is a nuclear exchange, the decision to launch U.S. missiles will be made, as it was in those cases, by the President and a few advisers. The public will be shut out of the process and deliberately kept uninformed by an intricate web of secrecy and deceit. The current Iran/*contra* scandal hearings before Congressional select committees should be understood as exposing not an aberration but a steady state of foreign policy.

It was not constitutional checks and balances but an aroused populace that prodded Lyndon Johnson and then Richard Nixon into deciding to extricate the United States from Vietnam. In the immediate future, our lives will depend not on the existence of the Constitution but on the power of an aroused citizenry demanding that we not go to war, and on Americans refusing, as did so many G.I.s and civilians in the Vietnam era, to cooperate in the conduct of a war.

The Constitution, like the Bible, has some good words. It is also, like the Bible, easily manipulated, distorted, ignored and used to make us feel comfortable and protected. But we risk the loss of our lives and liberties if we depend on a mere document to defend them. A constitution is a fine adornment for a democratic society, but it is no substitute for the energy, boldness and concerted action of the citizens.

DISCUSSION QUESTIONS

1. What is Zinn's main point about the relationship of the Constitution to political change and the expansion of democracy?
2. Identify the five issues of justice and liberty discussed by Zinn and explain how each relates to his main point about the Constitution.

PART II

POLITICS AND INSTITUTIONS

The formal institutions of the U.S. government exercise considerable influence over all of us. They touch our lives in many ways, quite independently of whether or not we want them to. Americans remain uneasy about the impact of government institutions. Surveys conducted since the 1960s reveal an erosion of trust in all government institutions. Americans generally do not trust the federal government to "do the right thing." One survey found that "an environment in which a majority of Americans believe that most people can't be trusted breeds attitudes that hold all politicians as corrupt, venal, and self-serving, and government action as doomed to failure."

While recognizing widespread public distrust, government nonetheless does matter. Congress, for example, has the authority to spend more than $3.7 trillion in fiscal year 2012. This is a staggering sum of money. And it undoubtedly is the case that the expenditure of those funds, not to mention the taxes levied to create the budget in the first place, will have an impact on us, whether we drive on federally subsidized roads, work in federally regulated workplaces, receive Social Security payments, or, perhaps in your case, receive federal loans to attend college. Notwithstanding debates over the social and moral implications of the nation's budgetary priorities, and recognizing the often exaggerated nature of protests from conservatives against the alleged evils of "big government," the fact remains that we *have* a large and active national government. It makes good sense to try to understand it.

The five chapters in Part II examine key political institutions and processes and the three branches of the federal government: the mass media, political parties, and elections, as well as Congress, the presidency, and the courts—the three cornerstones of the constitutional separation of powers. Although conventional political science texts include discussions of these institutional "nuts and bolts," we locate them against the backdrop of the structure of power analyzed in Part I. Thus we are stressing that political processes and government institutions do not make decisions in a vacuum; policymakers operate within the confines of economic and ideological boundaries that sharply limit the range of the possible.

We contend that your capacity to see the system clearly depends on your willingness to focus *first* on the structure and *second* on the processes and institutions. That is why we have organized the book this way. This distinction between primary focus and secondary focus may seem like hairsplitting, but actually it is crucial. Mainstream accounts of American politics downplay or ignore outright the deeper structural concerns, thus amplifying the institutions. To do so is to give analytic priority to the parts of government that are most directly accountable to the public, which in turn makes the system appear fairer and more democratic than it really is. Such a conventional focus on institutions also offers hope that if we can just elect the candidate with the best personality or the right party affiliation, our political problems can be effectively addressed with minimal, if any, changes.

While relatively comforting, this hope is not warranted. Significant progress in meeting the needs of the people requires questioning the structure itself. This obviously confronts you with a less comfortable and more daunting task, but it rests on an honest admission of what lies ahead for the student who seeks to interpret, and perhaps change, the political world we inhabit. In the final analysis, then, do our political institutions and the policy process deserve careful scrutiny? Absolutely. Part II will help you in this regard, but always be critically aware of the playing field where the clash of institutions takes place.

CHAPTER 4

Mass Media and Politics

As a looming presence in contemporary America, the mass media are inescapable. Indeed, Americans are eager consumers of media products and spend countless hours in contact with some form of media. Enhanced by technological breakthroughs of the late twentieth century, cable TV and the Internet allow access to more sources of information than ever before. Certainly the media have the potential to serve democratic ends by providing citizens with high-quality electoral and policy information as well as by acting as a watchdog over government and other powerful institutions. In practice, however, the mass media, driven by corporate profit imperatives, all too often contribute to cynicism, depoliticization, and a truncated and illusory view of the way the world works. The result, in the words of communications scholar Robert W. McChesney, is a "rich media" and a "poor democracy." Articles in this chapter provide the analytical tools to critically dissect the role of the mass media in politics today.

13 *Robert W. McChesney and John Nichols*

THE DEATH AND LIFE OF AMERICAN JOURNALISM

Today the media landscape of the United States is dominated by a handful of conglomerate corporations led by "the big six": General Electric (NBC), Walt Disney (ABC), News Corporation (FOX, Wall Street Journal), TimeWarner (CNN), VIACOM and CBS. Through mergers and acquisitions over the past two decades, these media giants have led the movement toward extreme concentration in media ownership. Throughout this time, media scholar and activist Robert McChesney and journalist John Nichols have led a counter movement, the fight against this level of concentration of corporate power. In this article, which is drawn from the "Preface" to the paperback edition of their book The Death and Life of American Journalism, *McChesney and Nichols update their call for media reform by once again advocating for "a great national debate about the future of journalism in America." They highlight the dramatic decline in the reporting and editing capacity of newspapers during the past decade, even as these "old media" sources continue to generate the vast majority of original news stories picked up by new digital media. Contrary to the popular perception, the Internet and web journalism generally have not, and probably will not come close to supplanting conventional journalism as a source of popular news. Moreover, the authors demonstrate that the "news" increasingly is dominated by the viewpoints of PR and official sources (government and corporate) that spin the "news" to their advantage, with the result that "news is fast becoming propaganda." Finally, McChesney and Nichols are careful to link their advocacy of media reform to a strengthening of democracy, noting the link between a truly free press and democratic self-government. To that end they call for robust public subsidy of journalism outlets to embrace "the public good nature of journalism."*

Source: Robert W. McChesney and John Nichols, *The Death and Life of American Journalism* (New York: Nation Books, 2011), Preface to 2011 paperback edition.

In April 2010 one of the most thoughtful and well-regarded figures in American journalism, Karen Dunlap, the president of the Poynter Institute, testified before a Federal Communications Commission panel on the state of American journalism. She pointed to a fresh analysis of the media business by a Poynter scholar "who calculated that the newspaper industry has lost $1.6 billion in reporting and editing capacity since 2000 or about 30 percent over that period. This comes from the sector that produces the vast majority of original reporting in local, national and international news. Even the many news start-ups replace only a small fraction of editorial capacity, and they, too, must find long-term sustainability." Then Dunlap repeated the conclusion of a just-finished Project for Excellence in Journalism report: "Unless some system of financing the production of content is developed, it is difficult to see how reportorial journalism will not continue to shrink, regardless of the potential tools offered by technology."

For writers and activists who spend long periods trying to sound the alarm about a crisis, there come rare moments when their complaints are echoed in the corridors of power, when voices in the wilderness are suddenly integrated into the national discourse. In the spring and summer of 2010, as we toured the country and provided our own testimony to members of the FCC, the Federal Trade Commission and the U.S. House and Senate, we experienced such a moment. But we are not so naïve as to believe that recognition equals transformation. And if there is a core message it is that the circumstance of journalism in the United States continues to degenerate and that the degeneration threatens not just our ability as a nation to communicate fully and functionally but also democracy itself. The fact that concerns we have raised for many years, which are outlined in this book, are now shared by those who once dismissed them encourages us.

But we are more determined than ever to move from recognition to action. The crisis we describe swept in with the force of a tsunami in the last years of George W. Bush's presidency,

and it continues, unabated, deep into Barack Obama's presidency. Hundreds of weekly and daily newspapers went out of business between 2007 and 2011. According to one industry survey, 300 newspapers folded in 2009 and another 150 went under in 2010. Broadcast news scaled back operations. The number of working journalists plummeted. Foreign news bureaus shuttered at the most rapid rate in history. Washington D.C. bureaus shut down and downsized just as rapidly, leaving vast sectors of the federal government uncovered. Statehouse bureaus went dark. Much of American public life—the legislative committees, courts, agencies, schools boards, local commissions that a free press must cover effectively for our governing system to work—went uncovered or was noted only so superficially as to serve the vested interests of political and economic power. For years media critics like ourselves have deplored the woeful quality of American journalism; now, not only is the quality of the news suffering, but the quantity of the news—indeed, the very existence of journalism as a field with paid practitioners, editors, fact-checkers, competing newsrooms and public accountability—is also in jeopardy.

Journalism cannot lose 30 percent of its reporting and editing capacity and continue to provide the information needed to maintain a realistic democratic discourse, open government and the outlines of civil society at the federal, state and local levels. And, nothing, absolutely nothing, that has occurred in the period since we finished the hardcover edition of this book leads us to believe the circumstance is improving—in fact, quite the opposite.

The United States is not experiencing a brief recession for journalism, as the silliest commentators continue to suggest; newsrooms will not be repopulated, let alone restored to their previous vigor, with an economic recovery. Instead, it is an existential crisis, one decades in the making, and as we argue herein, it goes directly to the issue of whether this nation can remain a democratic state with the liberties and freedoms many take for granted. This is not a crisis in which we are predicting almost unimaginable dire conse-quences a generation down the road unless the United States shifts course. The crisis is right here, right now, and unless there is forceful pol-icy intervention, an unacceptable circumstance will grow dramatically worse.

How much worse? A study that encapsu-lated the crisis was released literally days after the hardcover edition of this book. The report by the Pew Center for the People and the Press examined in exhaustive detail the "media ecol-ogy" of the city of Baltimore for one week in 2009. The object was to determine how, in this chang-ing media moment, "original" news stories were being generated and by whom. They tracked old media and new, newspapers, radio, television, Web sites, blogs, even Twitter "tweets" from the police department. What did they find? The first conclusion from the researchers was an unset-tling one: Despite the seeming proliferation of media, the researchers observed that "much of the 'news' people receive contains no original reporting. Fully eight out of ten stories studied simply repeated or repackaged previously pub-lished information." And where did the "original" reporting come from? Old media, particularly The *Baltimore Sun* newspaper, still generated around 95 percent of original news stories. In other words, a great many of the much-heralded online sites—even some that proudly labeled themselves as "news" operations—simply disseminated what traditional old media produced. But don't imag-ine that the dinosaurs are marching around in all their former glory. The *Sun*'s production of original news stories was itself down more than 30 percent from 10 years ago and down a whop-ping 73 percent from 20 years ago. And don't imagine that Baltimore is distinct. Indeed, note that 30 percent figure. It is precisely the same one that the Pew Project for Excellence in Journalism settled on in its assessment of the loss of report-ing and editing capacity at American newspapers since 2000. Our own research for this book and related projects on the future of journalism dem-onstrates that what has happened in Baltimore is happening in every corner of the country. In

city after city we visited in 2010 and 2011, from Portland, Seattle, Denver and San Francisco to Philadelphia, Boston, the Twin Cities and Milwau-kee, the number of paid journalists is down dra-matically from where it was one or two decades ago. And the trends for television and radio are no better than they are for newspapers. The bottom line is this: Old media outlets are downsizing and abandoning journalism and new media are not even beginning to fill the void.

For an example of what this means tangibly, consider this: Reporters instigated to a significant extent the spectacular corruption scandals over the past decade that brought down Jack Abramoff, Tom DeLay and Randall "Duke" Cunningham, among others, and these reporters were subse-quently "downsized" and/or their positions no longer exist. The United States is losing its most experienced and engaged investigative reporters—even Pulitzer Prize winners are getting layoff notices. This pattern is great news for the next generation of Abramoffs, DeLays and Cunning-hams, as corrupt public officials' transgressions will be less and less likely to be reported, and when the reporting stops, so too in all likelihood will the prosecutions. The implications for our governing system are self-evident and shocking.

But that's not the scariest part of Pew's Baltimore study. Of the "original" stories Pew identified, whether old media or new generated them, only 14 percent were developed by jour-nalists defining an issue and pursuing it. A stag-gering 86 percent of the stories originated with official sources and press releases pushing stories to the news media, saying, hey, this is the news you should be covering. In other words, those with power are getting the stories told that they want to have told. This is not the way it used to be. Official sources and public relations have been big players in news for a long time, and the best reporters always struggled so that they would not be taken at face value. But the old ratio of sto-ries generated by PR and official sources versus stories created by journalists used to be closer to 40–60 or 50–50, not 86–14. As the Pew study con-cludes: "the official version of events is becoming more important. We found official press releases often appear word for word in first accounts of events, though often not noted as such."

As journalism declines, there will still be plenty of "news," but it will be increasingly unfiltered PR. The hallmark of great PR is that the public does not recognize it as manipulation of the facts; it is surreptitious. To develop this point, although people can debate intelligently the 10 greatest advertising campaigns of all time, it is impossible to do so for public relations. If people understand a PR campaign exists, by definition it has failed. We are supposed to think it is genuine news. And there are a lot more corporations spending a lot more money to make sure we never do see through the spin. In 1960 there was less than one PR agent for every working journalist, a ratio of 0.75-to-1. By 1990 the ratio was just over 2-to-1. In 2011 the ratio stands at four PR people for every working journalist. At the current rates of change the ratio may well be 6-to-1 within a few years. Thus, there are far fewer reporters to interrogate the spin and the press releases, so the likelihood that these press releases get presented as legitimate "news" has become much greater.

In 2010 Wendell Potter published *Deadly Spin*, his memoir of his career in public relations, during much of which he worked with the health insurance industry to undermine any efforts at health care reform. Potter may be the first—and we hope not the last—high-level PR executive to leave the field and expose its seamy underside. What is striking about Potter's account—even to these experienced eyes—is how effective corporate PR is at dominating the news concerning the relevant industries, all the way from energy and banking and agri-business to telecommunications and health insurance and pharmaceuticals. There's a reason why phrases like "death panels" and "government takeover of health care" got more traction in 2009 and 2010 than phrases like "insurance-industry profiteering" and "Medicare for All." As Potter notes, with the decline of journalism, the ease with which PR operatives get their messages out increases exponentially. That means that on issue after issue, the

special interests have a decided advantage over the public.

Consider the economic crisis that hit the fan in 2008 and shows too many signs of continuing not just for a few years but for a generation. The economic perspective of corporations and investors, rather than that of workers and consumers, has defined much of the news media (and business news media) coverage of the crisis. The brief moment at which politicians and journalists seriously considered defects in the financial system and the overall economy quickly passed. The same bankers that directed the economy over a cliff—and the politicians and "experts" who lucratively rewrote the rules of the game to allow unprecedented chicanery and fraud—have been rehabilitated and have resumed their positions of power and influence. Wall Street bonuses soared toward record levels in 2010 and 2011. The expert economists who presciently warned that the deregulation of the financial sector and the dangerous growth of economic inequality portended disaster have been returned to their Siberian outposts. Signs point to a permanent unemployment rate—even during "boom times" for corporate profits—at levels not seen regularly since the 1930s. The downward pressure on wages and living standards is enormous. The immense social cost, the staggering damage done to American workers and families and the entire generation of people entering the workforce, barely registers as news, but let one major bank or billionaire investor fear that the rate of inflation might approach 3 or 4 percent annually, and a portion of the business news media begins to hyperventilate.

In contemporary America, getting economic issues right is a guarantee of obscurity, as major media outlets keep serving up the usual suspects. And the tragedy of this moment is that a little attention to someone whose views do not directly parallel those of the Wall Street speculators can go a long way. Consider the case of Elizabeth Warren, the Harvard professor whose comments regarding the mortgage crisis, credit card debt and the collapse of the middle class on the old PBS program *Bill Moyers' Journal* gave her a platform and a national following. She was so well regarded that the Obama administration charged her with the responsibility for setting up the new Consumer Financial Protection Bureau. Moyers is no longer on the air and Warren's platforms for serious interviews were therefore appreciably fewer in 2011 when, not coincidentally, the banking and financial services industries began attacking her. If the United States had financial journalism that actually examined and interrogated banking power, Elizabeth Warren would be on solid ground and Treasury Secretary Tim Geithner would be looking for a job. As it is, Geithner's background as a Wall Street insider earns him far more generous coverage in major media than does Warren's background as someone who has stood up to Wall Street and who, invariably, has been proven correct for having done so.

That calculus is as damaging as it is ridiculous. This is not how a free press is supposed to work in democratic theory. The job of a free press is to provide citizens with the information they need to understand and address problems, not to construct false and frequently dysfunctional choices. Because we're on the subject of false choices, let's consider American elections, the *sine qua non* of American constitutional democracy. News media are absolutely central to maintaining meaningful and competitive electoral processes in which citizens can accurately assess candidates. The heavily subsidized American press system of the late eighteenth and nineteenth centuries emerged first and foremost as a means for political parties and factions to organize citizens and draw them into public life. Without romanticizing election coverage of a generation or two ago, it is fair to say that the American people made a smart call when they lost faith in political journalism as the twentieth century gave way to the twenty-first. Many elections are barely covered at all, and when there is coverage, it is so superficial as to be of little value. In Illinois in 2010, for example, so little attention was paid to the Democratic primary for the state's No. 2 job, lieutenant governor, that a pawnbroker who spent heavily on

TV ads was nominated. The ads failed to mention that he had been arrested in 2005 for domestic abuse or that he had failed to pay back taxes and child support. When those details were revealed, a scandal developed that would ultimately force Scott Lee Cohen from the ticket. So why didn't voters know about Mr. Cohen's, er, problems, before the election? As Mark Brown of *The Chicago Sun-Times* explained it: "We in the news media failed the voters by missing the story." But the story wasn't really "missed." Like so many political stories these days, it was left uncovered by mainstream media outlets that no longer hire enough reporters to cover all the races, leaving most voters in the dark most of the time.

In the aftermath of the Supreme Court's decision in the case of *Citizens United v. FEC*, which allowed corporations to spent limitless amounts to buy election results, money has flooded the political process at such a rate that few eyes blink when it is suggested that as much as $10 billion will be spent on the 2012 federal elections or that a substantial portion of that amount will come from secretive donations from multinational corporations. That is twice the total amount spent in 2008 and four times the price tag for the 2000 election. Most of the money will pay for TV political ads, which tend to be of dubious value. At the same time, the media corporations that will rake in this booty have largely discontinued campaign coverage by their news divisions and have stopped broadcasting most candidate debates during primetime, with the exception of the presidential debates that party managers organize as little more than joint press conferences. So the same industries that pay PR firms to spin the news media now bankroll political campaigns and delight in the fact that there is precious little independent journalism left to examine their business or political machinations. The "bottom line," pun intended, is that news is fast becoming propaganda.

But, wait, isn't the Internet going to sort this mess out? In this book we spend considerable time assessing the Internet, considering both its role in precipitating the present crisis and the hope that it provides as a basis for a rejuvenated commercial journalism online. In particular, we assess the claims of those who hail the web as new, innovative source for news, such as Jeff Jarvis, who asserts that "Thanks to the web . . . journalism will not only survive but prosper and grow far beyond its present limitations." To the view of observers like Jarvis, all Americans must do is let the Internet work its magic in combination with the market, and the country's problems will be solved. Regrettably, we have found no more evidence to support that wishful thinking over the past 18 months than when we completed the first edition of this book. Let us speak plainly: No one has developed models for making web journalism profitable at anywhere near the level necessary for a credible popular news media.

Great journalism, as Ben Bagdikian put it, requires great institutions. Like any complex undertaking, a division of labor is required to achieve success: Copy editors, fact checkers and proofreaders are needed in addition to reporters and assigning editors. Great journalism also requires institutional muscle to stand up to governments and corporate power. It requires competition, so if one newsroom misses a story, someone else will expose it. It requires people covering stories they would not cover if they were doing journalism on a voluntary basis.

This point deserves additional comment. Invariably, during our travels now individuals approach us, presenting their own or someone else's new plan for online journalism that will, in their view, solve many of the problems we outline. Sometimes these have been ambitious national and international projects. Some have been more focused ventures providing advertising-supported "hyper-local" journalism online. All of them, at the start-up stage and into the visible future, tend to rely on volunteer labor or extremely underpaid and exploited labor. Americans would never turn their national defense or education system or medical care or airplane piloting over to self-appointed volunteers. Why should anyone think this approach could plausibly succeed with journalism?

One exchange in particular captured the absurdity of the situation. When we visited a prominent Midwest university, one of the journalism professors disputed our claim that the Internet was not providing a sufficient basis for a new era of journalism. He told us how he and several friends who had been laid off by the local daily newspaper had begun a Web site on which they covered movies, music, restaurants and the art scene in their city. He claimed the coverage was superior to what the "old media" produced, even at its peak. It was largely a volunteer operation, with revenues from donations and a few ads. We asked this professor how good a job his Web site did covering the county board meetings, when every now and then crucial zoning issues were decided, increasingly with no press attention. "The county board?" he replied. "We don't cover stuff like that. You'd have to pay me." Precisely.

Not much of that is happening online. Today we have a few thousand paid online news workers, interpreted liberally to include many aggregators who do little or no news gathering or reporting or even writing. More often than not, some old medium that provides the bank supports the best-known bloggers and online journalists. (John Nichols blogs voluminously, but his digital contributions would diminish sharply were he not on the payroll of *The Nation*.) When these old media go down, the number of paid digital journalists is likely to shrink, not grow. To the extent that the corporate news media giants are locating a profitable niche online, it increasingly looks like it may be as a commercial "app" in the rapidly emerging wireless market. Rupert Murdoch announced his iPad-only newspaper, *The Daily*, in 2011, and the *New York Times* announced its long-anticipated plan for an online payment system in March 2011. But there is no reason to believe these developments will ever come close to providing the resources for a full-throttle popular journalism or that this commercial product will avoid the limitations of commercial professional journalism as it has devolved over the past few decades. Instead, they will likely accentuate them. An internal memo on journalism from AOL CEO

Tim Armstrong captured the commercial logic: He ordered the company's editors to evaluate all future stories on the basis of "traffic potential, revenue potential, edit quality and turnaround time." All stories, it stressed, are to be evaluated according to their "profitability consideration."

What happens when a story—like that of a distant war or the privatization of a local water utility—fails to achieve proper "traffic potential, revenue potential"? Does it disappear off radar? And with it the prospect that citizens will know what is being done in their name but without their informed consent? That might be an acceptable Brave New World for the CEOs, but it's a loser for a democratic society. At the heart of too many of the emerging corporate online journalism undertakings is an understanding that the wages paid to journalists can be slashed dramatically while at the same time their workloads are increased to levels not seen for generations, if ever. Armstrong's memo states that all of AOL's journalistic employees will be required to produce "five to 10 stories per day." Tim Rutten of *The Los Angeles Times* captured this in his assessment of AOL's 2011 purchase of *The Huffington Post*: "To grasp the *Huffington Post*'s business model, picture a galley rowed by slaves and commanded by pirates." In the "new-media landscape," he wrote, "it's already clear that the merger will push more journalists more deeply into the tragically expanding low-wage sector of our increasingly brutal economy." With massive unemployment and dismal prospects, the extreme downward pressure on wages and working conditions for journalists is the two-ton elephant that just climbed into democracy's bed. "In the new media," Rutten concludes, "many of the worst abuses of the old economy's industrial capitalism—the sweatshop, the speedup and piecework; huge profits for the owners; desperation, drudgery and exploitation for the workers. No child labor, yet, but if there were more page views in it. . . ."

As one 2011 media industry assessment of the future of journalism put it, the future of news media will be to move the corporate "brands" to the digital realm, although "the future is still a little murky as to how these brands will turn a profit in terms of online advertising, paywalls and computer tablet apps." The report says this is "good news for public relations professionals who are trying to pitch stories" because "these sites will be looking for more content to fill their pages." The report concludes: "As a direct result of changing media platforms, PR pros are now a part of the media in a way they have never been before." Increasingly, it is difficult to avoid the conclusion that what makes the most sense for the profitability of news media firms is entirely inadequate, even dangerous, for the requirements of a free and self-governing people. Okay, things are not looking so great for working journalists, but what about the blogosphere and the newfound ability of people—rechristened "citizen journalists"—to go online, launch new Web sites, do their own thing, tell it like it is, and have the same caliber of Internet access to the world's attention as the mightiest media conglomerate? Won't that combine with the commercial journalism online to solve the journalism problem in the digital world? We devote considerable time herein assessing that claim and looking at the record. However, the evidence is thin, at best. Here Matthew Hindman's extraordinary *The Myth of Digital Democracy* offers confirmation of our worst fears and a valuable new resource. Although there are an infinite number of Web sites, human beings are only capable of meaningfully visiting a small number of them on a regular basis. The Google search mechanism strongly encourages implicit censorship, in that sites that do not end up on the first or second page of a search effectively do not exist. As Michael Wolff puts it in Wired: "the top 10 Web sites accounted for 31 percent of US page views in 2001, 40 percent in 2006, and about 75 percent in 2010." "Big sucks the traffic out of small," Wolff quotes Russian Internet investor Yuri Milner. "In theory you can have a few very successful individuals controlling hundreds of millions of people. You can become big fast." And once you get big, you stay big. In this regard Hindman's research on journalism, news media, and political Web sites is striking. What has emerged is "power law" distribution in which a small number of political or news media Web sites get the vast majority of traffic. The traditional giants with name recognition and resources dominated them. There is a "long tail" of gazillions of Web sites that exist but get little or no traffic, and few people have any idea that they exist. There is also no "middle class" of robust, moderately sized Web sites; that aspect of the news media system has been wiped out online. It leads Hindman to conclude that the online news media are more concentrated than the old media world. This is true too of the vaunted blogosphere, which has effectively ossified. Its traffic is highly concentrated in a handful of sites that people with elite pedigrees operate.

Don't get us wrong, here. Free speech is alive and well on the web, at least for the time being. But as Hindman has put it, we should not confuse the right to speak with the ability to be heard. We appreciate the long tail of obscure blogs, Web sites and Facebook pages as much as anyone, and we spend an inordinate amount of time on them—we dread to imagine a world without them—but they do not a free press make. Most of them languish at a certain point in time, as the lack of readership diminishes the enthusiasm to keep the project going, and there are no funds, so it must remain a volunteer operation. But the long tail points to a crucial point that the framers of the Constitution understood: There is a difference between free speech and having a free press. This is why they are distinct entries in the First Amendment. Without a strong journalism—a credible independent news media—the right to freedom of speech, as indispensable as it is, loses some of its power and value. In the worst case scenario it is a digital circle jerk where people can write to their hearts' content and possibly locate kindred spirits but not know what they are talking about—or what to talk about.

We are not vulgar materialists who run around claiming that merely accumulating resources is enough to create great journalism.

Even at the zenith of the old system . . . journalism relied excessively on official sources—people in government and corporate power—to set the agenda and define the range of legitimate debate. We think that we can have a journalism far better than that. It will require not only resources but also a new structure. And it will be digital. Although recent accounts suggesting the digital revolution is a mixed blessing that warrants public consideration intrigue us, the news system going forward needs to embrace the new technologies, not resist them. (That train has left the station; the distinction between old and new media is increasingly quaint.) So here's our bottom line: What America needs is a well-paid journalism sector that digital citizen journalism both complements and enhances.

In our view the evidence is overwhelming: If Americans are serious about reversing course and dramatically expanding and improving journalism, the only way this can happen is with massive public subsidies. The market is not getting it done, and there is no reason to think it is going to get it done. It will require a huge expansion of the nonprofit news media sector as well. It is imperative to discontinue the practice of regarding journalism as a "business" and evaluating it with business criteria. Instead, embracing the public good nature of journalism is necessary. That is the argument we make in this book.

Let's be clear on what we mean by the "public good" nature of journalism: That means journalism is something society requires but that the market cannot produce in sufficient quality or quantity. Readers or final news consumers have never provided sufficient funds to subsidize the popular journalism system that self-government requires. For the first century of American history the public good nature of journalism was understood implicitly and massive postal and printing subsidies addressed this understanding. For the past century, however, the infusion of advertising to provide the vast majority of revenues supporting the news masked the public good nature of journalism. But advertising had no specific attachment to journalism and is jumping ship as better alternatives present themselves in the digital universe, especially as news media appear less commercially attractive. Journalism increasingly is left standing naked in an unforgiving market, and it is shriveling in the cold gusts. The future of journalism left to the market will likely approach what education would be like if all public subsidies were removed. With no subsidies, our education system would remain excellent for the wealthy who could afford private schools in the first place, mediocre at best for the middle and upper-middle class, and nonexistent or positively frightening for the increasingly impoverished lower-middle and working class—the majority of the nation. This would be a nightmare for any credible democratic or humane society, and it would be a major step back toward the middle ages. The same logic applies to journalism. The U.S. Supreme Court has repeatedly affirmed that the duty—not merely the right—of the democratic state is to assure a viable news media. In the landscape of 2010s America, that means enlightened public subsidies.

Understanding "journalism as a public good" also helps explain one of the persistent questions we are asked when we discuss the crisis of journalism. "Isn't the basic problem," the question generally begins, "that most people are morons who either have no interest in journalism or are only interested in idiotic stories about celebrities? If people wanted good journalism, isn't it logical to expect the commercial news media to give it to them?" On the surface this seems like such a convincing premise that it is generally posed as a rhetorical question, to which all who have any hope left for the human species are expected to retreat in shame. Public good theory explains that no matter how strong the consumer demand, it will never be sufficient to provide the resources for a popular democratic journalism. Even when Americans have been most rabid about news and politics, there was not sufficient demand to subsidize a popular news media.

But public good theory is important in another way: It also highlights that it is impossible for the market to accurately gauge popular support for the news. The market cannot express all of our values; we cannot individually "purchase" everything we value. Our experience discussing the crisis of journalism with tens of thousands of people over the past 18 months has reinforced our view that a preponderance of Americans, and especially younger Americans notorious for their lack of interest in newspapers and conventional news media, want to have credible reporting on corporate and government affairs, even if they do not necessarily plan to read or view the news reports thereby produced. But they want to know that the work is being done and people in power are being held accountable, issues are being covered—and they are willing use their tax dollars to pay for journalism even if they themselves prefer to watch a reality TV show or listen to their iPods. And, who knows, to return rhetorical question fire, maybe if there was better and more compelling journalism, people might not find it so irrelevant to their lives?

Of course, the notion of government support for journalism strikes many as downright un-American, a dangerous measure that will be far more likely to increase the likelihood of a dystopian future rather than enhance journalism, freedom and self-government. Everywhere we travel we hear this; it has become so deeply ingrained in American political consciousness—across the political spectrum—that it requires no evidence to be asserted categorically and end all further debate—which is fitting because there is no evidence. We demonstrate in what follows that press subsidies are as American as apple pie; indeed, our democratic culture was built on them. If the U.S. government subsidized journalism today at the same level of GDP that it did in the 1840s, the government would have to spend in the neighborhood of $30–35 billion annually. This is probably the single most striking empirical point we make in the book, and it has proven, more than anything else, to be a game-changer for how Americans understand their own free press tradition.

What we demonstrate herein is not merely the size of these press subsidies but also that the framers who put them in place understood them as a necessary investment in democracy and as part of a commitment to a heterogeneous and vibrant participatory political culture. Thomas Jefferson, with the encouragement of his friend James Madison, proposed in 1791 that President George Washington name as the Postmaster General of the United States—overseer of the largest government agency by a wide margin—the most daring and controversial of its pamphleteers, Thomas Paine. It was a radical notion, too radical it would turn out for Washington, who was ill at ease with Paine's challenges to organized religion, consolidated wealth and authority in general. Jefferson turned to Paine, as do we, for inspiration and for the model of a take-no-prisoners, speak-truth-to-power journalism that has as its end not a recreation of the old order of empowered elites and cowering masses but a new order in which the will of an informed and emboldened people shall be the law of the land.

Federal press subsidies—for example, postal subsidies and paid government notices—have diminished in real terms to only a small fraction of their nineteenth-century levels, though they remain to the present day. Public broadcasting is the most visible contemporary media subsidy, and in 2010 it received approximately $1.1 billion in public support annually. State and local governments as well as public universities provide much of this public subsidy as well as some $420 million from the federal government.

We share the concern about government control over the content of journalism and reject any subsidies that would open the door to that outcome. We also understand that a government with a massive military and national security complex like the United States could be especially dangerous with its mitts on the keys to the newsroom. But we would ask those who worry about major media becoming an amen corner for the government to consider the manner in which the corporate news media cheer on U.S. foreign policy and militarism, often, as in the case of the 2003 Iraq invasion, with disastrous consequences. Remarkably, the same

no-questions-asked approach was in evidence as major media covered President Obama's unilateral decision to involve U.S. forces in the bombing of Libya in the spring of 2011—a decision made without seriously consulting Congress, let alone a request for the declaration of war required in the U.S. Constitution. As steadfast advocates for a free and independent media that speaks truth to power, we believe that the current circumstance is unacceptable; our major media do not speak truth to power. More often than not, especially in matters or war and peace, they provide an uncritical sounding board for those in power. For the purpose of ending this abuse of the public trust, we advocate new models for funding journalism, models that maintain ironclad protections against government censorship and direction of journalists while at the same time freeing those journalists from the grip of corporate interests and commercial pressures. More importantly, we are confident enough in America to believe that our people and their elected representatives can get the job done.

The United States, for all of its flaws, remains a democratic society in the conventional modern use of the term. Our state is capable of being pushed to make both progressive as well as regressive moves. This is a crucial distinction. We will be the first to argue that if a dictatorship or authoritarian regime subsidizes journalism, the "news" will more likely than not be propaganda that is designed to maintain an antidemocratic circumstance. But that does not mean the same outcome necessarily occurs when democratic nations institute press subsidies. Indeed, there is little evidence that press subsidies in democratic societies comparable to the United States increase government propaganda or that they grease the wheels for a transition to a dictatorship by the dominant party and a loss of freedom. Most of the evidence—in fact, the overwhelming preponderance of evidence—is precisely the opposite. Accordingly, the problem with categorically rejecting public subsidies is that doing so not only ignores the actual history of massive democratic journalism subsidies in the United States but it also does grave injustice to the existing track record of other democratic nations.

.   .   .

We seek to open a great national debate about the future of journalism in America. Although we have ideas about where that discussion should go, we are excited about the debate itself. Let us close with a story from our visit to the University of Virginia on our book tour in the winter of 2010. In a restaurant several blocks from the campus that Thomas Jefferson laid out, before our evening talk we met with a group of exceptional journalism students who had read the book and wanted to talk about our proposals. They especially liked our proposal for a "Journalism for America" initiative that would provide young people with stipends to cover underserved communities in the United States. But they had questions. Several women asked whether we had considered expanding the program so that young people with the background to do so might provide international coverage that was relevant to immigrant

communities in the United States. By the end of the dinner they had framed out a plan for linking the "Journalism for America" initiative to the Peace Corps so that young journalists could cover an immigrant community in the United States for a year and then travel with the Peace Corps to foreign lands with connections to the American communities. Thus, an Ethiopian-American community in Minnesota could get coverage by a Journalism for America/Peace Corps writer who had lived and worked in that community from Ethiopia. And the young writer could get both domestic and international reporting experience that might position her for the job she hopes to attain as an international correspondent. We loved the vision. But, above all, we loved the evidence that, when Americans are invited to outline a future for journalism, when they are brought into the process rather than pushed to the sidelines, they are ready and willing to do so in the most dynamic, creative and meaningful ways. We came away with confidence that, when this great debate opens up, as it has begun to do, American journalism and American democracy will flourish.

DISCUSSION QUESTIONS

1. Identify and reflect upon McChesney and Nichols's connection between a vibrant press and the quality of democracy. Why is this connection so vital and what has been threatening it?
2. Conventional wisdom says that the Internet has vastly democratized the gathering and reporting of the news. From the perspective of the authors, why is this not the case?
3. What are the main arguments the authors use in their advocacy of increased public subsidies of journalism? Many would view such subsidies as a direct threat to democracy, while the authors make precisely the opposite point. What do you make of this particular aspect of reform?

14 *W. Lance Bennett*

NEWS CONTENT AND ILLUSION
Four Information Biases that Matter

Debates about the quality of news coverage in the United States often revolve around assertions that the mass media are either too liberal or too conservative, depending on the politics of the critic. In this article, taken from his popular book News: The Politics of Illusion, *political scientist W. Lance Bennett argues that this liberal versus conservative controversy about journalistic bias is a "dead-end debate." Rather than focusing on the ideological slant of the news, Bennett asks us to consider "universal information problems" that lead journalists to frame stories in such a way that familiar political narratives come to replace hard-hitting investigative coverage. These "information biases" transcend ideology, debasing the quality of public information while contributing to the transformation of news into a "mass-produced consumer product." The four characteristics of the news include personalization, dramatization, fragmentation, and the authority-disorder bias. They developed as an outgrowth of the connection between evolving communications technologies and the profit motive that drives the corporate media. Taken together, while these four traits heighten the dramatic tension of news reports, they also feed the public's disenchantment with the news, accentuating already rampant public cynicism and furthering the distance between citizens and their leaders. Ultimately, Bennett contends, democracy is weakened by the way news stories are presented—the information biases inherent in the dominant news format—regardless of any ideological tilt that may or may not actually exist. Coupled with the forgoing analysis of McChesney and Nichols, the troubling issue we are left to ponder is whether our cherished notion of the "free press" retains any semblance of reality in the twenty-first century.*

It is a writer's obligation to impose narrative. Everyone does this. Every time you take a lump of material and turn it into something you are imposing a narrative. It's a writer's obligation to do this. And, by the same token, it is apparently a journalist's

Source: W. Lance Bennett, *News: The Politics of Illusion,* 5th edition. New York: Longman, 2003, pp. 41–50 and 75–76.

obligation to pretend that he never does anything of the sort. The journalist claims to believe that the narrative emerges from the lump of material, rises up and smacks you in the face like marsh gas.

—Nora Ephron

When George W. Bush announced his presidential candidacy a breathtaking seventeen months before the 2000 presidential election, he did so on a movie-set stage in Iowa, surrounded by bales of hay and a shiny red forklift behind him. The day's news coverage anointed him the front-runner. As if to prove their point, reporters noted that Bush attracted by far the greatest press entourage, even though three other prominent candidates were also campaigning in the state that day. Mr. Bush wittily acknowledged that news organizations have choices about where they assign reporters, as he took the microphone on his campaign plane shortly after it took off for Iowa that morning. He quipped to the crowd of reporters on board: "Thanks for coming. We know you have a choice of candidates when you fly, and we appreciate you choosing Great Expectations." Great Expectations was the nickname he gave the plane as part of a larger spin effort to defuse the typical pattern of news building up expectations about candidates only to dramatize their next fall. Mr. Bush again played flight attendant when he asked the reporters to "Please stow your expectations securely in your overhead bins, as they may shift during the trip and can fall and hurt someone—especially me."

This campaign 2000 story was written more in an entertainment format than as a means to deliver serious political information; it was personality-centered, well-scripted, and set as a comedy scene in which Mr. Bush played a flight attendant doing the pre-takeoff announcement. The story was also artificial in the sense of being disconnected from larger questions about the race, the issues, or Mr. Bush's qualifications for being president. Most importantly, there was no clear basis on which the Washington press had decreed him the front-runner. True, the ability to

deliver clever lines may be some qualification for being president, but the readers of the news story would be unable to know if Mr. Bush uttered that monologue spontaneously or if it was scripted as part his advisors' communication strategy to win over a skeptical press pack. Perhaps, in the mediated reality of contemporary politics, the distinction between an innate ability to think on one's feet and learning to deliver a scripted performance no longer matters.

A closer look at this front-runner story and the campaign news that surrounded it reveals one tangible political condition mentioned in passing that might explain why journalists granted Mr. Bush the early lead: money. Mr. Bush had already set a record for early campaign fund-raising. Raising the largest amount of money makes a candidate front-runner in the eyes of political insiders, as well as in the story lines of the prominent national journalists who cover politics from the perspectives of insiders. Pegging the political fortunes of candidates to the sizes of their war chests is not an idle measure of potential electoral success. It is money, after all, that indicates the strength of business and interest group belief that a candidate will support their political goals. And it takes money to bring a candidate's political messages to voters who are more expensive to reach than ever before. Yet one of the reasons that people are hard to reach is that they tend not to trust politicians or the journalists who cover them. And one of the reasons that people mistrust the political establishment is money. Both polls and public interest groups often identify money as one of the ills of politics.

The insider view that politics is bitter, partisan, personalized, manipulative and money-driven may be a defensible perspective (it is the inside view, after all), but this does not make it the only choice that news organizations have about how to cover government. This is not to argue that topics such as money should be ignored in campaign coverage. To the contrary, the question is how news organizations decide to play those topics in their stories.

Consider the choices that news organizations have in how to frame a campaign story in which money is a potential plot element. *Framing involves choosing a broad organizing theme for selecting, emphasizing, and linking the elements of a story such as the scenes, the characters, their actions, and supporting documentation.* For example the framing of the previous story might have been shifted from the *horse race* to the *money chase,* with a serious investigation of the interests to which Mr. Bush and the other candidates might be indebted. Yet the above story and hundreds more that followed it throughout the campaign told the tale of the horse race one more time. In the horse race plot, money is generally left poorly developed in the background, requiring us to decode the reasons why George W. Bush may be the leading candidate. Also typical of many political stories, this dramatized news fragment was implicitly negative. Money has become a code for what ails our public life, a disruptive or disordering principle in the democratic order of things.

The opening of the Bush presidential campaign thus displayed the information biases of many political news stories: (1) it was personality oriented, (2) with dramatic staging and scripting, (3) that left it fragmented or disconnected from underlying political issues and realities (such as Mr. Bush's issue positions or other qualifications for being named the leading candidate), and (4) its implicit message (about money in this case) is typically negative, suggesting threats to the normal order of things. The result is that while people may tune in to news for its entertainment value, they also find reason in many stories to doubt or dismiss politics in general.

This communication system appears to contribute to a public that is increasingly cynical and disillusioned with politics and government. The paradox is that journalists complain about the over-scripted campaigns, and, more generally, the staged events they cover, but they seem unable to find other ways to write stories or to replace the cynical tone with perspectives that might help citizens become more engaged. As a result of these and other factors, large numbers of people actively avoid politics, while watching the media spectacle with a mixture of disbelief and disapproval. Meanwhile more people escape from public affairs and political participation into ever more personalized media worlds that one observer has likened to the gated communities and suburban enclaves into which many people have physically migrated in society.

Let's move from the opening story of the 2000 election to the dramatic conclusion. To make a long story short, the *Bush as front-runner* story (with minor variations) swept through the news media for a time until it was replaced by other campaign *horse race* dramas, often with Mr. Gore as front-runner, each creating an episode to advance a long running story that must (if we are to call it news) continue to develop. Thus Mr. Bush and Democratic front-runner Al Gore jockeyed through the primaries, walked through heavily-scripted conventions, see-sawed through the debates, and finally headed to the finish line in one of the closest contests in American history. In an unexpected twist, the story was jarred from its predictable ending (an election night winner) because the electoral vote count was so close that it did not decide the result. The dispute over a handful of votes in Florida was eventually ended by a Supreme Court ruling that left many on both sides angry at the process that determined the result.

Did this photo finish in the presidential horse race of 2000 draw a large crowd of excited spectators? Hardly. The voter turnout reached a new modern era low beneath 50 percent. Continuous weekly polling of voters by *The Vanishing Voter,* a Harvard project led by Thomas Patterson and Marvin Kalb, revealed that a majority of voters did not become interested in the election until after it was over and the dispute in Florida broke out.

The point here is not to place the blame for civic disengagement on the news media. Journalists complained throughout the campaign that they had little to work with. How much more could they say about Al Gore's woodenness or George Bush's feeble grasp of foreign policy?

Yet this begs the question: Why were journalists acting like movie critics giving barely passing reviews to all those poorly-scripted and repetitively-acted political performances? Why was there so little innovative coverage that might stimulate citizen engagement with the election either on the level of the candidates (for example, the political and economic interests that they represented) or on the level of stirring involvement beyond the momentary act of voting in the most important democratic ritual in the civic culture?

It is remarkable that the leading news organizations not only converged in their horse race and campaign strategy coverage, but they stuck with those narrative choices in the face of clear voter disinterest. Even in the final weeks of the contest, stories with standardized dramatized framings such as the *horse race,* the *war room,* and other military metaphors outnumbered stories on all the issues in the race, combined, by a wide margin. For example, a study of *The Washington Post* and *The New York Times* in the final two weeks of the campaign showed that dramatized framings of the race or the strategic conflict outnumbered all policy issue stories by a margin of 69 to 45 in the *Post,* while the *Times'* melodrama-to-issue gap was even greater at 93 to 63. *Consider the possibility that the choices of such narrative framings of politics contain information biases that are far more serious and at the same time more difficult for the average person to detect than ideological biases.*

A Different Kind of Bias

This [article] takes a close look at news content. The concern is with information biases that make news hard to use as a guide to citizen action because they obscure the big picture in which daily events take place, and, in addition, they often convey a negative or cynical tone about politics that undermines citizen motivation for digging deeper to learn more or to become engaged. . . . Most debates about journalistic bias are concerned with the question of ideology. For example, does the news have a liberal or conservative, a Democratic or Republican, drift? To briefly review the

argument, some variations in news content or political emphasis may occur, but they can seldom be explained as the result of journalists routinely injecting their partisan views into the news. To the contrary, the avoidance of political partisanship by journalists is reinforced, among other means, by the professional ethics codes of journalists, by the editors who monitor their work, and by the business values of the companies they work for.

Another important point to recall is that people who see a consistent ideological press bias (that is, across most stories or over extended periods of time) are seeing it with the help of their own ideology. This generalization is supported by opinion research showing that people in the middle see the press as generally neutral, whereas those on the left complain that the news is too conservative, and those on the right think the news has a left-leaning bias. There are at least two ironies in this ongoing and inherently unresolvable debate about ideological bias. First, even if neutrality or objectivity could be achieved, citizens with strong views on particular issues would not recognize it. Second, even if the news contained strong ideological or issue biases, people with a point of view (who are most likely to detect bias in the first place) would be well equipped to defend themselves against such biases. Indeed many nations favor a partisan press system as the best way to conduct public debates and to explore issues . . .

So, many Americans are caught up in dead-end debates about a kind of news bias that is at once far less systematic and much less dangerous than commonly assumed. In the meantime, and this may be the greatest irony of all, these preoccupations with the politics of journalists detract attention from other information bias that really are worth worrying about. A more sensible approach to news bias is to look for those universal information problems that hinder the efforts of citizens, whatever their ideology, to take part in political life.

The task [of this article] is to understand the U.S. public information system at a deeper level than the endless debates over ideological bias. Fortunately most of the pieces to the news puzzle are right in front of us. For all of its defects, the news continues to be largely a public production, with government press offices, media organizations, and popular tastes all available for inspection. . . .

In turning to the workings of this system, it is important to understand that the news biases examined here have evolved over a long period of time. Their roots can be traced to the transition from a partisan to a commercial press in the 1800s. . . . It is thus helpful to think of the biases that we see at any point in time as historical products of the changing system of relations between people, press, and politicians. These relations continually shape and construct news and contribute to its evolving forms.

FOUR INFORMATION BIASES THAT MATTER: AN OVERVIEW

Our expectations about the quality of public information are rather high. Most of us grew up with history books full of journalistic heroism exercised in the name of truth and free speech. We learned that the American Revolution was inspired by the political rhetoric of the underground press and by printers' effective opposition to the British Stamp Act. The lesson from the trial of Peter Zenger has endured through time: *the truth is not libelous.* The goal of the history book journalists was as unswerving as it was noble: to guarantee for the American people the most accurate, critical, coherent, illuminating, and independent reporting of political events. Yet Peter Zenger would probably not recognize, much less feel comfortable working in, a modern news organization.

Like it or not, the news has become a massproduced consumer product, bearing little resemblance to history book images. Communication technologies, beginning with the wire services and progressing to satellite feeds and digital video, interact with corporate profit motives to create generic, "lowest-common-denominator" information formats. Those news story formulas often lack critical perspectives and coherent or useful organizing principles. . . . The illusions of coherence, diversity, and relevance have been achieved through packaging the news to suit the

psychological tastes of different segments of the market audience. It is necessary to look beyond ideology and the packaging of our favorite news source in order to see the remarkable similarities that run through most mainstream news content. In particular, there are four characteristics of news that stand out as reasons why public information in the United States does not do as much as it could to advance the cause of democracy: *personalization, dramatization, fragmentation,* and the *authority-disorder bias.*

PERSONALIZATION

If there is a single most important flaw in the American news style, it is the overwhelming tendency to downplay the big social, economic, or political picture in favor of the human trials, tragedies, and triumphs that sit at the surface of events. For example, instead of focusing on power and process, the media concentrate on the people engaged in political combat over the issues. The reasons for this are numerous, from the journalist's fear that probing analysis will turn off audiences to the relative ease of telling the human-interest side of a story as opposed to explaining deeper causes and effects.

It is easy for the news audience to react for or against the actors in these personalized humaninterest stories. When people are invited to take the news personally, they can find a wide range of private, emotional meanings in it, however, the meanings inspired by personalized news may not add up to the shared critical and analytical meanings on which a healthy democracy thrives. Personalized news encourages people to take an egocentric rather than a socially concerned view of political problems. The focus on personalities encourages a passive spectator attitude among the public. Moreover, the common media focus on flawed political personalities at the center of mistakes and scandals invites people to project their general anger and frustration at society or in their private lives onto the distant symbolic targets of politics. Either way, whether the focus is on sympathetic heroes and victims or hateful scoundrels and culprits, the media preference for personalized human-interest news creates a "can't-see-the-forest-for-the-trees" information bias that makes it difficult to see the big (institutional) picture that lies beyond the many actors crowding center stage who are caught in the eye of the news camera.

The tendency to personalize the news would be less worrisome if human-interest angles were used to hook audiences into more serious analysis of issues and problems. Almost all great literature and theater, from the Greek dramas to the modern day, use strong characters to promote audience identifications and reactions in order to draw people into thinking about larger moral and social issues. American news often stops at the character development stage, however, and leaves the larger lessons and social significance, if there is any, to the imagination of the audience. As a result, the main problem with personalized news is that the focus on personal concerns is seldom linked to more in-depth analysis. What often passes for analysis are opaque news formulas such as "he/she was a reflection of us," a line that was used in the media frenzies that followed the deaths of Britain's Princess Diana and America's John Kennedy, Jr. Even when large portions of the public reject personalized news formulas, as in the case of the year-long journalistic preoccupation with whether President Clinton's personal sexual behavior undermined his leadership, the personalization never stops. This systematic tendency to personalize situations is one of the defining biases of news.

DRAMATIZATION

Compounding the information bias of personalization is a second news property in which the aspects of events that are reported tend to be the ones most easily dramatized in simple "stories." As noted above, American journalism has settled overwhelmingly on the reporting form of stories or narratives, as contrasted, for example, to analytical essays, political polemics, or more scientific-style problem reports. Stories invite dramatization, particularly with sharply drawn actors at their center.

News dramas emphasize crisis over continuity, the present over the past or future, conflicts and relationship problems between the personalities at their center, and the impact of scandals on personal political careers. News dramas downplay complex policy information, the workings of government institutions, and the bases of power behind the central characters. Lost in the news drama (*melodrama* is often the more appropriate term) are sustained analyses of the persistent problems of our time, such as inequality, hunger, resource depletion, population pressures, environmental collapse, toxic waste, and political oppression. Serious though such human problems are, they just are not dramatic enough on a day-to-day level to make the news.

Important topics do come up, of course, such as when natural disasters strike, nuclear waste contaminates air or water supplies, or genocide breaks out in a distant land. Chronic conditions generally become news only when they reach astounding levels that threaten large-scale cataclysm through famine, depression, war, or revolution. But then the stories go away, again leaving the origins of and the solutions for those problems little-discussed in all but the biggest of stories. Most of these seemingly sudden "crises" are years in the making: deforestation that worsens flooding, neglected nuclear dumps festering in the Arctic or in Washington State, or bandit governments in African nations undermining the hope for civil society. With a steady flow of information provided by experts and issue advocacy organizations, these stories could be kept in the news as reminders to publics and politicians that there may be more important things than the glitzy media event of the day or the routine political skirmishing in Washington.

Crises, not the slow buildups to them, are the perfect news material, meaning that they fit neatly into the dramatization bias. The "crisis cycle" portrayed in the news is classic dramatic fare, with rising action, falling action, sharply drawn characters, and, of course, plot resolutions. By its very definition, a crisis is something that will subside on its own or reach dramatic closure through clean-up efforts or humanitarian relief operations. Unfortunately the crisis cycles that characterize our news system only reinforce the popular impression that high levels of human difficulty are inevitable and therefore accept-able. Crises are resolved when situations return to "manageable" levels of difficulty. Seldom are underlying problems treated and eliminated at their source. The news is certainly not the cause of these problems, but it could become part of the solution if it substituted illumination of causes for dramatic coverage of symptoms.

As in the case of personalization, drama-tization would not be a problem if it were used mainly as an attention-focusing device to intro-duce more background and context surrounding events. Drama can help us engage with the great forces of history, science, politics, or human rela-tions. When drama is used to bring analysis into mind, it is a good thing. When drama is employed as a cheap emotional device to focus on human conflict and travail, or farce and frailty, the larger significance of events becomes easily lost in waves of immediate emotion. The potential advantages of drama to enlighten and explain are sacrificed to the lesser tendencies of melodrama to excite, anger, and further personalize events. Thus the news often resembles real-life soap operas, only with far more important consequences than the ones on entertainment TV.

One of the things that makes the news dramatic—indeed, that may even drive news drama—is the use of visuals: photos, graphics, and live-action video. These elements of stories not only make the distant world seem more real, they make the news more believable. In many ways, particularly for television, the pictures may not only tell the stories but help editors and reporters decide which stories to tell and how to tell them.

In principle, there is nothing wrong with the emphasis on sights in news production. In fact one might argue that thinking visually is the best way to engage the senses more fully in com-municating about society and politics. Yet there is often a tension between not reporting impor-tant stories that are hard to picture and reporting

possibly unimportant stories simply because they offer great visual images. . . . The economics of audience attention often shade editorial decisions in the direction of starting with the pictures and then adding the words.

It is important to worry about the bases of such editorial decisions because in many ways they distinguish between good and bad uses of news drama. When stories are selected more for visuals than for larger political significance and context, the scripting of the story may bend information rather badly to suggest that the pic-tures do, in fact, reflect the larger situation. And since there is more than a grain of truth to the old adage that "seeing is believing," people may be compelled to see aspects of society that sim-ply are not there or that are not there in the ways they are dramatically portrayed in the news. The visually graphic coverage of crime on TV is an example of this. . . . At the very least, the selection of news stories primarily because they offer dra-matic images is one of several important reasons why the news is often so fragmented or discon-nected from larger political or economic contexts that would provide other ways to tell the story.

FRAGMENTATION

The emphasis on personal and dramatic qualities of events feeds into a third information charac-teristic of the news: the isolation of stories from each other and from their larger contexts so that information in the news becomes fragmented and hard to assemble into a big picture. The fragmen-tation of information begins by emphasizing indi-vidual actors over the political contexts in which they operate. Fragmentation is then heightened by the use of dramatic formats that turn events into self-contained, isolated happenings. The fragmentation of information is further exagger-ated by the severe space limits nearly all media impose for fear of boring readers and viewers with too much information.

Thus the news comes to us in sketchy dra-matic capsules that make it difficult to see the causes of problems, their historical significance, or the connections across issues. It can even be difficult to follow the development of a particular issue over time as stories rise and fall more in response to the actions and reactions of prominent public figures than to independent reporting based on investigation of events. In addition, because it is difficult to bring historical background into the news, the impression is created of a world of chaotic events and crises that appear and disappear because the news picture offers little explanation of their origins.

THE AUTHORITY-DISORDER BIAS

Passing for depth and coherence in this system of personalized, dramatized, and fragmented information is a fourth news tendency in which the authoritative voices of officials take center stage in many political news dramas to interpret the threatening and confusing events that threaten the order of social life. There is bias in placing so much news focus on the largely emotional questions of Who's in charge? and Will order be restored? (As opposed, for example, to What is the problem?, Why is it a problem?, What are the alternative explanations beyond the official ones?, and What can citizens do to make the situation better?)

It may be tempting to say that government, after all, is centrally about authority and order, so why shouldn't these concerns be central preoccupations of the news? The problem comes when journalists build themes about authority and order into the news as core dramatic emotional plot elements, rather than letting them pass through the news gates more formally when they arise in public debate, much the way partisan political views are generally reported. Instead, the focus on authority and order is often driven by considerations of what makes for bigger, more dramatic, more emotional stories.

Whether the world is returned to a safe, normal place, or the very idea of a normal world is called in question, the news is preoccupied with order, along with related questions of whether authorities are capable of establishing

or restoring it. It is easy to see why these generic plot elements are so central to news: They are versatile and tireless themes that can be combined endlessly within personalized, dramatized, and fragmented news episodes. When the dramatic balance between order and disorder is not a plausible focus for an event, the news quickly turns the plot pair around and challenges authority itself, perhaps by publicizing the latest scandal charge against a leader or by opening the news gates to one politician willing to attack another.

In the past, it could be argued that the news more often resolved the authority-order balance in favor of official pronouncements aimed at "normalizing" conflicted situations by creating the appearance of order and control. A classic scenario of politics, according to political scientist Murray Edelman, is for authorities to take central stage to respond to crises (sometimes after having stirred them up in the first place) with emotionally reassuring promises that they will be handled effectively. Today's authorities still play out their parts, but the news increasingly finds ways to challenge either the pronouncements of officials or the presumption of order in society, or both. In short, the biggest change in portrayals of authority and order in the news . . . is that the dominant news focus has shifted away from trusted authorities providing reassuring promises to restore chaotic situations to a state of order or normalcy. Such stories continue to appear, of course, but the growing news trend is to portray unsympathetic, scheming politicians who often fail to solve problems, leaving disorder in their wake.

What is the evidence for the proposition that news is more negative and less likely to paint reassuring pictures of the return to normalcy following dramatic crises and scandals? . . . For reasons having more to do with the news business than with external realities, the following changes have been charted in news content in recent years:

- increased levels of mayhem (crime, violence, accidents, health threats, freeway chases, and other images of social chaos)

- greater volume of criticism of government, politicians, and their policies, and less focus on the substance of policies
- higher journalistic tone of cynicism and negativity.

Many of these order-challenging news patterns are relatively subtle, reflecting the "hidden hand" of economic decisions within news organizations. For example, . . . the news recorded great increases in crime stories in the 1990s during a period in which officially reported rates of most violent crimes actually declined. This suggests that images of social disorder may be based on little more than choosing stories for their attention-getting effects. Images of disorder can be further amplified through subtle emphases in news writing. For example, is the traditional American family *threatened* by the increase in single-parent and two-working-parent households, or is the family in America simply *changing* in these ways as part of the normal course of social change?

The reason for thinking about authority and order as separable but related aspects of many news stories is that they are often set at odds with each other to create the dramatic tension in stories. Thus it would be too simple to say that authorities are almost always challenged and that disorder most often prevails. As news organizations take greater dramatic license with news plots, the two elements are mixed to achieve the greatest dramatic effect. A classic news plot represents authorities such as police, fire, and health officials as forces of good battling to restore order against social evils such as crime, violence, or disease. In one variation on this formula, crime or the latest health threat may seem to be running out of control, but officials appear in the news to tell us how we can be safe. Given the levels of mayhem and disorder in much of the news, the presence of at least some reassuring line of authority is a necessary dramatic counterpoint. Moreover, the question of what actually happened in a particular incident is often unclear at the time that news teams arrive. So we encounter the familiar news formula that goes: "The police

aren't exactly sure what happened here yet, but their investigation is in progress, and we expect a report soon."

When authorities are anchoring a scene, dramatic speculation about levels of disorder may soar in news scripts. A typical example comes from a local newscast in Orlando, Florida, where Channel 6 announced an "exclusive" and promised a report from their "live truck" at the scene. The newscast opened with the anchor describing "A shocking scene in a Lake Mary neighborhood tonight. A home surrounded by crime-scene tape. A death police are calling 'suspicious.' " As the anchor spoke, the screen flashed the words "Neighborhood Shocker." Cut to the reporter live from the scene who further dramatized the death of a sixty-six-year-old woman by saying that police did not know what happened. As if to document this claim, the reporter interviewed a police officer who said that there were no signs of violence, forced entry, or robbery. Although this statement could easily have supported either an order or a disorder plot for the story, the local news format clearly favored playing the murder mystery/shocker plot. The reporter announced that the police planned an autopsy the next day and did not know what they would find. The live feed ended with the reporter saying that, in the mean time, they "want to keep a very tight lid on what happened. . . . Live in Lake Mary, Nicole Smith, Channel 6 News." The next day, it turned out that the woman had died naturally of a heart attack. So much for the "Neighborhood Shocker." As one observer noted, "Journalism Shocker" would have been a more appropriate on-screen warning.

By contrast, other dramatic plot formulas challenge authority either by focusing on alleged personal failings of politicians or by finding examples of government failures. The political poster story of the 1990s was about wasteful government spending. Many news organizations, both local and national, have run prominent features on "How government is wasting your tax dollars." The lure of such dramatic accounts over more representative news descriptions is illustrated in a *Los Angeles Times* investigative series on government spending on computers in different agencies. Even though the investigation turned up many positive examples of taxpayer dollars well spent, here is how the story opened:

> WASHINGTON—After pumping $300 billion into computer systems in the last two decades, the federal government has compiled a record of failure that has jeopardized the nation's welfare, eroded public safety and squandered untold billions of dollars.

Whether or not most events fit the authority-disorder plot, it is easy enough to make them fit. A news show with a regular feature on government waste will, of course, find some alleged example of waste every time the feature is scheduled. Also, since there are few features on good things the government is doing, examples of government thrift (other than those forced by budget cuts) are less likely to be news.

.   .   .

Consider the picture so far: Each day news consumers are bombarded by dozens of compartmentalized, unrelated dramatic capsules. Some emotional satisfaction can be derived from forming strong identifications with or against the actors who star in these mini-dramas. But what about facts? What about knowledge and practical information? Unless the consumer has an existing interest or perspective on the subject, recalling facts from the news resembles a trivia game played alone. Most people cannot remember three-fourths of the stories in a TV news broadcast immediately after watching it, and information recall about the remembered quarter is sketchy at best.

Communication scholars have developed considerable empirical support for these four information biases in the news. There is now a sizable literature that reads like an inventory of these problems. The tendencies toward personalization, dramatization, and fragmentation have all been remarkably enduring over time, although they may have become more exaggerated with the economic pressures of the business. . . . While the focus on authority and order is also an enduring defining feature of the news, the shifting balance from order to mayhem and the unreflectively negative tone toward officials has left many observers puzzled and concerned. Indeed many politicians say they have left government because of the relentlessly negative media scrutiny, while others have surrounded themselves by legions of media consultants and handlers. At the same time that many journalists criticize their own product in these terms, they confess being helpless to change it under the current system of profit- and ratings-driven business values.

DISCUSSION QUESTIONS

1. Identify and explain the four information biases that Bennett explores. How do these biases affect what we see and hear as news? Can you think of ways any recent news stories have been influenced by these four biases?
2. In what way(s) is the quality of democracy imperiled by the continued consumption of news framed by information biases? Do you think that citizens would feel a stronger attachment to the political world if the news they received delved more honestly, analytically, and historically into the problems we face as a society?

15 John Atlas and Peter Dreier

WHY ACORN FELL
The Times, Lies, and Videotape

ACORN (Association of Community Organizations for Reform Now) was a nonprofit organization formed in the 1970s that worked on behalf of low and moderate income people. Because of ACORN's voter registration efforts, it became a regular target of the political right, who accused the group of perpetrating "voter fraud" during election campaigns. In 2008, ACORN claimed to have signed up 1.3 million new voters, and acknowledged some errors on the registration cards that it collected. However, there is no connection between problems in voter registration and voter fraud on Election Day. In fact, voter fraud is virtually nonexistent. By contrast, voter suppression and intimidation of eligible voters by public officials and private groups, often aimed at minority and low-income communities, are far larger problems than voter fraud, affecting tens if not hundreds of thousands of potential voters. Nevertheless, as John Atlas and Peter Dreier describe, ACORN became the object of a highly publicized right-wing sting operation that resulted in the organization losing funding sources and being forced to close in 2010. While the impetus to take down ACORN came from the right, Atlas and Dreier focus on the role played by the New York Times *in framing the ACORN story in seriously misleading and damaging ways. They also critique the mainstream media's very weak coverage of grassroots community organizing in general, in contrast to the attention showered on the smaller and arguably more orchestrated Tea Party movement.*

The *New York Times* hit ACORN with a one-two punch last weekend, making sure that the community organizing group—flattened by attacks from the right and withdrawal of funding from liberal foundations—stays knocked out. Both articles—Ian Urbana's Saturday story, "Acorn on Brink of Bankruptcy, Officials Say" and public editor Clark Hoyt's Sunday column, "The Acorn Sting Revisited"—reflect the paper's obsession with being so even-handed that the truth gets lost.

Both pieces reported conservative allegations against ACORN as if they were true, without

Source: John Atlas and Peter Dreier, "Why ACORN Fell: The Times Lies, and Videotapes," *Huffington Post*, 23 March 2010. Online location: http://www.huffingtonpost.com/peter-dreier/why-acorn-fell_b_510285.html

seeking to verify them. Yet since 2008 the paper has consistently ignored ACORN's community organizing successes while focusing on its enemies' accusations, belying its reputation as a "liberal" newspaper.

This reflects the *Times'* more general failure to cover grassroots organizing, except when groups engage in protest or otherwise disrupt business-as-usual.

Moreover, when the *Times* botched the ACORN story, as Hoyt now concedes, it acted as an unwitting co-conspirator with Fox News, Glenn Beck and the rest of the right wing echo chamber in scapegoating an organization that helps the working poor facing hard times to stay in their homes, make a living wage, and vote.

Because of its pivotal role in bringing down ACORN, until recently the nation's largest and most effective anti-poverty community organizing group, the *Times* owes the group an apology and the public a commitment to assign an experienced journalist to cover the complex world of community organizing, whose diverse practitioners mobilize poor and middle class people to win a voice in local, state, and national politics.

As the *Times'* public editor, Hoyt is supposed to be a kind of in-house inspector general, evaluating complaints from readers about the *Times'* news coverage to make sure it meets the standards of first-rate journalism. The crux of Hoyt's Sunday column is the following paragraph about the controversy over ACORN:

> "It remains a fascinating story. To conservatives, ACORN is virtually a criminal organization that was guilty of extensive voter registration fraud in 2008. To its supporters, Acorn is a community service organization that has helped millions of disadvantaged Americans by organizing to confront powerful institutions like banks and developers."

Hoyt seems to be saying: Take your pick. Or, according to journalistic convention: the truth lies somewhere in between. In doing so, he fails the test of his job description, which is to examine

whether the *Times* was accurate in its reporting. It is true, as Hoyt wrote, that conservatives have accused ACORN of being a "criminal organization" and "guilty of extensive voter registration fraud in 2008." But neither of these accusations against ACORN is correct, which Hoyt doesn't bother to explain.

The *Times* has never informed readers that the Republican Party's ongoing war against ACORN began in 2004 and accelerated during the 2008 presidential campaign. Karl Rove (President Bush's top political adviser) and conservative Republicans orchestrated an attack on ACORN for alleged "voter fraud," as part of a campaign to suppress the voting of minorities and the poor. As part of this effort, a U.S. Attorney was asked to investigate ACORN. The investigation came up empty-handed, but the GOP operatives persisted. The allegations of "voter fraud" hit a peak in October 2008, aided by Arizona Sen. John McCain's charge in a presidential debate with Barack Obama that ACORN "is now on the verge of maybe perpetrating one of the greatest frauds in voter history in this country, maybe destroying the fabric of democracy." He demanded that Mr. Obama disclose his ties to ACORN. McCain frequently repeated those accusations on the campaign trail.

Urbana repeats the misleading canard that, "Some chapters were also found to have submitted voter application forms with incorrect information on them during the lead-up to the 2008 presidential election, leading to blistering charges from conservative organizations linking Acorn's errors to the Obama campaign."

In fact, ACORN never engaged in voter fraud. When ACORN ramped up for its massive voter registration campaigns, it hired thousands of part-time staff, a few of whom tried to beat the system and get paid while handing in phony registrations. ACORN's quality-control procedures—phone-verifying every card, flagging problematic cards, and identifying offending workers for local officials—caught people trying to register under false names or multiple times. After ACORN reported these problems, politicians, mostly

Republicans, used them against ACORN in the media and in the legal process.

The statutes in the states where ACORN registered prospective voters required ACORN to submit all registration forms they received, even when ACORN believed they were faulty. In nine of the eleven states where ACORN's registration efforts were questioned, the law or voter-registration practice required ACORN to submit every voter-registration form, regardless of doubts about its authenticity. For any questionable form, ACORN's quality-control staff had attached a "problematic card report coversheet." As reported by McClatchy News Service and CNN, the law gave ACORN no choice but to flag the form and turn it in or face a thousand-dollar fine. ACORN neither had a policy nor an intention to engage in voter fraud. For all the publicity about some ACORN canvasser registering somebody in Florida who called himself "Mickey Mouse," Mickey Mouse didn't vote and couldn't vote. According to Barnard College professor Lorraine Minnite, voter registration and voter fraud are very rare.

Republican candidates and officials accused ACORN of voter fraud, and even filed lawsuits claiming it, but ACORN has never been found guilty of voter fraud. Last December, a report by the nonpartisan Congressional Research Service (CRS) noted that as of last October, ACORN had been subjected to at least forty-six federal, state, and local investigations, with only eleven still outstanding. In addition, the U.S. Attorney's office in Louisiana notified ACORN that it has closed its investigation. Only one state, Nevada, brought charges against ACORN, under an ambiguous law that prohibited paying staff to register voters.

The stories planted during and after the election season yielded a bountiful crop of misinformation. The mainstream news media was unwittingly complicit in the conservative campaign to frame ACORN. For example, a study of media coverage of ACORN found that over half (55%) of the all stories about ACORN during 2007 and 2008 focused on "voter fraud," while few stories reported on its grassroots organizing work.

Moreover, 80 percent of the print and broadcast stories about ACORN's alleged voter fraud (and 63 percent of the *Times*' stories) failed to mention that ACORN itself was reporting voter-registration irregularities to authorities, as required by law. The *Times*' coverage of ACORN was almost entirely negative; 56 percent of its stories focused on voter fraud and embezzlement.

Similarly, attacks against ACORN as a "criminal" organization have been a consistent mantra of the right and its business allies, who despise ACORN for its success at challenging the anti-consumer practices of banks and low-wage employers as well as its effective efforts to expand voting among the poor. But the fact that Rep. Darrel Issa and other ACORN opponents persistently claim that ACORN is criminal doesn't make it so—a distinction that gets lost in the *Times* reporting. This attack line gained prominence when two conservative activists, Hanah Giles (claiming she was a prostitute) and James O'Keefe (claiming he was her friend), visited 10 ACORN offices with a hidden video camera and tried to trap the group's housing counseling staff into giving them advice about buying a home to use for their prostitution ring.

Midway through his piece, Hoyt concedes the *Times* erred when it reported that O'Keefe entered the ACORN offices dressed as a pimp "in the outlandish costume—fur coat, goggle-like sunglasses, walking stick and broad-brimmed hat . . ." Hoyt excuses the error saying, "It is easy to see why The *Times* and other news organizations got a different impression. At one point, as the videos were being released, O'Keefe wore the get-up on Fox News, and a host said he was "dressed exactly in the same outfit he wore to these Acorn offices." He did not. O'Keefe spliced into the videos scenes of him in the pimp outfit, which Giles later admitted. Hoyt acknowledges that the *Times* was wrong to write that O'Keefe was dressed as a pimp. But, he says, "just because O'Keefe lied about his wardrobe doesn't mean that his videos don't reveal problems with the behavior of ACORN staffers argue."

Hoyt says, "But I am satisfied that The *Times* was wrong on this point, and I have been wrong in defending the paper's phrasing." Had the *Times* interviewed ACORN's staff and done some on the ground reporting it could have avoided that mistake.

Hoyt explains why he thinks the *Times* got the story wrong. "At least 14 reporters, reporting to different sets of editors, have touched it [the video controversy] since last fall. Nobody owns it. Bill Keller, the executive editor, said that, 'sensing the story would not go away and would be part of a larger narrative,' the paper should have assigned one reporter to be responsible for it." You'd think that, given its own internal disarray, the most powerful newspaper in the world would understand the management problems of an anti-poverty group—one that runs on a shoestring budget and whose staff earns relatively low salaries.

Yes, a handful of ACORN staffers exercise bad judgment in dealing with O'Keefe and Giles. ACORN CEO Bertha Lewis quickly dismissed the offending employees, launched an independent internal review and audit of the service programs, and instituted a complete review of ACORN's management operations to fix its weaknesses. Hoyt failed to emphasize that an investigation by the former Massachusetts Attorney General Scott Harshbarger found that to correct its management troubles ACORN's board fired its founder in May 2008. ACORN, he found "has made reforms in finances and governance a priority, including developing detailed bylaws, whistle-blower and document retention policies, and implementing independent auditing, codes of conduct and ethics, uniform and basic human resources and employment policies, and intensive board education and selection criteria."

Further, while ACORN has had oversight and management difficulties, they have been blown way out of proportion. For example, the *Times* failed to report that in only 3 or 4 of the 10 offices visited by the fake pimp and prostitute did ACORN's intake staff give patently outrageous advice and the videos covered only 10 of ACORN's 103 offices. In none of the offices visited by the video-tapers did ACORN employees create client files or bills, file tax returns, sign or submit loan documents, or arrange bank loans.

Hoyt also failed to report that O'Keefe and Giles targeted ACORN not because they wanted to expose problems with its housing or tax counseling programs, but because ACORN was a thorn in the side of Republicans and conservatives for its large-scale voter-registration drives among poor African Americans and Latinos who tend to cast ballots for Democrats. "Politicians are getting elected single-handedly due to this organization," O'Keefe told the press.

The *Times* played a critical role in damaging ACORN's reputation among both its reluctant and stalwart allies and gave aid and comfort to its enemies. A few days after Fox News and CNN played several of O'Keefe's misleading and doctored tapes over and over, the *Times* inaccurately reported that the fake pimp was "dressed so outlandishly that he might have been playing in a risqué high school play," thus giving its imprimatur to the video-tapers' lies. This image became implanted in the public mind, reinforcing the conservative view that ACORN was not only mismanaged but also that its African-American intake workers were buffoons and/or corrupt.

Two days later, the U.S. House of Representatives (including many Democrats) voted to de-fund the organization. In reality, less than 10 percent of ACORN's budget came from federal grants. But the symbolism of Congress' action was more important than the money itself. Congress' action provided ACORN's cautious foundation funders with an excuse to abandon their support. By the time other reports exonerated ACORN of wrongdoing, it was too late. Likewise, by the time a federal district court judge in New York found Congress' action to be an unconstitutional bill of attainder on March 10, ACORN could no longer use the money, since it was in the process of closing its offices. (The judge found no evidence that ACORN committed any crimes or violated federal contracts.)

Over the years, the *Times* has written about ACORN's battles with banks over redlining and payday lending, its campaigns for local living wage laws, and its efforts to protect affordable housing. In most stories ACORN was identified as the "community" or "consumer" voice in a story about a controversy. But since the 2008 presidential election campaign, *Times* stories about ACORN have typically been about the controversy swirling around the group itself.

Urbana's story is typical. He recounts how ACORN is close to bankruptcy because most of its major foundation supporters have withdrawn their grants. But because he doesn't really understand community organizing and the role of foundations, he never explains how difficult it is for a group that protests the policies of the rich and powerful on behalf of the poor to get cautious foundations to support them. Only a tiny proportion of all foundations provide grants to activist groups. Some of the funders who supported ACORN—such as the Ford Foundation, the Mott Foundation, and the Campaign for Human Development (an arm of the National Conference of Catholic Bishops)—had long been under attack by conservatives for their grants to ACORN. Some abandoned ACORN after a series of *Times* reports about ACORN's founder's brother embezzling almost $1 million from the organization's coffers in 2000 and internal fighting that ensued. Others cut off ACORN after the O'Keefe videos surfaced on Fox News and then elsewhere. Other funds abandoned ACORN after Congress voted to de-fund the organization.

Urbana fails to quote any foundation staff to understand why they withdrew their support or whether their perceptions of ACORN were accurate or based on false accusations that, repeated often enough, become what people believe.

ACORN could have survived the controversy over its founder's misdeeds and management problems. At that point, a handful of funders withdrew, but others simply asked ACORN to improve its management oversight and its new leader, Bertha Lewis, had already begun the process. It was the steady drumbeat of attacks on ACORN, repeated by the right-wing echo chamber and reported by the mainstream media that ultimately destroyed ACORN.

By October 2008, a national Rasmussen poll found that 60% of likely voters had a slightly unfavorable or very unfavorable opinion of ACORN. The same poll reported that 45% believed that ACORN was consciously trying to register people to vote multiple times in violation of election laws. By November 2009, another survey found that 26% of Americans—and 52% of Republicans—believed that ACORN had stolen the election for Obama. Overall 11% of Americans viewed ACORN favorably while 53% had a negative opinion of the group. ACORN has become well known, but what most Americans know about it is wrong, based on controversies manufactured by the group's long-time enemies.

Likewise, Urbana reports that "Darrell Issa of California, the ranking Republican on the House Committee on Oversight and Government Reform, described Acorn at a December hearing as a 'criminal organization' working hand-in-glove with the Obama administration. In February, committee Republicans released a report saying that Acorn 'exploits the poor and vulnerable' for political gain." It is definitely true that Issa said this and that the report by the Republican members of the committee (led by Issa, which Urbana doesn't mention) said that. But are they true? Do newspapers have to report any controversial statement by politicians, even if they are known to be false or misleading?

Many journalism schools teach students about the media's mistakes in covering Sen. Joseph McCarthy. In the early 1950s, at the height of the Cold War, newspapers routinely reported McCarthy's accusations that he had an exact count, and the names, of Communists working in the federal government. The numbers kept changing, and he never released the lists, but the media kept reporting his accusations. Haven't today's journalists learned any lessons from that experience?

Urbana apparently has not. His story acknowledges that ACORN did a great deal of good during its 40 years as a grassroots anti-poverty group. But he engages in the typical "he said/she said" journalistic balancing act that journalism watchdogs have long recognized distorts the reality. For example, Urbana quotes two low-income ACORN members who were helped by the organization's efforts. Then, Urbana writes: "But other supporters have grown disenchanted," quoting Rick Tingling-Clemmons, 66, a teacher in Washington, who was "an enthusiastic dues-paying member, but soured on the organization over the reports of embezzlement and dropped his affiliation last year." Based on Urbana's calculations, for every two ACORN members who continue to support the organization, one has quit in disenchantment. There is absolutely no evidence that more than a handful of ACORN members were prepared to leave the organization over the controversies.

Urbana reports that, "Republicans and conservatives attacked the group, in part because the group's registration efforts typically signed up voters who were believed to support Democrats." Yet he fails to inform readers that the voter fraud accusations were bogus.

Will the *Times* learn any lessons from its mistakes in its coverage of ACORN over the years?

The *Times* has no reporter whose beat covers community organizing or, more generally, liberal and progressive activism, but it overwhelms readers with stories about the Tea Party, whose numbers pale in comparison to membership in grassroots community organizing in cities across the country. Community organizing has changed dramatically since the days of Saul Alinsky—whose books, *Reveille for Radicals* (1946) and *Rules for Radicals* (1971) became bibles for activists in the 1960s and 1970s. There are now thousands of grassroots community organizing

groups around the country. There are also national networks and federations of community organizations that have significantly expanded and scale and scope of issue battles. These include National People's Action, the Center for Community Change, PICO, Gamaliel, DART, and the Industrial Areas Foundation (the latter founded by Alinsky in the 1940s). On myriad issues, these groups—often working in partnership with immigrant rights groups, environmentalists, labor unions, tenants organizations, and others—have waged effective campaigns for reform.

After Sarah Palin attacked Obama's community organizing experience in her acceptance speech at the GOP convention in St. Paul in 2008, there was a short increase—for about a week—of articles describing the work of community organizers. But since that peak, the mainstream media, including the *Times*, returned to its previous ignorance of this vital aspect of American democracy.

The *Times* does not have a community organizing "beat." Instead, they cover community organizing groups sporadically, typically in stories about controversial issues in which community groups are involved. But like the environment, health care, banking, real estate, City Hall, or the Pentagon, reporters need to develop sources and expertise to understand a subject. No *Times* reporter has developed expertise in covering community organizing groups, or developed the kind of sources necessary to understand what they do on a day-to-day basis and how they wage organizing campaigns that target some of the most powerful corporations and politicians in the country.

The *Times* is not alone is this serious failure, but as the nation's "paper of record" its failure is particularly glaring.

Indeed, the role of community organizing in American politics typically gets little attention in the mainstream media and is thus not well understood by the general public. Reporters know how to cover rallies, demonstrations, and riots, where protesters disrupt business-as-usual and get into the media's line of vision. But effective grassroots organizing is rarely so dramatic. It typically involves lots of one-on-one meetings, strategy discussions, phone calls, and training sessions that lead people to join together to channel their frustrations and anger into organizations that win improvements in workplaces, neighborhoods and schools. The *Times*, like other media outlets, is generally more interested in political theater and confrontation—when workers strike, when community activists protest, or when hopeless people resort to rioting. As a result, with a few exceptions, much of the best organizing work is unreported in the mainstream media.

This was particularly evident over the past year in the *Times'* coverage of the bottom-up campaign for health care reform. The paper covered the political dance among politicians and inside-the-Beltway industry lobby groups, and the attacks on Obama and other Democrats by Tea Party activists, but it virtually ignored the work of activist reform groups, such as Health Care for America Now!, even when they participated in protest and civil disobedience at insurance company offices, homes of insurance CEOs, and town meetings. On March 9, for example, at least 5,000 protesters picketed outside the Ritz-Carlton hotel in Washington, D.C., where America's Health Insurance Plans (AHIP), the powerful industry trade association, was holding its annual lobbying conference. About 50 public figures—including writer Barbara Ehrenreich, SEIU secretary-treasurer Anna Burger, AFL-CIO head Richard Trumka, the Center for Community Change's Deepak Bhargava, and former Congressman Bob Edgar—participated in civil disobedience. The following day, 24 insurance-industry victims—people who lost family members, are suffering because they were denied care, or went bankrupt due to premium costs—confronted reform opponents on Capitol Hill, including House Minority Whip Eric Cantor. Many major broadcast and newspaper outlets covered the protests, but not the *Times*.

This was not an isolated example. Throughout the health care debate, the *Times* published moving stories of families hurt by insurance industry malpractices, but overlooked the grassroots organizing among reformers that kept the issue alive when, several times, it appeared to be dead. Over the past year and half, it was HCAN and other grassroots activist groups that kept the pressure on the White House and on the Democrats in Congress, rallied the base, and kept public attention on the insurance industry.

ACORN was a key part of the HCAN coalition when it began in June 2008. As part of HCAN's strategy, ACORN planned to mobilize its members in states with key moderate Democrats, like Arkansas Sen. Blanche Lincoln, to push for a strong health reform package, including a public option. But by early 2009, ACORN was reeling from the attacks by conservative echo chamber and the Republicans, and had too few resources to adequately defend itself, exacerbated by the one-sided mainstream media coverage. As a result, ACORN played a marginal role in the health reform battles.

ACORN, which once had offices in 37 states will close all affiliated and field offices by April 1st. One of ACORN's legacies is the thousands of its former staff people who over many years learned organizing, research, and lobbying skills from ACORN and went on to work in many other public interest and grassroots activist and advocacy groups—unions, immigrant rights and environmental groups, health reform groups, consumer groups, and even as staffers to progressive legislators. Although no other community organizing group has reached the scale that ACORN had achieved at its peak two years ago, there are other local, state, and national groups that will continue to mobilize the poor for social change. Many of these groups will benefit by hiring some of ACORN's laid-off staffers. And the state branches of ACORN that recently broke off to form independent anti-poverty groups will no doubt emerge as serious advocates for the disadvantaged. But the loss of ACORN leaves a huge void in the nation's political landscape, one that won't be filled quickly.

The mainstream media, including the *New York Times*, played a pivotal role in ACORN's demise, but it has refused to acknowledge its role, as the two stories in the *Times* last weekend reveal. Hoyt, who rebuked the *Times'* editors last year for missing the right-wing attack on ACORN, now needs to urge the daily to assign a reporter to cover the important work of progressive community organizing groups.

DISCUSSION QUESTIONS

1. As an organization, ACORN was probably unknown to most Americans until 2008. According to Atlas and Dreier, what messages did the public receive about ACORN from the mainstream media in 2008–2010, and why do they think these messages were misleading?
2. Atlas and Dreier say the mainstream media do a poor job covering community organizing. Why do they think this occurs? Do you think there should be more reporting on this topic?

16 *Bill Moyers*

"FACTS STILL MATTER . . ."
The Need for an Independent Media

Award-winning author and journalist Bill Moyers has been involved in the media for well over 40 years. In this address to the journalism group History Makers, Moyers makes a strong case for an independent media driven by the pursuit of facts and the larger quest for truth. This mission is made all the more difficult by research that suggests that people often form their opinions based not on a rational assessment of the facts but on prior beliefs—beliefs that can "dictate the facts we choose to accept." This type of a "closed belief system" can be rendered almost impenetrable, particularly when biases are reinforced by a mass media that too often popularize false narratives as a weapon of political warfare. Drawing on his life in broadcast journalism making documentaries with PBS, Moyers discusses the difficulties of shining light on political corruption and the even-more challenging task of questioning the role of corporate power in our political life. He concludes with observations on WikiLeaks and the struggle for net neutrality. Throughout it all, Moyers makes a plea for the power of ideas and the crucial need for knowledge and facts if we are to nurture the critical thinking skills necessary for an informed democracy.

Thanks to all of you for your welcome—and for the chance to be here among so many kindred spirits. Your dedication to factual broadcasting, to our craft and calling; your passion for telling stories that matter; for connecting the present to the past, has created a community whose work is essential in this disquieting time when "what is happening today, this hour, this very minute, seems to be our sole criterion for judgment and action." It is a sad world that exists only in the present, unaware of the long procession that brought us here. As Milan Kundera's insight reminds us, the struggle against power "is the struggle of memory against forgetting."

I talked about this gathering when I was in California this past weekend and spent time with a good friend and supporter of my own work on television, Paul Orfalea. He's the maverick entrepreneur who founded Kinko's in a former hamburger stand with one small rented Xerox copier

Source: Bill Moyers, "Facts Still Matter . . ." Keynote speech at the History Makers convention, January 27, 2011, as published in *Truthout*, February 14, 2011. Online location: http://truth-out.org/index.php?option=com_k2&view=item&id=24:bill-moyers-facts-still-matter

and turned it into a business service empire with more than two billion dollars a year in revenue. After selling Kinko's, Paul became one of the most popular, if unorthodox, teachers of undergraduates at the University of California/Santa Barbara. When I told him what I would be doing today he applauded and understood immediately the importance of what you do. He described to me how he teaches history "backwards" to college students who have learned little about the past in high school, don't know that the past is even alive, much less that it lives in them and question its value today. He hands his students a contemporary story from some daily news source, tells them to begin with the "now" of it and to then walk the trail back down the chronology to trace the personalities, circumstances and choices that made it today's news. Their assignment, in effect, is to begin at the entrance to the cave and rewind Ariadne's thread in the opposite direction, back to the deep origins of the story. In an era marked by the lack of continuity and community between the generations, this strikes me as an inspired way to stretch young imaginations across the time zones of human experience.

And it's, of course, what you do so often in your work. No one I know does it more effectively than "Frontline," and I was pleased to learn that you are honoring its executive director, David Fanning, who is a genius, in my book, at story telling grounded in fact and presented with perspective. Over the past quarter century, I have been privileged to collaborate occasionally with David. But beyond my own personal and professional gratitude to him, all of us who produce current affairs and history programming know that he has kept the bar high while producing a body of work unequaled since [former CBS News President] Fred Friendly. Most of you are too young to have seen the whole arc of David's extraordinary career or to have known Fred Friendly's work. But some of us can never forget we're standing on the shoulder of those two giants.

Fred was right, as he so often was: independence meant the best hope for me to pursue journalism as a mission. Perhaps, we were naïve, but

in those days many of us still assumed that an informed public is preferable to an uninformed one. Hadn't Thomas Jefferson proclaimed that, "Whenever the people are well-informed, they can be trusted with their own government"? And wasn't a free press essential to that end?

Maybe not. As Joe Keohane reported last year in *The Boston Globe*, political scientists have begun to discover a human tendency "deeply discouraging to anyone with faith in the power of information." He was reporting on research at the University of Michigan, which found that when misinformed people, particularly political partisans, were exposed to corrected facts in new stories, they rarely changed their minds. In fact, they often became even more strongly set in their beliefs. Facts were not curing misinformation. "Like an underpowered antibiotic, facts could actually make misinformation even stronger."

I won't spoil it for you by a lengthy summary here. Suffice it to say that, while "most of us like to believe that our opinions have been formed over time by careful, rational consideration of facts and ideas and that the decisions based on those opinions, therefore, have the ring of soundness and intelligence," the research found that actually "we often base our opinions on our beliefs . . . and rather than facts driving beliefs, our beliefs can dictate the facts we chose to accept. They can cause us to twist facts so they fit better with our preconceived notions."

These studies help to explain why America seems more and more unable to deal with reality. So many people inhabit a closed belief system on whose door they have hung the "Do Not Disturb" sign, that they pick and choose only those facts that will serve as building blocks for walling them off from uncomfortable truths. Any journalist whose reporting threatens that belief system gets sliced and diced by its apologists and polemicists (say, the fabulists at Fox News, Rush Limbaugh and the yahoos of talk radio.) Remember when Limbaugh, for one, took journalists on for their reporting about torture at Abu Ghraib? He attempted to dismiss the cruelty inflicted on their captives by American soldiers as a little necessary "sport" for soldiers under stress, saying on air: "This is no different than what happens at the Skull and Bones initiation . . . you [ever] heard of need to blow some steam off?" As so often happens, the Limbaugh line became a drumbeat in the nether reaches of the right-wing echo chamber. So, it was not surprising that in a nationwide survey conducted by the *Chicago Tribune* on First Amendment issues, half of the respondents said there should be some kind of press restraint on reporting about the prison abuse. According to Charles Madigan, the editor of the *Tribune*'s Perspective section, 50 or 60 percent of the respondents said they "would embrace government controls of some kind on free speech, particularly when it has sexual content or is heard as unpatriotic."

No wonder many people still believe Obama was born in Kenya, not Hawaii, as his birth certificate shows; or that he is a Muslim, when in fact he is a Christian; or that he is a socialist when day by day he shows an eager solicitude for corporate capitalism. Partisans in particular—and the audiences for Murdoch's Fox News and talk radio—are particularly susceptible to such scurrilous disinformation. In a Harris survey last spring, 67 percent of Republicans said Obama is a socialist; 57 percent believed him to be a Muslim; 45 percent refused to believe he was born in America; and 24 percent said he "may be the antichrist."

The bigger the smear, the more it sticks. And there is no shortage of smear artists. Last year, *Forbes Magazine*, obviously bent on mischief, allowed the right-wing fantasist Dinesh D'Souza to tar Obama with a toxic brew so odious it triggered memories of racist babble—a perverted combination of half-baked psychology, biology and sociology—that marked the heyday of the Ku Klux Klan. Seizing upon the anti-colonial views of Obama's Kenyan father, who had deserted the family when the boy was two years old and whose absence from his life Obama meditated upon in his best-selling book *Dreams of My Father*, D'Souza wrote that, "Incredibly, the US is being ruled according to the dreams of a Luo tribesman of the 1950s. This philandering, inebriated African socialist, who raged against the world for denying

him the realization of his anticolonial ambitions, is now setting the nation's agenda through the reincarnation of his dreams in his son."

In a sane political world, you might think at least a few Republican notables would have denounced such hogwash by their own kind for what it was. But no. Newt Gingrich, once their speaker of the House, whose own fantasies include succeeding Obama in the White House, set the tone by praising D'Souza's claptrap as the "most profound insight I have read in the last six years about Barack Obama." D'Souza, said Gingrich, has made a "stunning insight" and had unlocked the mystery of Obama. I could find only one conservative who stood up against this trash. David Frum, the former speechwriter for George W. Bush, wrote on his blog: "The argument that Obama is an infiltrating alien, a deceiving foreigner—and not just any kind of alien, but specifically a Third World alien—has been absorbed to the very core of the Republican platform for November 2010." Once again, the right-wing media machine had popularized a false narrative and made of it a destructive political weapon.

Disinformation is not unique to the right, of course. Like other journalists, I have been the object of malevolent assaults from the "9/11 truthers" for not reporting their airtight case proving that the Bush administration conspired to bring about the attacks on the World Trade Center. How did they discover this conspiracy? As the independent journalist Robert Parry has written, "the truthers" threw out all the evidence of al-Qaeda's involvement, from contemporaneous calls from hijack victims on the planes to confessions from al-Qaeda leaders both in and out of captivity that they had indeed done it. Then, recycling some of the right's sophistry techniques, such as using long lists of supposed evidence to overcome the lack of any real evidence, the "truthers" cherry-picked a few supposed "anomalies" to build an "inside-job" story line. Fortunately, this Big Lie never took hold in the public mind. These truthers on the left, if that is where GPS can find them on the political map, are outgunned, outmatched and outshouted by the media apparatus on the right that pounds the public like drone missiles loaded with conspiracy theories and disinformation and accompanied by armadas of outright lies.

George Orwell had warned six decades ago that the corrosion of language goes hand in hand with the corruption of democracy. If he were around today, he would remind us that "like the rattling of a stick inside a swill bucket," this kind of propaganda engenders a "protective stupidity" almost impossible for facts to penetrate.

But you, my colleagues, can't give up. If you do, there's no chance any public memory of everyday truths—the tangible, touchable, palpable realities so vital to democracy—will survive. We would be left to the mercy of the agitated amnesiacs who "make" their own reality, as one of them boasted at the time America invaded Iraq, in order to maintain their hold on the public mind and the levers of power. You will remember that in Orwell's novel *1984*, Big Brother banishes history to the memory hole, where inconvenient facts simply disappear. Control of the present rests on obliteration of the past. The figure of O'Brien, who is the personification of Big Brother, says to the protagonist, Winston Smith: "We shall squeeze you empty and then we shall fill you with ourselves." And they do. The bureaucrats in the Ministry of Truth destroy the records of the past and publish new versions. These in turn are superseded by yet more revisions. Why? Because people without memory are at the mercy of the powers that be; there is nothing against which to measure what they are told today. History is obliterated.

The late scholar Cleanth Brooks of Yale thought there were three great enemies of democracy. He called them "The Bastard Muses": Propaganda, which pleads sometimes unscrupulously, for a special cause at the expense of the total truth; sentimentality, which works up emotional responses unwarranted by, and in excess of, the occasion; and pornography, which focuses upon one powerful human drive at the expense of the total human personality. The poet Czeslaw Milosz identified another enemy of democracy when, upon accepting the Noble Prize for Literature, he

said "Our planet that gets smaller every year, with its fantastic proliferation of mass media, is witnessing a process that escapes definition, characterized by a refusal to remember." Memory is crucial to democracy; historical amnesia, its nemesis.

Against these tendencies it is an uphill fight to stay the course of factual broadcasting. We have to keep reassuring ourselves and one another that it matters and we have to join forces to defend and safeguard our independence. I learned this early on.

When I collaborated with the producer Sherry Jones on the very first documentary ever about the purchase of government favors by political action committees, we unfurled across the Capitol grounds yard after yard of computer printouts listing campaign contributions to every member of Congress. The broadcast infuriated just about everyone, including old friends of mine who a few years earlier had been allies when I worked at the White House. Congressmen friendly to public television were also outraged, but, I am pleased to report, PBS took the heat without melting.

But shining the spotlight on political corruption is nothing compared to what can happen if you raise questions about corporate power in Washington, as my colleague Marty Koughan and I discovered when we produced a program for David Fanning and "Frontline" on pesticides and food. Marty had learned that industry was attempting behind closed doors to dilute the findings of the American Academy of Sciences study on the effects of pesticide residues on children. Before we finished the documentary, the industry somehow purloined a copy of our draft script—we still aren't certain how—and mounted a sophisticated and expensive campaign to discredit our program before it aired. Television reviewers and editorial pages of key newspapers were flooded with propaganda. Some public television managers were so unnerved by the blitz of misleading information about a film they had not yet broadcast that they actually protested to PBS with letters that had been prepared by the industry.

Here's what most perplexed us: the American Cancer Society—an organization that in no way figured in our story—sent to its 3,000 local chapters a "critique" of the unfinished documentary claiming, wrongly, that it exaggerated the dangers of pesticides in food. We were puzzled. Why was the American Cancer Society taking the unusual step of criticizing a documentary that it had not seen, that had not aired and that did not claim what the Society alleged? An enterprising reporter named Sheila Kaplan later looked into those questions for the journal *Legal Times*. It turns out that the Porter Novelli public relations firm, which had worked for several chemical companies, also did pro bono work for the American Cancer Society. Kaplan found that the firm was able to cash in some of the goodwill from that "charitable" work to persuade the compliant communications staff at the Society to distribute some harsh talking points about the documentary before it aired—talking points that had been supplied by, but not attributed to, Porter Novelli. *Legal Times* headlined the story "Porter Novelli Plays All Sides." A familiar Washington game.

Others also used the American Cancer Society's good name in efforts to tarnish the journalism before it aired, none more invidiously than the right-wing polemicist Reed Irvine, who pumped his sludge through an organization with the Orwellian name Accuracy in Media. He attacked our work as "junk science on PBS" and demanded Congress pull the plug on public broadcasting. Fortunately, PBS once again stood firm. The documentary aired, the journalism held up and the publicity liberated the National Academy of Sciences to release the study that the industry had tried to cripple.

However, there's always another round; the sharks are always circling. Sherry Jones and I spent more than a year working on another PBS documentary called "Trade Secrets," a two-hour investigative special based on revelations—found in the industry's own archives—that big chemical companies had deliberately withheld from workers and consumers damaging information about toxic chemicals in their products. These internal industry documents are a fact. They exist. They are not a matter of opinion or point of view. They state what the companies knew, when they knew it and what they did with what they knew (namely to deep-six it) at peril to those who worked with and consumed the potentially lethal products.

The revelations portrayed deep and pervasive corruption in a major American industry and raised critical policy implications about the safety of living under a regulatory system manipulated by the industry itself. If the public and government regulators had known what the industry knew about the health risks of its products when the industry knew it, America's laws and regulations governing chemical manufacturing would have been far more protective of human health. But the industry didn't want us to know. That's what the documents revealed and that was the story the industry fought to keep us from telling.

The industry hired as an ally a public relations firm in Washington noted for using private detectives and former CIA, FBI and drug enforcement officers to conduct investigations for corporations under critical scrutiny. One of the company's founders acknowledged that corporations may need to resort to "deceit" and other unconventional resources to counter public scrutiny. Given the scurrilous campaign that was conducted to smear our journalism, his comments were an understatement. To complicate matters, the Congressman, who for years had been the single biggest recipient of campaign contributions from the chemical industry, was the very member of Congress whose committee had jurisdiction over public broadcasting's appropriations. As an independent production firm, we had not used public funds to produce the documentary. But even our independence didn't stop the corporate mercenaries from bringing relentless pressure on PBS not to air the broadcast. The then president of PBS, Pat Mitchell, stood tall in resisting the pressure and was vindicated: one year later, The National Academy of Television Arts and Sciences awarded "Trade Secrets" an Emmy for outstanding investigative journalism.

Now, you can understand how it is that journalism became for me a continuing course in adult education. It enabled me to produce documentaries like "Trade Secrets" and out-of-the-box series like "Joseph Campbell and the Power of Myth." It enabled me to cover the summits of world leaders and the daily lives of struggling families in Newark. It empowered me to explain how public elections are subverted by private money, and to how to make a poem. Journalism also provided me a passport into the world of ideas, which became my favorite beat, in no small part because I never met anyone—philosopher or physicist, historian, artist, writer, scientist, entrepreneur or social critic—who didn't teach me something I hadn't known, something that enlarged my life.

Here's an example: One of my favorite of all interviews was with my sainted fellow Texan, the writer and broadcaster John Henry Faulk, who had many years earlier, been the target of a right-wing smear campaign that resulted in his firing by CBS from his job as a radio host here in New York, one of the low moments in that network's history. But John Henry fought back in court and won a landmark legal victory against his tormentors. After he returned home to Texas, I did the last interview with him before his death in 1990. He told me the story of how he and his friend Boots Cooper were playing in the chicken coop when they were about 12 years old. They spied a chicken snake in the top tier of nests, so close it looked like a boa constrictor. As John Henry put it, "All our frontier courage drained out our heels—actually it trickled down our overall legs—and Boots and I made a new door through that henhouse wall." Hearing all the commotion Boots' momma came out and said, "Don't you boys know chicken snakes are harmless? They can't harm you." And Boots, rubbing his forehead and behind at the same time, said, "Yes, Mrs. Faulk, I know that, but they can scare you so bad, it'll cause you to hurt yourself." John Henry Faulk told me that's a lesson he never forgot. Over and again I've tried to remember it, too, calling on it to restore my resolve and my soul.

I've had a wonderful life in broadcasting, matriculating as a perpetual student in the school of journalism. Other people have paid the tuition and travel and I've never really had to grow up and get a day job. I think it's because journalism has been so good to me that I am sad when I hear or read that factual broadcasting is passé—that television as a venue for forensic journalism is

on its way out and that trying to find out "what really happened"—which is our mandate—is but a quaint relic in an age of post-structuralism and cyberspace. But despite all our personal electronic devices, people are watching more television than ever. Much of this programming is posted online; I believe at least half the audience for my last two weekly series on Friday night came over the weekend via streaming video, iPods and TIVO. I was pleased to discover that the web sites most frequented by educators are those of PBS and that our own sites were among the most popular destinations. That's what keeps us going, isn't it? The knowledge that all the bias and ignorance notwithstanding, facts still matter to critical thinking, that if we respect and honor, even revere them, they just might help us right the ship of state before it rams the iceberg.

That's why, on balance, I count WikiLeaks a plus for democracy. Whatever side you take on the controversy, whether or not you think this information should be disclosed, all parties—those who want it released and those who don't—acknowledge that information matters. Partly because I grew up in the south and partly because of my experience in the Johnson White House, I'm on the side of disclosure, even when it hurts. The truth about slavery had been driven from the pulpits, newsrooms and classrooms during the antebellum days; it took a bloody civil war to drive the truth home. At the Johnson White House, we circled the wagons and grew intolerant of news that didn't conform to our hopes, expectations and strategies for Vietnam, with terrible, tragic results for Americans and Vietnamese, north and south. I say: "Never again!"

Here's a sidebar: I remember vividly the day President Johnson signed the Freedom of Information Act (FOIA): July 4, 1966. He signed it "with a deep sense of pride," declaring in almost lyrical language "that the United States is an open society in which the people's right to know is cherished and guarded." That's what he said. The truth is, the president had to be dragged kicking and screaming to the signing ceremony. He hated the very idea of journalists rummaging in government closets, hated them challenging the authorized view of reality, hated them knowing what he didn't want them to know. He dug in his heels and even threatened to pocket veto the bill after it reached the White House. Only the courage and political skill of a Congressman named John Moss got the bill passed at all and that was after a 12-year battle against his Congressional elders, who blinked every time the sun shined on the dark corners of power. They managed to cripple the bill Moss had drafted and, even then, only some last-minute calls to LBJ from a handful of influential newspaper editors overcame the president's reluctance. He signed "the f—— thing," as he called it and then, lo and behold, went out to claim credit for it.

It's always a fight to find out what the government doesn't want us to know. The official obsession with secrecy is all the more disturbing today because the war on terrorism is a war without limits, without a visible enemy or decisive encounters. We don't know where the clandestine war is going on or how much it's costing and whether it's in the least effective. Even in Afghanistan, most of what we know comes from official, usually military, sources.

Thus, a relative handful of people have enormous power to keep us in the dark. And when those people are in league with their counterparts in powerful corporations, the public is hit with a double whammy. We're usually told the issue is national security, but keeping us from finding out about the danger of accidents at chemical plants is not about national security; it's about covering up an industry's indiscretions and liabilities. Locking up the secrets of meetings with energy executives is not about national security; it's about hiding confidential memos sent to the White House showing the influence of oil companies on policies of global warming. We only learned about that memo from the Bush White House, by the way, thanks to the Freedom of Information Act.

Consider WikiLeaks, then, to be one big FOIA dump. Were some people in high places embarrassed? Perhaps. They did squeal, but I don't think they were stuck.

And even so, we learned some important things from WikiLeaks. For example, as Reza Alsan writes

in *The Atlantic*, the president of Iran, Mahmoud Ahmadinejad, may not be as fanatical as we think he is; the diplomatic cables released by WikiLeaks portray him as "a moderate reformer who'd like to cut deals with the West, but can't because hard-liners are calling the shots." One of them even slapped Ahmadinejad across the face when, at a high-level meeting, he proposed that the government allow more personal and press freedom at the height of the 2009 public protests in Iran. Such information can help us evaluate the incessant demands of neoconservative warmongers—the very people who rode the circuit with news of "weapons of mass destruction" in an effort to build support for invading Iraq—that we use military force against Iran to eliminate its nuclear capacity.

There are other uses of the disclosures from WikiLeaks admirably compiled by Greg Mitchell in the current edition of *The Nation*, where the one-time editor of *Editor and Publisher* performed an important public service by culling the gold from the dust.

I will close with an urgent appeal to you about one fight we won't win unless all of us join it. I'm sure everyone here agrees that we will eventually be moving to the web, all of us and that "free, instant, worldwide connectivity" is the future. But I'm sure you know that this incredible, free, open Internet highway is at risk, that corporations are on the brink of muscling their way to the front of the line. Media companies want the power to censor Internet content they don't like, to put toll booths on the web so they can charge more for the privilege of driving in the fast lanes, to turn it into a private preserve.

You may have heard that last month the FCC decided to protect free/open Internet access only on landline connections, not wireless—which is to say, there's no net neutrality in most of the online world. As Jenn Ettinger of the nonpartisan, nonprofit Free Press reported in *Yes!* magazine just two days ago:

> The rules that the FCC passed in December are vague and weak. The limited protections that were placed on wired connections, the kind you access through your

home computer, leave the door open for the phone and cable companies to develop fast and slow lanes on the Web and to favor their own content or applications.

Worse, the rules also explicitly allow wireless carriers . . . to block applications for any reason and to degrade and de-prioritize websites you access using your cell phone or a device like an iPad.

Perhaps the FCC is biding its time, waiting to see how things develop technologically, with the current FCC chair seemingly more open to citizen input than was his predecessor. Or, again, maybe the landline regulation was meant simply to get media reformers off the commission's back. We can't relax our vigilance. In Ettinger's words:

The FCC still has the opportunity to put in place a solid framework that would put the public interest above the profit motive of the phone and cable companies that it is supposed to regulate. And the FCC should take immediate steps to close the loopholes it created, to strengthen its rules and to include wireless protections. The fight is far from over. We can work to change the rules, demand better oversight and consumer protections and make sure that the big companies can't pad their bottom lines on the backs of their customers.

In this effort, we have a strong ally in FCC commissioner Michael Copps, who. on my broadcast last year, spelled out how "our future is going to ride on broadband. How we get a job is going to ride on broadband. How we take care of our health. How we educate ourselves about our responsibilities as citizens . . . And it's absolutely imperative that we have a place, that we have a venue to go to, to make sure that that Internet is kept open . . . That's our decision to make as a people, as citizens: who's going to control this ultimately?"

With all the media consolidation that's happening today, the web may be the last stand of independent factual broadcasters like you. The stakes are high and we have come to the decisive round. I'll leave you with a story Joseph Campbell told me years ago for my series "The Power of Myth." It seems a fellow rounding the corner saw a fight break out down the block. Running up to one of the bystanders, he shouted: "Is this a private fight or can anyone get in it?"

The Internet fight for democracy is a public fight. Come on in!

DISCUSSION QUESTIONS

1. In several parts of his speech, Moyers discusses his personal experiences as a journalist. What lessons did he learn during his career? How do those lessons illuminate his overall argument about the role of the media in our society?

2. According to Moyers, studies done by political scientists show that people selectively use (or ignore) facts to fit their preconceived beliefs and that as a result of "a closed belief system" many in America "seem more and more unable to deal with reality." Explain, using examples, the unreality of the worldview held by many Americans. What role do memory and history play in combating such a lack of reality?

3. What connection does Moyers make between the health of democracy and the health of a nation's media/information system? Given his analysis, how healthy would you say democracy is in the United States today? Explain.

CHAPTER 5

Parties and Elections

Elections and voting in America today reveal a wide gap between democratic ideals of citizen participation in the substantive discussion of issues and the realities of low voter turnout, the ascendancy of image and emotional manipulation in campaigns, and the distorting impact of big money. In principle, a broad franchise and regular elections (in which competing parties offer distinct approaches to important problems) should provide citizens with a link to government officials. This link should ensure responsiveness to public concerns and a measure of control over public policy. Indeed, many Americans have seen the very existence of elections and the right to vote as proof of the democratic nature of our political system. But many others are aware of the discrepancy between ideals and reality. This gap was underscored by the disputed presidential election of 2000, which was decided by a 5–4 Supreme Court ruling, and by the considerable volatility and alienation expressed in the congressional and presidential elections of 2006, 2008, and 2010. Readings in this chapter will help you understand this gap and what might be done to bridge it.

17 *Thomas Frank*

WHAT'S THE MATTER WITH AMERICA?

In this selection from his best-selling book of 2004 What's the Matter with Kansas? *author Thomas Frank explores what he considers the "preeminent question of our times," namely why ever-increasing numbers of working class and average-income Americans vote for conservative politicians whose policies intensify the economic hardships faced by those very same Americans. Frank attributes this "derangement" to the "Great Backlash," a cultural anger that emerged in the 1960s to be harnessed by Republican politicians who appeal to socially and culturally conservative issues in the service of economic ends that advance the fortunes of corporations and the wealthy. Or as Frank characterizes it, "The leaders of the backlash may talk Christ, but they walk corporate." The result has been a boon to the Republican Party. As they attract more angry, disaffected former Democrats with anti-abortion, anti-gay, anti-Hollywood, and other appeals central to the culture wars of our era, their economic agenda worsens the plight of those voters, whose anger intensifies even more, enhancing the power of Republicans in a kind of self-fulfilling spiral. While Frank views this political transformation through its impact on his home state of Kansas, this same "panorama of madness" pervades the entire nation. Indeed, it is the hallmark of party politics in the United States today.*

The poorest county in America isn't in Appalachia or the Deep South. It is on the Great Plains, a region of struggling ranchers and dying farm towns, and in the election of 2000 the Republican candidate for president, George W. Bush, carried it by a majority of greater than 80 percent.

This puzzled me when I first read about it, as it puzzles many of the people I know. For us it is the Democrats that are the party of workers, of the poor, of the weak and the victimized. Understanding this, we think, is basic; it is part of the ABCs of adulthood. When I told a friend of mine about that impoverished High Plains county so enamored of President Bush, she was perplexed. "How can anyone who has ever worked for someone else vote Republican?" she asked. How could so many people get it so wrong?

Her question is apt; it is, in many ways, the preeminent question of our times. People getting their fundamental interests wrong is what American political life is all about. This species

Source: Thomas Frank, *What's the Matter with Kansas?,* New York: Henry Holt, 2004, pp. 1–10.

of derangement is the bedrock of our civic order; it is the foundation on which all else rests. This derangement has put the Republicans in charge of all three branches of government; it has elected presidents, senators, governors; it shifts the Democrats to the right and then impeaches Bill Clinton just for fun.

If you earn over $300,000 a year, you owe a great deal to this derangement. Raise a glass sometime to those indigent High Plains Republicans as you contemplate your good fortune: It is thanks to their self-denying votes that you are no longer burdened by the estate tax, or troublesome labor unions, or meddling banking regulators. Thanks to the allegiance of these sons and daughters of toil, you have escaped what your affluent forebears used to call "confiscatory" income tax levels. It is thanks to them that you were able to buy two Rolexes this year instead of one and get that Segway with the special gold trim.

Or perhaps you are one of those many, many millions of average-income Americans who see nothing deranged about this at all. For you this picture of hard-times conservatism makes perfect sense, and it is the opposite phenomenon—working-class people who insist on voting for liberals—that strikes you as an indecipherable puzzlement. Maybe you see it the way the bumper sticker I spotted at a Kansas City gun show puts it: "A working person that *supports* Democrats is like a chicken that *supports* Col. Sanders!"

Maybe you were one of those who stood up for America way back in 1968, sick of hearing those rich kids in beads bad-mouth the country every night on TV. Maybe you knew exactly what Richard Nixon meant when he talked about the "silent majority," the people whose hard work was rewarded with constant insults from the network news, the Hollywood movies, and the know-it-all college professors, none of them interested in anything you had to say. Or maybe it was the liberal judges who got you mad as hell, casually rewriting the laws of your state according to some daft idea they had picked up at a cocktail party, or ordering your town to shoulder some billion-dollar desegregation scheme that they had dreamed up on

their own, or turning criminals loose to prey on the hardworking and the industrious. Or perhaps it was the drive for gun control, which was obviously directed toward the same end of disarming and ultimately disempowering people like you.

Maybe Ronald Reagan pulled you into the conservative swirl, the way he talked about that sunshiny, Glenn Miller America you remembered from the time before the world went to hell. Or maybe Rush Limbaugh won you over, with his daily beatdown of the arrogant and the self-important. Or maybe you were pushed; maybe Bill Clinton made a Republican out of you with his patently phony "compassion" and his obvious contempt for average, non-Ivy Americans, the ones he had the nerve to order into combat even though he himself took the coward's way out when his turn came.

Nearly everyone has a conversion story they can tell: how their dad had been a union steelworker and a stalwart Democrat, but how all their brothers and sisters started voting Republican; or how their cousin gave up on Methodism and started going to the Pentecostal church out on the edge of town; or how they themselves just got so sick of being scolded for eating meat or for wearing clothes emblazoned with the State U's Indian mascot that one day Fox News started to seem "fair and balanced" to them after all.

Take the family of a friend of mine, a guy who came from one of those midwestern cities that sociologists used to descend upon periodically because it was supposed to be so "typical." It was a middling-sized industrial burg where they made machine tools, auto parts, and so forth. When Reagan took office in 1981, more than half the working population of the city was employed in factories, and most of them were union members. The ethos of the place was working-class, and the city was prosperous, tidy, and liberal, in the old sense of the word.

My friend's dad was a teacher in the local public schools, a loyal member of the teachers' union, and a more dedicated liberal than most: not only had he been a staunch supporter of George McGovern, but in the 1980 Democratic primary he had voted for Barbara Jordan, the black U.S.

Representative from Texas. My friend, meanwhile, was in those days a high school Republican, a Reagan youth who fancied Adam Smith ties and savored the writing of William F. Buckley. The dad would listen to the son spout off about Milton Friedman and the godliness of free-market capitalism, and he would just shake his head. *Someday, kid, you'll know what a jerk you are.*

It was the dad, though, who was eventually converted. These days he votes for the farthest-right Republicans he can find on the ballot. The particular issue that brought him over was abortion. A devout Catholic, my friend's dad was persuaded in the early nineties that the sanctity of the fetus outweighed all of his other concerns, and from there he gradually accepted the whole pantheon of conservative devil-figures: the elite media and the American Civil Liberties Union, contemptuous of our values; the la-di-da feminists; the idea that Christians are vilely persecuted—right here in the U.S. of A. It doesn't even bother him, really, when his new hero Bill O'Reilly blasts the teachers' union as a group that "does not love America."

His superaverage midwestern town, meanwhile, has followed the same trajectory. Even as Republican economic policy laid waste to the city's industries, unions, and neighborhoods, the townsfolk responded by lashing out on cultural issues, eventually winding up with a hard-right Republican congressman, a born-again Christian who campaigned largely on an anti-abortion platform. Today the city looks like a miniature Detroit. And with every bit of economic bad news it seems to get more bitter, more cynical, and more conservative still.

This derangement is the signature expression of the Great Backlash, a style of conservatism that first came snarling onto the national stage in response to the partying and protests of the late sixties. While earlier forms of conservatism emphasized fiscal sobriety, the backlash mobilizes voters with explosive social issues—summoning public outrage over everything from busing to un-Christian art—which it then marries to pro-business economic policies. Cultural anger

is marshaled to achieve economic ends. And it is these economic achievements—not the forgettable skirmishes of the never-ending culture wars—that are the movement's greatest monuments. The backlash is what has made possible the international free-market consensus of recent years, with all the privatization, deregulation, and deunionization that are its components. Backlash ensures that Republicans will continue to be returned to office even when their free-market miracles fail and their libertarian schemes don't deliver and their "New Economy" collapses. It makes possible the policy pushers' fantasies of "globalization" and a free-trade empire that are foisted upon the rest of the world with such self-assurance. Because some artist decides to shock the hicks by dunking Jesus in urine, the entire planet must remake itself along the lines preferred by the Republican Party, U.S.A.

The Great Backlash has made the laissez-faire revival possible, but this does not mean that it speaks to us in the manner of the capitalists of old, invoking the divine right of money or demanding that the lowly learn their place in the great chain of being. On the contrary; the backlash imagines itself as a foe of the elite, as the voice of the unfairly persecuted, as a righteous protest of the people on history's receiving end. That its champions today control all three branches of government matters not a whit. That its greatest beneficiaries are the wealthiest people on the planet does not give it pause.

In fact, backlash leaders systematically downplay the politics of economics. The movement's basic premise is that culture outweighs economics as a matter of public concern—that *Values Matter Most,* as one backlash title has it. On those grounds it rallies citizens who would once have been reliable partisans of the New Deal to the standard of conservatism. Old-fashioned values may count when conservatives appear on the stump, but once conservatives are in office the only old-fashioned situation they care to revive is an economic regimen of low wages and lax regulations. Over the last three decades they have smashed the welfare state, reduced the tax burden on corporations and the wealthy, and generally facilitated the country's return to a nineteenth-century pattern of wealth distribution. Thus the primary contradiction of the backlash: it is a working-class movement that has done incalculable, historic harm to working-class people.

The leaders of the backlash may talk Christ, but they walk corporate. Values may "matter most" to voters, but they always take a backseat to the needs of money once the elections are won. This is a basic earmark of the phenomenon, absolutely consistent across its decades-long history. Abortion is never halted. Affirmative action is never abolished. The culture industry is never forced to clean up its act. Even the greatest culture warrior of them all was a notorious cop-out once it came time to deliver, "Reagan made himself the champion of 'traditional values,' but there is no evidence he regarded their restoration as a high priority," wrote Christopher Lasch, one of the most astute analysts of the backlash sensibility. "What he really cared about was the revival of the unregulated capitalism of the twenties: the repeal of the New Deal."

This is vexing for observers, and one might expect it to vex the movement's true believers even more. Their grandstanding leaders never deliver, their fury mounts and mounts, and nevertheless they turn out every two years to return their right-wing heroes to office for a second, a third, a twentieth try. The trick never ages; the illusion never wears off. *Vote* to stop abortion; *receive* a rollback in capital gains taxes. *Vote* to make our country strong again; *receive* deindustrialization. *Vote* to screw those politically correct college professors; *receive* electricity deregulation. *Vote* to get government off our backs; *receive* conglomeration and monopoly everywhere from media to meatpacking. *Vote* to stand tall against terrorists; *receive* Social Security privatization. *Vote* to strike a blow against elitism; *receive* a social order in which wealth is more concentrated than ever before in our lifetimes, in which workers have been stripped of power and CEOs are rewarded in a manner beyond imagining.

Backlash theorists, as we shall see, imagine countless conspiracies in which the wealthy, powerful, and well connected—the liberal media, the atheistic scientists, the obnoxious eastern elite—pull the strings and make the puppets dance. And yet the backlash itself has been a political trap so devastating to the interests of Middle America that even the most diabolical of string-pullers would have had trouble dreaming it up. Here, after all, is a rebellion against "the establishment" that has wound up abolishing the tax on inherited estates. Here is a movement whose response to the power structure is to make the rich even richer; whose answer to the inexorable degradation of working-class life is to lash out angrily at labor unions and liberal workplace-safety programs; whose solution to the rise of ignorance in America is to pull the rug out from under public education.

Like a French Revolution in reverse—one in which the sans-culottes pour down the streets demanding more power for the aristocracy—the backlash pushes the spectrum of the acceptable to the right, to the right, farther to the right. It may never bring prayer back to the schools, but it has rescued all manner of right-wing economic nostrums from history's dustbin. Having rolled back the landmark economic reforms of the sixties (the war on poverty) and those of the thirties (labor law, agricultural price supports, banking regulation), its leaders now turn their guns on the accomplishments of the earliest years of progressivism (Woodrow Wilson's estate tax; Theodore Roosevelt's antitrust measures). With a little more effort, the backlash may well repeal the entire twentieth century.

As a formula for holding together a dominant political coalition, the backlash seems so improbable and so self-contradictory that liberal observers often have trouble believing it is actually happening. By all rights, they figure, these two groups—business and blue-collar—should be at each other's throats. For the Republican Party to present itself as the champion of working-class America strikes liberals as such an egregious denial of political reality that they dismiss the whole phenomenon, refusing to take it seriously.

The Great Backlash, they believe, is nothing but crypto-racism, or a disease of the elderly, or the random gripings of religious rednecks, or the protests of "angry white men" feeling left behind by history.

But to understand the backlash in this way is to miss its power as an idea and its broad popular vitality. It keeps coming despite everything, a plague of bitterness capable of spreading from the old to the young, from Protestant fundamentalists to Catholics and Jews, and from the angry white man to every demographic shading imaginable.

It matters not at all that the forces that triggered the original "silent majority" back in Nixon's day have long since disappeared; the backlash roars on undiminished, its rage carrying easily across the decades. The confident liberals who led America in those days are a dying species. The New Left, with its gleeful obscenities and contempt for the flag, is extinct altogether. The whole "affluent society," with its paternalistic corporations and powerful labor unions, fades farther into the ether with each passing year. But the backlash endures. It continues to dream its terrifying dreams of national decline, epic lawlessness, and betrayal at the top regardless of what is actually going on in the world.

Along the way what was once genuine and grassroots and even "populist" about the backlash phenomenon has been transformed into a stimulus-response melodrama with a plot as formulaic as an episode of "The O'Reilly Factor" and with results as predictable—and as profitable—as Coca-Cola advertising. In one end you feed an item about, say, the menace of gay marriage, and at the other end you generate, almost mechanically, an uptick of middle-American indignation, angry letters to the editor an electoral harvest of the most gratifying sort.

From the air-conditioned heights of a suburban office complex this may look like a new age of reason, with the Web sites singing each to each, with a mall down the way that every week has miraculously anticipated our subtly shifting tastes, with a global economy whose rich rewards just keep flowing, and with a long parade of rust-free Infinitis purring down the streets of beautifully manicured planned communities. But on closer inspection the country seems more like a panorama of madness and delusion worthy of Hieronymous Bosch: of sturdy blue-collar patriots reciting the Pledge while they strangle their own life chances; of small farmers proudly voting themselves off the land; of devoted family men carefully seeing to it that their children will never be able to afford college or proper health care; of working-class guys in midwestern cities cheering as they deliver up a landslide for a candidate whose policies will end their way of life, will transform their region into a "rust belt," will strike people like them blows from which they will never recover.

DISCUSSION QUESTIONS

1. Frank argues that backlash conservatism creates numerous contradictions. Explore some of the contradictions. Why does he view them as "self-damaging"?

2. At one point, Frank offers the following semi-humorous contention: "With a little more effort, the backlash may well repeal the entire twentieth century." Explain what he means by that.

3. The thrust of Frank's argument rests on the belief that while backlash conservatism offers cultural issues to motivate voters, subsequent economic policy ruins the livelihoods of those same voters. In essence, he thinks economics should be more fundamental than social issues. Do you agree? Is it "deranged" for voters to allow concern for divisive social/cultural issues to trump economic concerns?

18 *Paul Street and Anthony DiMaggio*

THE MYTH OF THE TEA PARTY

Since the early days of the Obama presidency, the conservative, libertarian Tea Party movement has been a constant presence on the U.S. political landscape. Republican 2012 presidential candidates fall over themselves to get in the good graces of the Tea Party faithful. GOP (Grand Old Party) Congressional leaders, particularly in the House, craft policies to curry favor with the most extreme elements of the right wing. And the media cover every move of the Tea Party as if the future of the nation depends on it. Independent journalist Paul Street and political scientist Anthony DiMaggio have written a book about the Tea Party phenomenon, Crashing the Tea Party: Mass Media and the Campaign to Remake American Politics *(2011). In this article, they summarize some of their main themes. Chief among them is their argument that, contrary to popular portrayal, the Tea Party is not an insurgent protest movement tied to ultra conservative principles that have dragged "establishment" Republicans reluctantly to the far right. Rather, they view it as the culmination of the Republican Party's 30-plus year rightward drift, a party effort to cut taxes and slash spending so as to delegitimize the post–New Deal social welfare state and undermine the very notion of government itself, save for those aspects of the government that solidify the interests of big business. In almost all ways that matter, then, the Tea Party and the Republican Party share the same ideological and policy agenda.*

Elite pundits and other members of the political class love to blame the Tea Party for the ever more insane rightward drift of American politics and policy that has been on terrible display in 2011—culminating in the "debt ceiling deal" of August 2, 2011, when the conservative Democratic president Barack Obama signed on to a "deficit reduction" plan that included only spending cuts and no tax increases while setting up Social Security and Medicare for future near-term attacks. Conservative *New York Times* columnist David Brooks, reflecting on why the Republicans would fail to sign on to Obama's initial offer of a $4 trillion reduction in the deficit over ten years—a reduction that would have relied primarily on social spending

Source: "Beyond the Tea Party" by Paul Street and Anthony DiMaggio from *Z Magazine,* September 2011. Used by permission.

cuts for Social Security, Medicare, and other social programs—argued, "If the Republican Party were a normal party it would . . . seize the opportunity to put a long-term limit on the growth of government. It would seize the opportunity to put the country on a sound fiscal footing." But "over the past few years," Brooks argued, the Republican Party "has been infected by a faction that is more of a psychological protest than a practical, governing alternative. The members of this movement do not accept the logic of compromise, no matter how sweet the terms. . . . The members of this movement do not accept the legitimacy of scholars and intellectual authorities." Though he did not formally say so, this "protest movement" Brooks referenced was, of course, the Tea Party.

Three weeks later, *Washington Post* national correspondent Dan Balz pointed to "the hold the tea party movement continues to have on [the Republican] party"—the "biggest obstacle" House Speaker John Boehner had to "overcome" on the path to a "deal." At the outer reaches of blame-the-Tea Party madness, Brooks's fellow *Times* columnist Maureen Dowd waxed knowingly on how "the Tea Party drives [the government] Thunderbird off the cliff with the president and speaker of the House strapped in the back." Dowd was astonished at the power of "the towel-snapping Tea Party crazies," who have "changed the entire discussion. They've neutralized the White House. They've whipped their [GOP] leadership into submission. They've taken taxes and revenues off the table. They've withered the stock and bond markets," Dowd wrote, echoing Obama's claim that a small House "faction" of Tea Party "conservatives" was holding the U.S. economy "captive."

By the time of the manufactured debt-ceiling crisis that sparked Brooks's comment, it had become standard fare in media commentary to refer to extremism in Washington as being driven by the Tea Party "insurgency," which was thought to be pulling the more "establishment" and "moderately"-oriented Republican Party (and Democrats) to the right, in what represented a veritable "revolution" in U.S. politics. But Brooks and the rest of the media establishment were missing key points, as usual. The Republican Party didn't, and doesn't, care about "putting the country on a sound fiscal footing." Part of its ultra-rejectionism is, sadly, a normal hyper-partisanship of a GOP that refuses to accept any Democratic presidency, and resists anything Obama wants. Senate Minority Leader Mitch McConnell has explicitly stated more than once that the Republicans' top priority is to make Obama a one-term president—a rather brazen thing for him to announce as the country struggled with its worst economic crisis in 70 years.

Partisan goals and Tea Party histrionics aside, the Republican Party's official goal of "deficit reduction" has long been cover for its deeper, ideologically driven, and plutocratic agenda. Republicans have taken advantage of every opportunity over the last three decades to run up sky high deficits and debt in the name of promoting tax cuts for the rich, endless expansion of the militarist-imperialist state, and ever increasing corporate welfare, as seen in recent examples such as the bank bailout. Most of the nation's public debt is a creation of the Republicans themselves, who expect the public to believe that they have "found God" again, after they were thrown out of power in 2008.

The extraordinary cynicism of this practice is clear enough: pursue irresponsible fiscal policies while in power, then push forward with propagandistic initiatives such as the "cut, cap, and balance" amendment, which Republicans would never have considered passing when they controlled the White House and Congress. "Deficit reduction," after all, is not a serious policy in its own right, but a weapon to be called upon whenever Democrats take power. This is no small part of what former Vice President Dick Cheney meant when he said that "deficits don't matter," in response to the soon-to-be-fired Secretary of the Treasury Paul O'Neill's warning about the fiscal impact of massive tax cuts for the rich combined with giant increases in military spending.

Republicans want nothing less than complete destruction of the last remnants of the liberal state. They are driven by the desire to wage hard-right ideological warfare, demolish social welfare programs, smash workers' organizations, concentrate political power, and advance the interests of their big money backers. Observing that Obama had actually been pressing for greater deficit reduction than the Republicans last July, *Times* correspondent Jackie Calmes noted that the Republicans' "dynamic in the debt talks reflects the culmination of a 30-year evolution in Republican thinking, dating to the start of President Ronald Reagan's administration. The change is from emphasizing balanced budgets—or at least lower deficits—to what tax-cutting conservatives have called 'starve the beast,' that is, cut taxes and force government to shrink." Calmes forgot to mention that the Republicans only want to shrink what the left sociologist Pierre Bourdieu called the left hand of the state—the parts of the public sector that serve the social and democratic needs of the non-affluent majority, while the right hand of the state remains well fed.

THE TEA PARTY IS THE GOP

Brooks was further off base when he argued that the Republican Party had been taken over by the Tea Party "protest movement." As we show in our new book *Crashing the Tea Party: Mass Media and the Campaign to Remake American Politics*, the conventional mainstream description of the Tea Party phenomenon as a popular protest movement is dramatically off base. The Tea Party is a loose, elite-directed conglomeration of partisan interest groups set on returning the Republican Party to power. Despite protestations to the contrary, it is partisan Republican to the core, its leading activists and main supporters accurately described by one mainstream reporter as "super-Republicans." It is not an uprising or protest

against the existing political system. Rather, it is a reactionary, top-down manifestation of that system, dressed up and sold as an outsider rebellion set on changing the rules in Washington and across the country.

Consistent with the long-term rightward trajectory of the Republican Party and U.S. politics since the 1970s, its basic function, enabled by a corporate media, was to help the deeply unpopular (because so transparently plutocratic) Republican Party re-brand itself in deceptive grassroots and populist clothing to take political advantage of the widespread economic insecurity imposed by the epic recession of 2008–2009 during the mid-term congressional and state elections of November 2010. Matt Taibbi got it right last year: "The Tea Party today is being pitched in the media as this great threat to the Republican Party; in reality, the Tea Party is the GOP."

Tea Party/"super Republican" positions are consistent with the deeper and longer-term rightward drift of the Republican Party and American politics more broadly over the last 35 years of the neoliberal era. According to a common narrative in the mass media, the contemporary bipartisan political system is terribly polarized along a left/right continuum, with Democrats moving dramatically to the left and Republicans moving somewhat less dramatically to the right. This is a great illusion. Republican politicians have become far more reactionary than the Democrats have been "liberal" over the last half century and the rightward shift of the Republican Party is the main cause of such polarization. Democratic Party liberalism rose in the 1960s and 1970s—a reflection largely of the defeat and subsequent exodus of center-right southern Democrats from the party. From the Carter administration onward, however, Democrats have grown increasingly conservative in their embrace of neoliberalism and their declining support for worker protections and entitlement programs. The Democratic Party today is essentially a party of moderate conservatives, as reflected in Bill Clinton's celebration of his "Eisenhower Republican" orientation, and in

Obama's deep commitment to "compromise" and "middle ground." (Such an approach can't help but pull Obama and the rest of the party in an ever rightward direction.) Since the 1970s, by contrast, Republicans became nearly twice as conservative, never moving back to the center.

This dangerous rightward tilt has resulted from a number of factors in the neoliberal era, including:

- The ever-rising significance of big money in U.S. politics and policy at the same time that the U.S. has grown more savagely unequal.

- The rise of powerful new organizations (e.g. Americans for Tax Reform, the Club for Growth, the Christian Coalition, and many others groups) representing the right wing and business agendas.

- The atrophy of the U.S. labor movement (unions now represent less than 1 in 10 private sector workers, down from 1 in 3 in 1970) and mass membership in liberal and progressive organizations, formerly critical counterweights to an unmitigated business agenda in federal and state government.

- The increasingly immigrant-based composition of the U.S. workforce, which fuels nativist reaction at the same time as it robs labor of workers with citizenship rights and a long-term commitment to working and living conditions in the U.S.

- The Republican takeover of the formerly Democratic U.S. South and the rise of a more deeply reactionary, largely southern-led Republican Party in the wake of the Civil Rights legislation and judicial decisions of the 1960s and 1970s.

- The rising significance of primary elections (which tend to empower the GOP's hard right base relative to more Republican moderates) relative to general elections resulting from the escalated creation of solidly Republican and solidly Democratic legislative districts.

- The rise of mass voter apathy and demobilization, which favors highly organized right wing and right-leaning business interests.

- Corporate media consolidation, the decline of reliable and quality journalism willing and able to give the popular majority the accurate information it requires to be productively engaged in democracy, and the right wing's construction of a powerful media empire and noise machine that includes: newspapers like the *New York Post* and the *Washington Times; Fox News;* a range of "public affairs" broadcasts on cable television; and a vast talk radio network that leans far to the right and promotes a nearly constant assault on the supposedly socialist Democratic Party, on the allegedly "liberal" mainstream media, and on purportedly dangerous left activists, groups, and causes.

Our review of ideology in Congress (as revealed in analysis of voting records of the parties from the interest group Americans for Democratic Action) finds that the current crop of Tea Party Republicans are no more extreme in their voting than Republicans were in other extreme right-wing periods in the past—as in the highly polarized late Clinton and early George W. Bush years, and in the mid 1990s, when the "Republican Revolution" shut down government numerous times in the name of gutting the social welfare state. With the partial exception of the August vote to raise the debt-ceiling (supported by 53 percent of the House's Tea Party Caucus and 81 percent of non-Tea Party House Republicans), there have been no real differences in the voting records of "Tea Party Republicans" and "establishment" Republicans when it comes to key political-economic issues. Last July, to take one example, House Republicans pledged to vote for an increase in the national debt limit only if it was accompanied by a "cut, cap, and balance pledge." That pledge required supporters to vote for "substantial cuts in spending," "passage of a Balanced Budget Amendment," and "enforceable spending caps." As a hallmark of the Tea Party agenda, support for such an effort should have separated Tea Party and "moderate" Republicans to a significant degree. In fact, the bill was supported by 93 percent of the House's 60 Tea Party Caucus members and by 94 percent of its 180 non-Tea Party Republicans.

DISMAL DEMOBILIZING DEMOCRATS

Democrats have also consistently pointed to the Tea Party specter to rally voters to agree to cower under the umbrella of a lesser evil Democratic Party. "Sure," the Democrats' message to their liberal and progressive voting "base" runs: "we may not have lived up to our progressive campaign promises of democratic change, but look at who we have to deal with and who stands to win if we are voted out: the swamp-fed Tea Party monster."

Times columnist Ross Douthat put his finger on a key point: "The not-so secret secret is that the White House has given ground on purpose. Just as Republicans want to use the debt ceiling to make the president live with bigger spending cuts than he would otherwise support, Obama's political team wants to use those cra-a-a-zy Tea Partiers to make Democrats live with bigger cuts than they normally would support." Douthat thought the Administration wanted a "right-leaning deficit deal" in its effort to woo those all-powerful (in a winner-take-all two party elections system with a closely divided electorate) and supposedly ideology-averse independent voters for the 2012 election, who had been told again and again (falsely) that Obama is a left leaning big government liberal.

There may have been some truth in that formulation, but the bigger story was that the center-right Obama wanted to reward his big money backers and was more than willing to alienate much of his liberal base—even going to

the point of screwing with Medicare and Social Security (in by now standard defiance of his campaign pledges)—in order to serve his elite business class masters.

The wishes of those masters were confirmed in mid-July when Standard & Poor's and Moody's (the nation's and world's leading credit and bond-rating agencies) made it clear that they wanted to see roughly $4 trillion in spending cuts over 10 years in order for the U.S. government to be permitted to maintain its longstanding AAA rating.

Of course, "those cra-a-a-zy" Teapublicans owe no small part of their current powerful position in Washington to the Democratic Party's savage demobilization of its own progressive base as it acted in accord with its own longstanding identity as (in former Nixon strategist Kevin Phillips's phrase) "history's second most enthusiastic capitalist party." The left-liberal political scientist Sheldon Wolin easily foretold this pathetic Democratic performance in his chilling 2008 book, *Democracy Incorporated*: "The timidity of a Democratic Party mesmerized by centrist precepts points to the crucial fact that, for the poor, minorities, the working-class, anticorporatists, pro-environmentalists, and anti-imperialists, there is no opposition party working actively on their behalf. And this despite the fact that these elements are recognized as the loyal base of the Party. By ignoring dissent and assuming the dissenters have no alternative, the Party serves an important, if ironical, stabilizing function and in effect marginalizes any possible threat to the corporate allies of the Republicans. Unlike the Democrats, however, the Republicans, with their combination of reactionary and innovative elements, are a cohesive, if not a coherent, opposition force."

The electoral consequences of the dismal Democrats' centrist timidity were deadly. In the general midterm contest, the Democrats suffered from significant declines in voter participation on the part of segments of the electorate that played key roles in their triumphs in the 2006 (Congressional) and 2008 (Congressional and presidential) election cycles—union households, young voters, black voters. By contrast, voters who identified themselves as "conservative" increased their share of the active electorate significantly from 2006 and 2010. This was all it took for the highly energized and re-branded Republican Party to clean up in a mid-term election, when turnout is considerably smaller. As the left analyst and activist Charlie Post notes, no big "shift to the right" was required or took place. "An 8 percent shift in an election where only 40 percent voted— a shift of approximately three percent of the total eligible voters—accounts for the Republicans' victory."

YES, HE DID MEAN IT

As Wolin noted well before the contemporary Tea Party brand was formally launched, the word "conservative" merits quotation marks when used in connection to the radically regressive 21st century GOP. This is the hard right party that the deeply conservative Obama can't stop readily accommodating, much to the all-too-credulous dismay of many liberals and progressives who cling (against mountains of evidence) to the childish notion that the president is really one of them.

One of the more ridiculous aspects of the debt-ceiling drama has been the claim of Democratic pundits and spin doctors (e.g. MSNBC's Lawrence O'Donnell) that Obama never really meant to institute draconian Social Security, Medicare, and social spending cuts—that the "grand bargain" he offered was really just a clever ploy to expose the Republicans' partisan and arch-regressive agenda.

This was another preposterous narrative, as was seen when Obama subsequently signed on to the bipartisan "Gang of Six" budget plan, which "offered huge tax breaks for the wealthy, while lowering Social Security benefits for retirees and the disabled."

The Irrelevant Majority

The high stakes budget and debt-ceiling policy drama of 2011 stood in standard bold defiance of majority public opinion. Most Americans believed that:

- job creation should be a bigger government priority than deficit reduction;
- social protections should be expanded (not contracted);
- the rich are under-taxed;
- wealth inequality and poverty are the nation's leading moral issues;
- big business and the wealthy exercise far too much influence over government;
- government dollars should be significantly transferred from military to social programs (Obama's non-existent peace dividend);
- Social Security and Medicare benefits should be protected and expanded;
- public sector workers deserve and require full collective bargaining rights the very rights that have come under attack in numerous Republican-controlled state legislatures this year;

But none of this sort of longstanding majority progressive opinion ever seems to matter in the U.S., where, as the American philosopher John Dewey noted more than a century ago, "politics is the shadow cast on society by big business." The hope that anything progressive can be achieved within and through that system seems ever more dubious with each passing electoral extravaganza and political branding campaign. But elections and opinion polls are hardly the only or most effective method of expressing public sentiments over and against concentrated wealth and power. Mass street demonstrations and strikes and social movement formation beneath and beyond the dominant institutions are the more relevant popular avenues.

While serious progressives must surely fight for reforms and corrections like the expansion and protection of labor rights, carbon emission limits, and welfare benefits (and much more), they should also realize that reforms will not suffice. Dewey was surely correct when he warned that the nation's democratic institutions would never escape the giant capitalist "shadow" as long as power rests with "business for private profit through private control of banking, land, industry, reinforced by command of the press, press agents, and other means of publicity and propaganda."

DISCUSSION QUESTIONS

1. Explain how the media have covered the rise of the Tea Party movement and its relationship to "establishment" Republicans. From the vantage point of Street and DiMaggio, in what ways is this narrative flawed?
2. What are some of the key factors that have led to the rightward drift within the GOP? And where are the Democrats in all of this? Why haven't they been an effective counterpoint to the Tea Party movement generally, and in particular with reference to the debt ceiling crisis in the summer of 2011?
3. If Street and DiMaggio are correct in their analysis, do we really have a two-party system in the United States? Why or why not?

19 *Lawrence Lessig*

DEMOCRACY AFTER CITIZENS UNITED
The Supreme Court and Campaign Finance

On January 21, 2010, the U.S. Supreme Court shook up the world of American politics with its 5–4 decision in the case of Citizens United v. Federal Election Commission. *In its first significant decision concerning campaign finance since 1976 (in a case that equated campaign spending with speech), the Court overturned the 2002 McCain-Feingold restrictions placed on the ability of corporations and other groups to make independent campaign expenditures. Specifically the Court ruled that Congress, via its 2002 law, does not have the power to limit political free speech, unless the speech in question amounts to corruption. In his critical analysis of the case, Harvard law professor Lawrence Lessig draws an important distinction between personal corruption (wherein someone gets money to perform a political favor for someone else—essentially a bribe) and institutional corruption (wherein the influence of money weakens the overall effectiveness of an institution). Lessig chides the Court for viewing the legitimate role of Congress to include limiting political speech only if the former type of corruption is involved. In Lessig's opinion, the latter type of corruption—institutional corruption—is far more pervasive and far more damaging to the political process. He explores the Court's legal reasoning in depth, particularly the arguments of Justice Anthony Kennedy, who wrote the majority opinion. And Lessig contends that courts and legislatures need new, more expansive ways to think about how corruption works to undermine public faith in our political institutions. With corporations now free to devote unlimited amounts of money on independent political expenditures, the* Citizens United *decision promises to enhance the already enormous impact of corporations on congressional and presidential elections.*

Institutional corruption does not refer to the knowing violation of any law or ethical rule. This is not the problem of Rod Blagojevich, or, more generally, of bad souls acting badly. It instead describes an influence, financial or otherwise, within an economy of influence, that weakens

Source: "Democracy after Citizens United" by Lawrence Lessig from *Boston Review,* Volume 35, Number 5, September–October 2010, http://bostonreview.net/BR35.5/lessig.php. Copyright © 2010. Used by permission of the author.

the effectiveness of an institution, especially by weakening public trust in that institution. (An "economy of influence" rather than the simpler "system of influence" to emphasize the reciprocal character of such influence, often requiring little or no direct coordination.)

Congress is a paradigm case. Members of Congress run privately financed campaigns. The contributions that fund those campaigns are not illegal, or even unethical. To the contrary, they are protected speech under the First Amendment.

Yet arguably—or maybe obviously—those contributions are (1) an influence (2) within an economy of influence that has (3) (quite likely) weakened the ability of Congress to do its work, by (4) (certainly) weakening public trust in Congress. The vast majority of Americans believe money buys results in Congress; less than a quarter of Americans believe the institution worthy of their trust. When "free-market" Republicans vote to support milk subsidies or sugar tariffs, or when "pro-consumer" Democrats vote to exempt used-car dealers from consumer financial-protection legislation, it is easy to understand the mistrust and hard to believe that the influence of money hasn't weakened the ability of members to serve the principles, or even the interests, they were elected to represent.

This is "corruption" not because it describes the acts of evil or corrupted individuals. Members of Congress are insanely hard-working, decent souls, the overwhelming majority of whom entered public service to do good, as they see it. And indeed, the traditional corruption of politics—bribery—is likely at its lowest point in American history. From the perspective of criminal law, this is among the cleanest Congresses ever.

Instead, this is "corruption" because it weakens the integrity of the institution, of Congress itself. The framers intended Congress to be "dependent upon the People alone." But the private funding of public campaigns has bred within Congress a second, and conflicting, dependency. As with an alcoholic mother trying to care for her children, that conflicting dependency does not change the

good intentions of members of Congress—they still want to serve the public interest they thought themselves elected to serve. But as with an alcoholic mother trying to care for her children, that conflicting dependency distracts members from their good intentions, directing their focus more and more toward the challenge of raising money.

Such a dependency would distract any of us. Institutional corruption is not a particular weakness that affects a particular class within a particular institution. It is instead, as cognitive psychology and behavioral economics increasingly reveal, among the most human of reactions that evolution has produced. We all reward those whom we depend upon, whether or not such reward is consistent with our ideals or objectives. And we are especially prone to reward those whom we depend upon when our conduct is viewed as justified within the institution with which we are affiliated.

The solution to this form of corruption is not to extirpate human nature. Nor need we accept the corruption as simply part of the human condition. The solution, as the framers of the Constitution self consciously described, is to design institutions that avoid these conflicting dependencies. We can't presume that "angels [will] govern." But neither need we believe that every member of Congress is evil in order to recognize that a proper constitution prevents systems of dependence that draw representatives away from the interests they were elected to represent and the values they were chosen to serve. Indeed, when one studies the tiny dependencies that our framers sought obsessively to avoid (my favorite are the constitutional prohibitions intended to prevent dependence upon "foreign princes"—if only the framers had said "princes, foreign or domestic"), it is impossible to believe they wouldn't be astonished by the enormous dependencies that have evolved within their design. The one dependence they had in mind— "upon the People alone"—has almost become an afterthought.

On January 21, 2010, a year and a day after Barack "change the way Washington works" Obama was sworn into office, the Supreme Court rendered the environment for this institutional corruption much worse. By a five-to-four vote, the Court in *Citizens United v. Federal Election Commission* (FEC) secured to corporations a right that individuals have had since the last equally fundamental Supreme Court decision on campaign finance (*Buckley v. Valeo,* 1976): the right to spend an unlimited amount on independent campaign expenditures. "Independent *expenditures*"—not contributions to candidates. And "*independent* expenditures"—not coordinated with the campaign. No doubt, as corporations exercise this new right, candidates will become skilled in the dance necessary to get enormous corporate wealth spent for their political benefit.

At issue in *Citizens United* was a limitation in the Bipartisan Campaign Reform Act of 2002 (BCRA, commonly known as McCain-Feingold). BCRA forbade any company from using corporate funds to influence an election within 60 days of that election, even if the funds were being used simply to discuss an issue, although in a way that plainly demonstrated support for or opposition to a candidate. Citizens United, a nonprofit corporation, wanted to use funds from its own treasury to promote a film critical of Hillary Clinton. BCRA blocked that use because the film in effect advocated voting against Hillary Clinton. Citizens United challenged the law as an unacceptable abridgment of its freedom of speech.

Citizens United might have spoken through other channels—for example, by setting up a political action committee (PAC) with its own treasury to which individuals could contribute. And the individuals who had created Citizens United were still free (because of *Buckley*) to spend independently as much as they wanted to advance their interests. Nonetheless, the Court held that Congress had no power to block the corporation itself from spending funds on political speech.

Under our current system of campaign finance, there is a fundamental gap between the interests of voters and of contributors.

There is a core aspiration in the *Citizens United* opinion with which everyone ought to

agree, but there also is much to quibble with, and there is much more that is very confused.

The Court was right to raise a red flag about a law that purported to block political speech.

Such a law should face a significant burden of justification, regardless of whether the target is the Chamber of Commerce or the Chinese government, and even though the relevant "speech" is not the direct words of a citizen, but words and video purchased with corporate money. I don't believe vigilance against improper government regulation of speech should turn upon whether the regulated entity is a "person," or whether the speech is pure speech or money-as-speech. Nor did the Court. Instead, the Court focused its inquiry on Congress's power. Congress, the Court held, has no power to remove this liberty to speak, because, regardless of the speaker and irrespective of the means, Congress has no legitimate interest in silencing political speech.

Unless that speech amounts to corruption. But here the Court was extremely narrow, and mistaken in my view, in its understanding of corruption. The only corruption the Court found that justifies the suppression of political speech is "quid pro quo" corruption. And as independent expenditures are, by definition at least, made independently of a political campaign, they cannot constitute quid pro quo corruption. There may be a quid. There may be a quo. But because the two are independent, there is no pro.

This clarity was not cut from whole cloth. Since *Buckley* there has been a recurring suggestion that the only corruption that is constitutionally cognizable—the only kind that suffices for restricting political speech—is quid pro quo corruption. As the Court itself said in *FEC v. NCPAC* (1985): "Corruption is a subversion of the political process," and the "hallmark of corruption is the financial quid pro quo: dollars for political favors."

But in 1990 the Court suggested a more expansive definition of corruption. In *Austin v. Michigan Chamber of Commerce* the Court upheld a Michigan law that prevented corporations using money from their general treasuries to fund independent expenditures in candidate elections. The Court thus recognized another kind of corruption, beyond quid pro quo, that would come from the

> corrosive and distorting effects of immense aggregations of wealth that are accumulated with the help of the corporate form and that have *little or no correlation with the public's support for the corporation's political ideas.* (Emphasis added)

So a divided Court held that campaign spending could be regulated in order to prevent these effects as well. And after *Austin,* no opinion of the Court again said that quid pro quo was the only way to corrupt the political process capable of justifying a restriction on speech. Until, that is, *Citizens United,* which overruled *Austin.*

Yet *why* this is the only sense of corruption that might justify a restriction on speech is not clear. The argument on this essential point in Justice Kennedy's majority opinion in *Citizens United* seems almost an afterthought. It is perhaps best captured in two closely related passages.

First, to the suggestion that there may be a corruption beyond quid pro quo tied to the special influence that money has within our political system, Justice Kennedy quotes an earlier opinion of his:

> Favoritism and influence are not . . . avoidable in representative politics. It is in the nature of an elected representative to favor certain policies, and, by necessary corollary, to favor the voters and contributors who support those policies.

Notice the words "and contributors." Without those two words, the statement is certainly true. The claim could be made even more strongly: favoring the policies that one's constituents favor is the essence of representative democracy (on at least one dominant conception of it). It was for the purpose of establishing precisely this sort of dependency of representatives on constituents that the framers created frequent elections in the House. As *Federalist No. 57* put it, "The House

of Representatives is so constituted as to support in the members an habitual recollection of their dependence on the people."

But adding the words "and contributors" not only makes the statement not obvious (as Justice Kennedy seems to believe), but in my view, plainly wrong. The framers did not intend to make representatives dependent upon contributors. Representatives were to be dependent upon voters, or, more generally, "the People alone." It is conceivable—assuming many contingencies—that a dependence upon contributors could in effect be the same as a dependence upon voters. For example, to borrow an idea from Yale's Bruce Ackerman and Ian Ayres, if elections were funded by what we could call "democracy vouchers," where citizens could allocate up to $50 to any candidate and candidates could receive money only from citizens in their districts, then a dependency upon voters might well be the same as, or close enough to, a dependency upon contributors. Candidates would have to spend time talking to voters, if only to raise money from them. And because of the small size of the vouchers, the dependence would be relatively equal. In this system, the sort of thing you need to do to make voters happy is the same sort of thing you need to do to make contributors happy.

Under our current system of campaign finance, however, there is no such overlap between the interests of voters and of contributors. There is instead a fundamental gap. That gap has many dimensions, but the simplest to remark is the geographical source of campaign funds. In the most critical cases, the vast majority of contributions are not even from the voters. Opensecrets.org reports that 67 percent of contributions to John Kerry's 2008 senate-reelection campaign came from outside Massachusetts. His Republican opponent received 73 percent of his funding from out-of-state donors. Maplight.org reports that since January of 2007 79 percent of contributions to California state legislators have come from out-of-district contributors. This gap between contributors and voters means that responsiveness to one is not necessarily responsiveness to the other. Once more, the sort of thing you need to do to make contributors happy is not the sort of thing you need to do to make voters happy.

A vibrant free-speech tradition need not prevent the regulation of institutional corruption in Congress.

This leads to the second critical passage from *Citizens United,* casually dismissive of the problem of institutional corruption:

> The appearance of influence or access . . . will not cause the electorate to lose faith in our democracy.

Among constitutional lawyers, this sort of claim is called "Lochnerism," and the moniker is not high praise. It derives from an infamous 1905 case, *Lochner v. New York,* in which the Supreme Court struck down New York's Bakeshop Act of 1895. That progressive statute included a maximum-hours requirement for workers in the baking industry and established minimum conditions for plumbing, flooring, product storage, and sanitation. The Republican-dominated state legislature passed the regulation twice, each time unanimously. In defending this statute before the Supreme Court, lawyers for the State of New York said the regulation was a health measure, intended to improve the well-being of overworked bakers.

The Supreme Court, however, rejected New York's argument. On the Court's view, the regulation of hours worked had no bearing on a worker's health. The statute thus must have had a different motivation behind it. And as the Court sussed that motivation out, it claimed that New York's true aim was to benefit labor at the expense of capital. The law was simple redistribution, and the Fourteenth Amendment, the Court held, banned such a taking from A to give to B.

But the question of whether the regulation does or does not affect the health of bakers is a factual one, not a matter of constitutional interpretation. So one might rightly ask: on what factual basis did the Court rest its judgment?

The answer is none. The Court had no evidence for its claim, while the State of New York had plenty. An 1894 report by the New York State

Labor Commissioner found that baking was an especially dangerous occupation, in part because of the extended hours of the baker. After a 30-year war between courts and legislators, the Supreme Court finally decided firmly that it was no longer in the business of second-guessing state or federal legislatures about the social conditions they purported to regulate. As the Court said in *West Coast Hotel v. Parrish* (1937): "Even if the wisdom of the policy be regarded as debatable and its effects uncertain, still the Legislature is entitled to its judgment."

It is the view of every current justice on the Supreme Court that *Lochner* was mistaken, and that the Court has no business second-guessing legislatures, at least when they pass regulations that restrict the liberty of contract. But when it comes to the First Amendment, Lochnerism is alive and well, and Justice Kennedy's opinion in *Citizens United* may well mark an extreme. For whether or not "the appearance of influence or access" will "cause the electorate to lose faith in our democracy" is a factual issue. It is not resolved by the observation that the expenditures merely are intended to persuade voters, and thus that the system, as Kennedy put it, "presupposes that the [voters] have the ultimate influence over elected officials." "Ultimate influence" isn't necessarily the issue; it may be that relative influence is all that matters to whether "the electorate [will] lose faith in our democracy."

And given the radical inequality between interests and expenditures, a voter could well reason: "even if it is ultimately only votes that count, whether you get votes depends upon whether you can outspend your opponent; whether you can outspend your opponent in turn depends upon whether you can raise enough money or inspire others to spend enough money on your behalf; thus, it is the race for campaign money that is the real race in American democracy; and thus," this voter could well conclude, "there is every reason in the world to lose faith in this democracy— conceived of as a system in which representatives are to be dependent upon the people."

Kennedy's opinion puts the factual question off the table. He hasn't proven his conclusion.

He hasn't even offered evidence to suggest it is true. He has, like the Court in *Lochner,* simply asserted what those without life tenure on a federal bench would have to prove. And as empirical evidence certainly contradicts Justice Kennedy's assertion—many Americans have "lost faith in our democracy," and the role of money in elections is high on the list of reasons for their skepticism—this keystone to the Court's decision is not likely to survive very long.

To be clear: I am not saying that the Court should treat First Amendment questions the way it treats questions about the regulation of contracts. I, along with every justice on the Court, believe that free speech deserves a much more vigorous defense against improper legislation than the liberty of contract. But one could believe that more stringent standards for regulating speech are justified, yet also reject what the Court did in *Citizens United.* The Court should not be able to assert the facts that purportedly justify its negation of legislation with nothing more than analogical reasoning to back its claims. The rejection of *Lochner* could mean that, in most contexts, the legislature gets an almost-free pass from review. But the Court should never be entitled to a similar free pass. When invalidating legislation, courts should have to work harder than this.

Maybe Kennedy could have done better. Maybe his point is that legislatures only can regulate the First Amendment right to speak in the name of preventing quid pro quo corruption, that no other corruption of democracy justifies a regulation of speech. Bribery, Kennedy would say, is a special case. It is of course legitimate that a legislature forbid "speech" that amounts to bribery: regulations against quid pro quo corruption are thus acceptable, even though they restrict speech (and especially, the power of "money as speech"). But beyond that narrow class of corrupting speech there is no other that could weigh against the right to speak.

The point is clear enough. But is it true? Do the reasons for regulating speech that offers a bribe only justify regulating bribery? Or do the same reasons cover a wider range of conduct that is arguably at odds with the democratic process—with the exclusive dependence on the people intended by the framers?

We recognize the right of the state to ban bribery, even though bribery is speech. The interest of the state in banning this form of speech overwhelms the right of the briber or the bribed to engage in it. That is because bribery short circuits a deliberative or democratic process. When a congressman inserts an earmark into an appropriations bill in exchange for $10,000, we presume the reason he had for inserting that earmark had nothing to do with the merits of the earmark. We presume, in other words, that the legislative decision was guided by a venal interest rather than a public interest.

The Court was not oblivious to the ways in which expenditures might affect the political process. But the justices certainly were ignorant about them.

But why do we so presume? What if the congressman could prove that he would have inserted the earmark anyway? What if he said, "I only take bribes to do what I otherwise would have done"? And what if we could be certain that the venal interest was irrelevant to the inclusion of the earmark, that the congressman had only the public interest in mind?

I take it as uncontroversial that the law should reject such a defense. Maybe the congressman's claim is true. But as well as protecting against decisions by legislators that are in fact guided by venal rather than public reasons, it is perfectly appropriate for a legislature to protect against decisions that *appear* to be guided by venal rather than public reasons, even when they are not. As *Buckley* says, the concern is with "preventing corruption and the appearance of corruption." It would be too much to expect the public to ignore the potential venality of a bribe—no one believes the First Amendment requires that prosecutors prove that, but for the bribe, the decision would not have been made.

Bribes are thus instances of personal corruption. They are regulable because we presume they corrupt legislators by distracting them from their proper focus—on legislation that serves the public interest.

Institutional corruption brings this same concern to the level of the legislature. If a legislature can regulate to keep individual legislators from making decisions that are dependent upon venal rather than public interests, why can't it regulate to keep the legislature as a whole from making decisions based on improper dependencies? If it can act to assure that individual legislators don't act, or seem to act, on an obviously improper dependency, why can't it act to assure that the legislature itself not act, or seem to act, on a different, but equally improper, dependency?

A dependency, for example, upon funders rather than voters. If the framers were clear that legislators are to be dependent only on the people, is it permissible for a legislature to protect itself from other dependencies? Kennedy has not shown why not.

In short, bribery is regulable because it manifests personal corruption, the deviation from a public to a venal interest. Yet Kennedy has offered no argument as to why acts that constitute institutional corruption shouldn't likewise be regulable, as manifesting, improperly, a dependency upon funders rather than upon voters.

My suggestion is that we therefore recognize two kinds of corruption. One is personal, or venal. This is bribery. The legislator takes money for a decision, giving rise to the presumption that he was acting not for the public interest, but for his own private, venal interest.

The other is institutional, or what we could call, building on the work of Fordham University professor Zephyr Teachout, "dependency corruption." Dependency corruption happens when an institution develops a dependency that conflicts with its intended dependency. This corruption doesn't look to evil acts by evil individuals; it looks instead to the economies of influence that have developed within a designed system. Regulation of dependency corruption aims to prevent the deviation of an institution from its proper or intended focus, just as regulation of quid pro quo corruption aims to prevent individual deviation from proper focus.

The charge against the current system of funding congressional campaigns thus comes to this: not only has it eroded trust in Congress (the Pew Research Center's latest numbers indicate trust in government and faith in Congress both at historic lows), it has also engendered a focus on interests distinct from the interests of the voters. A people should have the power to avoid just this sort of distraction, a.k.a., corruption. A vibrant free-speech tradition need not disable that power.

Even if my analysis is correct, a defender of the decision in *Citizens United* could insist that the expenditures at issue in that case were still independent expenditures, a step removed from any economy of dependence. And if they are indeed independent, how could they generate an improper dependency?

They need not, of course. My argument is not an argument of grammar. It is perfectly possible that massive expenditures made independently of a decision-maker have no plausibly corrupting effect on the decision-maker. For example, millions are spent each year writing amicus briefs for the Supreme Court—sometimes on a single case. Yet no one thinks that the expenditures themselves, as distinct from the arguments in the briefs, affect the decisions of a justice. As the money spent there is irrelevant to the justice, the money does not in this sense corrupt.

But independent expenditures are not benign in every case. There was ample evidence presented in *Citizens United* that campaigns are aware of the independent expenditures made on their behalf. Indeed, there was plenty of evidence that the expenditures were reported directly to the campaigns. And while only the venally corrupt or the stupid would expressly link those expenditures to some kind of action, there are plenty of ways to coordinate without coordination. To paraphrase Boston political boss Martin Lomasney, Washington is the kind of city where one never writes if one can call, never calls if one can speak, never speaks if one can nod, and never nods if one can wink. Little doubt that in such a rich environment of reciprocity, open deals are rarely essential.

The Court, of course, was not completely oblivious to the ways in which such expenditures might affect the political process. But, with respect, the justices certainly were ignorant about them. The Court conceded that large expenditures by a corporation could raise questions. But the Court also insisted that those concerns could be addressed adequately by a regime of transparency in which all expenditures must be disclosed. The First Amendment, that is, need not be seen to deny the danger of corruption through independent expenditures; it instead simply limits the remedy to an acknowledged danger. And here, the Court thought, the constitutionally permissible remedy to a danger from large, tacitly coordinated expenditures is to require the speakers to disclose.

So long as First Amendment "Lochnerism" prevails on this Court, Congress will be unable to address institutional corruption.

But in this simple solution, the Court is overlooking an important way in which money—the right to spend—actually influences campaigns.

The assumption of the Court was that $1 million of influence would be disclosed as $1 million of influence and that voters could then reckon whether that level of influence should matter to their decision. Yet as economists Marcos Chamon and Ethan Kaplan have argued in their "iceberg theory" of campaign finance, the influence from campaign expenditures may be independent of the amount actually spent. The influence on any particular candidate, they maintain, also would depend on the credible threat of expenditures to benefit the candidate's opponent.

For example, the incentive effect of a $10,000 contribution to a candidate could be the equivalent to the incentive effect of a $2,000 contribution if the $2,000 contribution is bundled with a credible threat to contribute $8,000 to the candidate's opponent. The threat creates its own incentive. The more credible the threat, the greater the incentive.

These threats, however, are not reported on any campaign disclosure form. In the example above, the $2,000 contribution would have to be reported, but the $8,000 threat would not. The $2,000 is thus the visible tip of the iceberg, while the $8,000 is the bulk, hidden from the public's view.

Chamon and Kaplan wrote in the pre-*Citizens United* world, where the maximum "corporate contribution" through a corporate PAC was $5,000 per cycle. But the significance of their theory in a post-*Citizens United* world is much greater, for the power of a potential threat is limited by the maximum contribution allowed. After *Citizens United* those limits are removed. And while the threats must be of independent expenditures, there are obvious new ways in which corporate wealth can now translate into significant political influence.

Imagine, for example, that Exxon let it be known that it was willing to spend up to $1 million in any congressional district to promote candidates who are skeptical of global-warming science. Or imagine that Google let it be known that it would run up to $1 million in online ads to defeat global-warming skeptics. Neither position would necessarily be "coordination" sufficient to render the expenditures non-independent: both announcements could be made well before candidates are even chosen by parties. Yet, if the iceberg theory is correct, in neither case would all the money have to be spent in order to have its intended effect. Google might actually spend only a thousand dollars, and it would report that amount. But its influence would be far beyond what it reported, so long as its threat was credible.

Does the influence or threat of independent expenditures within the economy of influence that is privately funded campaigns further weaken the effectiveness of Congress to do its job? Does it further weaken public trust of Congress by confirming that "money buys results"?

Again, the answer depends on the facts. It is not simply a matter of logic, but instead hangs upon the actual expectations of an actual public. I have my intuitions. Maybe they are wrong. Maybe American cynicism is already so great that even a radical increase in a conflicting dependency won't further weaken public trust.

Lochnerism, however, will not permit us to know. So long as First Amendment Lochnerism prevails on this Court, so long as Justices are prepared to let their own factual speculations trump legislative fact-finding, and so long as judicial intuitions about the impact of disclosure requirements are permitted to decide the issue, Congress will be unable to address institutional corruption directly by limiting expenditures that create a reality or appearance of unacceptable dependency.

Yet Congress could still act in less-direct ways to prevent dependency corruption. It could, for example, adopt a voluntary, small-dollar contribution system under which candidates agree to take no more than, say, a hundred dollars from any citizen, and the government matches that amount with some multiple. Or Congress could enact the Ackerman-Ayres system of democracy vouchers. Both alternatives would provide important reform to the current system. The former is the idea behind the Fair Elections Now Act, whose sponsors estimate that it could raise more money for campaigns than the current system does. The latter would be even more dramatic. At $50 a voter, the voucher system would pump almost four times the amount spent on congressional campaigns in 2008 into a non-corrupting form of campaign finance.

But the blindness to this more fundamental corruption—a corruption that has likely done more damage to the United States in the last decade than all of the quid pro quo corruption in American history combined—will continue to limit the imagination and conduct of both courts and legislatures. We need a clearer way to mark this type of good-soul, institutional corruption. We need a broader recognition of its harms. Because the idea that the protections of the First Amendment would bend to allow punishment of small-time crooks like Rod Blagojevich and Duke Cunningham, yet block efforts to reform the economy of influence that has produced the Great Recession, or to confront global warming, is just crazy. We need a better lens to show why.

DISCUSSION QUESTIONS

1. Clearly identify what the Supreme Court said in its decision in *Citizens United v. Federal Election Commission.* How is it likely to change elections in the United States at the national level?
2. What shortcomings does Lessig find in Justice Kennedy's reasoning in the *Citizens United* case?
3. Explain the distinction Lessig makes between personal corruption and institutional corruption. Why is personal corruption such a relatively minor concern for Lessig's argument? And why is institutional corruption such a major concern?

20 *Katrina vanden Heuvel*

JUST DEMOCRACY
The Crisis and Opportunity in American Elections

Competitive political parties and frequent elections are part of the backbone of democracy. In this article, Katrina vanden Heuvel, Editor and Publisher of The Nation *magazine, surveys the health of democracy in America as the fall 2008 presidential election approaches. She finds some encouraging signs— millions of new voters registered and turned out in the spring 2008 presidential primaries at record levels in many states. She also sees rising hope and enthusiasm, generated in large part by the candidacy of Illinois Senator Barack Obama and his epic Democratic primary battle with New York Senator Hillary Clinton. Obscuring these bright spots, however, are ominous dark clouds of crisis, and vanden Heuvel highlights several key flash points in the electoral process, some relatively new, others long entrenched in the system. In order to address and hopefully overcome these dilemmas, vanden Heuvel then outlines an array of reforms—part of a "holistic democracy agenda"— that attempt to revive the promise of our electoral system, including changes in how we elect our leaders and how we fund their campaigns. The entire plan comes down to an effort to build a Just Democracy movement that aims to inspire people's confidence in our beleaguered political system—making an informed, engaged citizenry more likely.*

Democracy in America made a surprising—and welcome—comeback this spring. Many of us assumed the front-loaded primary season meant the contest would be less democratic than ever, but instead Barack Obama and Hillary Clinton were forced to fight the longest and most nationally inclusive race for a presidential nomination in history. About 3.5 million new voters registered and cast ballots, boosting participation among young people and people of color to new highs. More people voted in the Democratic primaries in North Carolina and Indiana than turned out for John Kerry in those states during the 2004 presidential race. The previously untapped potential of our democracy was on full display.

Source: Katrina vanden Heuvel, "Just Democracy," *The Nation,* Volume 287, Number 3, 21/28 July 2008, pp. 31–40.

No candidate has spoken to this potential more directly than Obama. Millions of Americans embraced the presumptive Democratic nominee's "firm conviction . . . that working together we can move beyond some of our old racial wounds, and that in fact we have no choice if we are to continue on the path of a more perfect union."

Obama's audacious hope is intoxicating, but that hope must be sustained by a vision of what a more perfect union would look like.

Essential to realizing that vision in the twenty-first century is a transformation that doesn't rank high in any poll or list of probable reforms.

If we are to realize the potential the primary season has revealed and begin moving toward that more perfect union, if we are to finally transcend our downsized politics of excluded alternatives, progressives will have to drive a bold agenda to invigorate democracy at home and capture greater power for the people. There may never be a better time than the next few years.

Some in Washington have touted the export of democracy abroad (often with disastrous results) while they neglect our own. The terrible irony is that they would not grant unconditional funding to a country whose democratic design looks like ours. The machinery of American democracy is broken: mistakes, chicaneries, snafus and disasters debilitate almost every race everywhere, every two years, with the result that an increasing number of Americans report feeling alienated by the voting process.

There are clear signs of the decline of our democracy: registration and voter turnout lag far behind other democracies; ever larger numbers of citizens are disenfranchised; the cost of running for office is spiraling out of control, excluding citizens of average means from participating in government; and our media, the forum for the healthy debate so essential to any democracy, are increasingly incapable of acting in the public interest.

This decline predates the 2000 presidential contest. Some of its roots are found in the invidious history of racial discrimination of which Senator Obama (all too briefly) reminded us. That unresolved election focused attention on our increasingly dysfunctional electoral system and the larger problems of our democracy. The past seven years of extremist Republican rule have stymied every effort to address the flaws that the 2000 election revealed.

Pollsters tell us that "process reforms" don't galvanize voters. Candidates slight them. Pundits often scorn them, assuming that money will always dominate and that corruption is simply a fact of nature. But the primary season just past—which saw Americans of every background and political persuasion becoming experts on superdelegates and tuning in to a live broadcast of the Democratic Party's rules and bylaws committee meeting—suggests that Americans do care about how our elections are run, and that they want them to be fair and functional. Obama—and, for that matter, Republican John McCain, who made his reputation as an election reformer—should, in this election year, address the concerns of millions of Americans about a broken system. And in 2009 progressives should recognize that it is vital to break from cynicism and advance a vision of government that is, in fact, of the people, by the people and for the people. It's time for Just Democracy.

THE CRISIS

American representative democracy is in trouble. New flash points arise daily; others have been with us for years:

- The Supreme Court recently upheld Indiana's harsh new law requiring voters to present a photo ID or be denied their right to vote, despite its potential to disenfranchise many people. That was a green light for building new barriers to voting.

- The Brennan Center for Justice at the New York University School of Law recently declared Florida to be "the most hostile state in the nation to new voters—particularly in traditionally underserved communities that might otherwise see record-breaking participation in this presidential election year." The number of registered voters in Florida has actually dropped seven percentage points since 2004, to only 65 percent of those eligible.

- Roughly one-third of all eligible Americans, 64 million people, are not registered to vote. This percentage is even higher for African-Americans (30 percent) and Hispanics (40 percent). Shockingly, for those between the ages of 18 and 24, it climbs to 50 percent. Registration rates are directly correlated with income: about 80 percent of those who make $75,000 or more a year are registered to vote, while only about 55 percent of those who make between $15,000 and $24,999 are registered. It's unacceptable for this country's registration rate to be so low.
- The United States is the only democracy in the world that strips the right to vote from citizens who have done time in prison. Fourteen states permanently disenfranchise some citizens; in 2004, these laws stripped 5.3 million Americans with felony convictions—disproportionately but by no means solely African-American and Latino—of the right to vote, even after they had paid their debt to society.
- Many Americans who are registered to vote don't make it to the polls. With only a single day on which to cast their ballot, working people often find themselves without the time to participate in the most basic ritual of our democracy.

Turnout is further suppressed by the increasing obstacles voters face when they try to cast their ballots: whether it's simply the failure to provide enough machines for voting to proceed quickly and efficiently, false notices instructing people to vote on the wrong day or at the wrong place, or bogus robo-calls to voters spreading disinformation and challenges at the polls—primarily targeting African-Americans—we confront a disturbing number of efforts to corrupt our democratic process.

The laws allowing voter challenges are the product of historic efforts to disenfranchise African-Americans. In Ohio the State Assembly first allowed challenges at polling places in 1831; by 1859 possessing a "visible admixture of African blood" was enough to endanger someone's right to vote. Florida allowed challenges for the first time just a year after federal law overruled a state law denying African-American men the right to vote. If these statutes and others like them have been purged of their overt racist bias, they still allow voters of any color to be excluded from the democratic process on the slimmest of pretexts.

Despite much of the mainstream media's eagerness to declare our elections since 2000 a success, too many of the problems that emerged during the 2000 debacle are still with us. In Columbus, Ohio, in 2004 African-American voters waited in line for hours before they could cast their ballots, while voters in white areas voted quickly and easily. In 2006 voters in one predominantly minority jurisdiction in Tennessee waited in line for as long as five and a half hours because of an insufficient number of voting machines. Similar reports were heard from states as diverse as Maryland, Colorado, Georgia, Ohio, Pennsylvania, Illinois, Utah and Massachusetts.

Even when voters are able to cast ballots, they do so without the confidence that their votes will be counted or, ultimately, count. Legitimate fears of easily hacked voting machines that leave no paper trail are exacerbated by a Supreme Court that ordered votes not to be counted in 2000.

That there have been so few serious efforts at the federal level to reform the Electoral College, which played a determining role in the 2000 selection of George W. Bush—who had fewer popular votes than Al Gore—is a disturbing sign that our democracy is unable to respond to the most basic consensus. In the aftermath of the Supreme Court's *Bush v. Gore* decision, which decided the election by awarding Florida's electoral votes to Bush, a Gallup poll summed up fifty years' worth of polling with the judgment that "a majority of Americans have continually expressed support for the notion of an official amendment of the U.S. Constitution that would allow for direct election of the president."

How we wound up with such a convoluted electoral process is a complicated story, but one of the key elements was the desire of the slave-holding states to preserve the influence they had gained through the infamous three-fifths compromise, in which slaves were counted as three-fifths of a person for the purpose of apportioning Representatives to the House. The Electoral College allowed those states to exert that same influence over the selection of the President.

Slavery is long gone, but time has done little to rid the Electoral College of its biases. Whether you live in the District of Columbia (whose citizens are denied voting rights in Congress) or New York City, Los Angeles or Chicago, the Electoral College blatantly privileges the votes of some citizens over others.

How much your vote counts should never depend on where you live. In a country where many of us live in "safe states"—states that aren't contested by the major-party candidates so voting can feel pointless—it is not surprising that in a worldwide survey of voter turnout for national elections since 1945, the United States placed 139th.

As Michael Waldman, executive director of the Brennan Center, observes in his new book, *A Return to Common Sense: Seven Bold Ways to Revitalize Democracy,* "In the United States, a typical off-year election sees turnout at 47 percent. Even in a presidential race, in recent years roughly four out of ten voting-age citizens haven't made it to the polls." Given the partisan divide among the voters who ultimately do make it to the polls, the President is often the choice of no more than a third of eligible American voters. This is not majority rule; it is plurality rule.

In a real democracy voters have a real choice. Under the Constitution, Congress was designed to reflect the diversity of the public, but now the power of incumbency limits the choices available to the people. In the 2004 House elections, only seven of the 399 incumbents running lost their seats. Subtract the four incumbent Texas Democrats whose districts were infamously dismantled by Texas Republican Tom DeLay, and only three incumbents lost—a North Korean-style 99 percent re-election rate. Four of the five national elections between 1996 and 2006 saw more than 98 percent of incumbents hang onto their seats. Even the "blue wave" of 2006 saw just twenty-nine seats in the House change hands. The power of incumbency has calcified our government into a duopoly.

Incumbents derive much of their staying power from the redistricting process, which has increasingly become a bipartisan farce in which the parties collaborate to draw district lines that will preserve their power (or, as DeLay demonstrated, gut the other guy).

Meanwhile, the citadels of incumbency are defended by arsenals of campaign cash. Even in a change election like 2006, the Center for Responsive Politics declared, "money was a clear winner." In 407 of 435 contests for the House, and twenty-four of thirty-three Senate contests, the winner simply outspent the loser. Given the recognition that incumbents already enjoy, they hold a massive advantage over challengers in fundraising; in the past three election cycles Congressional incumbents have raised hundreds of millions more than their opponents. At its source, the money flooding into our campaigns reflects unchecked and overwhelming corporate power; a recent study by the Campaign Finance Institute suggests that "bundlers," who will probably provide more than half the 2008 presidential candidates' staggering campaign contributions, represent only three industries: finance, law and real estate.

For too long, our politicians have been more focused on mobilizing money than the masses. Last November one analyst projected that the 2008 campaign would burn through $5 billion; we are already approaching the $2.5 billion mark.

At the same time, by creating an Internet-based infrastructure that has the potential to bypass the big-money establishment, Obama's campaign has revolutionized the way money is raised for elections. Its extraordinary ability to tap small donors, amassing more than 1.5 million individual donors, 90 percent of whom have given

$100 or less, promises to upend old, corrupt ways and make him (and other candidates) less mortgaged to wealthy special interests (even so, 55 percent Obama raised comes from large donors). And commendably, the campaign has cut off lobbyist donations to the Democratic National Committee and discouraged donors from helping "527" shadow operations, named after a provision in the tax code that allows groups to bypass restrictions on spending that is coordinated with parties or candidates. Still, Obama's decision in June to opt out of the public financing system for the general election is likely to boost the role of big special-interest contributions in the campaign.

Despite Obama's challenge to the old order, the system remains entrenched in other ways. The cost of television advertising is one of the most powerful engines of the money chase. Between 2002 and 2006 the already vast sums thrown at television advertising during elections nearly doubled, from $995.5 million to $1.7 billion. Broadcasters took that to the bank: spending on political ads accounted for half their revenue growth in 2001–02 and a jaw-dropping 80 percent of that growth in 2003–04. Not too long ago broadcasters were expected to operate as a public trust; they had a civic duty to promote public debate. Now elections seem to present little more than an opportunity for the networks to cash in on the crisis of our democracy.

The steadiest opposition to reforming a broken campaign finance system comes from big media companies, particularly those that own television stations, which now derive more than 12 percent of their income in election years from political advertising. As increasingly consolidated media dumb down political coverage—and, in the case of local elections, simply eliminate it—they enable a system in which information about candidates and campaigns comes only in the form of paid propaganda.

THE OPPORTUNITY

This is not the first time it's been clear that our electoral process demands renewal.

The Nation published clarion calls for change in 2001 and 2004. Now comes a confluence of events that offers an immense opportunity for reform. There's a chance that Obama will become President in 2009, and as a constitutional lawyer with a long record of teaching and action on electoral reform and voting rights, he may well be the best prepared President since the founders to take on the electoral process. And he could have a Congress in 2009 that is particularly well suited to act in alliance with a progressive administration.

Just a century ago progressive forces brought about a flurry of constitutional amendments, including women's suffrage and direct election of senators. We have a similar opportunity to pass the reforms that will build a more just democracy. A prodemocracy movement already has the grassroots and netroots in place, as well as the principles and concrete proposals. It will take political will, savvy strategy and hard-nosed organizing. That organizing should be integrated into the 2008 campaign, and it should continue after this year's voting is done.

The first challenge such a prodemocracy movement faces is crafting an agenda for people to rally behind, one to which they can hold their representatives accountable and one that captures the popular imagination. All too often democracy reformers find themselves fighting separate battles—over voting, campaign finance and media, to name a few—that are really part of a single war. When these issues are isolated from one another, arguments over policy quickly turn them into an insiders' fight—a fight that reformers have a tough time winning. Instead of repeatedly waging the same battles on ever narrower ground and debating the minutiae of policy, reformers must mobilize a popular movement that sees the links between these issues.

By developing a holistic democracy agenda, the larger public-interest and progressive community can unify and amplify particular issues—healthcare, the environment, an end to reckless wars and economic injustice. Of course, we all know how hard it is to break out of our silos. But if we are going to be stronger than the sum of our parts, it's crucial that we recognize our common stake in revitalizing our democratic process. That will free all of us to take on and defeat the powerful interests that dominate our broken democracy.

We need leaders like elder statesmen Bill Moyers and Al Gore as well as younger activists like Van Jones, Majora Carter and Stephanie Moore, who have emerged from a generation committed to a principled and participatory politics. We also need tough-minded commitment by activists on the ground and on the web to drive this agenda into the debate and out to the people, and the willingness to challenge the progressive organizations we've supported for years, our most trusted champions, to devote resources and energy to this cause and then use their power to hold politicians accountable.

All these measures are critical to changing our political landscape. And they are more possible in an era when tools like the Internet can promote change and connections among reformers. For a start, new online-offline combinations, using social networking, can create communities that would have been impossible to tap just a few years ago. Internet dynamo Lawrence Lessig's new group Change Congress (change-congress.org) has the potential to organize in new and pathbreaking ways. Linked to the online-offline strategy of building new communities and tapping into existing ones, building Just Democracy should be an integral part of the work done by a broad range of groups, from the NAACP to the League of Conservation Voters to the AFL-CIO to the League of Young Voters to Media Matters. Candidates who block reform should be challenged. We need an idealistic movement and a savvy operation with a long-term strategy.

What would a core agenda be? How about Just Democracy—a program to ensure that every voter can vote, that every vote gets counted, that money talks no louder than the many and that every challenger gets to make his or her case? Media reform is a piece of the puzzle, of course, as Robert McChesney and John Nichols have outlined in our pages. So too is party reform: how can a party that calls itself "Democratic" make unelected superdelegates defining players in its nominating process? There is no need to separate those necessary reforms, but my focus here is on the most important elements of a program to revitalize our electoral process.

Many of them are embodied in legislative proposals that have already been introduced in Congress. The long work of perfecting our democracy begins here.

Count Every Vote

The Help America Vote Act (HAVA) was intended to assuage Americans' fears that their votes might not be counted. Passed in 2002, it ranks somewhere between a disappointment and a fiasco. HAVA was a step in the right direction of establishing national standards—from voting machines to provisional ballots to paper trails to poll-worker training and voter protection—but it was not empowered to enforce crucial reforms, and it lacked a federal commitment to help states pay for elections.

There have been many legislative attempts to address the shortcomings of HAVA—including Senator Clinton and Representative Stephanie Tubbs Jones's Count Every Vote Act. So far, however, there has been no real movement on the issue. A new Congress, working with a committed President and an energized popular movement, could push through this legislation and, with it, genuine election reform.

Fix Black-Box Voting

Understandably, many prodemocracy advocates who make up the self-described Election Integrity Movement have focused their attention on the unreliability of voting machines manufactured by Diebold, Sequoia, ES&S and other corporations. HAVA supported states in updating voting machines (without specifying the type of machine) and provided funding to reach that goal. But in a glaring omission, it was left to the states to mandate a paper trail confirming for voters that their ballots had been cast as intended.

In December Ohio's new Secretary of State, Jennifer Brunner, issued a report declaring that "critical security failures" "could impact the integrity of elections in the Buckeye State." And she made some good recommendations for how to proceed. Most important, Brunner—as California Secretary of State Debra Bowen and Minnesota Secretary of State Mark Ritchie have already done—supports switching from touch-screens to optical-scan machines, which read ballots voters mark by hand like a standardized test. Optical scans are far more trustworthy and cost-effective than touch-screens—and they provide a record of each vote. A significant number of states still use touch-screen voting machines that do not produce paper trails—indispensable records that can be audited to double-check the results recorded by the computers. These systems are simply too unreliable to trust, given what we know about electronic voting. It's long past time for states and the federal government to standardize one publicly reviewed open-source hardware and software design for all voting machines and to end the grip of the corporate voting machine cartel on our elections.

We need a secure paper trail on all votes cast. As Representative Rush Holt points out, election results for six states and those for counties in another fourteen states could not be audited if the election were held today. His Emergency Assistance for Secure Elections Act (HR 5036) deserves support. It is an optional program that would allow states or jurisdictions to be reimbursed for the expense of providing paper ballots and/or conducting audits of election results. Despite initial bipartisan support for the bill, some of the same Republican Representatives who voted to release it from committee turned around and voted against the bill when it reached the House floor, in a gross display of the obstructionism with which the GOP has met nearly every effort at reform.

Holt has also proposed the Voter Confidence and Increased Accessibility Act (HR 811, with 216 sponsors—nearly half the House, including at least twenty Republicans), which would require all voting systems to provide a voter-verified paper trail to serve as the official ballot for recounts and audits, a valuable short-term measure worthy of support. The ultimate solution to the problem of electronic voting is a national law requiring voter-verified paper records, which should be the primary source for tabulating votes, backed up by mandatory recounts. This is Just Democracy.

Every bit as important as our unreliable voting systems is the relatively low-tech measure of ensuring that every polling place has an adequate number of machines and poll workers. That anyone should have to wait in line for five and a half hours is a disgrace. States should establish formulas for voting machine and poll worker allocation that take into account a variety of demographic and voting factors, not just the number of registered voters at some arbitrary cut-off date.

End the "Voter Fraud" Fraud

For too many years, American politics has been divided between two types of people: those who want more people to vote and those who want fewer people to vote. Recently the Bush-packed Supreme Court issued a disturbing ruling in favor of the kind of law we've become all too familiar with. This time the offending legislation was from Indiana, which has mandated that voters present an official ID at the polls, putting even more obstacles in the way of people who simply want to cast a ballot.

Not surprisingly, the Bush Administration's Justice Department sided with this thinly-veiled attempt to discourage election day turnout by folks believed to skew Democratic: the poor, the elderly, the young and minority voters. Arguing in support of the State of Indiana, the Administration claimed that "a state need not wait to suffer harm; it can adopt prophylactic measures to prevent it from occurring in the first place."

Talking loosely about "voter fraud" when we really mean election fraud helps reinforce the impression that the former is widespread. It is not. Voter fraud—the impersonation of a voter by another person—is extremely rare in the United States. Proposals to institute forms of voter identification, such as Arizona's requirement that people present proof of citizenship in order to register, do very little to curtail fraud. They can, however, do an excellent job of disenfranchising the 11 percent of citizens—more than 21 million people—who do not have a government-issued photo ID. The cost of acquiring such identification essentially constitutes an insidious poll tax. That's why we need a Summer 2008 project to get picture IDs to poor, elderly and minority voters.

The resurgence of election fraud rooted in the racist practices of the past is a far more imminent threat. A new Congress should pass Obama's Deceptive Practices and Voter Intimidation Prevention Act (S 453, with one Republican and nineteen Democratic sponsors). Passed in the House in June of last year as HR 1281, this legislation would not only make the dirty-trick politics of voter intimidation and misinformation illegal but, just as important, it would require election administrators to work with the community to ensure that corrected information is disseminated to voters in the affected area.

Passing this legislation would begin to redress the shameful neglect of civil rights shown by the Bush Administration. From 2001 to 2006, the voting section of the civil rights division of Bush's Justice Department brought only two voting discrimination cases on behalf of African-American voters, one of which was initiated during the Clinton years. A prodemocracy White House must appoint officials committed to protecting the right to vote.

Re-enfranchise Citizens

In the twenty-first century, the other America is behind bars, literally and figuratively: with one of every 100 Americans in prison, we are establishing a perverse parallel America—a predominantly nonwhite one—and making it permanent by stripping those consigned there of the right to vote. It's a hopeful sign that a growing number of states are re-enfranchising ex-felons. Vermont, Maine and Puerto Rico never deny citizens the right to vote and even allow prisoners to vote from jail, while sixteen other states as well as the District of

Columbia allow citizens to vote who are on probation or parole or who have been released from prison. Recognizing the right of ex-felons to vote would grant them the power to contest this status for others and help reintegrate them into society.

There are other second-class citizens in our country. Most egregiously, the mostly African-American population of the District of Columbia is denied representation in Congress. While the House voted in 2007 to allow the District a voting Representative in that chamber, the motion failed to pass the Senate by three votes.

Popularly Elect Our Presidents

The President is the only elected official whose office is intended to embody the will of the people as a whole. And yet we still maintain the Electoral College, which can override the people's will. We may have consigned the three-fifths compromise to history, but the Electoral College means that some people's votes count less than others'. Reform is long overdue, and the presidential election process has vast potential for transformative change right now.

The transpartisan push for a National Popular Vote for President is gaining traction. It would allow for the nationwide popular election for President to be implemented without amending the Constitution. States would pass identical laws by which they agree to award all their electoral votes to the presidential candidate who receives the most popular votes in all states and the District of Columbia. This interstate compact would go into effect only when it has been enacted by enough states—that is, those possessing a majority (currently 270) of the electoral votes. NPV has been endorsed by leading Republicans and Democrats, newspapers like the *New York Times* and *Los Angeles Times* and hundreds of legislators in forty states. In April 2007 Maryland became the first state to pass the legislation; since then, Illinois, New Jersey and Hawaii have followed suit. Eight states have passed NPV legislation in at least one chamber of their legislature. In June Florida Senator Bill Nelson proposed legislation to abolish the Electoral

College. FairVote's executive director, Rob Richie, who has championed NPV, believes "we'll have it by 2012"—finally modernizing what he calls "an eighteenth-century way of structuring elections."

This bold step into the twenty-first century would redraw and expand the horizons of the possible, immediately bringing in millions of voters routinely ignored when candidates focus on a few battleground states—sixteen in 2004—that increasingly settle modern presidential campaigns. Passage of NPV could also be the catalyst that advances many of the other proposals suggested here. For the first time in history, votes would be counted across state lines, providing further impetus for reform at the federal level.

Guarantee the Right to Vote

The right to vote is a rallying cry for a prodemocracy movement. Most Americans don't realize that the right to vote is not enshrined in our Constitution. Nor do they understand that our voting system is a shocking patchwork of rules. As Representative Jesse Jackson Jr. has written in *The Nation:* "Our voting system's foundation is built on the sand of states' rights and local control. We have fifty states, 3,141 counties and 7,800 different local election jurisdictions. All separate and unequal."

In the long term, a constitutional amendment guaranteeing every citizen the right to vote would finally place our democracy on a sturdy foundation. With the passage of such an amendment, citizens could use the courts to demand equal protection of that right—it would be an invaluable tool for establishing national standards for voting systems, fighting disenfranchisement and ultimately ensuring that every vote counts and is counted correctly. The organizing campaign around a constitutional amendment could also provide a valuable long-term strategy for achieving Just Democracy.

Say Farewell to Katherine Harris

Even as our right to vote has slowly been eroded, it has become increasingly evident that our system of election administration is riddled with flaws. That any state's top election official could also be the state chair for a presidential campaign—as was infamously the case in Florida in 2000 with Katherine Harris and in Ohio in 2004 with Kenneth Blackwell—is a gross conflict of interest that should be illegal. Election officials should be barred from participating in campaigns, and we need to establish strict conflict-of-interest laws. It's exciting that some recently elected secretaries of state are among the democracy movement's savviest allies. For example, Minnesota's Mark Ritchie, who ran the nonpartisan voter registration and mobilization group National Voice in 2003, won in 2006 on an inventive platform designed to repair—not exploit—the vulnerabilities of our electoral system.

Adopt Election Day Registration

Many voters are in effect stripped of their right to vote by our voter registration system. They discover only when they arrive at the polls that they're not on the rolls, or they're forced by bureaucratic bungling to cast a provisional ballot that isn't guaranteed to be counted. And yet local governments have little difficulty sending out notices for jury duty. Why don't we have the same capacity to register citizens to vote?

Under any opt-in system, even with the most comprehensive outreach plans, there will be citizens who neglect to register, to say nothing of botched registrations. Minnesota's Ritchie has a good idea: make registration at Departments of Motor Vehicles an opt-out process rather than opt-in. That is, you must check a box if you do *not* want to be registered to vote; if you don't check the box, you'll automatically be registered. Most states didn't even require voters to register before the 1870s; they instituted registration as new waves of immigrants arrived on our shores and former slaves joined the electorate. Many of the world's democracies practice universal registration, which assumes that it is the duty of the state to promote the involvement of its citizens, who are therefore automatically registered when they reach voting age. This idea isn't entirely foreign to the United States—while it's alone among the states, North Dakota has the distinction of not even requiring registration to vote. There's no reason this shouldn't be true in the other forty-nine states.

Steven Hill, director of the Political Reform Program with the centrist New America Foundation, projects that universal registration could give 50 million Americans the chance to vote. "Voting is a right, not a privilege," the Brennan Center's Michael Waldman observes. "We should recognize that individuals ought not to be charged with figuring out how to register and stay registered. And we should commit to the idea that in a democracy, the government has a duty, moral and legal, to make it possible for every eligible citizen to be able to vote." Waldman argues that universal registration could be the basis for a "grand bargain" between progressives and conservatives, simultaneously addressing the former's demand for access and the latter's desire for security (by making the government responsible for a national voter list). And while we're at it, let's lower the age for registering to vote to 16. We could even preregister young voters to ensure that they have the chance to make their voices heard. If we can register them for Selective Service, we can certainly register them to elect those who represent them in office. And how about retrieving Jesse Jackson's idea of every public high school student graduating with "a diploma in one hand and a voter card in the other"? It could start this fall, with the public school systems and their elected leaders, principals and union officials taking the lead on it this summer.

Short of abolishing registration entirely, allowing citizens to register up until—and even on—election day is one of the few measures guaranteed to boost turnout. Just over half the states cut off registration at least twenty-five days before an election, barring otherwise eligible voters from participating just when competition between candidates (and media coverage) intensifies.

Election Day Registration clearly demonstrates that many people who hope to vote on Election Day wind up being turned away at the polls.

For more than twenty-five years, states with EDR have consistently boasted higher turnout than states without it. In 2004 average turnout was 12 percent higher in states with EDR than in those without it; in 2006 the seven states with EDR averaged a 10 percent greater turnout. Senators Russ Feingold and Amy Klobuchar, with Representative Keith Ellison, have introduced legislation to allow EDR for all elections to federal office. Should the bill pass, the lack of EDR at the local and state level will be that much harder to justify.

And finally, why should Election Day be on Tuesday? That day was originally chosen because it was convenient; it gave a nation of farmers time to get to the polls without interfering with the three days of worship. We're no longer a nation of farmers, and having to go to the polls in the middle of a workweek is far from convenient. One possible solution would be to finally declare Election Day a national holiday. Such a "deliberation day," as one proposal has dubbed it, would not only ease crowds at the polls but also provide a powerful reaffirmation of the importance of voting and our commitment to democracy. Instead of making voting one more item on a list of errands, we could make it the most important act of a day devoted to democracy.

End the Party Duopoly

For the first time in nearly a century more than a quarter of American voters are not registered as either Republicans or Democrats. During the 2004 presidential campaign, one poll suggested 57 percent of voters thought candidates besides Bush and Kerry should be included in the debates. In the latest biannual survey from Harvard's Institute of Politics of 18- to 24-year-olds, 37 percent of young voters agreed that there was a need for a third party.

If majority rule is to be more than a hollow slogan and third parties more than "spoilers," we need to experiment with more accurate ways to represent the diversity of backgrounds, perspectives and opinions of the American people. Proportional representation—in which 10 percent of the vote wins 10 percent of the seats—is one way. But the United States is an outlier when it comes to PR. We're one of the few "advanced" democracies that don't use it in national elections. But PR isn't as alien as it might seem: Cambridge, Massachusetts, has used a proportional voting scheme to elect its City Council for seven decades. Illinois used a similar system to elect its lower house from 1870 to 1980, and it enjoys broad bipartisan support. As opposed to our winner-take-all system, in which a mere plurality of voters can carry an election, full representation allows for the expression of a broader range of interests.

The Democrats' use of proportional representation in their nominating process gives a sense of what it means: every vote counts, no matter how lopsided the result might be in any district or state.

Although not as radical a departure as proportional representation, instant runoff voting (IRV)—in which low-scoring candidates are eliminated and their supporters' second-choice votes are added to those that remain, until one candidate wins a majority—is another way to challenge the duopoly while protecting majority rule for all.

Backed by groups like FairVote and the New America Foundation, IRV also has the support of McCain and Obama, along with Democratic National Committee chair Howard Dean and third-party candidates like Libertarian Bob Barr, the Green Party's Cynthia McKinney and Ralph Nader.

And instant runoff voting has begun to catch on with the public. IRV has won thirteen of the last fourteen times it appeared on a ballot, winning landslides in cities like Oakland (69 percent), Minneapolis (65 percent), Sarasota (78 percent) and Santa Fe (65 percent). San Francisco just held its fourth IRV election, and exit polls have found it popular there with every measurable demographic. This fall, Pierce County, Washington, with a population of nearly 800,000, will use it for the first time for a hotly contested county executive election. And new cities voting to adopt it will include Glendale, California; St. Paul, Minnesota; and Memphis, Tennessee. A bill instituting IRV for Congressional elections in Vermont was vetoed by

that state's Republican governor but will be back next year.

Finally, fusion voting has the weight of long experience behind it. Before the twentieth century, it was a frequent tool of emerging parties, until major parties started banning it. Fusion allows two or more parties to nominate the same candidate on separate ballot lines. That simple change permits people to vote their values without "wasting" their vote or supporting "spoilers." The positive experience of New York's Working Families Party in the past decade shows you can build a viable minority party this way. And fusion has also helped progressives focus on the challenge of building majorities in a winner-take-all system. These options would dramatically open our electoral system to more choices, ensuring the representation of diverse views instead of seeing them co-opted or suppressed by the "least worst" options presented by the duopoly.

Money, Money, Money

Our representatives should represent all of us, not just big-money donors who can afford to buy access. Restoring accountability and responsiveness depends on cleansing politics of the influence of money. Full public financing for campaigns would free the best of our elected officials from that influence and increase the power of people over our representatives—or even let them *become* representatives; full public financing is almost the only way for citizens of average means to run for office.

The good news is that signs of discontent are clear. Americans of diverse backgrounds are fed up with politicians who don't listen to them, who don't care about them and who don't respond to their concerns. Clear majorities favor reforms such as public financing of campaigns. A survey conducted on behalf of pro-democracy groups like Public Campaign and Common Cause found that a full 74 percent of voters favor a voluntary system of public funding for elections (with only 16 percent opposed). This support stretches across party lines, netting 80 percent of Democrats, 78 percent of Independents and 65 percent of Republicans.

The not-so-good news: public financing in the form of matching funds has been available to presidential candidates since the mid-1970s, but as the primary season drags on ever longer and the cost of television airtime has skyrocketed, the need for campaign cash has become ever more desperate, causing candidates increasingly to opt out of the system. As Nick Nyhart, executive director of Public Campaign, put it, "The system is broken and badly needs an overhaul."

And we need to update the system: various modernizing reforms, among other provisions, are included in the Presidential Funding Act (S 436), introduced in the Senate by Russ Feingold and, ironically, Barack Obama. Because Obama is the first presidential candidate to opt out of public financing for a general election, it is incumbent on him to commit to making passage of comprehensive and updated public financing of all federal elections a top priority.

Short of introducing a system of full public financing, one modest proposal to reduce fundraising pressures would be to increase dramatically the amount a candidate receives for donations of $100 or less, by matching such donations on a 1:4 basis (this could be reinforced by eliminating matching funds for donations of more than $100). This simple formula could serve as the basis for a system of public financing of Congressional elections as well. Candidates would then have a greater incentive to cultivate small donors, restoring some degree of sanity to the fundraising process. Another way to decrease the pressure for campaign cash: guarantee free airtime to qualified candidates and make that airtime a condition for FCC renewal of lucrative TV and radio licenses.

For too long, the fundraising arms race has deterred Congress from taking meaningful steps to overhaul this dysfunctional system. Fortunately the convergence of democratic ideals and pragmatic considerations wrought by fundraising fatigue—key senators lament that they spend almost a third of their time raising money—has led to two excellent bills with impressive sponsorship.

Senators Dick Durbin and Arlen Specter's Fair Elections Now Act has garnered eight co-sponsors, including Obama (the first co-sponsor). In the House the Clean Money, Clean Elections Act of 2007 has fifty-five co-sponsors. Under both these bills, candidates who show a qualifying level of support and opt out of further private contributions would be supported by public funding.

Until now, however, the most promising and smartest experiments with voluntary systems of public financing have come from the states. In Arizona, where qualified candidates have been able to take advantage of public financing since the 2000 election, 42 percent of the State Legislature has been elected using public funds. In Maine, which inaugurated its public funding system four years earlier, 84 percent of the State Legislature has been elected using matching funds. Connecticut, New Jersey and New Mexico all have Clean Elections statutes.

Maine's experience with Clean Elections also suggests that these reforms successfully promote diversity. Eighteen percent more women have run for office since the reforms were enacted than in the decade before. In Arizona's 2006 primary, 69 percent of female candidates (as opposed to 52 percent of male candidates) took advantage of the state's public funding, and the percentage of minority candidates went from 6 percent in 2000 to 14 percent in 2006.

Meanwhile, analysis suggests that Latino communities and people with low incomes are much more actively involved as donors in Arizona's Clean Elections than they are in the privately financed campaigns in the state. The success of bringing more diverse, less affluent candidates into politics has led reform groups to downplay the fight against corruption and focus more on why change is necessary to give ordinary people more representation, voice and, yes, power in the electoral process.

THE WAY FORWARD

The Congressional Progressive Caucus could take the first step, calling on Democratic leaders to support the agenda detailed here. It could then be introduced in Congress as a package of bills, with the CPC demanding a roll-call vote on each. There should be a balance between paving the way for far-reaching change and reforms we can win now. Already Senator Bill Nelson's One Person, One Vote Initiative shows how a compelling package of reforms can enhance the case for each of its elements.

Meanwhile, campaigns should push this agenda in the states and at the grassroots, enlisting a broad coalition—beginning with voting, civil rights and media groups, along with the new secretaries of state—to organize in every district. (*AlterNet* is publishing a book, *Count My Vote,* that will be an invaluable resource for grassroots activists. It compiles the voting regulations of every state and offers sections exploring the unique situations of everyone from students to seniors to new voters.) Those politicians who vote against democracy should be targeted and made examples of, with the coalition fielding and supporting challengers to go after their seats. The muscle is there; it just has to be flexed.

Before the Voting Rights Act was passed, President Lyndon Johnson is said to have urged Dr. Martin Luther King Jr. to go out there and make it possible for him to do the right thing. Our elected representatives need pressure from a broad-based movement—reaching from the grassroots to the halls of Congress—if they're going to champion Just Democracy. Enlisting the netroots and the blogosphere, along with the progressive media, will be vital in getting the word out. The new democracy will come only when the defenders of the citadels of privilege find they are threatened on the terms of the old system. We're calling for radical democracy, birthed by bare-knuckled politics.

Admittedly, defining an agenda and building a movement is just a beginning; the fight will be long and hard. Few politicians have been willing to take the lead in calling for the measures proposed here. Trapped in the rapidly escalating race of campaign finance, who will set aside the weapons of dollars and incumbency to rebuild a truly representative democracy? If they won't do it, we will.

A Just Democracy movement will require idealism and diligent organizing; it will demand a broad coalition committed to making these reforms a high priority. Working together, we can repair the broken system we've been handed and confront the crisis of disenfranchisement that has overtaken our democracy. We want 100 percent registration. We want increased participation. We want full representation with majority rule. We want the right to vote. We want to vote without fear—that our votes will not count, or be counted by hacked machines.

It is long past time to place democracy at the center of our politics, where it belongs. We don't exist just to curse the political darkness but to craft solutions to make America a more perfect union.

DISCUSSION QUESTIONS

1. Explain the main contours of the crisis in the American electoral system, as discussed by vanden Heuvel. Delineate between deep-rooted historical issues and more recent ones. At one point she observes: "The machinery of American democracy is broken." Are you surprised by any of these problems? Have you encountered any of them?

2. According to vanden Heuvel, the "opportunity" we now have is to mobilize people to demand and support a broad agenda of electoral reform. Discuss her proposed reforms. Which seem most likely to succeed? Are any of these reforms more difficult to envision than others?

CHAPTER 6

Congress

Congress has frequently been described as the world's foremost legislative body, but its performance often disappoints Americans. Polls show consistently that we have less confidence in the legislative branch than in either the presidency or the judiciary. Indeed, a CBS News poll in October of 2011 found public approval of the job Congress is doing at an all-time low of 9%—with Americans giving a higher rating to polygamy, pornography, and "the U.S. going Communist." Ironically, the legislature is the first branch of government discussed in the Constitution, and there is no doubt that most of the Framers intended Congress to be the primary policy-making institution. In the nineteenth century, with the exception of several periods of strong presidential leadership, the Congress did in fact exert this kind of primacy in our political system. But beginning in the twentieth century, and particularly since the 1930s, increased assertion of presidential power has left the Congress as a reactive and fragmented body, though still with the power to block presidential initiatives.

Former Speaker of the House of Representatives Thomas P. "Tip" O'Neill used to say that all politics is local. Part of the problem with Congress is the mismatch between its local orientation and the increasingly national and international imperatives placed on the U.S. state to secure the domestic health and worldwide expansion of corporate capitalism. Members of Congress, especially in the House, are elected to represent states and districts with specific social needs, economic characteristics, and local power structures. Overlaying this local orientation and contributing to congressional indecision are weak party structures, the impact of campaign contributions, the typically great advantages for incumbents seeking reelection, and the ubiquitous impact of interest groups on policy-making. All of these pressures make it difficult for Congress to set an independent agenda for attaining the public good through taking on the myriad social and economic problems facing America. And these pressures are exacerbated by the bitter partisan divide in Congress evident in recent years.

21 *John C. Berg*

CONGRESS AND BIG BUSINESS

Political scientist John Berg frames this chapter with an article that places Congress within the context of a theory of society that views class structure, the needs of corporate capitalism, and our dominant liberal ideology as basic structural determinants that set the boundaries of debate on policy issues. Following in the tradition of Philip Brenner's pathbreaking 1983 book The Limits and Possibilities of Congress, *Berg analyzes how congressional politics can be seen as part of the larger ongoing social conflict in America. Contrary to the principles of pluralist theory (see our Introduction), this conflict privileges the interests of one key participant—giant multinational corporations—who exercise dominating class power, or "hegemony." Berg uses several examples to illustrate how and why Congress protects corporate interests with a swiftness and effectiveness that other classes and groups do not enjoy. He then details three ways in which corporate hegemony is built into the structure of Congress: through the legal system of the country, governmental separation of powers, and the power of specific congressional committees. Big business certainly does not win all the time, but the rules of the game are skewed so that their overall interests dominate policy debates and outcomes regardless of the party and personalities of congressional leaders. This remains as true today—in the face of continuing economic recession and the meltdown of the U.S. financial system from 2008 to 2012—as it was when Berg wrote in the early 1990s.*

Money talks. Everyone knows that. It talks a lot to Congress. Well-heeled lobbyists, political action committees (PACs), expense-paid junkets, multimillion-dollar campaigns, and juicy honoraria are abiding elements of American political lore. Everyone knows, too, that the rich do better than other people at getting their opinions heard and their interests accommodated by legislators. Average citizens, political scientists, and the members of Congress themselves join in bewailing the excessive importance of money in politics.

Source: John C. Berg, *Unequal Struggle: Class, Gender, Race, and Power in the U.S. Congress*, Boulder, CO: Westview Press, 1994, pp. 31–34 and 37–44.

Congressional politics is part of the fundamental social conflict in America. Congress is one arena in which this conflict takes place, but it is not an independent arena. Forces outside Congress influence what goes on inside it; in particular, if the Marxist theory is correct, Congress is influenced heavily by the economic structure of our society. Those who dominate the American economy dominate Congress as well. But Congress is also the most democratic part of our national government. Thus, oppressed social groups have found it the most permeable part of the state, often seeking to use congressional politics to advance their cause. . . .

We can see the effect of economic structure when we compare the way Congress handles different issues. In 1977, with the nation suffering from an energy shortage that restricted economic growth, hurt the balance of trade, inflated the cost of living, and forced many poor people to go without heat in winter, President Jimmy Carter presented a comprehensive national energy plan to Congress. After two years of hearings, backroom negotiations, and public debate, Congress managed to pass only one part of the plan: It removed price controls from natural gas, thus making energy even more expensive.

In 1989 the wreck of the oil tanker *Exxon Valdez* killed thousands of waterfowl, fish, marine mammals, and plants; threatened the ecological balance of Prince William Sound; and infuriated the public. Individual members of Congress responded with thousands of dramatic public speeches; but it was sixteen months before Congress as a legislative body managed to pass a bill raising the limits on liability of negligent oil shippers from $150 to $1,200 per ton of oil. Although the final bill was considered a victory by environmental lobbyists, several concessions had to be made to the oil industry before it could be passed. Double-hull requirements for oil tankers were deferred until 2010 (and to 2015 for most barges and for ships unloading offshore to lighters), oil companies shipping oil in tankers owned by others were exempted, and state governors lost any power to determine when a cleanup was complete.

In the early 1980s a large number of savings and loan associations—known as thrift institutions, or simply "thrifts"—began to lose money; by 1987 many were in danger of failing. The Federal Savings and Loan Insurance Corporation (FSLIC), which insured thrift deposits of $100,000 or less, warned that it might not be able to pay all the claims. Congress gave the FSLIC another $10 billion in 1987, but otherwise did nothing until after the 1988 election. Then, in early 1989, Congress moved with remarkable speed to enact a complicated—and expensive—reorganization plan for the thrift industry. President George Bush proposed a plan on February 6 and signed a new law on August 9. The S&L Bailout—as it became known—would cost $50 billion by the end of 1991, and at least $110 billion by 1999; some of the money would be paid to the holders of insured accounts, but much of it would be used to subsidize healthier, more profitable banks and thrifts in taking over unhealthy ones.

In this case Congress acted not only quickly but ingeniously. Since the passage of the Gramm-Rudman-Hollings Deficit Reduction Act (GRH) in 1985, new spending programs had been difficult to create. The bill deftly evaded this problem. It simply labeled $30 billion "off-budget" and assigned the remaining $20 billion to a fiscal year that had already begun—and which therefore had already passed the GRH test.

One could argue that Congress acted so quickly and smoothly in the savings and loan case because it simply had to. The nation faced a crisis, and failure to act would have had unthinkable consequences. However, this line of thought leads to further questions. What is a crisis? What sort of consequences are unthinkable? In 1991 a cholera epidemic broke out in Peru, threatening to spread throughout South and Central America; it was expected to be hard to stop because the projected cost of the necessary sanitary improvements was prohibitive—$200 billion over twelve years, or about the same as the savings and loan bailout.

Closer to home, it has been argued that American public education is in crisis. Millions of young people fail to complete high school; millions more graduate unable to read, to multiply fractions, or to understand the basic nature of atoms and molecules. These consequences are unthinkably tragic, but they are happening, and Congress has not found the will to prevent them.

Marxists use the concept of *hegemony* to explain the differences between these two crises. Hegemony refers to the dominating power of a social class (or part of one) whose class interests have come to be widely accepted as equivalent to the interests of society as a whole. The United States today is dominated in this way by the giant multinational corporations.

.   .   .

The American economy is not just capitalist; it is dominated by a small number of gigantic capitalist corporations. In 1988, the 500 largest industrial corporations in the United States—the so-called Fortune 500—had total sales of over $2 trillion. One-fifth of this amount, $402,183,000,000, was produced by just five companies: General Motors (GM), Ford, Exxon, International Business Machines (IBM), and General Electric (GE). In the same year, there were about 3.5 million corporations, and 14 million nonfarm proprietorships and partnerships, in the United States. The three major automobile makers alone employed 1,270,000 people, had assets of $356 billion, and earned profits of $11.2 billion. The ten largest commercial banks—all but one of them located in New York City—had assets of $860 billion, with nearly one-quarter of that, $207 billion, held by one bank, New York's Citicorp.

These giants are so big that the rest of the country needs them to be healthy. When Chrysler Corporation, only the third largest automobile maker, faced possible bankruptcy, the federal government stepped in to save it. It stepped in again to avert the failure of Chicago-based Continental Bank Corporation, the fourteenth largest commercial bank. As this practice has become more common, it has acquired a name, the "too big to fail" doctrine. It is one example of *hegemony*.

When Charles E. ("Engine Charlie") Wilson went from president of General Motors to secretary of defense in the Eisenhower administration, he told a Senate committee that he was not worried about any possible conflict of interest because he had always believed that "what was good for our country was good for General Motors, and vice versa. The difference did not exist. Our company is too big. It goes with the welfare of the country."

In the largest sense, Wilson was dead wrong. GM has been a cumbersome, inefficient enterprise that has contributed greatly to a whole range of national problems, from low productivity to air pollution to worker alienation. But in the short run—that is, given that GM already existed—Wilson was right. GM's huge labor force, its annual sales, and its impact as a customer on other major industries were so great that a failure of GM—or of another giant corporation—might well have plunged the whole economy into recession.

CORPORATE HEGEMONY

Until sometime in the early 1970s the giant financial and industrial corporations were able to dominate America and much of the rest of the world. This domination gave them a sense of security and led some to conclude that they were more interested in stability than in profits. Since that time, however, their dominance has been threatened by growing international competition. The best-known example is the auto industry, in which the big three U.S. automakers have lost market share to Japanese and European competitors both at home and abroad; but the same thing has occurred in many other industries as well.

This new global competition has changed both the composition and the interests of the hegemonic bloc. By reviving the emphasis on profits it has reinforced the dominance of finance capital over industrial corporations. Such once-mighty giants as IBM have learned that Wall Street would rather shift its investments to other companies and industries than support them in fighting to preserve their corporate position.

The willingness of many corporations to accept high wages and benefits and a certain amount of government regulation is likewise falling before international competitive pressure. These changes in the economic position of U.S. big business have had important political results; but the basic division between hegemonic and nonhegemonic sectors of the capitalist class remains.

Politics and ideology tend to reflect economics. Thus, the state (including Congress) tends to further the interests of the giant corporations; and public debate tends to be carried on in terms that incorporate those interests—as in 1990, when President Bush referred to protection of Exxon's oil supplies in the Persian Gulf as a defense of "our way of life." This is not automatically so. The nonhegemonic classes can and do organize themselves to contend for political power, and to change the terms of public discourse. But they find it harder to win; and unless they succeed in changing the economic structure as well, such political and ideological reforms are likely to be only temporary. Let us look at some concrete examples.

The crisis in the savings and loan industry threatened to destabilize the whole financial system, endangering giant banks along with small thrift institutions. It thus struck at the heart of corporate hegemony. The nature of this hegemony is missed by much left rhetoric. For example, Manning Marable has written recently:

> Is it right for a government to spend billions and billions for bailing out fat cats who profited from the savings and loan scam while millions of jobless Americans stand in unemployment lines desperate for work? Is it fair that billions of our dollars are allocated for the Pentagon's permanent war economy to obliterate the lives of millions of poor people from Panama to Iraq to Grenada to Vietnam, while two million Americans sleep in the streets and 37 million Americans lack any form of medical coverage?

The policies Marable decries are indeed neither right nor fair; but even those members of Congress who agree with this characterization fear that allowing the savings and loan industry to collapse, or (more debatably) cutting the military budget, would send even more millions to the unemployment lines or into the streets. For this reason, debate within Congress about the savings and loan crisis has centered on who should take the blame, not on whether to act.

By contrast, the crisis in education strikes at the U.S. working class, and cholera threatens workers and peasants in other countries. Millions of lives may be blighted, neighborhoods destabilized, and great human suffering caused, but most members of Congress still see a solution as optional—something we certainly ought to do if we can just find the money. Even the advocates of school reform find it useful to base their arguments on the need of capitalism for a more skilled labor force.

This is the theory of hegemony in its bare bones. Hegemonic interests are privileged in that Congress and the state act quickly and effectively to protect them; they find it more difficult to promote other interests that are equally vital in human terms. But students of politics must ask how this privilege is maintained. What is it about our political system—what is it about Congress—that makes it more responsive to hegemonic interests than to others?

In fact, the interests of the great corporations are well entrenched in the structure of American government. This structure is itself the product of past political struggles, dating back at least to the drafting of the Constitution. Some of these struggles have been won by the working class, farmers, and petty bourgeoisie; by women; by racial minorities; and by other democratizing forces. But on the whole, the trend has been toward the kind of state envisioned by Alexander Hamilton, a state dedicated to furthering business interests.

Corporate hegemony is built into the structure of Congress on at least three levels. First, it has become part of our basic legal order. Second, it is built into the separation of powers, which places the most crucial decisions outside of Congress's reach. Finally, it is part of the internal structure of Congress itself. The end result of decades of conflict is that Congress finds it easy to act on behalf of corporate interests and difficult to act against them. These structural features are reinforced by the nature of the American electoral system, and by the weakness of anticapitalist ideology.

Americans think of our legal order as founded on individual rights. However, the meaning of these rights has been transformed since the U.S. Constitution was first written. On the one hand, rights have been broadened and extended in such a way that the universalistic language of the Declaration of Independence is now applied to the propertyless, to women, and to the descendants of slaves, none of whom had been included at first. On the other hand, the language of rights has been applied to big business, becoming a fundamental restraint on the power of Congress and other democratic institutions to regulate business in the public interest.

Perhaps the most important business victory was the extension of individual civil rights to corporations. Today this extension has become such a basic feature of our legal system that we tend not to notice it, but it came about only in the latter half of the nineteenth century. Through a combination of state and federal legislation and Supreme Court decisions, two legal doctrines became firmly established. First, corporations—which had been conceived of originally as quasi-state agencies chartered by the state in order to achieve an important public purpose, such as building a bridge or a canal, settling Massachusetts Bay, or conquering India—were transformed into a means of concentrating capital without exposing its individual owners to excessive risk, for the sole purpose of making money.

Second, these corporations gained the status of *persons* under the law, and as such won the legal rights granted to persons by the Fourteenth Amendment. This amendment had been designed to give federal protection to the freed slaves; but the Supreme Court ignored this purpose for seventy years, while using the amendment to protect corporations from government regulation. The Court has since backed away from some of its more extreme interpretations, but the basic legal structure of corporate rights continues to

place many possible policies beyond the bounds of congressional or state legislative action.

Most recently, the Supreme Court has extended freedom of expression to corporate persons. The Court ruled in 1975 that the First Amendment applied to commercial advertising and, in 1980, extended it to cover political advocacy by businesses. A constitutional provision intended to protect human democracy and individualism thereby became a barrier to attempts to protect democratic discourse from the domination of capital.

The interests of giant corporations are also built into the operation of the constitutional separation of powers. Those who study the making of public policy know that the balance of power between Congress and the president varies with the issue at hand. The executive branch has the largest role in foreign policy, military action, and the regulation of the national economy. The president can order military action, recognize foreign governments, or sign Executive Agreements without congressional approval. Even when funds must be appropriated by Congress, he has considerable discretion to divert them to other purposes—and, as the Iran-*contra* case showed, he also has the *de facto* ability to exceed that discretion. He and his appointees also play the major role in attempts to regulate the national economy.

Congress, for its part, wields more detailed control over such issues as aid to education, environmental protection, housing, health, and welfare. In these areas, presidentially appointed officials must work with specific mandates and finite appropriations from Congress, and important issues are often decided by Congress, in committees or by floor amendments.

Some of these differences are rooted in the Constitution, whereas others have emerged since—as with the creation of the Federal Reserve System; but in general, those policy areas that are more vital to the interests of the great corporations are further removed from the influence of Congress.

Nonhegemonic classes and groups have better access to Congress than to the president and his inner cabinet, but this access does not give them proportional influence over those matters most important to the hegemonic fraction. The president can invade Grenada or Panama, go to war with Iraq, or sponsor terrorist attacks in Nicaragua, and Congress finds it hard to restrain him. The Federal Reserve System sets the nation's monetary policy, a key determinant of the fate of our economy, with little accountability to Congress or even to the president. In the case of foreign affairs, Congress's power is limited by the Constitution, which makes the president commander in chief of the armed forces; but it has been unable to resist the erosion of its own power to declare war. The United States fought both the Korean and Vietnam wars without formal declarations of war by Congress, and in the case of Vietnam the fighting continued long after Congress had turned against it. Finding itself unable to stop a war that was under way, Congress passed the War Powers Act of 1974; but this act has proved ineffective, having often been ignored by the president. However, the regulation of banking and currency are powers assigned to Congress; its loss of influence in these areas is the result of its own past decisions to create and maintain the Federal Reserve System. As a result, Congress must try to manage the economy—if it wishes to try at all—by raising or lowering federal taxes and spending, tools that are difficult to wield and uncertain in their effect. The powers to regulate interest rates and the money supply have proven more effective, but they have been removed from Congress and given to the Federal Reserve Board and the Federal Open Market Committee. In both cases, political struggles of the past have helped form structures that bias the political struggles of today.

The class basis of the separation of powers, and its changes over time, merit further study. As a simple approximation we could say that hegemonic interests dominate the presidency, whereas the influence of other social forces is confined to Congress. But hegemony operates within Congress as well. Congress has been unable to stop presidents from encroaching on its traditional powers partly because the interests that dominate the presidency also control the main levers of power within Congress.

Decisionmaking in each house of Congress is formally democratic, usually by majority vote. Yet small groups of members have always possessed the greatest share of power over decisions. Such power can come from control over the flow of bills to the floor, as with the party leaderships and the House Rules Committee; or from control over important legislative subject matter, as with the Appropriations, Tax-writing, and Budget Committees. The Appropriations, Rules, and Ways and Means Committees in the House are called "exclusive committees"—because they are so important that their members are not supposed to serve on other standing committees at the same time (a rule often broken, as it happens). The House Budget Committee is a special case; it is formed of selected representatives from other committees, and its chair, rather than being chosen by seniority, is elected by the House and considered a member of the House leadership. The Senate also recognizes certain committees as having extra importance: Appropriations, Budget, Finance (the Senate equivalent of House Ways and Means), and Foreign Relations (given special importance in the Senate because of that body's treaty ratification power). For ease of reference, all of these will be referred to from now on as *hegemonic committees*.

Both party leadership and hegemonic committee positions are almost always held by members who have incorporated the hegemonic ideology into their own outlooks. Several studies have shown that positions of power go to those members who have a "responsible legislative style," one of the essential elements of which is a willingness to put what is conceived of as the national interest ahead of narrow constituency interests.

For hegemonic committees, congressional leaders also prefer to pick members who come from seats that are relatively safe, so that they will be less subject to popular pressure on controversial decisions. There is also some self-selection of members. Richard Fenno, in a famous study of House committees, found that representatives were most likely to seek seats on the Ways and Means or Appropriations committees if they were more interested in achieving power as an end in itself than in promoting specific policies. Given the structure of American society, such power can best be pursued by choosing to side with big business.

These selection procedures do not work perfectly. However, potentially dissident committee members find themselves outnumbered and face strong pressure not to rock the boat. If they cooperate with hegemonic interests, they can use their committee positions to win significant benefits for their districts or for other interests they support; but if they come to be seen as troublemakers, such benefits are much harder to come by. Generally such pressures are enough to keep potential dissidents in line.

The hegemonic faction does not dominate Congress through sheer force; its power is maintained only by the tacit, and sometimes open, support of a majority of the members, who could vote to change the structure at any time. One of the strengths of Congress is that its leaders understand this contingency and act consciously to maintain their support. "Responsibility" includes "reciprocity" and "accommodation"—the willingness of a member of Ways and Means, for example, to serve as a voice for interests in his or her region that want particular concessions in the tax code, and to cooperate with members from other regions with like interests. The willingness to grant such concessions from time to time provides the solid foundation for the Ways and Means Committee's ability at other times to gain acceptance of an omnibus tax bill under a closed rule.

As Fenno observes, the power of the hegemonic committees is reinforced by institutional pride. House members want the Ways and Means Committee to be strong, because its power is, to some extent, theirs as well.

In addition to a generalized willingness to be accommodating, hegemony within Congress can involve specific accommodations of particular groups. For example, the Rayburn-McCormack leadership of the House Democrats—whose successors, known as the Austin-Boston Axis, remained in control of the House Democratic leadership through the 1980s—won and maintained power on the basis both of a moderate New Deal ideology and of a very specific agreement that amendments to the tax code that were regarded unfavorably by Southwestern oil interests would not be allowed on the floor. The oil industry has since been forced to fight harder for its interests, but it continues to be well represented in the House and Senate tax-writing committees, and still receives tax treatment more favorable than that accorded to most other industries. This arrangement is a reflection of the central position of the oil companies in the American economy—their inclusion in the hegemonic bloc—but it is not an automatic result of that economic importance. Rather, it is the consequence of a series of political victories by which the representatives of the oil companies have gained control of some of the levers of congressional power.

These three structural factors—the basic legal order, the division of powers among the branches of government, and the power of the hegemonic committees within Congress—provide the terrain on which pluralist conflict takes place. This conflict is fought out with the usual weapons of democratic politics—namely, votes and money; but the giant corporations enter the battle already in possession of the commanding heights and are therefore much more likely to win.

DISCUSSION QUESTIONS

1. What situations constitute a crisis to the U.S. Congress? According to what interests are crisis situations determined?
2. What evidence does Berg provide that corporations use our political system to exercise their hegemony? Relate this argument to Article 3 by Clawson, Neustadtl, and Weller by comparing the authors' perspectives on corporate hegemony.

22 *Common Cause*

DEMOCRACY ON DRUGS
How a Bill Really Becomes a Law

There's an old adage in politics that goes like this: The two things you shouldn't see in the process of being made are sausage and legislation. The following selection from Common Cause, a Washington-based non-partisan citizens' lobbying organization, offers a window into the legislative process. In late 2003, the House and Senate handed President Bush a huge legislative victory by passing a bill establishing a voluntary prescription drug program under Medicare, one of the centerpieces of the President's domestic agenda. The bill passed 220–215 in the House and 54–44 in the Senate. The Common Cause study chronicles a tale of deceit, manipulation, strong arm tactics, procedural violations, secrecy, and favoritism toward the pharmaceutical industry—all undertaken by the Republican leadership of Congress in the pursuit of private corporate profit under the guise of the public interest of the 40 million Medicare beneficiaries. So heavy-handed were the Republican tactics that in the fall of 2004, House Majority Leader Tom DeLay (R-TX) was officially admonished by the House Ethics Committee for his efforts to strong arm Rep. Nick Smith (R-MI) into changing his vote against the bill. As Common Cause points out, the sum total of irregularities and shenanigans involved in this story raises troubling questions about the democratic process and its promise of fairness and accountability. The result was a give-away to pharmaceutical companies with negligible, if any, benefits for the elderly. Moreover, the creation of Medicare Part D remains one of the major causes—along with the Bush era tax breaks for the wealthy and corporations, and unfunded wars in Iraq and Afghanistan—of the soaring budget deficit and rising national debt that continues to vex Congress as President Obama's first term winds down. Students of government might be left wondering: is this any way to run a legislature?

Source: Common Cause, *Democracy on Drugs. The Medicare/Prescription Drug Bill: A Study in How Government Shouldn't Work,* Washington, DC: Common Cause, May 18, 2004.

INTRODUCTION

Our Constitution reflects the over-arching concern of the Founding Fathers that the rights of the minority be jealously preserved and protected, even in the presence of a strong majority. From start to finish, the $535 billion Medicare bill passed by Congress and signed by President Bush late in 2003 has been a study in shutting out opposing voices and suppressing the flow of vital information.

This Common Cause report chronicles a series of incidents, large and small, that add up to a consistent effort by the Administration and Congressional leadership to bypass or undermine the rules and laws that are in place to ensure that our government works in an open and accountable manner and that all voices are heard on critical public policy issues.

The Medicare bill is the product of a process that included:

- Charges of bribery, delayed votes, inappropriate cabinet member lobbying and censoring of C-SPAN cameras.
- The Administration misleading Congress by withholding its own cost estimates for the prescription drug legislation—estimates that greatly exceeded what the President was telling the public. A career civil servant being threatened with his job if he told Congress the truth.
- Congressional Members excluded from the House-Senate conference committee that finalized the bill. Only a "coalition of the willing" was invited to participate.
- A principal author of the bill was forced to step down as head of a powerful House committee after it was reported that he was negotiating a $2 million a year lobbying job with the drug industry while he was moving the proposal through his committee. And a key Administration official involved in pushing the legislation was also offered lucrative private sector healthcare jobs.
- The drug industry showered Congress with campaign contributions and spent millions of

dollars on highly paid lobbyists who swarmed Capitol Hill while the bill was being considered.
- A propaganda campaign waged by the Department of Health and Human Services. The Administration paid people to pose as journalists in television segments that praised the benefits of the new Medicare law, and spent tens of millions of dollars on a campaign promoting the new program.

CHARGES OF BRIBERY ON THE HOUSE FLOOR

"directly or indirectly, corruptly gives, offers or promises anything of value to any public official . . . with intent to influence any official act."

—U.S. CODE. TITLE 18 SEC. 201. "BRIBERY OF PUBLIC OFFICIALS"

At the break of dawn on Nov. 22, 2003, Representative Nick Smith (R-MI) was about to cast his vote against a Medicare/prescription drug bill so flawed and controversial that the Republican House leadership held the vote open for three hours while they pressured their own Republican colleagues to vote for the bill. Votes in the House typically are open for 15 minutes.

Strong-arming Members of the House to vote with the leadership is routine business, but what went on in those early morning hours appears to have slid over the line from political pressure to outright bribery.

A Nov. 23, 2003 column written by Rep. Smith appearing on his website reads:

I was targeted by lobbyists and the congressional leadership to change my vote, being a fiscal conservative and being on record as a no vote. Secretary of Health and Human Services Tommy Thompson and Speaker of the House Dennis Hastert talked to me for a long time about the bill and about why I should vote yes. Other members and groups made offers of extensive financial campaign support and endorsements for my son Brad who is running for my seat. They also made threats of working against Brad if I voted no.

On Dec. 1, 2003, in a radio interview with Kevin Vandenbroek of WKZO in Kalamazoo, Mich., Rep. Smith said:

> They started out by offering the carrot, and they know what's important to every member, and what's important to me is my family and my kids. And I've term-limited myself, and so Bradley my son is running for [my congressional seat] and so the first offer was to give him $100,000-plus for his campaign and endorsement by national leadership. And I said No, I'm gonna stick to my guns on what I think is right for the constituents in my district.

Since Rep. Smith went public with his allegations, he has made several attempts to modify his original statement. Speaking to David Frownfelder of the *Daily Telegram* in Adrian, Mich. Rep. Smith said:

> I was told there would be aggressive, substantial support for my son, Brad [in his race for Congress] if I could vote yes on the bill. There were offers of endorsements and so maybe a member [of Congress] sitting close by said, 'Boy that really could be big money.' Tens of thousands or hundreds of thousands. But never was I offered any exact amount of money in exchange for my vote. Technically, in the legal description that I later reviewed on what a bribe is, probably it didn't meet the legal description of a bribe.

CENSORING C-SPAN

C-SPAN cameras perched above the House floor have for 25 years allowed the public to see for themselves how their representatives are carrying on the public's business. But the night of the vote on the prescription drug bill, the House leadership censored the public's view of the chamber.

In an interview on the 25th anniversary of C-SPAN's television coverage of Congress, the head of C-SPAN, Brian Lamb, noted that the congressional leadership has always controlled the cameras in the House and Senate chambers, generally focused on whoever is speaking, but also panning across the chamber to show activity on the floor. Lamb pointed out how the leadership's control of the cameras can subvert C-SPAN's studiously nonpartisan, objective coverage of Congress. Lamb said:

> You saw what happened in the middle of the night over the vote on Medicare on the floor of the House of Representatives, when they controlled the cameras. And I noticed that the camera wasn't moving from—it usually moves constantly from side to side. For almost the entire two or three hours that they had it open, the camera was showing the Democratic side. And that's where people don't get a fair shot.

In other words, the Republican leadership of the House intentionally diverted the C-SPAN cameras away from the Republican side of the House floor. Consequently, there is no visual record of who was talking to who that night while votes were sought by the leadership.

HHS SECRETARY ON THE HOUSE FLOOR

Rep. Smith said he was pressured during the three-hour vote by his own House leadership, but also, to his surprise, by the Department of Health and Human Services (HHS) Secretary Tommy Thompson, who made an unusual appearance on the House floor that night.

While House rules allow federal department heads to be in the House chamber, it is rare for such an official to be lobbying for legislation being considered by the House. According to *National Journal's CongressDaily*, Secretary Thompson defended the fact that he had broken House customs by lobbying members on the House floor during the final, three-hour roll call vote on the Medicare reform bill. "I spent five months working on this bill. I think it was only proper my being on the floor," Thompson said. But it appears Thompson's activities that night were a sharp departure from House customs.

MISLEADING CONGRESS AND WITHHOLDING PIVOTAL INFORMATION

"No government official should ever be muzzled from providing critical information to Congress."

—SENATOR CHUCK GRASSLEY (R-IA)
SENATE FINANCE COMMITTEE
CHAIRMAN

In 1997, Rep. Bill Thomas (R-CA) added language to the Balanced Budget Act conference report citing the importance of access by Congress to the estimates of HHS chief actuary (then, as now, Richard Foster). Some of that language in the conference report reads as follows:

It is important to emphasize that the Senate Committee on Finance, the House Committee on Ways and Means, and the House Committee on Commerce all rely on their ability to seek estimates and other technical assistance from the Chief Actuary, especially when developing new legislation. . . . The process of monitoring, updating and reforming the Medicare and Medicaid programs is greatly enhanced by the free flow of actuarial information from the Office of the Actuary to the committees of jurisdiction in the Congress. . . . When information is delayed or circumscribed by the operation of an internal Administration clearance process or the inadequacy of actuarial resources, the Committees' ability to make informed decisions based on the best available information is compromised.

Flying in the face of this statement, Foster, who has been the chief auditor in HHS for several years, said that he was threatened with dismissal if he released his official estimate of the cost of the prescription drug bill. His estimate added $156.5 billion to the estimated cost and likely would have led to several conservative Republicans voting against the bill.

In a public statement, Foster said:

For many years my office has provided technical assistance to the administration and Congress on a nonpartisan basis. But in June 2003, the Medicare administrator, Tom Scully, decided to restrict the practice of our responding directly to Congressional requests and ordered us to provide responses to him so he could decide what to do with them. There was a pattern of withholding information for what I perceived to be political purposes, which I thought was inappropriate.

Foster has said that he gave analyses in June 2003 to the White House and the Office of Management and Budget—which were not shared with Congress—predicting that prescription drug benefits being drafted on Capitol Hill would cost about $156 billion more than President Bush said he wanted to spend. Since Congress passed the Medicare bill, the Administration has revised its estimated 10-year cost of the program to $534 billion. Its original estimate was $395 billion.

Foster, the government's chief analyst of Medicare costs, says that he was warned repeatedly by his former boss, Thomas A. Scully, the Medicare administrator for three years, that he would be dismissed if he replied directly to legislative requests for information about prescription drug bills pending in Congress. In an email released by Foster, Scully's assistant, Jeffrey Flick, instructed the actuary to answer Republican queries regarding provisions in the Medicare bill but was warned—in bold font—not to provide information for Democratic requests "with anyone else until Tom Scully explicitly talks with you—authorizing release of information. The consequences for insubordination are extremely severe," Flick wrote in bold type. Interviews with federal officials, including Foster and Scully, make clear that the actuary's numbers were circulating within the Administration, and possibly among some Republican supporters of the bill on Capitol Hill, throughout the second half of last year, as Congress voted on the prescription drug bill, first in June and again in November.

At a hearing on Feb. 10, Secretary Thompson told lawmakers as much. Thompson said, "we knew all along" that the administration's cost estimates would be higher, but said he did not have a final figure until Dec. 24, 2003, after the bill was already signed into law.

On April 26, the Congressional Research Service issued a letter on the legality of Scully's decision to withhold information from Congress. Its conclusions read in part as follows:

> . . . actions which purposefully result in the transmission of knowingly false information to the United States Congress, and actions that involving the intentional and active prevention of the communication of accurate information to Congress in derogation of Federal law or responsibilities, might in certain circumstances involve activities which constitute violations of federal criminal provisions. . . . The issuance by an officer or employee in a department or agency of the Federal Government of a "gag order" on subordinate employees, to expressly prevent and prohibit those employees from communicating directly with Members or committees of Congress, would appear to violate a specific and express prohibition of federal law.

CONFERENCE COMMITTEE LOCKOUT

"This meeting is only open to the coalition of the willing."

—REP. BILL THOMAS (R-CA)
CHAIRMAN OF THE HOUSE WAYS AND
MEANS COMMITTEE

When the House and Senate each passed their own version of the Medicare bill, the Republican leadership at first followed routine procedure by appointing a 17-member conference committee to work out the differences between the two pieces of legislation. Seven Democrats were appointed to the committee. However, only two of those Democrats, Senators Max Baucus (MT) and John Breaux (LA), were included in the closed-door meetings that had actually produced the final legislation. Why? Because they were among the few Democrats who would not raise significant objections to the bill. According to conference members from both parties, when the bill was made available to the rest of the committee, they were given just one hour to review the 678-page document before they voted.

The ranking Democrat on the Ways and Means Committee, Rep. Charles Rangel (NY), was among the members of the original conference committee. However, he was excluded from the closed-door meetings. He arrived uninvited to one meeting, and Rep. Thomas, the conference chairman, stopped substantive discussion of the legislation until Rep. Rangel left.

Democrats and others have complained the tactics like those employed during the conference on the Medicare bill are becoming more common. Similar lockouts were staged during crucial conference committee meetings on huge energy and transportation bills. More and more the role of the full conference committee is perfunctory while the details of the legislation are hammered out in closed meetings that include only a small coterie handpicked by the party leadership.

SCULLY CASHES IN

In December 2003, as the ink of the President's signature was drying on the Medicare bill, Thomas A. Scully, the government official responsible for Medicare, announced that he was leaving the government for lucrative health care jobs in the private sector. He joined Alston & Bird, a law firm that represents hospitals, drug manufacturers and other companies in the health care industry. Scully also accepted a job with Welsh, Carson, Anderson & Stowe, a New York investment firm specializing in telecommunications and health care.

Surprisingly, even though federal law generally bars presidential appointees such as Scully from discussing possible employment with firms involved in matters handled by those officials, Scully obtained a waiver from the HHS ethics officer so that he could negotiate with potential employers while he helped write the Medicare law. These jobs did not just drop into his lap in December. He had apparently been negotiating with healthcare-related firms at the same time he was helping the Administration push the controversial prescription drug legislation through Congress, which directly affected those industries.

Apparently in response to criticism of Scully's waiver, the White House ordered federal agencies to cease issuing ethics waivers for senior Administration appointees that would allow them to pursue jobs with private companies while influencing federal policies that could affect those companies. A memo issued on Jan. 6, 2004 by the White House Chief of Staff stated that, effective immediately, such waivers could only be approved by the White House.

TAUZIN NEGOTIATES PHRMA JOB WHILE NEGOTIATING PRESCRIPTION DRUG BILL

As Medicare chief Scully was job searching while also helping pass the drug legislation, a powerful Member of Congress was also looking for a new job.

The Pharmaceutical Research and Manufacturers Association (PhRMA), the trade group for name-brand drug producers, reportedly offered Representative Billy Tauzin (R-LA) the top position at PhRMA and a compensation package that "would be the biggest deal given to anyone at a trade association," around $2 million a year, according to *The Washington Post*. The offer came just two months after Rep. Tauzin helped negotiate a $534 billion Medicare prescription drug bill widely viewed as a boon to pharmaceutical companies, which stand to make billions in profits while avoiding government price restrictions.

In February 2004, Common Cause called on Tauzin to resign his chairmanship of the powerful House Energy and Commerce Committee, saying "Even if your job negotiations with PhRMA began after your work on the Medicare bill was over, as you have reportedly said, it leaves one wondering whether you were trying to please PhRMA and what PhRMA may have promised you in return."

Tauzin denied there were any dealings with industry in exchange for his work on the bill, but he stepped down from the chairmanship of the House Energy and Commerce Committee in early February, while negotiations over the PhRMA lobbying post continued. The job remains open and Tauzin may still be eligible if it remains open at the end of his term.

DRUG INDUSTRY MONEY UNDERMINED THE PROCESS

As the Congressional fight on prescription drugs loomed, the drug industry drew up plans for raising millions of dollars to defeat efforts to reduce drug prices. The financial stakes were huge and the industry began to spend enormous amounts of money on campaign spending, lobbying, and advertising to influence the outcome of the legislation.

No group epitomized this more than PhRMA. PhRMA not only had a tremendous stake in the bill, but also turned out to be a major winner. The law prohibits the federal government from negotiating for lower drug prices and prohibits the reimportation of prescription drugs that are produced in the U.S. but sold for significantly less in other countries, which would also bring down the price of drugs.

PhRMA increased its yearly budget 23 percent to $150 million in anticipation of the upcoming Medicare fight. While PhRMA's interests range from international policy to local initiatives, industry protection in the Medicare reform bill was its top priority. According to published reports, PhRMA planned to spend $1 million for an "intellectual echo chamber of economists—a standing network of economists and thought leaders to speak against federal price control regulations through articles and testimony, and to serve as a rapid response team." Says one PhRMA document, "Unless we achieve enactment this year of market-based Medicare drug coverage for seniors, the industry's vulnerability will increase in the remainder of 2003 and in the 2004 election year."

PhRMA is well-known as one of Washington's most powerful lobbying forces. The trade group alone spent $16 million on lobbying in 2003, according to federal lobby disclosure reports filed with the Senate Office of Public Records. Including lobbying spent by all of PhRMA's companies, the group spent at least $72.6 million lobbying in 2003—or roughly $135,701 per member of Congress.

PhRMA has capitalized on hiring former Members of Congress and their staffs as part of its lobbying army. According to reports, PhRMA lobbyists include former Reps. Vic Fazio (D-CA), Vin Weber (R-MN) and Bill Paxon (R-NY). Other drug industry lobbyists include David W. Beier, former domestic policy advisor for Vice President Al Gore; Dave Larson, former health policy advisor to Senator Bill First (R-TN); and Edwin A. Buckham, former chief of staff to Rep. Tom DeLay.

The industry maintains a constant presence among policymakers. For example, in the weeks following the House and Senate's passage of their respective Medicare bills in June, pharmaceutical companies organized parties for congressional staffers that worked on the legislation. According to *The Washington Post*, the drug company Johnson & Johnson planned a cocktail party near the Capitol. The invitations read, "In recognition of your part in the historic passage of Medicare drug bills by both houses of Congress . . ." After Common Cause sent letters to Senate conferees and House leaders stating that attendance by staff members to the party could violate congressional ethics rules, the leadership discouraged their staff from going and the party was later cancelled. Congressional staff still had the opportunity, however, to attend a "Rooftop Rendezvous" thrown by PhRMA and hospital trade groups.

HHS Propaganda Campaign

Once legislation passes Congress and is signed into law by the President, it is the job of the executive branch to implement the new law, including informing the public of the effect or the benefits of the new law. HHS, charged with implementing the new prescription drug law, immediately launched a multi-million dollar campaign promoting the new prescription drug benefit under the guise of public service advertising.

Early this year, HHS created a TV ad designed to educate the public on the new drug benefits, but many criticized the ads as being political advertisements for the Administration that mislead the public about the facts of the new program. Adding to the concern about politicization of the prescription drug program was a contract for $9.5 million for producing and distributing the ads that went to a partisan media company, National Media, Inc.

HHS has also produced videos that were sent to broadcasters around the country touting the new program. The videos feature hired "reporters" who appear to be delivering straight news stories, but do not identify the government as the producer. Two videos end with the voice of a woman who says, "In Washington, I'm Karen Ryan reporting." The "reporter" in the commercial is reading from a script written by HHS.

The General Accounting Office (GAO) is now investigating these "fake video news" clips. The GAO will determine if they constitute illegal "covert propaganda." Federal law prohibits the use of federal money for "publicity or propaganda purposes" not authorized by Congress.

Conclusion

Posted on Congressional websites is a document called "How Our Laws Are Made." [http://thomas.loc.gov/home/lawsmade.toc.html] No one really believes the process meticulously detailed in the document is followed exactly—legislating is a messy process. But the laws, rules and procedures cited in the document are there to ensure that democratic principles are not empty words in the Constitution, but inform the way our government operates on a daily basis.

This report has told a tale of the rush to pass a thinly supported prescription drug bill that was a prime political goal of the Administration. In that rush, supporters showed disregard for the law, congressional rules, and other procedures and customs. We must reform and strengthen some of those laws and rules and, perhaps more importantly, those public officials must be held accountable. Americans must be assured that democracy is not just another word, but an integral part of how our government operates.

DISCUSSION QUESTIONS

1. What are the various ways the Republican leadership of Congress and the executive branch undermined the legislative process in pursuit of a Medicare and prescription drug reform bill? How is democracy threatened by such tactics?
2. Why do you think there is such a gulf between the appearance and reality of how a bill becomes a law within the U.S. Congress? Would the quality of citizenship be improved if the truth were more widely known? Explain.

23 *Matt Taibbi*

WALL STREET'S BIG WIN
The Charade of Financial Reform

In 2008, the U.S. economy was plunged into the worst recession since the Great Depression of the late 1920s and 1930s. Indeed, the economy still has not come close to a full recovery. Writing in the typical rough-and-tumble, populist rhetorical style for which Rolling Stone *is famous, congressional and finance reporter Matt Taibbi offers us a behind-the-scenes glimpse at the real world of congressional efforts to "reform" the sometimes shady practices of an out-of-control financial sector. Led by Wall Street investment bankers, their legion of lobbyists, corporate CEOs, assorted financial experts, and pro-business Senators and Representatives, financial deregulation since 1999 essentially "transformed Wall Street into a giant casino." This enabled Wall Street to earn huge profits from reckless and sometimes fraudulent practices, including the explosion of subprime home mortgages. When President Obama took over in 2009, he vowed to rein in such financial excesses and clean up the mess. But Taibbi details the actual inside give-and-take among key players in the Senate and House, the Obama administration, and corporate lobbyists that resulted in passage of the Dodd-Frank Wall Street Reform and Consumer Protection Act, which, while not totally toothless, turned out to largely benefit the industry it was supposed to regulate. None of the insider details Taibbi reveals are particularly unusual. Indeed, they were business as usual, as private power overcame public purpose. But the public seldom has this clear a glimpse into the inner workings of such congressional battles. When paired with the fight over the Medicare prescription drug program in Article 22, the picture that emerges raises serious questions about the nature of our representative democracy.*

Cue the credits: the era of financial thuggery is officially over. Three hellish years of panic, all done and gone—the mass bankruptcies, midnight bailouts, shotgun mergers of dying megabanks, high-stakes SEC investigations, all capped by a legislative orgy in which industry lobbyists

Source: Matt Taibbi, "Wall Street's Big Win: Finance Reform Won't Stop the High-Risk Gambling that Wrecked the Economy—and Republicans Aren't the Only Ones to Blame," *Rolling Stone Magazine*, Issue 1111, 19 August 2010.

hurled more than $600 million at Congress. It all supposedly came to an end one Wednesday morning a few weeks back, when President Obama, flanked by hundreds of party flacks and congressional bigwigs, stepped up to the lectern at an extravagant ceremony to sign into law his sweeping new bill to clean up Wall Street.

Obama's speech introducing the massive law brimmed with celebratory finality. He threw around lofty phrases like "never again" and "no more." He proclaimed the end of unfair credit-card-rate hikes and issued a fatwa on abusive mortgage practices and the shady loans that helped fuel the debt bubble. The message was clear: The sheriff was padlocking the Wall Street casino, and the government was taking decisive steps to unfuck our hopelessly broken economy.

But is the nightmare really over, or is this just another *Inception*-style trick ending? It's hard to figure, given all the absurd rhetoric emanating from the leadership of both parties. Obama and the Democrats boasted that the bill is the "toughest financial reform since the ones we created in the aftermath of the Great Depression"— a claim that would maybe be more impressive if Congress had passed any financial reforms since the Great Depression, or at least *any* that didn't specifically involve radically *undoing* the Depression-era laws.

The Republicans, meanwhile, were predictably hysterical. They described the new law— officially known as the Dodd-Frank Wall Street Reform and Consumer Protection Act—as something not far from a full-blown Marxist seizure of the means of production. House Minority Leader John Boehner shrieked that it was like "killing an ant with a nuclear weapon," apparently forgetting that the ant crisis in question wiped out about 40 percent of the world's wealth in a little over a year, making its smallness highly debatable.

But Dodd-Frank was neither an FDR-style, paradigm-shifting reform, nor a historic assault on free enterprise. What it was, ultimately, was a cop-out, a Band-Aid on a severed artery. If it marks the end of anything at all, it represents the end of the best opportunity we had to do

something real about the criminal hijacking of America's financial-services industry. During the yearlong legislative battle that forged this bill, Congress took a long, hard look at the shape of the modern American economy—and then decided that it didn't have the stones to wipe out our country's one dependably thriving profit center: theft.

It's not that there's nothing good in the bill. In fact, there are many good things in it, even some historic things. Sen. Bernie Sanders and others won a fight to allow Congress to audit the Fed's books for the first time ever. A new Consumer Financial Protection Bureau was created to protect against predatory lending and other abuses. New lending standards will be employed in the mortgage industry; no more meth addicts buying mansions with credit cards. And in perhaps the biggest win of all, there will be new rules forcing some varieties of derivatives—the arcane instruments that Warren Buffett called "financial weapons of mass destruction"—to be traded and cleared on open exchanges, pushing what had been a completely opaque market into the light of day for the first time.

All of this is great, but taken together, these reforms fail to address even a tenth of the real problem. Worse: They fail to even define what the real problem is. Over a long year of feverish lobbying and brutally intense backroom negotiations, a group of D.C. insiders fought over a single question: Just how much of the truth about the financial crisis should we share with the public? Do we admit that control over the economy in the past decade was ceded to a small group of rapacious criminals who to this day are engaged in a mind-numbing campaign of theft on a global scale? Or do we pretend that, minus a few bumps in the road that have mostly been smoothed out, the clean-hands capitalism of Adam Smith still rules the day in America? In other words, do people need to know the real version, in all its majestic whorebotchery, or can we get away with some bullshit cover story?

In passing Dodd-Frank, they went with the cover story.

During an otherwise deathly boring year spent covering this debate, I learned to derive some entertainment from watching politicians scramble to give floor speeches about financial reform without disclosing the fact that they didn't have the first fucking clue what a credit-default swap is, or how a derivative works. This was certainly true of Democrats, but the Republicans were way, way better at it. Their strategy was brilliant in its simplicity: Don't even bother trying to figure out the math-y stuff, and instead just blame the entire crisis on government efforts to make homeowners of lazy black people. "Private enterprise mixed with social engineering" was how Sen. Richard Shelby of Alabama put it, with a straight face, not long before the bill passed.

The argument favored by Wall Street lobbyists and Obama's team of triangulating pro-business Democrats was more subtle. In this strangely metaphysical version of recent history, the economy was ruined by bad luck and a few bad actors, not by any particular law or policy. It was the "guns don't kill people, people kill people" argument expanded to cover global financial fraud. "There is an assumption that math is evil," insisted Keith Hennessey, a member of the Financial Crisis Inquiry Commission, at a hearing in June. "Credit-default swaps are things, and things can't be culprits."

Both of these takes were engineered to avoid an uncomfortable political truth: The huge profits that Wall Street earned in the past decade were driven in large part by a single, far-reaching scheme, one in which bankers, home lenders and other players exploited loopholes in the system to magically transform subprime home borrowers into AAA investments, sell them off to unsuspecting pension funds and foreign trade unions and other suckers, then multiply their score by leveraging their phony-baloney deals over and over. It was pure financial alchemy—turning manure into gold, then spinning it Rumpelstiltskin-style into vast profits using complex, mostly unregulated new instruments that almost no one outside of a few experts in the field really understood.

With the government borrowing mountains of Chinese and Saudi cash to fight two crazy wars, and the domestic manufacturing base mostly vanished overseas, this massive fraud for all intents and purposes was the American economy in the 2000s; we were a nation subsisting on an elaborate check-bouncing scheme.

And it was all made possible by two major deregulatory moves from the Clinton era: the Gramm-Leach-Bliley Act of 1999, which allowed investment banks, insurance companies and commercial banks to merge, and the Commodity Futures Modernization Act of 2000, which exempted the entire derivatives market from federal regulation. Together, these two laws transformed Wall Street into a giant casino, allowing commercial banks to act like high-risk hedge funds, with a whole new galaxy of derivative bets to lay action on. In fact, the laws made Wall Street even crazier than a casino, because in a casino you have to put up actual money to make bets. But thanks to deregulation, financial companies like AIG could bet billions, if not trillions, without having any money at all to back up their gambles.

Dodd-Frank was never going to be a meaningful reform unless these two fateful Clinton-era laws—commercial banks gambling with taxpayer money, and unregulated derivatives being traded in the dark—were reversed. The story of how the last real shot at reining in Wall Street got routed tells you everything you need to know about how, and on whose behalf, our government works. It was Congress at its most cowardly, deceptive best, with both parties teaming up to subject reform to death by a thousand paper cuts—with the worst cuts coming, literally, in the final moments before the bill's passage.

The first of the two final battles coalesced around an effort by Sens. Carl Levin of Michigan and Jeff Merkley of Oregon to implement the so-called "Volcker rule," a proposal designed to restore the firewall between investment houses and commercial banks. At the heart of Merkley-Levin was one key section: a ban on proprietary trading.

"Prop trading" is just a fancy term for banks gambling in the market for their own profit. Thanks to the Clinton-era deregulation, giant commercial banks like JP Morgan Chase were not only allowed to serve as investment banks, accumulating mountains of privileged insider information, they were allowed to play the markets themselves. That meant that the prop-trading desk at Goldman Sachs could bet heavily against Greek debt not long after the bank had saddled Greece with toxic interest-rate swaps. It also meant that if any of these "too big to fail" banks went bust, American taxpayers would be expected to bail them out. The Volcker rule—pushed by Paul Volcker, the former Fed chief and current Obama adviser—aimed to lay down a simple law for big banks: If you want to gamble like a drunken sailor, fine. Just don't expect us to mop up the mess after you puke your guts out.

If Obama's team had had their way, last month's debate over the Volcker rule would never have happened. When the original version of the finance-reform bill passed the House last fall—heavily influenced by treasury secretary and noted pencil-necked Wall Street stooge Timothy Geithner—it contained no attempt to ban banks with federally insured deposits from engaging in prop trading. But that changed when Scott Brown, the Tea Party darling from Massachusetts, blindsided the Democrats by wresting away the seat of deceased liberal icon Ted Kennedy. With voters seething over Wall Street's rampant thievery and fraud, the Democrats suddenly got religion about reckless gambling by the financial industry.

Brown won his election on January 19th; just two days later, on January 21st, President Obama pulled a 180 and announced his support for the Volcker rule. Throughout the reform process, Volcker—a legendary figure whose demands for greater responsibility and transparency have alarmed Wall Street—had been forced to take a back seat to Geithner, at one point even sharply criticizing the House bill in open testimony. For the White House to suddenly throw its weight behind Volcker took the Hill by surprise. It was a "complete change of policy—a fundamental shift," observed Simon Johnson, an MIT economist and noted financial analyst. This was clearly the administration's attempt to get back on the right side of populist anger at Wall Street. So when Merkley and Levin took up the job of transforming Volcker's proposal into legislative reality, they assumed the Democratic leadership would be on their side.

It didn't work out that way. The counterattack began in May, when the Republicans objected to Merkley-Levin and invoked the Senate's unanimous-consent rule, by which no amendment comes to the floor unless all 100 members agree to let it be voted on. That left the Volcker rule in legislative purgatory right up to the initial Senate vote on the bill. In interviews, the soft-spoken, gregarious Merkley steadfastly refuses to point the finger at the Democratic leadership for failing to break the legislative logjam. But reading between the lines, it's obvious that he and Levin were on their own—no one with any juice in the key committees lifted a finger to help them. The two senators were like underage geeks who'd been told by Majority Leader Harry Reid that they had to come up with their own keg if they wanted to come to the party.

But come up with a keg they did. On the week of the first Senate vote, Merkley's staffers pored over Senate procedural rules and discovered an arcane clause that allowed them to attach their proposal to an amendment by Republican Sam Brownback of Kansas designed to exempt auto dealers from regulation by the new Consumer Financial Protection Bureau. The Brownback amendment had already been approved for a vote, so once Merkley's people used the remora-fish tactic of sticking to Brownback, there was seemingly no way to prevent Merkley-Levin from going to a vote.

Or so they thought. "We were plumbing the inner rules of the Senate," Merkley says. One of those rules is that when you attach your amendment to another, your measure has to be "germane" to the amendment you're attaching it to. Since Merkley-Levin's ban on prop trading and Brownback's auto-dealer exemption were completely different, this was not a simple thing to accomplish. So Merkley and Levin personally trekked down to one of the more obscure offices in the congressional complex.

"Carl Levin and I went on a trip down to the parliamentarian's office, where I'd never been," Merkley says. "They briefed us on what it took, and the team set about to make it work."

From there, Merkley and Levin hit the phones to lobby other members, including Republicans. Right up to the final vote on May 20th, they thought they had a real shot. "I got the sense that we might pick up quite a few Republican votes," says Merkley. "It was starting to look pretty good."

But that very fact that the Merkley-Levin amendment had such momentum is ultimately what did it in. "What killed us," says Merkley, "was that it was looking pretty good."

What happened next was a prime example of the basic con of congressional politics. Throughout the debate over finance reform, Democrats had sold the public on the idea that it was the Republicans who were killing progressive initiatives. In reality, Republican and Democratic leaders were working together with industry insiders and deep-pocketed lobbyists to prevent rogue members like Merkley and Levin from effecting real change. In public, the parties stage a show of bitter bipartisan stalemate. But when the cameras are off, they fuck like crazed weasels in heat.

With Merkley-Levin looking like a good bet to pass, the Republicans pulled a dual-suicide maneuver. Brownback withdrew his auto-dealer exemption, which instantly killed the ban on prop trading. What Merkley and Levin didn't know was that Brownback had worked out an agreement with the Democratic leadership to surreptitiously restore his auto-dealer exemption later on, when the final bill was reconciled with the House version. In other words, Democratic leaders had teamed up with Republicans behind closed doors to double-cross Merkley and Levin.

When the agreement was announced one day before the Senate vote, Merkley couldn't even make sense of what he was hearing. "You're

sitting there trying to understand what kind of deal has been struck," he says. "You know there's something there, but you're not really sure." Merkley almost objected to the deal, but unable to grasp that he had been sold out by his own party's leadership, he hesitated—a fatal mistake. The deal to reinstate Brownback went through, and Merkley's amendment to rein in Wall Street died.

That might have been the end of the Volcker rule—but soon after, Merkley and Levin made the most of their one last chance. According to Merkley, he and Levin convinced Rep. Barney Frank, who was overseeing the House bill, to reintroduce the amendment in conference talks. The Volcker rule was alive again—but it now began a journey into a new sort of hell, in which insiders from both parties chipped away at it until there was almost nothing left.

It started with Senate rookie Scott Brown, who demanded major changes to Merkley-Levin on behalf of big Massachusetts banks in exchange for his vote. But Senate sources I talked to insist that Chris Dodd, the powerful chair of the Senate Banking Committee, was just using Brown as a cover to gut the Volcker rule. "It became far more than accommodating the Massachusetts banks," says one high-ranking Senate aide. "It became a ruse for Treasury trying to get as far as they could, with Dodd's help."

From the start, Dodd had been opposed to the ban on proprietary trading. "Hey, I would gladly dump the Volcker rule," he reportedly told industry lobbyists. "But I can't, because of the pressure I'm getting from the left." Now, with Brown pressing for concessions, Dodd agreed to let Merkley-Levin be spattered with a wave of loopholes. If you can imagine a 4,000-pound lizard pretending to cower before a Cub Scout clutching a lollipop, then you've grasped the basic dynamic of a grizzled legislative titan like Dodd caving into Brown, the cheery GOP newbie with the Pez-dispenser face.

First, in what amounted to an open handout to the financial interests represented by Brown, insurers, mutual funds and trusts were exempted from the Merkley-Levin ban. Then, with the floodgates officially open, every financial company in America was granted a massive loophole—one that allowed them to skirt the ban on risky gambling by investing a designated percentage of their holdings in hedge funds and private-equity companies.

The common justification for this loophole, known as the *de minimis* exemption, was that banks need it to retain their "traditional businesses" and remain competitive against hedge funds. In other words, Congress must allow banks to act like hedge funds because otherwise they'd be unable to compete with hedge funds in the hedge-fund business. With the introduction of the *de minimis* exemption, Merkley-Levin went from being an absolute ban on federally insured banks engaging in high-risk speculation to a feeble, half-assed restriction that will be difficult, if not impossible, to enforce.

The driving force behind the exemption was not Scott Brown, but the Obama administration itself. By all accounts, Geithner lobbied hard on the issue. "Treasury's official position went from opposed to supportive," one aide told reporters. "They may have even overshot Brown's desires by a bit." Throughout the negotiations over the bill, in fact, Geithner acted almost like a liaison to the financial industry, pushing for Wall Street-friendly changes on everything from bailouts (his initial proposal allowed the White House to unilaterally fork over taxpayer money to banks in unlimited amounts) to high-risk investments (he fought to let megabanks hold on to their derivatives desks).

Geithner went all out for the *de minimis* exemption; one Senate aide was told flatly by "those who are in charge of counting noses" that the proposal was not subject to negotiation. This was the horse-head-in-the-bed moment of the Dodd-Frank bill—the offer that couldn't be refused. "We were told that there needed to be *de minimis* or there would be no bill," the aide says.

When Merkley first got the news about the exemption, he tried to keep it small. "I was hoping to limit it to one percent" of a company's tangible equity, he says. "The night before the conference, Geithner

was pushing for two percent. In the end, it got even worse—it was three percent." When Merkley tried to put a specific dollar limit of $250 million on high-risk gambling, Geithner shot him down. "He didn't want the sub-cap, and we lost," Merkley says.

Still, during the last round of negotiations, Merkley and Levin managed to pare back some of the worst of the exemptions. In one victory, they eliminated a proposal by Geithner that would have allowed banks to make unlimited trades "in facilitation of customer relations"—a loophole so laughably broad that it would cover, in the words of one Senate aide, "pretty much everything" that banks wanted to do. By June 25th, when the bill headed to its final meeting of the conference committee, it looked like Merkley and Levin would finally get their vote.

But that was before the senator from Wall Street showed up. In the final hours of negotiations, a congressional delegation from New York, led by Sen. Chuck Schumer, decided to take one last run at gutting the Volcker rule. It was as though someone had sent the scrubs off the court and called in the varsity. Schumer, a platitudinous champion of liberal social issues, moonlights as a pillbox-hat bellhop to Wall Street on economic matters. The self-aggrandizing New Yorker has not only fought to keep taxes low on hedge-fund billionaires, he got up onstage with Goldman Sachs CEO Lloyd Blankfein at a Democratic fundraiser in 2006 and performed "nostalgic furniture-store jingles."

This bears repeating: The person in whose hands America had placed its hopes for finance reform was someone who once sang furniture jingles onstage with Lloyd Blankfein.

Now, as the bill headed into final negotiations, the Schumer coalition suddenly decided that the *de minimis* exemption for banks simply wasn't big enough. In a neat trick, Schumer's crew agreed to keep the exemption at three percent—but they raised the limit dramatically by making it three percent of *something else*. Instead of being pegged to a bank's "tangible equity," the exemption would now be calculated based on a financial firm's "Tier 1" capital—a far bigger pool of money that includes a bank's common shares and deferred-tax assets instead of just preferred shares. In real terms, banks could now put up to 40 percent more into high-risk investments. "It was almost double what Geithner was talking about the night before," says Merkley. "For Bank of America alone, it comes to $6 billion."

Schumer himself entered the change in the Senate version of the bill—and then asked the House to sign off on it 15 minutes later. Rep. Paul Kanjorski of Pennsylvania, who had worked hard on the Volcker rule, tried to get a vote to block the change. But Barney Frank laid into him. "You had plenty of time with this," Frank barked. "You knew what was coming—*siddown.*"

Thus the Merkley-Levin across-the-board ban on risky proprietary trading became a partial ban in which insurers, mutual funds and trusts are completely exempt, and banks can still gamble three percent of their holdings. In practice, it will be up to future regulators to define how that limit will be calculated—and one can only imagine how far banks like Goldman Sachs will manage to stretch the loopholes in what's left of the Volcker rule. "It's not a *total* nothing burger," sighs one aide. "But, by the end, it didn't change a whole lot."

If the Volcker rule was a regulatory Godzilla threatening to stomp out Wall Street's self-serving investments, the proposal to shut down derivatives was nothing short of a planet-smashing asteroid headed straight at the heart of the financial industry's most reckless abuses. The key battle involved the so-called "Lincoln rule," put forward by Sen. Blanche Lincoln of Arkansas, which would have forced big banks to spin off their derivatives desks in the same way the Volcker rule would have forced them to give up proprietary trading. Banks would have to make a choice: Either forgo access to the cheap cash of the Federal Reserve, or give up gambling with dangerous instruments like credit-default swaps. Banks, in short, would have to go back to making money the old-fashioned way—making smart loans, underwriting new businesses, earning simple fees on customer trades. No more leveraged

gambling on whacked-out acid-trip derivatives deals, no more walking around with torches and taking out fire insurance on other people's houses, no more running up huge markers on the taxpayer's dime.

This, obviously, could not be permitted. Thanks to Clinton-era deregulation, the market for derivatives is now 100 times larger than the federal budget, and five of the country's biggest banks control more than 90 percent of the business. So the leadership of both parties pulled out all the stops to ensure that the Lincoln rule would be Swiss-cheesed to death before it ever saw the light of day.

The effort began with an extraordinary scene on the floor of the Senate—one that testifies to the nearly unanimous respect that senators hold for the human loophole machine known as Chris Dodd. In late May, the week the Senate voted on its version of the bill, Dodd came up with a hastily composed, five-page substitute to the Lincoln rule that would create a "financial stability" council with the power to unilaterally kill the rule. Faced with opposition from members of his own party, Dodd agreed to withdraw his substitute two days before the Senate vote—but given his track record of legislative maneuvering on behalf of big banks, his fellow Democrats weren't about to take him at his word. A group of senators from Dodd's own party—including Maria Cantwell of Washington—arranged to stay on the Senate floor in shifts, ensuring that there would be someone there to object in case Dodd tried to push his substitute through during one of those quiet, empty-hall, C-SPAN moments when no one was looking.

The fact that a group of Democrats had to come up with a scheme to prevent one of their own leaders from dropping a roofie in their legislative drinks pretty much sums up the state of affairs in Congress. "Yeah, that's the way it went down," says a Senate aide familiar with the Dodd Watch maneuver.

With Dodd unable to introduce his plan to gut the Lincoln rule, the measure actually passed in the Senate, to the extreme surprise of almost everyone on the Hill. This was a rare example of the Senate leadership not just allowing a vote on a financial reform guaranteed to cost major campaign contributors billions of dollars, but actually *passing* it.

But the ink was barely dry on the Senate bill before a full-blown mobilization against the Lincoln rule was under way. Just days after the Senate vote, Barney Frank came out and voiced opposition to the rule, saying it "goes too far." He trotted out Wall Street's lame, catchall justification for unfettered speculation: Banks need derivatives to balance their portfolios and "hedge their own risk." Not long after, a group of 43 conservative House Democrats calling themselves the "New Democrat Coalition" refused to support the reform bill unless the toughest part of the Lincoln rule—section 716—was gutted. "They were threatening to vote against the legislation unless accommodations were made for the banks, and the biggest accommodation was watering down 716," says Michael Greenberger, a Clinton-era financial regulator involved in the talks.

It seemed like every Democrat who mattered was against 716: Dodd, Frank, the New Democrats, the Treasury department, the influential FDIC chief Sheila Bair, even Paul Volcker. Schumer and other New Yorkers lobbied mightily against it, arguing that it would be a drain on the income of Wall Street banks; New York mayor Michael Bloomberg traveled to Washington specifically to lobby against the Lincoln rule. But the crowd had turned against Wall Street, and the populist scrubs seemed like they were about to win big.

But then Blanche Lincoln, the captain of the scrubs, coughed up the ball. Lincoln, who was never considered a particularly strong advocate of finance reform, had originally proposed her ban on derivatives—the most radical reform in the entire bill—during a re-election campaign in which she faced a stiff populist challenge from Bill Halter, the lieutenant governor of Arkansas. Rumors circulated in Washington that Democratic leaders were cynically holding off on gutting Lincoln's proposal until she got past Halter in the primary.

If that was the plan, it worked. In early June, only a week after she defeated Halter in the runoff, Lincoln set about gutting her own rule. First she offered a broad exemption for community banks. Then a group of conservative House Democrats led by Rep. Collin Peterson of Minnesota proposed an even bigger compromise—one that would exempt virtually every type of derivative from federal oversight. "I was told that Peterson offered this compromise and Lincoln quickly accepted it," says Greenberger.

That was the beginning of the end. The new deal allowed banks to keep their derivatives desks by moving them into subsidiary units and exempted whole classes of derivatives from regulation: interest-rate swaps (the culprits in disasters like Greece and Orange County), foreign-exchange swaps (which helped trigger a global crash after Long Term Capital Management imploded in 1998), cleared credit-default swaps (a big contributor to the AIG collapse) and currency swaps (also involved in the Greece mess). "About 90 percent of the derivatives market was exempted," says Greenberger.

In the end, this would be the entire list of derivatives that are subject to the new law: credit-default swaps that have not been cleared by regulators and swaps involving commodities other than silver and gold.

Hilariously, even the few new regulations on derivatives that remained in the bill don't seem to worry Wall Street. Just a few weeks after Lincoln agreed to gut the measure, famed JP Morgan executive Blythe Masters, often credited as one of the inventors of the credit-default swap—one insider calls her "the Darth Vader of the swaps market"—actually sounded psyched about the bill. The new law, she declared publicly, won't even hurt energy commodities, one of the few classes of derivatives that Lincoln *didn't* exempt.

"It's not a big change for commodities," Masters said. "It's fine-tuning more than a material impact." The so-called reforms, she concluded, "are actually going to be very beneficial for the industry."

And that, ladies and gentlemen, is what the Obama administration is touting as the toughest financial reform since the Great Depression.

The systematic gutting of both the Lincoln rule and the Volcker rule in the final days before the passage of Dodd-Frank was especially painful, in part, because so many other crucial reforms that would have spoken directly to the Big Fraud had already been whitewashed out of the bill. An amendment mandating the breakup of too-big-to-fail companies got walloped back in May, and Congress even rejected a ban on "naked" credit-default swaps—the financial equivalent of selling somebody a car with crappy brakes and then taking out a life-insurance policy on the driver.

The few reforms that Congress didn't reject outright it simply kicked into a series of "study groups" created by the bill. Along with promised studies on no-brainers like executive compensation and credit-rating agencies, the bill even punts on the fundamental question of how much capital banks should be required to keep on hand as a hedge against meltdowns, leaving the question to the Basel banking conferences in Switzerland later this year, where financial interests from all over the world will gather to hammer things out in inscrutable backroom negotiations.

"The next phase of all this—the regulatory phase—is going to be supertechnical and complex," says one Senate aide. "It raises questions about how journalists are going to keep the public the slightest bit interested. You might as well just hit the snooze button."

Worst of all, some analysts warn that the failure to rein in Wall Street makes another meltdown a near-certainty. "Oh, sure, within a decade," said Johnson, the MIT economist. "The question: Is it three years or seven years?"

Johnson was part of a panel sponsored by the nonpartisan Roosevelt Institute—including Nobel Prize-winning economist Joseph Stiglitz and bailout watchdog Elizabeth Warren—that concluded back in March that the reform bill wouldn't do anything to stop a "doomsday cycle." Too-big-to-fail banks, they said, would continue to borrow money to take massive risks, pay shareholders and management bonuses with the proceeds, then stick taxpayers with the bill when it all goes wrong. "Risk-taking at banks will soon be larger than ever," the panel warned.

Without the Volcker rule and the Lincoln rule, the final version of finance reform is like treating the opportunistic symptoms of AIDS without taking on the virus itself. In a sense, the failure of Congress to treat the disease is a tacit admission that it has no strategy for our economy going forward that doesn't involve continually inflating and reinflating speculative bubbles. Which sucks, because what happened to our economy over the past three years, and is still happening to it now, was not an accident or an oversight, but a sweeping crime wave unleashed by a financial industry gone completely over to the dark side. The bill Congress just passed doesn't go after the criminals where they live, or even make what they're doing a crime; all it does is put a baseball bat under the bed and add an extra lock or two on the doors. It's a hack job, a C-minus effort. See you at the next financial crisis.

DISCUSSION QUESTIONS

1. Why were the "Volcker rule" and the "Lincoln rule" eventually stripped from the Dodd-Frank financial reform bill? Why does it appear to be so difficult to seriously regulate the Wall Street financial sector when it is widely believed to be responsible for the financial crisis that has damaged severely the economy and the livelihood of millions of Americans since 2008?
2. Which political party do you feel is most to blame for this charade of financial reform, and why? What does Taibbi's analysis suggest about the current state of our two party system?

24 *Patricia Siplon and William F. Grover*

CONGRESSIONAL INERTIA
Iron Triangles Old and New

American citizens often complain about the performance of Congress. When Congress does act, citizens seldom view that action as benefiting the average middle-class and working-class American. In this article, political scientists Patricia Siplon and William Grover draw upon the time-tested concept of the "iron triangle" to explain the causes of congressional inertia. They trace the history of iron triangles to the earlier notion of the "military–industrial complex," which was articulated by President Dwight Eisenhower in his 1961 Farewell Address, and later expanded into an analysis of defense contracting by political scientist Gordon Adams. Adams defined the iron triangle as a symbiotic relationship among congressional committees and subcommittees, executive branch agencies, and private interest groups, particularly corporations. He was troubled by ever-rising defense budgets and how in U.S. defense policy, private corporate interests regularly came to be equated with the public interest. Moving beyond the example of military budgets, Siplon and Grover turn their attention to the role of iron triangles in HIV/AIDS policy. Since the early 1980s, the pharmaceutical industry has vigorously lobbied Congress, and worked closely with the Food and Drug Administration, to shape the nation's approach to the development, regulation, and pricing of drugs to fight the AIDS pandemic. The resulting pharmaceutical iron triangle dramatically impacted the development, pricing, and availability of the drugs azidothymidine (AZT) and Norvir. In the face of the deaths of millions suffering from AIDS worldwide, the fight to provide widespread access to cheap generic AIDS drugs continues, with occasional victories for social groups challenging this particular iron triangle. As with the example of defense contracting, when it comes to the life and death circumstances with HIV/AIDS policy, Congress far too often plays the role of a lapdog for corporate interests, instead of acting as a watchdog for the interests of American citizens.

Source: The authors have written this article specifically for *Voices of Dissent*.

What Congress does matters. As the new 110th Congress convened in January of 2007, it began the process of constructing the fiscal year 2008 budget, authorizing spending in the vicinity of $2.8 trillion when the new fiscal year begins October 1 (the corresponding figure for FY 2012 is more than $3.7 trillion). This is an incomprehensibly large amount of money—a sum that represents many things.[1] Most notably, it is a numerical statement about priorities; what we value as a society is indicated in how we allocate our budgetary resources. What do U.S. citizens think of those who allocate our budgetary resources? If we follow poll data, the answer clearly is: "not much." It has long been noted that while citizens routinely rate their own Senators and Representatives favorably, Congress as an institution gets very low marks. A *New York Times*/CBS news poll released in late September 2006 showed the approval rating for Congress at barely 25 percent, a dozen points below President George W. Bush's own anemic approval rating. The accompanying story observed that public "disdain for Congress is as intense as it has been since 1994," when Republicans captured both the House and Senate for the first time in decades. A full 77 percent of respondents in the *Times*/CBS poll said the 109th Congress had not done a good enough job to merit being reelected. Accordingly, voters expressed their displeasure with Republican control of Congress in November 2006, returning Democrats to power in the House and, more narrowly, in the Senate. Clearly something is afoot here. Opposition to the Bush administration's debacle in Iraq surely soured voters, as did corruption scandals involving some leading officials. But beneath those immediate issues lies a deeper sense that Congress does not deliver the goods—at least for ordinary Americans. As an institution, Congress is widely perceived to suffer from entrenched inertia that leaves it unable to

change course. Why is it so difficult for our legislative branch to change direction to respond to shifting priorities?

A BRIEF HISTORY OF A METAPHOR

Political science is awash in metaphors. The intent of a well-constructed metaphor is to capture some complex aspect of politics with an easily understood example. The opening paragraph above involves the most important and complicated function performed by Congress—readily conceptualized as controlling the national "purse strings." A multitude of metaphors winds its way through our political landscape: "horse races," "landslides," "pork," "log rolling," "hawks and doves," "quagmires"—these barely scratch the surface. Indeed, sociologist Max Weber once famously argued that a combination of passion and perspective is needed to succeed in politics, characterizing politics itself as, metaphorically, "a strong and slow boring of hard boards." Understanding the difficulty in getting Congress to change course, to address policy issues in a fresh way with the public interest at heart, involves one of the most apt metaphors used in congressional studies: the "iron triangle."

The origins of the iron triangle metaphor are rooted in the development of a closely related concept known as the "military–industrial complex." Although references to the military–industrial complex go back at least to the early part of the twentieth century, the most well-known usage came in President Dwight Eisenhower's Farewell Address on January 17, 1961. Eisenhower was a moderate Republican with vast military experience, having served as Supreme Commander of allied forces in World War II. He used his Farewell Address to issue a prescient warning about the combined power of the military bureaucracy

---

[1]Tellingly, among the things that figure does not include, however, is spending for the wars in Iraq and Afghanistan, which by the summer of 2008 had grown to about $850 billion, much of which the House and Senate have taken "off the books" with special emergency bills.

of the executive branch (particularly the Defense Department) and the arms industry:

This conjunction of an immense military establishment and a large arms industry is new in the American experience. The total influence—economic, political, even spiritual—is felt in every city, every state-house, every office of the federal government. We recognize the imperative need for this development. Yet we must not fail to comprehend its grave implications. Our toil, resources and livelihood are all involved; so is the very structure of our society. In the councils of government, we must guard against the acquisition of unwarranted influence, whether sought or unsought, by the *military–industrial complex*. The potential for the disastrous rise of misplaced power exists and will persist.

From President Eisenhower's perspective, the stakes involved could not have been higher. He went on to characterize the "huge industrial and military machinery of defense" as a potential threat to our liberties and to democracy itself. In a draft of his address, Eisenhower had referred to the "military–industrial–congressional complex," dropping the word "congressional" in deference to the sensitivities of members of Congress. But it was clear that he was concerned about the role Congress played in perpetuating the power of this alliance of the Pentagon and private corporate defense contractors.

It fell to Gordon Adams, a defense analyst and professor of international affairs, to more fully flesh out the political and economic implications of the iron triangle in his 1981 book *The Politics of Defense Contracting: The Iron Triangle*. Adams defined the iron triangle as a political relationship among three sets of participants in a specific policy area. This symbiotic relationship involves congressional committees and subcommittees, agencies within the executive branch bureaucracy, and private interest groups. In the case of defense policy, the relevant policy actors are the House and Senate Armed Services

Committees, as well as the House and Senate Defense Appropriations Subcommittees; for the executive branch the chief player is the Defense Department, although the Department of Energy and National Aeronautics and Space Administration (NASA) also might be involved; and the key interest groups are corporate defense contractors, their trade associations, and policy research institutions. In his study, Adams focused particularly on defense contractors such as Boeing, General Dynamics, Grumman, Lockheed, McDonnell Douglas, Northrop, several of which have long since merged. Working together to pursue a common set of interests, these three points of the triangle form a policy "subgovernment" whose political and economic power is exceptionally hard to challenge. Through lobbying and entertainment, campaign contributions, congressional hearings, shared personnel, and public policy articulation, these three sets of institutional actors develop a high level of expertise in the area of defense policy and a shared outlook on what constitutes "acceptable" debate on defense spending. From the perspective of those participating in the triangle, it looks as though the vital area of national defense policy is capably handled by this alliance of Congress, bureaucratic agencies, and interest groups. What could be wrong with a system that promotes shared knowledge and broadened expertise?

FROM WATCHDOG TO LAPDOG

As these triangular interactions grow, a set of mutually beneficial "sweetheart" relationships develop. Members of congressional committees and subcommittees constantly need campaign contributions and continually seek the perspective of Pentagon and corporate players for the latest information. Representatives and Senators from the defense-related committees protect their expertise and specialization, becoming insulated from views outside the triangle that might question their priorities and their definitions of national security. The Pentagon always seeks new weapons systems and more funding for troops to support the administration's defense strategy and fosters a particular outlook on foreign and military policy through research institutions that share a pro-military perspective. For their part, defense contractors want to market new and improved weapons systems, which are central to their pursuit of profit and the provision of millions of jobs. So all three sets of participants have a vested interest in the perpetuation of the triangle.

As Adams pointed out, the normal operation of the iron triangle has troubling implications for democracy, blurring if not eliminating the distinction between the public interest and private interests. Corporate views of "national security" merge with governmental views, as Congress and the Defense Department come to equate the private interests of contractors with the public interest. With the growing role of high-tech weapons systems in the U.S. economy, what emerges is, something critics of the military have long called a "permanent war economy," wherein the nation's economic health requires actual war and the continual threat of future wars—a situation that raises grave moral concerns and confirms one of President Eisenhower's worst fears. It is in the area of congressional politics, though, where we find perhaps the most unsettling impact, involving the interconnected role of *money*, *people*, and *oversight*.

The House and Senate are the governing institutions most closely aligned with the people. It is here that citizens have their most direct contact with national policy. The strength of the iron triangle can erode that contact. Earlier we mentioned that the most important function Congress performs is control of the nation's "purse strings." Each year Congress raises (through taxation) and spends (through appropriations) our hard-earned money. Money is the conduit for much of our politics. Campaign contributions from individuals and political action committees are the lifeblood of incumbent reelection campaigns. The Pentagon wants a larger portion of the budget each year from committees that authorize and spend money on national defense. Defense contractors spend millions of dollars lobbying Congress for

contracts that can run into the billions. By one estimate, there are some 35,000 registered lobbyists in Washington, DC, and collectively all types of interest groups spend upwards of $200 million per month to sway the opinions of federal policymakers. And who does the swaying? In addition to money, this is where personnel come in to play.

The iron triangle fosters close personal relations among people who sit at all three points of the triangle. It is common for, say, a Senator who serves on the Armed Services Committee to retire and go to work as a lobbyist for a defense contractor with whom he has worked on military policy for years. Thus he will be paid handsomely to lobby his former colleagues on the relevant Senate committee. Likewise, senior Pentagon officials are often drawn from the ranks of defense corporations, or from corporately funded policy research institutes with a shared, friendly view of military strategy. The degree to which personnel are interlocked is quite high. This revolving-door situation leads to the phenomenon of "recycled elites," people who move around to various points of the triangle, further insulating policymakers from outsider influences. The examples are many.

One especially clear current illustration of recycled elites within the iron triangle is Vice President Dick Cheney. Cheney worked in the administrations of both Presidents Nixon and Ford. In 1978, he was elected to Congress where he served as Wyoming's lone Representative for six terms, developing a reputation as an extremely pro-defense Congressman. He served as Secretary of Defense for President George H. W. Bush from 1989 to 1993 and joined a conservative think tank, the American Enterprise Institute, in 1993. From 1995 to 2000, he was Chair and CEO of Halliburton Energy Services. Halliburton is an oil services corporation that has been lavished with military contracts worth tens of millions of dollars to help rebuild Iraq during the war and is now charged with defrauding the federal government for its work on many of those contracts. During his Halliburton days, he also was a member of the conservative "Project for a New American Century," along with Donald

Rumsfeld and several other future architects of President George W. Bush's foreign and defense policy. And of course, he has been vice president in President Bush's administration since 2001. Cheney thus has held positions on all three points of the iron triangle. He is a prime example of how a community of interests, a way of looking at the world, is forged within the triangle. Such a worldview insulates the players from dissenting perspectives. While expertise surely is gathered over time, discussion of military policy is confined to a stiflingly narrow range of debate over the means of achieving a shared set of perspectives. Those perspectives themselves—the ends of policy—are not on the table. As a result, while policymakers may come and go, weapons systems are built, soldiers fight and die, and roots of U.S. foreign and military policy—the basic political and economic interests that underlie them—remain essentially unchanged.

In addition to money and personnel, a third factor to consider in exploring the impact of the iron triangle on congressional relations is oversight. If the most fundamental role of Congress is to control the nation's "purse strings," oversight is its second most pressing job. Oversight means that the House and Senate are charged with looking out for the public interest by overseeing the conduct of executive branch agencies that implement the policies Congress passes into law. Congress performs this role in many ways, for example, by holding congressional committee hearings and by conducting studies (armed with subpoena power) to investigate various agencies of the executive branch. The average citizen would have difficulty finding the time to single-handedly monitor the details of policy making and policy implementation. Congress is supposed to do that for us. In a sense, our elected representatives serve as our eyes and ears in Washington. It is this oversight role—the role of a "watchdog"— that is so valuable to a healthy democracy. But if Congress has been captured by the industry it is supposed to oversee and regulate—in the classic iron triangle case, the defense industry—then the watchdog becomes a mere lapdog of industry,

tethered to a set of interests from which it is ideally supposed to maintain some critical distance. When that critical distance has been lost, and the watchdog is tamed and transformed into a lapdog, the foundation of representative democracy is weakened.

The iron triangle began as a way to understand the intractability of an insulated way of approaching military budgets and national security policy. Yet the concept can be applied to virtually any policy area, as this case study demonstrates with regard to human immunodeficiency virus (HIV)/acquired immunodeficiency syndrome (AIDS)—another public policy issue where life and death literally hang in the balance.

NEW POLICY, NEW TRIANGLES

In 1981, scientists at the government agency in charge of monitoring the nation's health, the Centers for Disease Control and Prevention (CDC), realized that they were tracking a new and deadly disease. No one knew what caused it or how to treat it. They only knew that it seemed to be attacking people in the prime of their lives, whose condition then quickly deteriorated and who died of diseases such as rare types of pneumonia seldom seen among healthy populations. From people experiencing the new illness in themselves or a loved one, there was an urgent call for new drugs to fight the causative agent— which we now know as HIV—or at least the diseases and infections that HIV was facilitating. For ill and at-risk populations, new treatments were literally a matter of life and death. For drug companies, they were an opportunity to market an array of new products at the high prices that desperate people are willing to pay.

As a corporate interest group, it is hard to imagine one more well situated to achieve its aims in Washington than the pharmaceutical lobby. Although iron triangles work by making sure that members of key congressional committees and subcommittees are deeply beholden to the industry at hand, the pharmaceutical industry has hedged its bets by spreading its largess more widely. A 2005 report for the Center for Public Integrity found that it has spent more than $800 million in state and federal lobbying and campaign donations in the preceding seven years, making it second only to the insurance industry in combined expenditures (and first, when looking at lobbying only). The report also noted that most of this lobbying money was spent on the salaries of the three-thousand-strong lobbying force it has assembled, more than a third of which comes from the ranks of Congress and federal bureaucracies.

During the early 1980s, private and public laboratories raced to identify the new disease agent and find and mass-produce both treatments for infections caused by HIV and medicines designed to combat the virus itself. The pharmaceutical industry was already well placed to take advantage of the output of these laboratories. As the outlines of the AIDS pandemic began to take shape, a preexisting iron triangle, or more accurately, several iron triangles, anchored by the pharmaceutical industry absorbed this new policy area. The iron triangle most directly involved with the drug-related aspects of AIDS policy is the same iron triangle that operates around the development, regulation, and pricing of drugs generally. Like other iron triangles, it consists of a congressional committee or subcommittee, executive branch agencies, and private interests. On the House side, the congressional committee that most directly oversees the pharmaceutical industry is the House Energy and Commerce Committee, which is divided into six subcommittees, of which the Subcommittee on Health has most direct oversight of both public health and food and drugs. Of the executive branch agencies, the Food and Drug Administration (FDA), the organization charged with making sure that medicines are both safe and effective, has direct regulatory power over the pharmaceutical industry, although others, including the National Institutes of Health (NIH), also work very closely with the industry. The FDA also oversees the approval process of new drugs, a task that would prove extremely important as new drugs emerged in the

early years after the discovery of HIV. Finally, the pharmaceutical industry is well represented by a host of lobbyists and industry representatives: the two largest are Pharmaceutical Research and Manufacturers of America (PhRMA) and the Biotechnology Industry Organization. To say that these triangle elements are closely connected is a gross understatement: one telling indication of just how close is the fact that PhRMA's president is the former Chair of the Energy and Commerce Committee, twenty-four-year House veteran Billy Tauzin. This fact is all the more remarkable when one considers that Tauzin began negotiating the terms of his new employment with PhRMA (reported to include an annual salary in excess of $2 million) only weeks after he had achieved the passage of a Medicare reform bill he had helped to write (see Article 22). That bill had many provisions straight out of the PhRMA playbook, including prohibitions of government negotiations with pharmaceutical companies for lower prices and refusal to allow lower-cost imports from Canada. The cozy relationship was reinforced when Tauzin's successor as chair of the committee, fellow Republican James Greenwood, was snapped up for a similar position (and a high six-figure salary) by the pharmaceutical industry's other main lobbying group, the Biotechnology Industry Organization.

GOVERNMENT GIVEAWAYS AND THE FIRST AIDS DRUG

The first drug approved to combat HIV—azidothymidine (AZT), otherwise known as Retrovir—was licensed to the drug company Burroughs Wellcome (now two mergers later the international giant GlaxoSmithKline) in 1987. Although Burroughs Wellcome claimed the right to price the new drug—at the hefty price tag of $10,000 for a year's supply—the company had not actually discovered it. That distinction belonged to a researcher, Jerome Horwitz, who developed the compound as an anticancer drug in 1964, with funding from the National Cancer Institute (NCI). Nor did they conduct the original laboratory research that determined that AZT worked in a test tube against HIV. That was done by government-funded laboratories at Duke University and the NCI.

After Burroughs Wellcome got the good news from Duke and the NCI, the company quickly found a way to put its close relationship with the FDA to its advantage. David Barry, a virologist at Wellcome and a former researcher at the FDA, called Ellen Cooper, head of the Division of Antiviral Drug Products at the FDA, to see about expediting AZT's classification as an Investigational New Drug, the next stage in its approval process. Cooper suggested that preliminary data be sent as they were completed; when the final full application was sent, Cooper took less than a week to approve it. Burroughs Wellcome then put the drug through two of the three phases that the FDA traditionally requires for drug approval. Phase I ran for six weeks with nineteen subjects at the NCI and Duke University. Phase II followed, also at Duke and NCI, with 282 subjects, although only 27 participated in the full twenty-four weeks of the trial. Phase III trials were then waived, and the drug was approved on a 10–1 vote by an FDA advisory committee on January 16, 1987. By drug research standards, this one had been a relatively straightforward undertaking. It was formulated in a laboratory supported by a government grant and researched by two other publicly funded entities in small trials with few subjects, with steps explicitly expedited or waived along the way.

So why the $10,000 price tag? That question was asked, but not answered, during hearings of the House Subcommittee on Health and Environment (predecessor to the current Health Subcommittee) in March 1987. After pointing vaguely to the expenses that generally go into the development of any new drug, T. E. Haigler, the then CEO of Burroughs Wellcome, refused to divulge numbers to the more pointed questions of Democratic Congressman Ron Wyden, who asked for actual research and development costs. Though Wyden showed his exasperation (asking "why didn't you just set the price at $100,000 per patient?"), the direction of the power in this

relationship was clearly displayed. The government might finance the discovery of the drug and the research that went into it, but to question the price set for this publicly financed medication by a private company was clearly not within its power.

Eventually the price of AZT came down, though not through pressure from either the FDA or Congress. Rather, it was the work of enraged activists, banding together in a new group, the AIDS Coalition to Unleash Power (ACT UP), that forced the drop. Two weeks after Congress' ill-fated hearing, ACT UP staged the first protest of its existence on Wall Street, garnering headlines in major newspapers, and forcing Burroughs Wellcome to drop their prices by 20 percent to stem the tide of negative publicity. Two years later, with AZT still the only approved antiretroviral on the market and in the face of findings that AZT was helpful for those not yet suffering from full-blown AIDS, Burroughs Wellcome saw a ten-fold increase in its potential market, but once again resisted demands to lower its price. AIDS activists fought back, this time with an imaginative action within and outside the New York Stock Exchange that noisily shut down transactions for five minutes. Four days later, Burroughs Wellcome announced a second 20 percent price cut.

THE MORE THINGS CHANGE, THE MORE THEY STAY THE SAME

Two decades and millions of AIDS deaths later, the power of the pharmaceutical iron triangle appears to have remained intact. One thing that has changed is that, at least in wealthy countries, AIDS has moved from being a fatal disease to a chronic condition, manageable through a combination of drug therapies, often referred to as the "cocktail." Protease inhibitors are one type of drugs within the cocktail, and one of these is the drug ritonavir, more commonly known by its trade name, Norvir. The patent for Norvir is held by Abbott Laboratories, which now markets the drug not as a protease inhibitor but as a booster to be taken with the cocktail to heighten the effects of other protease inhibitors. But Abbott never actually developed Norvir. That was done with federal money in the form of a multimillion-dollar government grant from the NIH. The public interest group Consumer Project on Technology has estimated that, in all, Abbott's investment in clinical trials to test the drug it did not pay to develop was under $15 million, yet during its first five years on the market (1996–2001), Abbott's sales of Norvir totaled $1 billion. Yet despite these very healthy sales, none of which need to go to recoup costs of research and development (a common drug company justification for high prices), Abbott chose to raise its price again in 2003 by a whopping 400 percent. The price of the most common booster dose went from $1,600 to $7,800 per year. This price increase was particularly galling to AIDS activists in light of the fact that even before the increase, Norvir was selling in other wealthy countries for less than half the price, and the price increase meant that U.S. citizens were paying five to ten times more for a drug developed with their tax dollars than people in other wealthy countries.

Early attempts to sway Abbott were of the less confrontational variety: AIDS doctors around the country signed petitions asking Abbott to reexamine its pricing policies, and advocacy organizations organized similar petition drives on the same topic. When these failed, HIV-infected people and activists decided to use Norvir as a worst-case example for calling in a never-used power referred to as "march in" authority. This authority came from a piece of legislation passed in 1980 known as the Bayh–Dole Act, which gives the Secretary of Health and Human Services the power to open competition on a patent that was developed with federal funding (as Norvir was with an NIH grant) but is not available at a reasonable price to the public. Jamie Love, president of the nonprofit group Essential Inventions, made the formal petition to the government in January 2004. The NIH responded in May by holding a hearing, for which there is no official written record. Among those invited to testify was Birch Bayh, who had been one of the Senators who had

drafted the original law. As the national press noted, he testified *against* the march-in provision he had drafted, arguing that march-in could only be used if it were proven that the drug was not reaching the people who needed it. In his early August ruling, NIH Director Elias Zerhouni concurred, finding that Norvir was being made available to patients "on reasonable terms."

In the same year that the NIH was doing the bidding of the pharmaceutical industry at home, a newer government bureaucracy, the Office of the Global AIDS Coordinator, was serving it abroad. In 2003, President Bush had shocked many by announcing in his State of the Union a new global AIDS initiative, the President's Emergency Plan for AIDS Relief (PEPFAR), as a new five-year multibillion-dollar program to address the AIDS pandemic in some of the worst-affected countries on the planet. Equally surprising was his mention in the speech of the possibility of treating people for under $300 a year—a possibility that could only happen through the purchase of generic drugs adamantly opposed by the pharmaceutical lobby in the United States. Activists were cautiously optimistic, thinking the speech signaled that the Administration might be coming around to accept the use of these generic medicines being used by private humanitarian pilot programs in Africa. But these hopes were dashed when the Administration announced that it was opposed to using these products and called for a meeting in the African country of Botswana. At the meeting, the Office of the Global AIDS Coordinator argued that these generic drugs, some of which were four times cheaper than the most deeply discounted drugs offered by the U.S.-based companies, should not be given to sub-Saharan Africans because, though they had been through the World Health Organization's approval process, they had not been approved by the FDA. In the face of pressure from activist and humanitarian groups, the government eventually allowed some of the drugs to go through the FDA process, but in the months between the meeting and approval, they were not made available to the tens of thousands under treatment. During the interim, the shadow cast by the American iron triangle controlled by the pharmaceutical industry extended all the way to remote villages in Africa.

PROSPECTS AND CONCLUSIONS: EVEN IRON MELTS

Although iron triangles are incredibly strong, there is evidence to suggest that they are not indestructible. Secrecy, citizen ignorance and indifference, and the absence of countervailing forces all foster their development and maintenance. But conversely, public education, citizen monitoring, and mass mobilization are valuable tools in weakening these structures. President Eisenhower acknowledged as much in his aforementioned Farewell Address, noting that "an alert and knowledgeable citizenry" was needed to serve as a check on military-industrial ambitions. More specifically, two aspects of politics can weaken the solidity of iron triangles. First, budgetary restrictions can diminish the financial resources available to fund projects favored by corporate interests. In conditions of huge budget deficits or economic crisis, even privileged business groups can come up empty-handed. But this potential impediment to iron triangles tends to be transitory. When the financial cloud lifts, the priorities of private interests are quickly reasserted. And as we have learned in the aftermath of 9/11, even in situations of massive budgetary red ink, with deficits as far as the eye can see, certain corporate interests still can get what they want if their specific interest in profits comes to be tied directly to the general "national interest," as with private defense contractors like Halliburton and it subsidiaries, who continue to flourish while most competing domestic interests languish in Congress.

Beyond such budgetary considerations, though, lies a second, more long-term avenue for weakening iron triangles. Pressure from social movements can serve to challenge our legislators and the private interest groups whose priorities Congress too often serves. As the drug company Burroughs Wellcome discovered in our AIDS case study, it was easier to flout the authority of nominal holders of power—members of the Congressional subcommittee tasked to oversee their pricing policies—than it was to maintain their pricing in the face of an implacable social movement willing to take to the streets and colorfully demonstrate in front of television cameras that profits were taking precedence over access to life-saving medicines. If pressure such as this from democratic grassroots movements can be sustained over time by committed activists, it can have a lasting impact on our national priorities. In sum, at high enough temperatures (1,535°C, to be exact) even iron melts. And when it comes to iron triangles, "street heat" can be the catalyst.

DISCUSSION QUESTIONS

1. Identify the three components of the "iron triangle." Siplon and Grover list budgeting and oversight as two important powers that Congress could use to provide for the public interest. Why is it so difficult to use them to weaken iron triangles?
2. To what extent do you believe that the AIDS activist movement that has challenged the iron triangles related to pharmaceutical policy can be a model for others seeking to weaken iron triangles? Do you believe there were factors specific to AIDS that might not be replicable to other social movements, and if so, what are they?
3. If President Eisenhower was right in viewing an "alert and knowledgeable citizenry" as an effective check on the military–industrial complex (and by extension, other iron triangles), how might public education of the citizenry occur?

CHAPTER 7

The Presidency

The presidency has come to occupy the center stage of American government. Anyone who hopes to understand the American political system, especially as it has developed since the 1930s, must come to terms with the nature of the presidency. After World War II, the expansion of presidential power that began under President Franklin D. Roosevelt continued, and this growth was generally celebrated by scholars and other observers of the office who saw in the president a personification of the American system of government. But in the 1960s and 1970s, abuses symbolized by Vietnam and Watergate and the downfalls of Lyndon Johnson and Richard Nixon led to a more critical view of the "imperial presidency." Despite an upward trend in public trust in the presidency in the 1980s, the Iran-contra affair of 1986–1987, the impeachment and trial of President Bill Clinton in the late 1990s, and the hotly contested presidential election of 2000 call into question the ability of the presidency to resolve policy conflicts in an equitable and responsible way. This presidential challenge persisted after the post–9/11 "rally-'round-the-flag" response boosted George W. Bush's approval ratings to record levels, only to see them plummet to record low levels in 2008.

As president during the Great Depression and World War II, Franklin D. Roosevelt established the model of strong executive leadership that was venerated in postwar America. Indeed, even Ronald Reagan expressed his admiration for Roosevelt's leadership style at the very time he was attempting to reverse the liberal turn in public policy inaugurated by the New Deal. Still, given the recurrent crises that have beset the presidency in the past 40 years, many recent explanations of the presidency emphasize that the chief executive is, or should be, limited in powers by the constitutional structure and is not the free agent in policy decisions that the FDR model of presidential power suggested. In our view, it is no doubt important to put the president in the context of other government actors, but it is even more important to understand the interaction between the president and forces outside of government, such as the economy and the business community, social and political movements, and the role of the United States in the international political economy. The readings in this chapter should help you to put the presidency into context, as the first term of Barack Obama draws to a close.

25 *Michael A. Genovese*

THE LIMITS OF PRESIDENTIAL POWER

Political observers have commented frequently on the modern gulf between high public expectations of the American presidency and disappointing presidential performance. Michael Genovese, a scholar of the presidency, provides a deeper explanation of this gap by identifying two structural constraints that shape and limit presidential action. The first constraint is the economic framework of corporate capitalism. Drawing on the work of political scientist Charles Lindblom, Genovese notes that presidents who pursue reform agendas run the risk of losing business confidence. The need for business confidence has become an unexamined assumption of the modern presidency, an assumption with conservative implications for public policy and political change. Genovese also shows how the nature of the contemporary international economic system shapes presidential policy. Presidents operate in the context of global capitalism or "globalization," which involves powerful pressures towards market economies, open markets, free trade, and economic interdependence. Genovese contends that despite the superpower status of the United States and the benefits that derive from this status, economic globalism "takes power out of the hands of nations and places it in the hands of markets and corporations." Presidents are less free to pursue policies that do not succumb to the demands of the market.

Presidential politics operates within an economic framework of corporate capitalism. How does this reality shape and influence presidential behavior?

Two major functions of the modern capitalist state are (1) the stimulation of material accumulation and (2) the legitimization of the social order. The first function derives from the fact that the state is ultimately held responsible for meeting the material needs of the society; thus, at least in some minimal terms, economic deterioration is blamed on presidents. But in this regard the capitalist state is "weak," in that it does not own the means of production; they are privately held and will not be put in operation unless a return (profit) on investment is foreseen. Thus, the capitalist state must use the carrot more than

Source: Michael Genovese, *The Presidential Dilemma: Leadership in the American System*, 2nd edition. New York: Longman, 2003, pp. 73–79.

the stick, by helping the owning class in the accumulation of profit in order to promote production. Conversely, the owning class is in a strong position with presidents, who face the likelihood of an "investment strike" if policy is seen to hurt profits. This gives business a privileged position and places the president in a position of some dependency on what is referred to as "business confidence." In order to govern effectively, presidents must please the business community, lest they face a decline in business confidence and a deterioration of the overall economy, thus leading to a decline in presidential popularity and power.

It is just this situation that Charles Lindblom—though not referring specifically to the presidency—discusses in his article "The Market as Prison." Lindblom argues that political regimes with market systems have built-in defense systems that automatically trigger punishment whenever there is an attempt to tamper with or alter the basic structures of such systems. This built-in punishing mechanism makes market systems resilient and highly resistant to change because attempts at change bring quick and sure punishment. As Lindblom writes, "Many kinds of market reform automatically trigger punishments in the form of unemployment or a sluggish economy." This punishment is not the result of any conspiracy on the part of business; it is simply a built-in by-product of market-oriented systems. Lindblom writes:

> Business people do not have to debate whether or not to impose the penalty. They need do no more . . . than tend to their own business, which means that, without thought of effecting a punishment on us, they restrict investment and jobs simply in the course of being prudent managers of their enterprises.

While Lindblom does not focus on the presidency in this context, he does discuss the notion that the economic system is highly resistant to change by political leaders. He describes the situation thus:

What about government officials? It is critical to the efficiency of automatic punishment that it be visited on them. For it is they who immediately or proximately decide to persist in policy changes or to withdraw from such initiatives. The penalty visited on them by business disincentives caused by proposed policies is that declining business activity is a threat to the party and the officials in power. When a decline in prosperity and employment is brought about by decisions of corporate and other business executives, it is not they but government officials who consequently are retired from their offices.

That result, then, is why the market might be characterized as a prison. For a broad category of political/economic affairs, it imprisons policy making, and imprisons our attempts to improve our institutions. It greatly cripples our attempts to improve the social world because it afflicts us with sluggish economic performance and unemployment simply because we begin to debate or undertake reform.

Thus, with policy making being "imprisoned" in market-oriented systems, the leverage of presidents for reform is severely restricted by this self-regulating, self-punishing mechanism built into the system.

The other function, legitimization of the social order, derives from the need for the state to be seen as ruling in the interest of all, not in the interest of a dominant class. Welfare programs for the nonowning classes and entitlement programs for the middle class are examples of policies to satisfy this task. But when profits are squeezed, the revenues to support such programs become tight, and a crisis for the state can occur because it cannot reach an adequate balance between these contradictory goals.

Edward S. Greenberg develops the notion of the privileged position of business in policy making in these words:

> Presidents must act in such a way that they maintain the confidence of business leaders and ensure an economic environment conducive to profitable investment. The

president's popularity and thus much of his ability to effect a domestic program and foreign policy objectives is dependent on the state of the economy and the sense of well-being felt by the American people.

Since business people cannot be forced to make productive, job-creating investments in the American economy, government must induce them to do so. They are induced, in the main, by public policies that encourage and ensure profitability, especially among the most powerful economic actors and enterprises in the system. Thus, while no president can afford to respond to every whim of important business leaders, all his actions are bounded by the need to maintain "business confidence."

There is no active conspiracy on the part of business to "capture" the presidency. Rather, presidential success is intimately connected with business success. As presidential popularity rises and falls, in part due to economic conditions, presidents quickly learn that what is good for business is usually good for presidential popularity. When corporate capitalism gains, the president usually gains. Conversely, a sluggish economy is blamed on an administration's activities or lack thereof. Thus, the fate of the president is closely connected to fluctuations in the economy. Presidents help themselves by helping business.

In this way, presidents who do not have the confidence of business find themselves at a distinct political and economic disadvantage. As John Kennedy noted:

I understand better every day why Roosevelt, who started out such a mild fellow, ended up so ferociously antibusiness. It is hard as hell to be friendly with people who keep trying to cut your legs off . . . There are about ten thousand people in this country involved in this—bankers, industrialists, lawyers, publishers, politicians—a small group, but doing everything they can to say we are going into a depression because

business has no confidence in the administration. They are starting to call me the Democratic Hoover. Well, we're not going to take that.

But Kennedy recognized the other side of the business confidence coin as well, as he attempted to act as economic cheerleader:

This country cannot prosper unless business prospers. This country cannot meet its obligations and tax obligations and all the rest unless business is doing well. Business will not do well and we will not have full employment unless there is a chance to make a profit. So there is no long-run hostility between business and government. There cannot be. We cannot succeed unless they succeed.

Similarly, presidents who wish to pursue a reform agenda find themselves in a bind: "Do I sacrifice economic reforms for economic performance and personal popularity, or, do I play it safe and hope for incremental changes?" Which president would want to stir the embers of the market's self-punishing mechanism? Shortly after his election, Bill Clinton met with his top economic advisors to devise an economic stimulus package. After a lengthy discussion, a consensus was reluctantly arrived at that determined the first priority of the president: to rescue the bond market. Angry and frustrated that his reform agenda was being hijacked by the bond market, an exasperated Clinton threw his arms up in the air and said, "We've all become Eisenhower Republicans!" Which president could afford to stir the beast that will likely produce a sluggish economy and lower presidential popularity? Thus, presidential leverage in economic reform is severely limited by the invisible prison of the market.

Thomas Cronin, probably the most highly regarded of today's presidential scholars, begins to suggest a structural impediment in presidential choice vis-a-vis the business community when, in a lengthy reexamination of Richard Neustadt's

Presidential Power, he chides Neustadt for failing "to take into account the degree to which presidents are almost invariably stabilizers or protectors of the status quo rather than agents of redistribution or progressive change." Cronin adds that "all our presidents have had to prove their political orthodoxy and their acceptability to a wide array of established powers, especially to corporate leaders."

Political scientist Bruce Miroff notes that presidential scholars remain firmly committed to a "progressive" interpretation of the presidency. But as Miroff writes, "The Presidency, even (perhaps especially) in liberal hands, is best understood as the chief stabilizer—and not the leading force for change—in American politics." No president has "sought to question, much less assault, corporate power and its extraordinary skewing of resources and rewards. The present structure of the American economy has been accepted by modern Presidents as a given of American life."

In line with Charles Lindblom's concerns, Miroff writes:

> Because of their acceptance of the prevailing social and economic order, even the more liberal of recent Presidents have had little novel or profound that they really wanted to achieve in domestic affairs. Their most controversial domestic proposals have envisioned only modest reforms. Basically, these Presidents have sought to patch up remaining holes in the New Deal, and to stabilize and rationalize the corporate economy. None have acknowledged more fundamental problems in American society; none have proposed anything that resembles a program of social and economic reconstruction. Contrary to the conventional view, it has not been an obstructionist Congress or an apathetic public that has kept Presidents since FDR from major domestic accomplishments as much as it has been the orthodoxy of their own domestic vision.

Presidents are thus constrained by the needs of corporate capitalism. They are in part imprisoned, limited in what they can do, by the requirements of accumulation and legitimization.

The United States is the world's only superpower. In fact, it is a hyper-power. With military might second to none, a massive economy, and cultural penetration to all parts of the globe (I defy you to go to any large city in any country in the world and not find a McDonalds, Starbucks, or a local kid wearing a New York Yankee baseball cap or a "23" basketball jersey), the United States is the hegemonic power, or "big kid on the block." But if we are so strong, why do we seem so weak? Why, at a time when there are no rivals to power, is our grip on international events so fragile and tenuous?

When the Soviet Union imploded—marking the end of the Cold War—analysts wondered what international regime would replace the old order. For a time policymakers groped for an answer. George Bush (the first), in response to the invasion of Kuwait by Iraq, developed a multinationalist coalition based on a "new world order." But as the Gulf War ended, Bush abandoned this promising approach to international order and stability.

It was not until the Clinton years that the parameters of the new regime would come into view. Called "globalization," it encompassed an international acceptance of global capitalism—market economies, open markets, free trade, and integration and interdependence. Building on the institutions designed to oversee, coordinate, and stabilize the international economy—the International Monetary Fund (IMF), the World Bank, and the General Agreement on Tariffs and Trade (GATT), now the World Trade Organization (WTO)—these institutions have helped create a more integrated international economy.

The promise of globalism is political (countries that are connected by common bonds will better cooperate) and economic (a rising tide lifts all boats, although critics might argue that the rising tide lifts all yachts!). Those opposing the rise of globalism fear the widening gap between rich and poor nations, environmental degradation, and a decline in workers' rights.

In this age of globalization, what role and power would be assumed by the United States? And what role and power would be assumed by the presidency? Globalism takes power out of the hands of nations and places it in the hands of the market and corporations. National sovereignty is diminished as the requirements of the global economy drive policy. Globalism demands that market forces shape policy. Thus governments must please the international market or decline.

The United States is the most powerful actor in this system, and draws benefits from its leadership position. But this new system inhibits the freedom of a president to choose. Bound by the demands of a global economy, and the need to develop multinational responses to a variety of problems, the president is less free to pursue policies he chooses and increasingly compelled to succumb to the demands of the market.

Globalism is a two-edged sword. It brings some economic benefits but imposes further limits on choice. Non-Governmental Organizations (NGOs), international institutions, central banks, and market forces gain in power. Nations—and the U.S. president—lose power.

DISCUSSION QUESTIONS

1. How does Genovese use the theories of "accumulation" and "legitimization" to explain how the structure of our political economy imposes a squeeze on the office of president?
2. In what way does economic "globalization" place new limitations on the president's power? Has the international power of the American president changed as a result of the September 11, 2001, terrorist attacks?

26 *Bruce Miroff*

THE PRESIDENTIAL SPECTACLE

Public support has always been important to presidential governance, but modern presidents have "gone public" to an unprecedented degree in an attempt to shape public perceptions. Bruce Miroff, a political scientist who has written important books on the Kennedy presidency and on styles of presidential leadership, analyzes the relationship between the presidency and the public in a mass media age in which the presidency has assumed primacy in the political system. Drawing on cultural theory, Miroff argues that presidents actively shape public perceptions through the creation of images and the presentation of symbolic "spectacles." Miroff develops the notion of the presidency as spectacle through innovative case studies of Ronald Reagan and George W. Bush. Miroff's analysis of the "spectacular" nature of the presidency raises disturbing questions about American democracy. Popular sovereignty requires an accurate public understanding of the course and consequences of presidential action. But the presidential spectacle helps to obscure our understanding of actual presidential performance and relegates citizens to spectators at a performance.

One of the most distinctive features of the modern presidency is its constant cultivation of popular support. The Framers of the Constitution envisioned a president substantially insulated from the demands and passions of the people by the long term and dignity of the office. The modern president, in contrast, not only responds to popular demands and passions but also actively reaches out to shape them. The possibilities opened up by modern technology and the problems presented by the increased fragility of institutional coalitions lead presidents to turn to the public for support and strength. If popular backing is to be maintained, however, the public must believe in the president's leadership qualities.

Observers of presidential politics have come to recognize the centrality of the president's relationship with the American public. George Edwards has written of "the public presidency" and argued that the "greatest source of influence for the president is public approval." Samuel

Source: "The Presidential Spectacle" by Bruce Miroff from *The Presidency and the Political System,* 7th edition, edited by Michael Nelson. Copyright © 2002 CQ Press, an imprint of SAGE. Used by permission.

Kernell has suggested that presidential appeals for popular support now overshadow more traditional methods of seeking influence, especially bargaining. Presidents today, Kernell argues, are "going public," and he demonstrates their propensity to cultivate popular support by recording the mounting frequency of their public addresses, public appearances, and political travel. These constitute, he claims, "the repertoire of modern leadership."

This new understanding of presidential leadership can be carried further. A president's approach to, and impact on, public perceptions are not limited to overt appeals in speeches and appearances. Much of what the modern presidency does, in fact, involves the projection of images whose purpose is to shape public understanding and gain popular support. A significant—and growing—part of the presidency revolves around the enactment of leadership as a spectacle.

To examine the presidency as a spectacle is to ask not only how a president seeks to appear but also what the public sees. We are accustomed to gauging the public's responses to a president with polls that measure approval and disapproval of overall performance in office and effectiveness in managing the economy and foreign policy. Yet these evaluative categories may say more about the kind of information that politicians or academic researchers want than about the terms in which most members of a president's audience actually view the president. A public that responds mainly to presidential spectacles will not ignore the president's performance, but its understanding of that performance, as well as its sense of the overarching and intangible strengths and weaknesses of the administration, will be colored by the terms of the spectacle.

THE PRESIDENCY AS SPECTACLE

A spectacle is a kind of symbolic event, one in which particular details stand for broader and deeper meanings. What differentiates a spectacle from other kinds of symbolic events is the centrality of character and action. A spectacle presents intriguing and often dominating characters not in static poses but through actions that establish their public identities.

Spectacle implies a clear division between actors and spectators. As Daniel Dayan and Elihu Katz have noted, a spectacle possesses "a narrowness of focus, a limited set of appropriate responses, and . . . a minimal level of interaction. What there is to see is very clearly exhibited; spectacle implies a distinction between the roles of performers and audience." A spectacle does not permit the audience to interrupt the action and redirect its meaning. Spectators can become absorbed in a spectacle or can find it unconvincing, but they cannot become performers. A spectacle is not designed for mass participation; it is not a democratic event.

Perhaps the most distinctive characteristic of a spectacle is that the actions that constitute it are meaningful not for what they achieve but for what they signify. Actions in a spectacle are gestures rather than means to an end. What is important is that they be understandable and impressive to the spectators. Roland Barthes illustrates this distinction between gestures and means in his classic discussion of professional wrestling as a spectacle. Barthes shows that professional wrestling is completely unlike professional boxing. Boxing is a form of competition, a contest of skill in a situation of uncertainty. What matters is the outcome, and because that is in doubt, we can wager on it. But in professional wrestling, the outcome is preordained; it would be senseless to bet on who is going to win. What matters in professional wrestling is the gestures made during the match, gestures by performers portraying distinctive characters, gestures that carry moral significance. In a typical match, an evil character threatens a good character, knocks him down on the canvas, abuses him with dirty tricks, but ultimately loses when the good character rises up to exact a just revenge.

It may seem odd to approach the presidency through an analogy with boxing and wrestling— but let us pursue it for a moment. Much of what presidents do is analogous to what boxers do: they engage in contests of power and policy with other political actors, contests in which the outcomes are uncertain. But a growing amount of presidential activity is akin to pro wrestling. The contemporary presidency is presented by the White House (with the collaboration of the media) as a series of spectacles in which a larger-than-life main character and a supporting team engage in emblematic bouts with immoral or dangerous adversaries.

A number of contemporary developments have converged to foster the rise of spectacle in the modern presidency. The mass media have become its principal vehicle. Focusing more of their coverage on presidents than on any other person or institution in American life, the media keep them constantly before the public and give them unmatched opportunities to display their leadership qualities. Television provides the view most amenable to spectacle; by favoring the visual and the dramatic, it promotes stories with simple plotlines over complex analyses of causes and consequences. But other media are not fundamentally different. As David Paletz and Robert Entman have shown, nearly all American journalists "define events from a short-term, antihistorical perspective; see individual or group action, not structural or other impersonal long run forces, at the root of most occurrences; and simplify and reduce stories to conventional symbols for easy assimilation by audiences."

The mass media are not, to be sure, always reliable vehicles for presidential spectacles. Reporters may frame their stories in terms that undermine the meanings the White House intends to convey. Their desire for controversy can feed off presidential spectacles, but it also can destroy them. The media can contribute to spectacular failures in the presidency as well as to successful spectacles.

Spectacle has also been fostered by the president's rise to primacy in the American political system. A political order originally centered on institutions has given way, especially in the public mind, to a political order that centers on the person of the president. Theodore Lowi wrote, "Since the president has become the embodiment of government, it seems perfectly normal for millions upon millions of Americans to concentrate their hopes and fears directly and personally upon him." The "personal president" that Lowi described is the object of popular expectations; those expectations, Stephen Wayne and Thomas Cronin have shown, are both excessive and contradictory. The president must attempt to satisfy the public by delivering tangible benefits, such as economic growth, but these will almost never be enough. Not surprisingly, then, presidents turn to the gestures of the spectacle to satisfy their audience.

To understand the modern presidency as a form of spectacle, we must consider the presentation of presidents as spectacular characters, the role of their teams as supporting performers, and the arrangement of gestures that convey the meaning of their actions to the audience.

A contemporary president is, to borrow a phrase from Guy Debord, "the spectacular representation of a living human being." An enormous amount of attention is paid to the president as a public character; every deed, quality, and even foible is regarded as fascinating and important. The American public may not learn the details of policy formulation, but they know that Gerald Ford bumps his head on helicopter door frames, that Ronald Reagan likes jellybeans, and that Bill Clinton enjoys hanging out with Hollywood celebrities. In a spectacle, a president's character possesses intrinsic as well as symbolic value; it is to be appreciated for its own sake. The spectators do not press presidents to specify what economic or social benefits they are providing; nor do they closely inquire into the truthfulness of the claims presidents make. (To the extent that they do evaluate the president in such terms, they step outside the terms of the spectacle.) The president's featured qualities are presented as benefits in themselves. Thus John F. Kennedy's glamour casts his whole era in a romanticized glow, Ronald Reagan's amiability relieves the grim national mood that had developed under his predecessors, and George W. Bush's traditional marriage rebukes the cultural decay associated with Bill Clinton's sex scandals.

The president's character must be not only appealing in itself but also magnified by the spectacle. The spectacle makes the president appear exceptionally decisive, tough, courageous, prescient, or prudent. Whether the president is in fact all or any of these things is obscured. What matters is that he or she is presented as having these qualities, in magnitudes far beyond what ordinary citizens can imagine themselves to possess. The president must appear confident and masterful before spectators whose very position, as onlookers, denies them the possibility of mastery.

The presidential qualities most likely to be magnified will be those that contrast dramatically with the attributes that drew criticism to the previous president. Reagan, following a president perceived as weak, was featured in spectacles that highlighted his potency. The elder Bush, succeeding a president notorious for his disengagement from the workings of his own administration, was featured in spectacles of hands-on management. Clinton, supplanting a president who seemed disengaged from the economic problems of ordinary Americans, began his administration with spectacles of populist intimacy. The younger Bush, replacing a president notorious for personal indiscipline and staff disorder, presents a corporate-style White House where meetings run on time and proper business attire is required in the Oval Office.

Presidents are the principal figures in presidential spectacles, but they have the help of aides and advisers. The star performer is surrounded by a team. Members of the president's team can, through the supporting parts they play, enhance or detract from the spectacle's effect on the audience. For a president's team to enhance the spectacles, its members should project attractive qualities that either resemble the featured attributes of the president or make up for the president's perceived deficiencies. A team will diminish presidential spectacles if its members project qualities that underscore the president's weaknesses.

A performance team, Erving Goffman has shown, contains "a set of individuals whose intimate cooperation is required if a given projected definition of the situation is to be maintained." There are a number of ways the team can disrupt presidential spectacles. A member of the team can call too much attention to himself or herself, partially upstaging the president. This was one of the disruptive practices that made the Reagan White House eager to be rid of Secretary of State Alexander Haig. A team member can give away important secrets to the audience; Budget Director David Stockman's famous confessions about supply-side economics to a reporter for the *Atlantic* jeopardized the mystique of economic innovation that the Reagan administration had created in 1981. Worst of all, a member of the team can, perhaps inadvertently, discredit the central meanings that a presidential spectacle has been designed to establish. The revelations of Budget Director Bert Lance's questionable banking practices deflated the lofty moral tone established at the beginning of the Carter presidency.

The audience watching a presidential spectacle, the White House hopes, is as impressed by gestures as by results. Indeed, the gestures are sometimes preferable to the results. Thus, a "show" of force by the president is preferable to the death and destruction that are the results of force. The ways in which the invasion of Grenada in 1983, the bombing of Libya in 1986, and the seizing of the Panamanian dictator Manuel Noriega in 1990 were portrayed to the American public suggest an eagerness in the White House to present the image of military toughness but not the casualties from military conflict—even when they are the enemy's casualties.

Gestures overshadow results in a presidential spectacle. They also overshadow facts. But facts are not obliterated. They remain present; they are needed, in a sense, to nurture the gestures. Without real events, presidential spectacles would not be impressive; they would seem contrived, mere pseudoevents. Some of the facts that emerge in the course of an event, however, might discredit its presentation as spectacle. Therefore, a successful spectacle, such as Reagan's "liberation" of Grenada, must be more powerful than any of the facts on which it draws. Rising above contradictory or disconfirming details, the spectacle must transfigure the more pliant facts and make them carriers of its most spectacular gestures.

Presidential spectacles are seldom pure spectacles in the sense that a wrestling match can be a pure spectacle. Although they may involve a good deal of advance planning and careful calculation of gestures, they cannot be completely scripted in advance. Unexpected and unpredictable events will occur during a presidential spectacle. If the White House is fortunate and skillful, it can capitalize on some of those events by using them to enhance the spectacle. If the White House is not so lucky or talented, such events can detract from, or even undermine, the spectacle.

Also unlike wrestling or other pure spectacles, the presidential variety often has more than one audience. Its primary purpose is to construct meanings for the American public. But it also can direct messages to those whom the White House has identified as its foes or the sources of its problems. In 1981, when Reagan fired the air traffic controllers of the Professional Air Traffic Controllers' Organization (PATCO) because they engaged in an illegal strike, he presented to the public the spectacle of a tough, determined president who would uphold the law and, unlike his predecessor, would not be pushed around by grasping interest groups. The spectacle also conveyed to organized labor that the White House knew how to feed popular skepticism about unions and could make things difficult for a labor movement that became too assertive.

As the PATCO firing shows, some presidential spectacles retain important policy dimensions. One could imagine a continuum in which one end represents pure policy and the other pure spectacle. Toward the policy end one would find behind-the-scenes presidential actions, including quiet bargaining over domestic policies (such as Lyndon Johnson's lining up of Republican

support for civil rights legislation) and covert actions in foreign affairs (such as the Nixon administration's use of the CIA to "destabilize" a socialist regime in Chile). Toward the spectacle end would be presidential posturing at home (law and order and drugs have been handy topics) and dramatic foreign travel (from 1972 until the 1989 massacre in Tiananmen Square, China was a particular presidential favorite). Most of the president's actions are a mix of policy and spectacle.

THE TRIUMPH OF SPECTACLE: RONALD REAGAN

The Reagan presidency was a triumph of spectacle. In the realm of substantive policy, it was marked by striking failures as well as significant successes. But even the most egregious of the failures—public exposure of the disastrous covert policy of selling arms to Iran and diverting some of the profits to the Nicaraguan contras—proved to be only a temporary blow to the political fortunes of the most spectacular president in decades. With the help of two heart-warming summits with Soviet leader Mikhail Gorbachev, Reagan recovered from the Iran-contra debacle and left office near the peak of his popularity. His presidency, for the most part, floated above its flawed processes and failed policies, secure in the brilliant glow of its successful spectacles.

The basis of this success was the character of Ronald Reagan. His previous career in movies and television made him comfortable with and adept at spectacles; he moved easily from one kind to another. Reagan presented to his audience a multifaceted character, funny yet powerful, ordinary yet heroic, individual yet representative. His was a character richer even than Kennedy's in mythic resonance.

Coming into office after Jimmy Carter, a president who was widely perceived as weak, Reagan as a spectacle character projected potency. His administration featured a number of spectacles in which Reagan displayed his decisiveness, forcefulness, and will to prevail. The image of masculine toughness was played up repeatedly.

The American people saw a president who, even though in his seventies, rode horses and exercised vigorously, a president who liked to quote (and thereby identify himself with) movie tough guys such as Clint Eastwood and Sylvester Stallone. Yet Reagan's strength was nicely balanced by his amiability; his aggressiveness was rendered benign by his characteristic one-line quips. The warm grin took the edge off the toughness, removed any intimations of callousness or violence.

Quickly dubbed "the Great Communicator," Reagan presented his character not through eloquent rhetoric but through storytelling. As Paul Erickson has demonstrated, Reagan liked to tell tales of "stock symbolic characters," figures whose values and behavior were "heavily colored with Reagan's ideological and emotional principles." Although the villains in these tales ranged from Washington bureaucrats to Marxist dictators, the heroes, whether ordinary people or inspirational figures like Knute Rockne, shared a belief in America. Examined more closely, these heroes turned out to resemble Reagan himself. Praising the heroism of Americans, Reagan, as the representative American, praised himself.

The power of Reagan's character rested not only on its intrinsic attractiveness but also on its symbolic appeal. The spectacle specialists who worked for Reagan seized on the idea of making him an emblem for the American identity. In a June 1984 memo, White House aide Richard Darman sketched a reelection strategy that revolved around the president's mythic role: "Paint RR as the personification of all that is right with or heroized by America. Leave Mondale in a position where an attack on Reagan is tantamount to an attack on America's idealized image of itself." Having come into office at a time of considerable anxiety, with many Americans uncertain about the economy, their future, and the country itself, Reagan was an immensely reassuring character. He had not been marked by the shocks of recent U.S. history—and he denied that those shocks had meaning. He told Americans that the Vietnam War was noble rather than appalling, that Watergate was forgotten, that racial conflict was a thing of the distant past, and that the U.S. economy still offered the American dream to any aspiring individual. Reagan (the character) and America (the country) were presented in the spectacles of the Reagan presidency as timeless, above the decay of aging and the difficulties of history.

The Reagan team assumed special importance because Reagan ran what Lou Cannon has called "the delegated presidency." As the public knew, his team members carried on most of the business of the executive branch; Reagan's own work habits were decidedly relaxed. Reagan's team did not contain many performers who reinforced the president's character, as Kennedy's youthful, energetic New Frontiersmen had. But it featured several figures whose spectacle role was to compensate for Reagan's deficiencies or to carry on his mission with a greater air of vigor than the amiable president usually conveyed. The Reagan presidency was not free of disruptive characters—Alexander Haig's and James Watt's unattractive qualities and gestures called the president's spectacle into question. But Reagan removed these characters before too much damage had been done.

David Stockman was the most publicized supporting player in the first months of 1981. His image in the media was formidable. *Newsweek*, for example, marveled at how "his buzz-saw intellect has helped him stage a series of bravura performances before Congress" and acclaimed him "the Reagan Administration's boy wonder." There was spectacle appeal in the sight of the nation's youngest budget director serving as the right arm of the nation's oldest chief executive. More important, Stockman's appearance as the master of budget numbers compensated for a president who was notoriously uninterested in data. Stockman faded in spectacle value after his disastrous confession in fall 1981 that budget numbers had been doctored to show the results the administration wanted.

As Reagan's longtime aide, Edwin Meese III was one of the most prominent members of the president's team. Meese's principal spectacle role was not as a White House manager but as a cop. Even before he moved from the White House to the Justice Department, Meese became the voice and the symbol of the administration's tough stance on law-and-order issues. Although the president sometimes spoke about law and order, Meese took on the issue with a vigor that his more benign boss could not convey.

The Reagan administration developed an effective balance of images in foreign affairs in the persons of Secretary of Defense Caspar Weinberger and Secretary of State George Shultz. Weinberger quickly became the administration's most visible cold war hard-liner. As the tireless spokesperson and unbudging champion of a soaring defense budget, he was a handy symbol for the Reagan military buildup. Nicholas Lemann noted that although "Weinberger's predecessor, Harold Brown, devoted himself almost completely to management, Weinberger . . . operated more and more on the theatrical side." His grim, hawklike visage was as much a reminder of the Soviet threat as the alarming, book-length reports on the Russian behemoth that his Defense Department issued every year. Yet Weinberger sometimes could seem too alarming, feeding the fears of those who worried about Reagan's warmaking proclivities.

In contrast to Weinberger, Shultz was a reassuring figure. He was portrayed in the media in soothing terms: low-key, quiet, conciliatory. In form and demeanor he came across, in the words of *Time*, "as a good gray diplomat." Shultz was taken to be the voice of foreign policy moderation in an administration otherwise dominated by hard-liners. Actually, Shultz had better cold war credentials than Weinberger, having been a founding member of the hard-line Committee on the Present Danger in 1976. And he was more inclined to support the use of military force than was the secretary of defense, who reflected the caution of a Pentagon gun-shy after the Vietnam experience. But Shultz's real views were less evident than his spectacle role as the gentle diplomat.

The Reagan presidency benefited not only from a spectacular main character and a useful team but also from talent and good fortune in enacting spectacle gestures. The Reagan years were sprinkled with events—the PATCO strike, the Geneva summit, the Libyan bombing, and others—whose significance primarily lay in their spectacle value. The most striking Reagan spectacle of all was the invasion of Grenada. As the archetypal presidential spectacle, Grenada deserves a close look.

Reagan ordered American forces to invade the island of Grenada in October 1983. Relations had become tense between the Reagan administration and the Marxist regime of Grenada's Maurice Bishop. When Bishop was overthrown and murdered by a clique of more militant Marxists, the Reagan administration began to consider military action. It was urged to invade by the Organization of Eastern Caribbean States, composed of Grenada's island neighbors. And it had a pretext for action in ensuring the safety of the Americans—most of them medical students—on the island. Once the decision to invade was made, U.S. troops landed in force, evacuated most of the students, and seized the island after encountering brief but unexpectedly stiff resistance. Reagan administration officials announced that in the course of securing the island, U.S. forces had discovered large caches of military supplies and documents indicating that Cuba planned to turn Grenada into a base for the export of communist revolution and terror.

The details that eventually came to light cast doubt on the Reagan administration's claims of a threat to the American students and a buildup of "sophisticated" Cuban weaponry in Grenada. Beyond such details, there was the sheer incongruity between the importance bestowed on Grenada by the Reagan administration and the insignificance of the danger it posed. Grenada is a tiny island, with a population of 100,000, a land area of 133 square miles, and an economy whose exports totaled $19 million in 1981. That U.S. troops could secure it was never in question; as Richard Gabriel has noted. "In terms of actual combat forces, the U.S. outnumbered the island's defenders approximately ten to one." Grenada's importance did not derive from the military, political, and economic implications of America's actions, but from its value as a spectacle.

What was this spectacle about? Its meaning was articulated by a triumphant President Reagan: "Our days of weakness are over. Our military forces are back on their feet and standing tall." Reagan, even more than the American military, came across in the media as "standing tall" in Grenada.

The spectacle actually began with the president on a weekend golfing vacation in Augusta, Georgia. His vacation was interrupted first by planning for an invasion of Grenada and then by news that the U.S. Marine barracks in Beirut had been bombed. Once the news of the Grenada landings replaced the tragedy in Beirut on the front page and television screen, the golfing angle proved to be an apt beginning for a spectacle. It was used to dramatize the ability of a relaxed and genial president to rise to a grave challenge. And it supplied the White House with an unusual backdrop to present the president in charge, with members of his team by his side. As Francis X. Clines reported in the *New York Times:*

> The White House offered the public some graphic tableaux, snapped by the White House photographer over the weekend, depicting the President at the center of various conferences. He is seen in bathrobe and slippers being briefed by Mr. Shultz and Mr. McFarlane, then out on the Augusta fairway, pausing at the wheel of his golf cart as he receives another dispatch. Mr. Shultz is getting the latest word in another, holding the special security phone with a golf glove on.

Pictures of the president as decision maker were particularly effective because pictures from Grenada itself were lacking; the Reagan administration had barred the American press from covering the invasion. This move outraged the press but was extremely useful to the spectacle, which would have been subverted by pictures of dead bodies or civilian casualties or by independent sources of information with which congressional critics could raise unpleasant questions.

The initial meaning of the Grenada spectacle was established by Reagan in his announcement of the invasion. The enemy was suitably evil: "a brutal group of leftist thugs." America's objectives were purely moral—to protect the lives of innocent people on the island, namely American medical students, and to restore democracy to the people of Grenada. And the actions taken were unmistakably forceful: "The United States had no choice but to act strongly and decisively."

But the spectacle of Grenada soon expanded beyond this initial definition. The evacuation of the medical students provided one of those unanticipated occurrences that heighten the power of spectacle. When several of the students kissed the airport tarmac to express their relief and joy at returning to American soil, the resulting pictures on television and in the newspapers were better than anything the administration could have orchestrated. They provided the spectacle with historical as well as emotional resonance. Here was a second hostage crisis—but where Carter had been helpless to release captive Americans from Iran, Reagan had swiftly come to the rescue.

Rescue of the students quickly took second place, however, to a new theme: the claim that U.S. forces had uncovered and uprooted a hidden Soviet-Cuban base for adventurism and terrorism. In his nationally televised address, Reagan did not ignore the Iran analogy: "The nightmare of our hostages in Iran must never be repeated." But he stressed the greater drama of defeating a sinister communist plot. "Grenada, we were told, was a friendly island paradise for tourism. Well, it wasn't. It was a Soviet-Cuban colony being readied as a major military bastion to export terror and undermine democracy. We got there just in time." Grenada was turning out to be an even better spectacle for Reagan: He had rescued not only the students but the people of all the Americas as well.

As the spectacle expanded and grew more heroic, public approval increased. The president's standing in the polls went up. *Time* reported that "a post-invasion poll taken by the *Washington Post* and ABC News showed that 63% of Americans approve the way Reagan is handling the presidency, the highest level in two years, and attributed his gain largely to the Grenada intervention." Congressional critics, although skeptical of many of the claims the administration made, began to stifle their doubts and chime in with endorsements in accordance with the polls. An unnamed White House aide, quoted in *Newsweek*, drew the obvious lesson: "You can scream and shout and gnash your teeth all you want, but the folks out there like it. It was done right and done with dispatch."

In its final gestures, the Grenada spectacle actually commemorated itself. Reagan invited the medical students to the White House and, predictably, basked in their praise and cheers. The Pentagon contributed its symbolic share, awarding some eight thousand medals for the Grenada operation—more than the number of American troops that had set foot on the island. In actuality, Gabriel has shown, "the operation was marred by a number of military failures." Yet these were obscured by the triumphant appearances of the spectacle.

That the spectacle of Grenada was more potent and would prove more lasting in its effects than any disconfirming facts was observed at the time by Anthony Lewis. Reagan "knew the facts would come out eventually," wrote Lewis. "But if that day could be postponed, it might make a great political difference. People would be left with their first impression that this was a decisive President fighting communism." Grenada became for most Americans a highlight of Reagan's first term. Insignificant in military or diplomatic terms, as spectacle it was one of the most successful acts of the Reagan presidency.

THE SOURING OF SPECTACLE: GEORGE W. BUSH

George W. Bush scored the highest Gallup approval rating in history after the terrorist attacks on September 11, 2001—and the highest Gallup disapproval rating ever during his final year in office. Bush's was a spectacle that soared briefly, then soured worse than that of even his most beleaguered predecessors.

Although Bush promised the novelty of a "compassionate conservatism" during the campaign, his administration's original agenda mainly followed the familiar priorities of the Republican right. But Bush's conservatism ran deeper than his policy prescriptions. In its characters, its styles, and its gestures, the Bush administration was determined to reach back past the postmodern spectacle of Bill Clinton and restore the faded glories of contemporary conservatism.

One fund of recycled images and themes upon which Bush drew was the Reagan spectacle. As a presidential character, Bush enjoyed many affinities with Reagan. He presented himself as a Reagan-style nonpolitician whose optimism and bonhomie would brighten a harsh and demoralizing political environment. His principal policy prescriptions for the nation also recycled Reaganesque themes and gestures. Like Reagan, Bush rapidly pushed through Congress a massive tax cut that favored the wealthy in the guise of an economic stimulus, using "fuzzy math" to promise Americans the pleasure of prosperity without the pain of federal deficits. Like Reagan, Bush promoted a national missile defense system that would use cutting-edge (and still nonexistent) technology to restore the ancient dream of an innocent America invulnerable to the violent quarrels that beset the rest of the world. Even the Bush administration's most politically costly stance in its early months, presidential decisions favoring private interests over environmental protection, was couched in the Reagan-style claim of protecting the pocketbooks of ordinary citizens. Revising a Clinton rule that would have mandated higher efficiency for central air conditioners, Bush's secretary of energy, Spencer Abraham, indicated that his goal was to save low-income consumers from having to pay more to cool their homes or trailers.

Recycled images and themes from his father's administration were equally evident in the early months of Bush's presidency. They were especially useful as emblems of the new president's "compassionate" side. Like his father, "W" trumpeted his conciliatory stance toward congressional opponents. Like his father, he set out to be an "education president." The recycling of paternal gestures also was apparent in Bush's meetings with representatives of the groups that had opposed his election most strongly. Just as the father had met with Jesse Jackson after winning the White House, the son invited the Congressional Black Caucus. Neither Bush expected to win over African American voters through these gestures. Instead, each hoped to signal to moderate whites that he was a "kinder, gentler" conservative who exuded tolerance and good will.

On September 11, 2001, when al Qaida terrorists killed thousands of Americans in a twisted spectacle of their own by piloting hijacked airliners into the World Trade Center and the Pentagon, Bush was given the chance to stage a more politically potent spectacle. The recycled conservative became the warrior president. Clumsy in his first public responses to the horror of September 11, 2001, Bush quickly hit his stride in what would be remembered as iconic moments of his presidency: his visit with rescue workers at Ground Zero in New York and his impressive speech to Congress on September 20, which struck a delicate balance between a forceful response to terrorism, a compassionate response to tragedy, and a teaching of tolerance toward followers of the Islamic faith. These moments would be etched in the public mind during Bush's campaign for reelection. For example, in narrating Bush's 9/11 heroics near the site of the tragedy, the 2004 Republican convention in New York City was skillfully designed to link Bush inextricably with Americans' determination to defeat the nation's terrorist enemies.

After the initial success of the military campaign against al Qaida and the Taliban regime that harbored it in Afghanistan, the delicate balance in Bush's initial response to September 11 gave way to a consistently martial tone. Paced by Secretary of Defense Rumsfeld, the Bush administration began to feature a spectacle of muscular globalism. In his State of the Union address in January 2002, the commander in chief previewed an expansion of the war on terror to combat an "axis of evil" composed of North Korea, Iran, and especially Iraq. Bush's dramatic phrase, which made headlines around the world, rhetorically invoked the nation's Axis enemies in World War II and the Soviet "evil empire" of the cold war to amplify the peril posed by adversaries in the Middle East and Asia. In its emphasis on eliminating the regime of Saddam Hussein in Iraq, the phrase gestured toward the spectacular completion by the son of the mission in which the father, it now seemed, had sadly fallen short. The speech began the buildup to war against Iraq a year later, as the Bush administration mustered its political and rhetorical resources to portray Saddam's regime, with its alleged weapons of mass destruction and ties to al Qaida, as a sinister threat to American security.

The war in Iraq was far more serious and deadly than Reagan's invasion of Grenada, and Bush's spectacle specialists were on the lookout for even more gripping gestures that would display a president "standing tall." As Elisabeth Bumiller noted in the *New York Times*: "the Bush administration, going far beyond the foundations in stagecraft set by the Reagan White House, is using the powers of television and technology like never before."

Copiloting an S-3B Viking onto the deck of the aircraft carrier *Abraham Lincoln* on May 1, 2003, President Bush starred in what was instantly recognized as a classic of presidential spectacles; the press quickly dubbed it Bush's *Top Gun* affair, recalling the Tom Cruise movie. The White House used the carrier as its stage to announce that major combat operations in Iraq were over; a banner over the president's head was emblazoned, "Mission Accomplished." Every detail of the event was meticulously planned for how it would look on television and in newspaper photos. The landing at sea highlighted the degree of risk, with the Viking brought to a halt by the last of the four cables that catch planes on the carrier deck. Members of the *Lincoln* crew were garbed in varied but coordinated shirt colors as they surrounded the president (reminiscent of a football halftime ceremony). At the center of this massive stage was President Bush, who played his part with evident relish. Maureen Dowd described the moment: "He flashed that famous all-American grin as he swaggered around the deck of the aircraft carrier in his olive flight suit, ejection harness between his legs, helmet tucked under his arm, awe-struck crew crowding around."

Through these gestures, Bush's spectacle specialists implanted his image as a strong commander in chief, while eliding the grim realities on the ground in Iraq. Adhering to the tradition of civilian control of the military, Bush's predecessors had generally eschewed military garb. But his choice of clothing on the *Abraham Lincoln* and at the Baghdad airport played up his oneness with American armed forces. The copilot's tail-hook landing on the carrier and the secret flight into the dangerous Baghdad airport suggested that Bush was willing to share some of the risks to which his decisions as commander in chief exposed American troops. No matter how controversial the war in Iraq might be, the one aspect of it that aroused consensus among Americans was the steadfast courage of the armed forces. Associating himself with the troops through his warrior spectacles, Bush signified that this virtue was his, too.

Subsequent media inquiries unearthed details that potentially called into question this signification. Viewers of Bush's dramatic flight to the *Abraham Lincoln* had witnessed what appeared to be a risky jet landing at sea. Later it was revealed by the press that the aircraft carrier was close to San Diego and could have been reached by helicopter; in fact, the ship had sailed a bit further out into the Pacific so that the California coastline would not be visible on television. The president also was derided later on for the "Mission Accomplished" banner; whose sentiment turned out to be wildly premature.

Although the premises with which Bush had taken the nation to war in Iraq were soon shown

to be false, his 9/11 image as America's protector against terrorists and his identification through spectacle with American troops were formidable assets when he faced the voters in 2004. At the hands of the president's campaign managers (some of whom had designed his Iraq spectacles), John Kerry, a decorated war hero in Vietnam, was re-created as a foreign-policy weakling compared with George W. Bush, who had avoided Vietnam but had become a spectacle warrior.

Yet if Bush's spectacle specialists had hoped to portray the invasion and occupation of Iraq as an adventure tale, by the time of Bush's reelection, it was beginning to turn into a horror story instead. The "bad guys" in Iraq, with their suicide bombings and beheadings, perpetrated such sickening violence that Americans began to wonder what had happened to the Bush administration's prediction that Iraqis would greet U.S. forces as liberators. Even worse for the Bush spectacle was horror on the American side. American guards at the Abu Ghraib prison abused and sexually humiliated Iraqi prisoners. Meanwhile, American troops, many left poorly protected due to insufficient armor were subjected to grievous wounds from insurgent explosive devices in Iraq, and when they were shipped home, they were housed in shabby medical facilities. Most Americans continued to perceive the troops as virtuous, but it was increasingly difficult to find virtue in the civilian leaders who had sent them into such a hell.

September 11th, 2001, was an unexpected event that allowed Bush's spectacle to soar. Hurricane Katrina in 2005 was an equally unexpected event that compounded Bush's failures in Iraq and soured his presidency for the remainder of his term. The hurricane that devastated New Orleans and the Gulf Coast was among the worst natural disasters in America's history. But it was also a political disaster for the Bush presidency. Television, the tool of presidential spectacle, now savagely undermined it. Heart-wrenching pictures of hurricane victims, most of them poor and black, were powerful as well for what was absent: the federal rescue effort that could have saved many. Irate media commentators suggested that the president had abandoned his people.

President Bush's personal role in the Hurricane Katrina story contributed to that message. On vacation when the hurricane struck the Gulf Coast, Bush was urged by his top political adviser, Karl Rove, to fly over New Orleans and survey the damage. But unlike his "Mission Accomplished" landing, this was no *Top Gun* immersion in the thick of action. Photos of Bush soaring high above New Orleans in the comfort and safety of *Air Force One*, his press secretary Scott McClellan later observed, fostered "an image of a callous, unconcerned president." Accompanying stories of incompetence on the part of Bush's subordinates in response to the hurricane, the pictures suggested a president who poorly comprehended what was happening either at home or abroad.

Bush's team made its own contributions to the souring of his spectacle. The hapless supporting player in the Hurricane Katrina story was Michael Brown, the lightweight head of the Federal Emergency Management Agency. Leading roles in the Iraq fiasco were played by administration heavyweights, especially Vice President Dick Cheney and Secretary of Defense Donald Rumsfeld. Both Cheney and Rumsfeld became notorious in the media for the arrogance with which they wielded power and dismissed criticism. Cheney was prone to cheery pronouncements about Iraq that had no connection to events on the ground, as when he proclaimed that the insurgency was in its "last throes" just before it reached new depths of violence. Rumsfeld was inclined to disparage discontent in the military's ranks, replying to one soldier who bemoaned the lack of armor for trucks: "You go to war with the army you have, not the army you want . . ." Bush eventually dumped Rumsfeld, but he could not fire the vice president, whom critics compared to the grimmest authoritarian in modern film: Darth Vader.

Changes in the media also played a party in the souring of the Bush spectacle. Jeffrey Cohen has demonstrated that today's 24/7 news media, especially cable television, are not as favorable to

presidential prospects as the media were in the "golden age" of network television. Presidents now receive less coverage than before, the coverage they do receive is more likely to be negative in tone, and the audience for broadcast presidential speeches has shrunk. President Bush did have help from a cable network, FOX News, which tends to cheer on Republicans. On the other side of the ledger were numerous cable (and Internet) commentators who picked apart all of the Bush administration's flaws. Perhaps the deadliest blows to Bush were struck by Comedy Central's satirists of spectacle, Jon Stewart and Stephen Colbert.

By his final months in office Bush's spectacle had become so sour that the president was nearly ignored by the media. As the extraordinary election contest between Barack Obama and John McCain took center stage in 2008, Bush seemed more spectator than performer. A small and unexpected occurrence during the president's last visit to Iraq in December 2008 encapsulated the fate of his spectacle. Infuriated by what had happened to his country after Bush invaded it, an Iraqi journalist threw both of his shoes (a gesture of extreme contempt in his culture) at the American president during a news conference. At the heyday of his spectacle, aboard the *Abraham Lincoln*, Bush had emulated Reagan in "standing tall" as a warrior. Now, he was reduced to ducking footwear hurled by someone who represented many in their scorn for him.

CONCLUSION

It is tempting to blame the growth of spectacle on individual presidents, their calculating advisers, and compliant journalists. It is more accurate, however, to attribute the growth of spectacle to larger structural forces: the extreme personalization of the modern presidency, the excessive expectation of the president that most Americans have, and the media coverage that fixes on presidents and treats American politics largely as a report of their adventures. Indeed, presidential spectacles can be linked to a culture of consumption in which spectacle is the predominant form that relates the few to the many. Spectacle, then, is more a structural feature of the contemporary presidency than a strategy of deception adopted by particular presidents.

Is there any escape from spectacle, with its promotion of gesture over accomplishment, its obfuscation of presidential accountability, and its encouragement of passivity on the part of ordinary citizens? As the presidency of Barack Obama begins, the prospects are ambiguous. The failures of George W. Bush have set the stage for Obama to offer appealing contrasts in the realm of spectacle. More important, Obama appears to have the potential for the most impressive spectacle since Reagan. As the first black president, he represents a fundamental break with an exclusory racial tradition and an extraordinary affirmation of the American dream. His charisma and eloquence, so often on display during the 2008 election, have already made him a larger-than-life figure not only at home but around the world. In the enormous crowds that clock to see and hear Obama, presidential spectacle may even reach new heights.

On the other hand, Obama is the first president with a background as a community organizer. No previous president has expressed such a strong belief in grassroots politics and its axiom that change comes from the bottom up. His campaign for the White House featured innovative, web-and email-based methods to engage and activate millions of supporters, and he vows to seek input from ordinary citizens throughout his administration. The structural demands of presidential spectacle may prompt Obama to provide only lip service to these participatory values while cultivating the power that spectacle can bring when it is most successful. But if he upholds the political faith that he has professed in the past, a presidential spectacle may, for the first time, support and not supplant the democratic art of self-government.

DISCUSSION QUESTIONS

1. What examples does Miroff provide to support his view that the presidency as a spectacle "obfuscates presidential activity, undermines executive accountability, and encourages passivity on the part of citizens"?
2. After the September 11, 2001, attacks, President George W. Bush became preoccupied with the "war on terrorism." How did Bush invoke symbolic language to build support for this effort?

27 Tom Engelhardt

MILITARISM AND THE AMERICAN PRESIDENCY

Even as America's military role in Iraq winds down, U.S. military involvement in Afghanistan (and Pakistan) has been escalating. Tom Engelhardt is an author, editor, and co-founder of the TomDispatch website, launched after 9/11 to provide analysis and commentary on American politics and foreign policy from a wide range of "anti-imperial" perspectives. In this article from mid-2011, Engelhardt puts in perspective recent remarks by President Obama about the conflict in Afghanistan. In his view, Obama's statement was laced with a "triumvirate" of rhetorical idolatry in which no praise is too high for the U.S. military: America is seen as having a unique and exceptional world role, and God's blessing is ritually invoked for both. Engelhardt finds these and other statements by the president and his predecessor to be new in American history, at least in their fawning repetitiveness. In fact, he thinks they are "surreal" in the sense of being at odds with the harsh realities of the last decade, even if they are comprehensible as "strange, defensive artifacts of an imperial power in decline." Engelhardt points to evidence indicating a prolonged U.S. military campaign in Afghanistan that he believes is unsustainable. Without a deep rethinking of the meaning of American militarism, Engelhardt fears that our overstretched empire will lead to unravelling and decline.

It's already gone, having barely outlasted its moment—just long enough for the media to suggest that no one thought it added up to much.

Okay, it was a little more than the military wanted, something less than Joe Biden would have liked, not enough for the growing crew of anti-war congressional types, but way too much for John McCain, Lindsey Graham, & Co.

I'm talking about the 13 minutes of "remarks" on "the way forward in Afghanistan" that President Obama delivered in the East Room of the White House two Wednesday nights ago.

Tell me you weren't holding your breath wondering whether the 33,000 surge troops he ordered into Afghanistan as 2009 ended would be removed in a 12-month, 14-month, or 18-month span. Tell

Source: From "The Militarized Surrealism of Barack Obama" by Tom Engelhardt in TomDispatch.com, June 30, 2011, http://www.tomdispatch.com/blog/175412, © 2011. Used by permission.

me you weren't gripped with anxiety about whether 3,000, 5,000, 10,000, or 15,000 American soldiers would come out this year (leaving either 95,000, 93,000, 88,000, or 83,000 behind)?

You weren't? Well, if so, you were in good company.

Billed as the beginning of the end of the Afghan War, it should have been big and it couldn't have been smaller. The patented Obama words were meant to soar, starting with a George W. Bush-style invocation of 9/11 and ending with the usual copious blessings upon this country and our military. But on the evidence, they couldn't have fallen flatter. I doubt I was alone in thinking that it was like seeing Ronald Reagan on an unimaginably bad day in an ad captioned "It's never going to be morning again in America."

IDOLATOR PRESIDENT

If you clicked Obama off that night or let the event slide instantly into your mental trash can, I don't blame you. Still, the president's Afghan remarks shouldn't be sent down the memory hole quite so quickly.

For one thing, while the mainstream media's pundits and talking heads are always raring to discuss his policy remarks, the words that frame them are generally ignored—and yet the discomfort of the moment can't be separated from them. So start with this: whether by inclination, political calculation, or some mix of the two, our president has become a rhetorical idolator.

These days he can barely open his mouth without also bowing down before the U.S. military in ways that once would have struck Americans as embarrassing, if not incomprehensible. In addition, he regularly prostrates himself before this country's special mission to the world and never ceases to emphasize that the United States is indeed an exception among nations. Finally, in a way once alien to American presidents, he invokes God's blessing upon the military and the country as regularly as you brush your teeth.

Think of these as the triumvirate without which no Obama foreign-policy moment would

be complete: greatest military, greatest nation, our God. And in this he follows directly, if awkwardly, in Bush's footsteps.

I wouldn't claim that Americans had never had such thoughts before, only that presidents didn't feel required to say them in a mantra-like way just about every time they appeared in public. Sometimes, of course, when you feel a compulsion to say the same things ad nauseam, you display weakness, not strength; you reveal the most fantastic of fantasy worlds, not a deeper reality.

The president's recent Afghan remarks were, in this sense, par for the course. As he plugged his plan to bring America's "long wars" to what he called "a responsible end," he insisted that "[l]ike generations before, we must embrace America's singular role in the course of human events." He then painted this flattering word portrait of us:

"We're a nation that brings our enemies to justice while adhering to the rule of law, and respecting the rights of all our citizens. We protect our own freedom and prosperity by extending it to others. We stand not for empire, but for self-determination . . . and when our union is strong no hill is too steep, no horizon is beyond our reach . . . we are bound together by the creed that is written into our founding documents, and a conviction that the United States of America is a country that can achieve whatever it sets out to accomplish."

I know, I know. You're wondering whether you just mainlined into a Sarah Palin speech and your eyes are glazing over. But hang in there, because that's just a start. For example, in an Obama speech of any sort, what America's soldiers never lack is the extra adjective. They aren't just soldiers, but "our extraordinary men and women in uniform." They aren't just Americans, but "patriotic Americans." (Since when did an American president have to describe American soldiers as, of all things, "patriotic"?) And in case you missed the point that, in their extraordinariness and their outsized patriotism they are better than other Americans, he made sure to acknowledge them as the ones we "draw inspiration from."

In a country that now "supports the troops" with bumper-sticker fervor but pays next to no attention to the wars they fight, perhaps Obama is simply striving to be the premier twenty-first-century American. Still, you have to wonder what such presidential fawning, omnipresent enough to be boilerplate, really represents. The strange thing is we hear this sort of thing all the time. And yet no one ever comments on it.

Oh, and let's not forget that no significant White House moment ends these days without the president bestowing God's blessing on the globe's most extraordinary nation and its extraordinary fighters, or as he put it in his Afghan remarks: "May God bless our troops. And may God bless the United States of America."

The day after he revealed his drawdown plan to the nation, the president traveled to Ft. Drum in New York State to thank soldiers from the Army's 10th Mountain Division for their multiple deployments to Afghanistan. Before those extraordinary and patriotic Americans, he quite naturally doubled down.

Summoning another tic of this presidential moment (and of the Bush one before it), he told them that they were part of "the finest fighting force in the world." Even that evidently seemed inadequate, so he upped the hyperbole. "I have no greater job," he told them, "nothing gives me more honor than serving as your commander in chief. To all of you who are potentially going to be redeployed, just know that your commander in chief has your back . . . God bless you, God bless the United States of America, climb to glory."

As ever, all of this was overlooked. Nowhere did a single commentator wonder, for instance, whether an American president was really supposed to feel that being commander in chief offered greater "honor" than being president of a nation of citizens. In another age, such a statement would have registered as, at best, bizarre. These days, no one even blinks.

And yet who living in this riven, confused, semi-paralyzed country of ours truly believes that, in 2011, Americans can achieve whatever we set out to accomplish? Who thinks that, not having won a war in memory, the U.S. military is incontestably the finest fighting force now or ever

(and on a "climb to glory" at that), or that this country is at present specially blessed by God, or that ours is a mission of selfless kindheartedness on planet Earth?

Obama's remarks have no wings these days because they are ever more divorced from reality. Perhaps because this president in fawning mode is such an uncomfortable sight, and because Americans generally feel so ill-at-ease about their relationship to our wars, however, such remarks are neither attacked nor defended, discussed nor debated, but as if by some unspoken agreement simply ignored.

Here, in any case, is what they aren't: effective rallying cries for a nation in need of unity. Here's what they may be: strange, defensive artifacts of an imperial power in visible decline, part of what might be imagined as the Great American Unraveling. But hold that thought a moment. After all, the topic of the president's remarks was Afghanistan.

THE UNREAL WAR

If Obama framed his Afghan remarks in a rhetoric of militarized super-national surrealism, then what he had to say about the future of the war itself was deceptive in the extreme—not lies perhaps, but full falsehoods half told. Consider just the two most important of them: that his "surge" consisted only of 33,000 American troops and that "by next summer," Americans are going to be so on the road to leaving Afghanistan that it isn't funny.

Unfortunately, it just ain't so. First of all, the real Obama surge was minimally almost 55,000 and possibly 66,000 troops, depending on how you count them. When he came into office in January 2009, there were about 32,000 American troops in Afghanistan. Another 11,000 had been designated to go in the last days of the Bush administration, but only departed in the first Obama months. In March 2009, the president announced his own "new strategy for Afghanistan and Pakistan" and dispatched 21,700 more troops. Then, in December 2009 in a televised speech to the nation from

West Point, he announced that another 30,000 would be going. (With "support troops," it turned out to be 33,000.)

In other words, in September 2012, 14 months from now, only about half the actual troop surge of the Obama years will have been withdrawn. In addition, though seldom discussed, the Obama "surge" was hardly restricted to troops. There was a much ballyhooed "civilian surge" of State Department and aid types that more than tripled the "civilian" effort in Afghanistan. Their drawdown was recently addressed by Secretary of State Hillary Clinton, but only in the vaguest of terms.

Then there was a major surge of CIA personnel (along with U.S. special operations forces), and there's no indication whatsoever that anyone in Washington intends reductions there, or in the drone surge that went with it. As a troop drawdown begins, CIA agents, those special ops forces, and the drones are clearly slated to remain at or beyond a surge peak.

Finally, there was a surge in private contractors—hired foreign guns and hired Afghans—tens of thousands of them. It goes unmentioned, as does the surge in base building, which has yet to end, and the surge in massive citadel-style embassy building in the region, which is assumedly ongoing.

All of this makes mincemeat of the idea that we are in the process of ending the Afghan war. I know the president said, "Our mission will change from combat to support. By 2014, this process of transition will be complete, and the Afghan people will be responsible for their own security." And that was a foggy enough formulation that you might be forgiven for imagining more or less everything will be over "by 2014"—which, by the way, means not January 1st, but December 31st of that year.

If what we know of U.S. plans in Afghanistan plays out, however, December 31, 2014, will be the date for the departure of the last of the full Obama surge of 64,000 troops. In other words, almost five years after Obama entered office, more than 13 years after the Bush administration launched its invasion, we could find ourselves back to or just below something close to Bush-era troop levels. Tens of thousands of U.S. forces would still be in Afghanistan, some of them "combat troops" officially relabeled (as in Iraq) for less warlike activity. All would be part of an American "support" mission that would include huge numbers of "trainers" for the Afghan security forces and also U.S. special forces operatives and CIA types engaged in "counterterror" activities in the country and region.

The U.S. general in charge of training the Afghan military recently suggested that his mission wouldn't be done until 2017 (and no one who knows anything about the country believes that an effective Afghan Army will be in place then either). In addition, although the president didn't directly mention this in his speech, the Obama administration has been involved in quiet talks with the government of Afghan President Hamid Karzai to nail down a "strategic partnership" agreement that would allow American troops, spies, and air power to hunker down as "tenants" on some of the giant bases we've built. There they would evidently remain for years, if not decades (as some reports have it).

In other words, on December 31, 2014, if all goes as planned, the U.S. will be girding for years more of wildly expensive war, even if in a slimmed down form. This is the reality, as American planners imagine it, behind the president's speech.

OVERSTRETCHED EMPIRE

Of course, it's not for nothing that we regularly speak of the best laid plans going awry, something that applies doubly, as in Afghanistan, to the worst laid plans. It's increasingly apparent that our disastrous wars are, as Chairman of the Senate Foreign Relations Committee John Kerry recently admitted, "unsustainable." After all, just the cost of providing air conditioning to U.S. personnel in Iraq and Afghanistan—$20 billion a year—is more than NASA's total budget.

Yes, despite Washington's long lost dreams of a Pax Americana in the Greater Middle East, some of its wars there are still being planned as if for a near-eternity, while others are being intensified. Those wars are still fueled by overblown fears of terrorism; encouraged by a National Security Complex funded to the tune of more than $1.2 trillion annually by an atmosphere of permanent armed crisis; and run by a military that, after a decade of not-so-creative destruction, can't stop doing what it knows how to do best (which isn't winning a war).

Though Obama claims that the United States is no empire, all of this gives modern meaning to the term "overstretched empire." And it's not really much of a mystery what happens to overextended imperial powers that find themselves fighting "little" wars they can't win, while their treasuries head south.

The growing unease in Washington about America's wars reflects a dawning sense of genuine crisis, a sneaking suspicion even among hawkish Republicans that they preside ineffectually over a great power in precipitous decline.

Think, then, of the president's foreign-policy-cum-war speeches as ever more unconvincing attempts to cover the suppurating wound that is Washington's global war policy. If you want to take the temperature of the present crisis, you can do it through Obama's words. The less they ring true, the more discordant they seem in the face of reality, the more he fawns and repeats his various mantras, the more uncomfortable he makes you feel, the more you have the urge to look away, the deeper the crisis.

What will he say when the Great American Unravelling truly begins?

DISCUSSION QUESTIONS

1. Engelhardt refers to the president's pattern of making "greatest military, greatest nation, our God" statements. Why do you think President Obama, and before him President Bush, use this kind of rhetoric so often? What political and cultural functions are involved?
2. In what ways is the war in Afghanistan "unreal" and "unsustainable," according to Engelhardt? Do you agree?
3. Compare Engelhardt's perspective with that of Noam Chomsky in Chapter 9.

28 *Joseph G. Peschek*

THE OBAMA PRESIDENCY AND THE ECONOMIC CRISIS

Barack Obama campaigned for and was elected president on a program of "change" amidst an economic and financial crisis many called the worst since the 1930s and during a dramatic drop in support for the incumbent Bush administration. Many liberal and progressive voters hoped that the crisis of capitalism would lead to a sharp break with business-oriented "neoliberal" public policies on the domestic front, perhaps in the form of a "New New Deal." What have been the results of the Obama presidency's response to the economic crisis as we move toward the presidential campaign of 2012? In this article, political scientist Joseph G. Peschek explores the distinct nature of Obama's broad approach to questions of political economy and how it has shaped his handling of the economic stimulus, banking and financial regulation, and health care reform. Peschek argues that Obama's centrist approach, his quest for "business confidence," and the clout of powerful private economic interests ("capital") have resulted in as much continuity with, rather than departure from, the neoliberalism of his predecessors. If the kind of "change" many erstwhile supporters hoped for is to come about, radical changes in the way the U.S. political system currently functions are necessary—changes that go beyond the important question of who occupies the White House.

During the summer of 2011, in the wake of the debt ceiling agreement passed by Congress, the terms of discussion about economic policy among American political leaders increasingly centered on deficit reduction and spending cuts, rather than on job creation and reviving economic growth. This austerity-oriented shift to the right in official political discourse, including President Obama's, was far from what many liberal and progressive supporters of Obama's 2008 campaign had hoped for. It went against the advice of many mainstream economists, who worried about a reversion to pre-Keynesian thinking, and the public's consistently expressed preference for job

Source: Adapted from Joseph G. Peschek, "The Obama Presidency and the Great Recession: Political Economy, Ideology, and Public Policy." *New Political Science*, Volume 33, Number 4, December 2011.

creation policies, as well as opposition to entitlement cuts and support for tax increases on the wealthy to reduce the deficit.

What does the rightward trajectory of Obama's political economy tell us about the struggle for power in contemporary American politics? In his book *Who Rules America?* G. William Domhoff argues that, "The corporate community's ability to transform its economic power into policy influence and political access makes it the most important influence on the federal government." He goes on to contend that, "Despite their preponderant power in the federal government and the many necessary policies it carries out for them, leaders within the corporate community are constantly critical of it because of its potential independence and its ability to aid their opponents. They know they need government, but they also fear it, especially during times of economic crisis when they need it the most." In their book *American Society: How It Really Works*, scholars Erik Olin Wright and Joel Rogers note that challenges to corporate power in a capitalist democracy face both a "demand constraint" and a "resource constraint." The structural dependence of the state on the welfare of private capitalist firms—the demand constraint—helps to "ensure that in general, the only demands that get raised are those compatible with capitalist interests and a good business climate." But the demand constraint does not dictate specific policy outcomes. Bargaining over political demands enables the distribution of money and wealth, in more instrumental ways, to affect outcomes since "ordinary citizens operate under severe resource constraints in having their interests translated into public policy." While other determining factors are important in the current period, such as the relative coherence and intransigence of the Republican Party in opposition to Obama, I believe that these observations about the multi-dimensional powers of capital are helpful for understanding the influences and constraints that have shaped how the Obama administration has interpreted and responded to the economic crisis.

ECONOMIC CRISIS

By late 2008, many commentators were calling the economic crisis the worst since the 1930s. At stake were not just economic policies, but a basic model of the American social contract. This model is often referred to as "neoliberalism" or, misleadingly, "free-market capitalism." It involves freeing markets and business as much as possible from government regulation. According to economist Thomas Palley, the post-1980 neoliberal growth model severed the virtuous circle of growth that linked rising wages and productivity. "In place of wage growth as the engine of demand growth," Palley writes, "the new model substituted borrowing and asset price inflation. Adherents of the neo-liberal orthodoxy made controlling inflation their primary concern, and set about attacking unions, the minimum wage, and other worker protections. Meanwhile, globalization brought increased foreign competition from lower-wage economies and the prospect of offshoring of employment."

Associated with this macro-economic model was a massive accumulation of public and private debt, "feeding enormous financial profits and marking the growing financialization of capitalism (the shift in gravity from production to finance within the economy as a whole)." Simon Johnson, a former chief economist of the International Monetary Fund, notes that the growing wealth of the financial sector gave bankers enormous political weight, as well as "cultural capital," even without the exertion of overt pressure on government. According to Johnson, the banking-and-securities industry benefitted from the fact that Washington insiders already believed that large financial institutions and free-flowing capital markets were crucial to America's position in the world." One consequence of the acceptance of this model was the rapid inflation in housing prices—the "housing bubble," which would eventually burst with catastrophic effects.

It is important to recognize that the neoliberal capitalist model underlying the economic crisis was embraced by both Democrats and

Republicans for many years. It was not an invention of George W. Bush. Timothy Canova identifies continuities between the Clinton and Bush administrations, noting that both "embraced the so-called Washington Consensus, a policy agenda of fiscal austerity, central-bank autonomy, deregulated markets, liberalized capital flows, free trade and privatization." Moreover the turn to neoliberalism, globalization, and financialization appears to be evidence of deeply-rooted weaknesses in the U.S. capitalist economy itself. Seeming to offer plausible "escape routes" from the stagnation and overcapacity that marked the economic crisis of the 1970s, it proved to be unsustainable. As the economy tanked in 2008 a number of possible approaches to crisis management were possible, including an attempted resolution through a rebranded New Deal, as advocated by a number of progressive, Keynesian, and social democratic thinkers. What sort of approach to political economy did Barack Obama bring as he sought the presidency?

OBAMA'S CORPORATE CENTRISM

Making Connections

When Barack Obama returned to Chicago in the early 1990s after graduating from Harvard Law School, he began to form connections with influential law firms, political leaders, and business interests that went well beyond the circles in which he had moved as a community organizer in the mid-1980s. Several detailed profiles in the mainstream media demonstrate that a centrist, business friendly dimension of Obama's political orientation had been well-formed even before he announced his bid for the presidency. In the November 2006 issue of *Harper*'s, journalist Ken Silverstein showed that Obama had built a strong network of business supporters, including contributors from corporate law and lobbying firms, Wall Street financial firms, and large Chicago business interests. Silverstein acknowledged Obama's responsiveness to both his social activist and business constituents, noting that Obama

"quickly established a political machine funded and run by a standard Beltway group of lobbyists." In a 2007 article for the *New Yorker*, staff writer Larissa MacFarquhar maintained that Obama held a "Burkean" and "deeply conservative" view of history marked by a distrust of abstractions and an affirmation of continuity and stability. Focusing on Obama's economic policies for an August 2008 *New York Times Magazine* feature, economics columnist David Leonhardt described Obama as a "University of Chicago Democrat" who advocated policies that "often involve setting up a government program to address a market failure but then trying to harness the power of the market within that program. This, at times, makes him look like a conservative Democrat."

During the presidential campaign, Obama touted his base of small supporters, but he also received considerable support from the largest Wall Street firms and major corporate lobbyists. As Domhoff notes, "President Obama's network of donors is similar to those of most other successful candidates in the United States in that it builds on wealthy contributors." An August 2008 *New York Times* analysis showed that Obama received more donations of $1,000 or more than Hillary Clinton or John McCain. The article noted the role of more than five-hundred Obama "bundlers" who each collected contributions of $50,000 or more. "Many of the bundlers came from industries with critical interests in Washington. Nearly three dozen of the bundlers have raised more than $500,000 each, including more than a half-dozen who have passed the $1 million mark and one or two who have exceeded $2 million," reported Michael Luo and Christopher Drew. "An analysis of campaign finance records shows that about two-thirds of his bundlers are concentrated in four major industries: law, securities and investments, real estate and entertainment. Lawyers make up the largest group, numbering roughly 130, with many of them working for firms that also have lobbying arms. At least 100 Obama bundlers are top executives or brokers from investment businesses: nearly two dozen work for financial titans like

Lehman Brothers, Goldman Sachs or Citigroup. About 40 others come from the real estate industry." A post-election study by the Campaign Finance Institute found that while nearly fifty percent of Obama's donations came in individual contributions of $200 or less, only twenty-six percent of the money he collected through August 31 during the primary and twenty-four percent of his money through October 15 came from contributors whose total donations added up to $200 or less. This is because many donors contributed $200 or less several times during the campaign. When this is taken into account Obama's percentage of small donor contributions was similar to that of George W. Bush in 2004. Obama's established connections do not determine, but may help to explain, the mix of policies he accepted as president.

The Economy and the 2008 Election Campaign

The 2008 campaign for president was waged in an environment of deep dissatisfaction about the direction in which the country was headed, growing salience of economic issues, and a growing desire for basic change on the part of the public. By August, as Obama and Senator John McCain headed into their nominating conventions, voters remained focused on economic issues. Four in ten voters called the economy their top concern. When issues such as jobs, gas prices, and energy policy were added over half the respondents cited economy-related issues as most important. Only fifteen percent cited the Iraq war. In this poll sixty-five percent expressed confidence that Obama would make the right decisions on the economy, compared to fifty-four percent who expressed confidence in McCain on the economy.

In the Democratic primaries, Obama competed not only with Senator Hillary Rodham Clinton, but also with former Senator and vice presidential candidate John Edwards, who ran on a message of economic populism perhaps stronger than any major Democratic candidate since Jesse Jackson in 1988. Competing for the

support of working-class voters, Obama stated in February, "A country in which only a few prosper is antithetical to our ideals and our democracy." But Obama's economic and domestic policy positions at this stage were unclear and not to the left of Clinton's, let alone Edwards'. During the nomination fight the liberal economist and *New York Times* columnist, Paul Krugman, on several occasions described Obama's economic policies as less progressive than those of Edwards or Clinton. After Obama wrapped up the nomination, Krugman continued to argue that, "Progressive activists, in particular, overwhelmingly supported Mr. Obama during the Democratic primary even though his policy positions, particularly on health care, were often to the right of his rivals'. In effect they convinced themselves that he was a transformational figure behind a centrist façade. They may have had it backward." Shortly after Hillary Clinton ended her campaign Obama told CNBC, "Look. I am a pro-growth, free-market guy. I love the market."

During the general election campaign, Obama combined occasional populist attacks on Wall Street, the Bush administration, and John McCain with statements that reassured business leaders and mainstream economists that he was not a radical. Thus he stated at a campaign stop in Colorado, "I certainly don't fault Senator McCain for these problems. But I do fault the economic philosophy he subscribes to. It's the same philosophy we've had for the last eight years—one that says we should give more and more to those with the most and hope that prosperity trickles down to everyone else." On the other hand, in an interview on NBC's *Today* show Obama said that the cost of the bailout plan might limit his plans for spending on health care, energy, education and other domestic goals. "Does that mean that I can do everything that I've called for in this campaign right away?" he asked. "Probably not. I think we're going to have to phase it in. And a lot of it's going to depend on what our tax revenues look like." At a rally in Green Bay Obama said, "I am not a Democrat who believes that we can or should defend every government program just because it's there." He told the crowd "We will fire government managers who aren't getting results, we will cut funding for programs that are wasting your money and we will use technology and lessons from the private sector to improve efficiency across every level of government." Sounding notes of fiscal prudence Obama stated, "We cannot give a blank check to Washington with no oversight and accountability, when no oversight and accountability is what got us into this mess in the first place." By early October a survey of applied academic economists by *The Economist* found that a majority thought Obama had a better economic plan, a firmer grasp of economics, and would appoint better economic advisers than McCain. Obama scored better than McCain with the economists on nearly every issue: promoting fiscal discipline, energy policy, reducing the number of people without health insurance, reforming financial regulation and boosting long-term economic growth. Exit polls on Election Day showed that the economy dominated voters' concerns more than in any election since 1980, with sixty-three percent saying it was the most important issue, up from twenty percent in 2004. Three-quarters of those polled said the country was on the wrong track, more than nine in ten rated the economy in bad shape and at least seven in ten disapproved of President Bush's handling of the economy. As one analysis noted, "For McCain, who maintained his edge in the public's view as the stronger candidate on national security issues, the utter dominance of economic issues overwhelmed his campaign." While Obama's campaign of reassurance on economics may have been electorally shrewd, it also portended fateful choices that Obama, as president-elect, made on appointments to key economic policy positions.

Obama Assembles a Team

After the election Obama assembled an economic policy team that included many figures representing continuity with neoliberalism. Treasury Secretary Timothy Geithner, National Economic Council director Lawrence Summers, and Office of Management and Budget director Peter Orzag were associates of President Clinton's Treasury Secretary, Robert Rubin. In 2006 Obama was the only senator to address the inaugural meeting of the Hamilton Project, created by Clinton era Treasury Officials Robert Rubin and Roger Altman and others to formulate Democratic economic strategy. "Rubinomics" was a Wall Street-friendly approach to economic policy on the part of Democrats who supported balanced budgets, free trade, and financial deregulation. The *New York Times* observed that these selections signaled that "Obama intended to pursue aggressive, yet centrist policies, in finding ways to help jump-start the economy." *The Economist* found Obama's choices "reassuring especially for those who feared a shift to the left." The magazine quoted a hedge-fund manager who "breathed a sigh of relief" that there were "no Robert Reichs" in the cabinet, in reference to Bill Clinton's progressive labor secretary. Even Karl Rove found Obama's economic team "reassuring." Progressive journalist and economic analyst Robert Kuttner interpreted these key appointments differently: "Obama felt he needed men like Rubin and Summers for tutelage, access, and validation. That itself speaks volumes about where power resides in America."

Having reviewed Obama's relationship to economic and political elites, we might predict that, as president, Obama's record would be compromised in terms of his ability or willingness to create new models that break sharply with business-oriented, neoliberal orientations. At times Obama has adopted a populist pose. For example he attacked the Supreme Court's January 2010 *Citizens United* decision on campaign spending by corporations, stating, "This ruling opens the floodgates for an unlimited amount of special interest money into our democracy." But he has also taken pains to reassure and court the business community, perhaps in accord with the "demand constraint" of capitalist democracy noted previously. Obama told Bloomberg News that he did not "begrudge" JPMorgan Chase &Co. CEO, Jamie Dimon, his $17 million dollar bonus, nor Goldman Sachs Group Inc. CEO, Lloyd Blankfein, his $9 million award. "I know both these guys; they are very savvy businessmen. I, like most of the American people, don't begrudge people success or wealth. That is part of the free-market system," Obama explained. About two weeks later, in a speech to members of the Business Roundtable, Obama declared himself an "ardent believer in the free market." Acknowledging that government has a "vital, if limited, role to play in fostering economic growth," Obama maintained that, "I want everyone in this room to succeed. . . . Because I firmly believe that America's success in large part depends on your success."

One area of significant progressive achievement appears to be Obama's rebuilding of regulatory agencies such as the Environmental Protection Agency, the Occupational Health and Safety Administration, and the Securities and Exchange Commission. Other decisive breaks include the appointment of Hilda Solis as Labor Secretary and the recent recess appointment to the National Labor Relations Board of labor lawyer Craig Becker, whose nomination was strongly opposed by Republicans, some Democrats, and business groups. Obama's approaches to economic stimulus, health care, banking and financial regulation and health care reform are, in different ways, more problematic from a progressive perspective. As I will attempt to show briefly, they reflect both the limitations of Obama's market-deferential biases and the resource constraints that help to shape outcomes in key policy battles.

President Obama's Policy Initiatives

The Economic Stimulus

After the election Obama developed a stimulus plan that would provide up to $1 trillion to build infrastructure, provide assistance to debt-strapped state and local governments, invest in energy-efficiency projects, and other measures.

Obama's turn to the stimulus approach was greeted warmly by leading progressive economists as a neo-Keynesian measure to put the brakes on rising unemployment and stop the hemorrhaging of state and local government jobs and services. The American Recovery and Reinvestment Act (ARRA), which passed Congress in February 2009 with the support of three Republicans in the Senate and no Republicans in the House, included a mix of tax cuts, aid to state and local governments, emergency unemployment assistance, and spending for a variety of infrastructure projects. The cost was $787 billion. A number of studies and assessments concluded that the Recovery Act boosted employment. A November 2010 Congressional Budget Office (CBO) report estimated that as many as 3.6 million people were employed as a result of ARRA. In addition to saving and creating jobs, ARRA increased the number of hours worked, the CBO concluded. A summary of the CBO report noted, "Among ARRA's most effective provisions for saving and creating jobs, according to CBO estimates, are direct purchases of goods and services by the federal government, transfer payments to states (such as extra Medicaid funding), and transfer payments to individuals (such as increased food stamp benefits and additional weeks of unemployment benefits). CBO estimates indicate that tax cuts are less effective job producers, and tax cuts for higher-income people and corporations have very little bang for the buck." A study by Alan S. Blinder, a Princeton professor and former vice chairman of the Fed, and Mark Zandi, chief economist at Moody's Analytics, concluded that without the Obama administration's fiscal stimulus program and other measures, the U.S. GDP would have been about 6.5 percent lower in 2010, there would have been about 8.5 million fewer jobs, on top of the more than 8 million already lost, and the economy would have been experiencing deflation, instead of low inflation.

Unemployment was projected by the Obama administration to decline significantly in 2009 and 2010. But as unemployment rose in 2009 some on the left argued that, although the economy would be in much worse shape without the Recovery Act, the initial stimulus should have been larger and that a second stimulus package was needed. By early 2010, however, in the wake of Scott Brown's Senate victory in Massachusetts, while the Obama administration was willing to tout the relative success of the stimulus and push for a modest jobs bill, the president did not seem inclined to pursue a second stimulus package. The employment report of the Bureau of Labor Statistics showed that the drop in the unemployment rate from 9.2 percent to 9.1 percent was entirely due to a decline in labor force participation. 117,000 new jobs were created in July. To reach the pre-recession unemployment rate by mid-2014 would require the addition of 400,000 new jobs every month, three times as fast as occurred in July. Obama's commitment to a chimerical "fiscal responsibility" would seem to ensure that any forthcoming jobs initiatives will be extremely limited.

Health Care Reform

On March 23, 2010, President Obama signed a broad health care reform bill called the Patient Protection and Affordable Care Act. The legislation represented the largest expansion of health care coverage since the passage of Medicare and Medicaid forty-five years earlier. Among the goals of the reform were expanded coverage (ninety-five percent of non-elderly legal residents of the U.S. would have health insurance by 2019), reform of health insurance markets, and slowed growth of health care costs. The Congressional Budget Office estimated that the health care reform legislation would reduce budget deficits by $143 billion over 2010–2019.

The 2010 health care reform is a social policy achievement of historic magnitude, passed amidst hysterical cries about "socialism" and "death panels." In addition to being a victory for Obama and House Speaker Nancy Pelosi, the final push for health care reform saw the mobilization of liberal, left-wing, and labor groups such as Moveon .org, Health Care for America Now, the AFL-CIO

and Organizing for America in which, "the politics of maneuver within Washington was supplemented . . . by a politics of vigorous protest and advocacy." How was it received by progressives? Social policy experts Jonathan Oberlander and Theodore Marmor noted that, "the new health care law is anything but radical." They argued, "Despite such deep flaws in the U.S. health care system, the central assumptions of both the Obama administration and the Democratic leadership in Congress was that only legislation that did not radically change it has a chance of success."

Given the decision of the Obama administration to defer to Congress on the details of health care reform, the legislative process was marked both by intense bargaining and compromises among political leaders in search of votes and by a broad mobilization of health care lobbyists. One report found $133 million in lobbying by health insurance interests in the second quarter of 2009 alone. Another analysis found that statements of a dozen lawmakers had been ghostwritten by Washington lobbyists working for Genetech, one of the world's largest biotechnology companies. The *Washington Post* noted that health care interest groups "operate with opaque financing, often receiving hidden support from insurers, drugmakers, or unions." The final package excluded the public option that many progressives see as a compromise from a single-payer insurance system and in other ways protects the private insurance companies and other corporate interests from competition. Political scientist Jacob Hacker, an innovator of the public option, states, "The White House promised to protect hospitals and drug manufacturers from those (like me) who believed that government should play a stronger countervailing role. In return, the industries wouldn't kill reform." Here too the parameters of change were set by political clout of private economic interests.

Banking and Financial Reform

Perhaps the least progress has been in finance and banking reform where, to the chagrin of progressive critics, the approaches of Treasury Secretary Timothy Geithner, National Economic Council Director Lawrence Summers, and Federal Reserve Chair Ben Bernanke appear to have held sway during Obama's first year. In January 2010, accompanied by a good deal of populist rhetoric, Obama announced several new measures, including a new tax on the fifty largest U.S. financial institutions to recover losses from the financial bailout, endorsement of an independent consumer fiscal protection agency, and support for former Fed Chair Paul Volcker's plan to restrict the involvement of commercial banks in running hedge funds and engaging in proprietary trading. Economist Joseph Stiglitz called Obama's proposals "only a good beginning." By the spring of 2010, with business groups set to spend record amounts on lobbying in opposition to the plans, financial reform loomed as the next battleground in the struggle for power in Obama's America.

In July the administration's financial regulatory bill cleared Congress. Among its features was a "resolution authority" given to the Federal Deposit Insurance Corporation (FDIC) to be appointed as a receiver in the "orderly liquidation" of large financial companies as an alternative to bankruptcy court. The legislation expanded federal banking and securities regulation over a wider range of financial activities, created a council of federal regulators to detect financial risk, and established a new regulator to protect consumers of financial products. The so called Volcker rule was watered down in a compromise allowing banks to invest up to three percent of their capital in private-equity and hedge funds. Also weakened was a proposal by Senator Blanche Lincoln for tightened restrictions on the trading of financial instruments known as derivates. Lincoln's plan would have forced banks to move derivatives trading into a separately-capitalized institution within the larger bank holding company. In a last minute agreement, Congress decided to force banks to segregate their dealings in only the riskiest categories of derivatives. The *New York Times* noted, "The derivatives deal also headed off a last-minute rebellion by some

New York lawmakers concerned about the effect of Mrs. Lincoln's proposal on Wall Street businesses." Sheila Bair of the FDIC said of bankers, "I think they are breathing a sigh of relief today because the derivatives piece ended up being much less onerous than they originally expected. It could have been a lot worse." The implementation of the complicated bill will rely heavily on federal regulators, which in itself is a problem. As Robert Reich noted, "Reliance on the discretion of regulators rather than structural changes in the banking system plays directly into the hands of the big banks and their executives and traders who contribute mightily to Democratic and Republican campaigns."

Influencing the financial legislative process was a massive lobbying effort by Wall Street financial interests. In an example of the revolving door, at least seventy former members of Congress and fifty-six former congressional aides on the Senate or House banking committees were lobbying for the financial sector by 2009. According to the Center for Responsive Politics, members of the Senate Agriculture Committee, which took up the derivatives issue, received $22.8 million from people and organizations connected with financial, insurance, and real estate companies in the then-current election cycle, two and a half times what they received from agricultural donors. The House Financial Services Committee was also a major draw for Wall Street money. One report stated that executives and political action committees from Wall Street banks, insurance companies, hedge funds and other financial sectors had contributed $1.7 billion to congressional candidates in the last decade, with much of it going to members of the financial oversight committees. At a more structural level, the process of financial reform was probably affected by what John Bellamy Foster and Hannah Holleman call the "financialization of the capitalist class." They note that, by 2008, the ten largest U.S. financial conglomerates held more than sixty percent of U.S. financial assets, compared to only ten percent in 1990. They also contend that, in the Obama administration, "the figures who were selected to develop and execute federal policy, with respect to finance, were heavily drawn from executives of financial conglomerates." On April 13, 2011, the Senate Permanent Subcommittee on Investigations released a 650-page report entitled "Wall Street and the Financial Crisis: Anatomy of a Financial Collapse." Its executive summary states: "The investigation found that the crisis was not a natural disaster, but the result of high-risk, complex financial products; undisclosed conflicts of interest; and the failure of regulators, the credit rating agencies, and the market itself to rein in the excesses of Wall Street." In an interview, subcommittee co-chair Senator Carl Levin stated, "The overwhelming evidence is that those institutions deceived their clients and deceived the public, and they were aided and abetted by deferential regulators and credit ratings agencies who had conflicts of interest."

AFTER THE "SHELLACKING"

In the midterm elections of 2010, Republicans made a net gain of sixty-three seats in the House of Representatives. This was the largest gain for either party in a House election since 1948, and the largest in a midterm election since 1938. The GOP had lost fifty-five seats in the House in the two previous elections (2006 and 2008). President Obama described the results as a "shellacking." How are these results to be explained? A perhaps dominant "narrative" among political elites and in the mainstream media was that President Obama had "over-reached" on domestic policy in his first two years, and needed to move away from the "left" towards the "center" by embracing "pro-business" and deficit reduction policies. This interpretation rejects the possibility that Obama made less progress on the economy and job creation than many Americans expected precisely because he *did* pursue centrist and business-friendly policies that amounted to political insufficiency rather than overreach. In so doing he alienated many erstwhile supporters and conceded political mobilization to a highly disciplined right-wing.

Nevertheless, President Obama worked assiduously after the midterm elections to convince the business community that he was their friend and understood their pain. Thus, at a post-election press conference he stated, "You just had a successive set of issues in which I think business took the message that, well, gosh, it seems like we may be always painted as the bad guy. And so I've got to take responsibility in terms of making sure that I make clear to the business community as well as to the country that the most important thing we can do is to boost and encourage our business sector." In January, Obama penned an opinion piece for the *Wall Street Journal* in which he touted an executive order to "remove outdated regulations that stifle job creation and make our economy less competitive." An accompanying piece in the newspaper suggested the structural influence of capital on Obama's agenda: "The move is the latest effort by the White House to repair relations with corporate America. Business leaders say an explosion in new regulations stemming from the president's health-care and financial regulatory overhauls has, along with the sluggish economy, made them reluctant to spend on expansion and hiring. Companies are sitting on nearly $2 trillion in cash and liquid assets, the most since World War II." Obama followed up in early February with an address to the U.S. Chamber of Commerce, which spent many millions to defeat Democratic candidates in 2010. "I will tell you . . . I'll go anywhere to be a booster for American businesses, American workers, and American products. And I don't charge you commission," the President stated. "So if I've got one message, that message is: now is the time to invest in America."

Accompanying the campaign to win business confidence were such moves on the part of President Obama as the announcement of a two-year pay freeze for civilian federal workers, the acceptance of the extension of Bush-era tax cuts for all brackets for two years in a December 2010 compromise tax package with Congressional Republicans, and the appointments of William Daley as his chief of staff and Gene Sperling as head of the National Economic Council. Both Daley and Sperling worked in the Clinton administration where they championed deficit reduction and supported "free trade" policies such as NAFTA, and both have extensive connections to Wall Street and the business community. Obama's Fiscal Year 2012 budget proposal included about $1.1 trillion of deficit reduction measures over a decade, of which tax reforms and new revenue sources accounted for roughly one-third.

By mid-2011, political discussion was dominated by "deficit hawks" pushing fiscal austerity. With substantial economic reform forestalled, with severe problems of unemployment and mortgages confronting millions of Americans, and with a near total absence of presidential leadership for a fairer, more progressive approach to economic policy, a disciplined political conservatism has had much success in "framing" public understanding of the political environment, which is more skewed to the right and less conducive to progressive change than in November 2008. However, by "political environment" I do not mean "public opinion" in any direct sense. Opinion polls show high levels of public support for such progressive measures as tax increases on the wealthy and corporations, a "public option"

for health insurance, and reduced spending on the military and an end to the wars in Afghanistan and Iraq. In these ways public opinion is closer to the People's Budget put forward by the leaders of the Congressional Progressive Caucus, and is to the left of the budget plans of both Republican leaders and President Obama. Discussion of economic and budget policy in the mainstream media falls along a center-right axis in which progressive voices are largely side-lined. This finding underscores the need for progressives to champion media reform and in other ways open up public discussion to more facts and perspectives than the ideological myths currently filling the public sphere allow for. Even if supporting President Obama for reelection, the left also needs to maintain a clear critique of him and the political system that produced him. Under Obama, the country has moved in directions, in both domestic and foreign policy, that reveal at least as much continuity with, as departures from, the record of his predecessor. As I have tried to show, this has happened not in spite of, but in part because of, the choices and decisions that President Obama has made.

DISCUSSION QUESTIONS

1. Early in his article, Peschek refers to "resource constraints" and "demand constraints" in capitalist democracies. How are these concepts defined? How may they help explain what has happened with important economic and domestic policies under President Obama?
2. Peschek argues that the United States under President Obama, despite vows of "change," is continuing patterns of policy established by President George W. Bush. To what extent do you agree or disagree?

CHAPTER 8

Law and the Courts

L aw and courts play a central role in settling political conflicts in the United States, a point driven home by the Supreme Court decision that effectively decided the presidential election of 2000. In part, this reflects the dominance of classic liberal thought in America, with its emphasis on resolving disputes through formal procedures. Certainly there is no denying that we are a very litigious country, with a presence of lawyers and lawsuits that outstrips most, if not all, of the world's other nations. We also know that a good number of you, political science majors and students in political science courses, are on the road to law school. The articles in this chapter explore connections between law and politics in our legalistic culture and depict courts and judges as *political* actors whose values and practices usually reinforce the structure of power discussed in Part I.

Because we have a written Constitution that declares itself to be the supreme law of the land, who is authorized to interpret that Constitution becomes a crucial question. In our system, courts, especially the Supreme Court, have assumed this power of judicial review. The 1787 Constitution provided for a separate judicial branch of government but left its powers unclear. In *Federalist Paper 78,* Alexander Hamilton, an advocate of a strong central union, argued for a judiciary with the power to declare acts of the other branches of government unconstitutional. Thomas Jefferson, in contrast, feared the antidemocratic nature of Hamilton's argument, especially because the Constitution exempts the Court from direct democratic control. Jefferson argued that all three branches of government, within their assigned spheres of power, have important constitutional roles to play. The Court, he reasoned, is not the sole arbiter of constitutional questions. And government, ultimately, is answerable to the people. Hamilton's position triumphed when the Supreme Court under John Marshall, who was chief justice from 1801 to 1835, asserted the power of judicial review in the historic *Marbury v. Madison* case of 1803.

29 *Jeffrey Rosen*

SUPREME COURT INC.

One of the major themes of Voices of Dissent *is the need to critically examine the relationship between American politics and the capitalist economic system. Jeffrey Rosen is a law professor who frequently contributes analyses of legal affairs to news magazines and journals of opinion. In this article, Rosen chronicles the growing pro-business orientation of the Supreme Court. Hot button cultural issues like abortion, affirmative action, and the death penalty generate much attention when they reach the Court. But as Rosen argues, cases involving business "which include shareholder suits, antitrust challenges to corporate mergers, patent disputes and efforts to reduce punitive-damage awards and prevent product-liability suits—are no less important. They involve billions of dollars, have huge consequences for the economy and can have a greater effect on people's daily lives than the often symbolic battles of the culture wars." Rosen believes that the pro-business orientation of the current Court, which includes nominal liberals as well as conservatives, reflects an elite consensus about the virtues of private enterprise that is not necessarily shared by the wider public. It is a product as well of a decades-long campaign by conservative and business interests to shape the legal profession and the court system in pro–free market ways. Whereas Ralph Nader and the public-interest movement once made gains through the courts, today economic populists in robes are virtually an endangered species.*

I.

The headquarters of the U.S. Chamber of Commerce, located across from Lafayette Park in Washington, is a limestone structure that looks almost as majestic as the Supreme Court. The similarity is no coincidence: both buildings were designed by the same architect, Cass Gilbert. Lately, however, the affinities between the court and the chamber, a lavishly financed business-advocacy organization, seem to be more than just architectural. The Supreme Court term that ended last June was, by all measures, exceptionally

---

Source: Jeffrey Rosen, "Supreme Court Inc." *New York Times Magazine,* 16 March 2008.

good for American business. The chamber's litigation center filed briefs in 15 cases and its side won in 13 of them—the highest percentage of victories in the center's 30-year history. The current term, which ends this summer, has also been shaping up nicely for business interests.

I visited the chamber recently to talk with Robin Conrad, who heads the litigation effort, about her recent triumphs. Conrad, an appealing, soft-spoken woman, lives with her family on a horse farm in Maryland, where she rides with a fox-chasing club called the Howard County-Iron Bridge Hounds. Her office, playfully adorned by action figures of women like Xena the Warrior Princess and Hillary Rodham Clinton, has one of the most impressive views in Washington. "You can see the White House through the trees," she said as we peered through a window overlooking the park. "In the old days, you could actually see people bathing in the fountain. Homeless people."

Conrad was in an understandably cheerful mood. Though the current Supreme Court has a well-earned reputation for divisiveness, it has been surprisingly united in cases affecting business interests. Of the 30 business cases last term, 22 were decided unanimously, or with only one or two dissenting votes. Conrad said she was especially pleased that several of the most important decisions were written by liberal justices, speaking for liberal and conservative colleagues alike. In opinions last term, Ruth Bader Ginsburg, Stephen Breyer and David Souter each went out of his or her way to question the use of lawsuits to challenge corporate wrongdoing—a strategy championed by progressive groups like Public Citizen but routinely denounced by conservatives as "regulation by litigation." Conrad reeled off some of her favorite moments: "Justice Ginsburg talked about how 'private-securities fraud actions, if not adequately contained, can be employed abusively.' Justice Breyer had a wonderful quote about how Congress was trying to 'weed out unmeritorious securities lawsuits.' Justice Souter talked about how the threat of litigation 'will push cost-conscious defendants to settle.'"

Examples like these point to an ideological sea change on the Supreme Court. A generation ago,

progressive and consumer groups petitioning the court could count on favorable majority opinions written by justices who viewed big business with skepticism—or even outright prejudice. An economic populist like William O. Douglas, the former New Deal crusader who served on the court from 1939 to 1975, once unapologetically announced that he was "ready to bend the law in favor of the environment and against the corporations."

Today, however, there are no economic populists on the court, even on the liberal wing. And ever since John Roberts was appointed chief justice in 2005, the court has seemed only more receptive to business concerns. Forty percent of the cases the court heard last term involved business interests, up from around 30 percent in recent years. While the Rehnquist Court heard less than one antitrust decision a year, on average, between 1988 and 2003, the Roberts Court has heard seven in its first two terms—and all of them were decided in favor of the corporate defendants.

Business cases at the Supreme Court typically receive less attention than cases concerning issues like affirmative action, abortion or the death penalty. The disputes tend to be harder to follow: the legal arguments are more technical, the underlying stories less emotional. But these cases—which include shareholder suits, antitrust challenges to corporate mergers, patent disputes and efforts to reduce punitive-damage awards and prevent product-liability suits—are no less important. They involve billions of dollars, have huge consequences for the economy and can have a greater effect on people's daily lives than the often symbolic battles of the culture wars. In the current Supreme Court term, the justices have already blocked a liability suit against Medtronic, the manufacturer of a heart catheter, and rejected a type of shareholder suit that includes a claim against Enron. In the coming months, the court will decide whether to reduce the largest punitive-damage award in American history, which resulted from the *Exxon Valdez* oil spill in 1989.

What should we make of the Supreme Court's transformation? Throughout its history, the court has tended to issue opinions, in areas from free speech to gender equality, that reflect or consolidate a social consensus. With their pro-business jurisprudence, the justices may be capturing an emerging spirit of agreement among liberal and conservative elites about the value of free markets. Among the professional classes, many Democrats and Republicans, whatever their other disagreements, have come to share a relatively laissez-faire, technocratic vision of the economy and are suspicious of excessive regulation and reflexive efforts to vilify big business. Judges, lawyers and law professors (such as myself), drilled in cost-benefit analysis over the past three decades, are no exception. It should come as little surprise that John Roberts and Stephen Breyer, both of whom studied the economic analysis of law at Harvard, have similar instincts in business cases.

This elite consensus, however, is not necessarily shared by the country as a whole. If anything, America may be entering something of a populist moment. If you combine the groups of Americans in a recent Pew survey who lean toward some strain of economic populism—from disaffected and conservative Democrats to traditional liberals to social and big-government conservatives—at least two-thirds of all voters arguably feel sympathy for government intervention in the economy. Could it be, then, that the court is reflecting an elite consensus while contravening the sentiments of most Americans? Only history will ultimately make this clear. One thing, however, is certain already: the transformation of the court was no accident. It represents the culmination of a carefully planned, behind-the-scenes campaign over several decades to change not only the courts but also the country's political culture.

II.

The origins of the business community's campaign to transform the Supreme Court can be traced back precisely to Aug. 23, 1971. That was the day when Lewis F. Powell Jr., a corporate lawyer in Richmond, Va., wrote a memo to his friend Eugene B. Sydnor, then the head of the education committee of the U.S. Chamber of Commerce. In the memo, Powell expressed his concern that the American economic system was "under broad attack." He identified several aggressors: the New Left, the liberal media, rebellious students on college campuses and, most important, Ralph Nader. Earlier that year, Nader founded Public Citizen to advocate for consumer rights, bring antitrust actions when the Justice Department did not, and sue federal agencies when they failed to adopt health and safety regulations.

Powell claimed that this attack on the economic system was "quite new in the history of America." Ever since 1937, when President Franklin D. Roosevelt threatened to pack a conservative Supreme Court with more progressive justices, the court had largely deferred to federal and state economic regulations. And by the 1960s, the Supreme Court under Chief Justice Earl Warren had embraced a form of economic populism, often favoring the interests of small business over big business, even at the expense of consumers. But what Powell saw in the work of Nader and others was altogether more extreme: a radical campaign that was "broadly based and consistently pursued."

To counter the growing influence of public-interest litigation groups like Public Citizen, Powell urged the Chamber of Commerce to begin a multifront lobbying campaign on behalf of business interests, including hiring top business lawyers to bring cases before the Supreme Court. "The judiciary," Powell predicted, "may be the most important instrument for social, economic and political change." Two months after he wrote the memo, Powell was appointed by Richard Nixon to the Supreme Court. And six years later, in 1977, after steadily expanding its lobbying efforts, the chamber established the National Chamber Litigation Center to file cases and briefs on behalf of business interests in federal and state courts.

Today, the Chamber of Commerce is an imposing lobbying force. To fulfill its mission of serving "the unified interests of American business," it collects membership dues from more than three million businesses and related organizations; last year, according to the Center for Responsive Politics, the chamber spent more than $21 million lobbying the White House, Congress and regulatory agencies on legal matters. But its battle against the forces of Naderism got off to a slow start. In 1983, when Robin Conrad arrived at the chamber, the Supreme Court was handing Nader and his allies significant victories. That year, for example, the court held that President Reagan's secretary of transportation, Andrew L. Lewis Jr., acted capriciously when he repealed a regulation, inspired by Nader's advocacy, that required automakers to install passive restraints like air bags. In 1986, the chamber supported a challenge to the Environmental Protection Agency's aerial surveillance of a Dow Chemical plant. The chamber's side lost, 5–4.

But eventually, things began to change. The chamber started winning cases in part by refining its strategy. With Conrad's help, the chamber's Supreme Court litigation program began to offer practice moot-court arguments for lawyers scheduled to argue important cases. The chamber also began hiring the most-respected Democratic and Republican Supreme Court advocates to persuade the court to hear more business cases. Although many of the businesses that belong to the Chamber of Commerce have their own in-house lawyers, they would have the chamber file "friend of the court" briefs on their behalf. The chamber would decide which of the many cases brought to its attention were in the long-term strategic interest of American business and then hire the leading business lawyers to write supporting briefs or argue the case.

Until the mid-1980s, there wasn't an organized group of law firms that specialized in arguing business cases before the Supreme Court. But in 1985, Rex Lee, the solicitor general under Reagan, left the government to start a Supreme Court appellate practice at the firm Sidley Austin. Lee's goal was to offer business clients the same level of expert representation before the Supreme Court that the solicitor general's office provides to federal agencies. Lee's success prompted other law firms to hire former Supreme Court clerks and former members of the solicitor general's office to start business practices. The Chamber of Commerce, for its part, began to coordinate the strategy of these lawyers in the most important business cases.

At times, the strategic calculations can be quite personal. Because Supreme Court clerks have tremendous influence in making recommendations about what cases the court should hear, Conrad told me, having well-known former clerks involved in submitting a brief can be especially important. "When Justice O'Connor was on the bench and we knew her vote was very important, we had a case where the opposition had her favorite clerk on the brief, so we retained her next-favorite clerk," she said with a laugh. "We won."

In our conversation, Conrad was especially enthusiastic about Maureen Mahoney, a former clerk for Chief Justice Rehnquist and one of the top Supreme Court litigators who coordinate strategy with the chamber. When Mahoney agreed in 2005 to represent an appeal by the disgraced accounting firm Arthur Andersen, which was convicted in 2002 of obstructing justice by shredding documents related to the audit of Enron, few people thought the Supreme Court would take the case. "The climate was very anti-Enron," Mahoney told me, "and it was viewed as a doomed petition."

Mahoney rehearsed her Supreme Court argument in a moot court sponsored by the chamber. ("She was absolutely dazzling," Conrad recalls.) On April 27, 2005, Mahoney stood calmly before the justices and delivered one of the best oral arguments I've ever seen at the Supreme Court. She argued that because Arthur Andersen's accountants had followed a standard document-destruction procedure before receiving the government's subpoena, they couldn't be guilty of a crime; they weren't aware what they were doing was criminal. The Supreme Court unanimously agreed and reversed the conviction, 9–0.

The Arthur Andersen case is a good example of how significantly the Supreme Court has changed its attitude about cases involving securities fraud—and business cases more generally—from the Warren to the Roberts era. In a case in 1964, the court ruled that aggrieved investors and consumers could file private lawsuits to enforce the securities laws, even in cases in which Congress hadn't explicitly created a right to sue. In the mid-1990s, however, Congress substantially cut back on these citizen suits, and the court today has shown little patience for them. Mahoney says she sees her victory in the Arthur Andersen case as significant because it applied the same principle in criminal cases involving corporate wrongdoing that the court had already been recognizing in civil cases: namely, "refusing to create greater damage remedies or criminal penalties than Congress has explicitly specified." She describes the case as "a very important win for business."

This term, the Supreme Court has continued to cut back on consumer suits. In a ruling in January, the court refused to allow a shareholder suit against the suppliers to Charter Communications, one of the country's largest cable companies. The suppliers were alleged to have "aided and abetted" Charter's efforts to inflate its earnings, but the court held that Charter's investors had to show that they had relied on the deceptive acts committed by the suppliers before the suit could proceed. A week later, the court invoked the same principle when it refused to hear an appeal in a case related to Enron, in which investors are trying to recover $40 billion from Wall Street banks that they claim aided and abetted Enron's fraud. As a result, the shareholder suit against the banks may be dead.

III.

In addition to litigating cases before the court, the Chamber of Commerce also lobbies Congress and the White House in an effort to change the composition of the court itself. (Unlike many other government officials, the justices themselves are not, of course, subject to direct corporate lobbying.) The chamber's efforts in this area were inspired by Robert Bork's thwarted nomination to the court in 1987. Business groups were enthusiastic about Bork—not because of his conservative social views but because of his skepticism of vigorous antitrust enforcement. "In reaction to the Bork nomination, it struck us that we didn't even have a process in place to be a player," Conrad said.

So the chamber set up a formal process for endorsing candidates after their nominations. The process was designed to be bipartisan; and the chamber has encouraged Democratic as well as Republican presidents to appoint justices. Nominees are evaluated solely through the prism of their views about business. "We're very surgical in our analysis," Conrad said.

After the election of Bill Clinton, for example, the chamber endorsed Ruth Bader Ginsburg, who in addition to her pioneering achievements as the head of the women's rights project at the A.C.L.U. had specialized, as a law professor, in the procedural rules in complex civil cases and was comfortable with the finer points of business litigation. The chamber was especially enthusiastic about Clinton's second nominee, Stephen Breyer, who made his name building a bipartisan consensus for airline deregulation as a special counsel on the judiciary committee; and who, as a Harvard law professor, advocated an influential and moderate view on antitrust enforcement.

During Breyer's confirmation hearings his sharpest critic was Ralph Nader, who testified that his pro-business rulings were "extraordinarily one-sided." Another critic, Senator Howard Metzenbaum of Ohio, said that the fact that the chamber was the first organization to endorse Breyer indicated that "large corporations are very pleased with this nomination" and "the fact that Ralph Nader is opposed to it indicated that the average American has a reason to have some concern." The chamber's imprimatur helped reassure Republicans about Breyer, and he was confirmed with a vote of 87 to 9. "Frankly, we didn't feel like we had anyone on the court since Justice Powell who truly understood business issues," Conrad told me. "Justice Breyer came close to that."

The Breyer and Ginsburg nominations also came at a time when liberal as well as conservative judges and academics were gravitating in increasing numbers to an economic approach to the law, originally developed at the University of Chicago. The law-and-economics movement sought to evaluate the efficiency of legal rules based on their costs and benefits for society as a whole. Although originally conservative in its orientation, the movement also attracted prominent moderate and liberal scholars and judges like Breyer, who before his nomination wrote two books on regulation, arguing that government health-and-safety spending is distorted by sensational media reports of disasters that affect relatively few citizens.

Since joining the Supreme Court, Breyer has also been an intellectual leader in antitrust and patent disputes, which often pit business against business, rather than business against consumers. In those cases, many liberal scholars sympathetic to economic analysis have applauded the court for favoring competition rather than existing competitors, innovation rather than particular innovators. "The court deserves credit for trying to rationalize a totally irrational patent system, benefiting smaller new competitors rather than existing big ones," says Lawrence Lessig, an intellectual-property scholar at Stanford.

Clinton's nominations of Ginsburg and Breyer may have been welcomed by the chamber, but with the election of George W. Bush, the chamber faced a dilemma. Ever since the Reagan administration, there had been a divide on the right wing of the court between pragmatic free-market conservatives, who tended to favor business interests, and ideological states-rights conservatives. In some business cases, these two strands of conservatism diverged, leading the most staunch states-rights conservatives on the court, Antonin Scalia and Clarence Thomas, to rule against business interests. Scalia and Thomas were reluctant to second-guess large punitive-damage verdicts by state

juries, for example, or to hold that federally regulated cigarette manufacturers could not be sued in state court. As a result, under Conrad's leadership, the chamber began a vigorous campaign to urge the Bush administration to appoint pro-business conservatives.

When it came time to replace Chief Justice William Rehnquist and Justice Sandra Day O'Connor, the candidate most enthusiastically supported by states-rights conservatives, Judge Michael Luttig, had a record on the Court of Appeals for the Fourth Circuit that some corporate interests feared might make him unpredictable in business cases. ("One of my constant refrains is that being conservative doesn't necessarily mean being pro-business," Conrad told me.) The chamber and other business groups enthusiastically supported John Roberts, who had been hired by the chamber to write briefs in two Supreme Court cases in 2001 and 2002. At the time of Roberts's nomination, Thomas Goldstein, a prominent Supreme Court litigator, described him as "the go-to lawyer for the business community," adding "of all the candidates, he is the one they knew best." When Roberts was nominated, business groups lobbied senators as part of the campaign for his confirmation.

The business community was also enthusiastic about Samuel Alito, whose 15-year record as an appellate judge showed a consistent skepticism of claims against large corporations. Ted Frank of the American Enterprise Institute predicted at the time of the nomination that if Alito replaced O'Connor, he and Roberts would bring about a rise in business cases before the Supreme Court. Frank's prediction was soon vindicated.

"There wasn't a great deal of interest in classic business cases in the last few years of the Rehnquist Court," Carter Phillips, a partner at Sidley Austin and a leading Supreme Court business advocate, told me. In 2004, Judge Richard Posner, a founder of the law-and-economics movement, argued that the Rehnquist Court's emphasis on headline-grabbing constitutional cases had politicized it, and called on the court to hear more business cases. The Roberts court has unambiguously answered the call. As Phillips told me, Roberts "is more interested in those issues and understands them better than his predecessor did."

IV.

Exactly how successful has the Chamber of Commerce been at the Supreme Court? Although the court is currently accepting less than 2 percent of the 10,000 petitions it receives each year, the Chamber of Commerce's petitions between 2004 and 2007 were granted at a rate of 26 percent, according to Scotusblog. And persuading the Supreme Court to hear a case is more than half the battle: Richard Lazarus, a law professor at Georgetown who also represents environmental clients before the court, recently ran the numbers and found that the court reverses the lower court in 65 percent of the cases it agrees to hear; and when the petitioner is represented by the elite Supreme Court advocates routinely hired by the chamber, the success rate rises to 75 percent.

Faced with these daunting numbers, the progressive antagonists of big business are understandably feeling beleaguered and outgunned. "The fight before the court is generally not an even one," said David Vladeck, who once worked for the Public Citizen Litigation Group and now teaches law at Georgetown. "There's us on one side, with a brief or two, and industry on the other side, with a well-coordinated campaign of 10 or 12 briefs, with each one written by a member of the elite Supreme Court bar that address an issue in enormous depth." He added, ruefully, "You admire their handiwork, but it's frustrating as hell to deal with."

To gauge the degree of the frustration, I recently paid a visit to Ralph Nader, a few weeks before he announced his most recent campaign for president of the United States. It was a surprise to find that his office, the Center for Study of Responsive Law, shares an address in a grand building with the Carnegie Institution for Science. But the office itself, reassuringly, is buried on the ground floor, where Nader received me

at a conference table surrounded by file cabinets stuffed with faded back issues of *Mother Jones* and *The Nation.*

Nader was uncontrite about his 2000 run against Al Gore—which is often credited with helping George W. Bush win the presidency—and he insisted that because Clinton appointed justices like Breyer, Gore would have done the same. "Breyer hasn't been worse than I feared, because I had real concern when he was nominated," Nader told me. He conceded that, like Breyer, Democratic justices appointed by President John Kerry would presumably have been better on civil rights and liberties than John Roberts and Samuel Alito. Nevertheless, he disparaged Breyer as a "deregulation quasi-ideologue" who was able to weave a "tapestry of illusion" in his arguments by dealing in abstractions.

The main casualty of the 2000 run, Nader said, is that he is no longer collaborating with America's trial lawyers. They would ordinarily be his natural allies in representing consumer interests, but they donated heavily to Gore's campaign. After 2000, the trial lawyers "have been vitriolic," Nader explained. He blames them for not using their money to help counteract the influence of the Chamber of Commerce and other business groups before the federal courts. In part as a result of their stinginess, he said, his colleagues at Public Citizen are underfinanced and worn down. "There were some lawyers who left Public Citizen because they got tired of losing," he said. "Everyone is desperately trying to hold on to whatever issues are left, and then they become demoralized and discouraged."

Thirty years after the Chamber of Commerce founded its litigation center to counteract his influence, Nader all but conceded defeat in the battle for the Supreme Court. With the decline of economic populism in Congress, the weakening of trade unions and the rise of globalization, the political climate, he lamented, was passing him by. "I recall a comment by Eugene Debs," Nader said, looking at me intensely. "He said: The American people live in a country where they can have almost anything they want. And my regret is that it seems that they don't want much of anything at all."

Nader chuckled quietly and shook his head. "I say ditto."

V.

If there is an anti-Nader—a crusading lawyer passionately devoted to the pro-business cause—it is Theodore Olson. One of the most influential Supreme Court advocates and a former solicitor general under President George W. Bush, Olson is best known for his winning argument before the Supreme Court in *Bush v. Gore* in 2000. But Olson has devoted most of his energies in private practice to changing the legal and political climate for American business. According to his peers in the elite Supreme Court bar, he more than anyone else is responsible for transforming the approach to one of the most important legal concerns of the American business community: punitive damages awarded to the victims of corporate negligence.

Punitive damages—money awarded by civil juries on top of any awarded for actual harm that victims have suffered—are designed to penalize especially egregious acts of corporate misconduct resulting from malice or greed, and to deter similar wrongdoing in the future. In the nineteenth century, courts generally demanded a clear assignment of fault in cases where victims sued for injuries caused by malfunctioning products. It was hard for plaintiffs to recover in personal-injury cases unless the corporation was obviously at fault. But in the twentieth century, in liability cases involving a rapidly expanding class of potentially dangerous products like cars, drugs and medical devices, courts increasingly applied a standard of "strict liability," which held that manufacturers should pay whether or not they were directly at fault.

The animating idea was that manufacturers were in the best position to prevent accidents by improving their products with better design and testing. They and their insurance companies (rather than society as a whole) would shoulder the costs of accidents, thus giving them an incentive to make their products safer. Encouraged by Ralph Nader's book, *Unsafe at Any Speed,* published in 1965, courts began to see car accidents as predictable events that better car design could have prevented. In 1968, for example, a federal court held that car manufacturers could be sued for failing to make cars safe enough for drivers to survive crashes, even if the driver was at fault for the crash.

A series of well-publicized awards in the 1980s and 1990s culminated in the largest punitive damage award in American history—the $5 billion levied against Exxon after the *Exxon Valdez* oil spill in 1989. This was hardly typical: the median punitive award actually fell to $50,000 in 2001 from $63,000 in 1992. Nevertheless, critics like Olson claimed that multimillion-dollar punitive-damage verdicts were threatening the health of the economy. They resolved to fight back on several fronts. In his first Supreme Court argument, in 1986, Olson set out the broad contours of his argument: for most of English and American history, private litigants were entitled to be compensated for whatever damages they suffered, including pain and suffering, but any public wrongs like the failure of American business to make cars safer by adopting air bags should be addressed by legislation or regulation, not by the courts.

Olson decided that his clients deserved not just a lawyer who could argue a case but a lawyer who could change the political culture. "You had to attack it in a broad-scale way in the legislatures, in the arena of public opinion and in the courts," he told me recently. "I felt the business community had to approach this in a holistic way." He set out, in lectures and op-ed pieces, to publicize especially egregious examples. The poster child for punitive-damage abuse, widely derided in TV and radio ads paid for by the business community, was a New Mexico grandmother who, in 1994, was awarded $2.7 million in punitive damages when she scalded herself with hot McDonald's coffee. Consumer advocates countered that she had originally asked for $20,000 for medical expenses, which McDonald's refused to pay, and the award appeared to have the effect of persuading McDonald's to serve its coffee at a safer temperature. Nonetheless, the campaign to vilify plaintiffs' lawyers has been effective enough that the American Association of Trial Lawyers recently changed its name to the fuzzier American Association for Justice.

The business community made other inroads against punitive damages. Corporations financed campaigns against pro-punitive-damage state judges who had been elected with the assistance of large contributions from plaintiffs' lawyers. The business community also helped persuade more than 30 states to either impose caps on punitive-damage awards or direct substantial portions of the awards to be paid into special state funds. In 1996, it helped persuade the Republican Congress, led by Newt Gingrich, to pass legislation that would cap punitive-damage awards in product-liability cases in every state court in the country. But in 1996, President Clinton, with what must have been perverse pleasure, vetoed the bill on the grounds that it violated principles of federalism and states rights to which conservatives claimed to be devoted.

Thwarted by Clinton, and unable to persuade Congress to override the veto, opponents of punitive damages turned their attention back to the Supreme Court, looking for a victory they were unable to win in the political arena. Here, they were remarkably successful. As late as 1991, the court had refused to impose limits on a large punitive-damage award. But in a case in 1996, the court held for the first time that punitive-damage awards had to be proportional to the actual damage incurred by the plaintiff. The case involved a man who said he was deceived by BMW when it sold him a supposedly "new" car that was, in fact, used and had received a $300 touch-up job. The court, in a 5–4 opinion, overturned a $2 million punitive-damage award as "grossly excessive." In 2003, the court clarified what it meant: a single-digit ratio between punitive damages and compensatory damages was likely to be acceptable.

Last year, the business community watched with anticipation as Roberts and Alito revealed their views about punitive damages. The case involved the estate of a heavy smoker who sued Philip Morris for deceitfully distributing a "poisonous and addictive substance." A jury had awarded the estate $821,000 in compensatory damages and $79.5 million in punitive damages—a ratio of about 100 to 1. In a 5–4 opinion written by Breyer, the court held that it was unconstitutional for a jury to use punitive damages to punish a company for its conduct toward similarly affected individuals who are not party to the lawsuit.

This spring, the court will decide the *Exxon Valdez* punitive-damage case, which many consider the culmination of the business community's decades-long campaign against punitive damages. In 1989, the *Exxon Valdez* tanker, whose captain had a history of alcoholism, ran into a reef and punctured the hull; 11 million gallons of oil leaked onto the coastline of Prince William Sound. A jury handed down a $5 billion punitive-damage award.

After the verdict, Exxon began providing money for academic research to support its claim that the award for damages was excessive. It financed some of the country's most prominent scholars on both sides of the political spectrum, including the Nobel laureate Daniel Kahneman and Cass Sunstein, a law professor at the University of Chicago. (Sunstein says he accepted only travel grants, not research support, from Exxon; and Kahneman stresses that the financing had no influence on the substance of his work.) In a 2002 book, *Punitive Damages: How Juries Decide,* Sunstein studied hundreds of mock-jury deliberations and concluded that jurors are unpredictable and often irrational in punitive-damage cases. Jury deliberations, he found, increase the unpredictability, as well as the dollar amount of the final awards. Sunstein concluded that a system of civil fines determined by experts, rather than punitive damages determined by juries, might be more sensible. When Exxon appealed the $5 billion verdict in 2006, it was reduced by an appellate court to $2.5 billion. The reduced verdict is once again being challenged as excessive.

Walter Dellinger, the lawyer now arguing Exxon's case before the Supreme Court, is no Republican activist. Like Sunstein, he is one of the most respected Democratic constitutional scholars, as well as a former acting solicitor general for President Clinton. Last month, in his argument before the court, Dellinger argued that because Exxon has already paid $3.4 billion in fines, cleanup costs and compensation connected with the *Exxon Valdez* spill, and because it didn't act out of malice or greed in failing to monitor the alcoholic captain, additional punitive damages would serve no "public purpose."

During the argument, Breyer noted that the $2.5 billion punitive damage award represents a less than 10-to-1 ratio between punitive damages and compensatory damages, which is in the single-digit range that the Supreme Court has considered acceptable in the past. But Breyer also seemed concerned at other points that punitive-damage awards have not been routine in maritime cases like this one, and that the award might create "a new world for the shipping industry." Alito, who owns Exxon Mobil stock, did not participate, and because a tie would affirm the $2.5 billion punitive-damage award, the plaintiffs who are opposing Exxon need only four votes to prevail. But whether Dellinger gets five votes, a significant triumph is already behind him: he persuaded the court to take the case in the first place.

VI.

Ted Olson and the Chamber of Commerce aren't only trying to persuade the Supreme Court to cut back on large punitive-damage awards; they're also arguing that consumers injured by dangerous or defective medical devices and drugs in some cases shouldn't be able to file product-liability suits at all. Because there is no national product-liability law that allows federal suits for personal injuries, consumers who are injured by, say, defective heart valves or artificial hips have to sue in state courts under state tort law. By asking the Supreme Court to prevent injured consumers from suing in state court, the business community, supported by the Bush administration, is trying to ensure that these consumers often have no legal remedy for their injuries. And the Supreme Court has been increasingly sympathetic to the business community's arguments.

In a Supreme Court case Olson argued in December, he stood before the justices and argued that the manufacturers of defective medical devices—like heart valves, breast implants and defibrillators—should be immune from personal-liability suits because the federal Food and Drug Administration had approved the devices before they were marketed and the manufacturers had complied with all federal requirements. The case involved Charles Riegel, who had an angioplasty in 1996 during which the catheter used to dilate his coronary artery burst. Riegel, who needed advanced life support and emergency bypass surgery, eventually sued the manufacturer of the catheter, Medtronic. The company is colloquially referred to in the business community as "the pre-emption company" because of its practice of arguing that the Food and Drug Administration's "premarket approval" of its products pre-empts product-liability suits in state courts.

The lawyer representing Riegel's estate before the Supreme Court, Allison Zieve of Public Citizen, countered that Congress never intended to ban state product-liability suits when Senator Edward Kennedy sponsored a bill regulating medical devices in 1976. (Kennedy himself filed a brief in the case noting that he indeed intended no such thing.) "Lawyers think this is a close issue, but any time I talk to a nonlawyer about it, they're shocked," Zieve told me after the argument. "People think: of course, if somebody makes a defective product you can sue."

It's one thing to argue that the federal government's "premarket approval" of food, drugs and medical devices should pre-empt clearly inconsistent state laws and regulations. After all, if states imposed safety requirements that conflicted with the federal standard, the resulting regulatory confusion would make a national (and global) market impossible. But Olson's claim that federal regulation of medical devices and drugs should also pre-empt product-liability suits under state tort law is one of the more creative and far-reaching legal arguments of the business groups that litigate before the Supreme Court.

This type of argument arose out of the tobacco litigation of the 1980s and 1990s, which culminated in a $206 billion settlement paid by the top tobacco companies to a consortium of 46 state attorneys general in exchange for dropping tort suits against the companies. The tobacco litigation began modestly: in 1983, Rose Cipollone, a New Jersey woman dying of lung cancer, sued several of the country's largest tobacco companies for their failure to give adequate warnings about the dangers of smoking. After spending tens of millions of dollars fighting the verdict, the companies decided to take their defense to the next level. They argued that because the federal government required cigarette companies to have warning labels, tobacco companies couldn't be subject to tort suits in state courts. Jury verdicts, they argued, are no less a form of regulation than laws explicitly adopted by state legislatures.

In a decision in 1992, the Supreme Court endorsed part of the companies' argument. The decision unleashed a torrent of similar "pre-emption" claims by the manufacturers of dangerous drugs, defective medical devices and cars without air bags. And after the election of President Bush in 2000, the business community's crusade was aggressively supported by the White House. At the same time that the White House was scaling back on federal health-and-safety enforcement, it insisted that consumers should not be able to sue federally regulated industries in state court. Bush appointed as the general counsel of the Food and Drug Administration a former drug- and tobacco-company lawyer named Daniel Troy. With Troy's support, the F.D.A. reversed its position, held for 25 years, and argued for the first time that its premarket approval of medical devices should prevent injured consumers from bringing product-liability suits in state court.

After her Supreme Court argument in the Medtronic case, Zieve told me she wasn't sure

what to expect. Until the arrival of Chief Justice Roberts, groups like Public Citizen had found that they had a better chance of winning pre-emption cases before the Supreme Court than in the lower courts. But during the first two years of the Roberts Court, the justices had decided two pre-emption cases in favor of the corporate defendants.

The trend has continued. On Feb. 21, the Supreme Court handed Zieve a crushing defeat: an 8–1 opinion immunizing the makers of defective medical devices from product-liability suits. The lone dissent was written by Ruth Bader Ginsburg, who objected that Congress could not have intended such a "radical curtailment" of state personal-injury suits when it regulated medical devices in 1976. Ginsburg, who is devoted to liberal judicial restraint, has consistently opposed efforts to second-guess punitive-damage awards or expand federal pre-emption. I called Zieve soon after the Supreme Court issued its opinion, and she sounded shocked. "It's really unfathomable to me," she said. "I wasn't sure that this was a business-friendly court, but now I'm finding it harder not to view it that way." Zieve said that, as a result of the decision, "I think the industry will keep unsafe devices on the market longer and be slower to improve products."

In the eyes of advocates like Zieve and Public Citizen, the public is now caught in a Catch-22: at the very moment that agencies like the F.D.A. are being strongly reproved by critics—including the agency's own internal science board—for being unwilling or unable to protect public health, the court is making it harder for people to receive compensation for the injuries that result. On rare occasions, the Roberts Court has held that the Bush administration's deregulatory efforts circumvent the will of Congress—like the 5–4 decision last year holding that the Environmental Protection Agency acted capriciously when it adopted a rule that said it had no legal authority to regulate greenhouse gases. But by and large, the Supreme Court defers to agencies that refuse to regulate public health and safety. "The industry has a lot of money, and they can routinely hire the biggest names in the biggest firms, while we're doing it on our own," Zieve told me. "We don't charge anything—we're free. It didn't cost $250,000 to get us to write the brief."

VII.

The Supreme Court is unlikely to reconsider its pro-business outlook anytime soon. Nevertheless, there are several currents in American political life that run counter to the court, even if they may not be strong enough, or suitably directed, to reverse it. There are, for example, economic populists in both political parties—John Edwards Democrats and Mike Huckabee Republicans, to cite just two types—who express concern about growing economic inequality and corporate corruption, and blame unchecked corporate power for America's escalating economic problems. These populists tend to be from the working and middle classes rather than the professional classes, and their numbers may be growing. In recent Pew surveys, 65 percent of Americans agreed that corporations make excessive profits—the highest number in 20 years. Moreover, about half the country now asserts that America is divided on economic lines into two groups—the "haves" and "have nots"—up from only 26 percent two decades ago. And the number of Americans who view themselves as "have nots" has doubled to 34 percent today from 17 percent in 1988. Responding to pressures from this demographic, a Democratic Congress—bolstered by states-rights conservatives—might well try to pass legislation to counteract the court's recent decisions barring product-liability suits for defective medical devices.

What about the executive branch? It seems unlikely that John McCain, if he were elected president, would push back against the court: he has already pledged to appoint "judges of the character and quality of Justices Roberts and Alito," rather than justices more devoted to states rights, like Scalia and Thomas. As for Barack Obama and Hillary Clinton, both have sounded increasingly populist notes in an effort to attract union and blue-collar supporters, ratcheting up their attacks on corporate wealth and power, singling out the drug, oil and health-insurance industries and promising to renegotiate the North American Free Trade Agreement. But despite their rhetoric, it is not clear that either candidate would actually appoint justices any more populist than Bill Clinton's nominees. "I would be stunned to find an anti-business appointee from either of them," Cass Sunstein, who is a constitutional adviser to Obama, told me. "There's not a strong interest on the part of Obama or Clinton in demonizing business, and you wouldn't expect to see that in their Supreme Court nominees."

Still, the possibility does exist. If the economy continues to decline and blue-collar voters end up being crucial in the election, a Democratic president might appoint an economic populist to the Supreme Court as a kind of payback. Earlier this month, on the campaign trail in Ohio, Obama mentioned Earl Warren, who served as governor of California before becoming chief justice, as a model of the kind of justice he hoped to appoint. "I want people on the bench who have enough empathy, enough feeling, for what ordinary people are going through," Obama said. He praised Warren for understanding that segregation was wrong because of the stigma it attached to blacks, rather than because of the precise nature of its sociological impact. Appointing a former politician to the court would almost certainly introduce a more populist element: the Supreme Court that in 1954 decided *Brown v. Board of Education* included, in addition to a former governor, three former senators, a former Securities and Exchange Commission member and two former attorneys general. (By contrast, the Roberts court is composed of nine former judges.)

Whatever happens in November, Robin Conrad says the Chamber of Commerce is prepared to lobby as hard as ever for the appointment of pro-business justices. "If we do have a Democrat president, and that president has opportunities to nominate to the court," she said in our meeting as I glanced at her Hillary Clinton action figure, "we want to be able to express ourselves and work with that president." Regardless of how many justices retire in the next presidential term, Conrad is confident that, having helped to transform the Supreme Court in less than 30 years, she and her colleagues can assure American business of a sympathetic hearing for decades to come.

When I told Conrad that Ralph Nader told me that lawyers were leaving Public Citizen because they were tired of losing, she achieved a look of earnest concern. "I hope if they feel they've lost," she said, "they lost for a good reason—not because they've been overpowered or muscled by the big, bad business community, but they've lost because reason won."

Conrad looked at me squarely, and then added, "I guess if Ralph Nader wants to say we did him in"—she paused to weigh her words—"so be it."

DISCUSSION QUESTIONS

1. What steps have the Chamber of Commerce and other business groups taken to build a stronger pro-business presence in the American legal system?
2. Rosen calls Theodore Olson an "anti-Nader." Who is Theodore Olson and what is the significance of the term "anti-Nader" in terms of Rosen's overall argument?
3. Who are the winners and losers in the Supreme Court's business decisions? Is the Court saying that what is good for business is good for America?

30 *Saul Cornell*

NEW ORIGINALISM
A Constitutional Scam

As noted in Chapter 2, the U.S. Constitution holds an iconic place in American political culture, even though many citizens disagree about its meaning or display little knowledge of its content. While Americans across the political spectrum seek to anchor their politics in the Constitution, conservatives have been especially vociferous in recent years in claiming that the 1787 document is foundational for their limited government and protection of private property views. In this selection, legal historian Saul Cornell sharply criticizes an interpretation of the Constitution that is increasingly influential in conservative legal circles—"originalism." Originalists claim that the Constitution should be interpreted from the standpoint of the "original intent" of the Founders or, with the "new originalists," of the original "public meaning" of the Constitution as understood by a hypothetical "rational man on the street." Cornell maintains that actual historical inquiry reveals widespread disagreement about the meaning of the Constitution among both political elites and ordinary citizens in 1787–1788, with strong support for future generations employing the Constitution as a "living document." He finds it ironic that originalist constitutional arguments often dovetail with the views of the Anti-Federalist opponents of the Constitution in the 1780s. Cornell does not mince words as he accuses new originalists of engaging in an "intellectual shell game in which contemporary political preferences are shuffled around and made to appear part of the Constitution's original meaning."

Americans are deeply divided over how to interpret the Constitution. Originalism, the view that judges should interpret the Constitution by discovering the original intent or the original meaning of the text, has a strong hold on the public. Yet the opposing view, that judges ought to interpret the Constitution as a living document and read it in light of contemporary values or an evolving tradition, is also well entrenched in American culture. Not surprisingly, support for originalism is strongest among Tea Party activists, conservatives, and Republicans. Although

Source: From *Dissent Magazine,* May 3, 2011, online www.dissentmagazine.org. Used by permission.

the vast majority of legal academics are not originalists, the theory of originalism has never been stronger among law professors. Indeed, originalism now has adherents not only among conservative but also liberal legal scholars. There is really only one group in American society that remains largely immune to the lure of originalism: historians.

At first glance, this fact might seem strange. Historians devote their lives to understanding the past, so one would surmise that they, above all others, would be drawn to the theory of originalism. One might attribute the resolute anti-originalism of most historians to the fact that they are generally more liberal than the population at large and thus oppose originalism for political reasons. Although political orientation may account for some of this animus, their hostility to originalism has less to do with politics and more to do with questions of historical interpretation and method. When most historians look closely at originalist arguments, what they usually find is bad history shaped to fit an ideological agenda—what historians derisively call "law office history."

Originalist constitutional theory developed during the Reagan years as a critique of activist judges. Its theorists argued that a jurisprudence focused on the original intent of the Founders would serve as a means of limiting the discretion of judges. This theory proved controversial from the start and was subjected to a number of withering criticisms. One of the many problems with the theory stemmed from its shaky historical foundations. Simply put, the Founders did not speak with a single voice on most constitutional questions. Thus, traditional originalism collapsed as evidence accumulated that the Founding generation disagreed on most of the major constitutional issues they confronted. If Madison and Hamilton could not agree on how to interpret the Constitution, how could modern judges claim to have found an objective means to discern the true meaning of its text?

"New Originalism" has grown over the last decade, largely spurred by right-wing scholars, judges, and generous support from the Federalist Society, the wealthy conservative legal group that has become a farm team for conservative judges and academics. In contrast to traditional originalism, new originalism emerged at a time when the Supreme Court was dominated by a conservative majority, as it is today. The goal of new originalism is not to constrain judges, but to empower them to further the agenda of conservatives. (A few liberals have embraced a version of this theory, hoping to use it to revive and expand aspects of the Fourteenth Amendment, but this is a small minority within the originalist movement.) For right-wing scholars and judges, new originalism serves as a type of constitutional camouflage. It allows "conservatives" to create their own living constitution and advance a form of judicial activism, while claiming to be simply engaged in an act of constitutional redemption.

New originalism eschews a focus on original intent and instead concentrates on the public meaning of the Constitution. Yet, if one looks carefully at the murky methodology and dubious practices of new originalism, it is clear that its historical foundations are even shakier than that of old originalism. The new theory is little more than an intellectual shell game in which contemporary political preferences are shuffled around and made to appear part of the Constitution's original meaning.

New originalists are dismissive of history. They argue that original meaning, as they construe it, is simply different from historical meaning. If this claim were true, then historians would have no special expertise when it comes to understanding the original meaning of the Constitution. This view is utter nonsense. Different historical methods can certainly yield different answers to the question of what the Constitution meant. Social historians might give preference to what ordinary Americans thought the Constitution meant, while legal or constitutional historians might lay greater stress on the opinions of legal and judicial elites. It might well be the case that there was no consensus in the Founding era on what a specific provision of the Constitution meant. What is clearly false is the new originalist claim that original meaning is not subject to the rules of verification that apply to all historical works.

New originalists are especially fond of Justice Scalia's majority opinion in *District of Columbia v. Heller*, the controversial case that stuck down Washington's handgun ban. John McGinnis and Michael Rappaport, law professors who are proponents of new originalism, applaud Scalia for applying the Founding era's original methods to the problem of the Second Amendment. In *Heller*, Scalia cast aside the preamble of the Second Amendment, which declares that the purpose of the amendment is to protect a well-regulated militia. According to Scalia, the Founders believed that preambles should only be used to clarify an ambiguity in the text. This approach was so odd that Justice Stevens' dissent chided Scalia for interpreting the latter part of the Second Amendment first, and considering the preamble second—in essence reading the text backward. The sources Scalia cites for this bizarre approach turn out to have no connection to the Founding era at all. Scalia cited two legal treatises written in the nineteenth century and a single early-eighteenth-century English case that had come into disrepute by the time the Second Amendment was written.

The reason for Scalia's neglect of Founding-era sources is obvious if one actually reads sources from the period, which support Stevens', not Scalia's, reading. Take, for example, the views of then–Chief Justice John Jay, one of the coauthors of the *Federalist*, who opined in a 1790s decision that "a preamble cannot annul enacting clauses; but when it evinces the intention of the legislature and the design of the act, it enables us, in cases of two constructions, to adopt the one most consonant to their intention and design." Jay's method, the orthodox approach favored by judges and lawyers in the Founding era, flatly contradicts Scalia's view of preambles. (It also contradicts the new originalist claims about intent.)

John Yoo, a prominent new originalist legal scholar who helped to frame the Bush administration's novel views on torture, goes even further in circumventing historical understandings of the Constitution. (The Founders, it is worth recalling, were strong supporters of the principle of international law and took a dim view of torture.) For Yoo, the actual history of the Founding era poses few constraints on the modern lawyer or judge. Yoo accomplishes this sleight of hand by ignoring the conflicts and disagreements among the Founders. If one ignores those conflicts, one can cherry-pick evidence to construct whatever theory one likes. Most historians would point out that the Founding era was not only characterized by conflicts within the elite, such as the argument between Jefferson and Hamilton, but also an even more basic conflict between elites and ordinary Americans. Yoo and other new originalists not only ignore the tensions within the elite, they assume that common people in the Founding era lacked the knowledge necessary to understand the Constitution and played no role in the constitutional history of the period. (Yoo clearly did not bother to look at the Pennsylvania Constitution, newspapers from the period, or any text written by ordinary Americans.)

Yoo's theory is idiotic in the eighteenth-century sense of the word: it treats ordinary Americans as if they had no public voice—in other words, as idiots. Ignoring the real voices of eighteenth-century Americans is an important part of new originalism's methodological obfuscation. Yoo and other new originalists suggest instead that we interpret the Constitution from the point of view of an "informed, objective reader in 1787–1788." Gary Lawson, another prominent conservative new originalist, calls this fictive reader "a fully informed reader," while Georgetown's Randy Barnett, one of the most vocal public intellectuals in the new originalist movement, dubs his fictive reader "a typical rational man on the street."

Using fictive readers in place of actual historical ones effectively turns constitutional interpretation into an act of historical ventriloquism. The fictive readers imagined by new originalists somehow always seem to read the Constitution in exactly the same way that a modern right-wing law professor would read the document—a strange coincidence indeed! Even more remarkable is the claim made by some new originalists that we should not give any special weight to what people at the time actually said because, unlike new originalists, Madison, Jay, Hamilton, or any other actual person from that period would have had political motives. In their constitutional fantasy world, historical evidence cannot be used to impeach originalist claims because it would involve claims about actual practices by historical actors who were often blinded by their biases. By contrast, new originalists believe they have transcended their own political interests and created a methodology that reveals the objective meaning of the Constitution. Having cast the vast majority of Americans as idiots, and discounted the views of elites for their political biases, one might wonder what is left to the concept of original meaning. The answer is new originalist meaning ultimately has nothing to do with history: it is a modern ideology dressed up in historical clothing.

In order to determine original constitutional meaning, some new originalists have turned to philosophy. Lawrence Solum, a law professor and popular law blogger, argues that modern ordinary language philosophy provides a means of discerning the objective meaning of the Constitution's text. Reading Solum's originalist theory, one might be tempted to conclude that philosophers of language had reached a clear consensus on issues of meaning, but the reality is that philosophers remain deeply divided over these questions. Even if philosophical consensus existed, one would still need to develop some type of historical methodology to apply one's philosophical theory to the past. Rather than take the time to do the history right, Solum and other new originalists prefer history-lite, endorsing a method favored by Justice Scalia, who advises that we consult old dictionaries to ascertain the original meaning of the Constitution.

One problem with this approach is that the earliest American dictionaries were written after the Constitution and were not produced according to the rules of modern lexicography. More often than

not these texts were prescriptive, not descriptive. They were idiosyncratic products of their authors, who often had ideological, political, and linguistic agendas. Thus it is simply anachronistic to argue that one ought to consult historical dictionaries from the Founding era to elucidate a set of fixed linguistic facts that can be used to unravel the meaning of the text of the Constitution.

One wonders if any theory drawn from modern ordinary language philosophy could yield an objective theory of constitutional interpretation given that the Founders were themselves deeply divided over the nature of constitutional interpretation. Indeed, one of the most basic divisions within the Founding generation was between those who believed that the Constitution had to be interpreted according to the rules of ordinary language and those who believed that the Constitution ought to be interpreted according to a formal set of rules gleaned from Anglo-American jurists such as Sir William Blackstone. Even if one decided which version of ordinary language philosophy to use, and one perfected a historical method to implement this approach, the result would not be objectivity; what one would have done is simply taken sides in one of the Founding era's most basic disputes. Philosophy cannot replace history and cannot erase the fact that any theory of constitutional interpretation begins with a political choice about interpretive method.

There is something deeply ironic about new originalism that its advocates have missed because they lack an understanding of Founding-era history. Focusing on the public meaning of the Constitution, the chief insight of new originalism, is really not new at all. Such an approach was championed by the Anti-Federalist opponents of the Constitution more than two hundred years ago. Following new originalist methodology would not lead to a restoration of the original meaning of the Constitution, but it would give us an Anti-Federalist Constitution that never existed. This is an odd result, given that the Constitution was largely written by Federalists and ratified by state conventions dominated by Federalist majorities, not Anti-Federalist minorities.

Indeed, in *Heller*, Justice Scalia used an Anti-Federalist text written by the "Dissent of the Pennsylvania Minority" as one of the keys to unlocking the meaning of the Second Amendment. His methodology makes it easy for him to take a text articulating the beliefs of the dissent of the minority of a single state ratification convention and transform it into a proxy for public meaning. In the wacky world of new originalism, dissent becomes assent, minorities become majorities, and the interpretive method of the Anti-Federalist losers supplants the methods of the Federalist winners. Such creative rewriting of the past makes for interesting alternate histories, but it is not a serious scholarly methodology for understanding the historical meaning of the Constitution. It is a legal scam.

The periodic revival of Anti-Federalist constitutional ideas is in some sense hardwired into the structure of American constitutionalism. While such a process has often been self-conscious, at other times Americans have unknowingly reinvented an essentially Anti-Federalist critique of the Constitution. Given the expansion of federal power in modern America, particularly of executive and judicial authority, a revival of Anti-Federalist criticism seems inevitable. In this sense, new originalism is unremarkable; it is simply the latest in a long line of dissenting movements to revive an Anti-Federalist critique of the Constitution. What is a bit embarrassing is that its authors do not seem to be aware of the Anti-Federalist origins of their theory.

There is one significant difference between new originalism and the original Anti-Federalist focus on public meaning. The Anti-Federalists were motivated by a desire to reduce the power of lawyers and judges. Ultimately their goal was to allow the people to have a larger say in interpreting the Constitution. Public meaning was a form of popular constitutionalism designed to limit federal judicial review, not empower it. As originally understood, this theory was not designed to freeze the meaning of the Constitution at the Founding moment, but actually was closer in spirit to modern theories of a living constitution. The supreme irony of new originalism is that, if one follows the original version of this theory, it leads to something like the modern theory of the living constitution—the antithesis of new originalism.

Justice Scalia may believe we have a dead Constitution, the legal equivalent of a fly in amber. This was not how most Americans in the Founding era would have viewed the matter. Originalists, both old and new, argue that the theory of the living constitution lacks the legitimacy of their own theory. In fact, the historical pedigree of the theory of the living constitution is at least as good as traditional originalism, and far better than that of new originalism. The fact that Americans are deeply divided today over the relative merits of originalism and the rival theory of the living constitution ought to come as no surprise—Americans were divided over the very same issue when the Constitution was first proposed more than two hundred years ago.

DISCUSSION QUESTIONS

1. According to Cornell, what is the difference between "originalism" and "new originalism"? What does he see as the main weaknesses of both schools of constitutional interpretation?
2. Cornell notes that many Americans think that "judges ought to interpret the Constitution as a living document and read it in light of contemporary values or an evolving tradition." What are the strengths and weaknesses of the "living Constitution" view?

31 *Patricia J. Williams*

THIS DANGEROUS PATRIOT'S GAME

In the aftermath of the September 11 bombings of the World Trade Center and the Pentagon, political leaders enacted a series of sweeping laws, which restricted traditional constitutional liberties in the name of enhanced security. Columnist and Columbia University law professor Patricia Williams offers her assessment of the cost and benefits of this darkened legal landscape in this probing selection. For Williams, the devastation of September 11 left in its wake many profound, long-term tests for America. These challenges stem from the need to balance our response to the threat of terrorism with the need to preserve the rights of citizens. From her perspective, the balance has tipped dramatically away from civil rights and freedoms, toward "the 'comfort' and convenience of high-tech totalitarianism." As a result, today we face "one of the more dramatic Constitutional crises in United States history." She explores this crisis as it impinges on three areas of constitutional protection: freedom of the press, freedom from unreasonable searches and seizures, and the right to due process of law (including the right to adequate counsel, the right to a speedy public and impartial trial, and the right against self-incrimination). In each area, of course, defenders of the shrinkage of civil liberties justify it in the name of fighting "terrorism," assuring us that only those justly suspected of being a terrorist, or aiding terrorists, need have any fear. But given the elastic nature of the term "terrorist" and the nation's history of abusing rights during the panic of wartime, Williams fears that expansive use of executive and judicial power may go largely unchecked.

Things fall apart, as Chinua Achebe put it, in times of great despair. The American nightmare that began with the bombing of the World Trade Center and the Pentagon, has, like an earthquake, been followed by jolt after jolt of disruption and fear. In the intervening three months, yet another airplane crashed, this time into a residential section of New York City. Anthrax contamination succeeded in closing, for varying lengths of time, all three branches of government. From the tabloids to *The New York Times,* major media outlets have had their centers of operation evacuated repeatedly. The United States Postal Service is tied in knots. Hundreds of anthrax hoaxes have

Source: Patricia J. Williams, "This Dangerous Patriot's Game." *The Observer* (U.K.), 2 December 2001.

stretched law enforcement beyond all capacity. Soldiers guard all our public buildings.

Around four thousand Americans have died in planes, collapsing buildings or of anthrax toxin since that morning in September; tens of thousands more have lost their jobs. Some 5000 Arab residents between the ages of 18 and 33 have been summoned for interrogation by the FBI. And twenty million resident aliens live suddenly subject to the exceedingly broad terms of a new martial law. Even while we try to follow the president's advice to pick ourselves up in time for the Christmas shopping season, punch-drunk and giddily committed to soldiering on as before, we know that the economic and emotional devastation of these events has only begun to register.

As the enormity of the destruction settles in and becomes less dreamlike, more waking catastrophe, American society begins to face those long-term tests that inevitably come after the shock and horror of so much loss. We face the test of keeping the unity that visited us in that first moment of sheer chaos. We face the test of maintaining our dignity and civility in a time of fear and disorder. Above all, we face the test of preserving the rights and freedoms in our Constitution and its Bill of Rights.

Few in the United States question the necessity for unusual civil measures in keeping with the current state of emergency. But a number of the Bush administration's new laws, orders and policies are deservedly controversial: the disregard for international treaties and conventions; strict controls on media reports about the war; secret surveillance and searches of citizens' computers; widespread ethnic profiling; indefinite detention of non-citizens; offers of expedited American citizenship to those who provide evidence about terrorists; and military tribunals with the power to try enemies in secret, without application of the usual laws of evidence, without right of appeal, yet with the ability to impose the death penalty. Opportunity for legislative or other public discussion of these measures has been largely eclipsed by the rapidity with which most of them have been pushed into effect. This speed, one must accede, is

in large part an exigency of war. It is perhaps also because Mr. Bush has always preferred operating in a rather starkly corporate style. In any event, the President has attempted to enlarge the power of the executive to an unprecedented extent, while limiting both Congressional input as well as the check of the judiciary.

Overall, we face one of the more dramatic constitutional crises in United States history. First, while national security mandates some fair degree of restraint, blanket control of information is in tension with the Constitution's expectation that freedom of a diverse and opinionated press will moderate the tyrannical tendencies of power. We need to have some inkling of what is happening on the battlefield in our name. On the domestic front, moreover, the First Amendment's protection of free speech is eroded if even peaceful dissent becomes casually categorized as dangerous or unpatriotic, as it has sometimes been in recent weeks. This concern is heightened by the fact that the war has been framed as one against "terror"—against unruly if deadly emotionalism—rather than as a war against specific bodies, specific land, specific resources.

A war against terrorism is a war of the mind, so broadly defined that the enemy becomes anybody who makes us afraid. Indeed what is conspicuous about American public discourse right now is how hard it is to talk about facts rather than fear.

In a struggle that is coloured by a degree of social panic, we must be very careful not to allow human rights to be cast as an indulgence. There is always a certain hypnosis to the language of war—the poetry of the Pentagon a friend calls it—in which war means peace, and peace-mongering invites war. In this somewhat inverted system of reference, the bleeding heart does not beat within the corpus of law but rather in the bosom of those whose craven sympathies amount to naive and treacherous self-delusion. Everywhere one hears what, if taken literally, amounts to a death knell for the American dream: rights must be tossed out the window because "the constitution is not a suicide pact."

By accepting rational reasons to be afraid, the unalloyed ideology of efficiency has not only chilled free expression, but left us poised at the gateway of an even more fearsome world in which the "comfort" and convenience of high-tech totalitarianism gleam temptingly; a world in which our Americanness endures only with hands up so that our fingerprints can be scanned, and our nationalized-identity scrutinised for signs of suspicious behaviour.

This brings me to the second aspect of our Constitutional crisis—that is, the encroachment of our historical freedom from unreasonable searches and seizures. The establishment of the new Office of Homeland Security and the passage of the so-called USA Patriot Act have brought into being an unprecedented merger between the functions of intelligence agencies and law enforcement. What this means might be clearer if we used the more straightforward term for intelligence—that is, spying. Law enforcement agents can now spy on us, "destabilizing" citizens not just non-citizens.

They can gather information with few checks or balances from the judiciary. Morton Halperin, a defense expert who worked with the National Security Council under Henry Kissinger, was quoted, in *The New Yorker* magazine, worrying that if a government intelligence agency thinks you're under the control of a foreign government, "they can wiretap you and never tell you, search your house and never tell you, break into your home, copy your hard drive, and never tell you that they've done it." Moreover, says Halperin, upon whose own phone Kissinger placed a tap, "Historically, the government has often believed that anyone who is protesting government policy is doing it at the behest of a foreign government and opened counterintelligence investigations of them."

This expansion of domestic spying highlights the distinction between punishing what has already occurred and preventing what might happen in the future. In a very rough sense, agencies like the FBI have been concerned with catching criminals who have already done their dirty work, while agencies like the CIA have been involved in predicting or manipulating future outcomes—activities of prior restraint, in other words, from which the Constitution generally protects citizens.

The third and most distressing area of Constitutional concern has been Mr. Bush's issuance of an executive order setting up military tribunals that would deprive even long-time resident aliens of the right to due process of law. The elements of the new order are as straightforward as trains running on time. The President would have the military try non-citizens suspected of terrorism in closed tribunals rather than courts. No requirement of public charges, adequacy of counsel, usual rules of evidence, nor proof beyond a reasonable doubt. The cases would be presented before unspecified judges, with rulings based on the accusations of unidentified witnesses. The tribunals would have the power to execute anyone so convicted, with no right of appeal. According to polls conducted by National Public Radio, *The Washington Post,* and ABC News, approximately 65 percent of Americans wholeheartedly endorse such measures.

"Foreign terrorists who commit war crimes against the United States, in my judgment, are not entitled to and do not deserve the protections of the American Constitution," says Attorney General John Ashcroft in defense of tribunals. There are a number of aspects of that statement that ought to worry us. The reasoning is alarmingly circular in Ashcroft's characterization of suspects who have not yet been convicted as "terrorists." It presumes guilt before adjudication. Our system of innocent-until-proven-guilty is hardly foolproof, but does provide an essential, base-line bulwark against the furious thirst for quick vengeance, the carelessly deadly mistake—albeit in the name of self-protection.

It is worrisome, too, when the highest prosecutor in the land declares that war criminals do not "deserve" basic constitutional protections. We confer due process not because putative criminals are "deserving" recipients of rights-as-reward. Rights are not "earned" in this way. What makes rights rights is that they ritualize the importance of solid, impartial and public consensus before we take life or liberty from anyone, particularly those whom we fear. We ritualize this process to make sure we don't allow the grief of great tragedies to blind us with mob fury, inflamed judgments and uninformed reasoning. In any event, Bush's new order bypasses not only the American Constitution but the laws of most other democratic nations. It exceeds the accepted conventions of most military courts. (I say all this provisionally, given that the Bush administration is urging the enactment of similar anti-terrorism measures in Britain, Russia, and that troublesome holdout, the European Union.)

As time has passed since the order was published, a number of popular defenses of tribunals have emerged: we should trust our president, we should have faith in our government, we are in a new world facing new kinds of enemies who have access to new weapons of mass destruction. Assuming all this, we must wonder if this administration also questions whether citizens who are thought to have committed heinous crimes "deserve" the protections of American citizenship. The terrorist who mailed "aerosolised" anthrax spores to various Senate offices is, according to the FBI, probably a lone American microbiologist. Although we have not yet rounded up thousands of microbiologists for questioning by the FBI, I wonder if the government will be hauling them before tribunals—for if this is a war without national borders, the panicked logic of secret trials will surely expand domestically rather than contract. A friend observes wryly that if reasoning behind the order is that the perpetrators of mass death must be summarily executed, then there are some CEOs in the tobacco industry who ought to be trembling in their boots. Another friend who works with questions of reproductive choice notes more grimly that that is exactly the reasoning used by those who assault and murder abortion doctors.

"There are situations when you do need to presume guilt over innocence," one citizen from Chattanooga told *The New York Times*. The conservative talk show host Mike Reagan leads

the pack in such boundlessly-presumed guilt by warning that you might think the guy living next door is the most wonderful person in the world, you see him playing with his children, but in fact "he might be part of a sleeper cell that wants to blow you away." We forget, perhaps, that J. Edgar Hoover justified sabotaging Martin Luther King and the "dangerous suspects" of that era with similar sentiment.

In addition to the paranoia generated, the importance of the right to adequate counsel has been degraded. Attorney General Ashcroft's stated policies include allowing federal officials to listen in on conversations between suspected terrorists and their lawyers. And President Bush's military tribunals would not recognize the right of defendants to choose their own lawyers. Again, there has been very little public opposition to such measures. Rather, one hears many glib, racialized references to O.J. Simpson—who, last anyone heard, was still a citizen: "You wouldn't want Osama Bin Laden to have O.J.'s lawyer, or they'd end up playing golf together in Florida."

The tribunals also challenge the right to a speedy, public and impartial trial. More than 1000 immigrants have been arrested and held, approximately 800 with no disclosure of identities or location or charges against them. This is "frighteningly close to the practice of disappearing people in Latin America," according to Kate Martin, the director of the Center for National Security Studies.

Finally, there has been an ominous amount of public vilification of the constitutional right against self-incrimination. Such a right is, in essence, a proscription against the literal arm-twisting and leg pulling that might otherwise be necessary to physically compel someone to testify when they do not want to. It is perhaps a rather too-subtly-worded limitation of the use of torture.

While not yet the direct subject of official sanction, torture has suddenly gained remarkable legitimacy. Callers to radio programs say that we don't always have the "luxury of following all the rules"; that given recent events, people are "more understanding" of the necessity for a little behind-the-scenes roughing up. The unanimity of international conventions against torture notwithstanding, one hears authoritative voices—for example, Robert Litt, a former Justice Department official—arguing that while torture is not "authorized," perhaps it could be used in "emergencies," as long as the person who tortures then presents himself to "take the consequences."

Harvard Law School Professor Alan Dershowitz has suggested the use of "torture warrants" limited, he insists, to cases where time is of the essence. Most alarming of all, a recent CNN poll revealed that 45 percent of Americans would not object to torturing someone if it would provide information about terrorism. While fully acknowledging the stakes of this new war, I worry that this attitude of lawless righteousness is one that has been practiced in oppressed communities for years. It is a habit that has produced cynicism, riots and bloodshed. The always-urgently-felt convenience of torture has left us with civic calamities ranging from Abner Louima—a Haitian immigrant whom two New York City police officers beat and sodomized with a broom handle because they mistook him for someone involved in a barroom brawl—to Jacobo Timerman in Argentina to Alexander Solzhenitsyn in the Soviet Union—all victims of physical force and mental manipulation, all people who refused to speak or didn't speak the words their inquisitors wanted to hear, but who were "known" to know something. In such times and places, the devastation has been profound. People know nothing so they suspect everything. Deaths are never just accidental. Every human catastrophe is also a mystery and mysteries create ghosts, hauntings, "blowback," and ultimately new forms of terror. The problem with this kind of "preventive" measure is that we are not mindreaders. Even with sodium pentathol, whose use some have suggested recently, we don't and we can't know every last thought of those who refuse to speak.

Torture is an investment in the right to be all-knowing, in the certitude of what appears "obvious." It is the essence of totalitarianism. Those who justify it with confident proclamations of "I have nothing to hide, why should they," overlap substantially with the class of those who have never been the persistent object of suspect profiling, never been harassed, never been stigmatized or generalized or feared just for the way they look.

The human mind is endlessly inventive. People create enemies as much as fear real ones. We are familiar with stories of the intimate and wrong-headed projections heaped upon the maid who is accused of taking something that the lady of the house simply misplaced. Stoked by trauma, tragedy and dread, the creativity of our paranoia is in overdrive right now. We must take a deep collective breath and be wary of persecuting those who conform to our fears instead of prosecuting enemies who were and will be smart enough to play against such prejudices.

In grief, sometimes we merge with the world, all boundary erased in deference to the commonality of the human condition. But traumatic loss can also mean—sometimes—that you want to hurt anyone in your path. Anyone who is lighthearted, you want to crush. Anyone who laughs is discordant. Anyone who has a healthy spouse or child is your enemy, is undeserving, is frivolous and in need of muting.

When I served as a prosecutor years ago, I was very aware of this propensity among victims, the absolute need to rage at God or whoever is near—for that is what great sorrow feels like when the senses are overwhelmed. You lose words and thus want to reinscribe the hell of which you cannot speak. It is unfair that the rest of the world should not suffer as you have.

This is precisely why we have always had rules in trials about burdens of proof, standards of evidence, the ability to confront and cross-examine witnesses. The fiercely evocative howls of the widow, the orphan, the innocently wronged—these are the forces by which many a lynch mob has been rallied, how many a posse has been motivated to bypass due process, how many a holy crusade has been launched. It is easy to suspend the hard work of moral thought in the name of Ultimate Justice, or even Enduring Freedom, when one is blindly grief-stricken. "If you didn't do it then your brother did," is the underlying force of blood feuds since time began. "If you're not with us, you're against us," is the dangerous modern corollary to this rage.

I have many friends for whom the dominant emotion is anger. Mine is fear, and not only of the conflagration smouldering throughout the Middle East. I fear no less the risks closer to home: this is how urban riots occur, this is how the Japanese were interned during World War II, this is why hundreds of "Arab-looking" Americans have been attacked and harassed in the last weeks alone.

I hear much about how my sort of gabbling amounts to nothing but blaming the victim. But it is hardly a matter of condoning to point out that we cannot afford to substitute some statistical probability or hunch for actual evidence. We face a wrenching global crisis now, of almost unimaginable proportion, but we should take the risks of precipitous action no less seriously than when the grief with which we were stricken drove us to see evil embodied in witches, in Jews, in blacks or heathens or hippies.

Perhaps our leaders have, as they assure us, more intelligence about these matters than we the people can know at this time. I spend a lot of time praying that they are imbued with greater wisdom. But the stakes are very, very high. We cannot take an evil act and use it to justify making an entire people, an entire nation or an entire culture the corpus of "evil."

Give the government the power to assassinate terrorists, comes the call on chat shows. Spare us the circus of long public trials, say the letters to the editor.

I used to think that the most important human rights work facing Americans would be a national reconsideration of the death penalty. I could not have imagined that we would so willingly discard even the right of *habeus corpus*. I desperately hope we are a wiser people than to unloose the power to kill based on undisclosed "information" with no accountability.

We have faced horrendous war crimes in the world before. World War II presented lessons we should not forget, and Nuremberg should be our model. The United States and its allies must seriously consider the option of a world court. Our greatest work is always keeping our heads when our hearts are broken. Our best resistance to terror is the summoning of those principles so suited to keep us from descending into infinite bouts of vengeance and revenge with those who wonder, like Milton's Stygian Counsel.

Will he, so wise, let loose at once his ire,
Belike through impotence, or unaware,
To give his Enemies their wish, and end
Them in his anger, whom his anger saves
To punish endless . . . .

DISCUSSION QUESTIONS

1. Williams writes, "A war against terrorism is a war of the mind . . . " Explain. In what way(s) might the constitutional crises engendered by the Patriot Act affect the minds of Americans?
2. The essay poses a distinction between a criminal justice system based on reason, as represented in rules of procedure, and a system rooted in collective fear, prejudice, and hatred. What are the differences? Is collective fear a threat to individual rights? To democracy?
3. Williams warns us against the temptations of "the 'comfort' and convenience of high-tech totalitarianism." What are some contemporary examples of the technology of surveillance and control? How might these technologies collide with the basic values embodied in the First Amendment to the U.S. Constitution? The Fourth Amendment? The Fifth and Sixth Amendments?

32 R. Claire Snyder-Hall

NEO-PATRIARCHY AND THE ANTI-HOMOSEXUAL AGENDA

In the past decade, same-sex marriage had perhaps equaled abortion as a contentious and divisive social issue in American politics. Even as lesbians and gay men wed legally in Massachusetts, the first state to legalize gay marriage, a constitutional amendment to ban homosexual marriage was becoming a kind of political litmus test among conservatives. In this article, political scientist R. Claire Snyder-Hall explores and criticizes opposition to same-sex marriage. In many ways, the liberal principle of legal equality would seem to support the case for gay marriage. However, an overlapping coalition of religious and political conservatives, "pro-family" activists, and political theorists has developed an antigay agenda powered by a rhetoric that "resonates with many of our most cherished cultural narratives and personal fantasies." Snyder-Hall, author of Gay Marriage and Democracy: Equality for All, *finds that these arguments are "based on an idealized, inegalitarian heterosexual family with rigid gender roles." She argues that the antihomosexual agenda threatens valuable aspects of the liberal democratic tradition, including the separation of church and state, legal equality, and personal freedom. In this way Snyder-Hall demonstrates that the stakes in the battle debate over sexual orientation and marriage involve the core values of democracy itself.*

Starting in the late 1990s a series of court cases began raising the possibility that the civil right to marriage might soon be accorded to all citizens, not just to heterosexuals. The first important decision came in November 2003, when Massachusetts became the first state in the union to legalize same-sex marriage. It began issuing marriage licenses to same-sex couples on May 17, 2004, but not before then-Governor Mitt Romney revived a 1913 anti-miscegenation law to prevent non-residents from marrying in Massachusetts. This law was repealed by the state legislature four years later. The second landmark case came in 2008, when the California Supreme Court ruled that as a fundamental right, marriage could not be restricted to opposite-sex couples only. Since

Source: Revised and updated by the author from R. Claire Snyder-Hall "Neo-Patriarchy and the Anti-Homosexual Agenda." *Fundamental Differences: Feminists Talk Back to Social Conservatives,* Cynthia Burack and Jyl J. Josephson, eds., Lanham, MD: Rowman & Littlefield, 2003, pp. 157–171.

California, like most states, has no residence requirement for marriage, the California decision essentially extended the right to marry to all American citizens for the first time. The decision, however, was rescinded when voters passed Proposition 8, which was subsequently ruled unconstitutional by the California Supreme Court. The case is currently being litigated at the federal level, and same-sex marriage is on hold. Subsequently, however, the states of Connecticut (2008), Iowa (2009), Vermont (2009), and New Hampshire (2010) also legalized gay marriage because of court rulings. Then, in a third key turning point, same-sex marriage was legalized through the legislative process for the first time in the District of Columbia in 2009, followed by New York in 2011.

In direct opposition to legal equality for lesbian and gay couples, conservative forces have mobilized across the country in "defense" of heterosexual-only marriage. The Massachusetts decision fuelled calls for the passage of the Federal Marriage Amendment, originally introduced in 2001 yet still not passed as of 2008, which states "Marriage in the United States shall consist only of the union of a man and a woman. Neither this Constitution, nor the constitution of any State, shall be construed to require that marriage or the legal incidents thereof be conferred upon any union other than the union of a man and a woman." The Amendment would make permanent the 1996 Defense of Marriage Act (DOMA)—"no State shall be required to give effect to a law of any other State with respect to a same-sex 'marriage'"—which might be found to violate the Constitution's "full faith and credit clause." Even without the Amendment, however, DOMA prohibits the extension of federal benefits to legally married same-sex couples, thus denying them full equality before the law. While conservative forces have not been able to amend the U.S. Constitution, they have been able to pass anti-gay marriage amendments in 29 states, including California, as mentioned above.

In their attempt to prevent the logical extension of liberal principles to lesbian and gay citizens, anti-homosexual activists have made common cause with a number of other reactionary movements that want to undo the progress of feminism and reestablish the patriarchal nuclear family as the dominant family form. This essay examines the interconnected arguments advanced by a number of conservative constituencies committed to the politics of neo-patriarchy, including the religious particularism of the Christian Right, the homophobic anti-feminism of Concerned Women for America, the "family values" of James Dobson, the Fatherhood movement spearheaded by David Blankenhorn, and the conservative democratic theory of William Galston. While the details of these arguments differ, all have a similar form and use the same authorities, and all are both homophobic and anti-feminist. Thus, all undermine the principles of liberal democracy, despite rhetorical assertions to the contrary.

Lesbian/Gay Civil Rights and the Logic of Liberalism

Legal equality constitutes one of the most important founding principles of liberal democracy in the United States. While the equal rights of the Declaration of Independence were largely aspirational at the time they were written, over the course of the twentieth century, American society has become increasingly imbued with a liberal public philosophy that values individual choice, civil rights, legal equality, and a "neutral state" that leaves individuals free to pursue their own vision of the good life in civil society and the private sphere without interference from the government.

The revolutionary principle of legal equality has been successfully used to justify progressive change. African-Americans utilized this principle during the Civil Rights Movement in their struggle to end segregation. While violently opposed by the Right at the time, the principle of color-blind law has been largely accepted by contemporary conservatives. The struggle for gender-blind law has also been largely successful. Although feminists lost the battle for the Equal Rights Amendment (ERA) during the 1970s, since that time the principle of legal equality for women has been implemented through the Courts, which are charged with following the logic of liberalism as they apply the principles of the Constitution to new areas. While progress has not been inevitable or without setbacks, overall the level of legal equality within American society has advanced over time.

Despite the compelling logic of philosophical liberalism, the American Right actively opposed the extension of legal equality in every instance. The Old Right was explicitly racist and violently fought to stop the extension of civil rights to African-Americans. By 1965, however, Gallup polls "showed that 52 percent of Americans identified civil rights as the 'most important problem' confronting the nation, and an astonishing 75 percent of respondents favored federal voting rights legislation." With explicit racism on the decline, in 1965 right-wing leaders began developing a more marketable message, "mainstreaming the ideological positions of the Old Right and developing winnable policies" that "highlighted a protest theme" against a wide range of cultural changes inaugurated by the new social movements of the 1960s. This "New Right" successfully created a coalition between cultural conservatives, including Christian fundamentalists, and anti-government, fiscal conservatives (*aka* neo-liberals).

Feminism constituted precisely the enemy the New Right needed to consolidate its base. Anti-feminism "provided a link with fundamentalist churches," focused "the reaction against the changes in child rearing, sexual behavior, divorce, and the use of drugs that had taken place in the 1960s and 1970s," and "mobilized a group, traditional homemakers, that had lost status over the two previous decades and was feeling the psychological effects of the loss." The conservative mobilization against feminism solidified the New Right during the 1970s and played a "very important" role in its success: the election of Ronald Reagan in 1980 and the rightward shift of American politics.

The women's movement and the lesbian/gay civil rights movement were linked theoretically and through common struggle, and the Right used this connection to its advantage. For example, in the 1970s Phyllis Schlafly's Eagle Forum argued that "militant homosexuals from all over America have made the ERA issue a hot priority. Why? To be able finally to get homosexual marriage licenses, to adopt children and raise them to emulate their homosexual 'parents,' and to obtain pension and medical benefits for odd-couple 'spouses.' . . . Vote *NO on 6!* The Pro-Gay E.R.A." In its rise to power, the New Right successfully manipulated homophobia to increase opposition to gender equality and explicitly condemned all attempts to accord lesbians and gay men the equal protection of the law.

While the Christian Right continues to pose a serious threat to civil rights and has achieved unprecedented levels of power since 1980, the logic of liberalism in American society is hard to deny. Public opinion polls vary; however, a number of polls conducted in 2010 and 2011 show majority support for same-sex marriage among the general public. And among young people (18–29) who have come to age during an era of nearly hegemonic liberalism support is particularly and consistently high. Nevertheless, a coalition of religious, secular, and academic activists and organizations continue to oppose, and organize around their opposition to, the rights of gays and lesbians to marry—or even to form civil unions.

RELIGIOUS PARTICULARISM AND THE ANTI-HOMOSEXUAL AGENDA

The Christian Right opposes legal equality for lesbians and gay men when it comes to marriage because it defines marriage as a sacred religious institution, and its particular version of Christianity views homosexuality as a particularly grave sin. According to the Family Research Council (FRC) marriage is "the *work of heaven and every major religion* and culture throughout world history." Concerned Women for America (CWA) proclaims "we believe that marriage is *a covenant established by God* wherein one man and one woman, united for life, are licensed by the state for the purpose of founding and maintaining a family." Focus on the Family (FOF) opposes even "civil unions" because they "would essentially legalize homosexual marriage and therefore undermine the *sanctity* of marriage." Indeed because of this religious worldview, all three groups have made opposition to same-sex marriage a centerpiece of their political agenda.

The Christian Right's vision of heterosexual marriage directly relates to its understanding of gender differences, which it bases on its particular interpretation of the Christian Bible. More specifically, this reading focuses on the second creation story in Genesis, in which God created Eve out of Adam's rib to be his helper and declared that the man and his wife would become "one flesh" (Genesis 18:21–24), rather than on the first story in which "God created man in His image, in the image of God He created him; *male and female He created them*" (Genesis 1:26–27, emphasis added). Additionally, instead of reading the latter version as establishing gender equality at the origin, or even androgyny, as some religious scholars do, the Christian Right interprets it to mean "God's purpose for man was that there should be two sexes, male and female. Every person is either a 'he' or a 'she.' God did not divide mankind into three or four or five sexes." The Christian Right bolsters its interpretation with a few New Testament verses stating that woman is the "weaker vessel" (1 Peter 3:7), that man is "joined to his wife, and the two become one flesh" (Eph. 5:31–32), and that the "husband is the head of the wife" (1 Cor. 11:4; Eph. 5:23).

For the Christian Right, the Bible not only proclaims a natural gender hierarchy but also condemns homosexuality as a sin. It bases its interpretation on two sentences in Leviticus that proclaim "do not lie with a male as one lies with a woman; it is an abhorrence" (Leviticus 18:22) and "if a man lies with a male as one lies with a woman, the two of them have done an abhorrent thing; they shall be put to death" (Leviticus 20:13), completely ignoring the fact that the Ten Commandments did not include a prohibition on homosexuality. The Christian Right also stresses an interpretation of the Sodom and Gomorrah story (Genesis 18:16–19:29) that depicts the city's destruction as God's punishment for homosexuality, an interpretation that is highly contested by religious scholars. Finally, right-wing Christians justify their condemnation of lesbian and gay sexuality on three passages in Paul's writings—two words and two sentences total (I Corinthians 6:9–10, I Timothy 1:8–10, and Romans 1:26–27). They cannot base it on what Jesus said because he never even mentioned homosexuality. Although the meanings of all these passages have been debated at length by religious scholars, and no consensus exists as to their meanings, nevertheless, conservative Christians insist that God's will is as clear as it is specific: man and woman are naturally different, designed by God for heterosexual marriage and the establishment of the patriarchal family.

As far as their own religious rites are concerned, Christian Right churches certainly have the religious liberty to define marriage any way they see fit. However, when the faithful of the Christian Right ask the U.S. government and the governments of the states to restrict the right to civil marriage because of their particular interpretation of revealed religion, they violate the separation of church and state mandated by the First Amendment. Not all religions share the Christian Right's definition of marriage. For example, Reform Judaism not only favors civil marriage for gays and lesbians but also allows for religious unions, and many Muslims practice polygamy. In fact, even within Christianity, no clear consensus exists on the question of same-sex marriage. Nevertheless, despite the diversity of beliefs within America's religiously pluralistic society, the Christian Right group Alliance for Marriage has introduced a Federal Marriage Amendment that declares "Marriage in the United States shall consist only of the union of a man and a woman." Clearly this Amendment asks the federal government to establish one particular religious definition of marriage as the law of the land, thus violating the separation of church and state.

THAT '70S ARGUMENT: THE ANXIETY OF RIGHT-WING WOMEN

The Christian Right group Concerned Women for America, which claims to be the largest women's group in the country, consistently asserts that the struggle of lesbians and gay men for the right to marry is not an attempt to participate in the institution of marriage but rather an attempt to "undermine marriage" and destroy the family. In strictly logical terms this makes no sense. Aren't lesbians and gays actually *reinforcing* the legitimacy of marriage as an institution through their struggle for the right to marry? Indeed many within the LGBT community have criticized this struggle for doing precisely that and not much more. While same-sex marriage would not undermine the institution of marriage in general, it would undermine the *traditional patriarchal heterosexual vision of marriage* in particular, which is precisely what the Christian Right desperately wants to re-establish.

Concerned Women for America wants heterosexual marriage to maintain its privileged status in American society and to continue to function as the justification for special rights. This line of argumentation plays on a number of anxieties expressed by the first generation of New Right women who mobilized in opposition to the ERA and abortion rights during the 1970s. Status was a key concern for those women. "At the beginning of the contemporary women's movement, in 1968, women of all classes found themselves in something like the same boat." Most were homemakers and/or low-level employees. However, over the course of the next two decades "homemakers suffered a tremendous loss in social prestige" as "high-status women" began choosing careers over homemaking. Consequently, conservative homemakers—who, after all, had done the *right thing* for their time—now found themselves facing "status degradation," and they resented it. Twenty-five years later, the special status of

heterosexual marriage is being threatened by lesbians and gays, and many right-wing women again feel diminished.

Opposed to government-sponsored programs to support women and children, Christian Right women favor laws that force individual men to take responsibility for the children they father and for the mothers who bear those children. The 1970s generation feared that the changes inaugurated by feminism—the ERA, reproductive freedom, no-fault divorce, and the loosening of sexual mores—would make it easier for men to get out of their familial commitments. As opposed to liberal feminist women who wanted the right to compete equally with men, many anti-feminist women did not have the educational level or job skills that would allow them to pursue satisfying careers if forced to work outside the home. They feared that the ERA would eliminate the traditional legal requirement for husbands to support their wives financially. Phyllis Schlafly told homemakers that the ERA would say "Boys, supporting your wives isn't your responsibility anymore." At the same time, the rise of "no-fault" divorce laws during this period further threatened the economic security of traditional "housewives." As Schlafly put it, "even though love may go out the window, the obligation should remain. ERA would eliminate that obligation." To this day, Christian Right women condemn no-fault divorce, which "allows one person to decide when a relationship can be severed," often catapulting women into poverty. While higher wages for women, safe and affordable childcare, and universal health insurance constitute a progressive solution to the problems caused by the fragility of marriage and callousness of deadbeat dads, right-wing women demand the return of a traditional patriarchal vision of marriage, ignoring the reality of social change.

In the 1970s, conservative women worried that if sex became widely available outside of marriage, they would have difficulty keeping their husbands interested in them. Kristin Luker's interviews with the first generation of "pro-life" women revealed the following insight:

> If women plan to find their primary role in marriage and the family, then they face a need to create a "moral cartel" when it comes to sex. . . . If many women are willing to sleep with men outside of marriage, then the regular sexual activity that comes with marriage is much less valuable an incentive to marry. . . . [For] traditional women, their primary resource for marriage is the promise of a stable home, with everything it implies: children, regular sex, a "haven in a heartless world."

For the first generation of Christian Right women, the sexual liberation of many feminist women threatened to destabilize the marital bargain that many traditional women relied upon. Given the option, their husbands might abandon them for younger or more exciting women.

Do today's Christian Right women fear that if given the choice their husbands might choose other men? Perhaps. After all, anti-gay activist Dr. Paul Cameron tells them that "the evidence is that men do a better job on men, and women on women, if all you are looking for is orgasm." If you want "the most satisfying orgasm you can get," he explains, "then homosexuality seems too powerful to resist. . . . It's pure sexuality. It's almost like pure heroin. It's such a rush." In opposition, "marital sex tends toward the boring" and generally "doesn't deliver the kind of sheer sexual pleasure that homosexual sex does." Although the American Psychological Association expelled Cameron for ethics violations in 1983, he still serves as an oft-quoted right-wing "expert" on homosexuality. In light of his comments, it would be understandable if Christian Right women feel anxious about their ability to keep their husbands interested in heterosexual marriage.

Because homosexuality severs the connection between sex and reproduction, CWA sees homosexual relationships as necessarily fleeting, as driven by sexual gratification alone. For example, Beverly LaHaye insists that "homosexual relationships are not only the antithesis to family, but also threaten its very core. It is *the compulsive desire for sexual gratification without lasting commitment,* the high rate of promiscuity, and the self-defined morality among homosexuals that sap the vitality of the family structure, making it something less than it was, is, and should be." Clearly the desire of many gay and lesbian couples to marry and to raise children belies this argument. Nevertheless, Christian Right groups like CWA purposely depict the struggle for lesbian/gay civil rights in a reductive and patently distorted way in order to manipulate the anxieties of traditional women, secure their own special interests and advance their larger political agenda.

NEO-PATRIARCHY AND THE FATHERHOOD MOVEMENT

Joining the opposition to same-sex marriage are advocates of the fatherhood movement who seek to restore traditional gender roles and reestablish the patriarchal family as the dominant family form in America. Because no evidence exists that same-sex couples are less functional than heterosexual ones, or that their children are more likely to suffer negative effects, allowing same-sex couples to marry and have children would clearly undermine the myth that the patriarchal heterosexual family is the superior family form. Consequently, the fatherhood activists repeatedly assert that children need both a masculine father and a feminine mother in order to develop properly.

The fatherhood movement blames feminism and single mothers for the social problems caused by men and teenaged boys. While the packaging of their arguments varies slightly, advocates of this school of thought generally make a similar claim: Refusing to respect natural gender differences, feminists have pathologized masculinity and futilely attempted to change the behavior of men and boys. They have undermined the rightful authority of men as heads of the household, attempted to change the natural division of labor that exists between mothers and fathers, and propagated the idea that a woman can fulfill the role traditionally played by a man, thus rendering fathers superfluous to family life. Consequently, men have lost interest in fulfilling their traditional family responsibilities, and boys have no one to teach them how to become responsible men. Detached from the civilizing influence of the traditional patriarchal family, males increasingly cause a wide array of social problems, and everybody suffers.

Focus on the Family president James Dobson makes this argument from a Christian Right perspective. In *Bringing Up Boys,* he argues that traditional gender roles are natural and cannot be changed. He points to the continued power of men in society as evidence of their natural, "biochemical and anatomical," dominance. Dobson strongly opposes attempts to change the gender socialization of children and explicitly links this "unisex" idea to "the powerful gay and lesbian agenda," whose propagandists are teaching a revolutionary view of sexuality called "gender feminism," which insists that sex assignment is irrelevant. While Dobson sees this as dangerous for both sexes, it is particularly harmful for boys: "Protect the masculinity of your boys, who will be under increasing political pressure in years to come."

Dobson believes that a breakdown of traditional gender roles within the family fosters homosexuality in children. The prevention of homosexuality among boys requires the involvement of a properly masculine heterosexual father, especially during the early years. Dobson relies on the work of Dr. Joseph Nicolosi, a leading proponent of the Christian Right's "ex-gay" movement, who urges parents to monitor their children for signs of "prehomosexuality," so professionals can step in before it is too late. While "feminine behavior in boyhood" is clearly a sign, so is "nonmasculinity" defined as not fitting in with male peers. "The father," Nicolosi asserts, "plays an essential role in a boy's normal development as a man. The truth is, Dad is more important than Mom." In order to ensure heterosexuality, the father "needs to mirror and affirm his son's maleness. He can play rough-and-tumble games

with his son, in ways that are decidedly different from the games he would play with a little girl. He can help his son learn to throw and catch a ball. . . . He can even take his son with him into the shower, where the boy cannot help but notice that Dad has a penis, just like his, only bigger."

Based solely on the work of Nicolosi, Dobson concludes, "if you as a parent have an effeminate boy or a masculinized girl, I urge you to get a copy [of Nicolosi's book] and then seek immediate professional help." Beware, however, of "secular" mental health professionals who will most certainly "take the wrong approach—telling your child that he is homosexual and needs to accept that fact." Instead, Dobson recommends a referral from either Exodus International, the leading organization of the ex-gay ministries, or the National Association for Research and Therapy of Homosexuality, "formed to oppose the 1973 decision by the American Psychological Association to no longer classify homosexuality as an emotional or mental disorder."

Dobson's emphasis on the important role played by fathers bolsters the arguments of the "fatherhood movement," which emerged during the 1990s. One of the first organizations to spearhead this movement was the Promise Keepers (PK), founded by Bill McCartney in 1990 as a "Christ-centered ministry dedicated to uniting men through vital relationships to become godly influences in their world." This organization wants to restore fathers to their rightful place at the head of the patriarchal family.

Institute for American Values president David Blankenhorn advances a similar agenda using secular arguments. His book *Fatherless America* (1995) and the follow-up volume *The Fatherhood Movement* (1999)—co-edited with Wade Horn (George W. Bush's Secretary of Health and Human Services) and Mitchell Pearlstein—blames the "declining child well-being in our society," not on growing levels of poverty, deteriorating public services, lack of safe and affordable childcare, the lower income of women, child abuse, racism or misogyny, but rather on fatherlessness. Fatherlessness, he tells us, is "the engine driving our most urgent social problems, from crime to adolescent pregnancy to child sexual abuse to domestic violence against women." While some conservatives argue that "the best anti-poverty program for children is a stable, intact family," Blankenhorn demands more: "a married father on the premises."

Like those on the Christian Right, Blankenhorn insists that children need not just two involved parents but more specifically *a male father and a female mother enacting traditional gender roles.* Citing two anthropologists, Blankenhorn claims that "gendered parental roles derive precisely from children's needs." During childhood "the needs of the child compel mothers and fathers to specialize in their labor and to adopt gender-based parental roles." Consequently, men and women should stick with traditional roles, Blankenhorn insists, even if this conflicts with their "narcissistic claims" to personal autonomy.

Like Dobson, Blankenhorn condemns attempts to equalize the roles of mothers and fathers in childrearing, and derides what he calls the new "like-a-mother father." While Blankenhorn barely mentions lesbians and gay men in his analysis, his argument clearly justifies an opposition to same-sex marriage. Obviously, his insistence that proper childhood development requires heterosexual parents who enact traditional gender roles implies that, in his view, homosexual couples cannot raise healthy children. In addition, however, Blankenhorn specifically advocates laws to prohibit unmarried women from accessing sperm banks. Perhaps he shares the fear of CWA that gender equality would mean that "lesbian women would be considered no different from men," especially once they get access to male seed. If that were to happen, where would that leave men?

"SEEDBEDS OF VIRTUE": WHAT LESSONS DOES THE PATRIARCHAL FAMILY TEACH?

Building directly on the body of literature outlined above, a growing number of right-wing activists, respectable scholars, and well-known political theorists have begun connecting the neo-patriarchal movement to the survival and revitalization of American democracy. This approach claims, in short, that liberal democracy requires virtuous citizens, and virtue is best learned at home in a traditional family with two married parents. The Institute for American Values sponsored a conference on this topic that resulted in the publication of *Seedbeds of Virtue: Sources of Competence, Character, and Citizenship in American Society* that Blankenhorn edited with Mary Ann Glendon who so strongly opposes same-sex unions that she helped draft both the Federal Marriage Amendment and a similar amendment to the Massachusetts constitution.

While many conservative thinkers support the "seedbeds of virtue" approach to justifying the patriarchal heterosexual family—many in exactly the same terms as the fatherhood movement—I will concentrate on the arguments advanced by political theorist William Galston, who served as Deputy Assistant to the President for Domestic Policy under Bill Clinton, a *Democratic* president. While Galston's defense of the family does not explicitly specify the patriarchal heterosexual family form in particular, one can only infer that he endorses that vision for several reasons. First, he makes arguments similar to those of the neo-patriarchalists *without any caveats.* Second, he explicitly praises Mary Ann Glendon and Jean Bethke Elshtain for having "already said nearly every thing that needs saying on [the subject of the family]." While Glendon works politically in opposition to same-sex marriage, Elshtain's scholarship specifically proposes "a normative vision of the family—mothers, fathers, and children" and claims that this particular family form "is not only *not* at odds with democratic civil society but is in fact, now more than ever, a prerequisite for that society to function." Third, Galston himself signs *A Call to Civil Society: Why Democracy Needs Moral Truths* that says the number one priority for American democracy should be "to increase the likelihood that more children will grow up with their two married parents."

In addition, the lack of explicit references to homosexuality should not be interpreted as a lack of homophobia. As Jean Hardisty has discovered, since the mid-1980s, Christian Right organizations have tended to "highlight the religious principles undergirding their anti-homosexual politics only when they are targeting other Christians. When organizing in the wider political arena, they frame their anti-gay organizing as a struggle for secular ends, such as 'defense of the family.' " Thus you get James Dobson in Christian Right circles, David Blankenhorn in secular circles, and William Galston in academic circles. Despite variations on the theme, one thing remains constant: the normative vision presented by these conservatives gives lesbians and gay men absolutely no place in family life, and, by extension, no place in democratic society.

Working from a firm foundation in the history of political thought, Galston argues that liberal democracy requires individuals who have the virtues necessary for life in a free society. The claim is simple: "that the operation of liberal institutions is affected in important ways by the character of citizens (and leaders), and that at some point, the attenuation of individual virtue will create pathologies with which liberal political contrivances, however technically perfect their design, simply cannot cope." Cataloguing the wide array of virtues necessary for liberal democracy, Galston only implies that the traditional family best teaches these virtues to youngsters; he never argues it explicitly.

An examination of how the particular virtues cited by Galston relate to the traditional family produces three different arguments. First, many of the virtues Galston emphasizes, while originally acquired in a family, do not require a patriarchal heterosexual family form in particular. For example, important virtues like civility, the work ethic, delayed gratification, adaptability, discernment, and "the ability to work within constraints on action imposed by social diversity and constitutional institutions" could certainly be instilled in children by any functional family, including one headed by same-sex parents. Galston makes no argument for the superiority of heterosexuals in fostering these characteristics in children, and such an argument is not supported by empirical evidence.

Second, the traditional patriarchal family could actually undermine a number of important virtues extolled by Galston. For example, he argues that a liberal society is characterized by two key features—individualism and diversity. While children certainly need to learn independence, how does the traditional patriarchal family, in which wives are dependent upon their husbands' leadership and economic support, teach the virtue of independence to future *female* citizens? Galston must be focusing on boys only. Additionally, Galston cites "loyalty" as a central virtue for liberal democracy, defining it as "the developed capacity to understand, to accept, and to act on the core principles of one's society." This "is particularly important in liberal communities," he argues, because they "tend to be organized around abstract principles rather than shared ethnicity, nationality, or history." But if one of the fundamental principles of liberal democracy is legal equality for all citizens, again we must ask: What lessons does a child learn about equality growing up in a patriarchal nuclear family in which *men lead and women submit?* While the traditional family may provide certain benefits to children, it is unclear how it teaches them the universal principle of equality for all citizens, when this family form models gender inequality.

Third, a number of the democratic virtues Galston emphasizes could be undermined by the normative vision of the Christian Right. For example, Galston emphasizes "the willingness to *listen seriously to a range of views*" and the "willingness to set forth one's own views intelligibly and candidly as the basis of a *politics of persuasion rather than manipulation or coercion*." This directly relates to the virtue of *tolerance*. While Galston stresses that tolerance does not mean a belief that all lifestyles are "equally good," it does mean that "the pursuit of the better course should be (and in some cases can only be) the consequence of *education or persuasion rather than coercion.*" While open-mindedness, tolerance, and non-coercion certainly constitute important virtues for any democratic society, they are not hallmarks of the Christian Right, especially when it comes to its anti-homosexual agenda.

CONCLUSION

The fight against the extension of civil rights to lesbians and gay men forms a central component of the larger battle against women's equality. While the rhetoric deployed by conservatives resonates with many of our most cherished cultural narratives and personal fantasies, their overarching agenda actually undermines our most precious political values, including the separation of church and state, legal equality and personal liberty. While liberal democracy has its limitations, its virtue is that it maximizes the freedom of all by allowing individuals to organize their personal lives as they see fit. While a liberal state may respond to the will of its citizens by providing a default set of legal entanglements that make it easier for individuals to establish families (i.e., civil marriage), it may not legitimately deny equal protection of the laws to particular groups of citizens, no matter how unpopular they are. The conservative arguments against same-sex marriage, whether religious, secular, or academic, are all similarly structured and based on an idealized, inegalitarian heterosexual family with rigid gender roles. Justified by references to the well-being of children, these arguments are unsustainable when subjected to close scrutiny.

DISCUSSION QUESTIONS

1. Snyder-Hall argues that the founding principles of liberal democracy lend support to the struggle for equality of lesbians and gay men. How compelling do you find her argument?
2. Identify the leading arguments against homosexual equality and gay marriage. What are Snyder-Hall's arguments against each of these positions? Do you agree that these anti-gay perspectives serve to uphold rigid gender roles or "neo-patriarchy"?

PART **III**

POLITICS AND VISION

Politics is everywhere. Although you may not think of yourself as a political person, you are surrounded by, bombarded by, and inescapably influenced by politics. There is no shelter from the storm.

We firmly believe that as citizens you have an enormous stake in the direction American politics takes in the twenty-first century. We further assume that you do not automatically agree that the direction we are heading is the direction we ought to take. If our assumption is correct, and your views are not cast in stone, you may want to question critically the possible future options open to us. Given the structural context we have sketched in Part I, and the discussion of political institutions in Part II, it follows that we think conventional political leaders lack the creative vision necessary to move us beyond status quo conceptions of "problems" and "solutions." In our judgment, we face a potentially stifling lack of national political imagination.

In Part III, we offer you chapters that attempt to spark your interest in and imagination on two fronts. First, we look at some particularly important policy challenges involving issues of class and inequality, gender, race, and U.S. foreign policy. Our selection of these issues does not pretend to be exhaustive, but we do think that these articles will give you a clearer sense of how an alternative critical perspective looks at difficult political questions.

After exploring these issues, we conclude with a chapter that amounts to a call for action. Government, corporate, and media elites routinely defend their behavior by saying they act with people's best interests at heart. In their minds, this may well be true, for they often equate their class interests and political interests with a broader public interest. We are quite skeptical of this equation. Nevertheless, there is a sense in which we are all indirectly responsible for the actions of political and economic elites, at least to the extent that we remain silent in the face of actions we find morally wrong.

We are implicated in behavior we oppose if we have the freedom to oppose that behavior, but we choose not to. This is especially true for those of us who have gone to college and presumably have had the time and resources to develop the skills to think critically in an academic environment where alternative information should be readily available. The final chapter of our anthology thus encourages you to take responsibility in a political world that too often fosters apathy and disengagement.

CHAPTER 9

Political Challenges at Home and Abroad

We live in a changing world. Our values, ideologies, politics, society, economics, and the larger world outside America are being challenged and transformed, often in directions we only dimly understand. In Chapter 10, we stress that the shape of the future partly depends on choices we make and interpretations we reach. In this chapter we wish to indicate, without any attempt to be comprehensive, some of the major policy challenges facing Americans in the twenty-first century. By now it should be clear that we do not believe these challenges can be resolved on a humane and democratic basis unless we make far-reaching economic, political, and social changes. Confronted with crises, many of us react by withdrawing from politics or by hoping to muddle through. But opinion polls and other evidence convince us that millions of Americans have a sober-minded desire to comprehend and grapple with the dangers and opportunities we face. Each of the four readings in this chapter prepares us for the critical choices ahead.

33 *Barbara Ehrenreich*

KICKING PEOPLE WHEN THEY'RE DOWN
Poverty in America

Barbara Ehrenreich is an acclaimed author, activist, feminist, and social critic. Writing at the intersection of inequality, class, gender, and work, this article appeared as the Afterword to the tenth anniversary edition of her bestselling book Nickel and Dimed. *In that now-classic 2001 book, Ehrenreich explored the hellish world of low-wage work in America by joining the ranks of such workers in several different service sector occupations and writing about her experiences from the inside. Here she revisits her original work, only now against the backdrop of more pressing hardships ordinary blue collar workers and their families face in the midst of the even-steeper economic decline that began in 2008 and continues today. It is a world of contingent work, rampant poverty, and often overwhelming insecurity, marked by mounting bills, overcrowded living conditions (or outright homelessness), and lack of health insurance. Moreover, the traditional way of addressing such hardships since the 1930s—via provision of a government safety net—lies in tatters, with that safety net having become a "dragnet," as poverty increasingly has been criminalized in the United States. Ehrenreich's research and analysis raises chilling questions about what we have become as a nation facing both economic hard times and a political climate insensitive to the struggles of the working poor.*

I completed the manuscript for *Nickel and Dimed* in a time of seemingly boundless prosperity. Technology innovators and venture capitalists were acquiring sudden fortunes, buying up McMansions like the ones I had cleaned in Maine and much larger. Even secretaries in some hi-tech firms were striking it rich with their stock options. There was loose talk about a permanent conquest of the business cycle, and a sassy new spirit infecting American capitalism. In San Francisco, a billboard for an e-trading firm proclaimed, "Make love not war," and then—down at the bottom—"Screw it, just make money."

When *Nickel and Dimed* was published in May 2001, cracks were appearing in the dot-com bubble and the stock market had begun to falter,

Source: Nickel and Dimed: On (Not) Getting By in America, Afterword to the 10th Anniversary Edition, published August 2nd by Picador USA. New afterword © 2011 by Barbara Ehrenreich. Excerpted by arrangement with Metropolitan Books, an imprint of Henry Holt and Company, LLC. All rights reserved.

but the book still evidently came as a surprise, even a revelation, to many. Again and again, in that first year or two after publication, people came up to me and opened with the words, "I never thought . . ." or "I hadn't realized . . ."

To my own amazement, *Nickel and Dimed* quickly ascended to the bestseller list and began winning awards—and I am particularly proud of the Christopher Award, from a Catholic group, for books that "affirm the highest values of the human spirit." The book inspired an A&E documentary called *Wage Slaves* and was transformed by playwright Joan Holden into a fast, funny play that has been performed in major theaters as well as many smaller venues throughout the country. It has been adopted as a "community read" in dozens of communities, including Rochester, Minnesota; Appleton, Wisconsin; Concord, New Hampshire; and Peoria, Illinois.

Criticisms, too, have accumulated over the years. In 2006, Adam Shepard, a recent graduate who had been forced to read *Nickel and Dimed* in college, undertook to refute it with his own experiment as a low-wage worker. He turned out to be far more financially successful than I had been, ending up, after ten months, with an apartment and several thousand dollars saved. It should be pointed out, however, that he spent his first seventy days living off charity in a homeless shelter that also offered meals, a strategy that provided him with a considerable subsidy. He also enjoyed the advantage of being male, which meant he could work in industries such as moving and construction that pay better than the kinds of jobs that were open to me. But in his book, *Scratch Beginnings*, Shepard accused me, somewhat unchivalrously I think, of lacking the motivation to succeed.

A more common criticism is that *Nickel and Dimed* harbors a deep prejudice against Christians. This, anyway, has been one interpretation of the tent revival scene in Maine and my criticism of "visible Christians"—wearing Christian-themed T-shirts or "WWJD" bracelets—who tipped so poorly in Florida. Well, let me say that as an admirer of the Jesus of the Book of Matthew,

I hold Christians to a pretty high standard. Rather than just appealing for donations, the tent revival preachers should have acknowledged the poverty of their audience. And when confronted with a server earning $2 and change an hour, the answer to the questions "What Would Jesus Do?" is that when the time came to leave a tip, he would empty out his wallet, should the real Jesus have carried one.

The most dramatic attack on *Nickel and Dimed* occurred in 2003, when the University of North Carolina at Chapel Hill assigned the book to all incoming students. This prompted a group of conservative students and state legislators to hold a press conference denouncing *Nickel and Dimed* as a "classic Marxist rant" and a work of "intellectual pornography with no redeeming characteristics." The group proceeded to take out a full page ad in the *Raleigh News & Observer,* which had little to say about the book, but charged me with being a Marxist, an atheist, and a dedicated enemy of the American family—this last proven by my longstanding conviction that families headed by single mothers are as deserving of support as those headed by married couples. I was greeted on North Carolina radio talk shows by hosts asking, "What does it feel like to the antichrist of North Carolina?" and similarly challenging inquiries.

But while I was enjoying the free publicity, housekeepers on the UNC-CH campus put the brouhaha to good use by showing up at work wearing T-shirts and buttons reading, "Ask ME about being nickel and dimed." The housekeepers, it turned out, had been fighting for union recognition for years—against the very administration that had apparently approved *Nickel and Dimed* as freshman reading material. My involvement came to a glorious conclusion when the housekeepers and graduate student employees invited me to come to campus—on my own dime, of course—and speak at rallies for campus workers, although these unfortunately did not lead to union recognition.

But for the most part, the book has been far better received than I could have imagined it would be, with an impact extending well into the more comfortable classes. A Florida woman wrote to tell me that, before reading it, she'd always been annoyed at the poor for what she saw as their self-inflicted obesity. Now she understood that a healthy diet wasn't always an option. Another woman told me she'd always assumed that "unskilled" workers earned at least $15 an hour, which is what she paid her housekeeper. My sister in Colorado, who is by no means affluent herself, was so struck by the homeless workers I wrote about that she organized a local chapter of Habitat for Humanity. And if I had a quarter for every person who's told me he or she now tipped more generously, I would be able to start my own foundation.

What is even more gratifying to me, the book has been widely read among low-wage workers. In the last few years, hundreds of people have written to tell me their stories: the mother of a newborn infant whose electricity had just been turned off, the woman who had just been given a diagnosis of cancer and has no health insurance, the newly homeless man who writes from a library computer. To quote from a few of the e-mails I have received over the years:

Nickled and Dimed is far from fiction. It is pretty much my life. With 2 college degrees, I have struggled, and with no health insurance, I've incurred a ton of debt. I have not done as well as my parents, who came out of the Depression. Our government says there are jobs, but they are low-pay jobs with no benefits. Not livable wage jobs. Not jobs that will give you a house and savings for retirement. Nothing glimmers in this dust.

Hello, Barbara, I am a downsized federal employee, not white collar, blue collar [whose] income was less than $20,000. . . . After my 20 years in Data with the I.R.S. for $10.00 an hour, $6000.00 in 401K I can't locate, I took a job as a Direct Care Counselor, sort of like the nursing aide position you had in *Nickel and Dimed*. Well, I was hurt 4 months into this horrible, physical degrading job basically cleaning up after Mentally Ill/Disabled population while doing a Take Down for violent clients as

we called them, and I messed up my knee, three surgeries later needing knee replacement and out of work for almost 5 years now I collect $65.75 a week from worker's compensation insurance, from originally $256.00 a week after surgery #1. Now I have to find a job that I can do with a bad knee, because I can't survive any longer.

I just finished reading your book entitled "Nickel and Dimed." I appreciate the fact that you were willing to experience first hand what many of us live with day to day. . . . You witness the "pariah" syndrome the working poor experience daily. Very few people get the chance to delve into that other realm where you feel like a lesser being just for being.

Even more gratifying to me, the book has been widely read among low-wage workers. In the last few years, hundreds of people have written to tell me their stories: the mother of a newborn infant whose electricity had just been turned off, the woman who had just been given a diagnosis of cancer and has no health insurance, the newly homeless man who writes from a library computer.

At the time I wrote *Nickel and Dimed*, I wasn't sure how many people it directly applied to—only that the official definition of poverty was way off the mark, since it defined an individual earning $7 an hour, as I did on average, as well out of poverty. But three months after the book was published, the Economic Policy Institute in Washington, D.C., issued a report entitled "Hardships in America: The Real Story of Working Families," which found an astounding 29% of American families living in what could be more reasonably defined as poverty, meaning that they earned less than a barebones budget covering housing, child care, health care, food, transportation, and taxes—though not, it should be noted, any entertainment, meals out, cable TV, Internet service, vacations, or holiday gifts. Twenty-nine percent is a minority, but not a reassuringly small one, and other studies in the early 2000s came up with similar figures.

The big question, 10 years later, is whether things have improved or worsened for those in the bottom third of the income distribution, the people who clean hotel rooms, work in warehouses, wash dishes in restaurants, care for the very young and very old, and keep the shelves stocked in our stores. The short answer is that things have gotten much worse, especially since the economic downturn that began in 2008.

Post-Meltdown Poverty

When you read about the hardships I found people enduring while I was researching my book—the skipped meals, the lack of medical care, the occasional need to sleep in cars or vans—you should bear in mind that those occurred in the *best* of times. The economy was growing, and jobs, if poorly paid, were at least plentiful.

In 2000, I had been able to walk into a number of jobs pretty much off the street. Less than a decade later, many of these jobs had disappeared and there was stiff competition for those that remained. It would have been impossible to repeat my *Nickel and Dimed* "experiment," had I had been so inclined, because I would probably never have found a job.

For the last couple of years, I have attempted to find out what was happening to the working poor in a declining economy—this time using conventional reporting techniques like interviewing. I started with my own extended family, which includes plenty of people without jobs or health insurance, and moved on to trying to track down a couple of the people I had met while working on *Nickel and Dimed*.

This wasn't easy, because most of the addresses and phone numbers I had taken away with me had proved to be inoperative within a few months, probably due to moves and suspensions of telephone service. I had kept in touch with "Melissa" over the years, who was still working at Wal-Mart, where her wages had risen from $7 to $10 an hour, but in the meantime her husband had lost his job. "Caroline," now in her 50s and partly disabled by diabetes and heart disease, had

left her deadbeat husband and was subsisting on occasional cleaning and catering jobs. Neither seemed unduly afflicted by the recession, but only because they had already been living in what amounts to a permanent economic depression.

Media attention has focused, understandably enough, on the "nouveau poor"—formerly middle and even upper-middle class people who lost their jobs, their homes, and/or their investments in the financial crisis of 2008 and the economic downturn that followed it, but the brunt of the recession has been borne by the blue-collar working class, which had already been sliding downwards since de-industrialization began in the 1980s.

In 2008 and 2009, for example, blue-collar unemployment was increasing three times as fast as white-collar unemployment, and African American and Latino workers were three times as likely to be unemployed as white workers. Low-wage blue-collar workers, like the people I worked with in this book, were especially hard hit for the simple reason that they had so few assets and savings to fall back on as jobs disappeared.

How have the already-poor attempted to cope with their worsening economic situation? One obvious way is to cut back on health care. The *New York Times* reported in 2009 that one-third of Americans could no longer afford to comply with their prescriptions and that there had been a sizable drop in the use of medical care. Others, including members of my extended family, have given up their health insurance.

Food is another expenditure that has proved vulnerable to hard times, with the rural poor turning increasingly to "food auctions," which offer items that may be past their sell-by dates. And for those who like their meat fresh, there's the option of urban hunting. In Racine, Wisconsin, a 51-year-old laid-off mechanic told me he was supplementing his diet by "shooting squirrels and rabbits and eating them stewed, baked, and grilled." In Detroit, where the wildlife population has mounted as the human population ebbs, a retired truck driver was doing a brisk business in raccoon carcasses, which he recommends marinating with vinegar and spices.

The most common coping strategy, though, is simply to increase the number of paying people per square foot of dwelling space—by doubling up or renting to couch-surfers.

It's hard to get firm numbers on overcrowding, because no one likes to acknowledge it to census-takers, journalists, or anyone else who might be remotely connected to the authorities.

In Los Angeles, housing expert Peter Dreier says that "people who've lost their jobs, or at least their second jobs, cope by doubling or tripling up in overcrowded apartments, or by paying 50 or 60 or even 70 percent of their incomes in rent." According to a community organizer in Alexandria, Virginia, the standard apartment in a complex occupied largely by day laborers has two bedrooms, each containing an entire family of up to five people, plus an additional person laying claim to the couch.

No one could call suicide a "coping strategy," but it is one way some people have responded to job loss and debt. There are no national statistics linking suicide to economic hard times, but the National Suicide Prevention Lifeline reported more than a four-fold increase in call volume between 2007 and 2009, and regions with particularly high unemployment, like Elkhart, Indiana, have seen troubling spikes in their suicide rates. Foreclosure is often the trigger for suicide—or, worse, murder-suicides that destroy entire families.

"TORTURE AND ABUSE OF NEEDY FAMILIES"

We do of course have a collective way of ameliorating the hardships of individuals and families—a government safety net that is meant to save the poor from spiraling down all the way to destitution. But its response to the economic emergency of the last few years has been spotty at best. The food stamp program has responded to the crisis fairly well, to the point where it now reaches about 37 million people, up about 30% from pre-recession levels. But welfare—the traditional last resort for the down-and-out until it

was "reformed" in 1996—only expanded by about 6% in the first two years of the recession.

The difference between the two programs? There is a right to food stamps. You go to the office and, if you meet the statutory definition of need, they help you. For welfare, the street-level bureaucrats can, pretty much at their own discretion, just say no.

Take the case of Kristen and Joe Parente, Delaware residents who had always imagined that people turned to the government for help only if "they didn't want to work." Their troubles began well before the recession, when Joe, a fourth-generation pipe-fitter, sustained a back injury that left him unfit for even light lifting. He fell into a profound depression for several months, then rallied to ace a state-sponsored retraining course in computer repairs—only to find that those skills are no longer in demand. The obvious fallback was disability benefits, but—catch-22—when Joe applied he was told he could not qualify without presenting a recent MRI scan. This would cost $800 to $900, which the Parentes do not have; nor has Joe, unlike the rest of the family, been able to qualify for Medicaid.

When they married as teenagers, the plan had been for Kristen to stay home with the children. But with Joe out of action and three children to support by the middle of this decade, Kristen went out and got waitressing jobs, ending up, in 2008, in a "pretty fancy place on the water." Then the recession struck and she was laid off.

Kristen is bright, pretty, and to judge from her command of her own small kitchen, probably capable of holding down a dozen tables with precision and grace. In the past she'd always been able to land a new job within days; now there was nothing. Like 44% of laid-off people at the time, she failed to meet the fiendishly complex and sometimes arbitrary eligibility requirements for unemployment benefits. Their car started falling apart.

So the Parentes turned to what remains of welfare—TANF, or Temporary Assistance to Needy Families. TANF does not offer straightforward cash support like Aid to Families with

Dependent Children, which it replaced in 1996. It's an income supplementation program for working parents, and it was based on the sunny assumption that there would always be plenty of jobs for those enterprising enough to get them.

After Kristen applied, nothing happened for six weeks—no money, no phone calls returned. At school, the Parentes' seven-year-old's class was asked to write out what wish they would present to a genie, should a genie appear. Brianna's wish was for her mother to find a job because there was nothing to eat in the house, an aspiration that her teacher deemed too disturbing to be posted on the wall with the other children's requests.

When the Parentes finally got into "the system" and began receiving food stamps and some cash assistance, they discovered why some recipients have taken to calling TANF "Torture and Abuse of Needy Families." From the start, the TANF experience was "humiliating," Kristen says. The caseworkers "treat you like a bum. They act like every dollar you get is coming out of their own paychecks."

The Parentes discovered that they were each expected to apply for 40 jobs a week, although their car was on its last legs and no money was offered for gas, tolls, or babysitting. In addition, Kristen had to drive 35 miles a day to attend "job readiness" classes offered by a private company called Arbor, which, she says, were "frankly a joke."

Nationally, according to Kaaryn Gustafson of the University of Connecticut Law School, "applying for welfare is a lot like being booked by the police." There may be a mug shot, fingerprinting, and lengthy interrogations as to one's children's true paternity. The ostensible goal is to prevent welfare fraud, but the psychological impact is to turn poverty itself into a kind of crime.

How the Safety Net Became a Dragnet

The most shocking thing I learned from my research on the fate of the working poor in the recession was the extent to which poverty has indeed been criminalized in America.

Perhaps the constant suspicions of drug use and theft that I encountered in low-wage workplaces should have alerted me to the fact that, when you leave the relative safety of the middle class, you might as well have given up your citizenship and taken residence in a hostile nation.

Most cities, for example, have ordinances designed to drive the destitute off the streets by outlawing such necessary activities of daily life as sitting, loitering, sleeping, or lying down. Urban officials boast that there is nothing discriminatory about such laws: "If you're lying on a sidewalk, whether you're homeless or a millionaire, you're in violation of the ordinance," a St. Petersburg, Florida, city attorney stated in June 2009, echoing Anatole France's immortal observation that "the law, in its majestic equality, forbids the rich as well as the poor to sleep under bridges . . ."

In defiance of all reason and compassion, the criminalization of poverty has actually intensified as the weakened economy generates ever more poverty. So concludes a recent study from the National Law Center on Poverty and Homelessness, which finds that the number of ordinances against the publicly poor has been rising since 2006, along with the harassment of the poor for more "neutral" infractions like jaywalking, littering, or carrying an open container.

The report lists America's ten "meanest" cities—the largest of which include Los Angeles, Atlanta, and Orlando—but new contestants are springing up every day. In Colorado, Grand Junction's city council is considering a ban on begging; Tempe, Arizona, carried out a four-day crackdown on the indigent at the end of June. And how do you know when someone is indigent? As a Las Vegas statute puts it, "an indigent person is a person whom a reasonable ordinary person would believe to be entitled to apply for or receive" public assistance.

That could be me before the blow-drying and eyeliner, and it's definitely Al Szekeley at any time of day. A grizzled 62-year-old, he inhabits a wheelchair and is often found on G Street in Washington, D.C.—the city that is ultimately responsible for the bullet he took in the spine in Phu Bai, Vietnam, in 1972.

He had been enjoying the luxury of an indoor bed until December 2008, when the police swept through the shelter in the middle of the night looking for men with outstanding warrants. It turned out that Szekeley, who is an ordained minister and does not drink, do drugs, or cuss in front of ladies, did indeed have one—for "criminal trespassing," as sleeping on the streets is sometimes defined by the law. So he was dragged out of the shelter and put in jail.

"Can you imagine?" asked Eric Sheptock, the homeless advocate (himself a shelter resident) who introduced me to Szekeley. "They arrested a homeless man *in a shelter* for being homeless?"

The viciousness of the official animus toward the indigent can be breathtaking. A few years ago, a group called Food Not Bombs started handing out free vegan food to hungry people in public parks around the nation. A number of cities, led by Las Vegas, passed ordinances forbidding the sharing of food with the indigent in public places, leading to the arrests of several middle-aged white vegans.

One anti-sharing law was just overturned in Orlando, but the war on illicit generosity continues. Orlando is appealing the decision, and Middletown, Connecticut, is in the midst of a crackdown. More recently, Gainesville, Florida, began enforcing a rule limiting the number of meals that soup kitchens may serve to 130 people in one day, and Phoenix, Arizona, has been using zoning laws to stop a local church from serving breakfast to homeless people.

For the not-yet-homeless, there are two main paths to criminalization, and one is debt. Anyone can fall into debt, and although we pride ourselves on the abolition of debtors' prison, in at least one state, Texas, people who can't pay fines for things like expired inspection stickers may be made to "sit out their tickets" in jail.

More commonly, the path to prison begins when one of your creditors has a court summons issued for you, which you fail to honor for one reason or another, such as that your address has changed and you never received it. Okay, now you're in "contempt of the court."

Or suppose you miss a payment and your car insurance lapses, and then you're stopped for something like a broken headlight (about $130 for the bulb alone). Now, depending on the state, you may have your car impounded and/or face a steep fine—again, exposing you to a possible court summons. "There's just no end to it once the cycle starts," says Robert Solomon of Yale Law School. "It just keeps accelerating."

The second—and by far the most reliable—way to be criminalized by poverty is to have the wrong color skin. Indignation runs high when a celebrity professor succumbs to racial profiling, but whole communities are effectively "profiled" for the suspicious combination of being both dark-skinned and poor. Flick a cigarette and you're "littering"; wear the wrong color T-shirt and you're displaying gang allegiance. Just strolling around in a dodgy neighborhood can mark you as a potential suspect. And don't get grumpy about it or you could be "resisting arrest."

In what has become a familiar pattern, the government defunds services that might help the poor while ramping up law enforcement. Shut down public housing, then make it a crime to be homeless. Generate no public-sector jobs, then penalize people for falling into debt. The experience of the poor, and especially poor people of color, comes to resemble that of a rat in a cage scrambling to avoid erratically administered electric shocks. And if you should try to escape this nightmare reality into a brief, drug-induced high, it's "gotcha" all over again, because that of course is illegal too.

One result is our staggering level of incarceration, the highest in the world. Today, exactly the same number of Americans—2.3 million—reside in prison as in public housing. And what public housing remains has become ever more prison-like, with random police sweeps and, in a growing number of cities, proposed drug tests for residents. The safety net, or what remains of it, has been transformed into a dragnet.

It is not clear whether economic hard times will finally force us to break the mad cycle of poverty and punishment. With even the official level of poverty increasing—to over 14% in 2010—some states are beginning to ease up on the criminalization of poverty, using alternative sentencing methods, shortening probation, and reducing the number of people locked up for technical violations like missing court appointments. But others, diabolically enough, are tightening the screws: not only increasing the number of "crimes," but charging prisoners for their room and board, guaranteeing they'll be released with potentially criminalizing levels of debt.

So what is the solution to the poverty of so many of America's working people? Ten years ago, when *Nickel and Dimed* first came out, I often responded with the standard liberal wish list—a higher minimum wage, universal health care, affordable housing, good schools, reliable public transportation, and all the other things we, uniquely among the developed nations, have neglected to do.

Today, the answer seems both more modest and more challenging: if we want to reduce poverty, we have to stop doing the things that make people poor and keep them that way. Stop underpaying people for the jobs they do. Stop treating working people as potential criminals and let them have the right to organize for better wages and working conditions.

Stop the institutional harassment of those who turn to the government for help or find themselves destitute in the streets. Maybe, as so many Americans seem to believe today, we can't afford the kinds of public programs that would genuinely alleviate poverty—though I would argue otherwise. But at least we should decide, as a bare minimum principle, to stop kicking people when they're down.

DISCUSSION QUESTIONS

1. Compare and contrast Ehrenreich's account of the working poor with the image of the American Dream discussed in Articles 5 and 6 in Chapter 2. Does her account strengthen or weaken the analysis in those articles?

2. In keeping with the individualism of our political culture and ideology, many Americans believe the poor are exclusively to blame for their own situation. Assess this claim against the backdrop of Ehrenreich's article. Does the persistence of poverty in the United States (even among working Americans) challenge the principle of democracy? Why or why not?

3. Poverty does not get a great deal of attention as a political issue in American public life. Why is this the case? Should poverty and inequality be a greater concern?

RACE, GENDER, AND CLASS IN U.S. POLITICS

The battle for the 2008 presidential nomination of the Democratic Party came down to Senators Hillary Rodham Clinton and Barack Obama. What is the significance of a white woman and an African American man seriously contending for the presidential nomination of a major American political party for the first time? Writing while the nomination was still contested, English professor Walter Benn Michaels provides a provocative response. Michaels, the author of a much-debated book The Trouble with Diversity: How We Learned to Love Identity and Ignore Inequality *(2006), argues that struggles for racial and sexual equality have made real progress. Yet paradoxically, this progress has been accompanied by greater, not lesser, social and economic inequality. The reason for this, Michaels contends, is that champions of diversity have for the most part accepted the premises of "neoliberal" capitalism, with the inequalities and exploitation it entails. Despite Obama's remark during the campaign about "bitter" workers, class was the great unmentionable in the Obama–Clinton campaigns, in Michaels' view. For him, "Clinton and Obama are the emblems of a liberalism which has made its peace with a political ethics that will combat racist and sexist inequalities, while almost ignoring inequalities that stem not from discrimination but from exploitation."*

There have been two defining moments related to race in the Obama campaign, and more generally in United States progressive politics. The first was in January on the night of the Illinois senator's victory in South Carolina when, in response to comments by Bill Clinton about the size of the black vote, the Obama crowd started chanting: "Race doesn't matter."

"There we stood," said the novelist and Obama activist Ayelet Waldman, "in the heart of the old South, where Confederate flags still fly next to statues of Governor Benjamin Tillman, who famously bragged about keeping black people from the polls ('We stuffed ballot boxes. We shot them. We are not ashamed of it'), chanting race doesn't matter, race doesn't matter. White

Source: Walter Benn Michaels, "Some Democrats Are More Equal Than Others," *Le Monde Diplomatique*, June 2008, English Edition. Web Location: http://mondediplo.com/2008/06/05equality/

people and black people. Latinos and Asians, united in our rejection of politics as usual. United in our belief that America can be a different place. United. Not divided."

The second moment was in March when, in response to the controversial sermons of his former pastor, the Rev. Jeremiah Wright, Obama gave his "more perfect union" speech, declaring: "Race is an issue this nation cannot afford to ignore right now" and inaugurating what many commentators described as a supposedly much-needed "national conversation on race."

I say supposedly because Americans love to talk about race and have been doing so for centuries, even if today the thing we love most to say is that "Americans don't like to talk about race." What we aren't so good at talking about is class, as Obama himself inadvertently demonstrated when he tried to talk about class on 6 April at a closed-door San Francisco fundraiser ("Bittergate"). He tried to explain the frustrations of some small-town Pennsylvanians: "It's not surprising that they get bitter, they cling to guns or religion or antipathy to people who aren't like them or anti-immigrant sentiment or anti-trade sentiment."

"Change We Can Believe In"

There seems to be an obvious contradiction here. First, the chant of race doesn't matter; then the speech about why race does matter. But after reflection the contradiction fades, since the need for the speech, the history of American racism, is what prompted the promise of the chant: the idea that electing a black man would be a major step toward overcoming that history. Which, of course, it would.

It is the promise of overcoming the long history of racial division, the promise of solving in the twenty-first century what W. E. B. Du Bois described as the overwhelming problem of the twentieth century, the problem of the color line, that gives the Obama campaign its significance. The "change we can believe in" is not ideological, it's cultural (Obama and Clinton are ideologically almost identical; if people had wanted ideological

change, we'd be talking about John Edwards). And at the heart of that cultural change is the fact that it cannot be proclaimed. It must be embodied, and only a black person can embody it. We can elect white people who say that race shouldn't matter, but only the election of a black person can establish that it really doesn't.

So the Obama campaign is and has always been all about race, and especially about anti-racism as progressive politics. Whether or not he ultimately wins, and especially if he doesn't, we are still being shown the "progressive" wing of the Democratic Party leading Americans toward an increasingly open and equal society, for African-Americans and also for Asians and Latinos and women and gays.

But the problem with this picture—a problem that is also a crucial part of its attraction—is that it is false. There has been extraordinary, albeit incomplete, progress in fighting racism, but the picture is false because that progress has not made American society more open or equal. In fundamental respects it is less open and equal today than it was in the days of Jim Crow when racism was not only prevalent but was state-sponsored.

The hallmark of a neo-liberal political economy is rising sensitivity about differences of identity—cultural, ethnic, sometimes religious—and rising tolerance for differences of wealth and income. Readers who are familiar with the jargon of economic inequality will have an immediate sense of what it means to say that equality in America has declined when I tell you that in 1947, at the height of Jim Crow and the segregationist laws in the South, the U.S. Gini coefficient was .376 and that by 2006, it had risen to .464. Since on the Gini scale 0 represents absolute equality (everyone makes the same income as everyone else) and 1 represents absolute inequality (one person makes everything), this is significant.

Back then, the U.S. was in the same league as the countries of western Europe, albeit a little more unequal than them; today we're up there with Mexico and China. In 1947, the top 20% of the U.S. population made 43% of all the money the nation earned. In 2006, after years of struggle against racism, sexism and heterosexism, the top 20% make 50.5%. The rich are richer.

LEGITIMATE THE ELITE

So the struggle for racial and sexual equality— the relative success of which has been incarnated in the race and gender politics of the Democratic Party over the past six months—has not produced greater economic equality, but been compatible with much greater economic inequality, and with the formation of an increasingly elitist society. There is a reason for this. The battles against racism and sexism have never been to produce a more equal society; or to mitigate, much less eliminate, the difference between the elite and the rest; they were meant to diversify and hence legitimate the elite.

This is why policies such as affirmative action in university admissions serve such a crucial symbolic purpose for liberals. They reassure them that no one has been excluded from places like Harvard and Yale for reasons of prejudice or discrimination (the legitimating part) while leaving untouched the primary mechanism of exclusion: wealth (the increasing-the-gap between the rich and everyone else part). You are, as Richard Kahlenberg put it, "25 times as likely to run into a rich student as a poor student" at 146 elite colleges, not because poor students are discriminated against but because they are poor. They have not had the kind of education that makes it plausible for them even to apply to elite colleges, much less attend them.

What affirmative action tells us is that the problem is racism and the solution is to make sure the rich kids come in different colours; this solution looks attractive long after graduation, when the battle for diversity continues to be fought among lawyers, professors and journalists—in fact, any profession with enough status and income to count as elite. The effort is to enforce a model of social justice in which proportional representation of race and gender counts as success.

If what you want is a more diverse elite, electing a black president is about as good as it gets. Electing a woman president would be a close second. But if you want to address the inequalities we have, instead of the inequalities we like to think we have (inequalities produced by inherited wealth and poverty); if you want a political program designed to address the inequalities produced not by racism and sexism, which are only sorting devices, but by neo-liberalism, which is doing the sorting, neither the black man nor the white woman have much to offer.

They are two Democrats who can't even bring themselves to acknowledge publicly, in their last debate in April, that Americans making between $100,000 and $200,000 a year hardly qualify as middle class. Clinton committed herself "to not raising a single tax on middle-class Americans, people making less than $250,000 a year" and Obama (who was, as a commentator put it, "a lot squishier" about it) also committed himself to not raising taxes on people making under $200,000.

ROOT OF INEQUALITY

But only 7% of U.S. households earn more than $150,000; only 18% earn more than $100,000; more than 50% earn under $50,000. Once you have Democrats who consider people on $200,000 as middle class and in need of tax relief, you don't need Republicans any more. Clinton and Obama are the emblems of a liberalism which has made its peace with a political ethics that will combat racist and sexist inequalities, while almost ignoring inequalities that stem not from discrimination but from exploitation. The candidates' death match prominently features charges of racism and sexism.

In 1967, after the passage of the Civil Rights Act of 1965 and at the beginning of the effort to make the rights guaranteed by that act a reality, Martin Luther King was already asking "where do we go from here?"

King was a great civil rights leader but he was more than that, and the questions he wanted to raise were not, as he pointed out, civil rights questions. They were, he told the Southern Christian Leadership Conference, "questions about the economic system, about a broader distribution of wealth."

There were then, as there are now, more poor white people than poor black people in the U.S. and King was acutely aware of that. He was aware that anti-racism was not a solution to economic inequality because racism was not the cause of economic inequality, and he realized that any challenge to the actual cause, "the capitalistic economy", would produce "fierce opposition."

King did not live to lead that challenge and the fierce opposition he expected never developed because the challenge never did. Instead, not only the anti-racism of the civil rights movement but also the rise of feminism, of gay rights and of all the new social movements proved to be entirely compatible with the capitalistic economy King hoped to oppose.

It is possible but unlikely that Barack Obama or Hillary Clinton might some day take up King's challenge. Neo-liberalism likes race and gender, and the race and gender candidates seem to like neo-liberalism.

DISCUSSION QUESTIONS

1. Michaels writes that "The battles against racism and sexism have never been to produce a more equal society; they were meant to diversify and hence legitimate the elite." What does he mean by this statement? In your view, is it too sweeping? How might anti-racism and anti-sexism activists respond?

2. How is it possible for racial and sexual inequality to narrow, while economic inequality widens? What would Michaels say?

35 *Naomi Oreskes and Erik Conway*

MERCHANTS OF DOUBT

> *Today, it is not particularly controversial to claim that tobacco consumption, especially cigarette smoking, is a large contributor to the incidence of lung cancer. Yet this claim was fought tooth and nail for decades by tobacco companies, who sought to undermine and raise doubts about the scientific basis of the finding. In this selection from their book* Merchants of Doubt, *Naomi Oreskes and Erik Conway refer to a "tobacco strategy" in which scientific evidence is targeted by companies who work with industry lawyers, public relations experts, and marginal scientists in order to create public doubt. They see climate change denial as involving very similar processes. They use the case of Ben Santer, a U.S. Department of Energy employee at the Lawrence Livermore National Laboratory who has long been alert to the human causes of global warming. Santer was subject to a deliberate campaign that sought to discredit his findings. His accusers were given generous space to make their case in the pages of the* Wall Street Journal. *Moreover, some of the same accusers against Santer had been active in earlier years in disputing the tobacco-cancer linkage. The "tobacco strategy" is dangerous, for it is "used to attack science and scientists, and to confuse us about major, important issues affecting our lives—and the planet we live on."*

Ben Santer is the kind of guy you could never imagine anyone attacking. He's thoroughly moderate—of moderate height and build, of moderate temperament, of moderate political persuasions. He is also very modest—soft-spoken, almost self-effacing—and from the small size and non-existent décor of his office at the Lawrence Livermore National Laboratory, you might think he was an accountant. If you met him in a room with a lot of other people, you might not even notice him.

But Santer is no accountant, and the world has noticed him.

He's one of the world's most distinguished scientists—the recipient of a 1998 MacArthur "genius" award and numerous prizes and distinctions from his employer—the U.S. Department of Energy—because he has done more than just about anyone to prove the human causes of global warming. Ever since his graduate work in the mid-1980s, he has been trying to understand

Source: Excerpted from *Merchants of Doubt: How a Handful of Scientists Obscured the Truth on Issues from Tobacco Smoke to Global Warming* by Erik Conway and Naomi Oreskes, © 2010, Bloomsbury Publishing Plc.

how the Earth's climate works, and whether we can say for sure that human activities are changing it. He has shown that the answer to that question is yes.

Santer is an atmospheric scientist at the Lawrence Livermore National Laboratory's Model Diagnosis and Intercomparison Project, an enormous international project to store the results of climate models from around the globe, distribute them to other researchers, and compare the models, both with real-world data and with each other. Over the past twenty years, he and his colleagues have shown that our planet is warming—and in just the way you would expect if green house gases were the cause.

Santer's work is called "fingerprinting"—because natural climate variation leaves different patterns and traces than warming caused by green house gases. Santer looks for these fingerprints. The most important one involves two parts of our atmosphere: the troposphere, the warm blanket closest to the Earth's surface, and the stratosphere, the thinner, colder part above it. Physics tells us that if the Sun were causing global warming—as some skeptics continue to insist—we'd expect both the troposphere and the stratosphere to warm, as heat comes into the atmosphere from outer space. But if the warming is caused by green house gases emitted at the surface and largely trapped in the lower atmosphere, then we expect the troposphere to warm, but the stratosphere to cool.

Santer and his colleagues have shown that the troposphere is warming and the stratosphere is cooling. In fact, because the boundary between these two atmospheric layers is in part defined by temperature, that boundary is now moving upward. In other words, the whole structure of our atmosphere is changing. These results are impossible to explain if the Sun were the culprit. It shows that the changes we are seeing in our climate are not natural.

The distinction between the troposphere and the stratosphere became part of the Supreme Court hearing in the case of *Massachusetts et al. v. the EPA*, in which twelve states sued the federal government for failing to regulate carbon dioxide as a pollutant under the Clean Air Act. Justice Antonin Scalia dissented, arguing that there was nothing in the law to require the EPA to act—but the honorable justice also got lost in the science, at one point referring to the stratosphere when he meant the troposphere. A lawyer for Massachusetts replied, "Respectfully, Your Honor. It is not the stratosphere. It's the troposphere." The justice answered, "Troposphere, whatever. I told you before I'm not a scientist. That's why I don't want to deal with global warming."

But we all have to deal with global warming, whether we like it or not, and some people have been resisting this conclusion for a long time. In fact, some people have been attacking not just the message, but the messenger. Ever since scientists first began to explain the evidence that our climate was warming—and that human activities were probably to blame—people have been questioning the data, doubting the evidence, and attacking the scientists who collect and explain it. And no one has been more brutally—or more unfairly—attacked than Ben Santer.

The Intergovernmental Panel on Climate Change (IPCC) is the world's leading authority on climate issues. Established in 1988 by the World Meteorological Organization and the United Nations Environment Program, it was created in response to early warnings about global warming. Scientists had known for a long time that increased green house gases from burning fossil fuels could cause climate change—they had explained this to Lyndon Johnson in 1965—but most thought that changes were far off in the future. It wasn't until the 1980s that scientists started to worry—to think that the future was perhaps almost here—and a few mavericks began to argue that anthropogenic climate change was actually already under way. So the IPCC was created to evaluate the evidence and consider what the impacts would be if the mavericks were right.

In 1995, the IPCC declared that the human impact on climate was now "discernible." This wasn't just a few individuals; by 1995 the IPCC had grown to include several hundred climate scientists from around the world. But how did they know that changes were under way, and how did they know they were caused by us? Those crucial questions were answered in *Climate Change 1995: The Science of Climate Change*, the Second Assessment Report issued by the IPCC. Chapter 8 of this report, "Detection of Climate Change and Attribution of Causes," summarized the evidence that global warming really was caused by green house gases. Its author was Ben Santer.

Santer had impeccable scientific credentials, and he had never before been involved in even the suggestion of impropriety of any kind, but now group of physicists tied to a think tank in Washington, D.C., accused him of doctoring the report to make the science seem firmer than it really was. They wrote reports accusing him of "scientific cleansing"—expunging the views of those who did not agree. They wrote reports with titles like "Green-house Debate Continued" and "Doctoring the Documents," published in places like *Energy Daily* and *Investor's Business Daily*. They wrote letters to congressmen, to officials in the Department of Energy, and to the editors of scientific journals, spreading the accusations high and wide. They pressured contacts in the Energy Department to get Santer fired from his job. Most public—and most publicized—was an op-ed piece published in the *Wall Street Journal*, accusing Santer of making the alleged changes to "deceive policy makers and the public." Santer had made changes to the report, but not to deceive anyone. The changes were made in response to review comments from fellow scientists.

Every scientific paper and report has to go through the critical scrutiny of other experts: peer review. Scientific authors are required to take reviewers' comments and criticisms seriously, and to fix any mistakes that may have been found. It's a foundational ethic of scientific work: no claim can be considered valid—not even potentially valid—until it has passed peer review.

Peer review is also used to help authors make their arguments clearer, and the IPCC has an exceptionally extensive and inclusive peer review process. It involves both scientific experts and representatives of the governments of the participating nations to ensure not only that factual errors are caught and corrected, but as well that all judgments and interpretations are adequately documented and supported, and that all interested parties have a chance to be heard. Authors are required either to make changes in response to the review comments, or to explain why those comments are irrelevant, invalid, or just plain wrong. Santer had done just that. He had made changes in response to peer review. He had done what the IPCC rules required him to do. He had done what science requires him to do. Santer was being attacked for being a good scientist.

Santer tried to defend himself in a letter to the editor of the *Wall Street Journal*—a letter that was signed by twenty-nine co-authors, distinguished scientists all, including the director of the U.S. Global Change Research Program. The American Meteorological Society penned an open letter toaster affirming that the attacks were entirely without merit. Bert Bolin, the founder and chairman of the IPCC, corroborated Santer's account in a letter of his own to the *Journal*, pointing out that accusations were flying without a shred of evidence, and that the accusers had not contacted him, nor any IPCC officers, nor any of the scientists involved to check their facts. Had they "simply taken the time to familiarize [themselves] with IPCC rules of procedure," he noted, they would have readily found out that no rules were violated, no procedures were transgressed, and nothing wrong had happened. As later commentators have pointed out, no IPCC member nation ever seconded the complaint.

But the *Journal* only published a portion of both Santer and Bolin's letters, and two weeks later, they gave the accusers yet another opportunity to sling mud, publishing a letter declaring that the IPCC report had been "tampered with for political purposes." The mud stuck, and the charges were widely echoed by industry groups, business-oriented newspapers and magazines, and think tanks. They remain on the Internet today. If you Google "Santer IPCC," you get not the chapter in question—much less the whole IPCC report—but instead a variety of sites that repeat the 1995 accusations. One site even asserts (falsely) that Santer admitted that he had "adjusted the data to make it fit with political policy," as if the U.S. government even had a climate policy to adjust the data to fit. (We didn't in 1995, and we still don't.)

The experience was bitter for Santer, who spent enormous amounts of time and energy defending his scientific reputation and integrity, as well as trying to hold his marriage together through it all. (He didn't.) Today, this normally mild-mannered man turns white with rage when he recalls these events. Because no scientist starts his or her career expecting things like this to happen.

Why didn't Santer's accusers bother to find out the facts? Why did they continue to repeat charges long after they had been shown to be unfounded? The answer, of course, is that they were not interested in finding facts. They were interested in fighting them.

A few years later, Santer was reading the morning paper and came across an article describing how some scientists had participated in a program, organized by the tobacco industry, to discredit scientific evidence linking tobacco to cancer. The idea, the article explained, was to "keep the controversy alive." So long as there was doubt about the causal link, the tobacco industry would be safe from litigation and regulation. Santer thought the story seemed eerily familiar.

He was right. But there was more. Not only were the tactics the same, the people were the same, too. The leaders of the attack on him were two retired physicists, both named Fred: Frederick Seitz and S. (Siegfried) Fred Singer. Seitz was a solid-state physicist who had risen to prominence during World War II, when he helped to build the atomic bomb; later he became president of the U.S. National Academy of Sciences. Singer was a physicist—in fact, the proverbial rocket

scientist—who became a leading figure in the development of Earth observation satellites, serving as the first director of the National Weather Satellite Service and later as chief scientist at the Department of Transportation in the Reagan administration.

Both were extremely hawkish, having believed passionately in the gravity of the Soviet threat and the need to defend the United States from it with high-tech weaponry. Both were associated with a conservative think tank in Washington, D.C., the George C. Marshall Institute, founded to defend Ronald Reagan's Strategic Defense Initiative (SDI or "Star Wars"). And both had previously worked for the tobacco industry, helping to cast doubt on the scientific evidence linking smoking to death.

From 1979 to 1985, Fred Seitz directed a program for R. J. Reynolds Tobacco Company that distributed $45 million to scientists around the country for biomedical research that could generate evidence and cultivate experts to be used in court to defend the "product." In the mid-1990s, Fred Singer coauthored a major report attacking the U.S. Environmental Protection Agency over the health risks of secondhand smoke. Several years earlier, the U.S. surgeon general had declared that secondhand smoke was hazardous not only to smokers' health, but to anyone exposed to it. Singer attacked this finding, claiming the work was rigged, and that the EPA review of the science—done by leading experts from around the country—was distorted by a political agenda to expand government control over all aspects of our lives. Singer's anti-EPA report was funded by a grant from the Tobacco Institute, channeled through a think tank, the Alexis de Tocqueville Institution.

Millions of pages of documents released during tobacco litigation demonstrate these links. They show the crucial role that scientists played in sowing doubt about the links between smoking and health risks. These documents—which have scarcely been studied except by lawyers and a handful of academics—also show that the same strategy was applied not only to global warming, but to a laundry list of environmental and health concerns, including asbestos, secondhand smoke, acid rain, and the ozone hole.

Call it the "Tobacco Strategy." Its target was science, and so it relied heavily on scientists—with guidance from industry lawyers and public relations experts—willing to hold the rifle and pull the trigger. Among the multitude of documents we found in writing this book were *Bad Science: A Resource Book*—a how-to handbook for fact fighters, providing example after example of successful strategies for undermining science, and a list of experts with scientific credentials available to comment on any issue about which a think tank or corporation needed a negative sound bite.

In case after case, Fred Singer, Fred Seitz, and a handful of other scientists joined forces with think tanks and private corporations to challenge scientific evidence on a host of contemporary issues. In the early years, much of the money for this effort came from the tobacco industry; in later years, it came from foundations, think tanks, and the fossil fuel industry. They claimed the link between smoking and cancer remained unproven. They insisted that scientists were mistaken about the risks and limitations of SDI. They argued that acid rain was caused by volcanoes, and so was the ozone hole. They charged that the Environmental Protection Agency had rigged the science surrounding secondhand smoke. Most recently—over the course of nearly two decades and against the face of mounting evidence—they dismissed the reality of global warming. First they claimed there was none, then they claimed it was just natural variation, and then they claimed that even if it was happening and it was our fault, it didn't matter because we could just adapt to it. In case after case, they steadfastly denied the existence of scientific agreement, even though they, themselves, were pretty much the only ones who disagreed.

A handful of men would have had no impact if no one paid any attention, but people did pay attention. By virtue of their earlier work in the Cold War weapons programs, these men were well-known and highly respected in Washington, D.C., and had access to power all the way to the White House. In 1989, to give just one example, Seitz and two other players in our story, physicists Robert Jastrow and William Nierenberg, wrote a report questioning the evidence of global warming. They were soon invited to the White House to brief the Bush administration. One member of the Cabinet Affairs Office said of the report: "Everyone has read it. Everyone takes it seriously."

It wasn't just the Bush administration that took these claims seriously; the mass media did, too. Respected media outlets such as the *New York Times*, the *Washington Post*, *Newsweek*, and many others repeated these claims as if they were a "side" in a scientific debate. Then the claims were repeated again and again and again—as in an echo chamber—by a wide range of people involved in public debate, from bloggers to members of the U.S. Senate, and even by the president and the vice president of the United States. In all of this, journalists and the public never understood that these were not scientific debates—taking place in the halls of science among active scientific researchers—but misinformation, part of a larger pattern that began with tobacco.

This book tells the story of the Tobacco Strategy, and how it was used to attack science and scientists, and to confuse us about major, important issues affecting our lives—and the planet we live on. Sadly, Ben Santer's story is not unique. When scientific evidence mounted on the depletion of stratospheric ozone, Fred Singer challenged Sherwood Rowland—the Nobel laureate and president of the American Association for the Advancement of Science who first realized that certain chemicals (CFCs) could destroy stratospheric ozone. When a graduate student named Justin Lancaster tried to set the record straight on [scientist] Roger Revelle's views in the face of the claim that Revelle had changed his mind about global warming, he became the defendant in a libel lawsuit. (Lacking funds to defend himself, Lancaster was forced to settle out of court, leaving both his personal and professional life in tatters.)

Fred Seitz and Fred Singer, both physicists, were the most prominent and persistent scientists involved in these campaigns. William Nierenberg and Robert Jastrow were physicists, too. Nierenberg was a one-time director of the distinguished Scripps Institution of Oceanography and member of Ronald Reagan's transition team, helping to suggest scientists to serve in important positions in the administration. Like Seitz, he had helped to build the atomic bomb, and later was associated with several Cold War weapons programs and laboratories. Jastrow was a prominent astrophysicist, successful popular author, and director of the Goddard Institute for Space Studies, who had long been involved with the U.S. space program. These men had no particular expertise in environmental or health questions, but they did have power and influence.

Seitz, Singer, Nierenberg, and Jastrow had all served in high levels of science administration, where they had come to know admirals and generals, congressmen and senators, even presidents. They had also dealt extensively with the media, so they knew how to get press coverage for their views, and how to pressure the media when they didn't. They used their scientific credentials to present themselves as authorities, and they used their authority to try to discredit any science they didn't like.

Over the course of more than twenty years, these men did almost no original scientific research on any of the issues on which they weighed in. Once they had been prominent researchers, but by the time they turned to the topics of our story, they were mostly attacking the work and the reputations of others. In fact, on every issue, they were on the wrong side of the scientific consensus. Smoking does kill—both directly and indirectly. Pollution does cause acid rain. Volcanoes are not the cause of the ozone hole. Our seas are rising and our glaciers are melting because of the mounting effects of green house gases in the atmosphere, produced by burning fossil fuels. Yet, for years the press quoted these men as experts, and politicians listened to them, using their claims as justification for inaction. President George H. W. Bush once even referred to them as "my scientists." Although the situation is now a bit better, their views and arguments continue to be cited on the Internet, on talk radio, and even by members of the U.S. Congress.

Why would scientists dedicated to uncovering the truth about the natural world deliberately misrepresent the work of their own colleagues? Why would they spread accusations with no basis? Why would they refuse to correct their arguments once they had been shown to be incorrect? And why did the press continue to quote them, year after year, even as their claims were shown, one after another, to be false? This is the story we are about to tell. It is a story about a group of scientists who fought the scientific evidence and spread confusion on many of the most important issues of our time. It is a story about a pattern that continues today. A story about fighting facts, and merchandising doubt.

DISCUSSION QUESTIONS

1. Oreskes and Conway write about "merchants of doubt." What are the roles of business interests in creating doubt about scientific findings?
2. In what ways is merchandising doubt an effective political strategy? Are there ways to improve the scientific literacy of the public? Would a more scientifically literate public make any difference?

36 *Noam Chomsky*

9/11 AND THE IMPERIAL MENTALITY

The year 2011 witnessed the tenth anniversary of the 9/11 attacks on the United States as well as the assassination of their apparent planner, Osama bin Laden, by American special forces in Pakistan. In this selection, Noam Chomsky challenges dominant understandings of the meaning of 9/11 by holding the United States to the same moral and legal standards it professes to apply to others. For Chomsky, the 9/11 attacks were "horrendous atrocities" that have rightly been called a "crime against humanity." But in assessing their aftermath, Chomsky reminds us of inconvenient facts that are often dismissed as of no importance for thinking about terrorism and the role of the United States today. For example, he points to the "first 9/11"—the overthrow of the democratic government in Chile on September 11, 1973—a coup in which the United States was deeply implicated and whose consequences were at least as inhumane as the 2001 attacks inside America. The 2003 attack on Iraq was defended as a logical and necessary step in the war on terrorism by the Bush administration. From the standpoint of international law, as it was defended by the United States in the Nuremberg trials, the Iraq war was a crime of aggression. But such accurate descriptions are muted in official discourse about American foreign policy, which at most acknowledges "mistakes" and "blunders." For Chomsky, looking at ourselves clearly must involve rejecting an "imperial mentality" that leads to an American "exceptionalism," sanctioning actions by our country that we would condemn if done by others.

We are approaching the 10th anniversary of the horrendous atrocities of September 11, 2001, which, it is commonly held, changed the world. On May 1st, the presumed mastermind of the crime, Osama bin Laden, was assassinated in Pakistan by a team of elite US commandos, Navy SEALs, after he was captured, unarmed and undefended, in Operation Geronimo.

A number of analysts have observed that although bin Laden was finally killed, he won some major successes in his war against the U.S. "He repeatedly asserted that the only way to drive the U.S. from the Muslim world and defeat its satraps was by drawing Americans into a series of small but expensive wars that would ultimately bankrupt them," Eric Margolis writes. " 'Bleeding the U.S.,'

Source: Noam Chomsky, "Was There an Alternative?: Looking Back on 9/11 a Decade Later" adapted from *9-11: Was There an Alternative?*, an Open Media Book. Copyright © 2001, 2002, 2011 by Noam Chomsky. Reprinted with permission of The Permissions Company, Inc., on behalf of Seven Stories Press, www.sevenstories.com.

in his words. The United States, first under George W. Bush and then Barack Obama, rushed right into bin Laden's trap . . . Grotesquely overblown military outlays and debt addiction . . . may be the most pernicious legacy of the man who thought he could defeat the United States"—particularly when the debt is being cynically exploited by the far right, with the collusion of the Democrat establishment, to undermine what remains of social programs, public education, unions, and, in general, remaining barriers to corporate tyranny.

That Washington was bent on fulfilling bin Laden's fervent wishes was evident at once. As discussed in my book *9-11*, written shortly after those attacks occurred, anyone with knowledge of the region could recognize "that a massive assault on a Muslim population would be the answer to the prayers of bin Laden and his associates, and would lead the U.S. and its allies into a 'diabolical trap,' as the French foreign minister put it."

The senior CIA analyst responsible for tracking Osama bin Laden from 1996, Michael Scheuer, wrote shortly after that "bin Laden has been precise in telling America the reasons he is waging war on us. [He] is out to drastically alter U.S. and Western policies toward the Islamic world," and largely succeeded: "U.S. forces and policies are completing the radicalization of the Islamic world, something Osama bin Laden has been trying to do with substantial but incomplete success since the early 1990s. As a result, I think it is fair to conclude that the United States of America remains bin Laden's only indispensable ally." And arguably remains so, even after his death.

THE FIRST 9/11

Was there an alternative? There is every likelihood that the Jihadi movement, much of it highly critical of bin Laden, could have been split and undermined after 9/11. The "crime against humanity," as it was rightly called, could have been approached as a crime, with an international operation to apprehend the likely suspects. That was recognized at the time, but no such idea was even considered.

In *9-11*, I quoted Robert Fisk's conclusion that the "horrendous crime" of 9/11 was committed with "wickedness and awesome cruelty," an accurate judgment. It is useful to bear in mind that the crimes could have been even worse. Suppose, for example, that the attack had gone as far as bombing the White House, killing the president, imposing a brutal military dictatorship that killed thousands and tortured tens of thousands while establishing an international terror center that helped impose similar torture-and-terror states elsewhere and carried out an international assassination campaign; and as an extra fillip, brought in a team of economists—call them "the Kandahar boys"—who quickly drove the economy into one of the worst depressions in its history. That, plainly, would have been a lot worse than 9/11.

Unfortunately, it is not a thought experiment. It happened. The only inaccuracy in this brief account is that the numbers should be multiplied by 25 to yield per capita equivalents, the appropriate measure. I am, of course, referring to what in Latin America is often called "the first 9/11": September 11, 1973, when the U.S. succeeded in its intensive efforts to overthrow the democratic government of Salvador Allende in Chile with a military coup that placed General Pinochet's brutal regime in office. The goal, in the words of the Nixon administration, was to kill the "virus" that might encourage all those "foreigners [who] are out to screw us" to take over their own resources and in other ways to pursue an intolerable policy of independent development. In the background was the conclusion of the National Security Council that, if the U.S. could not control Latin America, it could not expect "to achieve a successful order elsewhere in the world."

The first 9/11, unlike the second, did not change the world. It was "nothing of very great consequence," as Henry Kissinger assured his boss a few days later.

These events of little consequence were not limited to the military coup that destroyed Chilean democracy and set in motion the horror story that followed. The first 9/11 was just one act in a drama which began in 1962, when John F. Kennedy shifted the mission of the Latin American military from "hemispheric defense"—an anachronistic holdover from World War II—to "internal security," a concept with a chilling interpretation in U.S.-dominated Latin American circles.

In the recently published Cambridge University *History of the Cold War*, Latin American scholar John Coatsworth writes that from that time to "the Soviet collapse in 1990, the numbers of political prisoners, torture victims, and executions of non-violent political dissenters in Latin America vastly exceeded those in the Soviet Union and its East European satellites," including many religious martyrs and mass slaughter as well, always supported or initiated in Washington. The last major violent act was the brutal murder of six leading Latin American intellectuals, Jesuit priests, a few days after the Berlin Wall fell. The perpetrators were an elite Salvadorean battalion, which had already left a shocking trail of blood, fresh from renewed training at the JFK School of Special Warfare, acting on direct orders of the high command of the U.S. client state.

The consequences of this hemispheric plague still, of course, reverberate.

FROM KIDNAPPING AND TORTURE TO ASSASSINATION

All of this, and much more like it, is dismissed as of little consequence, and forgotten. Those whose mission is to rule the world enjoy a more comforting picture, articulated well enough in the current issue of the prestigious (and valuable) journal of the Royal Institute of International Affairs in London. The lead article discusses "the visionary international order" of the "second half of the twentieth century" marked by "the universalization of an American vision of commercial prosperity." There is something to that account, but it does not quite convey the perception of those at the wrong end of the guns.

The same is true of the assassination of Osama bin Laden, which brings to an end at least a phase in the "war on terror" re-declared by President George W. Bush on the second 9/11. Let us turn to a few thoughts on that event and its significance.

On May 1, 2011, Osama bin Laden was killed in his virtually unprotected compound by a raiding mission of 79 Navy SEALs, who entered Pakistan by helicopter. After many lurid stories were provided by the government and withdrawn,

official reports made it increasingly clear that the operation was a planned assassination, multiply violating elementary norms of international law, beginning with the invasion itself.

There appears to have been no attempt to apprehend the unarmed victim, as presumably could have been done by 79 commandos facing no opposition—except, they report, from his wife, also unarmed, whom they shot in self-defense when she "lunged" at them, according to the White House.

A plausible reconstruction of the events is provided by veteran Middle East correspondent Yochi Dreazen and colleagues in the *Atlantic*. Dreazen, formerly the military correspondent for the *Wall Street Journal*, is senior correspondent for the National Journal Group covering military affairs and national security. According to their investigation, White House planning appears not to have considered the option of capturing bin Laden alive: "The administration had made clear to the military's clandestine Joint Special Operations Command that it wanted bin Laden dead, according to a senior U.S. official with knowledge of the discussions. A high-ranking military officer briefed on the assault said the SEALs knew their mission was not to take him alive."

The authors add: "For many at the Pentagon and the Central Intelligence Agency who had spent nearly a decade hunting bin Laden, killing the militant was a necessary and justified act of vengeance." Furthermore, "capturing bin Laden alive would have also presented the administration with an array of nettlesome legal and political challenges." Better, then, to assassinate him, dumping his body into the sea without the autopsy considered essential after a killing—an act that predictably provoked both anger and skepticism in much of the Muslim world.

As the *Atlantic* inquiry observes, "The decision to kill bin Laden outright was the clearest illustration to date of a little-noticed aspect of the Obama administration's counterterror policy. The Bush administration captured thousands of suspected militants and sent them to detention camps in Afghanistan, Iraq, and Guantanamo Bay. The Obama administration, by contrast, has focused on eliminating individual terrorists rather than attempting to take them alive." That is one significant difference between Bush and Obama. The authors quote former West German Chancellor Helmut Schmidt, who "told German TV that the U.S. raid was 'quite clearly a violation of international law' and that bin Laden should have been detained and put on trial," contrasting Schmidt with U.S. Attorney General Eric Holder, who "defended the decision to kill bin Laden although he didn't pose an immediate threat to the Navy SEALs, telling a House panel . . . that the assault had been 'lawful, legitimate and appropriate in every way.' "

The disposal of the body without autopsy was also criticized by allies. The highly regarded British barrister Geoffrey Robertson, who supported the intervention and opposed the execution largely on pragmatic grounds, nevertheless described Obama's claim that "justice was done" as an "absurdity" that should have been obvious to a former professor of constitutional law. Pakistan law "requires a colonial inquest on violent death, and international human rights law insists that the 'right to life' mandates an inquiry whenever violent death occurs from government or police action. The U.S. is therefore under a duty to hold an inquiry that will satisfy the world as to the true circumstances of this killing."

Robertson usefully reminds us that "[i]t was not always thus. When the time came to consider the fate of men much more steeped in wickedness than Osama bin Laden—the Nazi leadership—the British government wanted them hanged within six hours of capture. President Truman demurred, citing the conclusion of Justice Robert Jackson that summary execution 'would not sit easily on the American conscience or be remembered by our children with pride . . . the only course is to determine the innocence or guilt of the accused after a hearing as dispassionate as the times will permit and upon a record that will leave our reasons and motives clear.' "

Eric Margolis comments that "Washington has never made public the evidence of its claim that Osama bin Laden was behind the 9/11 attacks," presumably one reason why "polls show that fully a third of American respondents believe that the U.S. government and/or Israel were behind 9/11," while in the Muslim world

skepticism is much higher. "An open trial in the U.S. or at the Hague would have exposed these claims to the light of day," he continues, a practical reason why Washington should have followed the law.

In societies that profess some respect for law, suspects are apprehended and brought to fair trial. I stress "suspects." In June 2002, FBI head Robert Mueller, in what the *Washington Post* described as "among his most detailed public comments on the origins of the attacks," could say only that "investigators believe the idea of the Sept. 11 attacks on the World Trade Center and Pentagon came from al Qaeda leaders in Afghanistan, the actual plotting was done in Germany, and the financing came through the United Arab Emirates from sources in Afghanistan."

What the FBI believed and thought in June 2002 they didn't know eight months earlier, when Washington dismissed tentative offers by the Taliban (how serious, we do not know) to permit a trial of bin Laden if they were presented with evidence. Thus, it is not true, as President Obama claimed in his White House statement after bin Laden's death, that "[w]e quickly learned that the 9/11 attacks were carried out by al-Qaeda."

There has never been any reason to doubt what the FBI believed in mid-2002, but that leaves us far from the proof of guilt required in civilized societies—and whatever the evidence might be, it does not warrant murdering a suspect who could, it seems, have been easily apprehended and brought to trial. Much the same is true of evidence provided since. Thus, the 9/11 Commission provided extensive circumstantial evidence of bin Laden's role in 9/11, based primarily on what it had been told about confessions by prisoners in Guantanamo. It is doubtful that much of that would hold up in an independent court, considering the ways confessions were elicited. But in any event, the conclusions of a congressionally authorized investigation, however convincing one finds them, plainly fall short of a sentence by a credible court, which is what shifts the category of the accused from suspect to convicted.

There is much talk of bin Laden's "confession," but that was a boast, not a confession, with as much credibility as my "confession" that

I won the Boston marathon. The boast tells us a lot about his character, but nothing about his responsibility for what he regarded as a great achievement, for which he wanted to take credit.

Again, all of this is, transparently, quite independent of one's judgments about his responsibility, which seemed clear immediately, even before the FBI inquiry, and still does.

CRIMES OF AGGRESSION

It is worth adding that bin Laden's responsibility was recognized in much of the Muslim world, and condemned. One significant example is the distinguished Lebanese cleric Sheikh Fadlallah, greatly respected by Hizbollah and Shia groups generally, outside Lebanon as well. He had some experience with assassinations. He had been targeted for assassination: by a truck bomb outside a mosque, in a CIA-organized operation in 1985. He escaped, but 80 others were killed, mostly women and girls as they left the mosque—one of those innumerable crimes that do not enter the annals of terror because of the fallacy of "wrong agency." Sheikh Fadlallah sharply condemned the 9/11 attacks.

One of the leading specialists on the Jihadi movement, Fawaz Gerges, suggests that the movement might have been split at that time had the U.S. exploited the opportunity instead of mobilizing the movement, particularly by the attack on Iraq, a great boon to bin Laden, which led to a sharp increase in terror, as intelligence agencies had anticipated. At the Chilcot hearings investigating the background to the invasion of Iraq, for example, the former head of Britain's domestic intelligence agency MI5 testified that both British and U.S. intelligence were aware that Saddam posed no serious threat, that the invasion was likely to increase terror, and that the invasions of Iraq and Afghanistan had radicalized parts of a generation of Muslims who saw the military actions as an "attack on Islam." As is often the case, security was not a high priority for state action.

It might be instructive to ask ourselves how we would be reacting if Iraqi commandos had landed at George W. Bush's compound, assassinated him, and dumped his body in the Atlantic

(after proper burial rites, of course). Uncontroversially, he was not a "suspect" but the "decider" who gave the orders to invade Iraq—that is, to commit the "supreme international crime differing only from other war crimes in that it contains within itself the accumulated evil of the whole" for which Nazi criminals were hanged: the hundreds of thousands of deaths, millions of refugees, destruction of much of the country and its national heritage, and the murderous sectarian conflict that has now spread to the rest of the region. Equally uncontroversially, these crimes vastly exceed anything attributed to bin Laden.

To say that all of this is uncontroversial, as it is, is not to imply that it is not denied. The existence of flat earthers does not change the fact that, uncontroversially, the earth is not flat. Similarly, it is uncontroversial that Stalin and Hitler were responsible for horrendous crimes, though loyalists deny it. All of this should, again, be too obvious for comment, and would be, except in an atmosphere of hysteria so extreme that it blocks rational thought.

Similarly, it is uncontroversial that Bush and associates did commit the "supreme international crime"—the crime of aggression. That crime was defined clearly enough by Justice Robert Jackson, Chief of Counsel for the United States at Nuremberg. An "aggressor," Jackson proposed to the Tribunal in his opening statement, is a state that is the first to commit such actions as "[i]nvasion of its armed forces, with or without a declaration of war, of the territory of another State. . . ." No one, even the most extreme supporter of the aggression, denies that Bush and associates did just that.

We might also do well to recall Jackson's eloquent words at Nuremberg on the principle of universality: "If certain acts in violation of treaties are crimes, they are crimes whether the United States does them or whether Germany does them, and we are not prepared to lay down a rule of criminal conduct against others which we would not be willing to have invoked against us."

It is also clear that announced intentions are irrelevant, even if they are truly believed. Internal records reveal that Japanese fascists apparently did believe that, by ravaging China, they were laboring to turn it into an "earthly paradise." And although it may be difficult to imagine, it is conceivable that Bush and company believed they were protecting the world from destruction by Saddam's nuclear weapons. All irrelevant, though ardent loyalists on all sides may try to convince themselves otherwise.

We are left with two choices: either Bush and associates are guilty of the "supreme international crime" including all the evils that follow, or else we declare that the Nuremberg proceedings were a farce and the allies were guilty of judicial murder.

THE IMPERIAL MENTALITY AND 9/11

A few days before the bin Laden assassination, Orlando Bosch died peacefully in Florida, where he resided along with his accomplice Luis Posada Carriles and many other associates in international terrorism. After he was accused of dozens of terrorist crimes by the FBI, Bosch was granted a presidential pardon by Bush I over the objections of the Justice Department, which found the conclusion "inescapable that it would be prejudicial to the public interest for the United States to provide a safe haven for Bosch." The coincidence of these deaths at once calls to mind the Bush II doctrine—"already . . . a de facto rule of international relations," according to the noted Harvard international relations specialist Graham Allison—which revokes "the sovereignty of states that provide sanctuary to terrorists."

Allison refers to the pronouncement of Bush II, directed at the Taliban, that "those who harbor terrorists are as guilty as the terrorists themselves." Such states, therefore, have lost their sovereignty and are fit targets for bombing and terror—for example, the state that harbored Bosch and his associate. When Bush issued this new "de facto rule of international relations," no one seemed to notice that he was calling for

invasion and destruction of the U.S. and the murder of its criminal presidents.

None of this is problematic, of course, if we reject Justice Jackson's principle of universality, and adopt instead the principle that the U.S. is self-immunized against international law and conventions—as, in fact, the government has frequently made very clear.

It is also worth thinking about the name given to the bin Laden operation: Operation Geronimo. The imperial mentality is so profound that few seem able to perceive that the White House is glorifying bin Laden by calling him "Geronimo"—the Apache Indian chief who led the courageous resistance to the invaders of Apache lands.

The casual choice of the name is reminiscent of the ease with which we name our murder weapons after victims of our crimes: Apache, Blackhawk. . . We might react differently if the Luftwaffe had called its fighter planes "Jew" and "Gypsy."

The examples mentioned would fall under the category of "American exceptionalism," were it not for the fact that easy suppression of one's own crimes is virtually ubiquitous among powerful states, at least those that are not defeated and forced to acknowledge reality.

Perhaps the assassination was perceived by the administration as an "act of vengeance," as Robertson concludes. And perhaps the rejection of the legal option of a trial reflects a difference between the moral culture of 1945 and today, as he suggests. Whatever the motive was, it could hardly have been security. As in the case of the "supreme international crime" in Iraq, the bin Laden assassination is another illustration of the important fact that security is often not a high priority for state action, contrary to received doctrine.

DISCUSSION QUESTIONS

1. Chomsky refers to an "imperial mentality" within the United States. In what ways does this mentality serve as a set of blinders that distort the political realities of the world in which we live?
2. In the last section of his article, Chomsky refers to Orlando Bosch. Who was Bosch and how does his fate speak to the American understanding of the threat of "terrorism"?

CHAPTER 10

Visions of a New Democracy

Your actions, and inactions, have an impact on the world. The status quo, the political norm, is either challenged or left unchallenged by what you do with your life. In this way no one, not even the most ardent hater of things "political," is politically neutral.

Though in different ways, the readings in this final chapter all have at their core a belief that you can and should be politically involved in the United States through careful reflection and sustained action. Citizenship demands that we attempt to "do the right thing," even in the face of a political culture that too often seems mired in lethargy and disengagement. Obviously unanimity does not exist on what constitutes the "right thing." Political and economic elites may say that political participation is a good thing, for example, while actually being suspicious of the impact of citizen involvement on societal stability. And, of course, ordinary citizens themselves disagree on many issues. The point is that there is a place for *you* in debating, and perhaps changing, the priorities of the nation you live in. Discussion and debate over the ends of public life, the give-and-take, is what politics is all about.

37 *Martin Luther King, Jr.*

LETTER FROM BIRMINGHAM JAIL

"Letter from Birmingham Jail" is a classic statement of the civil rights movement. Written on scraps of paper found in his jail cell, this 1963 essay by the Reverend Dr. Martin Luther King, Jr., crystallizes many of the themes that served as catalysts to the movement for racial equality he helped lead. The letter was written in response to a statement issued by eight white Alabama clergymen who criticized King and other demonstrators for causing violence with their protests against segregation. King's searing moral response in support of nonviolent civil disobedience makes a powerful and impassioned call for democracy and human freedom. Among the many compelling points he makes, King criticizes political moderates— in this case the "white moderate" who, in King's words, "is more devoted to 'order' than to justice." To people who follow the doctrinaire belief that the truth always lies in the middle, his position may be surprising. He suggests that we should question the wisdom of assuming that gradual change and piecemeal reforms are the best way to approach a problem.

April 16, 1963

My Dear Fellow Clergymen:

While confined here in the Birmingham city jail, I came across your recent statement calling my present activities "unwise and untimely." Seldom do I pause to answer criticism of my work and ideas. If I sought to answer all the criticisms that cross my desk, my secretaries would have little time for anything other than such correspondence in the course of the day, and I would have no time for constructive work. But since I feel that you are men of genuine good will and that your criticisms are sincerely set forth, I want to try to answer your statement in what I hope will be patient and reasonable terms.

I think I should indicate why I am here in Birmingham, since you have been influenced by the view which argues against "outsiders coming in." I have the honor of serving as president of the Southern Christian Leadership Conference, an organization operating in every southern state, with headquarters in Atlanta, Georgia. We have some eighty-five affiliated organizations across the South, and one of them is the Alabama Christian Movement for Human Rights. Frequently we share staff, educational and financial resources

Source: Reprinted by arrangement with The Heirs to the Estate of Martin Luther King Jr., c/o Writers House as agent for the proprietor, New York, NY. Copyright © 1963 Dr. Martin Luther King Jr.; copyright renewed © 1991 Coretta Scott King.

with our affiliates. Several months ago the affiliate here in Birmingham asked us to be on call to engage in a nonviolent direct-action program if such were deemed necessary. We readily consented, and when the hour came we lived up to our promise. So I, along with several members of my staff, am here because I was invited here. I am here because I have organizational ties here.

But more basically, I am in Birmingham because injustice is here. Just as the prophets of the eighth century B.C. left their villages and carried their "thus saith the Lord" far beyond the boundaries of their home towns, and just as the Apostle Paul left his village of Tarsus and carried the gospel of Jesus Christ to the far corners of the Greco-Roman world, so am I compelled to carry the gospel of freedom beyond my own home town. Like Paul, I must constantly respond to the Macedonian call for aid.

Moreover, I am cognizant of the interrelatedness of all communities and states. I cannot sit idly by in Atlanta and not be concerned about what happens in Birmingham. Injustice anywhere is a threat to justice everywhere. We are caught in an inescapable network of mutuality, tied in a single garment of destiny. Whatever affects one directly, affects all indirectly. Never again can we afford to live with the narrow, provincial "outside agitator" idea. Anyone who lives inside the United States can never be considered an outsider anywhere within its bounds.

You deplore the demonstrations taking place in Birmingham. But your statement, I am sorry to say, fails to express a similar concern for the conditions that brought about the demonstrations. I am sure that none of you would want to rest content with the superficial kind of social analysis that deals merely with effects and does not grapple with underlying causes. It is unfortunate that demonstrations are taking place in Birmingham, but it is even more unfortunate that the city's white power structure left the Negro community with no alternative.

In any nonviolent campaign there are four basic steps: collection of the facts to determine whether injustices exist; negotiation; self-purification; and direct action. We have gone through all these steps in Birmingham. There can be no gain saying the fact that racial injustice engulfs this community. Birmingham is probably the most thoroughly segregated city in the United States. Its ugly record of brutality is widely known. Negroes have experienced grossly unjust treatment in the courts. There have been more unsolved bombings of Negro homes and churches in Birmingham than in any other city in the nation. These are the hard, brutal facts of the case. On the basis of these conditions, Negro leaders sought to negotiate with the city fathers. But the latter consistently refused to engage in good-faith negotiation. . . .

You may well ask: "Why direct action? Why sit-ins, marches and so forth? Isn't negotiation a better path?" You are quite right in calling for negotiation. Indeed, this is the very purpose of direct action. Nonviolent direct action seeks to create such a crisis and foster such a tension that a community which has constantly refused to negotiate is forced to confront the issue. It seeks so to dramatize the issue that it can no longer be ignored. My citing the creation of tension as part of the work of the nonviolent resister may sound rather shocking. But I must confess that I am not afraid of the word "tension." I have earnestly opposed violent tension, but there is a type of constructive, nonviolent tension which is necessary for growth. Just as Socrates felt that it was necessary to create a tension in the mind so that individuals could rise from the bondage of myths and half-truths to the unfettered realm of creative analysis and objective appraisal, so must we see the need for nonviolent gadflies to create the kind of tension in society that will help men rise from the dark depths of prejudice and racism to the majestic heights of understanding and brotherhood.

The purpose of our direct-action program is to create a situation so crisis-packed that it will inevitably open the door to negotiation. I therefore concur with you in your call for negotiation. Too long has our beloved Southland been bogged down in a tragic effort to live in monologue rather than dialogue.

. . . My friends, I must say to you that we have not made a single gain in civil rights without determined legal and nonviolent pressure. Lamentably, it is an historical fact that privileged groups seldom give up their privileges voluntarily. Individuals may see the moral light and voluntarily give up their unjust posture; but, as

Reinhold Niebuhr has reminded us, groups tend to be more immoral than individuals.

We know through painful experience that freedom is never voluntarily given by the oppressor; it must be demanded by the oppressed. Frankly, I have yet to engage in a direct-action campaign that was "well timed" in the view of those who have not suffered unduly from the disease of segregation. For years now I have heard the word "Wait!" It rings in the ear of every Negro with piercing familiarity. This "Wait" has almost always meant "Never." We must come to see, with one of our distinguished jurists, that "justice too long delayed is justice denied."

We have waited for more than 340 years for our constitutional and God-given rights. The nations of Asia and Africa are moving with jetlike speed toward gaining political independence, but we still creep at horse-and-buggy pace toward gaining a cup of coffee at a lunch counter. Perhaps it is easy for those who have never felt the stinging darts of segregation to say, "Wait." But when you have seen vicious mobs lynch your mothers and fathers at will and drown your sisters and brothers at whim; when you have seen hate-filled policemen curse, kick and even kill your black brothers and sisters; when you see the vast majority of your twenty million Negro brothers smothering in an airtight cage of poverty in the midst of an affluent society; when you suddenly find your tongue twisted and your speech stammering as you seek to explain to your six-year-old daughter why she can't go to the public amusement park that has just been advertised on television, and see tears welling up in her eyes when she is told that Funtown is closed to colored children, and see ominous clouds of inferiority beginning to form in her little mental sky, and see her beginning to distort her personality by developing an unconscious bitterness toward white people; when you have to concoct an answer for a five-year-old son who is asking: "Daddy, why do white people treat colored people so mean?"; when you take a cross-country drive and find it necessary to sleep night after night in the uncomfortable corners of your automobile because no motel will accept you; when you are humiliated day in and day out by nagging signs reading "white" and "colored"; when your first name becomes "nigger,"

your middle name becomes "boy" (however old you are) and your last name becomes "John," and your wife and mother are never given the respected title "Mrs."; when you are harried by day and haunted by night by the fact that you are a Negro, living constantly at tiptoe stance, never quite knowing what to expect next, and are plagued with inner fears and outer resentments; when you are forever fighting a degenerating sense of "nobodiness"—then you will understand why we find it difficult to wait. There comes a time when the cup of endurance runs over, and men are no longer willing to be plunged into the abyss of despair. I hope, sirs, you can understand our legitimate and unavoidable impatience.

You express a great deal of anxiety over our willingness to break laws. This is certainly a legitimate concern. Since we so diligently urge people to obey the Supreme Court's decision of 1954 outlawing segregation in the public schools, at first glance it may seem rather paradoxical for us consciously to break laws. One may well ask: "How can you advocate breaking some laws and obeying others?" The answer lies in the fact that there are two types of laws: just and unjust. I would be the first to advocate obeying just laws. One has not only a legal but a moral responsibility to obey just laws. Conversely, one has a moral responsibility to disobey unjust laws. I would agree with St. Augustine that "an unjust law is no law at all."

Now, what is the difference between the two? How does one determine whether a law is just or unjust? A just law is a man-made code that squares with the moral law or the law of God. An unjust law is a code that is out of harmony with the moral law. To put it in the terms of St. Thomas Aquinas: An unjust law is a human law that is not rooted in eternal law and natural law. Any law that uplifts human personality is just. Any law that degrades human personality is unjust. All segregation statutes are unjust because segregation distorts the soul and damages the personality. It gives the segregator a false sense of superiority and the segregated a false sense of inferiority. Segregation, to use the terminology of the Jewish philosopher Martin Buber, substitutes an "I-it" relationship for an "I-thou" relationship and ends up relegating persons to the status of things. Hence segregation is not only politically, economically and sociologically unsound, it is morally wrong and sinful. Paul Tillich has said that sin is separation. Is not segregation an existential expression of man's tragic separation, his awful estrangement, his terrible sinfulness? Thus it is that I can urge men to obey the 1954 decision of the Supreme Court for it is morally right; and I can urge them to disobey segregation ordinances, for they are morally wrong.

Let us consider a more concrete example of just and unjust laws. An unjust law is a code that a numerical or power majority group compels a minority group to obey but does not make binding on itself. This is *difference* made legal. By the same token, a just law is a code that a majority compels a minority to follow and that it is willing to follow itself. This is *sameness* made legal.

Let me give another explanation. A law is unjust if it is inflicted on a minority that, as a result of being denied the right to vote, had no part in enacting or devising the law. Who can say that the legislature of Alabama which set up that state's segregation laws was democratically elected? Throughout Alabama all sorts of devious methods are used to prevent Negroes from becoming registered voters, and there are some counties in which, even though Negroes constitute a majority of the population, not a single Negro is registered. Can any law enacted under such circumstances be considered democratically structured?

Sometimes a law is just on its face and unjust in its application. For instance, I have been arrested on a charge of parading without a permit. Now, there is nothing wrong in having an ordinance which requires a permit for a parade. But such an ordinance becomes unjust when it is used to maintain segregation and to deny citizens the First Amendment privilege of peaceful assembly and protest.

I hope you are able to see the distinction I am trying to point out. In no sense do I advocate evading or defying the law, as would the rabid segregationist. That would lead to anarchy. One who breaks an unjust law must do so openly, lovingly, and with a willingness to accept the penalty. I submit that an individual who breaks a law that conscience tells him is unjust, and who willingly accepts the penalty of imprisonment in order to arouse the conscience of the community over its injustice, is in reality expressing the highest respect for law.

Of course, there is nothing new about this kind of civil disobedience. It was evidenced sublimely in the refusal of Shadrach, Meshach and Abednego to obey the laws of Nebuchadnezzar, on the ground that a higher moral law was at stake. It was practiced superbly by the early Christians, who were willing to face hungry lions and the excruciating pain of chopping blocks rather than submit to certain unjust laws of the Roman Empire. To a degree, academic freedom is a reality today because Socrates practiced civil disobedience. In our own nation, the Boston Tea Party represented a massive act of civil disobedience.

We should never forget that everything Adolf Hitler did in Germany was "legal" and everything the Hungarian freedom fighters did in Hungary was "illegal." It was "illegal" to aid and comfort a Jew in Hitler's Germany. Even so, I am sure that, had I lived in Germany at the time, I would have aided and comforted my Jewish brothers. If today I lived in a Communist country where certain principles dear to the Christian faith are suppressed, I would openly advocate disobeying that country's antireligious laws.

I must make two honest confessions to you, my Christian and Jewish brothers. First, I must confess that over the past few years I have been gravely disappointed with the white moderate. I have almost reached the regrettable conclusion that the Negro's great stumbling block in his stride toward freedom is not the White Citizen's Counciler or the Ku Klux Klanner, but the white moderate, who is more devoted to "order" than to justice; who prefers a negative peace which is the absence of tension to a positive peace which is the presence of justice; who constantly says: "I agree with you in the goal you seek, but I cannot agree with your methods of direct action"; who paternalistically believes he can set the timetable for another man's freedom; who lives by a mythical concept of time and who constantly advises the Negro to wait for a "more convenient season." Shallow understanding from people of good will is more frustrating than absolute misunderstanding from people of ill will. Lukewarm acceptance is much more bewildering than outright rejection.

I had hoped that the white moderate would understand that law and order exist for the purpose of establishing justice and that when they fail in this purpose they become the dangerously structured dams that block the flow of social progress. I had hoped that the white moderate would understand that the present tension in the South is a necessary phase of the transition from an obnoxious negative peace, in which the Negro passively accepted his unjust plight, to a substantive and positive peace, in which all men will respect the dignity and worth of human personality. Actually, we who engage in nonviolent direct action are not the creators of tension. We merely bring to the surface the hidden tension that is already alive. We bring it out in the open, where it can be seen and dealt with. Like a boil that can never be cured so long as it is covered up but must be opened with all its ugliness to the natural medicines of air and light, injustice must be exposed, with all the tension its exposure creates, to the light of human conscience and the air of national opinion before it can be cured.

In your statement you assert that our actions, even though peaceful, must be condemned because they precipitate violence. But is this a logical assertion? Isn't this like condemning a robbed man because his possession of money precipitated the evil act of robbery? Isn't this like condemning Socrates because his unswerving commitment to truth and his philosophical inquiries precipitated the act by the misguided populace in which they made him drink hemlock? Isn't this like condemning Jesus because his unique God-consciousness and never-ceasing devotion to God's will precipitated the evil act of crucifixion? We must come to see that, as the federal courts have consistently affirmed, it is wrong to urge an individual to cease his efforts to gain his basic constitutional rights because the quest may precipitate violence. Society must protect the robbed and punish the robber.

I had also hoped that the white moderate would reject the myth concerning time in relation to the struggle for freedom. I have just received a letter from a white brother in Texas. He writes: "All Christians know that the colored people will receive equal rights eventually, but it is possible that you are in too great a religious hurry. It has taken Christianity almost two thousand years to accomplish what it has. The teachings of Christ take time to come to earth." Such an attitude stems from a tragic misconception of time, from the strangely irrational notion that there is something in the very flow of time that will inevitably cure all ills. Actually, time itself is neutral; it can be used either destructively or constructively. More and more I feel that the people of ill will have used time much more effectively than have the people of good will. We will have to repent in this generation not merely for the hateful words and actions of the bad people but for the appalling silence of the good people. Human progress never rolls in on wheels of inevitability; it comes through the tireless efforts of men willing to be co-workers with God, and without this hard work, time itself becomes an ally of the forces of social stagnation. We must use time creatively, in the knowledge that the time is always ripe to do right. Now is the time to make real the promise of democracy and transform our pending national elegy into a creative psalm of brotherhood. Now is the time to lift our national policy from the quicksand of racial injustice to the solid rock of human dignity.

You speak of our activity in Birmingham as extreme. At first I was rather disappointed that fellow clergymen would see my nonviolent efforts as those of an extremist. I began thinking about the fact that I stand in the middle of two opposing forces in the Negro community. One is a force of complacency, made up in part of Negroes who, as a result of long years of oppression, are so drained of self-respect and a sense of "somebodiness" that they have adjusted to segregation; and in part of a few middle-class Negroes who, because of a degree of academic and economic security and because in some ways they profit by segregation, have become insensitive to the problems of the masses. The other force is one of bitterness and hatred, and it comes perilously close to advocating violence. It is expressed in the various black nationalist groups that are springing up across the nation, the largest and best-known being Elijah Muhammad's Muslim movement. Nourished by the Negro's frustration over the continued existence of racial discrimination, this movement is made up of people who have lost faith in America, who have absolutely repudiated Christianity, and who have concluded that the white man is an incorrigible "devil."

I have tried to stand between these two forces, saying that we need emulate neither the "do-nothingism" of the complacent nor the hatred and despair of the black nationalist. For there is the more excellent way of love and nonviolent protest. I am grateful to God that, through the influence of the Negro church, the way of nonviolence became an integral part of our struggle.

If this philosophy had not emerged, by now many streets of the South would, I am convinced, be flowing with blood. And I am further convinced that if our white brothers dismiss as "rabble-rousers" and "outside agitators" those of us who employ nonviolent direct action, and if they refuse to support our nonviolent efforts, millions of Negroes will, out of frustration and despair, seek solace and security in black-nationalist ideologies—a development that would inevitably lead to a frightening racial nightmare.

Oppressed people cannot remain oppressed forever. The yearning for freedom eventually manifests itself, and that is what has happened to the American Negro. Something within has reminded him of his birthright of freedom, and something without has reminded him that it can be gained. Consciously or unconsciously he has been caught up by the *Zeitgeist*, and with his black brothers of Africa and his brown and yellow brothers of Asia, South America and the Caribbean, the United States Negro is moving with a sense of great urgency toward the promised land of racial justice. If one recognizes this vital urge that has engulfed the Negro community, one should readily understand why public demonstrations are taking place. The Negro has many pent-up resentments and latent frustrations, and he must release them. So let him march; let him make prayer pilgrimages to the city hall; let him go on freedom rides—and try to understand why he must do so. If his repressed emotions are not released in nonviolent ways, they will seek expression through violence; this is not a threat but a fact of history. So I have not said to my people: "Get rid of your discontent." Rather,

I have tried to say that this normal and healthy discontent can be channeled into the creative outlet of nonviolent direct action. And now this approach is being termed extremist.

But though I was initially disappointed at being categorized as an extremist, as I continued to think about the matter I gradually gained a measure of satisfaction from the label. Was not Jesus an extremist for love: "Love your enemies, bless them that curse you, do good to them that hate you, and pray for them which despitefully use you, and persecute you." Was not Amos an extremist for justice: "Let justice roll down like waters and righteousness like an ever-flowing stream." Was not Paul an extremist for the Christian gospel: "I bear in my body the marks of the Lord Jesus." Was not Martin Luther an extremist: "Here I stand: I cannot do otherwise, so help me God." And John Bunyan: "I will stay in jail to the end of my days before I make a butchery of my conscience." And Abraham Lincoln: "This nation cannot survive half slave and half free." And Thomas Jefferson: "We hold these truths to be self-evident, that all men are created equal . . . " So the question is not whether we will be extremists, but what kind of extremists we will be. Will we be extremists for hate or for love? Will we be extremists for the preservation of injustice or for the extension of justice? In that dramatic scene on Calvary's hill three men were crucified. We must never forget that all three were crucified for the same crime—the crime of extremism. Two were extremists for immorality, and thus fell below their environment. The other, Jesus Christ, was an extremist for love, truth and goodness, and thereby rose above his environment. Perhaps the South, the nation and the world are in dire need of creative extremists.

I had hoped that the white moderate would see this need. . . .

Before closing I feel impelled to mention one other point in your statement that has troubled me profoundly. You warmly commended the Birmingham police force for keeping "order" and "preventing violence." I doubt that you would have so warmly commended the police force if you had seen its dogs sinking their teeth into unarmed, nonviolent Negroes. I doubt that you would so quickly commend the policemen if you were to observe their ugly and inhumane treatment of Negroes here in the city jail; if you were to watch them push and curse old Negro women and young Negro girls; if you were to see them slap and kick old Negro men and young boys; if you were to observe them, as they did on two occasions, refuse to give us food because we wanted to sing our grace together. I cannot join you in your praise of the Birmingham police department.

It is true that the police have exercised a degree of discipline in handling the demonstrators. In this sense they have conducted themselves rather "nonviolently" in public. But for what purpose? To preserve the evil system of segregation. Over the past few years I have consistently preached that nonviolence demands that the means we use must be as pure as the ends we seek. I have tried to make clear that it is wrong to use immoral means to attain moral ends. But now I must affirm that it is just as wrong, or perhaps even more so, to use moral means to preserve immoral ends. Perhaps Mr. Connor and his policemen have been rather nonviolent in public, as was Chief Pritchett in Albany, Georgia, but they have used the moral means of nonviolence to maintain the immoral end of racial injustice. As T. S. Eliot has said: "The last temptation is the greatest treason: To do the right deed for the wrong reason."

I wish you had commended the Negro sitinners and demonstrators of Birmingham for their sublime courage, their willingness to suffer and their amazing discipline in the midst of great provocation. One day the South will recognize its real heroes. They will be the James Merediths, with the noble sense of purpose that enables them to face jeering and hostile mobs, and with the agonizing loneliness that characterizes the life of the pioneer. They will be old, oppressed, battered Negro women, symbolized in a seventy-two-year-old woman in Montgomery, Alabama, who rose up with a sense of dignity and with her people decided not to ride segregated buses, and who responded with ungrammatical profundity to one who inquired about her weariness: "My feets is tired, but my soul is at rest." They will be the young high school and college students, the young ministers of the gospel and a host of their elders, courageously and nonviolently sitting in at lunch counters and willingly going to jail for conscience' sake. One day the South will know that when these disinherited children of God sat down at lunch counters, they were in reality standing up for what is best in the American dream and for the most sacred values in our Judaeo-Christian heritage, thereby bringing our nation back to those great wells of democracy which were dug deep by the founding fathers in their formulation of the Constitution and the Declaration of Independence.

.   .   .

Yours for the cause of Peace and Brotherhood, Martin Luther King, Jr.

DISCUSSION QUESTIONS

1. Explain why Martin Luther King, Jr., may have come to the conclusion that the white moderate's devotion to order has been "the Negro's great stumbling block" rather than the persecutions of the "White Citizen's Counciler or the Ku Klux Klanner."
2. In what way does King criticize the white moderate? What does he mean by the statement "justice too long delayed is justice denied"?
3. Why would King object to the pluralist understanding of American politics as explained in the introduction to this reader? How is the kind of action that King calls for viewed in our society today?

38 *Naomi Klein*

RECLAIMING THE COMMONS

One of the most striking developments in U.S and world politics in recent years has been the growth of a diverse and broad-based movement against corporate domination of the global economy. Misleadingly labeled the "antiglobalization" movement, this new wave of activism reached mass awareness with the protests in Seattle at the meeting of the World Trade Organization in 1999. One of the most articulate thinkers of the movement is the Canadian writer and activist Naomi Klein, author of No Logo (2000) *and* The Shock Doctrine (2007). *In this article, Klein clarifies the nature and goals of the movement, which opposes the privatization and commodification of everyday life rather than globalization as such. She explains that activists have targeted "free-market" trade agreements as a way of resisting "McGovernment"—the "happy meal" of cutting taxes, privatizing services, slashing regulations, busting unions, and removing any obstacles to the unfettered reign of the market, which is the hidden agenda of the free-trade agenda. Far from seeing democracy and the free-market as synonymous, Klein asserts that the dominant form of corporate globalization amounts to "a crisis in representative democracy." For her, the spirit of the oppositional campaigns and movements is one of "reclaiming the commons"—acting to create a public sphere in which grassroots democracy can flourish and resist the boundless drive of the corporate project.*

What is "the anti-globalization movement"? I put the phrase in quote-marks because I immediately have two doubts about it. Is it really a movement? If it is a movement, is it anti-globalization? Let me start with the first issue. We can easily convince ourselves it is a movement by talking it into existence at a forum like this—I spend far too much time at them—acting as if we can see it, hold it in our hands. Of course, we have seen it—and we know it's come back in Quebec, and on the U.S.–Mexican border during the Summit of the Americas and the discussion for a hemispheric Free Trade Area. But then we leave rooms like this, go home, watch

Source: Naomi Klein, "Reclaiming the Commons." *New Left Review,* 9, May–June 2001, pp. 81–89.

some TV, do a little shopping and any sense that it exists disappears, and we feel like maybe we're going nuts. Seattle—was that a movement or a collective hallucination? To most of us here, Seattle meant a kind of coming-out party for a global resistance movement, or the "globalization of hope," as someone described it during the World Social Forum at Porto Alegre. But to everyone else Seattle still means limitless frothy coffee, Asian-fusion cuisine, e-commerce billionaires and sappy Meg Ryan movies. Or perhaps it is both, and one Seattle bred the other Seattle—and now they awkwardly coexist.

This movement we sometimes conjure into being goes by many names: anti-corporate, anti-capitalist, anti-free trade, anti-imperialist. Many say that it started in Seattle. Others maintain it began five hundred years ago—when colonialists first told indigenous peoples that they were going to have to do things differently if they were to "develop" or be eligible for "trade." Others again say it began on 1 January 1994 when the Zapatistas launched their uprising with the words *Ya Basta!* on the night NAFTA became law in Mexico. It all depends on whom you ask. But I think it is more accurate to picture a movement of many movements—coalitions of coalitions. Thousands of groups today are all working against forces whose common thread is what might broadly be described as the privatization of every aspect of life, and the transformation of every activity and value into a commodity. We often speak of the privatization of education, of health care, of natural resources. But the process is much vaster. It includes the way powerful ideas are turned into advertising slogans and public streets into shopping malls; new generations being target-marketed at birth; schools being invaded by ads; basic human necessities like water being sold as commodities; basic labour rights being rolled back; genes are patented and designer babies loom; seeds are genetically altered and bought; politicians are bought and altered.

At the same time there are oppositional threads, taking form in many different campaigns and movements. The spirit they share is a radical reclaiming of the commons. As our communal spaces—town squares, streets, schools, farms, plants—are displaced by the ballooning marketplace, a spirit of resistance is taking hold around the world. People are reclaiming bits of nature and of culture, and saying "this is going to be public space." American students are kicking ads out of the classrooms. European environmentalists and ravers are throwing parties at busy intersections. Landless Thai peasants are planting organic vegetables on over-irrigated golf courses. Bolivian workers are reversing the privatization of their water supply. Outfits like Napster have been creating a kind of commons on the internet where kids can swap music with each other, rather than buying it from multinational record companies. Billboards have been liberated and independent media networks set up. Protests are multiplying. In Porto Alegre, during the World Social Forum, José Bové, often caricatured as only a hammer of McDonald's, travelled with local activists from the Movimento Sem Terra to a nearby Monsanto test site, where they destroyed three hectares of genetically modified soya beans. But the protest did not stop there. The MST has occupied the land and members are now planting their own organic crops on it, vowing to turn the farm into a model of sustainable agriculture. In short, activists aren't waiting for the revolution, they are acting right now, where they live, where they study, where they work, where they farm.

But some formal proposals are also emerging whose aim is to turn such radical reclamations of the commons into law. When NAFTA and the like were cooked up, there was much talk of adding on "side agreements" to the free trade agenda, that were supposed to encompass the environment, labour and human rights. Now the fight-back is about taking them out. José Bové—along with the Via Campesina, a global association of small farmers—has launched a campaign to remove food safety and agricultural products from all trade agreements, under the slogan 'The World is Not for Sale.' They want to draw a line around the commons. Maude Barlow, director of the Council of Canadians, which has more members than most political parties in Canada, has argued that water isn't a private good and shouldn't be in any trade agreement. There is a lot of support for this idea, especially in Europe since the recent food scares. Typically these anti-privatization campaigns get under way on their own. But they also periodically converge—that's what happened in Seattle, Prague, Washington, Davos, Porto Alegre and Quebec.

BEYOND THE BORDERS

What this means is that the discourse has shifted. During the battles against NAFTA, there emerged the first signs of a coalition between organized labour, environmentalists, farmers and consumer groups within the countries concerned. In Canada most of us felt we were fighting to keep something distinctive about our nation from "Americanization." In the United States, the talk was very protectionist: workers were worried that Mexicans would "steal" away "our" jobs and drive down "our" environmental standards. All the while, the voices of Mexicans opposed to the deal were virtually off the public radar—yet these were the strongest voices of all. But only a few years later, the debate over trade has been transformed. The fight against globalization has morphed into a struggle against corporatization and, for some, against capitalism itself. It has also become a fight for democracy. Maude Barlow spearheaded the campaign against NAFTA in Canada twelve years ago. Since NAFTA became law, she's been working with organizers and activists from other countries, and anarchists suspicious of the state in her own country. She was once seen as very much the face of a Canadian nationalism. Today she has moved away from that discourse. "I've changed," she says, "I used to see this fight as saving a nation. Now I see it as saving democracy." This is a cause that transcends nationality and state borders. The real news out of Seattle is that organizers around the world are beginning to see their local and national struggles—for better funded public schools, against union-busting and

casualization, for family farms, and against the widening gap between rich and poor—through a global lens. That is the most significant shift we have seen in years.

How did this happen? Who or what convened this new international people's movement? Who sent out the memos? Who built these complex coalitions? It is tempting to pretend that someone did dream up a master plan for mobilization at Seattle. But I think it was much more a matter of large-scale coincidence. A lot of smaller groups organized to get themselves there and then found to their surprise just how broad and diverse a coalition they had become part of. Still, if there is one force we can thank for bringing this front into being, it is the multinational corporations. As one of the organizers of Reclaim the Streets has remarked, we should be grateful to the CEOs for helping us see the problems more quickly. Thanks to the sheer imperialist ambition of the corporate project at this moment in history— the boundless drive for profit, liberated by trade deregulation, and the wave of mergers and buyouts, liberated by weakened anti-trust laws— multinationals have grown so blindingly rich, so vast in their holdings, so global in their reach, that they have created our coalitions for us.

Around the world, activists are piggy-backing on the ready-made infrastructures supplied by global corporations. This can mean cross-border unionization, but also cross-sector organizing—among workers, environmentalists, consumers, even prisoners, who may all have different relationships to one multinational. So you can build a single campaign or coalition around a single brand like General Electric. Thanks to Monsanto, farmers in India are working with environmentalists and consumers around the world to develop direct-action strategies that cut off genetically modified foods in the fields and in the supermarkets. Thanks to Shell Oil and Chevron, human rights activists in Nigeria, democrats in Europe, environmentalists in North America have united in a fight against the unsustainability of the oil industry. Thanks to the catering giant Sodexho-Marriott's decision to invest in Corrections Corporation of America, university students are able to protest against the exploding U.S. for-profit prison industry simply by boycotting the food in their campus cafeteria. Other targets include pharmaceutical companies who are trying to inhibit the production and distribution of low-cost AIDS drugs, and fast-food chains. Recently, students and farm workers in Florida have joined forces around Taco Bell. In the St. Petersburg area, field hands—many of them immigrants from Mexico—are paid an average $7,500 a year to pick tomatoes and onions. Due to a loophole in the law, they have no bargaining power: the farm bosses refuse even to talk with them about wages. When they started to look into who bought what they pick, they found that Taco Bell was the largest purchaser of the local tomatoes. So they launched the campaign *Yo No Quiero Taco Bell* together with students, to boycott Taco Bell on university campuses.

It is Nike, of course, that has most helped to pioneer this new brand of activist synergy. Students facing a corporate take-over of their campuses by the Nike swoosh have linked up with workers making its branded campus apparel, as well as with parents concerned at the commercialization of youth and church groups campaigning against child labour—all united by their different relationships to a common global enemy. Exposing the underbelly of high-gloss consumer brands has provided the early narratives of this movement, a sort of call-and-response to the very different narratives these companies tell every day about themselves through advertising and public relations. Citigroup offers another prime target, as North America's largest financial institution, with innumerable holdings, which deals with some of the worst corporate malefactors around. The campaign against it handily knits together dozens of issues—from clear-cut logging in California to oil-and-pipeline schemes in Chad and Cameroon. These projects are only a start. But they are creating a new sort of activist: "Nike is a gateway drug," in the words of Oregon student activist Sarah Jacobson.

By focusing on corporations, organizers can demonstrate graphically how so many issues of social, ecological and economic justice are interconnected. No activist I've met believes that the world economy can be changed one corporation at a time, but the campaigns have opened a door into the arcane world of international trade and finance. Where they are leading is to the central institutions that write the rules of global commerce: the WTO, the IMF, the FTAA, and for some the market itself. Here too the unifying threat is privatization—the loss of the commons. The next round of WTO negotiations is designed to extend the reach of commodification still further. Through side agreements like GATS (General Agreement on Trade and Services) and TRIPS (Trade-Related Aspects of Intellectual Property Rights), the aim is to get still tougher protection of property rights on seeds and drug patents, and to marketize services like health care, education and water-supply.

The biggest challenge facing us is to distil all of this into a message that is widely accessible. Many campaigners understand the connexions binding together the various issues almost intuitively—much as Subcomandante Marcos says, "Zapatismo isn't an ideology, it's an intuition." But to outsiders, the mere scope of modern protests can be a bit mystifying. If you eavesdrop on the movement from the outside, which is what most people do, you are liable to hear what seems to be a cacophony of disjointed slogans, a jumbled laundry list of disparate grievances without clear goals. At the Democratic National Convention in Los Angeles last year, I remember being outside the Staples Centre during the Rage Against the Machine concert, just before I almost got shot, and thinking there were slogans for everything everywhere, to the point of absurdity.

MAINSTREAM FAILURES

This kind of impression is reinforced by the decentralized, non-hierarchical structure of the movement, which always disconcerts the traditional media. Well-organized press conferences are rare, there is no charismatic leadership, protests tend to pile on top of each other. Rather than forming a pyramid, as most movements do, with leaders up on top and followers down below, it looks more like an elaborate web. In part, this web-like structure is the result of internet-based organizing. But it is also a response to the very political realities that sparked the protests in the first place: the utter failure of traditional party politics. All over the world, citizens have worked to elect social democratic and workers' parties, only to watch them plead impotence in the face of market forces and IMF dictates. In these conditions, modern activists are not so naive as to believe change will come from electoral politics. That's why they are more interested in challenging the structures that make democracy toothless, like the IMF's structural adjustment policies, the WTO's ability to override national sovereignty, corrupt campaign financing, and so on. This is not just making a virtue of necessity. It responds at the ideological level to an understanding that globalization is in essence a crisis in representative democracy. What has caused this crisis? One of the basic reasons for it is the way power and decision-making has been handed along to points ever further away from citizens: from local to provincial, from provincial to national, from national to international institutions, that lack all transparency or accountability. What is the solution? To articulate an alternative, participatory democracy.

If you think about the nature of the complaints raised against the World Trade Organization, it is that governments around the world have embraced an economic model that involves much more than opening borders to goods and services. This is why it is not useful to use the language of anti-globalization. Most people do not really know what globalization is, and the term makes the movement extremely vulnerable to stock dismissals like: "If you are against trade and globalization why do you drink coffee?" Whereas in reality the movement is a rejection of what is being bundled along with trade and so-called globalization—against the set

of transformative political policies that every country in the world has been told they must accept in order to make themselves hospitable to investment. I call this package "McGovernment." This happy meal of cutting taxes, privatizing services, liberalizing regulations, busting unions—what is this diet in aid of? To remove anything standing in the way of the market. Let the free market roll, and every other problem will apparently be solved in the trickle down. This isn't about trade. It's about using trade to enforce the McGovernment recipe.

So the question we are asking today, in the run up to the FTAA, is not: are you for or against trade? The question is: do we have the right to negotiate the terms of our relationship to foreign capital and investment? Can we decide how we want to protect ourselves from the dangers inherent in deregulated markets—or do we have to contract out those decisions? These problems will become much more acute once we are in a recession, because during the economic boom so much has been destroyed of what was left of our social safety net. During a period of low unemployment, people did not worry much about that. They are likely to be much more concerned in the very near future. The most controversial issues facing the WTO are these questions about self-determination. For example, does Canada have the right to ban a harmful gasoline additive without being sued by a foreign chemical company? Not according to the WTO's ruling in favour of the Ethyl Corporation. Does Mexico have the right to deny a permit for a hazardous toxic-waste disposal site? Not according to Metalclad, the U.S. company now suing the Mexican government for $16.7 million damages under NAFTA. Does France have the right to ban hormone-treated beef from entering the country? Not according to the United States, which retaliated by banning French imports like Roquefort cheese—prompting a cheese-maker called Bové to dismantle a McDonald's; Americans thought he just didn't like hamburgers. Does Argentina have to cut its public sector to qualify for foreign loans? Yes, according to the IMF—sparking general strikes against the social consequences. It's the same issue everywhere: trading away democracy in exchange for foreign capital.

On smaller scales, the same struggles for self-determination and sustainability are being waged against World Bank dams, clear-cut logging, cash-crop factory farming, and resource extraction on contested indigenous lands. Most people in these movements are not against trade or industrial development. What they are fighting for is the right of local communities to have a say in how their resources are used, to make sure that the people who live on the land benefit directly from its development. These campaigns are a response not to trade but to a trade-off that is now five hundred years old: the sacrifice of democratic control and self-determination to foreign investment and the panacea of economic growth. The challenge they now face is to shift a discourse around the vague notion of globalization into a specific debate about democracy. In a period of "unprecedented prosperity," people were told they had no choice but to slash public spending, revoke labour laws, rescind environmental protections—deemed illegal trade barriers—defund schools, not build affordable housing. All this was necessary to make us trade-ready, investment-friendly, world-competitive. Imagine what joys await us during a recession.

We need to be able to show that globalization—this version of globalization—has been built on the back of local human welfare. Too often, these connexions between global and local are not made. Instead we sometimes seem to have two activist solitudes. On the one hand, there are the international anti-globalization activists who may be enjoying a triumphant mood, but seem to be fighting far-away issues, unconnected to people's day-to-day struggles. They are often seen as elitists: white middle-class kids with dreadlocks. On the other hand, there are community activists fighting daily struggles for survival, or for the preservation of the most elementary public services, who are often feeling burnt-out and demoralized. They are saying: what in the hell are you guys so excited about?

The only clear way forward is for these two forces to merge. What is now the anti-globalization movement must turn into thousands of local movements, fighting the way neoliberal politics are playing out on the ground: homelessness, wage stagnation, rent escalation, police violence, prison explosion, criminalization of migrant workers, and on and on. These are also struggles about all kinds of prosaic issues: the right to decide where the local garbage goes, to have good public schools, to be supplied with clean water. At the same time, the local movements fighting privatization and deregulation on the ground need to link their campaigns into one large global movement, which can show where their particular issues fit into an international economic agenda being enforced around the world. If that connexion isn't made, people will continue to be demoralized. What we need is to formulate a political framework that can both take on corporate power and control, and empower local organizing and self-determination. That has to be a framework that encourages, celebrates and fiercely protects the right to diversity: cultural diversity, ecological diversity, agricultural diversity—and yes, political diversity as well: different ways of doing politics. Communities must have the right to plan and manage their schools, their services, their natural settings, according to their own lights. Of course, this is only possible within a framework of national and international standards—of public education, fossil-fuel emissions, and so on. But the goal should not be better far-away rules and rulers, it should be close-up democracy on the ground.

The Zapatistas have a phrase for this. They call it "one world with many worlds in it." Some have criticized this as a New Age non-answer. They want a plan. "We know what the market wants to do with those spaces, what do *you* want to do? Where's your scheme?" I think we shouldn't be afraid to say: "That's not up to us." We need to have some trust in people's ability to rule themselves, to make the decisions that are best for them. We need to show some humility where now there is so much arrogance and paternalism. To believe in human diversity and local democracy is anything but wishy-washy. Everything in McGovernment conspires against them. Neoliberal economics is biased at every level towards centralization, consolidation, homogenization. It is a war waged on diversity. Against it, we need a movement of radical change, committed to a single world with many worlds in it, that stands for "the one no and the many yesses."

DISCUSSION QUESTIONS

1. How does Klein characterize the "corporate agenda" in the age of globalization? Why does she think that this agenda is a threat to democracy in any meaningful sense?
2. Contemporary political discourse often speaks of "free-market democracy" as an ideal that all countries strive to attain. Why would the movements that Klein discusses take issue with this easy equation of democracy and free markets?

39 *Jared Bernstein*

ALL TOGETHER NOW
Common Sense for a Fair Economy

Our general introduction was framed by a quote from the quintessential American revolutionary Thomas Paine: "A long habit of not thinking a thing wrong, gives it the superficial appearance of being right" was his call to arms in his 1776 pamphlet Common Sense. *In this article, we offer you a selection animated by the spirit captured in a different quote from Paine: "We have it in our power to begin the world again." Economist Jared Bernstein offers his vision for a new democracy that springs from a conviction that beginning the world again is necessary and possible if we move forward with a common sense commitment to basic fairness for all. Bernstein's proposition is straightforward: our political culture is steeped in the ideology of individualism—a core value that has hardened into an extreme version of hyperindividualism that he captures in the acronym YOYO, meaning "You're on your own." Although the roots of YOYO reach back at least to 1900, the policy thrust of YOYO lies beneath virtually every conservative initiative of the past 25 years. The conservative mantra boils down to the assumption that everything public is bad, everything private is good. Government is to be feared and attacked; private business is to be praised and expanded. Against the chorus of YOYO supporters demonizing the common good, Bernstein articulates an alternative vision he calls WITT—the philosophy that "We're in this together." The WITT philosophy is collaborative in nature, using the federal government to help us achieve important public purposes. Bernstein argues that without a renewed sense that "We're in this together," our most vexing problems—from globalization, to health care, to environmental degradation—will remain unsolved.*

READY OR NOT, YOU'RE ON YOUR OWN

I once heard an allegory about mealtime in heaven and hell. It turns out that in both places, meals are served at a huge round table with lots of delicious food in the center. The food is out of reach, but everyone's got really long forks.

In hell, everyone starves because, while people can reach the food with their forks, the forks are much longer than their arms, so nobody can turn a fork around and eat what's on the end of it.

In heaven, faced with the same problem, people eat well. How?

By feeding each other.

Protecting the rights of individuals has always been a core American value. Yet in recent years the emphasis on individualism has been pushed to the point where, like the diners in hell, we're starving. This political and social philosophy is hurting our nation, endangering our future and that of our children, and, paradoxically, making it harder for individuals to get a fair shot at the American dream.

This extreme individualism dominates the way we talk about the most important aspects of our economic lives, those that reside in the intersection of our living standards, our government, and the future opportunities for ourselves and our children. The message, sometimes implicit but often explicit, is, *You're on your own.* Its acronym, YOYO, provides useful shorthand to summarize this destructive approach to governing.

The concept of YOYO, as used in this book, isn't all that complicated. It's the prevailing vision of how our country should be governed. As such, it embodies a set of values, and at the core of the YOYO value system is hyper-individualism: the notion that whatever the challenges we face as a nation, the best way to solve them is for people to fend for themselves. Over the past few decades, this harmful vision has generated a set of policies with that hyper individualistic gene throughout their DNA.

The YOYO crowd—the politicians, lobbyists, and economists actively promoting this vision— has stepped up its efforts to advance its policies in recent years, but hyper-individualism is not a new phenomenon. I document archaeological evidence of YOYO thinking and policies from the early 1900s, along with their fingerprint: a sharp increase in the inequality of income, wealth, and opportunity. The most recent incarnation can be found in the ideas generated by the administration of George W. Bush, but the YOYO infrastructure—the personnel with a vested interest in the continued dominance of these policies—will not leave the building with

Bush. Unless, that is, we recognize the damage being done and make some major changes.

One central goal of the YOYO movement is to continue and even accelerate the trend toward shifting economic risks from the government and the nation's corporations onto individuals and their families. You can see this intention beneath the surface of almost every recent conservative initiative: Social Security privatization, personal accounts for health care (the so-called Health Savings Accounts), attacks on labor market regulations, and the perpetual crusade to slash the government's revenue through regressive tax cuts—a strategy explicitly tagged as "starving the beast"—and block the government from playing a useful role in our economic lives. You can even see this go-it-alone principle in our stance toward our supposed international allies.

While this fast-moving reassignment of economic risk would be bad news in any period, it's particularly harmful today. As the new century unfolds, we face prodigious economic challenges, many of which have helped to generate both greater inequalities and a higher degree of economic insecurity in our lives. But the dominant vision has failed to develop a hopeful, positive narrative about how these challenges can be met in such a way as to uplift the majority.

Instead, messages such as "It's your money" (the mantra of the first George W. Bush campaign in 2000), and frames such as "the ownership society," stress an ever shrinking role for government and much more individual risk taking. Yet global competition, rising health costs, longer life spans with weaker pensions, less secure employment, and unprecedented inequalities of opportunity and wealth are calling for a much broader, more inclusive approach to helping all of us meet these challenges, one that taps government as well as market solutions.

To cite one potent example, 46 million people lack health coverage, and the share of our economy devoted to health care is headed for unsustainable levels. We urgently need to begin planning a viable alternative, such as a system of universal coverage as exists in every other advanced economy. In every case, these countries insure their citizens, control health costs better than we do, and have better overall health outcomes. Yet our leaders want to solve the problem with an individualistic, market-based system of private accounts designed to cut costs by shifting risk from the insurer to the patient, unleashing more of the very market forces that got us into this mess in the first place.

As I stress throughout, those crafting such policies are trapped in the YOYO paradigm, one where common-sense solutions, even those embraced by the rest of the advanced world, are out of bounds. This book has but a few central messages, but this is one of them: we simply can no longer afford to be led by people wearing ideological blinders. We must seriously investigate a new way of thinking if we are to successfully craft an equitable approach to growth, risk, and the distribution of opportunity and income.

For decades in the post-WWII era, the income of the typical family rose in lockstep with the economy's performance. As the bakers of the economic pie—the workforce—grew more productive, they benefited commensurately from their work: between the mid-1940s and the mid-1970s, both productivity and real median family income doubled.

Since the mid-1970s, however, family income has grown at one third the rate of productivity, even though families are working harder and longer than ever. Recently, the problem has grown more severe. In late 2003, we finally pulled out of the longest "jobless recovery" on record, going back to the 1930s. Our economy expanded, but we were losing jobs. Moreover, despite solid overall growth since the recession of 2001, the typical family's income has consistently fallen and poverty has gone up. The gap between the growth in productivity, which has been quite stellar, and the very flat pace at which the living standards of most families are improving has never been wider. This is a characteristic of YOYO economics: the economy does fine; the people in the economy do not.

How has this occurred, and what role do the people and politics of YOYO play? While the whole story might be made more interesting by a

right-wing conspiracy, the rise of YOYO isn't one. Though conservatives have introduced recent YOYO initiatives like Social Security privatization and private accounts for health care and unemployment, this is not a story of good Democrats and bad Republicans. It is the story of the ascendancy of a largely bipartisan vision that promotes individualist market-based solutions over solutions that recognize there are big problems that markets cannot effectively solve.

We cannot, for example, constantly cut the federal government's revenue stream without undermining its ability to meet pressing social needs. We know that more resources will be needed to meet the challenges of prospering in a global economy, keeping up with technological changes, funding health care and pension systems, helping individuals balance work and family life, improving the skills of our workforce, and reducing social and economic inequality. Yet discussion of this reality is off the table.

WE'RE IN THIS TOGETHER

We need an alternative vision, one that applauds individual freedom but emphasizes that such freedom is best realized with a more collaborative approach to meeting the challenges we face. The message is simple: *We're in this together.* Here, the acronym is *WITT.*

Though this alternative agenda uses the scope and breadth of the federal government to achieve its ends, this book is not a call for more government in the sense of devoting a larger share of our economy to government spending. In fact, there is surprisingly little relationship between the ideological agenda of those in charge and the share of the economy devoted to the federal government. To the contrary, some of the biggest spenders of federal funds have been purveyors of hyper-individualism (with G. W. Bush at the top of the list). But, regardless of what you feel the government's role should be in the economy and society, an objective look at the magnitude of the challenges we face shows we must restore the balance between individual and collective action. We simply cannot effectively address globalization, health care, pensions, economic insecurity, and fiscal train wrecks by cutting taxes, turning things over to the market, and telling our citizens they're on their own, like the gold prospectors of the 1800s, to strike it rich or bust.

All Together Now aims to set us on a new path. At the heart of the WITT agenda is the belief that we can wield the tools of government to build a more just society, one that preserves individualist values while ensuring that the prosperity we generate is equitably shared. Importantly, under the WITT agenda, this outcome occurs not through redistributionist Robin Hood schemes, but through creating an economic architecture that reconnects our strong, flexible economy to the living standards of all, not just to the residents of the penthouse. As the pie grows, all the bakers get bigger slices.

Where YOYO economics explains why we cannot shape our participation in the global economy to meet our own needs, or provide health coverage for the millions who lack that basic right, or raise the living standards of working families when the economy is growing, WITT policies target these challenges head on.

As YOYOism rolls on, the amplitude of our national discomfort, the vague sense that something is fundamentally wrong in how we conduct our national and international affairs is climbing. In poll after poll, solid majorities view our country as headed in the wrong direction, and there are signs that the YOYO infrastructure is not impenetrable. Though the administration may ultimately get its way, some members of Congress have unexpectedly been resisting White House demands for billions more in tax cuts for the wealthy. In a totally uncharacteristic reversal, the Bush administration was forced to reinstate the prevailing wage rule it suspended in the wake of Hurricane Katrina. In the off-year 2005 elections, a few closely watched races revealed that simply pledging to cut taxes wasn't enough. In a couple of important cases, candidates and initiatives that delivered more WITTisms than YOYOism prevailed. The climate of a few years ago has changed, and resistance is no longer futile.

A growing chorus is calling for a more balanced role of government in our lives. In the words of Iowa governor Tom Vilsack, "Government is nothing more nor less than the instrument whereby our people come together to undertake collectively the responsibilities we cannot discharge alone." If enough of us add our voices, we can reject messages like "It's your money" and "You're on your own" as divisive and counterproductive.

We can move the pendulum away from a politics that excessively focuses on individuals—the YOYO agenda toward an approach wherein we work together to craft solutions to the challenges we face. Embedded in these solutions is a healthy respect for markets and individuals. But that respect is not excessive. It does not lead us to stand idly by while the economy expands year after year as poverty rises and the real incomes of working families stagnate. Neither does it impel us to shy away from our goal: building a society where the fruits of economic growth are broadly shared with those who create that growth each day of their working lives.

A RETURN TO COMMON SENSE

The subtitle of this book invokes *Common Sense,* the most famous work of the American revolutionary Thomas Paine. What's the connection?

It's partly, of course, the issue of whom our government represents. Paine was ready to throw off the yoke of British tyranny well before most of the nation's founders were. In this spirit, part of what follows is a common-sense critique of the United States' current situation. Hyper-individualism has held sway numerous times in our history, and a characteristic of these periods is the extent to which they favor the chosen few over the majority.

But what makes Paine so relevant today was his ability to see outside the box. While the majority of the colonists were unhappy with the Crown, most were unable to envision ending their relationship with England and seriously consider independence. *Common Sense,* which starts right off with a vitriolic personal attack on King George III, offered the colonists a radically different view of their options. Paine told the colonists that their humanity was a gift from God, not from the king. Thus, they had a responsibility to themselves and their children to construct a system of government that would free them from the constraints of the Crown to pursue their "natural rights." We can see this philosophy clearly embedded in the Declaration of Independence, where the right to life, liberty, and the pursuit of happiness was enshrined as a God-given, self-evident right of humanity.

We have drifted too far from Paine's vision. Many of us share a sense of deep discomfort and insecurity about the direction our country is taking. But there do not seem to be any signposts pointing to a better way. Why not?

It's easy to blame the lack of leadership, and there's something to that. The quality of many of our leaders does seem particularly suspect these days. Opportunists can always be found in politics, but their influence is often countered by those truly motivated to promote the public good (which is not to say that such people agree on how to do so, of course). Right now, the ratio of opportunists to idealists may be unusually high.

But the problem cuts deeper. The emphasis on individualism will always be a core American value, but it has been stressed to the breaking point. As the YOYO influence has spread, assisted by the muscular application of contemporary economics, the YOYOs have implemented a philosophy of hyper-individualism that disdains using the tools of government to seek solutions. More than anything else, this policy has led to our current predicament. Under the banner of "You're on your own," we have lost a sense of common ownership of our government, an institution that many of us now distrust as feckless at best and corrupt at worst.

This abandonment of our faith in government to help meet the challenges we face—social, economic, and international—has been costly. We have shut off our critical faculties that under normal circumstances would lead us to be deeply angered by much of what's going on. Despite the events of September 11, 2001, we are less prepared for a national disaster now than we were a few years ago. Our citizens are dying in an underfunded war launched on false pretenses, and our actions have helped to unleash powerful forces that are both lethal and destabilizing. A majority of our representatives are addicted to tax cuts with no regard for their future impact. Shortsighted vested interests are at the table, constructing self-enriching energy policies instead of incentives to conserve; polluters are editing the science out of environmental protection acts.

These are front-page stories. Yet in the absence of a broadly shared vision in which we see that each one of these calamities poses a deep threat to our common fate, it's not clear how we should react. We have a vague sense that something important is off-kilter, but since the YOYOs have taken government solutions off the table, we have no means of crafting a suitable response. When the answer for every problem is a market-based solution—a private account, leavened with a tax cut for the wealthiest—we are trapped.

Clearly, we need to escape from that restrictive, cynical vision. Pursuing our collective, rather than strictly personal, interests will help. The plan I offer is straightforward: diagnose the point at which we got off course and chart the way forward.

DISCUSSION QUESTIONS

1. Discuss the core vision of the YOYO and WITT positions. How do these positions connect with the analysis of liberal individualism offered by Hochschild and Speth in Articles 5 and 6 in Chapter 2? Is Bernstein against individualism?
2. Which message—You're on your own" or "We're in this together"—makes the most political sense to you, and why? Based on his essay in Article 37, do you think that Martin Luther King, Jr., would have agreed with you?

40 *Bill McKibben*

DEEP ECONOMY
Reimagining Growth and Progress

With the worldwide success of Al Gore's 2006 documentary film An Inconvenient Truth, *climate change became a mainstream issue. Yet years before that, in his 1989 classic* The End of Nature, *environmentalist and author Bill McKibben first brought the concept of climate change into popular consciousness. McKibben's 2007 best seller* Deep Economy *has popularized his analysis even further. In this selection from* Deep Economy, *McKibben lays out the boundaries of his argument for a new political economy, asking his readers to imagine a world beyond our conventional worship of economic growth and consumption. He catalogs three "fundamental challenges to the fixation on growth." First, he contends that growth, conventionally understood, creates unacceptably high levels of inequality, with negative consequences both politically and economically. Second, growth is exhausting our resources, including energy supplies, leaving us with an unsustainably stressed (and warming) natural environment. We are, he argues, simply "running out of planet." Finally, McKibben says that the traditional link between economic growth and personal happiness has been severed. In other words, "More no longer is Better." His article challenges us to confront what he thinks is the most pressing issue of our time. The good news is, he thinks we can avoid the worst impacts of global climate change—and in the process strengthen democracy—if we act, now.*

For most of human history, the two birds More and Better roosted on the same branch. You could toss one stone and hope to hit them both. That's why the centuries since Adam Smith have been devoted to the dogged pursuit of maximum economic production. The idea that individuals, pursuing their own individual interests in a market society, make one another richer and the idea that increasing efficiency, usually by increasing scale, is the key to increasing wealth has indisputably produced More. It has built the unprecedented prosperity and ease that distinguish the lives of most of the people reading this book. It is no wonder and no accident that they dominate our politics, our outlook, even our personalities.

Source: Bill McKibben, *Deep Economy: The Wealth of Communities and the Durable Future,* New York: Times Books/Henry Holt, 2007, pp. 1–4, 11–19, 29–42, 45.

But the distinguishing feature of our moment is this: Better has flown a few trees over to make her nest. That changes everything. Now, if you've got the stone of your own life, or your own society, gripped in your hand, you have to choose between them. It's More or Better.

Some of the argument I'll make in these pages will seem familiar: growth is no longer making most people wealthier, but instead generating inequality and insecurity. And growth is bumping against physical limits so profound—like climate change and peak oil—that continuing to expand the economy may be impossible; the very attempt may be dangerous. But there's something else too, a wild card we're just now beginning to understand: *new research from many quarters has started to show that even when growth does make us wealthier, the greater wealth no longer makes us happier.*

Taken together, these facts show that we need to make a basic shift. Given all that we now know about topics ranging from the molecular structure of carbon dioxide to the psychology of human satisfaction, we need to move decisively to rebuild our local economies. These may well yield less stuff, but they produce richer relationships; they may grow less quickly, if at all, but they make up for it in durability.

Shifting our focus to local economies will not mean abandoning Adam Smith or doing away with markets. Markets, obviously, work. Building a local economy will mean, however, ceasing to worship markets as infallible and consciously setting limits on their scope. We will need to downplay efficiency and pay attention to other goals. We will have to make the biggest changes to our daily habits in generations—and the biggest change, as well, to our worldview, our sense of what constitutes progress.

Such a shift is neither "liberal" nor "conservative." It borrows some elements from our reigning political philosophies, and is in some ways repugnant to each. Mostly, it's *different.* The key questions will change from whether the economy produces an ever larger pile of stuff to whether it builds or undermines community—for community, it turns out, is the key to physical survival in our environmental predicament and also to human satisfaction. Our exaltation of the individual, which was the key to More, has passed the point of diminishing returns. It now masks a deeper economy that we should no longer ignore.

In choosing the phrase "deep economy," I have sought to echo the insistence, a generation ago, of some environmentalists that instead of simply one more set of smokestack filters or one more set of smokestack laws, we needed a "deep ecology" that asked more profound questions about the choices people make in their daily lives. Their point seems more valid by the month in our overheating world. We need a similar shift in our thinking about economics—we need it to take human satisfaction and societal durability more seriously; we need economics to mature as a discipline.

This shift will not come easily, of course. Focusing on economic growth, and assuming it would produce a better world, was extremely convenient; it let us stop thinking about ends and concentrate on means. It made economics as we know it now—a science of means—extraordinarily powerful. We could always choose our path by fixing our compass on More; we could rely on economists, skilled at removing the obstacles to growth, to act as guides through the wilderness. Alan Greenspan was the wisest of wise men.

But even as that idea of the world reigns supreme, with the rubble of the Iron Curtain at its feet as deserved proof of its power, change is bubbling up from underneath. You have to look, but it's definitely there. A single farmers' market, for instance, may not seem very important compared to a Wal-Mart, but farmers' markets are the fastest-growing part of our food economy. They've doubled in number and in sales and then doubled again in the last decade, suggesting new possibilities for everything from land use patterns to community identity. Similar experiments are cropping up in many other parts of the economy and in many other places around the world, driven not by government fiat but by local desire and necessity. That desire and necessity form the scaffolding on which this new, deeper economy will be built, in pieces and from below. It's a quiet revolution begun by ordinary people with the stuff of our daily lives. Eventually it will take form as legislation, but for now its most important work is simply to crack the consensus that what we need is More.

A word of caution, however. It's easy for those of us who already have a lot to get carried away with this kind of thinking. Recently I was on a reporting trip to China, where I met a twelve-year-old girl named Zhao Lin Tao, who was the same age as my daughter and who lived in a poor rural village in Sichuan province—that is, she's about the most statistically average person on earth. Zhao was the one person in her crowded village I could talk to without an interpreter: she was proudly speaking the pretty good English she'd learned in the overcrowded village school. When I asked her about her life, though, she was soon in tears: her mother had gone to the city to work in a factory and never returned, abandoning her and her sister to their father, who beat them regularly because they were not boys. Because Zhao's mother was away, the authorities were taking care of her school fees until ninth grade, but after that there would be no money to pay. Her sister had already given up and dropped out. In Zhao's world, in other words, it's perfectly plausible that More and Better still share a nest. Any solution we consider has to contain some answer for her tears. Her story hovers over this whole enterprise. She's a potent reality check.

And in the end it's reality I want to deal with—the reality of what our world can provide, the reality of what we actually want. The old realism—an endless More—is morphing into a dangerous fantasy. (Consider: if the Chinese owned cars in the same number as Americans, the world would have more than twice as many vehicles as it now does.) In the face of energy shortage, of global warming, and of the vague but growing sense that we are not as alive and connected as we want to be, I think we've started to grope for what might come next. And just in time.

·   ·   ·

Let's begin with the simplest objection, the one that fits most easily into our current political debates. *Though our economy has been growing, most of us have relatively little to show for it.* The median wage in the United States is the same as it was thirty years ago. The real income of the bottom 90 percent of American taxpayers has declined steadily: they earned $27,060 in real dollars in 1979, $25,646 in 2005. Even for those with four-years college degrees, and even though productivity was growing faster than it has for decades, earnings fell 5.2 percent between 2000 and 2004 when adjusted for inflation, according to the most recent data from White House economists. Much the same thing has happened across most of the globe; in Latin America, for instance, despite a slavish devotion to growth economics, real per capita income is the same as a quarter century ago. More than eighty countries, in fact, have seen per capita incomes fall in the last decade.

The mathematics that makes possible this seeming contradiction between rapid growth and individual stagnation is the mathematics of inequality. Basically, almost all the growing wealth accumulates in a very few (silk-lined) pockets. The statistics are such that even an arch-conservative commentator like Dinesh D'Souza calls them "staggering." Between 1997 and 2001, according to a pair of Northwestern University economists, the top 1 percent of wage earners "captured far more of the real national gain in income than did the bottom 50 percent." Economists calculate a "Gini coefficient" to measure income inequality across a society; the U.S. coefficient has risen steadily since the late 1960s, to the point where many economists believe wealth is more stratified today than any time since the Gilded Age. And that gap will continue to grow: the 2006 round of tax cuts delivers 70 percent of its benefits to the richest 5 percent of Americans, and 6.5 percent to the bottom 80 percent.

Economists can't explain all the underlying reasons for this spreading gap. The decline of unions had something to do with it, and so did the advent of computerization. Clearly, in a globalized economy, workers in the rich world now find themselves competing with far more people than they used to—and since per capita income is $1,700 in China, it will be a long time before that playing field levels. With the spread of the Internet, the number of jobs that can be transferred across continents has grown exponentially.

Beyond all that, though, there's the simple ideology of growth. Bill Clinton signed us up for the North American Free Trade Agreement (NAFTA), the General Agreement on Tariffs and Trade (GATT), and all the rest with the promise that international trade would spur efficiency and thereby increase growth. George W. Bush sold his massive tax cut with the argument that it would "get the economy moving." Every argument for raising minimum wages or corporate taxes, on the other hand, meets the response that such measures would stifle our economic growth. Growth is always the final answer, the untrumpable hand, and its logic keeps inequality growing, too.

Any debate on these issues has been muffled in the last few decades; the growth consensus usually carried the day without much trouble, in part because elite journalists and pundits found themselves on the happy side of the economic chasm. The extremes have become so enormous, though, that debate can't help but emerge, even if only by accident. Take, for example, the juxtaposition of two stories on a recent front page of the *New York Times*. One concerned the record-setting Christmas bonuses Wall Street executives had received. It quoted a real estate broker who said clients were suddenly shopping for apartments in "the $6 million range" instead of contenting themselves with $4 million digs. "One senior trader is building a sports complex for triathlon training at his house in upstate New York," the article reports. "It will include a swim-in-place lap pool, a climbing wall, and a fitness center." Another investment banker seemed flummoxed by his windfall: " 'I have a sailboat, a motor boat, an apartment, an SUV. What could I possibly need?' After brief reflection, however, he continued: 'Maybe a little Porsche for the Hamptons house.' " Meanwhile, a few columns away, there was a picture of a Mexican farmer in a field of sickly tomatoes. His small cooperative, post-NAFTA, had tried to sell its produce to the global supermarket giants like Ahold, Wal-Mart, and Carrefour, which had moved into the country with their vast capital and their vast commitment to efficiency. Lacking the money to invest in greenhouses and pesticides, however, he and his neighbors couldn't produce the perfectly

round fruit the chains' executives demanded. "The stark danger," the reporter Celia Dugger notes, "is that millions of struggling small farmers . . . will go bust and join streams of desperate migrants to America and to the urban slums of their own countries." She closes her story by interviewing José Luis Pérez Escobar, who after twenty years as a Mexican potato farmer, went under and then left for the United States, without his wife and five children. He now earns $6 an hour, working the graveyard shift tending grass at a golf course. Alongside the exhilaration of the flattening earth celebrated by Thomas Friedman, the planet (and our country) in fact contains increasing numbers of flattened people, flattened by the very forces that are making a few others wildly rich.

Even when the question of inequality has been engaged, though, the standard liberal line is to question not expansion but only the way that the new money is spread around. Leftwing "social critics continue to focus on income," says the sociologist Juliet Schor. "Their goals are redistribution and growth." In fact, critics in the Democratic party and the union movement typically demand even faster growth. They're as intellectually invested in the current system as the average CEO.

I agree with the argument for fairness, that we should distribute wealth more equitably both here and around the globe. (In fact, there's persuasive evidence that if all you cared about was growth, the best way to speed it up would be to redistribute income more fairly.) And it's extremely important to bear in mind that we're *not,* despite the insistence of our leaders, growing wealthier. *Growth simply isn't enriching most of us.*

But I'm not going to tarry long here, because I also think that a program of redistribution, however wise or moral, will do relatively little to deal with the even more fundamental, and much less discussed, problems that a growth-centered, efficiency-obsessed economy faces. It's to those problems, and to the physical world, that we now turn.

It's useful to remember what Thomas Newcomen was up to when he launched the Industrial Revolution. He was using coal to pump water out of a coal mine. The birth of the Industrial Revolution was all about fossil fuel, and so, in many ways, was everything that followed. We've learned an enormous amount in the last two centuries—our body of scientific knowledge has doubled so many times no one can count—but coal and oil and natural gas are still at the bottom of it all.

And no wonder. They are miracles. A solid and a liquid and a gas that emerge from the ground pretty much ready to use, with their energy highly concentrated. Of the three, oil may be the most miraculous. In many spots on the face of the earth, all you have to do is stick a pipe in the ground and oil comes spurting to the surface. It's compact, it's easily transportable, and it packs an immense amount of energy into a small volume. Fill the tank of my hybrid Honda Civic with ten gallons—sixty pounds—of gasoline and you can move four people and their possessions from New York to Washington, D.C., and back. Coal and gas are almost as easy to use, and coal in particular is often even cheaper to recover—in many places it's buried just a few feet beneath the surface of the earth, just waiting to be taken.

That simple, cheap, concentrated power lies at the heart of our modern economies. Every action of a modern life burns fossil fuel; viewed in one way, modern Western human beings are flesh-colored devices for combusting coal and gas and oil. "Before coal," writes Jeffrey Sachs, "economic production was limited by energy inputs, almost all of which depended on the production of biomass: food for humans and farm animals, and fuel wood for heating and certain industrial processes." That is, energy depended on how much you could *grow*. But *fossil* energy depended on how much had grown eons before, on all those millions of years of ancient biology squashed by the weight of time till they'd turned into strata and pools and seams of hydrocarbons, waiting for us to discover them.

.   .   .

As everyone knows, the last three years have seen a spate of reports and books and documentaries insisting that humanity may have neared or passed the oil peak—that is, the point where those pools of primeval plankton are half used up, where each new year brings us closer to the

bottom of the bucket. The major oil companies report that they can't find enough new wells most years to offset the depletion of their old ones; worrisome rumors circulate that the giant Saudi fields are dwindling faster than expected, and, of course, all this is reflected in the rising cost of oil. The most credible predict not a sharp peak but a bumpy ride for the next decade along an unstable plateau, followed by an inexorable decline in supply. So far that seems to be spot-on—highly variable prices, trading higher over time.

One effect of those changes, of course, can be predicted by everyone who's ever sat through Introductory Economics. We should, theory insists, use less oil, both by changing our habits and by changing to new energy sources. To some extent that's what has happened: SUV sales slowed once it appeared high gas prices were here to stay, and the waiting lists for Toyota Priuses were suddenly six months long. Buses and subways drew more riders. People turned down their thermostats a touch, and sales of solar panels started to boom. This is a classic economic response. But it's hard for us to simply park our cars, precisely because cheap oil coaxed us to build sprawling suburbs. And Americans can switch to hybrids, but if the Chinese and the Indians continue to build auto fleets themselves, even if they drive extremely small cars, then the pressure on oil supplies will keep building. Meanwhile, solar power and the other renewables, wondrous as they are, don't exactly replace coal and oil and gas. The roof of my home is covered with photovoltaic panels, and on a sunny day it's great pleasure to watch the electric meter spin backward, but the very point of solar power is that it's widely diffused, not compacted and concentrated by millennia like coal and gas and oil.

It's *different:* if fossil fuel is a slave at our beck and call, renewable power is more like a partner. As we shall eventually see, that partnership could be immensely rewarding for people and communities, but can it power economic growth of the kind we're used to? The doctrinaire economist's answer, of course, is that no particular commodity matters all that much, because if we run short someone will have the incentive to develop a substitute. In general, this has proved true in the past—run short of nice big sawlogs and someone invents plywood—but it's far from clear that it applies to fossil fuel, which in its ubiquity and its cheapness is almost certainly a special case. Wars are fought over oil, not over milk, not over semiconductors, not over timber. It's plausible—indeed, it's likely—that if we begin to run short, the nature of our lives may fundamentally change as the scarcity wreaks havoc on our economies.

.   .   .

The diminished availability of fossil fuel is not the only limit we face. In fact, it's not even the most important. Even before we run out of oil, we're running out of planet.

One consequence of nearly three hundred years of rapid economic growth has been stress on the natural world: we've dug it up, eroded it away, cut it down. You could point to a thousand different types of environmental damage, and taken together the toll has been enormous. In the spring of 2005, a panel of 1,300 scientists assembled by the United Nations issued a "Millennium Ecosystem Assessment" report. They found that "human actions are depleting Earth's natural capital, putting such strain on the environment that the ability of the planet's ecosystems to sustain future generations can no longer be taken for granted." And you could list a dozen such warnings. A majority of the living Nobel laureates in the sciences recently warned that, "if not checked, many of our current practices . . . may so alter the living world that it will be unable to sustain life in the manner we know." This is the planetary equivalent of the doctor clearing his throat and asking you to sit down.

Furthermore, there's every reason to think the situation will deteriorate further as the rest of the world begins to develop. If you want to argue that an economy structured like ours makes sense for the whole world, here are the kind of numbers you need to contend with: given current rates of growth in the Chinese economy, the 1.3 billion residents of that nation alone will, by 2031, be about as rich as we are. If they then eat meat, milk, and eggs in the same quantities as we do, calculates the

eco-statistician Lester Brown, they'll consume 1,352 million tons of grain, or two-thirds of the world's entire 2004 grain harvest. They'd use 99 million barrels of oil a day, 20 million more barrels than the entire world consumes at present. If China's coal burning were to reach the current U.S. level of nearly two tons per person, says Brown, the country would use 2.8 billion tons annually—more than the current world production of 2.5 billion tons. They'd use more steel than all the West combined. Paper? At the American rate, they'd consume 303 million tons, roughly double the current world production. Cars? They'd have 1.1 billion on the road, half again as many as the current world total. And that's just China. By then, India will have a higher population, and its economy is growing almost as fast. And then there's the rest of the world.

.   .   .

Our momentum is enormous. So enormous, in fact, that to most of us the health of the economy seems far more palpable, far more real, than the health of the planet. Think of the terms we use—the economy, whose temperature we take at every newscast via the Dow Jones average, is "ailing" or "on the mend." It's "slumping" or "in recovery." We cosset and succor it with enormous devotion, even as we more or less ignore the increasingly urgent fever that the globe is now running. The ecological economists have an enormous task ahead of them.

Thankfully, however, they have unexpected allies, who are raising an even deeper question, an even more powerful challenge to the reigning orthodoxy. They ask, What does richer mean? Even if I am getting richer, am I getting happier? Those are the *really* radical questions, and the ones to which we now turn.

Traditionally, ideas like happiness and satisfaction are the sorts of notions that economists wave aside as poetic irrelevancies, questions that occupy people with no head for numbers who have to major in something else at college. An orthodox economist can tell what makes someone happy by what they do. If they buy a Ford Expedition, then ipso facto a Ford Expedition is what makes them happy. That's all you need to know.

The economists calls this behavior "utility maximization"; in the words of the economic historian Gordon Bigelow, "The theory holds that every time a person buys something, sells something, quits a job, or invests, he is making a rational decision about what will . . . provide him 'maximum utility.' 'Utility' can be pleasure (as in, 'Which of these Disney cruises will make me happiest?') or security (as in 'Which 401(k) will let me retire before age 85?') or self-satisfaction (as in, 'How much will I put in the offering plate at church?'). If you bought a Ginsu knife at 3 A.M., a neoclassical economist will tell you that, at that time, you calculated that this purchase would optimize your resources." The beauty of this notion lies in its simplicity: it reassures the economist that all the complex math he builds on top of the assumption adds up to something real. It reassures the politician that all his efforts to increase GNP are sensible and rational even when they may seem otherwise. It is perhaps the central assumption of the world we live in: you can tell who I really am by how I spend.

But is the idea of utility maximization simple, or simple-minded? Economists have long known that people's brains don't work quite as rationally as the model might imply. When Bob Costanza was first edging into economics in the early 1980s, for instance, he had a fellowship to study "social traps," for example, a nuclear arms race, "where short-term behavior can get out of kilter with longer broad-term goals." It didn't take long to demonstrate, as others had before him, that, if you set up an auction in a certain way, people will end up bidding $1.50 to take home a dollar. Other economists have shown that people give too much weight to "sunk costs"— that they're too willing to throw good money after bad, or that they value items more highly if they are thinking of acquiring them. Building on such insights, a school of "behavioral economics," pioneered by researchers like Princeton's Daniel Kahneman, Stanford's Amos Tversky, and Harvard's Andrei Shleifer, has emerged as a "robust, burgeoning sector" of mainstream economics, "opening the way for a richer and more realistic model of the human being in the marketplace."

The real wonder, in a sense, is that it took so long. Each of us knows how irrational much of our behavior is, and how unconnected to any real sense of what makes us happy. I mean, there you are at 3 A.M. thinking about the Ginsu knife. You're only thinking about it in the first place because someone is advertising it, devoting half an hour of infomercial time to imagining every possible way to make you think that your life will be more complete with this marvel of the cutler's trade—that you will be hosting dinner parties full of witty conversation and impressing potential mates with your suave carving ability, your paper-thin tomato slices. There you are at the car lot thinking about the Ford Expedition. If you are like 95 percent of other buyers, you will never drive it off a paved road. By any objective and rational assessment, the Expedition is a very poor decision, given that it will harm the earth in irreparable ways, and given the fact that it's more dangerous than a car, not only to everyone else on the road but even to yourself—not to mention what its thirst for fuel will cost you. But you are wondering, in some back part of your cortex, if the manliness inherent in such a very large conveyance will perhaps win you new and robust friends, as has been suggested by a number of recent commercials you have had the pleasure of observing. Or maybe you were completely freaked out by 9/11 and there's something mysteriously comforting about the yards of unnecessary sheet metal surrounding you. Such thoughts are not rational; in fact, they set us up for as much unhappiness as pleasure.

So the orthodox economist's premise that we can figure out what constitutes a good economy by summing the *rational individual* actions of consumers is suspect. "Rational" is a stretch; and, as we shall see, "individual" may cause even more trouble. But until fairly recently, that orthodox economist had a pretty good comeback to these kinds of objections, namely "Well, what other way is there?" I mean, it seems unlikely that you'd get any closer by appointing someone (me, say) to decide that everyone had to have a Juiceman in the kitchen and that if they did, happiness would reign. The misery of centrally planned economies testifies to that.

In recent years, however, something new has happened. Researchers from a wide variety of disciplines have begun to figure out how to assess satisfaction more directly, and economists have begun to sense the implications that ability holds for their way of looking at the world. In 2002, Daniel Kahneman won the Nobel Prize in economics even though he was trained as a psychologist. To get a sense of some of his preoccupations you can pick up a book called *Well-being* in which, with a pair of coauthors, he announces the existence of a new field called hedonics, defined as "the study of what makes experience and life pleasant and unpleasant. It is concerned with feelings of pleasure and pain, of interest and boredom, of joy and sorrow, and of satisfaction and dissatisfaction. It is also concerned with the whole range of circumstances, from the biological to the societal, that occasion suffering and enjoyment." If you are worried that there might be something altogether too airy about this, be reassured that Kahneman thinks like an economist. Indeed, in the book's very first chapter, "Objective Happiness," as he attempts to figure out how accurately people can determine their own mental states, Kahneman describes an experiment that compares "records of two patients undergoing colonoscopy." Every sixty seconds, he insists they rate their pain on a scale of 1 to 10, and eventually he forces them to "make as hypothetical choice between a repeat colonoscopy and a barium enema." Dismal science, indeed.

.   .   .

In the words of the economist Richard Layard, "We now know that what people say about how they feel corresponds closely to the actual levels of activity in different parts of the brain, which can be measured in standard scientific ways." Indeed, people who call themselves happy, or who have relatively high levels of electrical activity in the left prefrontal region of the brain, are also "more likely to be rated as happy by friends," "more likely to respond to requests for help," "less likely to be involved in disputes at work," and even "less likely to die prematurely." In other words, conceded one economist, "It seems that what the psychologists call subjective well-being is a real phenomenon. The various empirical measures of it have high consistency, reliability, and validity."

The idea that there is a state called happiness, and that we can dependably figure out what it feels like and how to measure it, is extremely subversive. It would allow economists to start thinking about life in far richer terms, allow them to stop asking "What did you buy?" and to start asking "Is your life good?"

It won't happen overnight, but it will happen eventually. Because if you can ask someone "Is your life good?" and count on the answer to mean something, then you'll be able to move to the real heart of the matter, the question haunting our moment on earth: *Is more better?*

.   .   .

In some sense, you could say that the years since World War II in America have been a loosely controlled experiment designed to answer this very question. The environmentalist Alan Durning found that in 1991 the average American family owned twice as many cars, drove two and a half times as far, used twenty-one times as much plastic, and traveled twenty-five times farther by air than did the average family in 1951. Gross domestic product per capita has tripled since 1950. We are, to use the very literal vernacular, living three times as large. Our homes are bigger: the size of new houses has doubled since 1970, even as the average number of people living in each one has shrunk. Despite all that extra space, they are stuffed to the rafters with belongings, enough so that an entire new industry—the storage locker—has sprung up and indeed has reached huge size itself. We have all sorts of other new delights and powers: we can communicate online, watch a hundred cable stations, find food from every corner of the world. Some people have clearly taken more than their share of all this new stuff, but still, on average, all of us in the West are living lives materially more abundant than most people did a generation ago. As the conservative writer Dinesh D'Souza noted recently, we have created not just the first middle class but "the first mass affluent class in world history."

What's odd is, none of this stuff appears to have made us happier. All that material progress—and all the billions of barrels of oil and millions of acres of trees that it took to create it—seems not to have moved the satisfaction meter an inch. In 1946, the United States was the happiest country among four advanced economies; thirty years later, it was eighth among eleven advanced countries; a decade after that it ranked tenth among twenty-three nations, many of them from the third world. There have been steady *decreases* in the percentage of Americans who say that their marriages are happy, that they are satisfied with their jobs, that they find a great deal of pleasure in the place they live. Ever since World War II, the National Opinion Research Council has once a year polled Americans with the fundamental question: "Taken all together, how would you say things are these days—would you say that you are very happy, pretty happy, or not too happy?" (It must be somewhat unsettling to receive this phone call.) The proportion of respondents saying they were very happy peaked sometime in the 1950s and has slid slowly but steadily in the years since. Between 1970 and 1994, for instance, it dropped five full percentage points, dipping below the mark where one-third of Americans were able to count themselves as very happy. As Richard Layard points out, this trend is even more remarkable than it seems. "People must seek anchors or standards for such evaluations, and it is natural for them to compare their current situation with their situation in the recent past: if last year was bad, then an average current year would appear to be good. Such annual corrections would tend to wipe out any trend." Yet there the trend is, as plain as can be and continuing to the present. In the winter of 2006, the National Opinion Research Center published data about "negative life events" covering the years 1991 to 2004, a period dominated by the rapid economic expansion of the Clinton boom. "The anticipation would have been that problems would have been down," the study's author said. Instead the data showed a rise in problems—the percentage of respondents who reported breaking up with a steady partner doubled, for instance. As one reporter summarized the findings, "There's more misery in people's lives today."

The phenomenon isn't confined to the United States; as other nations have followed us into mass affluence, their experiences have begun to yield similar, though less dramatic, results. In the United Kingdom, for instance, per capita gross domestic product grew 66 percent between 1973 and 2001, yet people's satisfaction with their lives changed not at all. Japan saw a fivefold increase in per capita income between 1958 and 1986 without any reported increase in satisfaction. In one place after another, in fact, rates of alcoholism, suicide, and depression have gone up dramatically even as the amount of stuff also accumulated. The science writer Daniel Goleman noted in the *New York Times* that people born in the advanced countries after 1955 are three times as likely as their grandparents to have had a serious bout of depression. Indeed, one report in 2000 found that the *average* American child reported now higher levels of anxiety than the average child *under psychiatric care* in the 1950s: our new normal is the old disturbed. The British researcher Richard Douthwaite noted that between 1955 and 1988, the doubling of the UK's national income had coincided with increases in everything from crime to divorce. That's not to say that getting richer caused these problems, only that it didn't alleviate them. All in all, we have more stuff and less happiness. *The experiment we've undertaken has yielded a significant, robust, and largely unexpected result . . .*

·   ·   ·

We're richer, but we're not happier. We have more music, more education, more communication, and certainly more entertainment than any people who have ever lived—we can be entertained literally around the clock, and we can carry our entertainment with us wherever we go as long as we remember the Nano and the earbuds. But if satisfaction was our goal, then the unbelievable expenditures of effort and resources since 1950 to accomplish all this (and by most measures humans have used more raw materials since the end of World War II than in all of prior human history) have been largely a waste. "Estimates suggest," said one team of economists, "that 20 percent of the American population are flourishing and over 25 percent are languishing, with the rest somewhere in between."

In fact, the more we study the question, the less important affluence seems to be to human happiness. In one open-ended British questionnaire, people were asked about the factors that make up "quality of life." They named everything from "family and home life" to "equality and justice," and when the results were totted up, 71 percent of the answers were non-materialistic. The best predictor of happiness was health, followed by factors like being married. Income seemed not to matter at all in France, Holland, or England, and it was only the seventh or eighth most important predictor in Italy, Ireland, and Denmark. In one classic study of how various "domains" contributed to life satisfaction, "goods and services you can buy" came in twelfth among thirty areas, behind even "political attitudes" and swamped by "feelings about recreation and family."

How is it, then, that we became so totally, and apparently wrongly, fixated on the idea that our main goal, as individuals and as nations, should be the accumulation of more wealth?

The answer is interesting for what it says about human nature. *Up to a certain point,* none of what I've just been saying holds true. *Up to a certain point,* more really does equal better.

Consider the life of a very poor person in a very poor society. Not, perhaps, a hunter-gatherer—it may not make much sense to think of hunter-gatherers as poor. But, say, a peasant farmer in China, trying to survive on too little land. (China has one-third of the world's farmers, but one-fifteenth of its arable land; in many places the average holding is less than a sixth of an acre, an area smaller than the footprint of the average new American home.) You lack very basic things, including any modicum of security for when your back finally gives out, your diet is unvaried and nutritionally lacking; you're almost always cold in the winter.

To compensate you for your struggles, it's true that you also likely have the benefits of a close and connected family, and a village environment where your place is clear. Your world makes sense. Still, in a world like that, a boost in income delivers tangible benefits. I remember one reporting trip when I visited a shower-curtain factory in rural China, staffed by people who had grown up on such farms. I wandered through the

workrooms, watching kids—almost everyone was between eighteen and twenty-two, as if the factory was some kind of shower-curtain college—smooth out long bolts of polyester on huge cutting-room tables, and sew hems and grommets, and fold them up in plastic bags, and pack them into cartons. It's hard to imagine a much simpler product than a shower curtain, basically, a big square of fabric with a row of holes along the top.

The workday here was eight hours; because of the summer heat everyone was working from seven-thirty to eleven-thirty in the morning and then again from three to seven in the afternoon. I'd been there a few minutes when all labor ceased and everyone poured down the stairs into the cafeteria for lunch. Rice, green beans, eggplant stew, some kind of stuffed dumpling, and a big bowl of soup: 1.7 yuan, or about 20 cents. While the workers ate, I wandered into the dormitory rooms. Each one had four sets of bunkbeds, one set of which stored suitcases and clothes. The other beds were for sleeping, six to a room. MP3 players sat on most pillows; in the girls' rooms, big stuffed animals graced most beds. There were posters of boy bands, and stacks of comic books, and lots of little bottles of cosmetics. One desk to share, one ceiling fan. Next to the dormitory, a lounge housed a big-screen TV and twenty or thirty battered chairs; the room next door had a Ping-Pong table.

Virtually all the workers came from Junan county in Shandong province, a few hundred kilometers to the south, where the factory owner had grown up. He let me select at random and interview as many workers as I liked. He was especially pleased with my first pick, Du Pei-Tang, who was twenty years old—a goofy grin, nervous, but with very bright and shining eyes. His father had died and his mother had remarried and moved away, so he'd grown up with his grandparents. His first job had been as a guard at an oil company in Shandong province, but it only paid a few hundred yuan a month and there was no food or dormitory. One of his relatives had introduced him to the shower-curtain factory owner, who had the reputation of being nice to his workers, so he'd come to work, earning about 1,000 yuan a month. From that, he'd been able to save 12,000 yuan in a little less than two years. And here's the thing you need to understand: 12,000 yuan—call it $1,200—is actually a pretty big sum of money, enough to be life changing. In a year or two more, he said, he'd have enough to build a small house back in his hometown and to get married. For fun, Du played table tennis and watched videos on the factory TV—which was good because, as the owner pointed out, buying a single Coke every night would come near to halving his savings. I asked him if he'd seen any movie that showed him a life he might aim for. He got very quiet, and said yes, he'd recently seen a film "about a young man successful in both business and family life. That's important to me because I grew up lacking the family atmosphere. I hope I would have that kind of life—not be that person, but have a good wife, a good family, a good business."

.   .   .

It may well be that moving away to the factory for a few years will disrupt the lives of these young people in unforeseen ways and leave them rootless and unhappy; it may well be that the world can't afford the ecological implications of everyone in China making lots of plastic stuff, or lots of money. The only point I'm trying to make is that China's relentless economic growth—9 percent a year for the last couple of decades, the fastest in the history of the planet—was indeed lifting lots of people out of poverty and in the process making their lives somewhat happier.

And it wasn't, as it turns out, just my anecdotal impression. In general, researchers report that *money consistently buys happiness right up to about $10,000 per capita income, and that after that point the correlation disappears*. That's a useful number to

keep in the back of your head—it's like the freezing point of water, one of those random numbers that just happens to define a crucial phenomenon on our planet. "As poor countries like India, Mexico, the Philippines, Brazil, and South Korea have experienced economic growth, there is some evidence that their average happiness has risen," Richard Layard reports. But *past the $10,000 point*, there's a complete scattering: when the Irish were making a third as much as Americans they were reporting higher levels of satisfaction, as were the Swedes, the Danes, the Dutch. Costa Ricans score higher than Japanese; French people are about as satisfied with their lives as Venezuelans. In fact, past the point of basic needs being met, the "satisfaction" data scramble in mind-bending ways. A sampling of *Forbes* magazine's "richest Americans" has happiness scores identical with those of the Pennsylvania Amish and only a whisker above those of Swedes, not to mention Masai tribesmen. The "life satisfaction" of pavement dwellers—that is, homeless people—in Calcutta was among the lowest recorded, but it almost doubled when they moved into a slum, at which point they were basically as satisfied with their lives as a sample of college students drawn from forty-seven nations. And so on.

.   .   .

We need, in short, a new utilitarianism. When More and Better shared a branch, we could kill two birds with one stone. Since they've moved apart, we can't. We in the rich countries no longer inhabit a planet where straight-ahead Newtonian economics, useful as it has been, can help us. We need an Einsteinian economics, a more complicated and relativistic science that asks deeper questions.

Discussion Questions

1. Explain more fully each of the three arguments McKibben makes about the limits of economic growth as we know it today. What might have to change (politically, economically, socially) if we were to address each of these challenges?
2. Discuss one or two of the many examples McKibben uses from other countries around the world. How might the experiences of people in those countries illuminate ours?
3. Would you characterize McKibben's analysis as optimistic or pessimistic? Explain.

Credits

Chapter 1: Page 11, Frances Moore Lappé, *Getting a Grip: Clarity, Creativity, and Courage in a World Gone Mad*, Cambridge, MA: Small Planet Media, 2007, pp. 3–18. Used by permission. Page 18, Susan George, "A Short History of Neo-liberalism," from Lecture at the Conference on Economic Sovereignty in a Globalizing World. Bangkok, Thailand, March 24–26, 1999. Copyright © 1999 by Susan George. George is Board Chair of the Transnational Institute, Amsterdam. Used by permission. Page 25, Material excerpted from "Follow the Money" from *Dollars and Votes: How Business Campaign Contributions Subvert Democracy* by Dan Clawson, Alan Neustadtl, and Mark Weller. Used by permission of Temple University Press. Copyright © 1998 by Temple University. All Rights Reserved. Page 35, From *Monthly Review*, January 2010, Volume 61, No. 10, http://monthlyreview.org/2010/03/01/what-every-environmentalist-needs-to-know-about-capitalism. Used by permission.

Chapter 2: Page 48, From *Facing Up to The American Dream* by Jennifer Hochschild. Copyright © 1995 Princeton University Press, 1996 paperback edition. Reprinted by permission of Princeton University Press. Page 62, Originally published as "What Is the American Dream: Dueling Dualities in the American Tradition" by James Gustave Speth in *Grist*, June 24, 2011. Used by permission of the author. Page 68, "The Theology of American Empire" by Ira Chernus from *Foreign Policy In Focus*, September 12, 2007. Used by permission of the author. Page 74, From *Citizens of the Empire: The Struggle to Claim Our Humanity* by Robert F. Jensen. Copyright © 2004 by Robert Jensen. Reprinted by permission.

Chapter 3: Page 82, Joshua Cohen and Joel Rogers, *Rules of the Game: American Politics and the Central American Movement*, pp. 4–16. Copyright © 1986 by South End Press. Reprinted by permission. Page 89, Kenneth Dolbeare and Linda Medcalf, "The Dark Side of the Constitution" from *The Case Against the Constitution: From the Antifederalists to the Present*, pp. 120–124, 126–133, and 136–141. Copyright © 1987 by M. E. Sharpe. Reprinted by permission. Page 101, Excerpt from "Our Godless Constitution" by Brooke Allen from the February 21, 2005, issue of *The Nation*. Reprinted with permission. www.thenation.com. Page 106, "Some Truths Are Not Self-Evident" by Howard Zinn from the July 18, 1987, issue of *The Nation*. Reprinted with permission. www.thenation.com.

Chapter 4: Page 112, From the Preface to *The Death and Life of American Journalism* by Robert McChesney and John Nichols. Reprinted by permission of Nation Books, a member of the Perseus Books Group. Page 123, From *News: The Politics of Illusion*, Fifth Edition by W. Lance Bennett. Copyright © 2003 Longman, Inc. Reprinted by permission of Pearson Education, Inc. Page 133, "Why ACORN Fell: The Times, Lies, and Videotape" by John Atlas and Peter Dreier from *Huffington Post*, March 23, 2010. Used by permission. Page 141, "Facts Still Matter . . ." Speech by Bill Moyers to History Makers, New York City, January 27, 2011. Used by permission.

Chapter 5: Page 150, "What's the Matter with America?" from the book *What's the Matter with Kansas?* by Thomas Frank. Copyright © 2004 by Thomas Frank. Reprinted by permission of Henry Holt and Company, LLC. Page 155, "Beyond the Tea Party" by Paul Street and Anthony DiMaggio from *Z Magazine*, September 2011. Used by permission. Page 162, "Democracy After Citizens United" by Lawrence Lessig from *Boston Review*, Volume 35, Number 5, September–October 2010, http://bostonreview.net/BR35.5/lessig.php. Copyright © 2010. Used by permission of the author. Page 171, "Just Democracy" by Katrina vanden Heuvel from the July 21, 2008 issue of *The Nation*. Reprinted with permission. www.thenation.com.

Chapter 6: Page 185, John C. Berg, *Unequal Struggle: Class, Gender, Race, and Power in the U.S. Congress*. Copyright © 1994 by John C. Berg. Reprinted by permission. Page 192, Common Cause, *Democracy on Drugs. The Medicare/Prescription Drug Bill: A Study in How Government Shouldn't Work*. Copyright © 2004 by Common Cause. Reprinted by permission. Page 200, "Wall Street's Big Win" by Matt Taibbi from *Rolling Stone*, August 19, 2010. Copyright © 2010 Rolling Stone LLC. All Rights Reserved. Reprinted by permission. Page 209, Patricia Siplon and William F. Grover, "Congressional Inertia: Iron Triangles Old and New." Used by permission.

Chapter 7: Page 219, From *The Presidential Dilemma: Leadership in the American System*, Second Edition, by Michael Genovese. Copyright © 2003 by Pearson Education, Inc. Reprinted by permission of Pearson Education, Inc. Page 224, "The Presidential Spectacle" by Bruce Miroff from *The Presidency and the Political System*, Seventh Edition, edited by Michael Nelson. Copyright © 2002 CQ Press, an imprint of SAGE. Used by permission. Page 237, From "The Militarized Surrealism of Barack Obama" by Tom Engelhardt in TomDispatch.com, June 30, 2011, http://www.tomdispatch.com/blog/175412, © 2011. Used by permission. Page 242, Joseph G. Peschek, "The Obama Presidency and the Great Recession: Political Economy, Ideology, and Public Policy." *New Political Science*, Volume 33, Number 4, December 2011.

Chapter 8: Page 253, "Supreme Court Inc." by Jeffrey Rosen from *New York Times*, March 16, 2008, © 2008 The New York Times. All rights reserved. Used by permission and protected by the Copyright Laws of the United States. The printing, copying, redistribution, or retransmission of this Content without express written permission is prohibited. Page 266, From *Dissent Magazine*, May 3, 2011, online www.dissentmagazine.org. Used by permission. Page 271, Patricia J. Williams, "This Dangerous Patriot's Game" from *The Observer*, December 2, 2001. Used by permission of the author. Page 277, "Neo-Patriarchy and the Anti-Homosexual Agenda" by R. Claire Snyder-Hall in *Fundamental Differences*, edited by Cynthia Burack and Jyl J. Josephson. Copyright © 2003 Rowman and Lifftlefield Publishers, Inc. Used by permission.

Chapter 9: Page 289, "Afterword" excerpted from *Nickel and Dimed* by Barbara Ehrenreich. Copyright © 2001 by Barbara Ehrenreich. Reprinted by permission of Henry Holt and Company, LLC. Page 297, From "Some Democrats Are More Equal Than Others" from *Le Monde Diplomatique*, June 2008, English Edition. Reprinted by permission. Page 301, Excerpted from *Merchants of Doubt: How a Handful of Scientists Obscured the Truth on Issues from Tobacco Smoke to Global Warming* by Erik Conway and Naomi Oreskes, © 2010, Bloomsbury Publishing Plc. Page 307, Noam Chomsky, "Was There an Alternative?: Looking Back on 9/11 a Decade Later" adapted from *9–11: Was There an Alternative?*, an Open Media Book. Copyright © 2001, 2002, 2011 by Noam Chomsky. Reprinted with permission of The Permissions Company, Inc., on behalf of Seven Stories Press, www.sevenstories.com.

Chapter 10: Page 314, Reprinted by arrangement with The Heirs to the Estate of Martin Luther King Jr., c/o Writers House as agent for the proprietor, New York, NY. Copyright © 1963 Dr. Martin Luther King Jr.; copyright renewed © 1991 Coretta Scott King. Page 321, Naomi Klein, "Reclaiming the Commons," *New Left Review*, 9 May–June 2001, pp. 81–89. Reprinted by permission of the author. Page 328, Reprinted with permission of the publisher. From *All Together Now*, copyright © 2006 by Jared Bernstein, Berrett-Koehler Publishers, Inc., San Francisco, CA. All rights reserved. www.bkconnection.com. Page 333, Excerpts from "Deep Economy: Reimagining Growth and Progress" from the book *Deep Economy: The Wealth of Communities and the Durable Future* by Bill McKibben. Copyright © 2007 by Bill McKibben. Reprinted by permission of Henry Holt and Company, LLC.